MEDIA NOW

Communications Media in the Information Age

Second Edition

D1400901

Joseph Straubhaar
University of Texas, Austin

Robert LaRose
Michigan State University

Australia • Canada • Denmark • Japan • Mexico
New Zealand • Philippines • Puerto Rico
Singapore • South Africa • Spain • United Kingdom
United States

Media now : communications media in the informa
HE 7775 .S79 2000 62120
Straubhaar, Joseph D.

Acquisitions Editor: Karen Austin
Executive Editor: Deirdre Cavanaugh
Development Editor: Sherry Symington
Associate Development Editor: Ryan E. Vesely
Editorial Assistant: Dory Schaeffer
Project Editor: Cathy Linberg
Print Buyer: Barbara Britton
Permissions Editor: Susan Walters
Production: Thompson Steele, Inc.

Text and Cover Designer: Stephen Rapley
Copy Editor: Thompson Steele, Inc.
Cover Images: Tony Cordoza/Photonica, Tony Stone Images, and PhotoDisc
Cover Printer: Phoenix Color
Compositor: Thompson Steele, Inc.
Printer: World Color Book Services, Taunton, Massachusetts

COPYRIGHT © 2000 by Wadsworth, a division of Thomson Learning

For permission to use material from this text, contact us:
web www.thomsonrights.com
fax 1-800-730-2215
phone 1-800-730-2214

Printed in the United States of America
1 2 3 4 5 6 7 03 02 01 00 99

Wadsworth/Thomson Learning
10 Davis Drive
Belmont, CA 94002-3098
USA
www.wadsworth.com

International Headquarters
Thomson Learning
290 Harbor Drive, 2nd floor
Stamford, CT 06902-7477
USA

UK/Europe/Middle East
Berkshire House
168-173 High Holborn
London, WC1V 7AA,
United Kingdom

Asia
Thomson Learning
60 Albert Street #15-01
Albert Complex
Singapore 189969

Canada
Nelson/Thomson Learning
1120 Birchmount Road
Scarborough, Ontario M1K 5G4
Canada

All rights reserved. No part of this work covered by the copyright hereon may be reproduced or used in any form or by any means—graphic, electronic, or mechanical, including photocopying, recording, taping, or information storage and retrieval systems—without the written permission of the publisher.

Library of Congress Cataloging-in-Publication Data
Straubhaar, Joseph D.
Media now : communications media in the information age / Joseph Straubhaar, Robert LaRose.—2nd ed.
p. cm.
Rev. ed. of: Communications media in the information society
Updated ed. c1997.
ISBN 0-534-54828-8 Instructor's Edition ISBN 0-534-54830-X
1. Telecommunication—United States. 2. Information technology—United States. 3. Mass media—United States.
I. LaRose, Robert. II. Straubhaar, Joseph D. Communications media in the information society. III. Title
HE7775.S79 2000
364.0973—dc21 99-26908

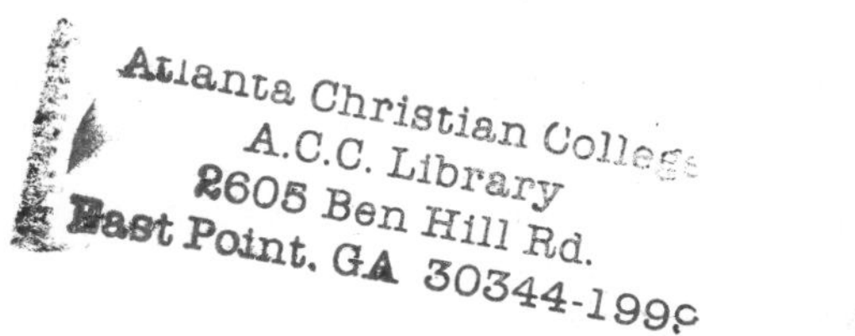
Atlanta Christian College
A.C.C. Library
2605 Ben Hill Rd.
East Point, GA 30344-1999

Brief Contents

INTRODUCTION **MEDIA AND THE INFORMATION SOCIETY**

CHAPTER 1 **Changing Media Environment** 2
CHAPTER 2 **Media Theory** 30

THE MEDIA

CHAPTER 3 **Books and Magazines** 56
CHAPTER 4 **Newspapers** 92
CHAPTER 5 **Radio and Recorded Music** 128
CHAPTER 6 **Film and Video** 168
CHAPTER 7 **Television and Cable** 202
CHAPTER 8 **Computer Media and the Internet** 248
CHAPTER 9 **Communications Infrastructure** 280
CHAPTER 10 **Public Relations** 312
CHAPTER 11 **Advertising** 346

MEDIA ISSUES

CHAPTER 12 **Media and the Individual** 382
CHAPTER 13 **Media and Society** 416
CHAPTER 14 **Media Policy, Law, and Ethics** 450
CHAPTER 15 **Globalization of Communications Media** 484

Contents

PREFACE xviii

CHAPTER 1

CHANGING MEDIA ENVIRONMENT 2

What Is Media Convergence? 5

The Rise of the Internet 5
Converging Technologies 6
Converging Industries 7
Changing Lifestyles 7
Changing Careers 7
Changing Regulations: The Telecommunications Act of 1996 8
Shifting Social Issues 9
The World Wide Web and Mass Media Studies 10
New Term: Communications Media 10
PROFILE: Mr. AOL 11

The Development of Communications Media 12

Preagricultural Society 12
Agricultural Society 12
Industrial Society 13
Information Society 14

Conventional View of Mass Media 15

The SMCR Model 15

Contemporary View of Mass Communication 17

The Audience Is Powerful 17
Emphasis on Interactivity 19
Production to the Desktop, Power to the People? 20

The Digital Revolution 20

Advantages of Digital Media 20
TECHNOLOGY DEMYSTIFIED: A Digital Media Primer 21
TECHNOLOGY DEMYSTIFIED: Sharing with Packet Switching 22
Communications Media Make the Switch to Digital 23
MEDIA WATCH: Watch the Industries Merge and Converge 26

Summary and Review 27

MEDIA IMPACT: The Scandal of the Year 28

INTRODUCTION: MEDIA AND THE INFORMATION SOCIETY

CHAPTER 2

MEDIA THEORY 30

Media Economics 33

Mass Production, Mass Distribution: The Keys to Economic Success 33
Ownership Patterns 35
MEDIA WATCH: Follow the Money 37
The Profit Motive 37

Sources of Media Revenue 38
From Mass Markets to Market Segments 41

Critical Studies 42
Political Economy 42
Setting the Agenda 43
Gatekeeping and Framing 44
Opinion Leaders 45
Literary Criticism 45
The Active Audience 46

Societal Functions of the Media 47
Functions of the Mass Media 47
MEDIA IMPACT: **Where Have All the Theories Gone? 48**
Functions of New Communications Media 49

Social Learning Theory 49
Social Learning of Media Behavior 49
Social Learning vs. Uses and Gratifications 50

Diffusion of Innovations 51
PROFILE: **The Most Widely Cited Living Social Scientist 51**

Summary and Review 53

CHAPTER 3

THE MEDIA

BOOKS AND MAGAZINES 56

A Brief History of Print Communication 58
Early Print Media 58
The Gutenberg Revolution 60
Early Print Media in America 61
MEDIA IMPACT: **Early Magazines and Books 63**
PROFILE: **Savior or Destroyer of The New Yorker? 68**
Modern Publishing 69
MEDIA WATCH: **'Zines 70**

Technology Trends in Books and Magazines 71
Publishing Changes with the Internet 73
TECHNOLOGY TRENDS: **Internet Magazines Get Serious 73**
TECHNOLOGY TRENDS: **Cuddling Up with a Nice Electronic Book 75**

Print Genres and Forms 77
Book Publishing 77
Magazines Genres: Where Does Segmentation Stop? 78

Industry Organization 80
Magazine Industry Consolidation 80
Magazine Distribution 81
Publishing Houses and Groups 81
Bookstores 82
Selling Books and Magazines On-Line 83

Audiences for Books and Magazines 83

Policy Issues for Print Media 85

Consolidation and Concentration of Ownership 85
Intellectual Property and Copyright 86
Censorship, Freedom of Speech, and the First Amendment 87
MEDIA ETHICS: "Sexing Up" Cosmo 88

Summary and Review 89

CHAPTER 4

NEWSPAPERS 92

A Brief History of Newspaper Publishing 94
The Colonial and Revolutionary Periods 94
Newspapers in the 1800s 96
Ethnic and Minority Press 96
The Penny Press and the Rise of Mass Newspapers 97
MEDIA WATCH: The Tweed Ring and the Dangers of the Advertising Bottom Line 100
Pulitzer vs. Hearst: The Rise of Yellow Journalism 100
MEDIA WATCH: Citizen Hearst and the Spanish-American War 101
Newspapers Peak and Decline after 1900 103
Investigative Reporting and Watergate 106

Trends in Newspaper Technology 107
Technology in Newsgathering 108
Technology in Newspaper Production 108
TECHNOLOGY TRENDS: The Fax Gazette: Back to the Future of Newspapers 109
Technology in Newspaper Distribution 109
Technology in Newspaper Advertising 111

Newspaper Industry Organization 112
Newspaper Economics 112
The Newspaper Publishing Industry 112
MEDIA WATCH: Television and McPaper 114

Newspaper Content Genres 116
Newspaper Sections and Contents 116

Audiences for Newspapers 117

Newspaper Policy and Ethical Issues 118
Newspaper Consolidation, Chains, and Shakeout 118
Freedom of Speech and the First Amendment 118
Libel 119
Privacy of Newsmakers 119
Reporting and Content 119
MEDIA ETHICS: The Ethics of "Tabloidization" 120
Accuracy and Truthfulness 120
Coverage of Sex and Scandal 121
MEDIA IMPACT: Matt Drudge Shakes Up the Press 122
Journalism Education 123
Newspapers, Gatekeeping and "Information Glut" 123
PROFILE: Breaking Down Walls 124

Summary and Review 125

CHAPTER 5

RADIO AND RECORDED MUSIC 128

A Brief History of Audio Media 130

Wireless Radio Telegraphy 132
MEDIA IMPACT: **Radio and the Sinking of the *Titanic* 133**
Early Sound Broadcasting 133
MEDIA IMPACT: **David Sarnoff and the Radio Music Box 134**
The Rise of Radio Networks 136
MEDIA WATCH: **BBC, License Fees, and the Road Not Taken 137**
MEDIA IMPACT: **Frank Sinatra, Teen Heart-Throb 138**
The Fall of the Radio Networks 139
The Boom in Recorded Music 139
MEDIA IMPACT: **Allen Freed and the DJ Era 140**
The Rise of FM Radio and Specialized Formats 141

Trends in Audio Technology 144

Audio Recording 144
The Basics of Radio Transmission and Reception 146
TECHNOLOGY DEMYSTIFIED: **Experiments with Electromagnetism 148**

Forms and Genres 149

Radio Musical Genres 149
MEDIA IMPACT: **Teen Idols and Rock 'n' Roll 150**
Music Genres and Radio Formats 151
MEDIA IMPACT: **As Alternative Becomes Dominant 154**

Industry Organization 155

Record Companies 156
Radio Stations 157

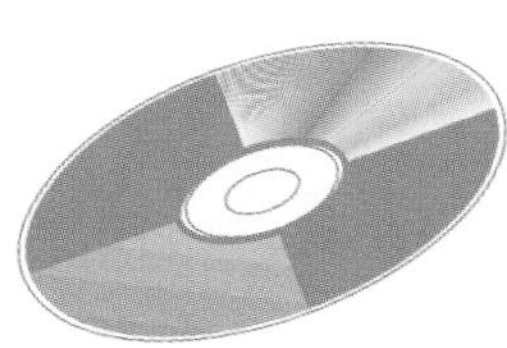

Audiences for Audio Media 158

MEDIA IMPACT: **Is Radio Listening on the Wane? 160**

Policy and Ethical Issues 160

Radio Licensing and Regulation 160
Radio Ownership and Control Rules 161
Networks and Program Control 162
The First Amendment and Freedom of Speech 162
Intellectual Property in Recordings and Radio 163

Summary and Review 163

CHAPTER 6

FILM AND VIDEO 168

A Brief History of Film 170

The Rise of Stars and the Studio System, 1919–1927 172
Revolutionary Talking Pictures 173
The Movie Industry During the Studio Era 174

MEDIA WATCH: Orson Welles's Citizen Kane 175
MEDIA WATCH: Beyond Disney: Chuck Jones's Animation at Warner Brothers 176
Film and Television, 1948–1960 177
Studio Changes and Independent Filmmakers 179
Films on Cable and Video 180
PROFILE: George Lucas 182

Trends in Film Technology 182
Technology of Movie Sound 183
Improving Film Visual Technology 183
Film Special Effects 184
Computer Revolution in Film 184
TECHNOLOGY TRENDS: Steve Jobs's Virtual Film Studio 185
Movie Theater Technology 186

Film Genres 187
Silent Films Set the Patterns 188
Film Genres That Exploit Sound 188
Later Films Expand the Variety of Genres 189

Industry Organization 190
The Film Industry 190
Independent Filmmakers 191
Film Distribution 191
Consolidation and Change in Film Industry Ownership 193

Audiences for Film 194

Policy, Social, and Ethical Issues 195
Violence, Sex, Profanity, and Film Ratings 195
Vertical and Horizontal Integration 196
Film Piracy 196
Film Preservation 197
MEDIA ETHICS: Do Filmmakers Need to Think about Social Impacts? Should Viewers Edit Movies? 198

Summary and Review 199

CHAPTER 7

TELEVISION AND CABLE 202

A Brief History of Television, Cable, and Satellite TV 204
From Radio Networks to Television 205
MEDIA IMPACT: Born on a Mountaintop—Community Antenna TV 206
MEDIA IMPACT: TV from New York to Hollywood 207
MEDIA IMPACT: Murrow, McCarthy, Blacklists, and Politics on TV 208
MEDIA IMPACT: Television and Vietnam 209
Diversifying the Television "Vast Wasteland" 210
MEDIA WATCH: Hollywood Recycles 211

Network Television Faces the Competition in the 1980s–1990s 215
MEDIA ETHICS: Corporate Takeovers and News Emphasis 216
PROFILE: World Media Baron 218

Trends in Television Technology 219
Television Transmission and Reception 219
Cable TV 222
New Multichannel Competition 223
Home Video 223
Digital Television 223

TV Genres 225
From Radio and Film to Television 225
How TV Genres Developed 227
Genres and Forms in Multichannel Programming 228

Industry Organization 230
The Television Industry 230
Cable Industry Structure 234
Network Ownership and Group Station Owners 236
Cable Ownership and Control 236

Audiences for Television 237
Audiences for Multichannel Media 238

Policy and Ethical Issues 239
Ownership Rules 239
Owner Interference with TV News 240
Violence Warnings and Controls 241
Diversity and Minority Ownership 242
Fairness Doctrine 243
MEDIA ETHICS: What Do You Do When the Truck Doesn't Blow Up? 243
The Need to Visualize TV News 244

Summary and Review 244

CHAPTER 8

COMPUTER MEDIA AND THE INTERNET 248

A Brief History of Computer Media 250
The Dawn of the Computer Age 250
Preparing for Doomsday: The First Computer Networks 251
The Rise of the Personal Computer 252
The Birth of On-Line Services 253
Shifting Fortunes, Shifting Technology in Personal Computing 253
The Evolution of the World Wide Web 254

Trends in Computer Media Technology 254
Trends in Computer Media Hardware 254
Computer Media Software Trends 256
PROFILE: Mother of the Computer 257
Future Directions in Computer Media 257

TECHNOLOGY TRENDS: Computers Read My Mind, Caressed My Flesh! 258
Web Technology Trends 261

Computer Media Genres 261
Internet Functions, Internet Protocols 261
TECHNOLOGY DEMYSTIFIED: Make Your Own Web Page! 262
What's on the Web? 264
Computer Software Genres 266

Using Computer Media 267
MEDIA IMPACT: Who are the "Have-Nots"? 267

Structure of the Computer Media Industry 268
Computer Hardware Industry 268
Computer Software Industry 269
Content Providers 269
Who Runs the Internet? 270

Policy, Social, and Ethical Issues 270
Ownership and Control 270
Internet Governance 271
MEDIA IMPACT: Join in the Debate 271
Censorship 272
Antisocial Behavior 273
Encryption 274
User Privacy 274
MEDIA ETHICS: Ethical Internet Surfing 275
Intellectual Property 276
MEDIA IMPACT: Finding Safe Harbor in Copyright Bay 277

Summary and Review 278

CHAPTER 9

COMMUNICATIONS INFRASTRUCTURE 280

Historical Development of the Information Infrastructure 282
From Telegraph to Telephone 282
The Government vs. AT&T 284
The Video Infrastructure: Cable Television 285
The Government vs. Cable 285
The Wireless Infrastructure 285
The Rise of the Internet 286
The Government Steps Aside 287
MEDIA IMPACT: Monitoring the Telecom Act 287

Trends in Infrastructure Technology 288
The First Telephone 288
Overcoming Distance 289
Untangling the Wires—Advances in Transmission Technology 289
TECHNOLOGY DEMYSTIFIED: Satellites 291
TECHNOLOGY DEMYSTIFIED: Fiber Optics: Why You Can Hear a Pin Drop 292

Getting Where You Want to Go: Switching 292
Becoming Digital: Trends in Digital Networks 293
MEDIA WATCH: **The Fight of the (Next) Century: Cable Telephone or Telco TV? 294**
TECHNOLOGY TRENDS: **Keep Track of Your Internet Options 296**
Communicating Anywhere: Mobile Communication Trends 297

Infrastructure Services 298
Residential Services 298
Business Services 299

Using the Infrastructure 300

Industry Organization 300
Telephone Carriers 301
Internet Service Providers 302
PROFILE: **The Convergence Cowboy 302**
Internet Organization 303
Cable Television 303
Mobile Carriers 303
Satellite Carriers 303
Private Networks 304
Equipment Manufacturers 304

Issues in the Infrastructure Industry 305
Ownership and Control 305
Content Control 306
Subsidies 306
Universal Service 307
Spectrum Allocation 308
Network Security 308
Piracy 309

Summary and Review 310

CHAPTER 10

PUBLIC RELATIONS 312

History of Public Relations 314
Hail Caesar! 314
The Origins of Modern Public Relations 315
The American Way 316
Public Relations in the Age of Robber Barons 316
PR Pioneers 317
Public Relations Matures 320
Rise of Public Relations Ethics 320

Trends in Public Relations Technology 321
New Mass Media—TV Leads the Way 321
Videoconferencing 322
Satellite Broadcasting 322
Video News Releases 323
MEDIA WATCH: **Tips for Effective Video News Releases 324**
Personal Computer 325

Advanced Telephony 326
The Internet—A New Dimension for Public Relations 327

Forms of Public Relations 329
MEDIA WATCH: **Cyber Crisis–A New Public Relations Worry 330**
The Publics of Public Relations 333
Good vs. Bad PR: A Commentary 333
PROFILE: **The Personal Touch 334**
MEDIA IMPACT: **A Year in the Life of a Public Relations Campaign 335**
Elements of Successful Public Relations 335
Industry Demographics 337

Public Relations Issues 339
Private Interests vs. the Public Interest 339
MEDIA ETHICS: **From the PRSA Code of Professional Standards for the Practice of Public Relations 341**
Professional Ethics 341
Professional Development 342
Use of Research and Evaluation 342
Public Relations and Society 343

Summary and Review 343

CHAPTER 11

ADVERTISING 346

A Brief History of Advertising 348
Advertising in America 349
The Rise of the Advertising Profession 350
Hard Sell vs. Soft Sell 352
The Era of Integrated Marketing Communication (IMC) 353

Trends in Advertising Technology 353
TECHNOLOGY TRENDS: **Advertising Agencies of Tomorrow: How One Company Is Integrating New Media 355**

Advertising Industry Organization 357
Advertisers 358
Inside the Advertising Agency 359
MEDIA WATCH: **Elements of an Advertising Plan or Campaign 360**
PROFILE: **Creative Philosopher 361**
Advertising Media 361
Research 363

Advertising Genres 366
One-Voice Marketing 366
Use of Popular Culture 367
Relationship Marketing 368
Direct Marketing 368
MEDIA WATCH: **Other Forms of Marketing Communication Related to Advertising 369**

Other Forms of Advertising Communication 370
The Key to Success: Understanding Consumer Needs 371

The Advertising Audience 371
The Media Evaluation Model 373

Advertising Issues 374
Ethics 374
Promotion of "Consumption Values" 374
Advertising and Children 375
Stereotyping of Women and Minorities 376
Privacy and Intrusiveness 377
Deception and "Puffery" 377
MEDIA ETHICS: Advertising and "Ethics" 378
Media Literacy 379

Summary & Review 380

MEDIA ISSUES

CHAPTER 12

MEDIA AND THE INDIVIDUAL 382

Research on Effects of the Media 386
The Deductive Approach 386
The Inductive Approach 386
Quantitative vs. Qualitative Methods 386
MEDIA IMPACT: Critical Communication Theory 387
Content Analysis 387
TECHNOLOGY TRENDS: On-Line Research Methods 389
Experimental Research 389
Survey Research 391
MEDIA ETHICS: Would You Mind Answering a Few of Our Questions? 392
Ethnographic Research 393
TECHNOLOGY DEMYSTIFIED: The Science of Sampling 394

Theories of Media Effects 395
Media as Hypodermic Needle 395
The Multistep Flow 397
Selective Processes 397
Social Learning Theory 398
Cultivation Theory 398
Priming 399
Other Perspectives 399

Communications Media and Antisocial Behavior 399
Violence 399
MEDIA IMPACT: A Critical View of Media, Violence, and Culture 400
Prejudice 401
Sexual Behavior 403
Drug Abuse 404
The Effects of Computer Media 405
MEDIA IMPACT: The Social Effects of the Internet 407

Communications Media and Prosocial Behavior 408
Information Campaigns 408
Informal Education 410

The Effects of Advertising 411

The Effects of Political Communication 412

Summary and Review 414

CHAPTER 13

MEDIA AND SOCIETY 416

Understanding Societal Effects 418
Individual Effects vs. Societal Effects 418
Social Criticism 419
MEDIA WATCH: Forecasting the Telephone 420

Communications Media and Social Inequality 421
Political Economy 422
The Knowledge Gap 423
A Hidden Curriculum? 424
MEDIA IMPACT: Women and Telephones: A Feminist Critique 425
Race and Gender 426

Communications Media and Community 426
The Global Village 427
TECHNOLOGY DEMYSTIFIED: Joining the Luddites 428
Social Fragmentation 428
Being There 429
Health and Environment 429

Communications Media and Culture 430
Technological Determinism 431
Cultural Determinism 431
Mass Media and Mass Culture 432
PROFILE: The Thoroughly Postmodern Postman 433

Communications Media and Social Institutions 433
Communications Media and Educational Institutions 434
Communications Media and Political Institutions 435
Communications Media and Economic Institutions 437
TECHNOLOGY TRENDS: Home, Sweet Office 444
MEDIA WATCH: What About *Your* Job? 447

Summary and Review 448

CHAPTER 14

MEDIA POLICY, LAW, AND ETHICS 450

Policy, Law, and Ethics in Communications 452

Key Communications Policies 453
Freedom of Speech and the First Amendment 453
Limits on the First Amendment 455

MEDIA ETHICS: A Question of Ethics 455
MEDIA IMPACT: George Carlin and "Seven Dirty Words" 458
The Fourth Amendment and Privacy 460
MEDIA IMPACT: Consumer Privacy Tips 461
MEDIA IMPACT: Consumer Privacy Rights 462
Patent and Copyright Law: Protecting Intellectual Property 463
Ownership Issues 464
Concentration of Ownership 466
Access to Media and Universal Service 467
The Radio Acts and Frequency Allocation 468
Defining Technical Standards for Media 469

The Policymaking Process 470
Federal Regulation and Policy Making 471
State and Local Regulation 474
Lobbies 474
The Fifth Estate: The Media in the Policy Process 475

Ethics in the Communications Media 475
General Considerations in Individual Ethics 476
Codes of Ethics 476
MEDIA IMPACT: Social Responsibility and Ethics 477
Ethical Issues for Media Professionals 477
MEDIA ETHICS: Society of Professional Journalists' Code of Ethics 478

Summary and Review 481

CHAPTER 15

GLOBALIZATION OF COMMUNICATIONS MEDIA 484

Media: Global, Regional, National, Local 486

Comparisons of National Communications Media Systems 489
MEDIA IMPACT: How Different Media Systems Would Handle a Major Nuclear Disaster 492

Media and Information Flows 493

Globalization of Media Companies and Operations 493
PROFILE: Global Media Giant 494
MEDIA WATCH: Top Mass Media Firms 495

Major Media Systems: National and Global 496
Newspapers 496
Magazines and Books 497
Radio Broadcasting 498
MEDIA IMPACT: The Cuban-American Radio War 499
Music 500
Film 501
MEDIA IMPACT: *Titanic* Sinks Iranian Culture? 502
Television 503
MEDIA IMPACT: Soap Operas around the World 506

Cable and Satellite TV around the World 506
Telecommunications Systems 507
Computers and Information Services Spreading Slowly Worldwide 509
MEDIA IMPACT: **Bangalore Joins the World Computer Economy 509**
The Internet 511
MEDIA IMPACT: **The Zapatista Revolution on the Internet 512**
Telecommunications Industries: Global Providers 513
TECHNOLOGY TRENDS: **Political Security: A Closed or an Open Internet—The Great Red Firewall of China 514**

Regulation of International Media 515

Issues in the Globalization of Media 516
Cultural Imperialism 516
Free Flow of Information versus Cultural Sovereignty 517
Trade in Media 517
Media and National Development 518

Summary and Review 519

CREDITS 522

GLOSSARY 523

REFERENCES 531

INDEX 543

Preface

We wrote this book to be the first in a new generation of textbooks about mass communications. Our focus is on the kinds of communications that are mediated by technology. We expanded that focus to include new media technologies that were rapidly becoming "mass" media, such as computers, the Internet, and telecommunications. Our theme is that the convergence of these technologies is creating a new communications environment. Our goal is to prepare students to thrive in that environment.

The specific reason we wrote this book is that we could not find an existing introductory mass communications textbook that adequately prepares our students for the real world as it stands today. Our new title for the second edition, *MEDIA NOW: Communications Media in the Information Age,* reflects our desire to focus on the cutting edge of both the traditional mass media (magazines, books, newspapers, radio, film, and television) and the new media (computer media, Internet, and telecommunications).

We saw too many students diligently studying mass media in the traditional way—only to discover after graduation that the vast majority of today's real jobs require skills and a knowledge base that their textbooks had barely touched on.

In the last few years, students in advertising, journalism, and public relations have often found jobs faster if they also know how to design and construct a Web page and how to find information on the Web. Students also find jobs in innovative places—at phone companies, in corporate communications divisions, and so on—but discover that they do not always know enough to succeed in these new environments. Their introductory textbooks paid little or no attention to the telecommunications and computer industries and to how industries that had always been disparate are now converging.

Since our first edition, the Telecommunications Act of 1996 changed the rules to further encourage convergence and competition across media industries. That has led to fairly traditional combinations, such as the merging of movie studios, television networks, and cable operations, and also to new alliances such as the one created when NBC and Microsoft joined forces to produce both a cable news channel and Web site.

Today's television production or journalism students are as likely to end up working for a media conglomerate controlled by an electronics company as they are for a stand-alone TV station or magazine. Those students need to understand the large, diverse interests of such firms if they are to rise in the company from their first jobs. Many of the best entry-level jobs in the Information Society, for which a well-prepared communications student can compete, are outside the traditional mass media—in Internet Service Providers, software design firms, or telephone companies.

This book shows where today's communications industries came from and how they got to where they are. But, more importantly, it also seriously assesses their trajectories into the future. It helps students understand how mass media are being transformed as they converge with technologies such as the computer, Internet, and telephone. It helps them create a vision of their future in the Information Society and information economy.

Our purpose is not to be cheerleaders for communication technology. In fact, we try to raise critical issues about the implications of information technologies parallel to our discussion of the implications of mass media. However, we have seen the lights turn on behind our students' eyes when we begin a class discussion with a headline from the morning paper. They realize that the convergence of technologies we are talking about is not dry history or mere speculation, but is really happening right now. Most of them already have some personal experience with it, and the rest have a strong curiosity about it. It is important to expose them to—and to demystify—communications technologies. This book is designed to help both professor and student do that.

NEW TO THIS EDITION

In this second edition, our goal is retain our book's innovative coverage of technology and convergence, but within a more traditional table of contents and with a streamlined narrative. We have expanded our coverage of traditional media, and now have separate full chapters for magazine and book publishing, newspapers, audio and radio, film, and TV.

New Chapters

There is more in-depth coverage of traditional media in four new chapters:

- Chapter 3, "Books and Magazines," has more extensive coverage of these media in a separate chapter.
- Chapter 4, "Newspapers," is now a separate chapter to give more in-depth coverage to that key industry, as it continues both traditional publishing and enters into new electronic forms.
- Chapter 6, "Film and Video," expands coverage of these media to a full new chapter.
- Chapter 7, "TV and Cable," expands and combines coverage of television and cable programming.

We have expanded and updated coverage of computer media with a new chapter:

- Chapter 8, "Computer Media and the Internet," focuses our coverage of computers on their communication uses and combines that with in-depth coverage of the Internet.

The dramatic shifts in communications infrastructure are the focus of a new chapter:

- Chapter 9, "Communications Infrastructure," covers the rapid convergence of telephony, cable, and satellite technologies as a basis for delivering a wide variety of media, including cable TV channels, telephone calls, e-mail, and Web pages. This chapter also traces the history of this dramatic convergence as well as the implications for us and our society.

The new edition also boosts the coverage of the relationship between media and society, media and the individual, and ethics with two new chapters:

- Chapter 12, "Media and the Individual," addresses media effects from both a behavioral and critical focus.
- Chapter 13, " Media and Society," looks at the broader context of how media interact with society from both a social science and critical perspective.

We have also considerably expanded our coverage of ethical issues and updated and revised information on policy and law in a new chapter:

- Chapter 14, "Media Policy, Law, and Ethics," examines formal media law on freedom of speech and other issues; the broad range of policy and regulation of privacy, ownership, and standards; as well as ethical issues for journalists and other communicators. We have also included more material on policy and ethics in each media chapter.

Integrated Coverage of Economics

We also now integrate economics coverage throughout rather than isolating it in a single chapter. Plus, in the revised Chapter 2, "Media Theory," we provide students with a broad foundation for understanding the economics of specific media covered later in the book.

Expanded History

As educators, we owe our students an introduction to mass communications that is both cutting-edge as well as historic, so Chapter 1, "Changing Media Environment," now includes the development of the Information Society and the basics of media convergence. For greater perspective, we have expanded our coverage of the history of communications media throughout the book.

Demystifying Technology

With the help of reviewer feedback, we increased the clarity of technical explanations, and continue to provide students with much better coverage of emerging technologies than is typical of other texts. In this edition, we assume no technical sophistication on the student's part. Our explanations of technology are easy to read while still providing vital detail. We also include a great deal of anecdotal material to bring the subject to life. The historical treatments begin with the very earliest forms of each technology or medium, since these are the easiest starting points for non-technical readers.

Global Media

The revised and updated Chapter 15, "Globalization of Communications Media," looks at how countries are developing media comparatively, the globalization of media companies, and the increasing flow of media around the world.

New Features

This book comes with a rich set of new features to aid in learning:

- *What's Ahead* Each chapter opens with a brief summary of the chapter.
- *Chapter Outline* A succinct chapter outline provides a quick view of the main topics.
- *Glossary* Key terms are defined in the margins, and a complete glossary is included in the back of the book.
- *Time Lines* Major events in each media industry are summarized in chart form.
- *Internet Links* Throughout the book, students are encouraged to use Internet links to learn more about the media.
- *Boxed Features* Six new boxed features are designed to target specific issues:

  Media Ethics analyzes an ethical issue in depth, followed by questions for reflection.

  Profile focuses on key media figures.

  Media Watch focuses on economics/business developments.

  Media Impact examines the impact of some key aspect of media on the individual and society.

  Technology Demystified explains technological background information simply.

  Technology Trends focuses on technological changes in the various media.

- *Electronic Resources* Many of the boxes and sources cited contain electronic resources—places to look on the Internet or in InfoTrac College Edition for further information. (See below for more information about this resource.)

New Resources for Students and Teachers

For this new edition, important new resources are now available:

- *Book-Specific Web Site* For instructors, this site provides sample syllabi, PowerPoint® slides, updated test item questions, suggested readings, a career hotlink, and a "contact the authors" section. For students and instructors, there are chapter-by-chapter interactive quizzes, an on-line glossary, relevant Internet links for further information on various topics, and updated and additional chapter information. http://communication.wadsworth.com/
- *CNN Mass Communication Video* To help stimulate class discussions, a series of CNN videos, with segments keyed to material in the text, is available to professors by arrangement with Wadsworth. Contact your local Wadsworth sales representative or call 1-877-999-2350, ext. 875.
- *InfoTrac® College Edition* A fully searchable, on-line database, which is updated daily, provides students access to complete articles from over 600 scholarly and popular periodicals, dating back 4 years. This database allows students to expand their knowledge of media issues with contemporary articles from all the major media and video clips from library and network news sources. Exercises for using InfoTrac College Edition are included in a variety of boxed features throughout the text. Additional questions will be featured on the book-specific Web site.
- *Revised Instructor's Manual* with Test Questions, Lecture Guides, Transparency Masters, and transition notes reflecting changes from the previous edition.
- *New PowerPoint® Presentation CD-ROM* Designed to work with PowerPoint®, this flexible presentation tool includes text and images to illustrate concepts in this text.

- *Thomson Learning Testing Tools*™ Test creation and grading for essay, multiple-choice, fill-in, and matching are available in cross-platform (Win/Mac) with these testing tools. Flexible delivery via print, diskette, LAN, WAN or Internet is featured. Instructors will have ability to scramble, test, and grade on-line, and create multiple versions of a test.

ACKNOWLEDGMENTS

We wish to thank our spouses, Sandy Straubhaar and Betty Whipple, for both their patience and valuable ideas. We also want to thank several helpful graduate students, Patrice Sheffer, Drew Bolyard, Jennifer Gregg, and David Weinstock, for research assistance and feedback, and a number of our undergraduate students, as well as Julia, Rolf, and Chris Straubhaar for insights into their culture and concerns.

We would also like too thank our team at Wadsworth Publishing: Sherry Symington, our development editor; Deirdre Cavanaugh, executive editor; Karen Austin, editor; Cathy Linberg, project editor; Ryan Vesely, associate development editor; and Andrea Fincke, our production editor at Thompson Steele.

We wish to thank the following reviewers for their thoughtful suggestions and guidance in the preparation of this book: Erik Bucy, Indiana University; Larry Campbell, University of Alaska–Anchorage; Richard Caplan, University of Akron; Meta Carstarphen, University of North Texas; John Chapin, Rutgers University; Dan Close, Wichita State University; David Donnelly, University of Houston; Tom Grimes, Kansas State University; Larry Haapanen, Lewis and Clark State College; Jack Hodgson, Oklahoma State University; Kevin Howley, Northeastern University; Howard Keim, Tabor College; Randall King, Point Loma Nazarene University; Seong H. Lee, Appalachian State University; William Lingle, Linfield College; Linda Lumsden, Western Kentucky University; Kyle Nicholas, University of Texas–Austin; Daniel Panici, University of Southern Maine; Arthur Raney, Indiana University; Joseph Russomanno, Arizona State University; Marc Ryan, Marist College; Tom Shaker, Northeastern University; Michael Ray Taylor, Henderson State University; Max Utsler, University of Kansas; Hazel Warlaumont, California State University–Fullerton; Clifford Wexler, Columbia–Greene Community College; Alan Winegarden, Concordia University; J. Emmett Winn, Auburn University; and Phyllis Zagano, Boston University.

We also thank the following individuals for their reviews of the previous edition: Sandra Braman, University of Illinois–Champaign; Joseph Chuk, Kutztown University of Pennsylvania; Michael Doyle, Arkansas State; Linda Fuller, Worcester State College; Ken Hadwiger, Eastern Illinois University; Rick Houlberg, San Francisco State University; James Hoyt, University of Wisconsin–Green Bay; Peter Pringle, University of Tennessee–Chattanooga; Humphrey Regis, University of South Florida; Marshall Rossow, Mankato State University; Gay Russell, Grossmont College; Roger Soenksen, James Madison University; and Don Tomlinson, Texas A&M University.

CHAPTER 1

Changing Media Environment

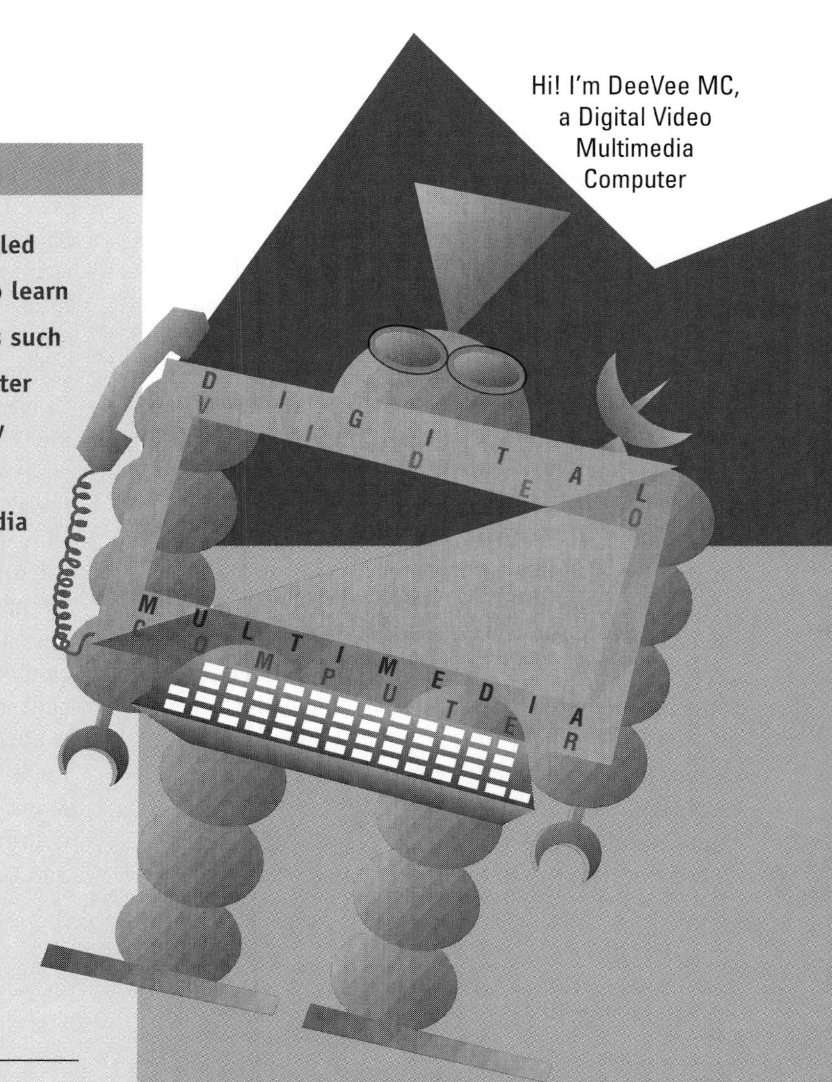
Hi! I'm DeeVee MC,
a Digital Video
Multimedia
Computer
DIGITAL
VIDEO
MULTIMEDIA
COMPUTER

WHAT'S AHEAD

To learn about what has been traditionally called mass communication, it's no longer enough to learn about the conventional mass media industries such as print, radio, television, and film. This chapter examines how traditional mass media and new computer and telecommunications media are converging to create new communications media that have profound effects on every aspect of our lives.

WWW

Access the MEDIA NOW site on the World Wide Web at:
http://communication.wadsworth.com/
Choose "Chapter 1" from the selection box to access electronic information and other sites relevant to this chapter.

A GLIMPSE INTO HELL

An evening at home in Hell, Michigan, with the Digital Video Multimedia Computer (DVMC) machine, 2010.

ESPN8—Detroit Sports—Pro-Am Sports—Southeast Michigan Sports—HellSports—

Honey, quit channel surfing and switch over to Interactive Movie Classics. I want to remake *Gone with the Wind* using Madonna and Leonardo deCaprio.

NFL—Volleyball—Synchronized Swimming—Water Polo—Scuba—Sportrivia—

D-a-a-a-d, I have to watch my calculus tutorial NOW, or I'll miss the live interactive feed from Ann Arbor!

Sportnews—Sportstalk—Baseball Card Auction—Sports Movie Classics—Sports Memorabilia Shopping—Sports Newsreel—Sports Music—

And I promised I'd video Gramma to show her my new talking sneakers!

Golf Virtuality Game—Old Tiger Stadium bleachers—Old Tiger Stadium press box—Old Tiger Stadium upper deck—

That does it! Kids, I'm taking charge with my remote control override. Lock out Dad's controller, NOW!

Your DVMC has detected family dysfunction. Tuning to the Family Counseling Channel.

Not again!!!

Chapter Outline

What Is Media Convergence?
The Rise of the Internet
Converging Technologies
Converging Industries
Changing Lifestyles
Changing Careers
Changing Regulations: The Telecommunications Act of 1996
Shifting Social Issues
The World Wide Web and Mass Media Studies
New Term: Communications Media
The Development of Communications Media
Preagricultural Society
Agricultural Society
Industrial Society
Information Society
Conventional View of Mass Media
The SMCR Model
Contemporary View of Mass Communication
The Audience Is Powerful
Emphasis on Interactivity
Production to the Desktop, Power to the People?
The Digital Revolution
Advantages of Digital Media
Communications Media Make the Switch to Digital
Summary and Review

The average American spends 2700 hours per year watching TV or listening to radio. That's 337 eight-hour days, a full-time job! We spend another 800 hours absorbed in other media, such as recorded music, books, newspapers, magazines, and the Internet (Dizard, 1997). That's 3500 hours of media use—more time than we spend on anything else, including working or sleeping (Hamlin, 1995).

The consumption of information is increasingly what sustains our economy. On the job, most of the economic activity in the United States now involves producing, processing, or distributing information, including the output of the mass media, telecommunications, and computer industries. **Information workers** now dominate the work force, and the proportion of workers engaged in information work has more than doubled in the space of a single generation (Dordick & Wang, 1993; Schement & Curtis, 1997). Information workers include computer programmers, television producers, journalists, advertising account executives, accountants, secretaries, and file clerks. Even in agricultural and manufacturing occupations, which dominated the world of work as late as the 1950s, information technologies are increasingly important. The impact of these changes is so sweeping that many observers have concluded that we now live in an **information society.**

Information workers produce, process, or distribute information as their primary work activity.

In the **information society,** exchange of information is the predominant economic and social activity.

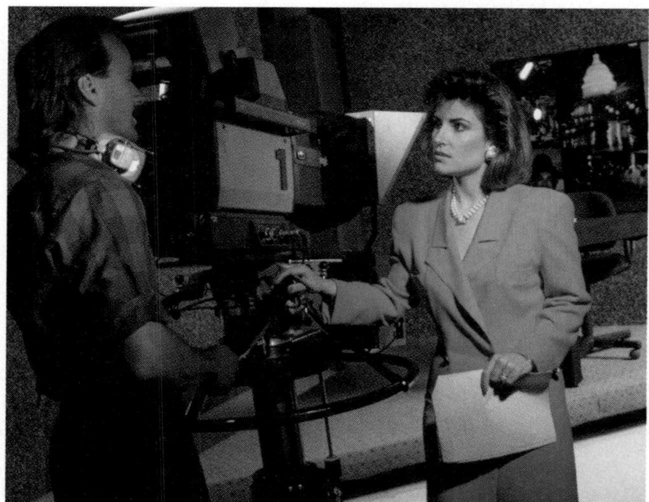

ACTION!
Information workers, such as this TV director, are now the dominant occupational group in American society.

COMPUTER MEDIA TIME LINE

4000 B.C.	Agriculture and writing originate in ancient Sumer
1712	Industrial Revolution begins with invention of steam engine
1833	First urban newspaper with mass circulation
1900	U.S. an agricultural society
1910	U.S. transition to industrial society; film mass medium
1927	Radio becomes mass medium
1948	Wilbur Schramm publishes SMCR model
1960	U.S. transition to information society
1962	First digital phone system
1967	Newspapers computerize
1975	First personal computer
1980	Nora and Minc originate convergence concept
1980	Critical communications perspective gains followers
1982	CD, first digital music recording medium
1993	World Wide Web
1995	*Toy Story,* the first all-digital movie
1996	Telecommunications Act reforms U.S. media policy; communications studies "discovers" the Internet
1998	First V-chip; Microsoft antitrust suit is filed; first U.S. HDTV broadcasts, merger mania hits telecommunications industry

WHAT IS MEDIA CONVERGENCE?

The transition to an information society is accelerating because of rapid changes in technology. It is no longer meaningful to talk about the various media of communication—print, radio, television, film, telephones, and computers—as though they were completely distinct entities. Advances in computers and telecommunications networks have led to their merging, or **convergence,** with conventional mass media.

This convergence is apparent in many different ways. We see it in the rise of the Internet, the integration of communications technologies, the merging of media empires, new lifestyles, new careers, changing regulations, and shifting social issues—even in the way we study the mass media.

Convergence is the integration of mass media, computers, and telecommunications into a common technological and institutional base.

The **Internet** is a network of computer networks used worldwide for electronic communication.

The Rise of the Internet

Recently, the **Internet** has become almost synonymous with the concept of the *information superhighway.* The Internet is a "network of networks" that connects computers worldwide so that they can exchange messages with one another and share access to files of computer data (December, 1996). The **World Wide Web** ("the Web," for short) is that portion of the Internet that is rich in graphics and that allows users to navigate between **Web pages** by selecting key words or graphical symbols.

Many Web pages offer audio and video as well as text and graphics and thus epitomize the convergence of conventional communications media and computer

The **World Wide Web** (the "Web," for short) is the portion of the Internet that links users to graphical, audio, and video information.

Web pages are the individual locations, or sites, where information is found on the Web.

The World Wide Web provides a model of the convergence of newspapers, radio, and television on high-speed data networks. Note the video and audio links on the toolbar, which lead to audio and video feeds.

technologies. The Internet is thus the model for the communications media environment of tomorrow: a high-speed computer network through which we can read news stories, watch video, listen to music, and converse with our family, friends, and co-workers with equal ease. With personal computer penetration now around 50 percent and prices plunging into the "impulse buy" range, the Internet is coming within reach of most Americans.

Converging Technologies

Digital means computer-readable.

Compact discs are digital recording media originally used for music, but now also used to store computer data and video as well as audio.

Digital television is television that is transmitted in a digital format.

All communications technologies are rapidly converging into a common computer-readable, **digital** form (Baldwin, McVoy, & Steinfield, 1996; Negroponte, 1995; Cairncross, 1997; Dizard, 1997). For example, music in the form of **compact discs** is one type of digital medium (see page 21) and the public long-distance telephone network is another digital medium. Even traditional print media such as books, magazines, and newspapers are usually created on computers and leave this digital environment only when printed out on paper. Furthermore, because increasing numbers of people are reading on-line versions of leading newspapers and magazines over the Internet, "print" media are, in effect, becoming part of the digital world. Radio, television, and home video are in the midst of a revolutionary conversion to digital technology that will have profound effects on the way we think of mass media in the future. The introduction of **digital television** could be the pivotal event that puts a computer processor—and the information society—in virtually every home. Conversely, every personal computer may soon be able to play television programs. Technological convergence is already quite advanced in the world of work, where high-capacity corporate networks freely mix digitized phone conversations, electronic documents, computer data, and video transmissions. The future evolution of the Internet may allow all of us access to the same array of services in our homes.

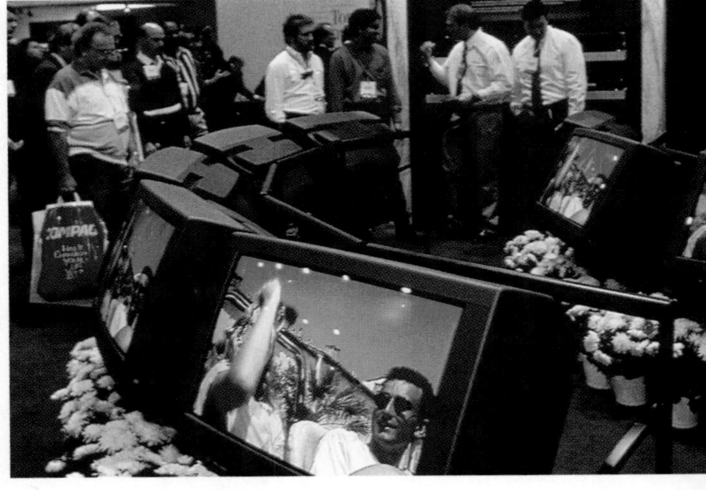

FUTURE TV.
High-definition television (HDTV) puts a computer in every television set and means a larger and sharper picture.

Converging Industries

Telephone, computer, cable television, and media firms are merging and forming partnerships at a dizzying rate in an effort to get the upper hand in the race to control the future of the media (see Figure 1.1). For example, computer software giant Microsoft Corporation has made investments in the broadcasting, cable television, satellite, publishing, and Internet service industries in an effort to be at the forefront of merging mass media and computer media. Long-distance telephone giant AT&T bought cable television giant Tele-Communications, Inc. (TCI). NBC Television and Disney both acquired their own Internet search engines to gain a more visible presence in the new computer medium. Formerly distinct channels of communication, such as telephone and television, can now be integrated into a single digital network, so it makes sense to forge alliances across formerly rigid industry boundaries. Meanwhile, large businesses and public institutions are reinventing themselves to take advantage of new ways of doing business made possible by the technological convergence (Dyson, 1997).

Changing Lifestyles

When computer media enter our homes, mass media consumption patterns tend to change. According to one study, a third of Internet users actually spend less time watching television than they did before (Miller & Clemente, 1997). Convergence is also introducing us to new ways to live, as millions now work (Dizard, 1997), form social relationships (Parks & Floyd, 1996), forge new identities (Turkle, 1997), and develop new cultures (Dery, 1996) “on the Net.” All this could mean more life choices, lower prices of goods and services purchased directly from suppliers, and a better quality of life for the average family. But it might also degrade human relationships by replacing them with impersonal computer transactions.

Changing Careers

For those considering a career in the information society, convergence will make jobs and careers highly volatile as companies continually re-engineer themselves and compete on a global scale. Most people entering the work force today will have four or five different *careers*—not just jobs, but careers—in their future. That means that the student considering a professional career in journalism, advertising, or television (or even computer science) will eventually have to retool for several very different professions—or join the “have-nots” in the lower strata of the information society.

FIGURE 1.1
Information technology and media are converging in the information society.

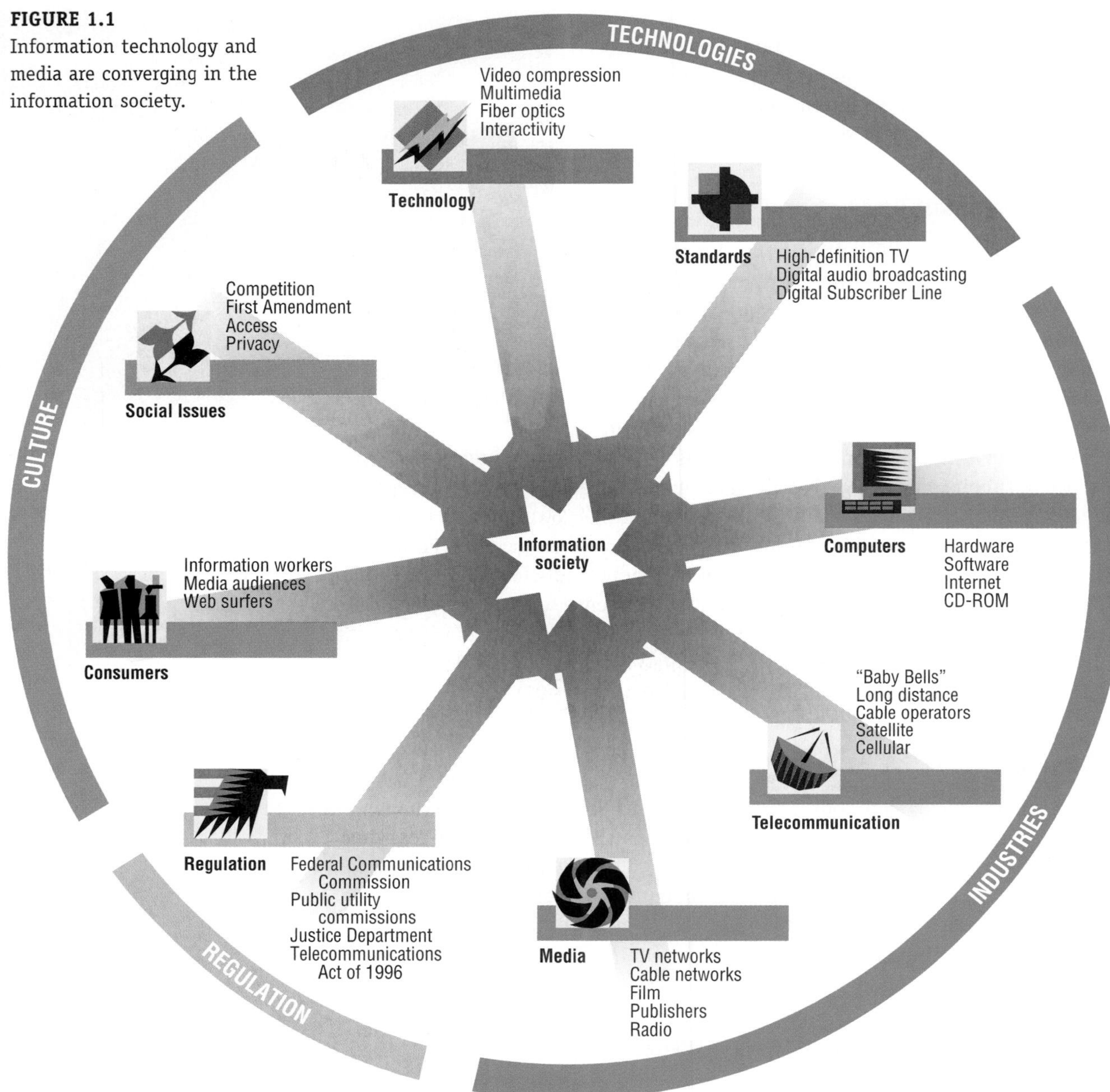

Changing Regulations: The Telecommunications Act of 1996

The convergence of traditional mass media with telephone and computer technologies is also now the official policy of the U.S. government. In the Telecommunications Act of 1996 (discussed in Chapter 14), Congress stripped away the regulations that had protected broadcasting, cable television, telephone, and other telecommunications companies from competition with one another (Baldwin,

McVoy, & Steinfield, 1996). With the new law, lawmakers hoped to spark competition, improve service, and lower prices in all communications media. Countries around the world are following suit in deregulating their own communications industries, as they race to build advanced communications networks that they hope will give them a competitive advantage in the global economy of the Information Age.

Shifting Social Issues

But this melding of media also gives rise to numerous social and political issues that force their way to the top of the public agenda. These issues range from the effects of new forms of violence, racism, and sexism that reach us via computer to the threats to personal freedoms engendered by the spread of advanced computer networks (Dyson, 1997). Converging technology also raises mounting concerns about job security within rapidly changing information industries, about equal opportunity for those with obsolete skills, about privacy in a world of computerized record keeping, about the health of those who overuse communications technology, and about the ever-widening gap between the rich who have access to those technologies and the poor who don't. Some fear that convergence may put us at the mercy of "digital robber barons," who will use their monopoly power over the new digital media to enrich themselves at our expense by charging high prices, destroying their competitors, and withholding innovations. The antitrust action filed by the U.S. government against Microsoft in 1998 is intended to stem its perceived monopoly in the computer software business. The issue is global, as well. The flow of information across international boundaries and the balance of trade in information technologies and communications services are increasingly sources of conflict in relations between nations (Cairncross, 1997). These issues will be discussed further in Chapters 14 and 15.

Meanwhile, the mass media have become social issues in themselves. They are criticized for contributing to violence, sexual promiscuity, economic exploitation, mindless consumption, and irresponsible government. Internet pornography now contends with television violence as the leading focus of concern about the media's impact on society. But the convergence of computers and conventional mass media also holds out the hope for new ways to correct old media ills. For example, the new V-chip allows parents to shield children from offensive programs, and a new content-rating system for the Internet might solve the pornography problem there. The Internet also offers access to more diverse political coverage and empowers entrepreneurs to cut out profit-draining middlepersons by communicating directly with their customers.

LANDMARK LEGISLATION. The Telecommunications Act of 1996 represents a radical shift in U.S. government policy toward communications media.

One Hundred Fourth Congress
of the
United States of America

AT THE SECOND SESSION

Begun and held at the City of Washington on Wednesday, the third day of January, one thousand nine hundred and ninety-six

An Act

To promote competition and reduce regulation in order to secure lower prices and higher quality services for American telecommunications consumers and encourage the rapid deployment of new telecommunications technologies.

Be it enacted by the Senate and House of Representatives of the United States of America in Congress assembled,

SECTION 1. SHORT TITLE; REFERENCES.

(a) SHORT TITLE.—This Act may be cited as the "Telecommunications Act of 1996".

(b) REFERENCES.—Except as otherwise expressly provided, whenever in this Act an amendment or repeal is expressed in terms of an amendment to, or repeal of, a section or other provision, the reference shall be considered to be made to a section or other provision of the Communications Act of 1934 (47 U.S.C. 151 et seq.).

SEC. 2. TABLE OF CONTENTS.

The table of contents for this Act is as follows:

Sec. 1. Short title; references.
Sec. 2. Table of contents.
Sec. 3. Definitions.

TITLE I—TELECOMMUNICATION SERVICES

Subtitle A—Telecommunications Services

Sec. 101. Establishment of part II of title II.

"PART II—DEVELOPMENT OF COMPETITIVE MARKETS

"Sec. 251. Interconnection.
"Sec. 252. Procedures for negotiation, arbitration, and approval of agreements.
"Sec. 253. Removal of barriers to entry.
"Sec. 254. Universal service.
"Sec. 255. Access by persons with disabilities.
"Sec. 256. Coordination for interconnectivity.
"Sec. 257. Market entry barriers proceeding.

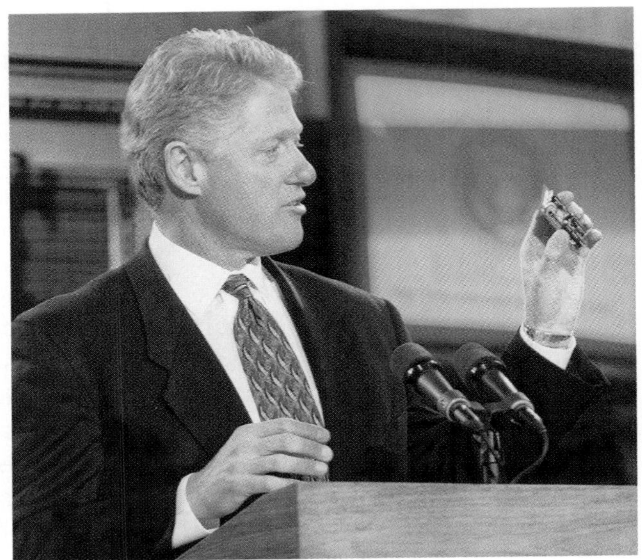

TECHNOPOLITICAL CONVERGENCE. President Clinton holds up the prototype of the V-chip, a technology mandated by Congress to help parents supervise their children's TV viewing.

The World Wide Web and Mass Media Studies

Convergence also has implications for communications scholars who study the role of media in society. The astounding growth of the World Wide Web means that the Internet can no longer be ignored as an important mass medium. As Morris and Ogan (1996) put it, if we ignore computer media, "Not only will the discipline [of mass communications] be left behind," but we "will also miss an opportunity to explore and rethink answers to some of the central questions of mass communications research." The convergence of conventional media and computer networks continues to yield new forms that combine elements of radio, television, film, and journalism in ways that defy conventional categorization and even blur such fundamental distinctions as that between interpersonal communication and mass communication (Negroponte, 1995; Dizard, 1997). In particular, the **interactive** quality of new media systems poses a challenge to theories about media consumption and media effects that were based on assumptions of essentially one-way communication to passive audiences.

Interactive communication uses feedback to modify a message as it is presented.

The convergence of information technologies and conventional communications media is a far-reaching development. It represents fundamental changes not only in the fabric of the communications media but also in our daily lives—changes fraught with both opportunity and peril.

New Term: Communications Media

Various terms have been used to describe this convergence of traditional mass media and computer technologies. In the late 1970s, two French scholars (Nora & Minc, 1980) coined the term *telematique.* The English equivalent, "telematics," has gained some currency but seems to lose something in the translation. Others prefer "informatics," to emphasize that information networks are involved in the convergence.

PROFILE

MR. AOL.
Steve Case worked his way up from the proprietor of a childhood lemonade business to chairman of America Online.

Mr. AOL

Name: Steve Case

Born: Oahu, Hawaii, 1958

Education: A graduate of Williams College

Current Position: Chairman, America Online

Style: Shy and unassuming, he favors polo shirts and turkey sandwiches.

Greatest Achievements: Founded America Online and made it into the number one on-line service in the world.

Most Dubious Achievements: Along with his marketing chief Jan Brandt, he pioneered the practice of distributing CDs with AOL software so widely that they seem as numerous (and as pesky) as cockroaches. Hence the nickname his critics have hung on him: "the cockroach of the Internet." In another dubious achievement, AOL's switch to flat-rate pricing from time-sensitive fees in 1996 prompted such a big jump in usage that it "browned out" the AOL network, infuriating millions of users.

Entry Level: Steve started with a lemonade business, and by age 11 he was selling Swiss watches with his brother Dan. His first job out of college was marketing hair conditioner for Procter & Gamble. Later, he traveled around the country testing pizza toppings for Pizza Hut and found that plain cheese was the most popular—a foreshadowing, some think, of his later on-line content strategy.

His Inspiration: Back in 1982, Steve had to spend thousands of dollars getting his sluggish modem and an old Kaypro portable computer connected to the leading on-line service of that era, *The Source.* At the time he thought, "the ability to sit at your desk and access information and connect to people all over the world—how could that not, over time, be a huge business?" His Big Idea was to make the service easy to try and easy to use.

How He Got to the Top: He founded AOL in 1985 out of the remains of an on-line computer game distributor he had joined two years earlier. He changed the name to America Online in 1991, made it into a public company in 1992, and in 1997 bought out his main competition, *CompuServe* (who had previously absorbed *The Source*). Until 1996, he inflated profits by treating all those CDs as tax deductions. After losing a billion dollars, he and his new president, Bob Pittman, finally figured out how to turn a profit—by cutting costs and selling exclusive access to their subscribers to marketers and providers of on-line content, such as Amazon.com. His 1998 acquisition of Netscape put him in a position to be a dominant force on the World Wide Web.

Where Does He Go from Here? Now, the challenge is to keep AOL profitable by striking new exclusivity deals and creating appealing new content. It will also be necessary to avoid alienating users with spreading commercialism and rate increases, falling victim to arch-rival William Gates of Microsoft, and getting into trouble with the U.S. Justice Department over AOL's own hardball business tactics.

SOURCE: Gunther, M. (1998, March 30). "The Internet is Mr. Case's neighborhood." *Fortune,* 137(6), p. 68.
Cooper, J. (1997, September 22). "How AOL lost the battles but won the war." *Time,* 150(12), p. 46.

Basically, the *information superhighway* is to the Information Age what the superhighway of roads was to the Industrial Age: a universal network on which all travelers may "ride," whether their communication purpose is commerce, public service, or the pursuit of happiness. The Internet is rapidly subsuming other networks that might lay claim to this title, from the consumer information services offered by America Online (AOL) to corporate computer networks (Cairncross, 1997). Many are using the Internet as their telephone network, too, taking advantage of "Internet telephony" services that make it possible to place calls all

1. **List four examples of the convergence phenomenon.**
2. **What is meant by the term *information society?***
3. **What are four traditional mass media?**
4. **What are some other examples of communications media?**

over the world at a fraction of the cost of conventional phone lines. Most mass media outlets now have some form of presence on the Web, and many use it as a channel to distribute print, radio, and video content. Thus, the Internet is rapidly turning into that information superhighway.

If this continues, as we mentioned earlier, there may well come to be only a single "medium," instead of distinct radio, TV, film, and print media. This will take the form of a sophisticated, high-speed computer network with its associated display and storage devices. Formerly neat distinctions between interpersonal communication and mass media are also breaking down, just as are the barriers among the telephone, broadcasting, publishing, computer, and cable industries. Therefore, in this text **communications media** will be used as an umbrella term for our new world of communications, in which the once-clear distinctions between conventional media are fading fast away.

Communications media include all forms of communication mediated through mechanical or electronic channels.

THE DEVELOPMENT OF COMMUNICATIONS MEDIA

To understand media convergence fully, it is important to place it in historical perspective. We will approach this topic by relating communications media developments to three stages of economic development shown in Figure 1.2: agricultural, industrial, and information societies (Bell, 1973; Dizard, 1990).

DOWN ON THE FARM. Agricultural societies are characterized by resource extraction. Written communication evolves as a specialized function.

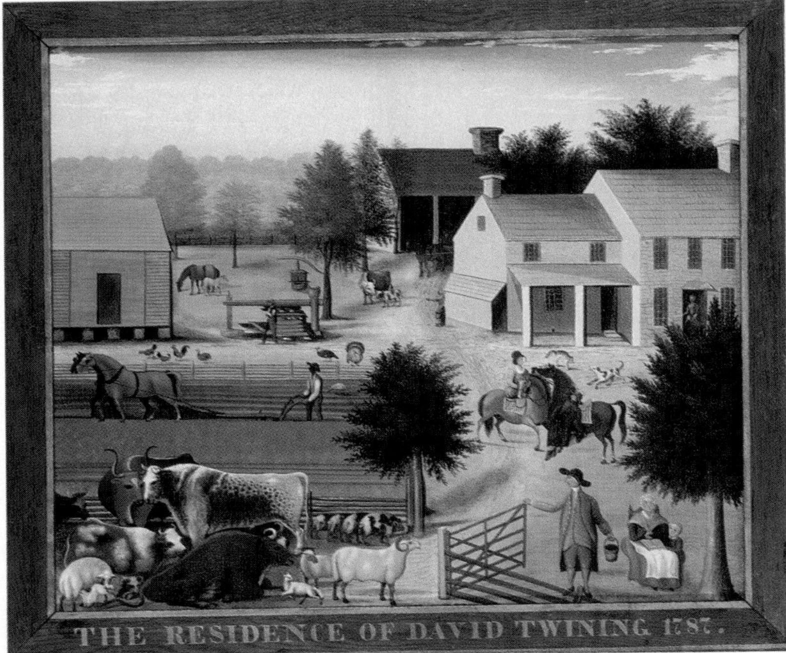

Preagricultural Society

In preagricultural societies, most people lived in small groups as hunters and gatherers. These cultures depend on the spoken word, rather than written language, to transmit their traditions from one generation to the next. The oral tradition lives on in contemporary societies—for example, among the growing numbers of illiterates who are unable to read books, newspapers, or street signs. And many of these are homeless people who have reverted to hunting and gathering, though in the urban jungle, not the "real" jungle (Dordick, 1997).

Agricultural Society

In agricultural economies most work is on farms or in resource extraction;

miners, those who fish for a living, and lumberjacks (or jills), for example. These societies are more settled and more complex, so their members pay a great deal of attention to communication, and bring written languages into being. Social stratification occurs, giving rise to specialized occupations such as those of doctors, teachers, and candlemakers. Communication is also a specialized function because most people—whether peasants or nobles—are unable to read or write. Members of religious orders and merchant classes are usually the first to specialize in correspondence, record keeping, and the copying of manuscripts. With most of the populace still illiterate, couriers skilled at memorizing long oral messages also emerge as communications specialists.

The primary mass medium in early agricultural societies was the hand-copied book, but circulation was limited. Hand copying was very laborious, and the ruling classes did not want the masses exposed to new ideas through reading. Thus most books were produced for a literate elite class of scholars and priests.

Agricultural societies and written communication date back to ancient Sumer, about 4000 B.C. But as late as 1900, the United States was still an agricultural economy, with agricultural employment the most prevalent. Today, the number of agriculturalists is dwindling rapidly, and they have sunk to about 2 percent of the U.S. population. However, many developing countries are still primarily agricultural economies.

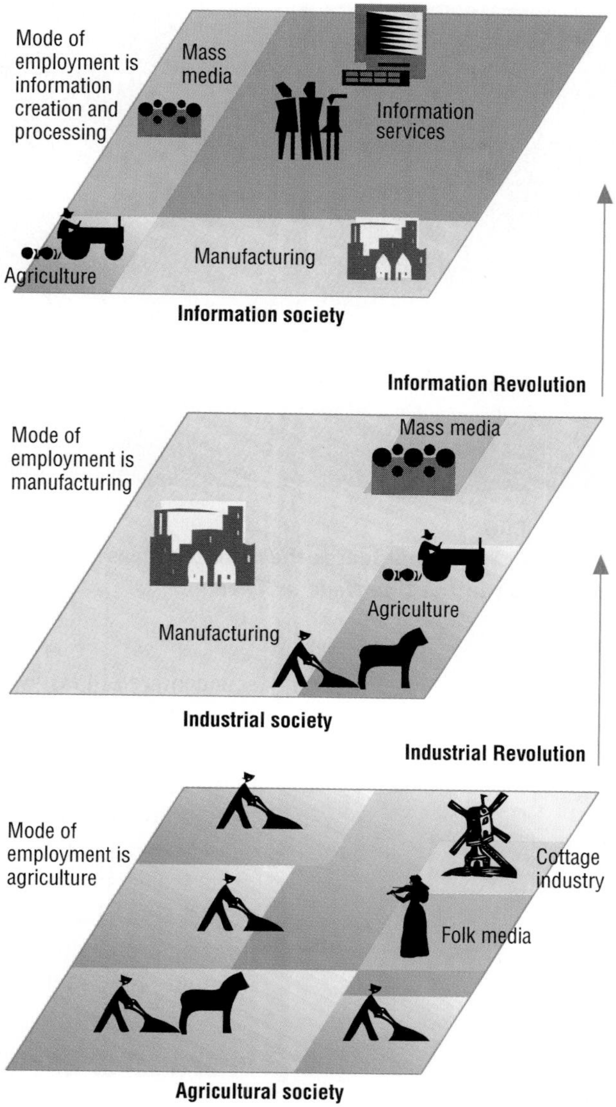

FIGURE 1.2
The three basic stages of economic development, from agricultural to industrial to informational.

Industrial Society

Although the Industrial Revolution is often dated to Thomas Newcomen's invention of the steam engine in 1712, an important precursor of the industrial method is found in the field of communication: the publication of the Gutenberg Bible in 1455. Gutenberg was the first to use movable metal type, an invention that dramatically improved the speed of book printing over the hand-copying methods that preceded that time. Now thousands of identical copies of a book could be made relatively cheaply. Mass production led to larger audiences as new types of books were printed.

In a sense, the Industrial Revolution extended Gutenberg's mass production methods to the manufacture of virtually all types of goods. Industrial production

ONLY A COG.
Charlie Chaplin experiences the pitfalls of mass production in the film *Modern Times*.

START THE PRESSES!
The advent of the printing press in the late fifteenth century was a precursor to mass literacy and the Industrial Revolution.

was centered in large cities, triggering a mass migration from country to city and from agricultural jobs to manufacturing. By 1910, the United States was an industrial society: Manufacturing outstripped agricultural employment for the first time. Industrialization also encouraged the spread of literacy to cope with more complex job requirements and the demands of urban life.

Urbanization, literacy, and the need to advertise new manufactured goods on a mass scale gave rise to the first truly mass medium, the urban newspaper, in the 1830s. Soon, industrial methods were applied to speed up and economize the printing process further and to invent newer amusements for the urban masses, including film, radio, and television.

Information Society

Information workers may be found even in preagricultural societies, in the persons of storytellers and shamans. As late as 1900, when the United States was still an agricultural society—in that farmers predominanted among the four basic categories of employment (agriculture, industry, services, and information)—only about 10 percent of those employed were information workers. At the pinnacle of the industrial society in 1950, this proportion grew to about 30 percent. But the point at which information work dominates the work force marks the transition to an information society. This happened in the United States in 1960, but only a handful of other nations have yet made the transition. Today, the proportion of information workers has leveled off at just under 50 percent, although these figures do not include the growing number of factory, retail, and agricultural employees who spend much of their day at computer terminals and who should perhaps be classified as information workers as well.

Because the media reflect the economic status of the societies that spawn them, it comes as no surprise that the dominant medium in an information society is one that helps to create, store, and process information: the computer. The conversion of all media to computer-readable forms is what drives the convergence of the mass media left over from the industrial era with computer media. Computer media transform the mass media experience in other ways as well, rendering them interactive and multimedia and making it possible to customize them to highly refined audience segments or even to individual tastes.

CONVENTIONAL VIEW OF MASS MEDIA

One way to appreciate more acutely the significance of converging communications media in the information society is to understand how views of mass media developed in the years before their convergence with computers.

The SMCR Model

The classic definition of the communication process was developed by Wilbur Schramm (1982), who has been credited as the founder of mass communication studies. He broke down the process of communication into eight major components to create what is known as the **Source-Message-Channel-Receiver (SMCR)** model (see Figure 1.3).

SMCR is a model of the communication process that analyzes the exchange of information as it passes back and forth from the *source* to the *message* to the *channel* to the *receiver,* and back to the source.

The *source* is the originator of the communication.

The *message* is the content of the communication, the information that is to be exchanged.

An *encoder* translates the message into a form that can be communicated—often a form that is not directly interpretable by human senses.

A *channel* is the medium or transmission system used to convey the message from one place to another.

FIGURE 1.3
The SMCR model is one way of describing the communication process.

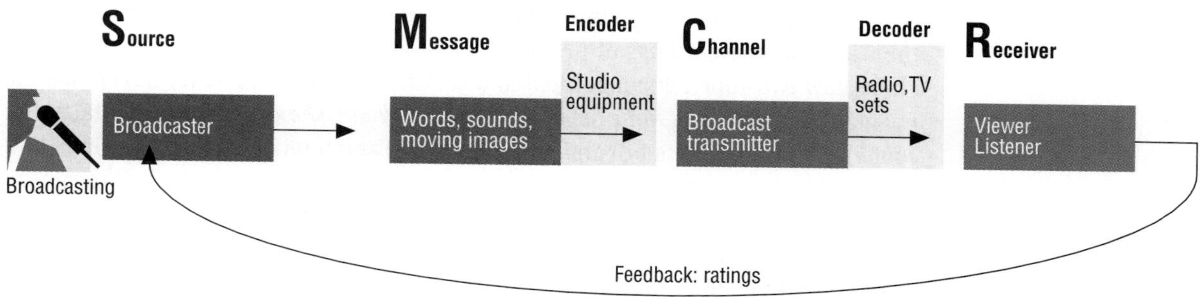

1. What are three basic stages of economic development?
2. What forms of communications media distinguish the basic states of economic development?
3. What do the letters SMCR stand for?
4. Use the SMCR model to describe what happens when you watch TV.

A *decoder* reverses the encoding process.

The *receiver* is the destination of the communication.

A *feedback* mechanism between the source and the receiver may be used to regulate the flow of communication.

Noise is any distortion or errors that may be introduced during the information exchange.

This model can be applied to all forms of human communication, but here we will just illustrate it with a mass communication example. When you are at home watching a television program, the television network (a corporate *source*) is the originator of the *message,* which is *encoded* by the microphones and television cameras in the television studio. In this case, the *channel* is not literally the number on the television dial to which you are tuned, but rather the entire chain of transmitters, satellite links, and cable television equipment required to convey the message to your home. Although we sometimes call a TV set a "receiver," it is really the *decoder* in this scheme of things, and the viewer is the *receiver. Feedback* from viewers is provided via television rating services and by cards, letters, and phone calls to the station. Electronic interference with the broadcast and the distractions of barking dogs or fighting neighbors are possible *noise* components in this situation.

Mass communication is one-to-many, with limited audience feedback.

In this classic view, **mass communication** is one-to-many, or *point-to-multipoint,* communication. That is, through a mass medium such as newspapers, radio, TV, or film, the *message* is communicated from a single *source* to hundreds or even thousands of *receivers,* with relatively restricted opportunities for the audience to communicate back to the source.

Gatekeepers decide what will appear in the media.

Agenda setting is the ability of the media to determine what is important.

In Wilbur Schramm's heyday, from the late 1940s to the early 1980s, mass media were produced by large, multilayered media corporations, where an elite corps of authoritative media commentators and professional producers acted as **gatekeepers,** deciding what the audience should receive and thereby serving an **agenda-setting** function. The editors and publishers, recognizing their own power, were aware of themselves as shapers of public opinion and popular tastes (Schramm, 1982).

Essentially, mass media messages were undifferentiated and were addressed to the largest possible audience. The underlying strategy was to *homogenize* tastes and opinions to further the goals of a mass market industrial economy. This meant using the media to promote tastes in consumer products that would generalize to the widest possible groups of people. For example, everyone would want to buy the shiny new two-tone persimmon red and classic white 1956 Mercury advertised on popular television programs such as *The Ed Sullivan Show.* The car manufacturer could then produce vats of persimmon red paint and tons of chrome at a time, lowering production costs and boosting profits.

In this classic view, the audience was an undifferentiated mass, anonymous to the source and a passive receptacle for the mass message. The economics of the media were such that audiences of thousands or millions were needed to attract the millions of advertising dollars needed to create and sustain mass media systems. Feedback was largely limited to reports from audience research bureaus, which took days or weeks to compile.

"NOW, ON WITH THE SHEW!" Our variety programs of the 1950s, such as *The Ed Sullivan Show,* were designed to appeal to a homogeneous mass market. (Ed is on the far left.)

CONTEMPORARY VIEW OF MASS COMMUNICATION

The convergence phenomenon has altered these conventional conceptions of the mass media, perhaps to the point where we can legitimately ask whether the mass media as Schramm and other early mass communications scholars saw them decades ago still exist. Not only the technology has changed, but also our understanding of the communication process.

The Audience Is Powerful

One of the major changes associated with new technologies is a shift by media toward smaller and smaller target audiences. Advanced audience research methods have helped the media cater to smaller audiences by enhancing the richness and speed of audience feedback. The result is that **narrowcasting**—dedicating channels to specific audience subgroups, or *market segments*—is now practical. *Demographic* characteristics (such as sex, age, and income), once the sole means of defining audiences, are being replaced by a focus on *lifestyles* and user needs and even individual preferences. Some print and electronic publications have gone the next step, using personal forms of address in their advertising copy. Also, many businesses now customize Web site content for the individual viewer. Rather than homogenize audiences, the new communications media try to cater to specialized groups and to define new niches. Furthermore, interactive technologies hold the promise of making the feedback virtually instantaneous. Perhaps more than any other change in the mass media, this strengthening of the feedback link alters the fundamental nature of the mass communication process, making the audience far more powerful.

Narrowcasting directs media channels to specific segments of the audience.

In the terms of the traditional SMCR model, the *source* of a Web home page is the person who authored the page, and the content of the page is the *message,* which the author encoded with the software she used to compose the page's content. The *channel* is the Internet, including the computer that the Web page is stored on, the network connections between that computer, called a server, and your own. Your computer acts as the decoder. It decodes the message with your browser software (such as Netscape or Internet Explorer), and you are the *receiver.*

The Web differs from conventional mass media in the direct and instantaneous feedback it delivers from the receiver to the source. As a receiver, you are giving the source feedback in the form of e-mail or any information you enter. Although it

TALKING BACK.
Today the audience takes an active role in many media, as is the case with live call-in shows on radio and TV.

is usually invisible to the user, there is also a constant stream of feedback inside the Internet, confirming the arrival of information and signaling readiness for the next block of data. In fact, you are continuously modifying the content of the media presentation as you select the parts of the site you wish to visit, play the audio and video files you find there, or move on to other pages through the page's *links.* Some sites even keep track of your interactions with them, and record that information secretly, so that they "get to know you." *Noise* is present in the form of network errors that occur during the exchange, or, if you prefer, in the form of your culturally determined perception that the page isn't "cool." The audience plays an active role in seeking out and assembling content, in effect taking on programming and filtering functions, formerly exclusively performed by the source in the mass media.

In the **cultural studies** view, communication is a process in which the source and the receiver jointly create the meaning of the message.

Culture is a system of images and symbols shared by a group.

The notion of a powerful audience is nothing new to those who subscribe to the **cultural studies** view; they hold that the communication process is a reciprocal activity involving the *joint creation of meaning* between the author or producer and the person who receives the message and makes sense of it (Downing, Mohammadi, & Sreberny-Mohammadi, 1990). From this perspective, communication takes place in the context of **culture.** Communication involves the exchange of meaning through the language and images that compose the shared culture of participants. The receiver of the communication plays an active role, filtering messages through the lens of his or her own culture, participation in significant groups, and personal experiences (Morley, 1986).

In the terms of the conventional SMCR model described in the previous section, the cultural studies approach emphasizes the feedback link and an active process of "decoding" the messages on the part of the receiver. Stuart Hall (1980) redefined encoding as creating a message with verbal, visual, or written codes or symbols that someone else decodes with her or his own understanding of those codes. The creator may intend the codes to mean one thing, but the receiver may interpret them quite differently. Although people often accept the intended meaning, they also negotiate different meanings or even reject the intended message entirely (Morley, 1992).

Note that unlike the cultural studies approach, the conventional SMCR model regards encoding and decoding as mechanical processes, performed by machines. Whereas in the critical studies approach, the interpretation of meaning resides in people: the source and the receiver. Thus, to understand what communication professors mean when they talk about encoding and decoding, you must ask them which school of thought they subscribe to, the critical studies approach or the conventional SMCR model.

Emphasis on Interactivity

As technology has allowed communications media to target audiences and get fast feedback, there has been increased emphasis on *interactivity*. We hear about interactive television, interactive cable, interactive telephones, interactive computer services, interactive games, interactive commercials, interactive compact discs, and even interactive soda cans (with computer chips that talk to you when you pull the tab). But just what is this "interactivity"?

Sometimes, *interactive* is used as a synonym for "two-way," but few of the systems developed to date are truly two-way in the same sense that a conversation between two people is. In a conversation, two people not only take turns responding to each other but also modify their interaction on the basis of preceding exchanges. Computer games that get harder as you score more points and transactional systems such as home banking systems perhaps come the closest to this sense of being interactive. That is because the content of the information exchange between you and the game or the bank is continually modified depending on your responses. The ultimate form of interactivity meets the so-called *Turing test,* named after the British mathematician and computer pioneer Alan Turing. To pass this test, an interactive system must convince users that they are interacting with a human being rather than a machine. For example, let's say you were playing computer chess on the Internet and became so impressed with your opponent's mastery of the game that you sent her an e-mail asking to meet face to face. If an e-mail came back from the system operator tactfully explaining that you had been playing a computer, *that* would be artificial intelligence.

At the other extreme, the term *interactivity* is sometimes used so broadly that it is applied to any situation in which the content of a media system is selectable or customizable by the user. That would mean, for example, that Web pages that let users assemble their own version of the daily newspaper from a vast library of digital information could be called interactive. Similarly, television systems that allow viewers to select alternative endings to soap operas or to switch between wide-angle and close-up shots while watching football games would be deemed interactive. However, this broad use of the word would mean that books with indexes, televisions with remote controls, and mechanical candy machines are interactive—the user can select the content.

Rather, *interactivity* is more meaningful when applied, somewhat more narrowly, to systems wherein feedback from the receiver is used by the source—whether human or computer—to continually modify the message as it is being delivered to the receiver. By this definition, on-line newspapers, interactive soap operas, and home banking systems are interactive, but TV remote controls and textbooks are not (no real-time feedback to the source). In the video game example where the game gets harder as you score more points, there is no real-time feedback to the source either, but we can still consider it "interactive" because the player is getting, in effect, real-time responses from the person who created the software for the game. The software acts just like another player would. What about the mechanical candy machine? No, it does not qualify because there is no ongoing transaction that is continually modified. A truly interactive candy machine would let

IMMATERIAL GRRRRL. Lara Croft, star of the popular *Tomb Raiders* computer game, is an example of a computer-synthesized character, an entirely new mode of media production.

you select how many peanuts you want in your candy bar and would ask whether you want to wash it down with a soda (cf. Rafaelli, 1988). Now that many candy machines have computer chips and small computer screens built in, they can make a claim to interactivity as well; they will keep asking you to add more money until you have enough of that snack—and then ask whether you want another selection.

Production to the Desktop, Power to the People?

Another change associated with new communications media is that new technologies have made it possible to strip away many of the middle layers of media organizations and to shrink the minimum size of mass media enterprises back to the size of small cottage industries (Negroponte, 1995). Certainly, giant media corporations are still with us, and indeed they are getting bigger than ever, but the number of people required to turn out a media product within them is shrinking. In the case of material published on a desktop computer, such as newsletters and underground magazines ("zines"), a staff of one may be sufficient. Then there is the Lara Croft phenomenon. Lara is the computer-generated star of the popular *Tomb Raider* computer games, but she now receives modeling contracts, offers of movie roles, and marriage proposals as though she were a real person. Lara reminds us that technology may eventually allow a single individual sitting at a powerful computer workstation to produce an entire movie without a studio, set, or actors.

Affordable portable TV cameras, audio recorders, and digital editing technology put people from all walks of life in the producer's chair. You no longer have to work for a huge media corporation to create professional media products. Even the dividing line between communications media and the receiver is getting weaker. For example, with radio call-in programs, TV programs based on home videos and Internet newsgroup "channels," the program is assembled from user contributions. In the process, the professionalism and authoritativeness of sources is eroding, as may their ability to define culture and dictate popular opinion.

THE DIGITAL REVOLUTION

As we begin the twenty-first century, communications media have entered a new era. The technological advances associated with our information society have resulted in a transition to digital transmission across all media forms—in fact, sometimes it seems that the entire world is "going digital."

Digital communication converts sound, pictures, and text into computer-readable formats by breaking them up into strings of ones and zeros.

Analog communication uses continuously varying signals corresponding to the light or sounds originated by the source.

Advantages of Digital Media

By **digital communication** we mean the conversion of sound, pictures, and text into computer-readable formats—by breaking them up into strings of ones and zeros that carry information in encoded form (see the Technology Demystified box). In contrast, **analog communication** relays *all* the information present in the original message in the form of continuously varying signals that correspond to the fluctuations of sound or light energy originated by the source of communication.

TECHNOLOGY **DEMYSTIFIED**

A Digital Media Primer

To see how communications are translated into computer-readable data, consider a simple telephone call. The digital conversion that makes the call possible occurs on a computer card that allows your telephone line to communicate with the telephone company's switch. First, brief excerpts, or samples, of the electrical waveform corresponding to your voice are taken from the telephone line, at a rate of 8000 samples per second. The size, or voltage level, of each sample is measured and "rounded off" to the closest of 256 different possible readings; then a corresponding eight-digit binary number is transmitted. All digital transmissions are composed of only two "digits"—1 and 0. These are actually a series of "on-off" electrical pulses. An electric current is turned on for a brief moment to indicate a 1 and turned off for a 0. The process is reversed at the receiving end. At 8000 samples a second and eight digits per sample, the on-off signals are very numerous—64,000 each second!

Thus, when two lovers are talking on the phone and there is complete (if meaningful) silence on the line, the voltage reading is zero. The binary number corresponding to this is eight zeros: 00000000. If the lovers then begin to quarrel and start shouting at each other, the voltage reading might jump temporarily to the maximum, and a binary number corresponding to the highest level would be sent: 11111111. To the couple, it seems that they are talking to each other, but in reality they are listening to computer emulations of their voices.

Another example of how communications are translated into computer-readable data is the transmission of pictures. To make computer graphics, the computer stores digital information about the brightness and color of every single point on the computer screen. On most computers, there are 640 points of light going across and 480 down.

Similarly, when we type text into a computer, there are no tiny A's and B's inside there; rather, each key corresponds to a unique sequence of seven computer bits (such as 1000001 for A). That is what is stored inside the computer or transmitted through the Internet, in the form of tiny surges of electricity, short beeps of sound, flashes of light, or pulses of magnetism.

The human senses are all analog communication systems, of course, so for humans to receive the message, we have to convert back from digital to analog.

1010101010101

There are some significant advantages to adopting digital systems.

Quality. Transmission quality is improved because the digital signals are less susceptible to interference and distortion. As long as the basic pattern of 1s and 0s can be identified, the original transmission can be restored, in crystal clear form. In contrast to the old-fashioned analog systems, a digital transmission can be "cleaned" of any noise that may creep in during transmission or recording. The older analog systems just keep adding to the noise, and even make any existing noise louder, each time we reproduce a media transmission. For example, if a tape recording of a concert is copied from one audio cassette onto another, and then another, as it is passed from person to person, the final version will include all of

TECHNOLOGY DEMYSTIFIED

Sharing with Packet Switching

How does the Internet work? The key is its underlying set of communication rules, or *protocols.* These are known collectively as Transmission Control Protocol/Internetworking Protocol. TCP/IP relies on a method of transmission that is common to many other types of data networks, packet switching. As communication media technologies converge, packet switching is slowly conquering the world of communication.

As the name implies, packet switching breaks up digital transmissions into small chunks of digits called packets. Each packet has additional bits to indicate the network addresses of the sending and receiving parties, the sequence number of each packet, and an error-checking code. The advantage is that many simultaneous messages can share a single circuit. By means of the address information and the sequence number, the message is reassembled at the receiving end.

An analogy can be made between packet switching and postal delivery. Imagine that you are on a Hawaiian vacation and have only a handful of postcards available to write on. If you had to send a long letter back home—perhaps to explain the symptoms of an exotic tropical disease that will postpone your return to work—you would divide the message among several postcards and mark them "1 of 3," "2 of 3," and so on, so that your boss would be sure not to miss any of your excuses. The Post Office might route each of your cards differently back to the mainland. One might go via a direct flight to your home city, another by tramp steamer through San Diego, another via a flight through San Francisco. If one card arrived late, your boss could wait for it and then reassemble your message from the sequence numbers. If the tramp steamer was lost at sea, your boss could wire you to retransmit the missing "packet." You could, of course, buy an express mail package for all your postcards, ensuring that they would all arrive together, but this "dedicated circuit" would obviously be a lot more costly. In contrast, packet networks are sometimes described as connectionless, because they do not require a dedicated connection between any two points on a network for communication to take place.

The future of packet-switching technology will be to increase transmission speeds by several orders of magnitude with fiber optics. Provision will also be made for prioritization of the packets so that voice and video packets that require immediate delivery will get preferential treatment over applications in which some delay can be accepted, such as electronic mail.

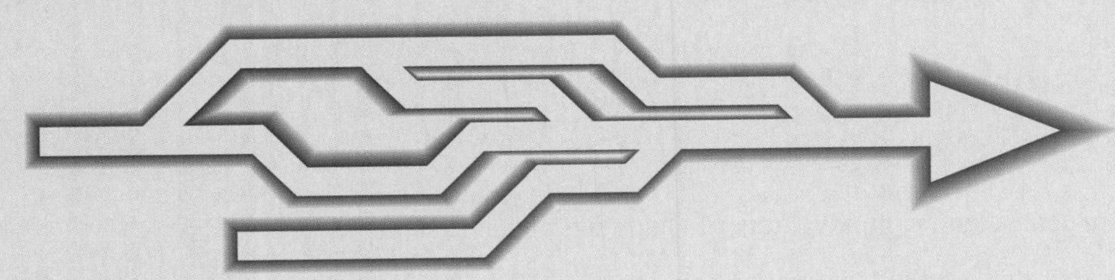

the "hiss" introduced by each of the recording heads it passed through. Digital systems can make perfect copies time after time, so the third-generation copy of the concert will sound exactly like the original.

Channel Abundance. When messages are digitally encoded, it becomes possible to use *digital compression.* This means subtracting redundant information from media content—such as stationary backdrops that do not change between frames of a TV picture—to allow multiple channels to be carried where only one was possible before. For example, video compression makes it possible to transmit ten programs simultaneously on channels that once carried only a single program. Cable television systems are boasting of this feat when they promise "lots more channels" with their digital cable service. Another related digital advantage is that many users can share the same transmission channel simultaneously by taking turns. This approach, which is called **packet switching** (see the Technology Demystified box), is how the Internet works.

Packet switching breaks digital information up into individually addressed chunks, or packets, so that many users can share a single channel.

Not only can more content be crammed into existing channel space, but the supply of channel space is also increasing. **Fiber optics** is a significant step forward; it relies on light energy rather than electricity to communicate information. Newer technology is multiplying the capacity of fiber optic networks already in place, even as fiber networks are extended closer and closer to the end user. And other new options are being developed, including satellites capable of broadcasting to miniature antennas on your home or automobile, telephone lines that can carry video signals as well as voices, and digital broadcast services with interactive capabilities.

Fiber optics uses light instead of electricity to communicate.

The culmination of these developments is likely to be a system of *video on demand*—or, more generally, media on demand. There will be so many channels available that users will be able to "call up" virtually any media product from anywhere in the world at any time without making a trip to the newsstand, library, or video store (Negroponte, 1995).

User Control. This abundance of choices has created a new challenge: how to navigate through all your options. One solution has been the development of Internet pages, called portals, that allow you to select just the content you wish ("First show me the weather; then the sports, but only the Dodgers' score; then the news, but only the society news; and then my electronic mail). Some radio broadcasts already include a digital format code, making it possible to program radios for such functions as "heavy metal seek." The *search engines* on the World Wide Web that let users search for content by keywords are indicative of the degree of user control that will probably be available in all media some day. So, too, are the *filtering programs* that allow parents to program their computers so their children are shielded from explicit sexual content on the Internet. The **V-chip** is a new electronic tool for automatically filtering out violent or adult programming on television, too. And now Web pages are getting new content codes that will not only help us to filter out what we don't want to see but also help us find material that we do want. Many Web sites ask you to log in and then address you by name or tailor their contents to you, adding a personal dimension to mass communication. New wrinkles include "agent" software that looks for information on the Web for you and *avatars* that let you construct images of yourself that interact with other avatars.

The **V-chip** is an electronic tool for automatically filtering out violence or adult programming on television.

Communications Media Make the Switch to Digital

All of these advantages have resulted in a gradual switch from analog to digital across the full spectrum of communications media.

Telephone. The first consumer communications medium to be digitized was the telephone, beginning in 1962 with the installation, in the heart of telephone

FIGURE 1.4
The analog-to-digital conversion process occurs in a variety of media.

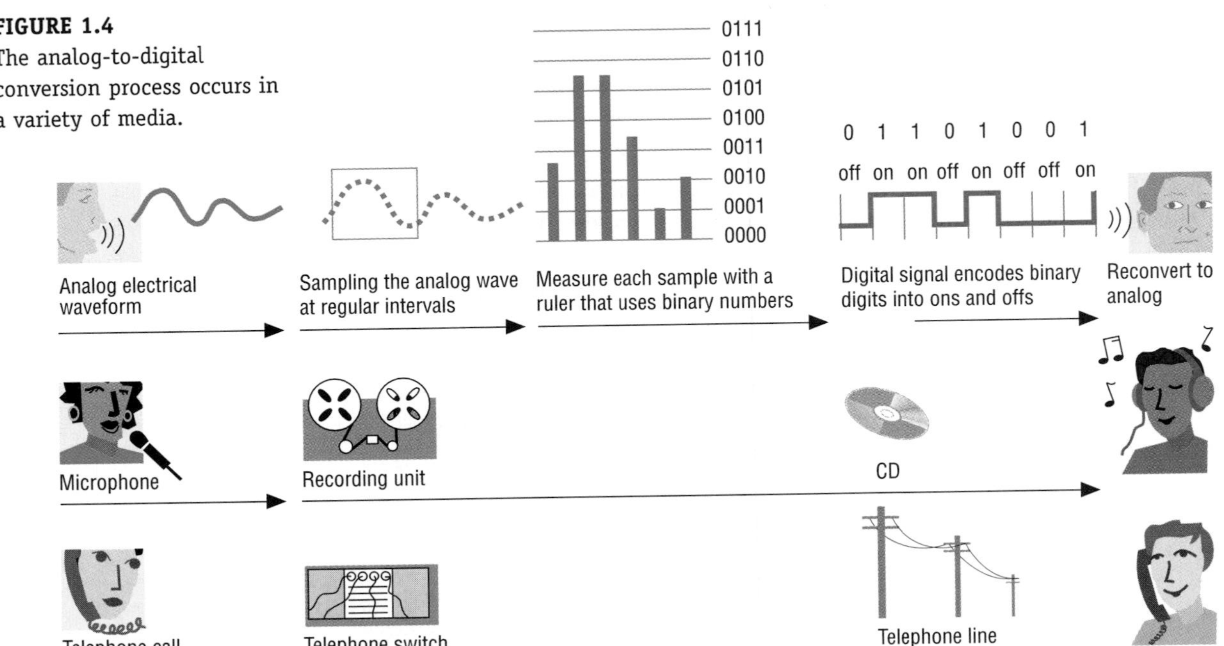

networks, of high-speed lines that were capable of carrying two dozen conversations simultaneously. Today, most telephone conversations are converted to digital form before they leave your neighborhood and are conveyed as computer data throughout the long-distance telephone networks (see Figure 1.4). The latest in mobile phones, *Personal Communication Services (PCS)*, also rely exclusively on digital transmission. Unlike the familiar cellular phones, the new digital systems convert your voice to computer digits right inside the handset.

But the telephone is no longer just for talking. It is also the connection to the Internet for most users. A new high-speed transmission technology, **Digital Subscriber Line (DSL)** is coming; it will make telephone lines a practical medium for high-quality audio and even video entertainment as well. A growing number of telephone calls are also being transmitted in the same *packet-switching* protocols used to carry data and images over the Internet.

Digital Subscriber Line (DSL) is a high-speed digital phone service that can transmit audio, video, and computer data over conventional phone lines.

Print Media. Digitization first hit the production rooms of print media in 1967–1969. Now, most print publications are computerized throughout their production cycle. It is only in the final printing process that the information is converted from computer code to the printed page. Hundreds of daily newspapers are now available electronically through the World Wide Web, a format that totally bypasses the final print step—unless readers choose to print out articles via their personal computers.

Digital versatile disc (DVD) technology is a higher-capacity descendant of compact disc (CD) technology that fully integrates computer, audio, and video storage.

Film. The movie industry followed a trajectory similar to that of print, with all of the digitization taking place behind the scenes. In Hollywood the computer movement started with the special effects created for *Star Wars* in 1974. Now most of the editing of "big films" is done on computer, and the first completely computer-generated film, *Toy Story,* debuted in 1995. On the home front, the newest rage in home video is the **digital versatile disc (DVD)** that stores entire movies on a single disc via the same basic technology found in digital audio recordings. DVD may well become a common storage medium for movies, video, audio, and computer data.

Recordings. The first phase of the evolution to digital media in the recording industry was the *compact disc (CD),* which digitally encodes music in the form of microscopic pits on the surface of a plastic disc. This method of digital encoding closely resembles that used in the telephone network, except that more digits are used to improve sound quality. Compact discs were first introduced in 1982. The latest tape-recording media also utilize digital formats, and most recording studios have made the digital transition. The Internet is an increasingly important source of recorded music for computer-savvy fans who download digital music files of the latest releases directly to their computer disc drives.

A SPECIAL ADVERTISING SUPPLEMENT FROM THE NEW YORK TIMES

The New York Times ON THE WEB

NYC Weather 63° F

FRIDAY, APRIL 30, 1999 | Site Updated 5:30 PM

QUICK NEWS
PAGE ONE PLUS
International
National/N.Y.
Politics
Business
Technology
Science/Health
Sports
Weather
Opinion
Arts/Living
Automobiles
Books
Diversions
Job Market
Magazine
Real Estate
Travel
SITE INDEX

NATO Hits Central Belgrade; Russian Diplomacy Continues

NATO jets hit the headquarters of the Yugoslav army, the interior ministry and a residential area in Belgrade on Friday. Russian leaders, meanwhile, continued their diplomatic campaign to end the crisis. Go to Article
•RELATED ARTICLE: Bombing Unites Serb Army

Economic Growth Continues Despite Record Trade Deficit

The U.S. economy grew at a strong 4.5 percent annual rate in the first three months of this year, even as the nation's foreign trade deficit soared to record levels. Go to Article

U.S. civil rights leader Jesse Jackson was in Belgrade visiting three caputured U.S. soldiers on Friday. Go to Article
•ISSUE IN DEPTH: The Conflict in Kosovo
•AUDIO: Sgt. Christopher Stone

INTERNATIONAL
Explosion in London Pub

ALL THE NEWS . . .
***The New York Times* is one of the thousands of newspapers worldwide that now publishes on the World Wide Web.**

Computers. At about the same time that compact discs for music came along in the early 1980s, personal computers were introduced into the home, marking another important step in the digitization of communications media. By the late 1980s, nonmusic compact discs started to be used with personal computers, where they served as high-capacity storage devices for audio, video, and graphics as well as computer text. With the burgeoning of the CD-ROM, **multimedia,** combining text, graphics, audio, and video in a single presentation, became a reality. But the biggest push for computer media came from the advent of the World Wide Web in 1993. More and more Internet users are finding not only radio stations but also video programming and a wealth of other information and entertainment services on the World Wide Web.

Multimedia systems integrate text, audio, and video and let the user select the presentation mode.

Cable and Satellite Television. Cable TV was the next to go digital. Although most cable systems still transmit analog television, in 1998 cable companies began to convert their video to digital form as a way to increase the number of channel offerings on their systems—through digital compression. Cable had to go digital in part to meet competition from the **Direct Broadcast Satellite (DBS)** industry, which began beaming hundreds of channels of digital programming directly to home dishes in 1995. Users in many parts of the country now enjoy high-speed Internet access courtesy of their local cable operator.

Direct Broadcast Satellite (DBS) is a system of transmitting television signals from satellites directly to compact home receivers.

Broadcasting. After years of wrangling over standards, broadcasting is now also set for a digital revolution. **High-definition television (HDTV),** television transmitters and receivers using digital formats, went on the air in the United States in 1998. The next generation of radio, **digital audio broadcasting (DAB),** will

High-definition television (HDTV) is a form of digital television that provides a wider and more detailed picture than conventional TV.

Digital audio broadcasting (DAB) is the transmission of radio programs in digital format.

1. How does the cultural studies approach differ from the SMCR approach?
2. Is an automated teller machine interactive? Explain.
3. What are three advantages of "going digital"?
4. Explain how far each of the following has progressed in making the transition to digital technology: telephone, print, film, recordings, cable TV, broadcasting.

complete the transition from the "old" analog mass media to the "new" digital media.

As we move into the future we are likely to see a continuation of the digital revolution that may lead not just to improved versions of traditional media, but also to new media forms. Future media of all kinds will almost certainly have multimedia extensions, so that we can view the lyrics of the songs we are listening to on our computer screen or view video clips from the latest plane crash in the middle of our electronic newspaper. When that day comes for you, newspaper, radio, television, and film as you now know them now will no longer exist.

MEDIA WATCH

Watch the Industries Merge and Converge

For Further Research:

WWW

New mergers, acquisitions, and partnerships in the multimedia industry are forming all the time—while old ones fall apart. Perform your own "convergence watch" by conducting an electronic search to track the action in the communications media industry. For example, to track convergence in television, enter "television industry" as a search term into InfoTrac College Edition and check "subject guide." A new page pops up with "television broadcasting industry" as one of the options and "see also nnn subdivisions" right under it. Click through to the subdivisions and look for "acquisitions, mergers, and divestments." Then continue on with the other communications media industries. For industry names, you can use the chapter titles in this book (e.g., television, radio, film, computer) and also the important segments within them found under "industry structure" in each chapter (cellular radio, home video, Internet Service Provider, for example).

An easy way to track gross convergence activity is to jot down the number of items listed in the "acquisitions, mergers, and divestments" category in each industry. Or, you can tabulate the number and size of specific deals by listing them in a table next to the dollar values of each transaction. (Note that many of the articles are duplicates about the same deals appearing in different publications.) Another interesting item to track is the reason given for each deal (to cut costs, to consolidate operations, to gain international presence, to enter a new market, for example). Or, build a "convergence matrix" to keep track of how many of the deals cut across industries; for example, telephone companies buying cable TV systems or TV networks buying Internet search engines.

SUMMARY AND REVIEW

WHAT IS THE INFORMATION SOCIETY?

The information society is one in which the production, processing, and distribution of information are the primary economic and social activities. In an information society, an ever-increasing amount of time is spent with communications media and using information technologies such as the telephone and the computer. More and more people are employed as information workers—people who produce, process, or distribute information as their primary work activity. The information society is a further step in the evolution of society from its former bases in agriculture and manufacturing into an information economy, in which the manipulation of information is the primary economic activity.

WHAT DO WE MEAN WHEN WE SAY THAT MASS MEDIA AND INFORMATION TECHNOLOGIES ARE CONVERGING?

More and more communication is created and distributed in computer-readable digital form. This means that the same basic technologies can be used to transmit all forms of communication—whether in the form of text, audio, or video—in an integrated communication system such as the Internet. Thus, separate channels are no longer needed for each medium. The organizations that produce and distribute communication are also merging as part of the convergence trend. Laws and public policies governing the media, career opportunities in communications industries, social and personal issues arising from media consumption, and even theories of the media and their role in society are all changing to reflect the convergence.

WHAT ARE THE COMPONENTS OF THE COMMUNICATION PROCESS?

All communication processes can be described in terms of a simple model in which a corporate or individual *source* encodes a *message* and transmits it through a physical *channel* to the person for whom the message is intended, the *receiver.* We call this the SMCR model. In most communication situations, feedback is also provided between the receiver and the source. Contemporary views of the process stress that it takes place in the context of a culture shared by the source and the receiver and that both source and receiver contribute to the creation of meaning.

WHAT IS MASS COMMUNICATION?

The conventional view is that mass communication involves hundreds or thousands of people, and there is no immediate feedback. Newspapers, magazines, radio, television, and film are all examples of mass media.

WHERE DID THE MASS MEDIA COME FROM?

While mass media had forerunners in agricultural and preagricultural societies, they are generally regarded as creations of the industrial age. Mass production methods coupled with the rise of large urban audiences for media during the industrial age led to the rise of print and later mass media.

WHAT IS INTERACTIVITY?

A variety of meanings have been attached to the term "interactive," ranging from the

IMPACT

MEDIA

The Scandal of the Year

For Further Research:

The media are often criticized for their potentially harmful effects on society. To identify the issues of current interest, do a keyword search on "television and behavior," "Internet and behavior," and the like. You can use each of the communications media in turn to widen your search. You can also vary the search terms. Social issues, society, ethics, policy, hearings, and protest are other keywords that are likely to yield the latest "hot issues" when combined with the names of specific media. You can combine these into a single search by judicious use of parentheses and "search operators" (*and, or, not*)—for example, "(television or Internet or radio or newspaper) and (behavior or society or ethics or hearings)." You might also keep track of the background or affiliation of the people calling attention to the issue (academic, religious, law enforcement, or political, for instance) and record what kinds of remedial action they suggest.

WWW

If you are using InfoTrac College Edition, do a Power Trac keyword search using the search terms mentioned.

simple ability to select content from a large number of options to devices that could pass the Turing test by faithfully mimicking human interaction. The term should be reserved for communication situations in which the user modifies the content by providing feedback to the source in real time.

HOW ARE MASS MEDIA CHANGING IN THE INFORMATION SOCIETY?

The convergence of computer, telecommunications, and mass media systems is bringing about some fundamental changes in the way the mass communications media function. Mass media sources are becoming more numerous, and also less authoritative and professionalized. Their ability to act as gatekeepers who set the agenda for public opinion is also being diminished. Messages are customized for smaller and smaller specialized audience segments, sometimes even using personal forms of address, and are narrowcast to these segments, rather than being broadcast to a homogeneous audience. Audiences are likewise becoming smaller and less anonymous than they were formerly and have improved and more expeditious means of providing feedback to the source of the media content—and even to participate in the creation of that content. In the process, the power of audiences increases as we move away from passive mass media to interactive new media.

WHAT ARE THE CHARACTERISTICS OF EMERGING COMMUNICATIONS MEDIA SYSTEMS?

Channels are proliferating not only to reach the new audience segments but also to target specific locations. However, the long-term trend is to integrate the many specialized channels into a single, all-purpose digital network that will provide access at the convenience of the audience. The new communications media systems that are emerging are digital, as opposed to analog. Familiar mass media forms such as radio and television are evolving into new forms, such as videotex, high-definition television (HDTV), and the World Wide Web section of the Internet, that are all-digital. Technical advances such as digital compression, broadband media, and fiber optic networks will greatly increase the number of channels coming into the home. New interactive capabilities will give users a new measure of control over the channels they view and the content of those channels, including the ability to order the media presentations they wish, on demand. Digital technology also makes it possible to mix text, audio, computer graphics, and video into integrated multimedia networks to produce entire media presentations from computer workstations, as with desktop publishing.

Electronic Resources

For up-to-the-minute URLs about *Changing Media Environment*, access the MEDIA NOW site on the World Wide Web at:

http://communication.wadsworth.com/

CHAPTER 2

Media Theory

WHAT'S AHEAD

There is nothing as practical as a good theory, or so our old professor said. Here we review important theories that explain the existence of the communications media—theories we will need in the chapters to come. We will work our way from broad explanations of media in society down to theories of how we, as individuals, use the various communications media.

WWW

Access the MEDIA NOW site on the World Wide Web at: **http://communication.wadsworth.com/** Choose "Chapter 2" from the selection box to access electronic information and other sites relevant to this chapter.

NEW YORK, NEW YORK, 2006

TO: EnterNet
FROM: John Q. Consumer
SUBJ: You stink
CC: president@whitehouse.gov, @SPCAlist

I just watched your new channel, America's Funniest Pet Gladiators, and I have never seen anything so tasteless. I don't find it at all amusing to see pets dressed up like knights in armor fighting each other. I am e-mailing the White House on this, and then I am going to spam all your sponsors and employees and get all the members of my SPCA chapter to add your network to their parental control lockout list. That's the Society for the Prevention of Cruelty to Animals, in case you don't know. And you probably don't.

TO: VP of Programming
FROM: Corporate Web Master
SUBJ: America's Funniest Pet Gladiators
CC: Legal, Payroll, Chairman's Office

This is an automatic notification to inform you that the number of e-mails criticizing the above program has reached 10,000 per day. Unless a satisfactory explanation is received by EnterNet's Chairman's Office by 5 P.M. today, your program will be canceled and your salary will be docked.

TO: Chairman's Office, EnterNet
FROM: VP of Programming
SUBJ: America's Funniest Pet Gladiators
CC: Legal, Payroll

We put the sponsor's target audience specification through the computer, had some creative conferences, hired a director, and found all this free talent at the dog pound. It costs us next to nothing, and it is really big with the macho dog owner-with-leather-jacket set. They buy TONS of dog food for their big angry mutts, it turns out. Our advertisers love it. Spreadsheet attached.

TO: VP of Programming
FROM: Chairman's Office
SUBJ: Americas Funniest Pet Gladiators
CC: Legal, Payroll, Public Relations

Congratulations on your big success with the above program. Payroll, give her a raise. Legal, take a Congresspperson to lunch. PR, spam all the big donors to the SPCA. Remind them we're the ones who put on the Adopt-a-Puppy Channel.

Chapter Outline

Media Economics
Mass Production, Mass Distribution: The Keys to Economic Success
Ownership Patterns
The Profit Motive
Sources of Media Revenue
From Mass Markets to Market Segments
Critical Studies
Political Economy
Setting the Agenda
Gatekeeping and Framing
Opinion Leaders
Literary Criticism
The Active Audience
Societal Functions of the Media
Functions of the Mass Media
Functions of New Communications Media
Social Learning Theory
Social Learning of Media Behavior
Social Learning vs. Uses and Gratifications
Diffusion of Innovations
Summary and Review

How can we explain the media? Why is there television? Why are there newspapers? Who decides "what's on" and "what's important," and what criteria do they use? Why do we watch it? Observers of the communications media have come up with many different answers to these questions over the years, reflecting a wide range of underlying assumptions about how society functions and how the individuals in society behave. When scholars analyze these assumptions about the media and formulate them into models of social action or human behavior, we call them **theories** of communications media. These theories can help us understand the media around us and how we respond to them.

As we move, in this chapter, from theories about society at large to the individual, we are changing what the scholars call the *unit of analysis.* At the broadest level of analysis, we consider the role of media in society at large. Next we examine how the media help form culture, and then we move to the media institutions that function within society. When, finally, we consider why individuals use the media, we make the individual the unit of analysis.

There are also grand theories that attempt to cut across all units of analysis. **Economics,** the study of the forces that allocate resources to satisfy competing needs (Picard, 1989), is one such theory. In this chapter, economics is treated at the level of society and media institutions, but it can also be applied to the individual level, as anyone who has ever had to pay the rent will attest. The field of **critical studies** embraces two other paradigms: *political economy,* which explains economic forces from a Marxist perspective, and *cultural studies,* which explains the interrelationships among audiences, media, and culture. **Functionalism** is an approach favored by sociologists, who try to explain media institutions—and also individual media behavior—according to the social functions they fulfill. At the end of the chapter, we will discuss **social learning theory** as an explanation of individual media behavior and will examine how it applies "upward" to media institutions and society at large.

In Chapter 15 we will study a theory that states that the function of media in society depends on the overall nature of the political systems in which they operate; it uses the entire social system as the unit of analysis.

Theories are general principles that can be used to explain things.

Economics is a theory that explains society in terms of the production, distribution, and consumption of goods and services.

Critical studies explains society in terms of the interrelationships among audiences, media, and culture.

According to that theory, in *authoritarian* countries such as Cuba, the government attempts to control not only all aspects of public life but also what individuals do and think. The present chapter focuses on communications media in the United States, where a pattern of private ownership and competition prevails in communications media, coupled with government oversight to prevent the abuses of excessive concentration of economic power. This arrangement, the *social responsibility model,* describes a rather complex interplay of forces that determines the content of the media and who consumes it.

Functionalism is the theory of communications media that explains them in terms of their basic social functions.

Social learning theory explains human behavior in terms of how we learn through our own experience or the experience of others.

MEDIA ECONOMICS

Economics seems to act like a force of nature. Classical economists like to speak of the "invisible hand" that makes societies, organizations, and individuals conform to the laws of economics. In their view, social structure, culture, and individual psychology merely reflect these economic forces. However, as we shall see further on, another group of economists, who call themselves *political economists,* view economic forces as the result of class struggles, rather than the other way around. Chapter 1 discussed how broad historical economic forces shaped society and created the communications media as we know them today. This chapter starts by examining how those same forces determine industry structure and then discusses how they mold the behavior of media institutions.

Mass Production, Mass Distribution: The Keys to Economic Success

As discussed in Chapter 1, throughout the history of communications media, mass production and mass distribution have been the keys to economic success. In this respect, mass media follow a conventional industrial economic model in which profits are reaped by producing many copies of the same basic product at the lowest possible cost (see Figure 2.1). As media companies get larger, expand their scope, and find more consumers, they can spread the *first-copy costs* over more and more consumers. They also may figure out ways to produce media products more efficiently—with lower labor costs, for example. Large media companies are better able to afford investments in such labor-saving technologies as electronic typesetting and robotic television cameras. Or they can buy and merge other media outlets and slash redundant staff. Collectively, we call these factors **economies of scale.**

Economies of scale result in reduced per-unit costs when large numbers of copies are manufactured.

What distinguishes the media from other industries is that the *marginal costs* are low. That is, the incremental, or marginal, cost of each additional copy is very low after that first copy is made. Consider a local newspaper, for example. The first-copy cost includes the cost of the printing presses and the newsroom facilities, the delivery trucks, the salaries for the reporters and the production staff, and all of the management overhead and investment costs associated with getting each edition on the street. But the incremental cost to the publisher for the second

FIGURE 2.1
Mass media develop by building on economies of scale to reap increasing profits from larger mass markets.

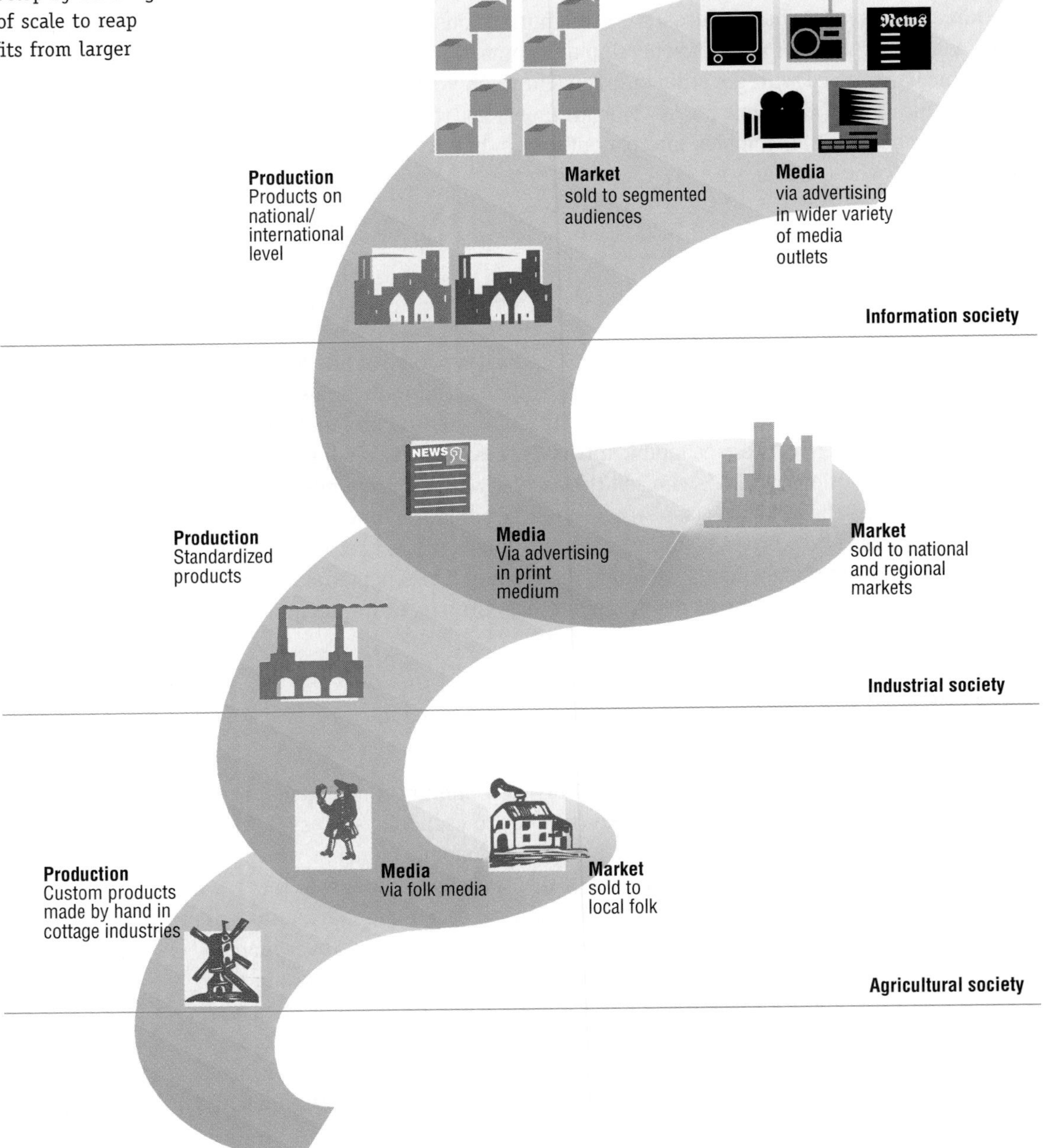

person who reads the paper is minimal over and above the cost of the first person. Although the marginal costs are minimal, they are not zero (printing each additional copy costs *something*), so publishers prefer to offset these incremental costs by charging subscription fees to supplement their advertising revenues.

The principle is essentially the same in advertising-supported media such as television and radio and in commercial Web sites, except that the cost of each additional copy of, say, a TV program, radio broadcast or a Web site, are virtually zero. That is, whether one person views or listens to it or a million people do, the cost to the source is the same. But production efficiencies are hard to come by, because each program or home page is an original product. Instead, advertising media such as radio and television rely on a different principle: They realize profits by distributing the same product to wider and wider audiences, which generates more advertising dollars because advertisers will pay more if they know they can reach a larger audience. The cost of broadcasting a program to 1000 homes is the same as broadcasting it to 2000 homes, but the value to the advertiser doubles. Mass-producing the media product for the widest possible audience thus tends to fatten profits.

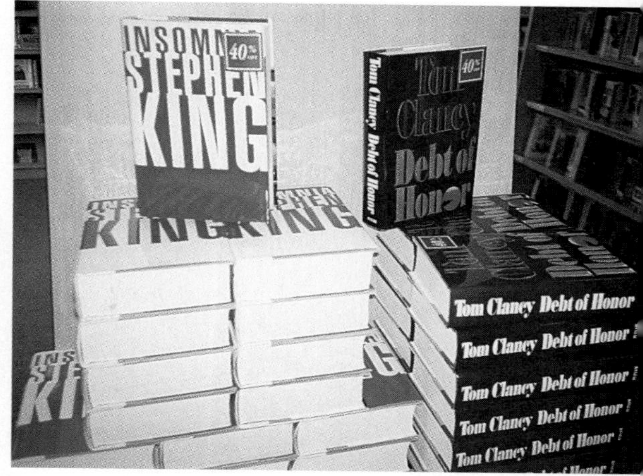

CHEAPER BY THE THOUSAND. The first-copy costs are offset by revenues from many thousands of identical copies.

The media can reinvest some of these profits to find ways to make improved products that consumers want more. For example, film companies invest their profits in new films that they hope will be hits. In the presence of competition, some of the cost savings may also be passed along to consumers. When this happens, the **law of supply and demand** dictates that more people will consume the product, leading to further economies of scale, further improvements in production and products, and so on. It is perhaps easiest to grasp these concepts in relation to standard consumer items such as color television sets. Continuous improvement in electronics and manufacturing techniques has reduced the price of a color TV set from $6000 in 1953 to less than $200, in today's dollars, today.

The **law of supply and demand** describes the relationship among the supply of products, profits, prices, and consumer demand.

Ownership Patterns

Even so, the system does not always work in the consumer's favor. The producer can pocket the cost savings in the form of higher profits—especially if there is no **competition** around to undercut the price or introduce attractive new products. In fact, why bother to become more efficient? Sometimes producers can make more money by simply raising prices, provided that the price is not so steep that consumers forgo making any purchase.

Competition exists when several companies supply the same market.

Although many countries, including the United States, try to prevent abuses such as price gouging, private ownership can still lead to ownership patterns that are not in the best interest of consumers. These patterns include **monopoly,** in which one company dominates an industry, and **oligopoly,** in which a few companies dominate (see Figure 2.2). Of course, big is not invariably bad. In fact, the greatest economies of scale should result when there is only a single provider of a product, because the initial costs are spread among the greatest possible number of consumers (Noam, 1983).

Monopoly exists when one company dominates or controls an industry.

Unfortunately, however, big companies can behave badly when they dominate a market. They use their *market power* to get away with underhanded tactics, such as slashing prices below costs to drive smaller competitors out of business. (For example, a large home video chain may rent movies for less than the local "mom and pop" video store can afford to charge.) After the giants have killed off competitors, they can raise prices again to boost profits. Another favorite strategy is to take profits from a business where a company enjoys monopoly dominance, such

Oligopoly exists when only a few companies dominate an industry.

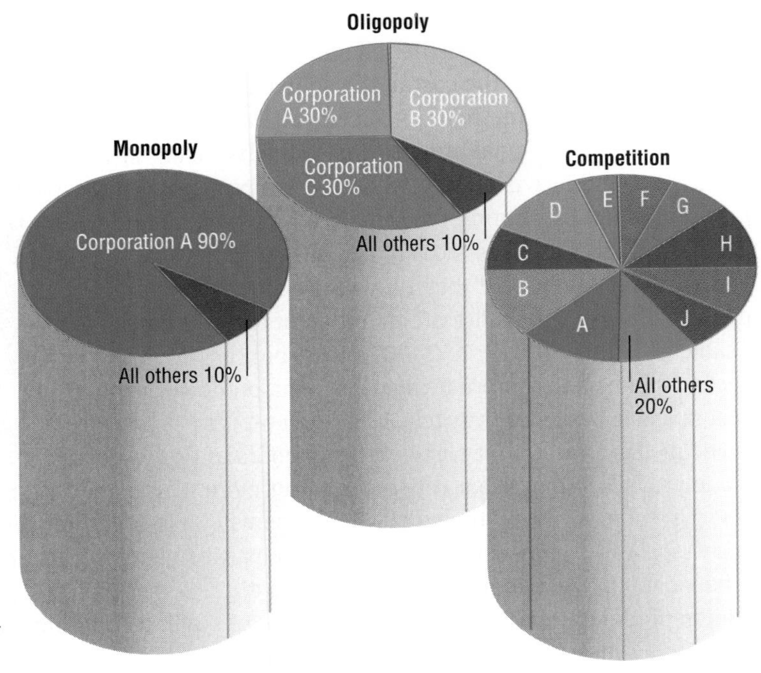

FIGURE 2.2
Media ownership patterns reflect the number of competing media and how they divide the market.

as personal computer operating system software, and use those profits to take over other competitive businesses, such as the market for Internet browser software. (This is what Microsoft is accused of doing in its battle with Netscape for dominance in the browser software market.) Monopolists may also hold back innovations like digital television because they are already making plenty of profits with the status quo. High entry costs can pose barriers to would-be competitors and reinforce narrow or concentrated patterns of ownership. Again, when they finally succeed in dominating the market, companies can raise their prices—and their profits—with impunity.

Monopolies in communications media are especially pernicious because they can result not only in an economic monopoly but also in a monopoly on information, as media owners promote their own views at the expense of diversity. Some communications media, such as the telephone—and, increasingly, cable television and the Internet—are regarded as such necessities that, to keep their service, consumers would be willing to pay far more than their actual costs. Even if there is an oligopoly, wherein several big companies share dominance, the firms can forge a "gentleman's agreement" to fix prices among themselves, with nearly the same effects on the consumer as a monopoly.

We will see in a later chapter that monopolies are capable of such abuses and that there are laws against them, but some still manage to survive. In the media field, for example, the major professional sports leagues enjoy monopoly status when they negotiate the sale of their broadcast rights to an oligopoly consisting of the major

BUSINESSMAN OR MONOPOLIST?
The dominance of the computer software industry by Microsoft Corporation, led by its chairman William Gates, led the U.S. Justice Department to investigate him for monopoly practices.

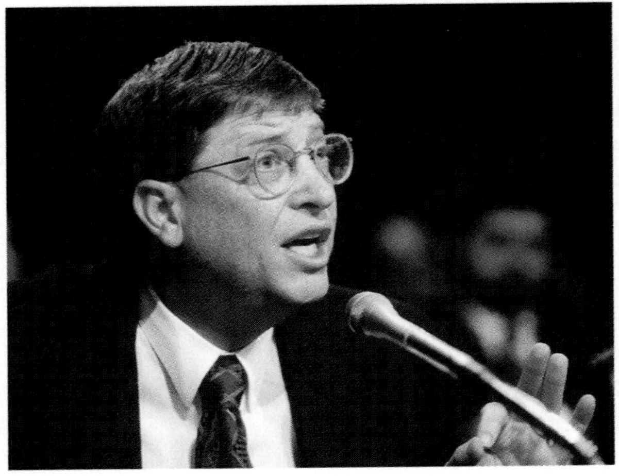

MEDIA WATCH

Follow the Money

For Further Research:

To gain some insight into broadcast economics, we can look at the latest on how much it costs to produce programs for TV—and how much broadcasters can earn from showing their programs by selling advertising time to their sponsors. The trade press publications that cover the industry like to publish stories about new highs in production costs. To get a sense of the going rates, try a keyword search on "production budget." (This may turn up some references to oil production costs; to eliminate them, add "not oil.") The fees that networks have to pay for the rights to broadcast live sporting events are another crucial aspect of television economics these days. Type in "sports rights" to learn the latest. To find out how much television networks are getting for their advertising, try "(up front) and advertising." The "up front" refers to the advertising rates that broadcasters try to get for their new programs when they sell them in advance (up front) to sponsors in the early fall. Many of these articles will indicate the impact of these figures on broadcasters' bottom line—their overall profit or loss. You can also get to that information by typing in the names of broadcast networks, along with money words such as "revenues or profits or net." If you are using InfoTrac College Edition, do a Power Trac keyword search using the search terms above.

advertising-supported networks. This has resulted in multibillion-dollar payments just for the right to transmit pictures of grownups playing children's games.

The Profit Motive

Now we will change our unit of analysis to see how these mighty economic forces that operate at the societal level affect the behavior of individual media organizations. Where private ownership is the norm, as it is in the United States, all else is ultimately subordinate to the flow of profits, which dictate the content of the media and the types of audiences that they seek. In other words, the owners of the media must turn a profit after paying all their operating costs and their taxes. They also have to pay the costs of creating their production and distribution apparatus, known as the *entry costs,* and pay back the money they borrowed from banks or their investors, with interest. Moreover, the profits that media return to their owners must match or exceed the returns that those investors could realize if they invested in other types of businesses or just left their money in the bank (Picard, 1989). The economic pressure is so great that media organizations sometimes have to compromise their public service obligations. For example, they may reduce their news staff to meet the profit goals set by management (Auletta, 1991).

But profits are not always paramount. In many parts of the world (see Chapter 15) public media systems are established to ensure that certain types of content, such as education, cultural arts, or government propaganda, are carried. The Public

Broadcasting Service (PBS) is the prime example of a not-for-profit organization in the United States, but in some countries public ownership extends to nearly all broadcast media and to print media as well. In these cases the government makes up the difference between operating costs and revenues from general tax funds or user fees. No profits are expected.

Sources of Media Revenue

The formula for staying profitable is really quite simple. The payments received from consumers and advertisers are the *economic base* (see Figure 2.3). The

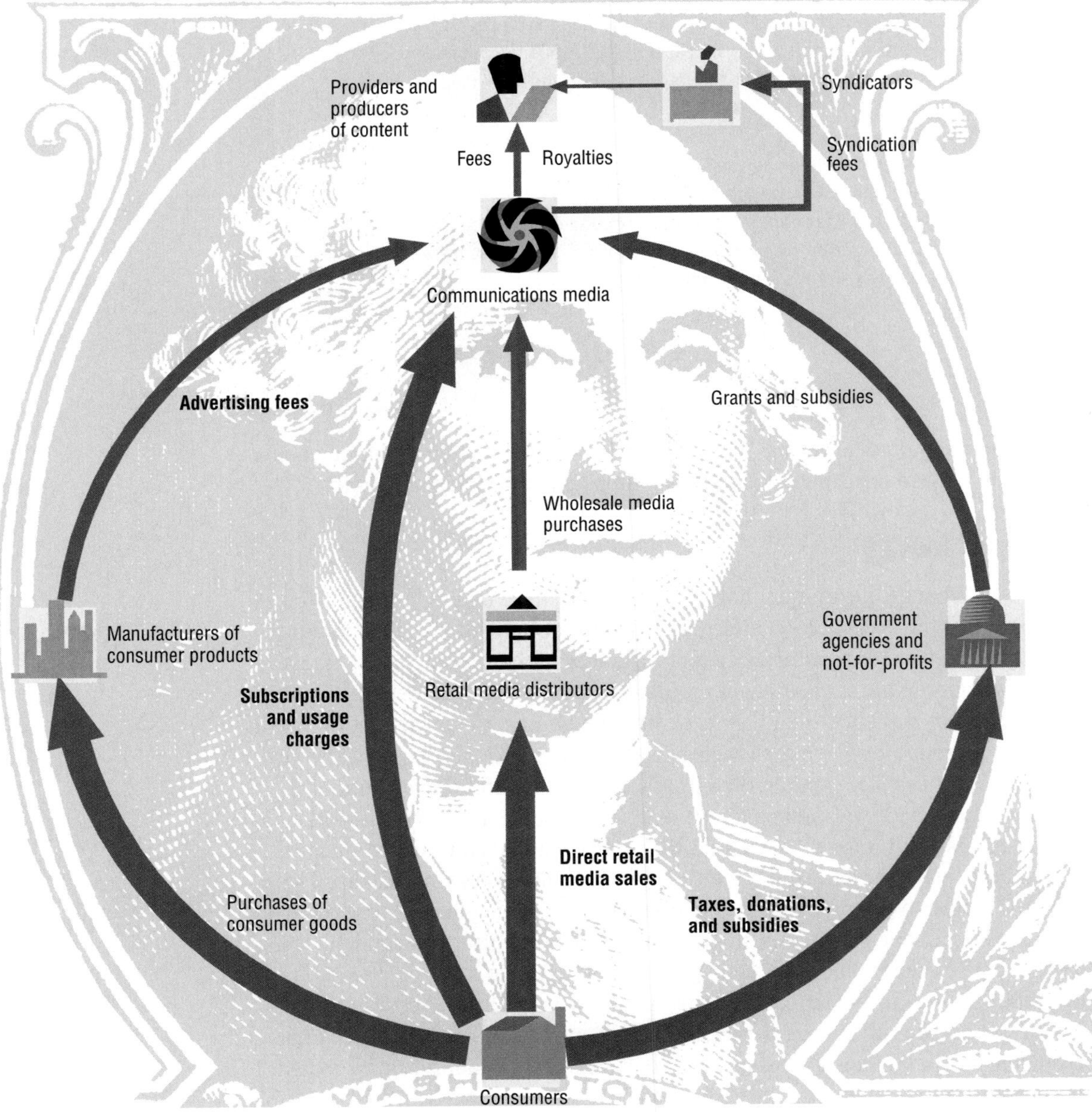

FIGURE 2.3
There are four main ways of paying for media: advertising, direct sales, subscriptions, and public subsidies. Media organizations in turn pay the producers of the content either directly or through syndication agreements and royalty fees.

money from these payments must exceed the total spent on content, distribution, daily operations, taxes, and investment. Payments are made in the following forms.

1. **Direct sales** occur whenever consumers pay out lump sums to purchase tangible cultural or information products that they can take home with them, just as they buy quarts of milk at a supermarket. College textbooks, compact discs, and computer programs are among the media that are commonly purchased in this way. Payments are usually made to a retailer, who passes the money along to the manufacturer through one or more intermediaries. For example, when you buy a compact disc in a music store, the store owner pays a record distribution company, who in turn pays the record company. When you buy a single issue of a newspaper or magazine at a newsstand, that is a direct sale, too.

2. **Rentals** also involve direct payment for a tangible product, except that the consumer only borrows the product and promises to return it after an agreed-upon period of time. Video tape and video game rentals are familiar examples. In these cases, the retail outlet often buys the media product directly from the manufacturer and then recoups the purchase price by renting it, just as a landlord profits by renting an apartment to a tenant.

3. **Subscriptions** are a different form of direct payment in which the consumer is buying a continuing service rather than a single product. The information service may be in the form of a series of publications or installments or access to a body of information for a certain period of time. Newspapers and magazines derive a great deal of their revenues from this source, as do telephone companies and companies that provide access to the Internet. The subscription payments typically go directly back to the provider of the service, although intermediaries may be involved, as when a cable company sends part of your monthly subscription fee back to the cable network that makes the programs you watch on cable.

4. **Usage fees** include admission fees to movies or theaters, as well as the per-minute fees you pay when you are on the telephone. Pay-per-view charges for cable movies are another example. Unlike direct sales, the product you "take home" is not a tangible one; all you come away with is memories of what you saw or heard. Additional charges are often added to the monthly subscription fee for usage beyond what is offered with the basic subscription.

5. **Advertising.** Communications media also have some economic bases all their own. Most important

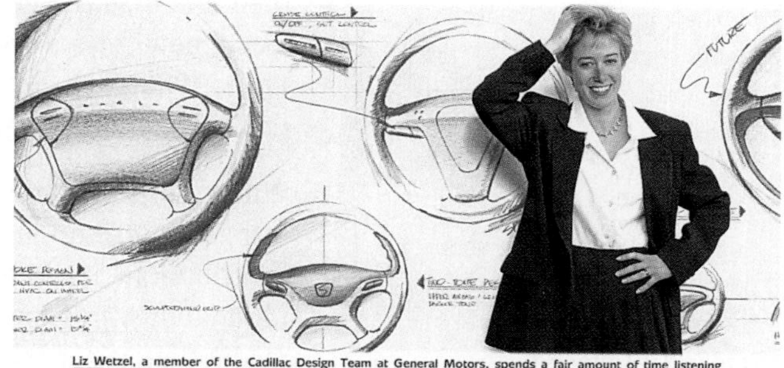

"Finding out what the customer wants is easy. Doing something about it, that's the hard part."
Liz Wetzel, a member of the Cadillac Design Team at General Motors, spends a fair amount of time listening to customers react to her ideas. This is not always fun. Human nature being what it is, most people instinctively want to discount views that don't square with their own. Sometimes responding to customer input means scrapping a beloved notion. It can mean a costly retooling or a delay in production. So be it. These days at General Motors, the customer isn't just somebody with an opinion. The customer is a colleague with a whole lot of clout.

SELLING THE AUDIENCE. Advertising is the major revenue source for mass media. The media sell advertising space on the basis of the size of the audience.

General Motors

In **advertising**, the media sell audience access to those who wish to pay to put their sales message before the audience.

of these is **advertising,** whereby the media "sell" their audiences to advertisers, who in turn wish to sell their products to those audiences. The main economic base for many American media, including all commercial television and radio stations, is advertising. In addition, advertising provides an important partial base for other media, such as newspapers and magazines and World Wide Web services, which have other sources of revenue as well. Advertisers pay for the privilege of placing ads in the hope that they can persuade those who use those media to purchase their products. The price is set in relation to the number of consumers that use the medium.

6. **Syndication** is the rental or licensing of media content to other media. It is an important means of support for producers of news, feature columns, comic strips, films, television, and music. The immediate consumer of the media product is not the end user, but rather other media outlets. For instance, most television programs that run on television networks are produced by independent production companies. After their first run on a network, these programs are often resold as reruns in syndication. There is also "first-run" syndication, wherein the producer sells the media product directly to individual media outlets instead of to a network. For example, a TV station might buy *Wheel of Fortune* in first-run syndication, rather than running a show supplied by its network. The production companies may handle the sales themselves or hand them over to intermediaries, known as syndicators (Eastman, 1993).

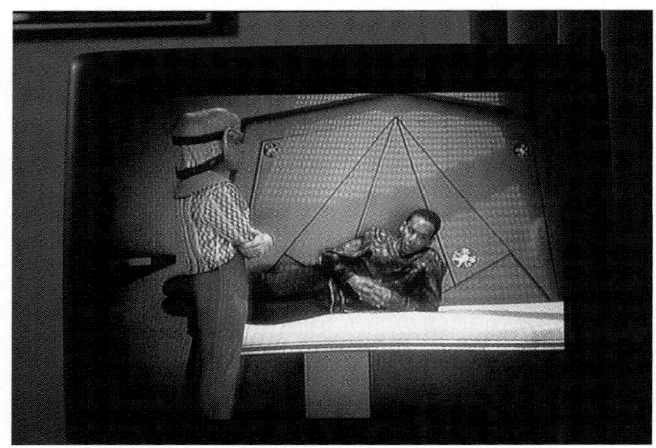

SYNDICATION. First-run syndicated programs such as *Star Trek: Deep Space Nine,* shown here, are sold directly to individual TV stations.

Syndication is a rental or licensing of media products by their producers to other media companies for broadcast, distribution, or exhibition.

7. **Copyright royalty fees** are ways of compensating the creators of media content for the use of their original ideas. For example, when a photograph is used by a newspaper, it pays the photographer for the right to use the photograph. These fees are the photographer's compensation for finding the right subject and taking the photo (Zelezny, 1993). In other cases it is hard to keep track of each use of the copyrighted product. In the music industry, for example, music artists' associations estimate how often songs are played, collect fees from radio stations and live performance venues, and pay the artists their share on the basis of these estimates. Now efforts are being made to create new rules to enforce copyright protection in digital media such as the World Wide Web, where it is extremely easy to make copies and extremely difficult to monitor when copies are made.

Copyright royalty fee is a payment legally required for use of another person's intellectual property.

8. **Public subsidies** are another economic base for media. These may take the form of contributions from individuals to communications media or collective contributions made through government institutions or private charitable foundations. In general, public subsidies are provided for communications media that society considers desirable but commercial interests do not find profitable. Public television is a prime example. The operas, educational programs, and Lawrence Welk reruns on PBS cost too much in relation to the

size of the audiences they attract to be supported by advertising. PBS is therefore subsidized by a combination of federal, state, and local taxes; contributions from private foundations and public institutions; and voluntary contributions from individual viewers like you. Those sponsorship blurbs that sometimes look like ads are technically "enhanced underwriting credits" acknowledging the generosity of private corporations who make large voluntary contributions.

Other examples of public communications subsidies are the so-called *access fees* and *universal service fees* that appear on your monthly telephone bill, which are intended to keep local telephone service affordable to all. There are also many hidden subsidies. For example, for many years business users have paid much more than the true cost of their telephone service so that residential phone service would cost less. And the Internet is subsidized by a wide variety of public sources, including tuition paid by college students whose universities offer "free" Internet access.

From Mass Markets to Market Segments

Economic factors may also dictate the relationships between media and their audiences. From the previous discussion of the benefits of mass production and distribution (pp. 33–35), it would seem natural that communications media would constantly strive to reach larger and larger markets with products that had the broadest possible appeal. Indeed, until recent changes in communications media, this was the case. Now, however, technological changes and receptivity by audiences and advertisers are all encouraging media to *narrowcast*—to target smaller, more specific segments with more specialized content (Owen & Wildman, 1992).

For example, let's go back to 1978 for a minute to consider the economics of television broadcasting. The three broadcast television networks, CBS, NBC, and ABC, ruled the television screens. The top shows could command the attention of up to half the people watching television. Their sponsors sold mass market products that appealed to a broad spectrum of viewers. For the sponsors, this was a good deal—a relatively inexpensive way to present a mass market item to a mass audience.

Fast-forward 20 years and we find that the top-rated television shows reach only a fraction of the audience they once did. Instead of touting the sheer size of the audience, network executives now talk about its "quality": their ability to target special groups of people, such as young consumers aged 18 to 34, that especially interest advertisers. But the media "products" have changed, too. They are no longer the "one-size-fits-all" products of the last generation. Turning to cable television, we find even narrower targeting. Entire channels, such as MTV, are now directed toward specific groups of consumers. We also see a proliferation of magazine titles addressed to almost every conceivable specialized interest, from dog grooming to fly fishing. And on the World Wide Web you can quickly find a Web page that caters to just about anything that might interest you—not just fly fishing, but fly fishing for trout in western Montana (www.montananet.com/rvrbend/fishing.htm).

1. What are economies of scale? Entry costs?

2. Why is the first copy of a mass media production the most expensive?

3. Why do economies of scale lead to mass audience media?

4. What are the basic types of media ownership patterns?

5. Name five sources of media revenues.

6. How do the mass media make profits? Why are profits necessary?

One factor that promotes narrowcasting is the use of information technologies to lower production and distribution costs. This is the move toward desktop production that was discussed in Chapter 1. Another factor that has encouraged narrower market segmentation is advertiser interest in zeroing in on specific groups. The new media outlets help advertisers target specific groups more effectively, making their advertising more efficient. Sophisticated computer techniques give advertisers the ability to think about consumers in new ways as well, making it practical to aggregate a mass audience across multiple media vehicles.

To today's marketers, consumers are no longer anonymous members of broad demographic groups (such as males aged 49–54) but are members of distinctive lifestyle groups (such as aging hippie college professors) and even individuals ("Hello, Mr. LaRose, we have a computer for YOU"). No longer does the advertiser hope to sell a computer to the aging hippie college professor among the millions who tune in to the evening news and view the 30-second computer commercial—the old mass media way of doing things. Instead, the computer company might pay an Internet search engine to display a link to its on-line computer store whenever someone types in "personal computer." Finally, audiences are gravitating toward more specialized media and consumer products. New genres, such as the music video channel and the Web chatrooms, are developing to reflect new trends that are suddenly important enough to excite the profit motive of media developers and consumer goods manufacturers alike. The new specialized media also permit more producers to pursue their own interests, exploring the profitability of catering to yet more specialized tastes. And so it continues . . . .

CRITICAL STUDIES

This brings us to the complex question of the interrelationship between the media and their content, their audiences and *culture*—the ideas by which we conduct our lives and through which we communicate with each other. Here, we will part company with classical economic theory and turn to the *critical studies approach,* another broad paradigm that begins at the societal level as the unit of analysis.

Political Economy

One important school of thought in critical studies looks at media economics from a very different perspective from the one we just presented, a view based on the philosophy of nineteenth-century *political economist* Karl Marx. This analysis of American media suggests that media reflect the interests of advertisers and, through the advertisers' corporations, the general nature of what the people in power want said (Altschul, 1984). According to this theory, we can predict much about the content of the mass media if we know who the owners are (Schiller, 1976; Bagdikian, 1993). As commercial interests become involved in the Internet, the same may be said of that medium as well (McChesney, 1996). In this view, the dominant groups in a society, which are usually those that own the major corporations, want to create an underlying consensus, or **hegemony,** of ideology favoring the system that serves their continued domination. Although consumer needs and the law of supply and demand are still a factor, they are secondary in an economic system devoted to preserving the interests of the ruling classes.

Hegemony is an underlying consensus of ideology that favors a system that serves the interests of a dominant group in society.

For example, although we may see news reports that criticize major corporations for their mistakes, we seldom see anything in the media that questions the basic premise of an economy in which a few large companies maintain social dominance. At the same time, the owners of media compete with various other interests, such as consumer groups, to form public opinion. In this view, any hegemony, or consensus of opinion, reflected in media is a potential source of group conflict (Gramsci, 1971) but the conflicts are usually resolved in favor of those who hold economic power—unless the lower classes revolt.

Critical studies scholars also point out that even media such as public television are actually not free of influence from economic interests. That is because businesses often support public media through direct donations, and large charitable foundations, such as the Ford Foundation, that donate money to public television are controlled by the same group of people who are prominent in the nation's economic and political life. It is usually necessary for major PBS productions to attract corporate or foundation sponsors. Because corporations are unlikely to sponsor programs that are critical of them, such critical programs are largely left unmade. Who would fund a hard-hitting exposé of corporate pollution of the environment, for example?

Communications media may also end up supporting the political and economic status quo in other ways. For example, the trend toward pay-per-use may eventually make what is currently free public information expensive and therefore less accessible (Schiller, 1986; Mosco, 1989). Many sporting events that were once available "free" on commercial TV are now on pay cable. Citizens who can afford the price of a cable TV subscription are empowered to participate more fully in the political process by virtue of watching C-SPAN broadcasts of congressional proceedings as well as broadcasts of local public meetings. Indeed, anyone who cannot afford a personal computer with an Internet connection is in danger of being shut out of the information society both politically and economically.

Setting the Agenda

Exactly how do the agendas of the media owners find their way into our culture? One of the main theories about how media influence society is that media help set the agenda for public and governmental discussions. According to this **agenda-setting** theory, what people identify as issues depends in large part on what the media cover as news and even as entertainment. For example, the O.J. Simpson trial, in which the African American football star defended himself against the allegation that he had murdered his caucasian wife, helped to push race relations to

Agenda setting is the ability of the media to determine what is important.

SETTING THE AGENDA. **Activist groups and organizations try to set the public agenda by staging "media events," such as this antiabortion group's press conference in Buffalo, New York.**

the top of the public agenda in the mid-1990s. Thus agenda setting bestows political power on the media, and the goals and intentions of media decision makers become an important aspect of the social system.

Gatekeeping and Framing

Gatekeeping is deciding what will appear in the media.

Gatekeeping theory (White, 1949; Shoemaker, 1991) emphasizes the crucial role of the so-called gatekeepers, the media executives who can either open or close "the gate" on a media message such as a story, a plot idea, or a song. Reporters also are gatekeepers; they decide whether or not to report an event and how to report it if they do. Editors are gatekeepers when they decide whether to run the story.

A related theory examines how writers frame a story (Atheide, 1974; Gitlin, 1983). Writers decide what to include within the view, or *frame,* of a story, and what to leave out—much as a painter chooses what to put in the frame of a painting. They must decide not only what facts to put in but also what conceptual framework to put them in, what context to include, and how to interpret the facts. In colloquial terms, all of these decisions affect the "spin," or bias, of the story.

French media critic Pierre Bourdieu (1998) contends that even in countries where there is supposedly freedom of expression, there is nonetheless a form of *invisible censorship* at work. Journalists, writers, and producers realize what it is permissible and what it is not permissible to carry in the media, and they pre-edit their own works to be consistent with those perceived norms—all in the interest of remaining employed in communications media companies.

Interestingly, both conservative and liberal critics of the U.S. mass media tend to accuse them of having a *bias* toward the opposite end of the political spectrum. For example, conservative critics complain that most reporters are Democrats, that Hollywood films tend to make military figures and businesspeople look bad, and that popular records undermine the morals of our youth. Liberals insist that media ignore underlying social problems such as poverty and ignorance in favor of safer "human interest" and crime stories that bolster ratings.

Opinion Leaders

Media professionals do not have a free hand to make up the news. They in turn respond to **opinion leaders,** people outside of media organizations who try to influence public opinion. For example, the government plays a role in setting the media's agenda, particularly in news about foreign policy. The media tend to focus on those countries and those issues that the president is talking about, visiting, negotiating with, or fighting (Gandy, 1982). Many other groups help set the agenda for media coverage by calling attention to issues they care about. Foundations commission studies, for example, hoping that the results will make media headlines, and *lobbying groups* such as the Audubon Society and the Sierra Club hold press conferences to publicize environmental problems. Extreme examples are terrorist groups who hijack airplanes or plant bombs to call attention to their grievances.

Opinion leaders are people who try to influence media coverage.

Sometimes the relationship between the media and the opinion leaders they cover can become quite cozy. Political reporters catch rides on the same plane as the politicians they cover, business reporters may go on all-expenses-paid travel junkets to witness the introduction of a new product. How can they avoid feeling pressure to give favorable coverage? This raises the issue of how media professionals are trained and developed (McQuail, 1987). Ultimately, it is the conscience of individual media professionals and their membership in professional societies that uphold those **ethics** that prevent abuse.

Ethics are moral rules of conduct that guide one's actions in specific situations.

While we are on that topic, we should point out that we are having this discussion in the context of the critical studies approach, which questions the motives of the media system. In fact, most journalists would probably deny that they are biased. Instead, they would insist that they are objective, unbiased reporters who adhere to the ethical precepts and standards of their profession (see Chapter 14). Agenda setting, gatekeeping, and opinion leadership can be all analyzed without reference to questions of hegemony or class domination that is implicit here.

Literary Criticism

Another critical studies approach to understanding the relationship among content, audiences, and culture is to look at electronic media as a new kind of literature and apply traditions of *literary* (or *cultural*) *criticism* (Newcombe, 1992; Allen, 1992). This approach tends to focus on *genres,* or types of formats, such as horror or science fiction. Within this tradition, media analysts examine styles of writing or production, storytelling conventions, themes, and characterizations. They probe for both verbal and visual symbols in media (Seiter, 1992; Berger, 1992a, 1992b). In this **semiotic analysis,** words, sounds, and images are interpreted individually as *signs,* or symbols of something other than the literal action. The sign has two components: a *concept,* or the thing signified, and a sound-image, or *signifier.* A media presentation can be thought of as a *text* that the author intends to be read in a

Semiotic analysis is the science of signs, of how meaning is generated in media "texts."

ROMANCE OF THE CENTURY? The hit movie *Titanic* revived the romance genre in contemporary film.

certain way. Berger (1992b) gives the example of a *Star Trek* episode in which a musical theme functions as a sign to announce that the starship *Enterprise* is about to come to the rescue.

However, the audience does not necessarily interpret signs in the same way the author intended. For example, the producers of an old movie may have added romantic violin music to convey passion and romantic tension. But if the audience for the old movie is modern teenagers, they may interpret the soundtrack as corny and funny, not romantic.

Genres are types of formats of media content.

The **genres** that are the focus of this theoretical approach are basically categories of literary or artistic works that have a particular style and format. They become formulas that evolve out of this interaction between the producers and the audience over time (Allen, 1992). For example, the centuries-old form of the novel in literature has been broken down into a number of genres, such as science fiction and gothic romances. Most genre novels are now labeled explicitly on their spines or covers and consigned to different shelves in the bookstore so that would-be readers know what they are getting. But few would be confused, anyway, because we know that the book with the rocket ship on the cover is science fiction and that the one with a bare-chested man and a woman in a long gown is probably a romance. With some minor variations and innovations, the genres of print were subsequently transported to film, radio, and then to television. In computer media as well, we find in games like Quake and Myst echoes of the action adventure and romantic novels of old.

At this point we begin to see that the audience has a role to play in the selection of content. Media creators have to follow certain conventions and produce media that fit the expectations of their audiences; otherwise, they risk alienating those audiences. So, the audience wields a great deal of power in the creative process.

The Active Audience

This introduces one of the most important questions we can ask about communications media: Just how powerful are the media relative to their audiences? Do audiences passively receive media content, or are they active in interpreting it? This debate dates back to the days of World War II. Some experts, such as Adorno and Horkheimer (1972), saw powerful media propaganda as an explanation for some of the brutal acts perpetrated during the war. Today, some see the media as powerful carriers of ideology that impose the interests of ruling groups on vulnerable audiences (Chomsky & Herman, 1988).

In a later chapter on media effects (Chapter 12), we will learn about the processes of *selective exposure, selective attention,* and *selective perception* that social scientists have found greatly reduce the power of the media over individuals. This parallels a popular notion in current cultural studies that media and audiences are *both* powerful and that it is the interaction of media and audiences that creates meaning and shapes culture. One such view of the audience reception process builds on the idea of *reading.* Media producers create *texts.* These include radio programs, music, television shows, and films as well as written text such as books, magazines, and newspapers. Creators of media content have a *preferred reading* that they would like the audience to take out of the text. However, the audience won't necessarily accept or even perceive that preferred reading. The audience might reject it, negotiate some compromise interpretation between what they think and what the text is saying, or contest what the text says with some alternative interpretation (Morley, 1992). For example, Cuban citizens who watch one of the marathon television speeches of President Castro extolling the achievements of communism in Cuba might fully accept Fidel's intended message. But they might instead look around at their own impoverished surroundings and reject Fidel's words. Or they might negotiate a meaning by agreeing with him that communism is good in principle but is, in practice, an ineffective way to run a country.

STOP & REVIEW

1. **What is a political economist?**
2. **What are signs or symbols in media content? List some examples.**
3. **What are the main kinds of "readings" that audiences might make of media?**
4. **Who are gatekeepers and who are agenda setters? What is the difference?**
5. **What are genres, and how do they develop?**
6. **What makes an audience active?**

SOCIETAL FUNCTIONS OF THE MEDIA

According to sociological theories of communications media, the mass media have important functions for us as a society and as individuals. For any society to exist, a number of communication functions have to be performed. We have to keep track of what is going on around us—what sociologists call *surveillance.* We have to put observations and ideas together, correlate them, and interpret what they mean—a process called *interpretation.* We have to *transmit values* from one generation or group to another in order to maintain society. And we need and want to be *entertained* and amused (Wright, 1974).

WATCHING THE WEB. For many, the World Wide Web now performs the surveillance function that was once the province of radio, TV, and newspapers.

Starr Report Skewers Clinton
Kenneth Starr's report to Congress
President Clinton of impeachable
include perjury and obstruction of
details repeated sexual encounters
president and Monica Lewinsky.
Full Story >
CBS
Link directly to these files:
THE STARR REPORT
THE WHITE HOUSE RESPONSE
Download files to your hard drive:
THE STARR REPORT:

Functions of the Mass Media

The following discussion of social functions of the media is based on theories developed by Charles Wright (1974) and other media sociologists. They see the function of media as preserving social stability by enabling people to meet important needs.

Surveillance. If you kept a diary of all the information that you need over the course of a day, you might be staggered by its complexity and diversity. Certain mass media specialize in providing information to help people with their surveillance of the environment. These media include newspapers, news magazines, TV news broadcasts, CNN, The Weather

MEDIA IMPACT

Where Have All the Theories Gone? 

For Further Research:

Communications theories continuously change over time as new facts are made and new paradigms emerge to replace old ones. If you have the InfoTrac College Edition, you can find out the latest developments by just typing in the name of a theoretical paradigm as an InfoTrac College Edition keyword search; you might try "uses and gratifications," "social learning," "cultivation analysis," or "agenda setting." To find out the latest in critical communications research, try "cultural studies" or "political economy," but keep in mind that these theories extend beyond the field of communications studies, so you might want to narrow your search—with "and communication," for example. The number of citations will give you a rough idea of how actively each of these theories is being pursued by researchers today, although InfoTrac does not index all the important communications media journals. Searches on the names of important researchers associated with each theory (such as Albert Bandura, Everett Rogers, and Karl Marx) should turn up some of the latest works they have written (if they are still alive), as well as researchers who refer to them by name.

Look especially for "full text" citations. The most recent studies will run down the latest theoretical developments in the first part of the paper, which is usually a review of previous research. They will give you a feel for the kinds of studies that contribute to theory building—and that you will learn to conduct if you choose a career in academia. Each new study is supposed to add new knowledge, so read a couple of them and write down exactly how each one breaks new ground or further confirms or extends an existing theory. Look for this information toward the end of the paper in the Discussion or Conclusion section, where the researchers make the case for the significance of their work.

Channel, and C-SPAN. We also use the telephone and, increasingly, electronic mail to keep up with what is going on in our personal lives. Many users of the World Wide Web find that it is an exceptionally powerful tool for surveillance, because it enables us to seek out information on topics of interest to us rather than passively waiting for the media to bring them to our door.

Interpretation. Information is not of much use until it is processed, interpreted, and correlated with what we already know. Although we do much of this analysis ourselves, aided by the groups we belong to, the media provide much of the interpretation and meaning. Television documentaries tell us why a situation or crisis developed; soap operas tell us what other lifestyles are supposed to look like. New information media like Internet news groups permit people with narrow common interests, such as the newest car or the latest teenage heart-throb, to discuss and share them, reinforcing world-views and values.

Values Transmission/Socialization. One of the most important functions of culture is to pass ideas from one generation to another. Anthropologists observe that as soon as human beings had language, they were using it to pass on ideas to their children. Mass media changed the process. When human societies were exclusively oral, individuals learned things directly from other people who lived near them—and who were probably very much like them. Each village might have its own unique dialect and myths. Today media have assumed many of the traditional roles of storytellers, teachers, and even parents, and they transmit the same cultural concepts all over the world. This function is not limited to media with an obvious educational or informational function, such as college textbooks or television news programs, but rather includes all media.

Entertainment. Perhaps the most common daily function of mass media is to entertain. With the exception of magazine-style information programs such as *60 Minutes* and *20-20,* the top ten programs on network television have always been predominantly entertainment programs. Americans spend enormous amounts of time and money on going to feature films, listening to music, renting videos, watching television comedies, and, now, "surfing" the Internet just for fun.

Functions of New Communications Media

In the past, scholars had only the mass media in mind when discussing the social functions of communications media. The rapid spread of the Internet now raises questions about its social functions. In particular, the Internet has attracted attention for its function in building and maintaining new "virtual" communities, even cultures (Dery, 1996). Research on that oldest of interactive media, the telephone, provides another perspective (LaRose, 1998). Though it is often thought of as a medium for interpersonal communication, the phone also appears to have an entertainment function, a social maintenance function, and a function in commerce—inasmuch as we are able to obtain products and services by completing transactions over it. The Internet has become a source of commerce too, as more products are bought on-line.

SOCIAL LEARNING THEORY

What accounts for individual media consumption behavior? How and why do we make the choices we do about which TV program to watch, which newspaper to read, and which new media to bring into our lives? For guidance in answering these questions, we turn to yet another theoretical perspective, *social learning theory* (Bandura, 1986), also known as *social cognitive theory.*

LEARNING TO LOVE THEM. According to social learning theory, we watch hit shows such as *Friends,* shown here, because they fulfill expectations we have formed about the desirable outcomes of viewing—such as a few laughs.

Social Learning of Media Behavior

According to social learning theory, our media consumption patterns are shaped by our own direct experience with them and also by the experiences of others that we observe. For example, if we see one of our friends laughing at a Donald Duck comic book, we may ask to borrow it. If we enjoy reading that particular Donald Duck comic book, we are likely to buy more of them or even try other comics for enjoyment. If we are bored by Donald or offended by his bad-tempered antics, we will avoid future issues. In other words, when we receive positive reinforcement for our comic book reading (we laugh or see others laugh), it is more likely that we will repeat the same media behavior in the future. When we get negative reinforcement (we are bored or offended), we are less likely to persist in that behavior.

The outcomes we expect from our media behavior are in a constant state of flux as we encounter new media. These changing perceptions alter our behavior. Our life situation may also change, and with it the criteria we use to select media. At some stages of our lives we may seek media that entertain; at other times information may be more of a priority. We may trade in our comic book collection for a pile of college textbooks, for example. We also learn from others by listening to what they have to say about the media. These individuals include both the "real" people in our daily lives and the writers and media personalities that we encounter in the media.

Social Learning vs. Uses and Gratifications

Uses and gratifications is the theory that predicts media usage according to the human needs that they satisfy.

For many years, the **uses and gratifications** perspective dominated thinking about media consumption behavior, which it explained in relation to the media's expected ability to gratify general human needs for new knowledge, social interaction, and diversion. Recently, the theory has been reformulated (Palmgreen & Rayburn, 1985) to focus on the match between the gratifications we seek and those we actually obtain from the media. For example, research on the uses and gratifications of the World Wide Web (Eighmey & McCord, 1998) has found that entertainment, information, and personal approach are important gratifications that people expect of Web pages. The Web sites that fulfill these expectations are likely to earn repeat visits. Thus the uses and gratifications theory winds up being the same as social learning theory, in the end.

But social learning theory is superior to the uses and gratifications theory in many ways. It better explains the avoidance of media, as in "I'd better not let Mom catch me watching the Playboy channel, or I'll be grounded." Here, the expectation of a negative consequence for media behavior dictates usage. The social learning perspective further adds the notion that media behavior may arise out of our own inner self-evaluations. "I'm not watching *Third Rock from the Sun* tonight because I am disgusted with how much of a couch potato I am." Another important factor that the uses and gratifications theory ignores is our perception of our own competency to complete the task in question, our *self-efficacy.* This is certainly a factor in computer media. And what computer user has not had an attack of *computer anxiety,* a fear of using computers (Kernan & Howard, 1990), after an especially frustrating day at the keyboard? Social learning theory explains how we may generalize these bad experiences and come to associate them with the medium rather than the message. Finally, as we will see in Chapter 13, social learning theory is one of the leading approaches for understanding the effects of mass media, as well as the consumption of the media.

Social learning theory also works well as we change the unit of analysis to the organization level or even the societal level. It has been proposed as a way to explain media usage in organizations, where it is known as the social influence model (Fulk, Schmitz, & Steinfield, 1990). Organizations learn which types of media are most effective at certain tasks and use them accordingly, although social influence—what the boss wants, mainly—also plays an important role. But aren't companies in business to turn a profit? Indeed they are, but they are run by people, and those people quickly learn that pleasing the boss is one way to increase their own personal rewards. In fact, social learning theory can explain the *profit motive* that we proposed at the beginning of this chapter. The quest for profit is just another way of saying that people tend to persist in behavior that they expect to have positive consequences for them.

DIFFUSION OF INNOVATIONS

Finally, social learning theory helps us understand why people decide to start using a new communications medium to begin with (Rogers, 1995). In the most general sense, **diffusion** is a process by which an innovation—a new way of doing things—is communicated through mass media and interpersonal channels over time among the members of a community. This approach has proved to be one of the most useful in describing how new media get accepted.

Diffusion is the process whereby innovations spread in a social system.

For example, researcher Everett Rogers (1986) observed that VCRs diffused very quickly in the United States, going from 1 percent of American households in

PROFILE

The Most Widely Cited Living Social Scientist

Name: Everett Rogers

Education: Ph.D., Iowa State University, 1957

Current Position: Professor, University of New Mexico, Department of Communication & Journalism

Style: Casually collegiate; sports jacket, no tie.

Most Notable Achievement: His work on the diffusion of innovations is widely recognized both within and outside the field of communications studies; it is the most widely cited work in social science.

Most Dubious Achievement: His early work on diffusion in developing countries was criticized for promoting the interests of developed nations and ruling elites at the expense of the peasants, a position that he has since modified in favor of a "grassroots-up" approach to development of communication.

Entry Level: After getting his Ph.D., Dr. Rogers first taught at Iowa State, then Ohio State, and then at Michigan State University's Department of Communication.

His Inspiration: During his time in Iowa, he learned of 1940s studies of how new varieties of seed corn spread from farm to farm. He realized that the same principles might apply to innovations of all types.

How He Got to the Top: Success came through the two things that major universities value most: numerous scholarly publications and lucrative grants. The number of times other scholars cite one's work is another way of "keeping score" in academia. Citations indicate how influential one's work is, and it is here that Ev, as he is known, reigns supreme. And, oh yes, teaching counts, too. He is a world-renowned lecturer. He also advanced his career through a series of appointments at prestigious universities, including the University of Michigan, Stanford, and the Annenberg School for Communication at the University of Southern California.

Where Does He Go from Here? His latest research examines the transfer of technology from university research centers to private industry and the diffusion of information about AIDS.

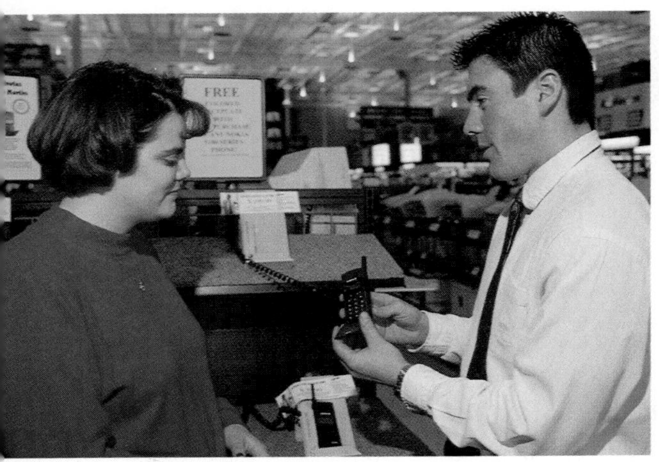

NOW I NEED ONE, TOO. The "diffusion of innovation" theory tells us how innovations, such as the cellular phone, spread from person to person—almost like a disease.

1980 to 20 percent in 1985 to 80 percent in 1998. Costs are important in diffusion. VCR prices declined rapidly, from $2200 in 1975 to $300 in 1985 to under $100 in 1998, which made VCRs more accessible. As a general rule, all new technologies follow a similar price pattern, the first few units sold costing 10 or more times as much as the last units sold—a direct consequence of the economies of mass production we discussed earlier.

How quickly an innovation diffuses depends on several factors. What are the relative advantages of the new idea compared to existing ways of doing things? What is the compatibility of the new idea with existing ways of doing things? How complex is the new idea? How difficult is the new technology to operate? How easy is it to try out the new way before committing a lot of time or money to it? Can people observe some other, similar situations wherein others are already successfully doing things this new way? In social learning terms, the information about the innovation that we acquire from the media and the observations we make of it "in action" form our expectations of how it will perform for us, persuading us whether to adopt it or not.

VCRs scored very highly on all these counts, and therefore their use spread rapidly. The VCR offered a clear expansion of viewing options, was compatible with both television hardware and movie/TV "software" or content, was similar in concept to older tape recorder technology, and was easy to use (except perhaps for time-delayed recording). And by the mid-1980s most people had a chance to watch family and friends using them.

Certain prior conditions can affect diffusion of innovations. One is the amount of previous practice or experience people have had with similar technologies. For example, among the first people to use portable cellular telephones in their cars

FIGURE 2.4
Some people adopt new ideas earlier than others. The majority of people tend to adopt only after innovators and early adopters have forged the way.

were those who had already used mobile radios. Another condition is the *innovativeness* of potential adopters; some people are naturally more inclined than others to try out new gadgets. Finally, the norms of the social system play a role. Cellular phones went from being associated with blue-collar delivery truck drivers to being chic for executives, a change that spurred adoption among white-collar workers.

Diffusion of new communication technology goes through a predictable sequence of stages. First, we gain knowledge about the new idea from the media and from people we know. Then we weigh the merits of trying it. Next, we decide to try it. Finally, we implement that decisionif we still believe that the innovation will do desirable things for us. Afterwards, we continue to reassess our experience with the innovation and either confirm, reject, or modify our use of it.

1. **What are the main social functions of the mass media?**
2. **How does social learning theory explain media usage?**
3. **What is the difference between social learning theory and uses and gratifications?**
4. **Using the "diffusion of innovations" paradigm, explain how the use of VCRs spread through society.**

People do not adopt new ideas at the same rates (see Figure 2.4). Those who first figure out how to use a new technology or idea to accomplish something are called *innovators.* People who follow up on innovative ideas through specialized media such as trade journals or interpersonal contacts are *early adopters.* Those who perceive a trend relatively early and decide to go with it make up the *early majority.* Those who wait to see what most people are going to do constitute the *late majority.* Those who wait until the very end have been called *laggards.*

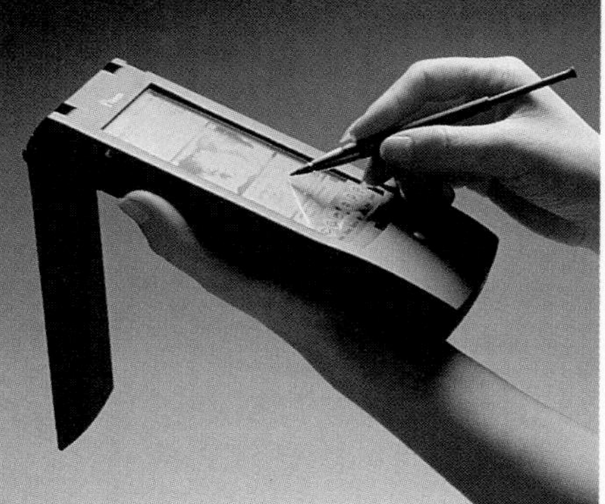

FAILURE.
Not all innovations succeed. Apple's early personal data assistant product, *Newton,* failed to catch on because of a faulty handwriting-recognition program.

Interactive communication technologies diffuse in a characteristic way. First, a certain minimum number, or *critical mass,* of adopters and users of a new technology are necessary for it to be useful enough for most people to go along with the trend (Markus, 1990). Because both computers and telecommunications technologies are relatively flexible tools, they tend to be used in new, unanticipated ways by their adopters. Rogers (1986) calls this *reinvention.* For instance, early adopters of personal home computers were often attracted by their potential to play educational software for children or manage family finances. But once they had them, most adopters used them to play computer games. Now the personal computer is being reinvented again, as a tool to send electronic mail and access information on the Internet.

SUMMARY AND REVIEW

HOW DO ECONOMICS INFLUENCE THE NATURE OF THE MASS MEDIA?

First-copy costs in mass media require virtually all the investment in the production of the work. Examples are the master print of a film, the printing plates of a newspaper or book, and the master recording of a song. Economies of scale occur when manufacturers make so many copies of something that they learn how to make each of those copies more cheaply. By the law of supply and demand, cheaper copies can reach far more people, creating a broader audience. Producers want to spread production costs and also their entry costs—the initial costs of establishing a media enterprise—across a broad audience in order to increase profits and satisfy their investors.

WHY ARE THE PATTERNS OF MEDIA OWNERSHIP SO IMPORTANT?

Media can be structured as monopolies, where one company dominates the industry; as oligopolies, where a few companies dominate; or in competition, where a number of companies vie for dominance. The patterns of ownership have a great deal to do with the diversity and nature of the media's content, their availability and accessibility to people, and their role in society. Generally speaking, the more the ownership of media is concentrated in the hands of a few, the less diverse and more expensive the media are.

WHAT ARE THE MAIN SOURCES OF REVENUE FOR COMMUNICATIONS MEDIA?

Most revenues come directly from the end user of media products. Direct sales of media products occur when consumers pay out a lump sum and take a tangible media product home with them, such as a book or a CD. Rentals also involve a payment for a tangible product, except that the consumer pays only to borrow it, as in a videotape rental. Subscriptions permit magazines and other media to be sold on a continuing basis over time for a standard fee. Usage fees are charged for access to intangible media products, such as movie theater admissions and telephone calls, that consumers can't literally go home with. The media collect advertising revenues by selling access to their audiences to advertisers, who in turn pay for advertising by charging higher prices to consumers.

WHAT IS SYNDICATION?

Some media producers sell what they produce primarily to other media companies for broadcast, distribution, or exhibition. The customers are other media outlets, rather than individual consumers. Syndication, or the rental or licensing of media content to other media, is an important means of support for the creators and producers of news, feature columns, comic strips, films, television, and music.

WHAT IS A COPYRIGHT? HOW DO MEDIA CREATORS USE IT TO GET PAID FOR THEIR WORK?

A copyright is a legal protection granted by the government to the creator of an artistic work. If a work is copyrighted, any use of that work requires permission of the copyright holder, who may charge a royalty fee for permission to use it. Royalty fees are sometimes the creator's only compensation for his or her work.

WHAT IS THE ROLE OF PUBLIC SUBSIDIES?

Public subsidies, from either voluntary contributions or taxes, are provided for socially desirable content that commercial interests do not find it profitable to provide. The educational and cultural programs on the Public Broadcasting Service (PBS) are prime examples. So are telephone user fees that subsidize access by the poor.

WHAT IS THE RELATIONSHIP BETWEEN SEGMENTATION AND NARROWCASTING?

Technological changes, industry changes, and receptivity by audiences and advertisers are all encouraging media to segment their audiences—that is, to focus on smaller, more specific audiences with more specialized programs or contents. The targeting of media content to appeal to the tastes of a particular narrow audience segment is called narrowcasting.

HOW DO POLITICAL ECONOMISTS EXPLAIN MEDIA CONTENT?

The dominant class in society uses its ownership of the media to influence their content. This class creates a consensus, or hegemony, of ideas that reinforces its position of dominance. In this view, maintaining class dominance is furthered by the profitability of media enterprises.

WHAT IS THE RELATIONSHIP AMONG OPINION LEADERS, GATEKEEPING, AND AGENDA SETTING?

Opinion leaders from government, businesses, and political interest groups try to influence what the media cover and what "spin" media give to that coverage. Within the media themselves, a variety of media professionals make decisions at different levels to decide what goes into and what stays out of news and entertainment media. They are the gatekeepers. Media help to set the agenda for society at large by virtue of the amount of coverage they give to different issues, so the battle to control media can be quite important.

WHAT IS SEMIOTICS, AND WHAT ARE SIGNS?

Semiotics is a systematic way of looking at media content to examine the symbols and signs contained in it. The signs in media communicate something of symbolic value to the audience; they include visual images, music, camera angles, words, and so on. The producer creates or encodes a meaning into the sign, but the audience may decode or interpret a different meaning.

WHAT ARE GENRES IN MEDIA?

In media content, formulas, or genres, evolve over time. These formulas are things like soap operas, mystery novels, and action cartoons. They represent an agreement between producer and audience on what kinds of stories ought to be told and how, or on how a music video ought to look, or on how a talk show host ought to act.

HOW ACTIVE IS THE AUDIENCE?

Audiences seem to read the "texts" of media in a fairly active way. Some audience members might accept the "preferred" meaning—the reading that the writer or producer intended them to get out of the text. Others might use their own experiences and ideas to negotiate their own meaning out of their reading of the material. Others might contest or even oppose the meaning that the author intended.

WHAT FUNCTIONS DO MEDIA SERVE FOR SOCIETY?

Among the functions sociologists have identified for communications media are surveillance (keeping track of our world or environment), interpretation (making sense of what we learn), value transmission (passing values on from one generation to the next), and entertainment.

WHY DO PEOPLE USE PARTICULAR MEDIA?

Through their interactions with the media and their observations of others, people learn expectations about the consequences of media use that shape their media behavior. Positive outcomes include learning new things, diversion, and social interaction. But they may also wish to avoid media that they find boring or offensive.

HOW DO NEW COMMUNICATIONS MEDIA SPREAD IN A SOCIETY?

New technologies spread like a disease, from person to person, slowly at first but gradually picking up speed. People consider an innovation's relative advantages, its compatibility with existing practices, its complexity, and any opportunities they have to observe the innovation in action before they try it out themselves. Some people are innovators, some are early adopters, followed by the majority of adopters, late adopters, and laggards. Interactive technologies seem to require a critical mass of users before large numbers will adopt it.

Electronic Resources

For up-to-the-minute URLs about *Media Theory,* access the MEDIA NOW site on the World Wide Web at:

http://communication.wadsworth.com/

CHAPTER 3

Books and Magazines

WHAT'S AHEAD

This chapter examines the development of books and magazines from hand copying by medieval monks to computer "books," and from early magazines to electronic "'zines" that exist only in cyberspace. It looks at how technologies, contents, and audiences have changed, and considers what ethical issues publishing professionals face as they keep up with technology and industry change.

WWW

Access the MEDIA NOW site on the World Wide Web at:
http://communication.wadsworth.com/
Choose "Chapter 3" from the selection box to access electronic information and other sites relevant to this chapter.

THE OFFICES OF MURDOCH-TURNER PUBLISHING ASSOCIATES, 2017

Good morning, Miss Bassey. I understand you have an idea for a new magazine?

Yes, Ma'am. I think I have spotted a new trend that nobody has a magazine for yet.

You realize, I hope, that there are 50,000 magazines now. And if you go on the Web, then almost everybody has some kind of "zine" about pet chihuahuas or something that they hope people will be interested in.

I know. I probably read a couple of dozen magazines a week myself.

So your idea better be pretty good, to break into all that competition.

Oh, it is. I want to do a magazine about what celebrities, like Hollywood stars, eat for breakfast. It would have gossipy stuff about the stars, nutritional advice, lots of great photos, great advertising potential—just think of the breakfast cereal companies.

Hmmnn. Not bad, it sounds a little silly on first thought, but I think we can put a little development money your way. I'll bet we can make a killing off Kellogg alone!

Chapter Outline

A Brief History of Print Communication
Early Print Media
The Gutenberg Revolution
Early Print Media in America
Modern Publishing
Technology Trends in Books and Magazines
Publishing Changes with the Internet
Print Genres and Forms
Book Publishing
Magazine Genres: Where Does Segmentation Stop?
Industry Organization
Magazine Industry Consolidation
Magazine Distribution
Book Publishing Houses and Groups
Bookstores
Selling Books and Magazines On-Line
Audiences for Books and Magazines
Policy Issues for Print Media
Consolidation and Concentration of Ownership
Intellectual Property and Copyright
Censorship, Freedom of Speech, and the First Amendment
Summary and Review

A BRIEF HISTORY OF PRINT COMMUNICATION

Early Print Media

The history of the print media is a repetitive cycle of technological innovation, competition as new forms and uses of media arise, increased demand for new services and abilities, changes in society wrought by media, and governmental attempts to restrict the media's political power.

The early development of writing, paper, and printing took place in the Middle East and China. In C.E. 105 the Chinese began making paper from rags, but it was not until C.E. 700 that Arab traders brought this new technology to the West. Using wooden blocks to print characters had been practiced earlier during the T'ang Dynasty in China (C.E. 618–906), followed by the development of movable clay type in 1000 and that of *movable metal type* in 1234 in Korea. These inventions did not spawn a large printing industry, however. It was not until the beginning of the Industrial Revolution in the fifteenth century that Johannes Gutenberg of Germany (re)discovered movable type and Europeans began to develop further and exploit the printing press (Carter, 1991).

Books have long been a "mass" medium, in the limited sense that manuscripts were hand-copied and distributed to audiences. Literacy and reading came five thousand years before the modern mass media. Until Gutenberg's press in 1455, however, books were a limited medium in Europe and the rest of the world. For thousands of years, printed materials were available only to an **elite,** the few best-educated and often most powerful people in society, such the Mandarin bureaucratic elite of China. In the civilizations of Greece, Egypt, China, Islam, and Rome, few people were highly educated and had access to libraries. In China and the Islamic nations, interest in literature and books on science and philosophy flourished among an educated few.

Elite are better educated, more affluent, higher status audiences who have earlier, wider access to media.

Books tended to build on earlier **oral traditions.** The Hebrew *Torah* (familiar to Christians as the first five books of the *Old Testament*), started out as oral tradition and was written down later. The same is true of early Greek epics such as *The Iliad* and of European literature such as the Icelandic sagas and the folk stories and fairy tales collected by the brothers Grimm.

Oral traditions are poetry, stories, ballads, and other pre-media forms of culture passed orally from one generation to another.

BOOKS AND MAGAZINES TIME LINE

C.E. 105	Rag-based paper invented in China
1000	Movable clay type invented in China
1234	Movable metal type invented in Korea
1455	Gutenberg Bible
1602	First modern lending library, the Bodley
1640	First book published in the American colonies
1731	First magazine published
1732	*Poor Richard's Almanack*
1790	First U.S. copyright law enacted
1846	Rotary press (type on cylinder) invented in the United States
1857	*Harper's Weekly* begins publication
1860	Heyday of the "Dime Novel" begins (through 1880)
1900	Magazine muckraking reporting
1909	Copyright Act of 1909
1923	*Time* magazine introduced
1936	*Life* magazine introduced
1960s	Computer-based photo composition and "typesetting" begins
1969	*Saturday Evening Post* succumbs to specialized competition
1980s	Desktop publishing begins
1980	Number of publishers doubles from 1970 to 12,000
1998	70,000 book titles by 50,000 publishers; Sonny Bono Copyright Term Extension Act

A key development in print media was the growth of literacy and the distribution of books in the **vernacular,** the everyday languages that Europeans spoke. Prior to 1100, written communication was nearly always in Latin, the language of the Catholic Church. Thus, to be literate, people had to learn a second language. By the 1200s, written versions of daily languages were more common. Books were being written in vernacular languages: Italian, French, German, English, and Swedish. In the 1300s and 1400s, literacy became more commonplace among the political elite, the commercial and trading class, and such professionals as the sea captain Columbus. Outside this group, though, most people remained illiterate.

Vernacular is the everyday language that people speak, like German, compared to official religious or governmental languages, like Latin in the European Middle Ages.

As European society gradually became more specialized, reading and writing were initially the job of clerks and priests. Monks often devoted their lives to copying books by hand. The books were often beautifully illustrated as well. Some surviving examples, among them the Irish *Book of Kells,* are considered major works of art. In Europe throughout the Middle Ages, few books other than the Bible and religious or philosophical commentaries were available. This began to change by the 1300s and 1400s. Universities were established to train more people as clerks, and nobles began to take an interest in learning to read.

A number of the most important books that were printed and circulated in Europe actually came from the Hebrew Middle East (*the Bible, the Torah*) or the Arab Middle East (books on science, math, astronomy, and navigation). Many came from ancient Greece (classic works of science, literature, and philosophy, such as Plato's *Republic,* which influenced European ideas of democracy). Printing these classic or ancient works gave people access to ideas from books that had

HAND MADE. Among the earliest books were illuminated manuscripts, carefully done by hand.

survived in hand-copied form for centuries. The existence of useful books on mathematics, science, and geography furthered interest in reading.

Europeans obtained access not only to Greek and Roman texts but also to works developed elsewhere in the world. For instance, in the late 1400s, Christopher Columbus learned from an Arab book on geography that he might be able to reach India and Southeast Asia by sailing west across the Atlantic Ocean. People such as Columbus would probably not have had access to such books a hundred years earlier. Clearly, the European explosion of print technology and printed contents built on a much larger world context.

The Gutenberg Revolution

The Gutenberg Bible first appeared in 1455, the result of the development of movable type and mechanical printing five years earlier by Johannes Gutenberg. His 1455 printing press and others that followed fueled an explosion in early book printing. Technology breakthroughs such as Gutenberg's press made possible new forms of mass production. The new press could print many more books, handbills, or newsletters at a much lower cost. By 1470 a French printed Bible cost one-fifth of what a **manuscript** version had cost, even though the printed one was a careful, relatively expensive duplication of the hand-copied original. As the Industrial Revolution gained momentum, printing and reading became a cyclical process that reinforced itself. As more people had sufficient money and interest to buy books, book production benefited from **economies of scale** (see Chapter 2) and became cheaper, which permitted even more people to buy books.

Manuscript originally meant written or copied by hand.

Economies of scale result in reduced per-unit costs when large numbers of copies are manufactured.

Chapbooks were cheaply bound books or pamphlets of poetry or prose aimed at a broader audience, much like early paperbacks.

Printers also quickly began turning out pictorial prints, posters, and pamphlets as well. Most of these were religious and didactic—that is, explicitly aimed at teaching people or changing their ideas about religion. The *Bible,* prayer books, and hymnals (songbooks) were among the earliest books.

Beyond the *Bible* and religious pamphlets, new products were often more entertainment-oriented and aimed at broader groups of people with less education. Broadside ballads were single sheets of words for popular songs. **Chapbooks** were cheaply bound books or pamphlets of poetry, ballads, or prose; they were aimed at a broader audience, much like current small-format paperbacks. Their contents included cautionary tales (*Dr. Faustus*), courtly adventures (*Charlemagne and the Twelve Peers*) and strange tales such as that of *Melusine,* the mermaid. The stage had been set for a wide variety of literature to follow.

Stories that turned into novels existed in both European and non-European cultures well before the development of the printing press. *Beowulf* and *The Odessey* were composed verbally, memorized, and passed from generation to generation long before they were ever written down. Likewise, hand-copied written versions of those same stories helped preserve them until printing could extend their reach. Still, book-length novels flourished with printing. Printing made literature far more affordable to a mass audience.

Libraries were one means of popularizing books and making them more accessible. The first modern lending library of printed books was started by Bodley in 1602 in Oxford, England. Later, as the cost of binding and paper came down further, publishers began to try to sell books directly to the public through bookstalls in railway stations. By 1850, collections like the Railway Library sold a number of books for a shilling. Book publishing accelerated rapidly: Two million titles were issued worldwide in the 1700s and eight million in the 1800s. By 1900, a best-selling novel could sell 600,000 copies in the English-speaking world (Dessauer, 1981), which reflects the fact that book publishing—much more than newspapers or magazines—has almost always been a transnational phenomenon.

STOP & REVIEW

1. **What key elements of print media developed first outside Europe?**
2. **What was Gutenberg's contribution?**
3. **What were the first subjects of printed books?**
4. **What were the first magazines concerned with?**
5. **Why did magazines develop?**

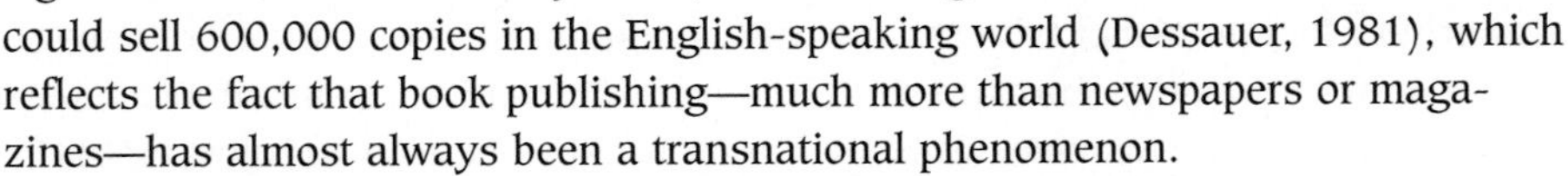

Magazines began to develop in the 1700s. They carried fiction and nonfiction in varying degrees, depending on the readership. The first British periodical to call itself a magazine was *The Gentleman's Magazine* of 1731, which deliberately left news to the papers and focused on elegant and amusing writing about literature, politics, biography, and criticism (Riley, 1993). This formula still characterizes much of magazine content: a periodical weekly or monthly selection of humor, fiction, and essays about politics, literature, sports, music, theater, and famous people.

Magazine was a colonial-era term for a warehouse; print magazines were storehouses of various materials from books, pamphlets, and newspapers.

Early Print Media in America

Print media in America also began with religious books, such as hymnals, and copies of the *Bible.* The *Bay Psalm Book* was printed in 1640 by the Puritans in Massachusetts on the first press the English brought to American colonies. Soon thereafter came newspapers in Boston, New York, and Philadelphia, as discussed in Chapter 4.

Benjamin Franklin was one of the major American colonial innovators in printing, publishing, politics, and even practical inventions. Franklin was involved with his brother James in the *Pennsylvania Gazette* newspaper. As a printer, he was experimenting to see what kinds of print media would find an audience. Franklin published one of the first successful nonreligious books, *Poor Richard's Almanack,* every year from 1732 to 1757. The *Almanack* was an annual volume. It contained moral advice, farming tips, and a variety of other information that was thought to be of interest. Along with educational primers, religious books, and law books, almanacs were among the most popular kinds of books.

Book printers also produced political pamphlets, which were an important way to galvanize support for the American Revolution. For example, Thomas Paine's *Common Sense,* which urged readers to support independence from Great Britain, sold 100,000 copies in 10 weeks.

In 1731 Franklin started the first **subscription library** in the future United States, beginning an American tradition in which lending libraries greatly helped popularize book reading. Before that, reading depended on private library collections, which in turn depended on private wealth. The Library of Congress was begun with Thomas Jefferson's private collection of 6500 volumes. The high cost of

Subscription libraries lent books to the public for a fee or a regular subscription.

books and the difficulty of gaining access to them also gave rise to magazines and newspapers.

Early American Magazines. Magazines started to develop in the early 1700s, at about the same time as newspapers. Philadelphia began as the nation's leader for magazines. The first American magazines published there were Bradford's *American Magazine* and Ben Franklin's *General Magazine and Historical Chronicle.* Both debuted in 1741, ten years after magazines originated in Great Britain. Franklin thought, perhaps prematurely, that the time was right for a magazine to serve a small audience that was reading the new British magazines. Bradford was a rival printer and publisher who raced to beat Franklin into print. Bradford's magazine lasted for 3 months, Franklin's for 6 months. Circulation remained local. Several other short-lived magazines were tried prior to the American Revolution, but all were limited by there being few potential readers and few writers and by the high costs of publishing and distribution.

During the American Revolution, from 1775 to 1789, many magazines also took a more political tone. Thomas Paine edited *Pennsylvania Magazine,* which urged revolution, in 1775–1776. Many magazines of the period were primarily political essays, though many also had humor and covered some other topics. For example, *The Royal American Magazine* (1774–1775) supported independence despite its title, had cartoons engraved by Paul Revere, and printed popular song lyrics (Riley, 1993). Despite the emphasis on politics, many magazines in the 1700s were called "**miscellanies**" because they carried such a variety of contents, trying to appeal to a small, far-flung, and diverse audience. Few magazines were widely read or long-lived until the 1800s (Tebbel, 1969).

Miscellanies were magazines that carried a wide variety of contents.

After the American Revolution, a new sense of cultural independence fostered new magazines. However, magazines took a while to succeed economically, as they were still limited by the relatively low literacy of the general public and by cost. Potential subscribers were thinly spread across a large geographical area. Magazines were given no cost break in postal rates until 1794, and local postmasters could refuse to carry them if the load of mail was too heavy (Riley, 1993).

The first U.S. Congress gave the fledgling American publishing industry a significant economic boost with the passage of the Copyright Act of 1790. It gave authors and their publishers exclusive rights to their publications for a period of 14 years (renewable for an additional 14 years). During that time, anyone who wished to reproduce the work would have to make a payment, called a royalty fee, to the copyright holder for the use of the work. The Copyright Act was thus intended to assure that new creative works would be made by guaranteeing a financial return to their originators.

Early American magazines were aimed at the better-educated and wealthy elite and a small but growing middle class. This was a small and marginally profitable audience, but some magazines succeeded. Many were still political, including *Port Folio* (1799), the first magazine to achieve substantial national circulation. It was a political organ of the Federalist movement, which advocated a strong central government. It contained essays such as Alexander Hamilton's *Federalist Papers.* It was opposed by anti-Federalist magazines, such as *The*

MEDIA IMPACT

Early Magazines and Books

For Further Research:

Facsimilies or reproductions of a number of early magazines and books are available on the Internet and in the on-line collections of college and university libraries. To get a better sense of what early publications actually looked like and the impact they had during their eras, try using the Internet to find images and illustrations. For example, if you use hotbot or altavista to search for *Harper's Weekly* Civil War illustrations, you will quickly find several sites. For instance, one search result showed that a likely source was:

WWW

OhioLINK - What's New?
New OhioLINK Services September 4, 1998 OhioLINK is proud to announce the addition of the HarpWeek database. It contains editions of *Harper's Weekly* from the Civil War era (1857–1865). *Harper's Weekly* was a leading national magazine during the . . . (http://www.ohiolink.edu/whats-new.html).

At that site, you have to exercise some logic and look at the bottom of the page for "Electronic Texts." Clicking that listing takes you to a page which has a link listed for "HarpWeek: The Civil War Era. The full text and images of *Harper's Weekly* from 1857 through 1865." Clicking that takes you to another site, http://app.harpweek.com/, which has the actual text and illustrations.

HARPER'S WEEKLY
A JOURNAL OF CIVILIZATION

THE CIVIL WAR, ILLUSTRATED. **The vivid illustrations of Civil War action in *Harper's Weekly* attracted large audiences in the 1860s.**

National Magazine of Richmond. That magazine was also notable for being one of the few published outside the dominant publishing centers of Philadelphia, Boston, and New York.

There was a new trend toward somewhat more specialized "literary miscellanies," whose editors wanted to popularize the emerging American literature. *The Saturday Evening Post* (1821–1969) is an example of the many literary weeklies that became popular. They covered weekly events, politics, and art and included reviews, travelogs, short stories, serialized fiction, and so on. "Special miscellanies" began to appear that focused on more specific topics and audiences. Sarah Josepha Hale's *Ladies' Magazine* of Boston (1828–1836) was the first successful American women's magazine; it was followed by *Godey's Lady's Book* (1830–1839).

By the 1840s, magazines began to shift their attention from the better-educated and wealthier elite toward broader and more sustainable mass audiences. *Harper's Weekly* (1857 to the present) is a surviving, successful, well-illustrated magazine from that era. For other magazine milestones, see Time Line.

Magazines in the Civil War Era. Approaching and during the Civil War, magazines began to have a much broader impact on public life. The powerful antislavery novel, *Uncle Tom's Cabin* (1852) first appeared serialized in a Washington D.C. magazine, the *National Era.* Several magazines grew to fame during the Civil War, largely on the basis of their print coverage and their illustrations dramatizing scenes of the war. *Leslie's Illustrated Newspaper* (which was really a weekly magazine) and *Harper's Weekly* created an important new form of publication, the illustrated news weekly; they are predecessors of today's *Newsweek* and *Time.*

135,000 SETS, 270,000 VOLUMES SOLD.
UNCLE TOM'S CABIN
FOR SALE HERE.
AN EDITION FOR THE MILLION, COMPLETE IN 1 Vol., PRICE 37 1-2 CENTS.
" " IN GERMAN, IN 1 Vol., PRICE 50 CENTS.
" " IN 2 Vols., CLOTH, 6 PLATES, PRICE $1.50.
SUPERB ILLUSTRATED EDITION, IN 1 Vol., WITH 153 ENGRAVINGS,
PRICES FROM $2.50 TO $5.00.
The Greatest Book of the Age.

AGAINST SLAVERY. Harriet Beecher Stowe's *Uncle Tom's Cabin* was a best-seller in its day and also helped set the agenda for opposition to slavery.

These newsmagazines were distinguished from newspapers by their format. Magazines were smaller and usually published weekly or monthly rather than daily. Daily newspapers evolved toward a short time horizon (today's headline news), whereas magazines had something different to offer: illustration and photos, high-quality images, more in-depth coverage, longer pieces, more investigative reporting, and a focus on trends rather than daily events.

Expanding Demand for Magazines and Books. In the mid-1800s, conditions became more favorable for the creation of a mass reading public for books and magazines. An expanding public education system taught more people to read. Wages increased, more people moved to the cities to work in the burgeoning industrial economy, and an urban middle class grew. Prices also fell with printing economies of scale, improved printing technology, and more demand for print media. Access to books increased as the number of public libraries tripled between 1825 and 1850.

Perhaps most important, however, was the **popularization** of book content. Many American novelists earned loyal fans by addressing the uniquely American national experience and interests.

> **Popularization** is the process of making a medium appeal to a much broader audience across social classes.

For example, James Fenimore Cooper wrote compelling novels about the struggles of both white settlers and indigenous people on the frontier, which still included western New York and Kentucky. In novels such as *The Last of the Mohicans,* Cooper dramatized the attraction of the West. Immigrants sometimes cited his novels as part of what they knew about America, part of what drew them. Cooper also contributed to magazines such as *Knickerbocker.* Nathaniel Hawthorne concentrated more on the manners and idiosyncracies of New England in books like *The Scarlet Letter.* English authors such as Charles Dickens and Sir Walter Scott were also popular.

Novels even had political effects; a prime example is Harriet Beecher Stowe's *Uncle Tom's Cabin,* which sold 300,000 copies in its first year and did much to inspire popular opposition to slavery (Davis, 1985). Cooper's novels, along with others about the frontier and the West, both catered to and contributed to public interest in American expansion westward beyond the original colonies, shaping opinions that affected the Mexican–American War in 1846–1848 and other national policies of expansion.

> **Dime novels** were inexpensive paperback novels that aimed at a mass readership.

From 1860 to 1880, even more popular material appeared in cheaper formats. The **dime novels** addressed a broader audience of middle-class and even working-class people. For instance, some 250 million Horatio Alger books were sold. This popular hero managed to rise out of poverty by hard work, thrift, planning, and other popular virtues. In fact, "Horatio Alger story" eventually became a popular synonym for a tale of hard work and social mobility.

The Growth of Magazines in the Nineteenth Century. Magazines kept expanding their readership by moving beyond general-interest magazines, such as *The Saturday Evening Post,* to more specialized **genres.** Another magazine genre with mass appeal consisted of women's magazines, such as *Ladies' Home Journal, Good Housekeeping,* and *McCall's* from the late 1800s. By 1910, both *The Saturday Evening Post* and *Ladies' Home Journal* circulated to over a million readers (Tebbel, 1969b).

Genres are formats of media content that enable writers and audiences to understand each others' expectations.

The rise of magazines into a major mass medium in the 1800s was propelled by some of the factors that also drove mass newspapers: increased literacy, improved print technology, greater personal income, lower production costs, and a growing urban population. However, magazines benefited particularly from a major change in their delivery system. The Postal Act of 1879 gave magazines special rates. This de facto subsidy to magazine distribution continues today: Publishers pay lower third-class rates for mailing, yet the magazines are treated as full-cost "first-class" mail. (Catalogs and newsletters also pay bulk-mail rates and benefit from low prices.) As a result, by 1900 there were 1800 magazines in the United States, a large increase from the 260 that existed in 1860 (Riley, 1993).

Twentieth-Century Magazines. As the new century dawned, magazines expanded their readership and gave consumers more choices than ever before. Many new kinds of magazines (investigative magazines, digests, newsmagazines, and pictorial magazines) competed with newspapers for position as the dominant mass medium. Since the 1830s, cheap, mass audience daily newspapers, known as the Penny Press, had emerged as the main mass medium of the time. (See Chapter 4.)

Muckraking and the Rise of Magazines. Magazines also began to overtake newspapers as platforms for investigative reporting and crusades for reform. Much of the investigative reporting known as **muckraking** in the early 1900s was done for magazines such as *McClure's* and *Collier's.* Muckraking was closely associated with the rise of nationally circulated, inexpensive magazines. Magazines now reached millions of readers and had a much greater impact on public opinion.

Muckraking is journalism that investigates scandal, "raking up the muck" of dirty details.

The term *muckraking* refers to reporters being willing to stir up and sift through the unpleasant aspects of public life that most people ignore, looking for misdeeds by public figures without worrying about offending sensibilities or insulting the people under investigation. These reporters helped promote legislation such as the Pure Food and Drug Act of 1907.

Magazines shifted into muckraking during the Progressive Era, 1890–1920. Along with a tide of concern about social issues, particularly among city dwellers, investigative reporting in both magazines and newspapers began to focus on problems connected with urban America. A number of reporters and editors also began to pursue an activist agenda of curbing the excesses of big business through government regulation.

Magazine journalism, then as now, attracted crusading reporters, but the new level of support for them was to some degree a by-product of changes in the magazine industry. Magazines were looking for controversial, striking content that would draw in a mass audience.

One frequent goal of muckraking investigative reporters was to attack big business and corrupt government and push for a more just society. For example, in 1902 Ida Tarbell wrote a classic muckraking exposé of Standard Oil Company under John D. Rockefeller for the magazine *McClure's.* The article, with its vivid descriptions of the abuses committed by the company, was very popular. Muckraking about monopolies continues. In 1997–1998, several books and numerous magazine articles charged monopoly abuses by Microsoft.

MUCKRAKER. Ida Tarbell gained prominence as one of the leading turn-of-the-century magazine writers by exposing the abuses of Standard Oil Company.

Another classic example of magazine muckraking was a Lincoln Steffens series on the "Shame of the Cities," also for *McClure's.* In three installments, it exposed the corruption that revolved around Minneapolis Mayor Albert Alonzo. (The articles led to the resignation of the mayor.) Books also were part of the muckraking trend. Upton Sinclair's *The Jungle,* a book about Chicago slaughterhouses, was published in 1905, and led to the Meat Inspection Act of 1906.

Muckraking reporting in magazines often led to landmark reform legislation. The Pure Food and Drug Act (1907) resulted from an article in *Collier's,* "The Great American Fraud" by Samuel Hopkins Adams. The Mann Act (1909), which prohibited transportation of females across states lines for immoral purposes, resulted from an article in *McClure's* by Burton J. Hendrick on "Daughters of the Poor." The term *muckraking* has now lost its crusading political sense and refers today more to investigation of sexual scandals and other "dirt" on public figures. However, contemporary journalists continue to target corruption and abuses of power with a crusading spirit that sometimes results in positive change. The Watergate hearings about illegal acts by government investigators, which led to the resignation of President Richard Nixon, was largely stimulated by the investigative reporting of Woodward and Bernstein for *The Washington Post* in 1972. Just as *McClure's* specialized in muckraking in the 1900s, some current magazines (*The Nation* and *Mother Jones* come to mind) still specialize in muckraking journalism.

Mass Audience Magazines. In the early 1900s, magazines that aimed at a genteel, better-educated audience continued to give way to more widely popular mass publications. *Century* and *Scribner's,* which did not adjust to the new mass market, disappeared. Their new competitors were much less expensive because they were expected to sell many more copies. That also required refocusing content on topics of mass appeal, such as "modern" life, current issues, and success stories (Payne, 1993). Some "quality" magazines like *Harper's Monthly* and *Atlantic Monthly* kept a loyal audience but barely survived.

STOP & REVIEW

1. What was the role of the print media in the Civil War?
2. How did the Civil War affect magazine development?
3. What is muckraking?
4. How did muckraking affect magazine development?

As with the earlier newspaper Penny Press (dating from the 1830s), part of the audience breakthrough for magazines was due to price. The cost of the new magazines was usually 15 cents a copy, less than half the price of the traditional magazine, which made for much higher circulation. However, typical day wages for a laborer were a dollar, and a meal could be had for 10 cents, so magazines were still not a medium for the working class or the poor.

Most of the new magazines stressed popular content, dealt with the "here and now," and focused on middle-class or mass audience interests. Some of these were truly major American mass media for a time. Benjamin Franklin started the *General Magazine* in January 1741, but it was short-lived. *The Saturday Evening Post* was founded in 1821. In 1897, it refocused on the accomplishments of American business, inspirational success stories, action stories, romance, and some factual reports. With this formula it reached a circulation of 3,000,000 in 1937, with a profitable advertising base (Murray, 1993). Its formula for appealing to a middle-class audience never adjusted to competition from television, however. Advertising shifted to television, and despite an enthusiastic readership and a circulation of 6.8 million, the *Post* lost money and went out of business in 1969. A quarterly version was eventually revived, but it had little impact.

The *Ladies' Home Journal* did much better with its more narrowly targeted audience. It circulated to 1,000,000 in 1905, compared with 4,544,000 in 1996. It survived and prospered, ranking sixteenth in advertising income among magazines in 1996 (Alsop, 1998, p. 929). But it has a great deal of competition from other women's magazines and has a much less important relative position among American national media.

Another very successful magazine from the 1920s is *The New Yorker* (1925–), which emphasized an audience that was "upper-class, highly educated, literate and sophisticated," but had only a modest circulation (Payne, 1993). *The New Yorker* was one of the first successful modern *targeted magazines,* in contrast to mass-oriented magazines such as *Reader's Digest, The Saturday Evening Post,* and even *Time.* By drawing advertisers who wanted to reach a select audience, it heralded a tendency toward **segmentation:** the targeting of substantial but still specific audiences.

Segmentation is when media focus on specific, smaller audiences with more specialized, targeted media formats.

Another example of a new successful, targeted magazine was *The New Republic* (1914–). It emphasized serious discussion of political issues, current affairs, and intellectual trends from a liberal point of view. It had a small reader-

PROFILE

TINA BROWN.

Savior or Destroyer of The New Yorker?

Name: Tina Brown

New Position: Brown is chairperson and part owner of a new multimedia company, in partnership with Miramax Films, that will launch a monthly magazine and produce movies, television programs, and books.

Recent Position: Editor of *The New Yorker* until 1998.

Style: Bold and assertive; has a multimillion-dollar New York apartment. Has a very strong personality, which people tend either to love or to hate.

Most Notable Achievement: She dramatically revamped, revived, and popularized *The New Yorker* magazine, increasing circulation nearly 40 percent, to more than 860,000.

Most Dubious Achievements: While at *The New Yorker,* Brown brought in very hot writers but did not nurture many new ones on the way up. She made *The New Yorker* flashier and more readable, but less distinctive, than the original version of the magazine and tilted the content away from the East Coast establishment toward the entertainment industry.

How She Got to the Top: She was editor of *Vanity Fair,* a notable magazine but not an institution of U.S. publishing. Showed wit, style, sophistication, and a taste for flamboyant photography.

Her Inspirations: The glamour of classic magazines of the 1930s and the desire to create the maximum buzz, or industry excitement, for her current magazine.

Where Does She Go from Here? She is eager to find out whether content can be leveraged back and forth among magazines, films, and television. Her new position will give her the opportunity to test one vision of industry convergence.

ship but succeeded because that readership was an influential one—political leaders, intellectuals, some business leaders, and college professors—that people wished to reach.

One of the most successful "new" magazine formulas, or genres, was the *newsmagazine.* These competed with the newspapers very directly, as well as with existing magazines. News magazines provided extensive news coverage, along with commentary. In 1923, Henry Luce and Briton Hadden started a magazine called *Time,* the first weekly news magazine. Luce and Hadden apparently felt that people were being bombarded with information but were still uninformed. *Time* promised to take all of the important events from *The New York Times* newspaper and compile them into a weekly publication that would sift through the clutter, summarize what was important, and offer a point of view on it, according to Walter Isaacson, managing editor of *Time* (March 9, 1998).

Time's success as a newsmagazine led Time, Inc. to introduce *Life,* an illustrated photojournalism magazine in 1936. *Life* met the public's desire for a photographic report of the world and was extremely successful. *Life* published photos of the week's events, with captions and a fairly short news analysis, creating a visual style of journalism that later fed into television news approaches. Newspapers recognized the new appeal of photographs and increasingly began adding them to their papers. Later, television news moved into this visual journalism niche. Competition from television led to the failure of *Life,* which was primarily focused on images, while

Time and *Newsweek,* which balanced photo images with extensive text and reporting, continued to do well. *Life* was subsequently resurrected as an irregularly published photo magazine focused on various topics.

Even after television came on the scene, visual reporting and visual appeal remained very important for magazines. Many magazines still depend on high-quality photography and illustration for a great part of their appeal. Reader studies show that photos in both articles and advertisements hold much attraction for magazine readers. However, visual magazines now tend to serve much more specific, segmented audiences. Bridal magazines, fashion magazines, sports magazines, and even rock music magazines depend a great deal on visual appeal. Annie Leibowitz became famous as a photographer for *Rolling Stone;* Richard Avedon gained fame through his photos in fashion magazines. More recently, *Wired* magazine has become well known for extravagant, even confusing visual layouts of photos and for striking typefaces and colors. Readers cite the high-quality photos and images in magazines as one reason why they still prefer reading print magazines to looking at the same content over the Internet.

GET A LIFE.
The colorful photojournalism of *Life* magazine pioneered a visual approach to the news that was later copied by television.

Magazines as a *mass* medium probably peaked in the 1940s and 1950s. Magazines such as *The Saturday Evening Post, Look,* and *Life* sold well into the 1960s, but they were losing money because much of their audience and their advertisers shifted their focus to television. Magazines gradually changed to become one of the first highly segmented, or targeted, media. Some mass circulation magazines died out, but many other kinds of magazines prospered. In 1950 there were 250 magazines with total sales of 147 million. In 1996 there were 605 regular or major magazines with total sales of 365 million (Alsop, 1998, p. 929).

The 1960s and 1970s saw a proliferation of more specialized magazines for more specific audiences. Traditional women's magazines, for example, were joined by a host of magazines aimed at younger girls (*Teen*), teen-agers (*Seventeen*), young women (*Details*), working women (*Working Woman*), young working women (*Cosmopolitan*), feminists (*Ms.*), and homemakers (*Good Housekeeping*).

The 1980s and 1990s saw a continuation of this trend. There are now several magazines covering most hobbies and interests, from canoeing to dairy farming. By the late 1990s, with desktop publishing, cheap photocopying, and "publication" of magazines in virtual form on the World Wide Web, there were much lower barriers to entry into the magazine business. People published their own personal "**'zines.**" Ambitious twenty-somethings aimed to make it big on a shoestring by publishing on the Web.

'Zines are very narrowly focused, even personal, magazines or Web sites usually produced by non-professionals.

Modern Publishing

Book publishing grew substantially in the twentieth century. As with magazines and newspapers, printing costs decreased. Demand, spurred by rising literacy and rising wages, increased.

Many publishing houses have been around since the early 1800s: Lippincott (1792), Wiley (1807), Harper & Row (1817), Houghton Mifflin (1832), Allyn & Bacon (1868), and Doubleday (1897). However, many of the most active American publishing houses started up since 1900. Most of the major hardback publishers,

MEDIA WATCH

'Zines

One of the gray areas between magazines and newsletters is occupied by the large number of publications called fanzines or simply 'zines. These tend to be created by people who are enthusiastic about a topic, usually a hobby, but sometimes something related to their work or education. Many 'zines discuss science fiction or other popular literature, movies, rock music, pop music, and other kinds of popular entertainment. 'Zines reflect the proliferation of diverse strains of popular culture and the segmentation of many people into small, distinct interest groups. 'Zines mirror groups of people whose life—or at least their spare time—revolves around things as distinct as listening to underground music, recreating the Middle Ages, reading science fiction, participating in role-playing games, collecting porcelain figures, restoring old cars, or enjoying folk music.

'Zines' creators don't usually see them as commercial ventures at first; most simply want to communicate their interests to like-minded people. However, many charge a subscription fee to become self-supporting. A number of these creations then evolve into commercially successful publications. Some of them even develop higher-quality production values, using more art, more color, and better paper. At that point, they become full-fledged magazines.

such as McGraw-Hill (1909), Prentice-Hall (1913), Simon & Schuster (1924), and Random House (1925), set up shop early in the century. As printing costs declined, more Americans could afford hardback books, and the publishing industry grew. Many major publishers increased the number of books available to the general public. However, the strongest segments of the pre–World War II publishing industry were still educational, professional, and reference books, not mass market fiction. A book selling 50,000 copies, particularly in nonfiction, could be judged a best-seller (Dessauer, 1981). After several decades of debate, legislation, and court cases, a lower "book rate" was established for mailing books, which made both mail-order sales and marketing via book clubs much easier. Mail-order clubs, such as the Book-of-the-Month Club and the Literary Guild, scared publishers at first, but ultimately benefited them by popularizing book reading and buying. New York gradually became the main publishing center, but in the late 1900s, publishers proliferated on both coasts, along with some in the Midwest and South.

Most of the later publishing houses, such as Pocket Books (1939), Bantam Books (1946), and New American Library (1948), grew up around *paperback* books. World War II ushered in the paperback era. Young people away from home at war read more, and as they returned home and entered college (assisted by educational benefits for veterans), they started to read even more, both textbooks and mass market paperbacks. *Chain bookstores* in new suburban shopping malls began to promote book purchases. In fact, chain bookstores, such as B. Dalton, now account for half of all bookstore sales. In response to demand for more serious literature, nonfiction, and textbooks, publishers brought out larger-format trade paperbacks to complement "pocket-size" paperbacks.

A number of more specifically targeted publishing companies also arose, particularly since the 1970s, when the number of publishing houses doubled from 6000 in 1972 to almost 12,000 in 1980 (Dessauer, 1981). Niche publishers, such as West, targeted specific industries, like the legal system. Small to medium-sized houses grew to serve specific segmented interest groups among the reading public; TOR and DAW, for example, publish large numbers of science fiction paperbacks. Some, such as the politically critical Monthly Review Press, represented specific political lines of interest.

STOP & REVIEW

1. What were some of the first general-public, nonelite magazines?
2. What were some of the first targeted, or segmented, magazines?
3. When did magazines begin to have to compete with other mass audience media?
4. When did segmentation become the dominant trend in magazines?
5. Give some current examples of magazines targeted to audience segments?

Although publishing houses have consolidated several times (one major wave of mergers occurred in the 1960s and another in the 1990s), small new publishers are constantly entering the field. By 1998 there were more than 50,000 American book publishers, if you count the small publishers that rely on desk-top publishing technology and publish only a few titles, often in very specialized areas. The number of titles produced annually grew from about 10,000 in the 1950s to more than 50,000 per year in the mid-1990s (Folkerts & Teeter, 1994) to over 70,000 by the late 1990s, again depending on what kinds of "books" from what kinds of presses you count. These qualifications are important, because small presses now do small press runs of everything from favorite family recipes to stories about Grandpa for Christmas presents.

TECHNOLOGY TRENDS IN BOOKS AND MAGAZINES

Earlier we recounted the origins of paper and printing in Asia and the origins of modern printing with Gutenberg in 1455 (Carter, 1991). For the next 500 years, most improvements in publishing technology revolved around finding faster ways to press ink on paper, although progress was slow for around 400 years. The first *rotary press,* invented in 1846, used rotating cylinders of type to print on both sides of large, continuous rolls of paper at the same time, instead of on single sheets, one side at a time. By the end of the century, a single press could print tens of thousands of copies per hour, a thousand-fold increase from the early 1800s.

Typesetting, however, remained a slow manual process requiring typesetters to locate and put in place individual letters of type to form each word, just as Gutenberg had done. *Linotype* machines, first introduced in 1868, cast entire lines of type instantly from molten lead so that one typesetter could do the work of five (Sloan, Stovall, & Startt, 1993).

Printed illustrations were a staple of magazines dating back to the Civil War period (1861–1865), but only a few publications could afford them because they required the painstaking engraving of wood or metal master plates. *Lithography,* brought over from France in the 1860s, speeded the printing of illustrated pages by substituting a type of chemical engraving for hand carving. *Photoengraving* transformed illustrated publications by chemically etching images onto the surface of metal plates through a photographic process, a vast improvement over handmade lithographs. By the 1890s, photographs were routinely reproduced in a wide range of print publications.

Offset printing, introduced after World War II, produced further advances in the quality, speed, and economy of printing. Now an entire page of print, complete with illustrations, could be photographed and the photographic image transferred to a smooth metal plate. The plate was treated so that only the desired areas attracted the ink and transferred them to a rubber roller and then to paper.

Computerization has occasioned many other changes in the print media. At first, in the 1960s, computers were put to work assisting the typesetters, automatically hyphenating and spacing the type on each line. In the 1970s, computers substituted for typesetting machines—and many typesetting people as well—by creating images directly on photographic film that could be transferred to metal printing plates. Later, the layout and paste-up of pages were computerized as well. This process was further simplified by **digitizing** photographs so that they too could be edited and placed on the page electronically. *Pagination* software enabled users to set type, add headings, put text into columns, make text "wrap around" photos or illustrations, and crop and place photos—all automatically.

Digitizing means making an image or text computer-readable, as with a scanner.

In the 1980s, more power and speed were packed into desktop computers. *Scanners* for digitizing photos into computer-readable form became cheaper. Software products like PageMaker enabled users to do layout and page makeup inside a personal computer. On the output end, high-speed *laser printing* and *photocopying* technology made typesetting unnecessary, at least in low-volume applications. Laser printers allowed computer-readable information to be printed onto paper, using the same basic approach as photocopying and yielding high-quality print and images. This package of elements, known as **desktop publishing,** has done much to decentralize print media. Almost anyone with a personal computer can now produce her or his own books, magazines, fanzines, flyers, and posters. Although computers are no substitute for writing talent, visual design ability, or editorial skills, the layout templates and text and grammar checkers that come with desktop publishing products have given many an amateur effort a professional appearance.

Desktop publishing is the composition, layout, and sometimes printing of materials using a personal computer.

In addition to the availability of cheap local offset printing, photocopying has enabled individuals to produce, and distribute inexpensively, materials created with desktop equipment. Printing a certain minimum number of copies is necessary to make offset or other higher-quality printing worthwhile—the cost of producing the master has to be spread over a large number of copies to be economical. Photocopying relies on a fundamentally different process, which uses the paper original as the master.

Custom publishing takes advantage of the flexibility of computer-based publishing to print selected parts of books. Publishers—including the publishers of this text—have long fought producers of photocopied college course packets by prosecuting them in the courts for copyright violations. By printing selections from popular textbooks themselves, publishers hope to reap the profits that formerly went to local copy shops.

Custom publishing refers to creating customized versions of print newspapers, magazines, or books for particular audiences.

Publishing Changes with the Internet

One of the most widely ballyhooed capabilities of the Internet, **electronic commerce,** or the ability to complete purchases on-line, is having a major impact on book publishing. With "virtual bookstores" like Amazon.com, users enjoy the convenience of searching for titles on-line with powerful search engines rather than waiting while harried bookstore clerks thumb through *Books in Print.* The virtual bookstores take note of your purchases and recommend other books that you might

Electronic commerce is the ability to offer goods, advertise, and complete purchases on-line.

TECHNOLOGY ***TRENDS***

Internet Magazines Get Serious

Internet magazines are an enormously varied breed. For many, designing such a magazine is a chance to speak directly to a relatively few people who are passionately interested in things such as raising bulldogs or reviving Old Norse religion. The World Wide Web seems to lend itself naturally to micropublishing.

On the other hand, some aspiring "e-'zine" editors have more ambitious plans for reaching an audience not much smaller than that of many regular magazines. Now several Internet-based magazines, with no print version, have finally broken into the big time, serving those with serious political interests.

Salon [www.salon.com], an Internet-based news and literary magazine, was founded by David Talbot, a one-time senior editor of the modern liberal, muckraking magazine *Mother Jones.* Talbot wanted to revitalize American literary culture, annoy liberals, anger conservatives, and create a quality product away from the "misguided bean counters" who, he says, have taken over news media. *Salon* hit the national news in the fall of 1998 by releasing information about the sexual indiscretions of Republican members of Congress who were calling for President Clinton's resignation or impeachment over the scandal of his sexual involvement with White House intern Monica Lewinsky. *Salon* was accused of passing along information leaked by White House staff who wanted to strike back at those persecuting Clinton. That raised a few ethical issues about the use of anonymous and politically motivated source—a practice that has been common in regular politics but had not focused directly on sexual behavior. *Salon* reached 547,000 people in June 1998, and the numbers shot up after the "Clinton versus the Republicans" pieces.

Another prominent electronic magazine is *Slate* [www.slate.com], which is edited by Michael Kinsley, former editor of the neoliberal opinion magazine *New Republic. Slate* initially looked a lot like the *New Republic,* but it has gradually found a different niche as a "meta-news" magazine, one that both summarizes the news and explains what is going on behind the scenes. *Salon* is free and supported by advertising. It costs about $7 million a year and was on the road to making money in 1998. *Slate* charged $19.95 a year to subscribe. It costs about $5 million a year and is backed by Microsoft. In 1998 it had only 27,000 subscribers and was losing money. In 1999, it resorted to being free to attract more readers.

Both *Salon* and *Slate* show that a significant audience for a serious magazine comparable to print magazines in quality can be found on the Web.

If you are interested in following trends in electronic magazines, you can start with a major portal to the Web such as Yahoo [www.yahoo.com] and look at the list there. If you are using the InfoTrac College Edition, you can also find good starting points, as well as interesting background. A search on the term "Magazines" found

Insight on the News, August 24, 1998 v14 n31 p10(11). Point, click and read net 'zines. (increasing popularity of Internet periodicals) Eli Lehrer.

like to read; it's almost like having a personal librarian! The vast inventories and searchable data bases also give new life to *backlists* of older books and to obscure titles from small publishers that cannot find shelf space in the "real" bookstore down the street (Carvajal, 1998). In fact, a growing number of authors are bypassing conventional publishers altogether, selling the books they produce on their desktops directly through the Web. About 10 percent of all new titles are published this way (Carvajal, 1996).

Another Information Age innovation is transforming the book industry through the compilation of its best-seller lists. The conventional method was to poll bookstore clerks by phone, a method that neglected some important book outlets and that also may have been influenced by the clerks' own tastes in literature. The new method gathers data directly from scanners at a wide range of retail book outlets, including the supermarkets and drugstores that cater to more less-refined tastes than bookstores do.

One innovation that has not yet worked out very well is publishing the books themselves on-line. The Gutenberg Project, an attempt to place the great works of world literature on the Internet, once threatened to end in failure. The tedious labor involved in typing, proofreading, and scanning into the computer lengthy works like *Don Quixote* is one deterrent, but reading the books on a computer screen seems to be the real problem (Frost, 1996). Computer text is harder—and about 60 percent slower—to read than ink on paper, and even the most portable laptop computer is not really welcome in bed or in a beach chair. Help may be on the way in the form of ubiquitous wireless connections to the Internet and new computer display technologies that users might feel comfortable curling up with in front of a fire.

Hypertext is a system for linking different texts and images within a computer document or over a network.

CD-ROM is a compact disc computer storage medium with read-only memory.

Another new technology direction is the interactive book, or **hypertext,** which combines literature with computer games in either Internet or **CD-ROM** format. Interactive novels allow multiple plot twists or enable readers to watch the story unfold from the perspective of different characters. Others resemble multiple-user gaming environments with literary pretensions (Blanton, 1996). Although gaming obviously works well with interactivity, the classic story-telling of the novel or film may not lend itself to interactivity. Attempts to transfer popular movie plots to games don't always result in experiences that feel "playable" or truly interactive. The author of one popular recent science fiction novel, *Snow Crash,* intended to craft an interactive experience but ended up writing a regular print novel about a futuristic Internet.

The *interactive textbook* is also in its early stages. Most publishers make on-line teaching and student guides available along with their best-selling textbook titles. To protect textbook sales, the full text will not be available until electronic commerce transactions become more commonplace. Instead, the "virtual student" gets access to updates of the text, exercises, chats with the authors, and sample exam items.

Publishing books in computer-readable form on *compact disc* has met with some success, but mostly for bulky reference titles or works that benefit from multimedia extensions. The technology is the same as that used in CD music players; in fact, the latest computers can handle music and data through the same built-in CD-ROM players. The latest *digital versatile disc* (DVD) technology

TECHNOLOGY **TRENDS**

Cuddling Up with a Nice Electronic Book?

There is something very sensuous to many people about a printed book. Even small paperbacks have their advantages: cheap, portable, no batteries required, durable. Nicely bound books with large type intrigue the romantic and the collector. Both entice us to curl up by a nice fire, in a warm bath, or in bed—and relax.

Can a high-tech plastic device weighing 1 to 3 pounds, with a limited battery life but a brighter screen, ever offer serious competition to print books, the oldest medium around? Several new electronic book readers, including NuvoMedia's RocketBook and the Softbook, appeared in 1998 to test the idea.

They have their appeal. No nightlight is required, although a battery is. You can mark passages electronically, search for keywords, or get constant updates for timely material, like tax laws. You can carry a pile of titles around with you a lot more easily. You can download titles from the Internet, as well as buying them at shops or by mail. However, both reader and "books" are likely to cost more than regular books for the foreseeable future.

This may well be one of the ultimate tests of just how well computers can interface with people. Can the advantages of electronic scanning, searching, and a built-in light compete with a book's simple interface, low cost, portability, and traditional charm?

If you want to keep track of how the electronic book does in competition with regular books, and if you are using the InfoTrac College Edition, try searching new sources with InfoTrac, with the keyword "publishing-electronic."

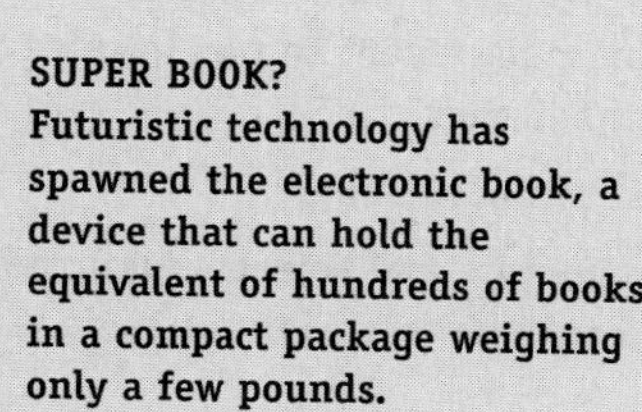

SUPER BOOK? Futuristic technology has spawned the electronic book, a device that can hold the equivalent of hundreds of books in a compact package weighing only a few pounds.

expands the storage capacity of CDs to the point where an entire bookcase worth of books can be stored on a single disc, complete with audio, graphics, and video clips.

The magazine industry has also jumped on the Internet bandwagon. Thousands of titles have planted their mastheads on the Web, although few have yet seen profits. Many of these publications offer electronic versions of their current issues, articles from past issues, or special features (pitched to Web surfers) that are not found in the print versions. There are also a growing number of periodicals that are available *only* on the Web. *Slate,* a publication of Microsoft Corporation, features commentary on public affairs. For academics, there is the *Journal of Computer Mediated Communication* (JCMC).

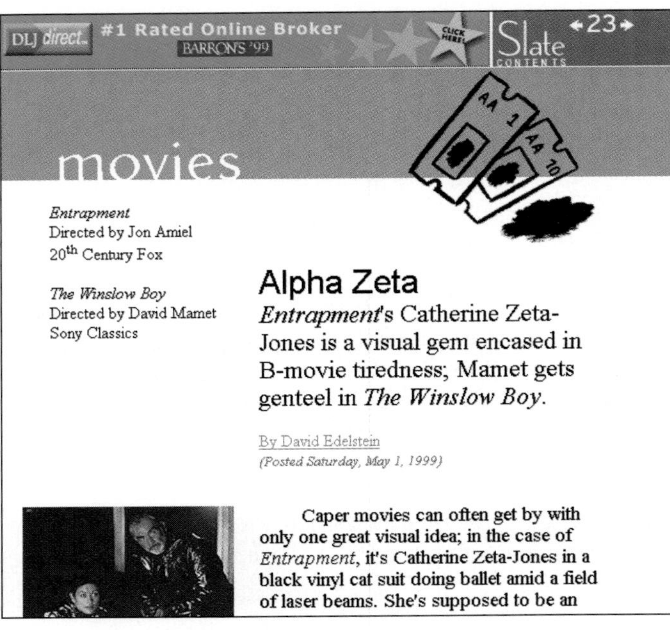

DLJ direct. #1 Rated Online Broker BARRON'S '99

CLICK HERE!

Slate CONTENTS ◂23▸

movies

Entrapment
Directed by Jon Amiel
20th Century Fox

The Winslow Boy
Directed by David Mamet
Sony Classics

Alpha Zeta

Entrapment's Catherine Zeta-Jones is a visual gem encased in B-movie tiredness; Mamet gets genteel in *The Winslow Boy*.

By David Edelstein
(Posted Saturday, May 1, 1999)

Caper movies can often get by with only one great visual idea; in the case of *Entrapment*, it's Catherine Zeta-Jones in a black vinyl cat suit doing ballet amid a field of laser beams. She's supposed to be an

ONLY ON THE WEB.
Backed by computer software giant Microsoft, *Slate* magazine is one of the first advertising-supported magazines available only on the World Wide Web.

This page first appeared in *Slate* magazine, www.slate.com. Reprinted with permission. Copyright © 1999 Microsoft Corporation.

No discussion of trends in publishing technology would be complete without considering what the library of tomorrow might be like. Libraries have been computerizing their card catalogs for decades now, and many catalogs are now accessible through the World Wide Web; some even let the user order books for convenient pickup or delivery. For the serious researcher, most of the paperbound keyword and author–title indices such as *Lexis-Nexis* and *Social Science Citation Index,* are now available through Web data bases or on CD-ROM. Increasingly, abstracts of articles, and even the full text of scholarly publications, are searchable via keywords from the researcher's computer workstation. The **search engines** of the Web are also becoming a staple of library research. Many local libraries now offer Internet access as one of their services to the public. In fact, many in the late 1990s see libraries as the preferred way to give poor or disadvantaged people access to the Web.

Search engines let the user search for specific text, audio, and video within a computer document or site, or over a network, like the World Wide Web.

What to do with those old stacks of books and journals? For now, we are just going to leave them there. Computerizing paperbound volumes requires *optical character recognition* (OCR) software that converts printed words to computer-readable characters. But OCR software is not foolproof, so the resulting text still has to be carefully proofread by a human. And graphics and illustrations require a separate pass through the scanner. The copyright holders, or their heirs, must be tracked down and compensated as well. In the long run, though, we will have to scan the old books or lose them as they yellow and crumble into dust.

1. **What was the impact of movable-type printing?**
2. **What was the impact of rotary printing?**
3. **What are the main recent trends in print media production technologies?**
4. **What are the main recent trends in print media delivery technologies?**
5. **What is desktop publishing?**
6. **How will computers and telecommunications affect the magazine of the future?**

PRINT GENRES AND FORMS

In the following sections, we examine some of the principal genres and forms in books, newspapers, and magazines.

Book Publishing

Technology facilitates publishing and influences what formats are possible in media, but it does not define their contents. For example, book-length **novels** flourished with printing because mechanical reproduction allowed quantities of books to be produced less expensively. However, the concepts and forms that characterize the novel originated much earlier. Greek poets before 1000 C.E. produced epic works. *The Tale of Genji,* recognizable as a novel by current standards, was written in Japan in the twelfth century. The antecedents of novels about daily life, romances, mysteries, and horror or terror existed well before the advent of printing. Although some story forms, or genres, have been around for a long time, they have still been changed by developments in technology and economics. The major events are summarized in the timeline at the beginning of this chapter.

Novels are long prose fiction narratives, dealing with human experience and a sequence of events.

In the twentieth century, markets for fiction became much more clearly defined by genre. For both books and pulp magazines that specialized in short stories, the first half of the century was a boom era for detective stories, science fiction, and westerns (Folkerts & Teeter, 1994).

Books are diverse and hard to characterize in general terms. Some books are sacred, some are sensational; some are eagerly read for pleasure, some are assigned reading in college courses.

The major categories of book genres, according to the Association of American Publishers, are as follows:

TOP OF THE CHARTS. Novelists such as Anne Rice dominate the market for trade fiction books.

Trade books. Hard or soft cover, including "serious" fiction (like Isabel Allende's *House of the Spirits*) and most nonfiction, such as cookbooks (like the soft-cover version of *The Joy of Cooking*), biographies, how-to books, and art books.

Professional books. Reference or professional education books aimed at doctors, lawyers, scientists, researchers, managers, and engineers (such as *The Programmer's Guide to Windows® 98*).

Elementary, high school, and college textbooks, such as *Media Now: Communications Media in the Information Age.*

Mass market paperbacks. Soft-bound books, generally smaller in format and less expensive than trade paperbacks (like *Mirror Image* by Danielle Steele).

Religious books. Bibles, other sacred texts, hymnals, prayer books, and commentaries.

Book club editions. Clubs that publish, sell, and distribute their own editions of mass market books, professional books, and other specialized books. The Quality Paperback Book Club, for instance, issues trade paperback versions of current hardcover best-sellers.

Mail-order publications. Books largely created by publishers to be sold by mail. These are usually classic novels or specialized series on such subjects as cooking, western history, wars, cars, and aviation (like the Time–Life series on *Cowboys*).

Subscription reference books. Books sold as a package or series, including encyclopedias, atlases, dictionaries, glossaries, and thesauruses (like *The Encyclopaedia Britannica*). (Many of these "books" are now often sold to computer owners as periodically updated CD-ROMs.)

Audiovisual and multimedia. Videotapes, CD-ROMs, computer diskettes, slides, and audiotapes marketed primarily to schools, companies, and training groups, but also to individuals, by both regular publishing houses and new multimedia publishing companies. (Microsoft's *Encarta* encyclopedia series is an example.)

University and scholarly presses. Scholarly or artistic books of primary appeal to scholars and libraries (such as Baldwin, McVoy, and Steinfield's *Convergence: Integrating Media, Information and Communication*).

SPECIAL INTEREST. Magazines are becoming much more specialized, appealing to narrow segments of the audience.

Magazines Genres: Where Does Segmentation Stop?

The trend in magazine design and contents has been toward specialization, or segmentation, of audiences with narrowly focused genres. If you look closely at a large newsstand, you will notice that although there are dozens of magazines about motorcycles, tennis, crocheting, and computers, most general-interest magazines have disappeared.

Most current magazines represent one of the following:

General-interest: *People, US, Reader's Digest*

Geographic: *New York, Arizona Highways, Southern Living*

Demographic: *Seventeen, Teen People, People en Español, Latina, Ebony*

Lifestyle: *Details, Rolling Stone, Martha Stewart Living*

Newsmagazines: *Time, Newsweek*

Special-interest: *Guitar Player, Road & Track, Country Kitchens*

Trade and Professional: *Broadcasting & Cable, NEA* (National Education Association) *Today*

Elite: *The New Yorker, The New York Review of Books*

Generally, magazines have several advantages as segmented media. For example, the number of magazines is not constrained by technical restrictions, such as a limited number of radio frequencies or cable channels, so magazines can continue expanding into more specialized topics and treatments until they saturate the audience. Their formats and their economic base are more flexible. A small-circulation magazine can still be profitable if those it reaches are interested enough in its contents to support it or if that audience is important to specific advertisers (Dominick, 1993).

For example, Table 3.1 shows that magazine circulation and advertising revenues do not coincide very reliably. Some magazines reach a slightly smaller, but highly sought-after audience, such as the men who read *Sports Illustrated.* Some popular magazines, such as *National Geographic,* depend much more on subscriptions than on advertising for their revenues.

ZINE SCENE.
Electronic magazines on the Web take segmentation to new highs. Zero City, a poetry e-zine, shows that a concept not commericially viable in a conventional magazine can exist as an e-zine.

Books and magazines perform an important set of communications functions for elite audiences. Political activists are served by a variety of magazines ranging from liberal, such as *The Nation,* to conservative, such as *The National Review.* Intellectual magazines, such as *The New York Review of Books,* try to set the stage and agenda for academic and political debates on various issues, often by reviewing and summarizing books that they hope will help shape the debate. Some government policy-oriented magazines, such as *Foreign Affairs,* pride themselves

TABLE 3.1 Magazine Circulation and Annual Advertising Revenues, 1996

Publication	Circulation	Advertising Revenues ($)
NRTA/AARP Bulletin	20,567,352	—not applicable
Modern Maturity	20,538,786	59,460,589
Reader's Digest	15,072,260	201,592,101
TV Guide	13,013,938	402,973,357
National Geographic	9,025,003	60,671,984
Better Homes and Gardens	7,605,325	335,490,904
Family Circle	5,239,074	174,362,534
Good Housekeeping	4,951,240	184,812,233
Ladies' Home Journal	4,544,416	159,527,008
Woman's Day	4,317,604	216,908,112
McCall's	4,290,216	102,974,274
Time	4,102,168	439,623,516
People Weekly	3,449,852	525,563,737
Prevention	3,311,244	—not available
Playboy	3,236,517	—not available
Newsweek	3,194,769	383,767,258
Sports Illustrated	3,173,639	522,173,037
Redbook	2,926,702	99,848,782

Source: Publisher's Information Bureau, Audit Bureau of Circulations and Magazine Publishers of America.

on having an influential readership and on their articles sometimes affecting policy debates.

Magazines, trade journals, newsletters, and newspapers also meet crucial needs of business audiences. Business magazines supply information on business areas, professional development, and current economic trends. Some publications are fairly general, such as *Business Week* and *Fortune.* Others cover specific industries, such as *Advertising Age* and *Broadcasting.* Some trade publications, such as *Variety,* blur the distinction between newspapers and magazines by having both daily and weekly editions. Most specific of all are newsletters, which often serve only a few hundred readers who are willing to pay hundreds of dollars a year for the information offered. An example is *Telecom AM,* an Internet-based daily newsletter by Warren Publishing on the telecommunications industry, which costs $16.95 a month.

However, the 1980s and 1990s showed that segmentation and specialization can reach insupportable extremes. Several niches, such as entertainment magazines, women's magazines, health magazines, and fashion magazines, have experienced shakeouts. Audience circulation and economic support by advertisers were divided among too many magazines. Some of the less popular magazines failed as readership levels plateaued or even shrank, and advertisers invested less as economic expansion slowed. Still, a number of new magazines have survived their first few years and have established stable or growing audiences, and new magazines still spring up all the time.

INDUSTRY ORGANIZATION

A number of trends can be seen in the ownership of both newspapers and magazines.

Magazine Industry Consolidation

Consolidation refers to a reduction in the number of media outlets and a concentration of the ownership of media among fewer owners.

The magazine industry has both proliferated and **consolidated.** Most major magazines are published by a few large groups. For example, the current Time-Warner Group, one of the largest media conglomerates, grew from a magazine group. In 1923, Henry Luce and Briton Hadden founded Time Inc., which condensed information from *The New York Times.* Then, during the Depression, they started *Fortune,* which sold for $1 and was very successful. Their photojournalism-oriented *Life* (1936) was so successful that the group became Time-Life, Inc. They later added *Sports Illustrated* (1954), *People Weekly* (1974), and *Money* (1972).

However, the magazine industry is also one of the media areas where a new entrant or competitor can best break in by appealing to a new segment of the market that is not yet served by other magazines. For instance, *Rolling Stone* went quickly from a small counterculture or "hippie" magazine in 1969 to a widely read rock music and counterculture lifestyle magazine in the 1970s. It has since become the mainstream popular music magazine. Magazine start-ups accelerated in the 1960s, a decade in which over 750 new magazines appeared (Folkerts & Teeter, 1994).

More recently, the Ziff-Davis Group has capitalized on the rapidly growing interest in personal computers to build a very profitable magazine empire by publishing magazines such as *PC Week, PC Magazine,* and *MacWeek.* The 1980s saw even more new magazines. Over 1200 new magazines were founded between 1985 and 1989. Although only 35 percent survived, that was a greater success rate than in the first half of the 1980s (Payne, 1993). In the 1990s, a number of start-up efforts were focused on World Wide Web-based magazines, but new print magazines continue to appear, too.

Magazine Distribution

Magazines are distributed directly by subscription and by retailers, such as supermarkets and newsstands. Mailing and subscription operations, such as Publisher's Clearinghouse, have become a major business. Magazine mailing lists are commodities of great value to other magazines, catalogs, and direct-mail marketers. There is a brisk trade in buying and selling mailing lists, whether they include subscribers to general-interest magazines or to highly specific and targeted trade journals and newsletters. Magazine wholesalers and distributors are a crucial link between publishers and retailers. Many retailers simply take what the wholesaler delivers, so the distributors have a great influence on whether a new magazine gets delivered to newsstands and thereby reaches the public.

Book Publishing Houses and Groups

Publishing houses are the organizations that supervise the overall production of books, including the development of new books, editing, printing, and marketing. There is a tendency to consolidate large established publishing houses, even while new small ones start.

Some publishers publish only books that will sell many copies, whereas others, such as many university presses, publish books because they think the works are intellectually or artistically important and ought to be read. There are over 50,000 book publishers in the United States; they include commercial publishers, universities, religious groups, trade associations, and vanity presses that will publish anything as long as the author provides the money. Even though the computerized publishing technologies discussed earlier make the publication of smaller, more specialized projects possible, major mass market books continue to become more expensive to produce because marketing and other costs have increased. As a result, many publishers feel that they have to concentrate on selling more copies of fewer books.

Concentration of ownership has been a cyclical trend in the American book publishing industry. But the actual degree of concentration does not seem to have changed much, according to Department of Commerce statistical analysis (Curwin,1986, p. 45).

Concentration of ownership occurs when media are owned by a small number of individuals, government agencies, or corporations.

As with other print media, a wave of consolidation occurred among the major publishing houses in the 1990s, but a number of small ones still exist, and new publishing houses continually spring up, focusing on new areas of interest and new audiences. Still, as Table 3.2 shows, the publishing business is dominated by a number of large houses.

TABLE 3.2 Top North American Book Publishers, 1998

Simon & Schuster	\$2.3 billion (in annual sales)
Bertelsmann/Random House	\$2.3 billion
Thomson Corporation	\$1.5 billion
McGraw-Hill	\$1.3 billion
Pearson	\$1.2 billion
Time-Warner	\$1.1 billion
Harcourt General	\$1.1 billion

Source: Data from *The New York Times.*

There is also a trend toward foreign acquisition of, or investment in, American publishing houses. The German company Bertelsmann bought Doubleday, Dell, and Random House; the French company Hachette bought Grolier; the British Maxwell company bought Macmillan; the British Penguin company bought New American Library and Dutton; and the Australian Rupert Murdoch bought Harper & Row. As of 1998, non-U.S. firms owned half of the top 20 U.S. publishing houses, controlling 28 percent of the market. The major U.S.-owned publishing houses now include Simon & Schuster, owned by Paramount Communications; Time Publishing Group, owned by Time-Warner; Harcourt Brace & Company, owned by General Cinema Corporation; Random House, owned by the print-oriented Advance Group; and the Reader's Digest Association.

Bookstores

Bookstores buy books directly from publishers to stock their shelves. Booksellers range in size from national chains to small, independent bookstores.

Several kinds of large *chain stores* sell a large number of books. General chain stores like Wal-Mart and Kmart sell a great many books and magazines. By stocking and promoting a book, they can add considerably to its sales. Conversely, if they decide not to carry or promote a book because it is too controversial or too specialized to be interesting to their clientele, they radically lower a book's chance of becoming a best-seller.

THE BOOKSTORE OF TOMORROW. Amazon.com is the leading Internet bookstore. Here's the order page for the previous edition of this textbook!

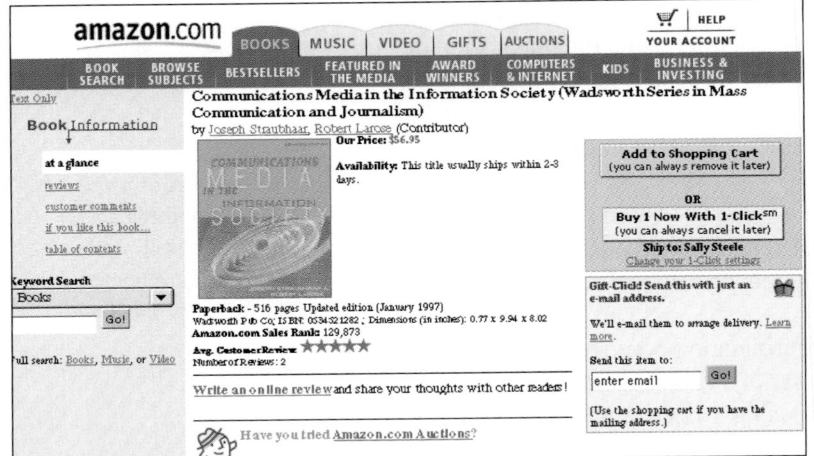

There are large chains of medium-sized stores, like Waldenbooks, that are typically located in malls. They sell great quantities of books. There are also growing chains of book and magazine superstores; Barnes & Noble and Borders are examples. These are typically large, stand-alone stores located near malls or other major commercial areas. They expanded quickly in the late 1990s and sell an increasing number of books and magazines as well.

Selling Books and Magazines On-Line

Virtual bookstores, like Amazon.com, sell books via the Internet and may have no physical retail stores at all.

"Virtual bookstores" like Amazon.com rival major bookstore chains as the largest book retailers and currently account for about 5 percent of all book sales in the United States. Amazon.com operates only via the Internet and has no physical retail stores at all. It claims an inventory of 2.5 million titles, although many of the books are not physically available in their own warehouse. Amazon.com often plays middleman, taking orders over the Internet and arranging to have books shipped to customers from publishers. The on-line stores can offer discounts by virtue of the volume discounts that they secure from publishers. The books show up a couple of days later in the mailbox.

Backlist books are those which are not being currently promoted by a publisher but are still in print.

Amazon.com's success has inspired competition. Barnes & Noble, a major retail book chain, now sells books over the Internet and stocks more than 350,000 titles in its distribution center. As of 1998, the German media conglomerate Bertelsmann entered into a joint venture with Barnes & Noble to compete with Amazon.com. In the long run, publishers could eliminate the intermediaries, selling books directly to the public via the Internet.

Internet book sales may mitigate the publishing industry trend, strongly reinforced by retail chains. Most stores, particularly the widely spread retail chains such as Waldenbooks, concentrate less on offering a wide variety of titles and more on pushing *blockbuster* best-sellers. Internet sales of books may benefit customers looking for more diverse or even obscure titles. And that may be a boon to authors and publishers of books other than best-sellers. According to *The New York Times* (March 9, 1998), many electronic customers prefer older **"backlist"** titles to current best-sellers. For example, often aided by electronic search engines, Amazon.com customers as a group bought at least one copy of 90% of the Penguin Group's backlist, which is devoted to pocketbook editions of classic fiction, plays, and nonfiction.

1. **What are the main trends in book publishing?**
2. **What are the effects of consolidation in the book publishing industry?**
3. **Which are the main publishing groups? To what conglomerates do they belong?**
4. **Does the trend toward foreign ownership affect U.S. publishing?**
5. **What are the main trends in magazines?**
6. **What are the trends in magazine genres?**
7. **How are computers and the Internet affecting book publishing and selling?**

AUDIENCES FOR BOOKS AND MAGAZINES

A mass audience still exists for print media, including best-selling paperback novels and self-help books and major general-interest magazines, such as *People Weekly.* There are also many fragments of the general audience now pursuing more specific personal interests, such as sports, glamour, business, hobbies, music, and entertainment, via a wide variety of specialized books and magazines.

On the average, people now read magazines about as often as books but quite a bit less than newspapers. With over 12,000 'zines, magazines, and related periodicals being published, magazine readership is quite fragmented. There are sizable subgroups, particularly among younger people, who read magazines but do not read newspapers or books. Magazine readership is highest among those of

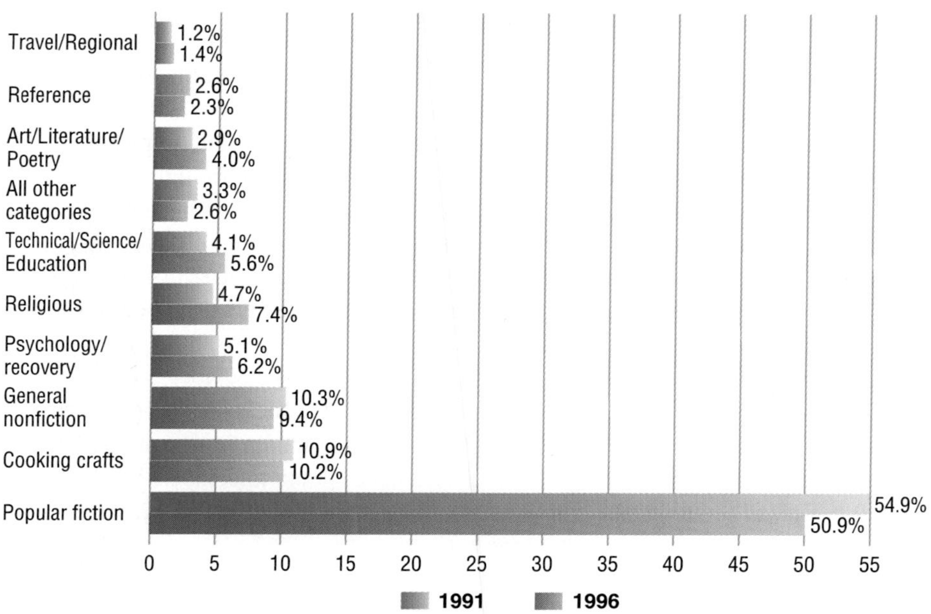

Source: Data from the *Wall Street Journal Almanac, 1998,* p. 930.

FIGURE 3.1
Popular fiction accounts for most book reading, although less in 1996 than in 1991.

ages 18–24 and 35–44; it is much lower among those over age 55 (Veronis, Suhler and Associates, 1997).

Although 70,000 book titles were published in 1998 and Americans bought about 3 billion books in 1998, the readership is uneven. Americans buy and read an average of four books a year, but that is deceptive. Many people do not read books. Some read the *Bible* or other religious works but few other books. Many read reference books for work purposes. And do cookbooks count? The United States tends to lag behind most other industrialized or information-oriented nations in books read per year. Figure 3.1 shows what kinds of books people read in 1996.

Table 3.3

Top Magazines for Men		Top Magazines for Women	
Title	**Readership (in Millions)**	**Title**	**Readership (in Millions)**
Sunday Comics (Puck)	41.6	Sunday Comics (Puck)	45.9
Parade	37.8	Parade	41.9
Reader's Digest	20.3	Reader's Digest	29.0
USA Weekend	20.0	Better Homes & Gardens	26.5
Sports Illustrated	17.8	People	23.9
National Geographic	16.7	USA Weekend	22.6
TV Guide	15.4	Good Housekeeping	21.3
Sunday Magazine	13.7	TV Guide	19.9
People	13.2	Family Circle	19.7
Consumer Reports	9.4	Woman's Day	19.6

Source: MediaMark Research, Inc. TopLine Reports, New York. Available: http://www.mediamark.com/mri/docs/TopLineReports.html

Note: These numbers reflect readership, not circulation (as in Table 3.1).

Both magazine and book readership are limited by the growing problem of adult illiteracy in the United States. Although the official literacy rate is 98 percent, many adults have low-level literacy skills. The National Adult Literacy Survey found that upwards of 15 percent of the adult population lacks the literacy skills required to function effectively in society. People with the lowest levels of literacy are unable to locate an item of information in a paragraph of a simple newspaper article, for example. And international surveys show that there are more functionally illiterate adults in the United States than in other industrialized nations.

1. Is there still a mass audience for magazines?
2. Who reads magazines, and who reads newspapers?
3. What are the trends among book readers?
4. What are the trends among magazine readers?
5. How are these trends related to overall literacy?

Who is illiterate? Recent immigrants who are not literate in English account for about a quarter of the total. Poverty is also a determining factor; two-fifths of those with the lowest level of literacy skills live below the poverty line. However, people with poor reading skills are found throughout the population. Most of them are in a state of denial; only about a third of those at the lowest literacy level admit they have difficulty reading (Bowen, 1999).

Throughout this chapter, we have seen that magazine publishers target their publications to segmented audiences. The impact of this strategy on the audiences for magazines can be seen in Table 3.3. In this table we see the most popular magazines for men and women, based on the numbers who say that they read each title. Note that a magazine targeted primarily to men, *Sports Illustrated,* is in the top 5 for men, while "women's magazines" such as *Better Homes and Gardens* are among the favorites for women. However, these figures also show that the age of the mass market magazine is still with us, but now in the form of magazines that are actually newspaper supplements. The *Sunday Comics, Parade,* and *USA Weekend* rank at the top for both men and women. *Reader's Digest, People,* and *TV Guide* are leading mass market magazines among those distributed through the conventional magazine channels of yearly subscriptions and newsstand sales.

POLICY ISSUES FOR PRINT MEDIA

Consolidation and Concentration of Ownership

A major policy issue in magazine and book publishing is how the tendency toward consolidation and concentration of ownership is affecting diversity and freedom of speech. U.S. media policy and most American thinking assume that competition among various media outlets is crucial. Print media, especially magazines and books, have also been among the most competitive, so there has never been any great concern about regulating them in the United States

Of course, before the Internet, relatively few people really had the freedom to speak to others via the media, but it has been assumed that competition will bring out diverse points of view and approximate a fairly free discussion among knowledgeable people. Even before the consolidation of media ownership, however, many people questioned the assumption that mass media reflected diverse points of view (McChesney, 1997). The more open and interactive nature of the Internet may change this for the growing portion of the U.S. population that has effective access to the Internet.

Conglomerates are companies made up of diverse parts, usually across several media industries.

Consolidation is apparent in the magazine and book publishing industries. Both domestic and foreign **conglomerates** have been buying up magazine and book publishers.

There has been a trend toward publishing houses being acquired by conglomerate publishing groups, such as Bertelsmann, Simon & Schuster, Pearson, and International Thomson Publishing. As in most other media, these conglomerate ownership groups are increasingly international, possibly taking them outside national control. The German company Bertelsmann made headlines in 1998 by buying Random House, one of the largest U.S. publishing houses.

Most readership of both magazines and books is concentrated on the output of a few publishers. Books are very important in national intellectual and political life. Does increasing concentration in the U.S. book publishing industry mean a reduction in the points of view expressed or in the ability of diverse people to find publishers for their ideas? The trend toward consolidation worries some writers and publishers, who fear that it will be hard for manuscripts other than probable blockbuster best-sellers to find a publisher if the number of houses continues to decline. This concern is partially met by a steady rise of new, small publishing houses. Another interesting phenomenon is the number of people self-publishing their own manuscripts on the World Wide Web.

There are also signals of growth and diversity. While some magazines and book publishers consolidate, new magazines and new publishing houses continue to spring up. Although they tend to be small and to reach far fewer people than the largest book and magazine publishers, collectively, new publishers are a significant force.

New electronic publishers and on-line sources of news and information certainly increase the potential for competition and greater diversity of viewpoints. Electronic publishing is still finding its way among interactive electronic novels and role-playing games, but on-line sources of information have been exploding. On-line information services include computer network access to wire services, magazine sites, magazines that publish only on-line (such as *Slate*), newspaper copy, and an increasing number of alternative Internet information sources, such as discussion groups focused on various issues and events. These services are covered further in Chapter 8.

Copyright is a legal privilege to use, sell, or license intellectual property, such as a book or a film.

Intellectual Property and Copyright

Intellectual property is the result of intellectual or creative work, owned by an individual, institution, or company.

Copyright issues have become crucial points of contention for print media. Book publishers and academic journals both have cracked down on photocopying, by students and professors, of material that has been copyrighted by publishers. Many informal newsletters and new electronic publications also "borrow" or sample images, sections of text, and headlines from newspapers, magazines, and books. As electronic distribution increases, new **intellectual property** rules may be required because publishers and authors are determined to collect royalties from such reproduction and use.

Individual authors have rights during their lifetimes, and their heirs have rights for 70 years after the writers' deaths, so any publication less than 125 years old has to be checked for its copyright status. The duration of copyright protection has increased steadily over the years, with the life-plus-70-year standard set by the Sonny Bono Copyright Extension Act of 1998, up from the 50-year limit established by the 1976 Copyright Act. Supporters like to defend the increase with tales of starving writers and their impoverished descendants, but in reality the beneficiaries are more likely to be transnational publishing conglomerates. And, copyright laws have a dual purpose. In addition to protecting the rights of authors so as to encourage the publication of new creative works, copyright is also supposed to place reasonable time limits on those rights so that outdated works may be incorporated into new creative efforts. The extended copyright protection, therefore, frustrates creative endeavors such as including poetry and song lyrics on Internet sites.

And what about starving students who have to pay higher fees for course packets and textbooks—who feels sorry for them? One of the basic precepts of copyright law is fair use—the notion that some copyright infringements serve a higher social purpose such as education, should be permitted. These include making single copies for personal use, citing short passages in scholarly works, and making multiple copies for classroom use. So, if a student makes her own copy of a course packet, that's fair use and no copyright royalty is owed. Now, what if the student is short on time and asks a copy shop to make the copies for her? That is a copyright violation, at least according to a landmark decision that the publishing industry won against Kinko's in 1991—a decision that sharply boosted course packet prices. The continual bolstering of copyright protection and the hardball legal tactics of transnational publishing giants has a chilling effect on the exercise of fair use rights.

And once a copyrighted text is available on-line, how do we control copying in a medium where multiple perfect copies can be made with a tap on a keyboard? Various technological fixes, including digital "watermarks," pay-as-you-go access to copyrighted works, and the encoding of copyrighted material, are some of the possibilities. In Chapters 8 and 14 we will consider these problems further.

Censorship, Freedom of Speech, and the First Amendment

First Amendment issues are also crucial. Freedom of speech and of expression in print media is well established, but a number of community and religious groups have objected to the contents of various books, magazines, and new Internet "publications." Usually people object because those published contents are seen as being overtly sexual or as inciting to violence or the sexual abuse of women or children. Since the turn of the century, most books have been exempt from overt **censorship,** although novels like *Lady Chatterley's Lover* (1928), by D.H. Lawrence, went through periods of censorship in the United States. By today's standards, many readers would consider Lawrence's sexually explicit passages fairly tame, but the book challenged the understood limits of its time.

First Amendment grants freedom from interference by government with speech or expression.

Censorship is control over media content by those in higher authority in a society.

MEDIA ETHICS

"Sexing Up" *Cosmo*

Bonnie Fuller is a sensation in the magazine world. After "sexing up" *Cosmopolitan* magazine, she moved to *Glamour* to do a makeover on it. She had previously reworked *Young Miss* into *YM: Young and Modern* and had reworked *Marie Claire,* all with substantial circulation increases. She left *Cosmo* with a very healthy circulation of 2.3 million (as of 1998). Something Fuller does is clearly working with the readers.

Part of *Cosmo*'s appeal on the newsstand was a sexy cover, a model with perfect cleavage and cover lines like "His secret moan zones . . . ." But another part was dramatic writing that offers, or seems to offer, real stories about real people. There was something intriguing to readers about tantalizing bits of the sex lives of real people. This raises questions about how far a magazine ought to go in using sex to draw in an audience. In particular, should a magazine pander to a sort of voyeurism that leads people to want to know real details about real people?

Another problem is that the people aren't always real. And sometimes the quotes are "sexed up" to make them more dramatic or more explicit, judging by several examples given by Katherine Rossman in "The Secret of Her Success," *Brill's Content* (November 1998), a magazine that aims to act as a watchdog about the press.

This has some writers worried. What should a writer do when an editor alters a quote? What should the fact-checking department do when the editor wants to make a story more dramatic by fictionalizing it slightly? The editors note that most of the stories are very personal accounts, often submitted by readers.

Factcheckers aren't going to call and ask such a contributor if he really "touched her there." Editors note that sometimes both people and experiences are composites, created by blending several real people and their quotes. That is different from complete fabrication. Or is it? A related point is that *Cosmo* may well be entitled to have different standards for talking about sex lives than *The New York Times* should adhere to when talking about a sex scandal such as that between President Clinton and Monica Lewinsky. People probably don't have quite the same expectations about *Cosmo*'s ethics on the use of quotes and factchecking, but exactly what standards do apply to a magazine like *Cosmo* is still an interesting question.

Books still get pulled from library shelves for various reasons. For example, *Catcher in the Rye* (1951), by J.D. Salinger, has been challenged for rough language and *The Adventures of Huckleberry Finn* (1885), by Mark Twain, for racial stereotypes and epithets.

The focal point for discussions about censorship of books is usually the local library or school system. Campaigns to ban books usually focus on what is assigned in schools or is available through libraries. Librarians have evolved a number of strategies for reconciling *freedom of access* with the desire to protect children or other vulnerable audiences from adult content. Some books are not shelved but have to be requested; access to others is restricted by age. For example, a number of libraries in 1992 restricted access to Madonna's book *Sex.*

The Internet poses similar challenges for libraries. The search engines of the Web are also becoming a staple of library research. However, those search engines can be used to seek out a wide variety of controversial material, including sex, violence, and hate speech. Many local libraries now offer Internet access as one of their services to the public. See Chapters 8 and 14 for discussions of recent initiatives to require libraries to use *filtering* programs to screen out controversial material.

Magazines have also been challenged in various communities and by various legal decisions. Most stores that distribute sexually explicit magazines now shelve them in a section that is off limits to those under age 18. Some stores, such as convenience store chains, have gone further, blocking off the covers of such magazines from open view or removing them altogether.

STOP & REVIEW

1. **What are the policy implications of concentration of ownership?**
2. **What are the main copyright issues for publishing?**
3. **What are the First Amendment issues in publishing?**
4. **What are the current threats to freedom of speech and of publishing?**

There have been fewer overt attempts to limit freedom of speech and of the press in political terms. During the 1950s, however, the anticommunist campaign of Senator Joseph McCarthy resulted in several authors being blacklisted—prohibited from writing or publishing. McCarthy's main focus was Hollywood screenwriters for films and television programs (see Chapters 6 and 7), but his efforts to denounce and blacklist writers he considered communist sympathizers affected some print media as well. Although he succeeded in swaying opinion in the early 1950s, most people reacted negatively to McCarthy's campaign by the mid-1950s, and modern efforts to suppress a writer are often denounced as "McCarthyism" (Altschull, 1984).

Like other media magnates, the owners of publishing houses do sometimes make attempts to influence the politics of what their houses publish. In 1997–1998, Rupert Murdoch, owner of HarperCollins, got his company to back out of a contract to publish a book by Chris Patton, the last British governor of Hong Kong. Patton was strongly disliked by the leadership of China for pushing democratization quickly, just before the Chinese takeover of the city in 1997. Murdoch feared that the book, *East and West: China, Power and the Future of Asia* (which was finally published by Times Books in 1998), would anger the Chinese leadership and damage Murdoch's efforts to introduce his satellite channel, Star TV, and other of his Asian media interests into China.

SUMMARY AND REVIEW

WHAT KEY ELEMENTS OF THE PRINT MEDIA WERE DEVELOPED FIRST OUTSIDE EUROPE?

A number of essential ideas were brought to Europe; for example, using rags to make paper was imported from China. Other printing techniques, such as movable metal type, developed in parallel form outside Europe but were probably not a direct influence on the development of European print media.

WHAT WAS THE IMPACT OF PRINTING IN EUROPE?

The advent of printing by Gutenberg greatly accelerated the growth of literacy by making books cheaper and more widely available. Education became more widespread because texts were easier to get. Printing affected religion by making the *Bible* widely available, politics by boosting news circulation, and economics by increasing knowledge and skills.

WHY AND HOW DID MAGAZINES DEVELOP?

In 1741 the first U.S. magazines, Bradford's *American Magazine* and Ben Franklin's *General Magazine,* appeared. During the American Revolution, many magazines took a more political tone. Few magazines were popular or long-lived. They covered weekly events, politics, and art and contained reviews, travelogs, short stories, and serialized fiction; they were aimed at an educated elite. By the 1820s, magazines of more general interest, such as *The Saturday Evening Post,* began to appear. The number of magazines increased during the Civil War, and they began to reach wider audiences. The Postal Act of 1879 made distribution cheaper.

WHAT WAS THE ROLE OF PRINT MEDIA IN THE CIVIL WAR? HOW DID THE WAR AFFECT THE MEDIA?

Books and magazines affected the issues debate that led up to the Civil War. *Uncle Tom's Cabin,* for example, is a book widely credited with helping influence northern U.S. opinion against slavery. Several magazines, such as *Harper's Weekly,* grew to fame during the Civil War as a result of their print coverage and also their illustrations, which dramatized scenes of the war. Illustration became prominent tools of magazine journalism. Circulations grew.

WHAT WAS "MUCKRAKING"?

Muckraking characterized the post–Civil War period, when crusading magazines turned their attention to scandals and corruption in government and among industry cartels.

WHEN DID MAGAZINES PEAK AS MASS AUDIENCE MEDIA?

After the Civil War, magazines expanded. After the 1890s, many new kinds of magazines sprang up. News photo magazines, such as *Life,* and general-interest magazines, such as *The Saturday Evening Post* and *Collier's,* continued to serve a broad audience up through the 1950s, when both their photojournalism roles and entertainment functions were undercut by television.

WHAT FORM HAVE MAGAZINES TAKEN AS MODERN MASS MEDIA?

They have become more targeted to more segmented audiences. Instead of addressing a broad mass audience, magazines now tend to focus on very specific audiences for politics, hobbies, interest groups, and demographic groups.

WHAT ARE THE MAIN RECENT TRENDS OR CHANGES IN PRINT MEDIA PRODUCTION TECHNOLOGIES?

Since the 1970s, computerization has done much to change print media. Computers first substituted for typesetting machines, and then most of the layout of a page came to be done on computers, particularly when photographs could be scanned or digitized so that they could be placed on the page electronically.

WHAT ARE THE MAIN RECENT TRENDS OR CHANGES IN PRINT MEDIA DELIVERY TECHNOLOGIES?

Books moved in bulk along railroads, but the mail was crucial for enabling magazines to reach a broad audience in an affordable manner. In the 1990s, electronic delivery by World Wide Web were becoming alternatives for magazine delivery.

WHAT IS DESKTOP PUBLISHING?

Desktop publishing is the creation of publication-quality documents using the increased power and speed of desktop computers, laser printers, and scanners that digitize photos or illustrations into computer-readable form. This has done much to decentralize print media. Lay people can now produce local or specialized media, and professional media use desktop publishing for their products as well. This has led to the proliferation of magazines, "'zines," and small book-publishing houses.

WHAT ARE THE MAIN TRENDS IN BOOK PUBLISHING?

Increasing numbers of books are being published and purchased by consumers, students, and businesses. Large publishing houses are consolidating even as smaller ones proliferate.

WHAT ARE THE TRENDS IN MAGAZINES?

General-interest magazines have declined as specialized, targeted magazines have grown in numbers and diversity.

IS THERE STILL A MASS AUDIENCE? WHO READS MAGAZINES, AND WHO READS NEWSPAPERS?

The average adult spends about as much time on newspapers as on books or magazines, but younger people read newspapers less and magazines more.

WHAT IS THE TREND AMONG PRINT MEDIA READERS RELATED TO OVERALL LITERACY?

There seems to be an overall trend toward less reading, in part because overall functional literacy seems to be declining, with more time spent on TV.

IS THERE A TREND TOWARD CONSOLIDATION AND CONCENTRATION OF OWNERSHIP IN PRINT MEDIA?

Book publishing has become more concentrated and internationalized. Magazine publishing has concentrated in a similar way, but more new magazine companies have continued to enter the field.

WHAT ARE SOME PEOPLE'S CONCERNS ABOUT CONSOLIDATION IN THE PUBLISHING INDUSTRY, PARTICULARLY AMONG BOOKS AND MAGAZINES?

Concentration in book or magazine publishing might reduce competition and the diversity of their contents. However, there is also an explosion of small publishing houses, magazines, and Internet sites.

WHAT CURRENT THREATS ARE THERE TO FREEDOM OF SPEECH AND OF THE PRESS?

Freedom of speech and of expression in print media is well established, although a number of groups object to the contents of various print media, usually because those contents are seen as overtly sexual. Freedom of speech is less clear for new media.

WHAT ARE THE MAIN COPYRIGHT ISSUES FOR PRINT MEDIA?

A major issue in print media is photocopying of material that has been copyrighted by publishers. The Sonny Bono Copyright Term Extension Act of 1998 extends the period of protection to the life of the author, plus 70 years. Many newsletters and new electronic "publications" also borrow or sample images, sections of text, and headlines from newspapers, magazines, and books. Computer-based production and electronic network distribution make such copying easy. Publishers and authors want to collect royalties in return for such reproduction and use. As electronic distribution increases, new intellectual property rules may be required.

Electronic Resources

For up-to-the-minute URLs about *Books and Magazines,* access the MEDIA NOW site on the World Wide Web at:

http://communication.wadsworth.com/

CHAPTER 4

Newspapers

WHAT'S AHEAD

This chapter reviews the historical trends that have characterized the development of American newspapers up to the present, where the number of newspapers has decreased but still attracts a profitable and influential readership. A review of technology trends finds that newspapers are increasingly embracing the Internet as a way to reach and serve readers and to compete with new on-line sources of news. Both of these industry trends, along with mergers and consolidation, ethical issues, and how to treat the privacy of public figures and private citizens, give newspaper professionals a great deal to think about.

Access the MEDIA NOW site on the World Wide Web at: **http://communication.wadsworth.com/** Choose "Chapter 4" from the selection box to access electronic information and other sites relevant to this chapter.

PARIS, OREGON (POPULATION 15), 2010

Say, Lefty, before you shut me down for the night, you wanted to revise your newspaper subscriptions for tomorrow.

That's right. Remind me what I'm getting now.

O.K. The papers are *Idaho Daily Statesman, American Farm Daily, High Desert Tattler,* and *Wall Street Journal.* Interests are farm equipment prices, beef prices, ranching, beef production, survivalism, local gossip, and local politics (local being Boise, Idaho, to Winnemucca, Nevada). Acceptable ads are farm equipment, light trucks, firearms, and local groceries.

Well, let's can that *Wall Street Journal.* Costs too much. And when I say local, I mean Nampa, Idaho, to Winnemucca—gettin' tired of reading about them city slickers in Boise.

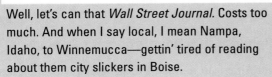

NEXT MORNING:

Mornin' Lefty. I found forty items, three photos. Do you want me to print this stuff, or do you want to screen it first?

Jest print the headlines and photos for now, extra large type. My eyes are still feelin' poorly. Maybe I'll look at the rest later.

If you'll accept three video farm equipment ads, they'll cover the costs of your papers. Want to see them?

Goldurn ads. Yeah, guess so. Run 'em now. Jest tell them fellers that I don't authorize resale of the information that I accepted these ads, O.K.?

They'll accept that condition, if you also accept a separate print ad, printing nonoptional.

[censored] O.K.

Chapter Outline

A Brief History of Newspaper Publishing
The Colonial and Revolutionary Periods
Newspapers in the 1800s
Minority Press Voices
The Penny Press and the Rise of Mass Newspapers
Pulitzer vs. Hearst: The Rise of Yellow Journalism
Newspapers Peak and Decline after 1900
Investigative Reporting and Watergate
Trends in Newspaper Technology
Technology in Newsgathering
Technology in Newspaper Production
Technology in Newspaper Distribution
Technology in Newspaper Advertising
Newspaper Industry Organization
Newspaper Economics
The Newspaper Publishing Industry
Newspaper Content Genres
Newspaper Sections and Contents
Audiences for Newspapers
Newspaper Policy and Ethics Issues
Newspaper Consolidation, Chains, and Shakeout
Freedom of Speech and the First Amendment
Libel
Privacy of Newsmakers
Reporting and Content
Accuracy and Truthfulness
Coverage of Sex and Scandal
Journalism Education
Newspapers, Gatekeeping, and "Information Glut"
Summary and Review

A BRIEF HISTORY OF NEWSPAPER PUBLISHING

Before there were newspapers, there were newsletters. Medieval banks published financial and trade-oriented newsletters, which probably count as the longest-running print medium apart from religious books and pamphlets. Newspapers were first developed as irregular news sheets in Holland, Great Britain, and France to carry news about foreign events, such as the Thirty Years War in Germany, Austria, and Holland (1618–1648) and commercial or economic issues. These news sheets, called **corantos,** were largely replaced by daily reports, or **diurnos,** that focused more on domestic events, such as the king and Parliament between 1640 and 1650 in Great Britain (Stephens, 1989).

The Colonial and Revolutionary Periods

The first American newspapers struggled with the question of control by colonial authorities. The first U.S. newspaper, *Publick Occurrences Both Foreign and Domestick,* published in 1690 by Benjamin Harris, contained stories that scandalized both the British Crown and Puritan authorities; it was shut down after one issue. In 1704, Boston postmaster John Campbell started the *Boston News-Letter,* which carried a notice that it was published "by authority" of the royal governor. Most of the news was straightforward, if dull: news from foreign papers (often months late), notices of ship departures and arrivals (important in a port city), summaries of sermons, and legal and death notices. Campbell's replacement as postmaster also started a newspaper. These two newspapers highlighted an early and continuing connection between print media and the means of delivery, postal or otherwise (Tebbel, 1969a).

Corantos, the ancestors of newspapers, were irregular news sheets that appeared around 1600 in Holland and England and covered foreign affairs.

Politicization of Newspapers. In 1721, James Franklin started the *New England Courant* with no "by authority" approval. It was intended to be independent. Franklin was jailed and forbidden to publish without prior approval, so James made his brother, Benjamin, the new editor. Ben Franklin was very successful as a newspaper editor. He soon moved to Philadelphia and started the *Pennsylvania Gazette.*

NEWSPAPER TIME LINE

1455	Gutenberg Bible published
1620	*Corantos,* first news sheets
1640s	*Diurnos,* first daily newspapers
1690	First American newspaper, *Publick Occurrences Both Foreign and Domestick*
1721	*New England Courant* begins publication
1733	Zenger libel case
1776	American Declaration of Independence promulgated by colonial newspapers
1783	First daily newspaper published in America, *Pennsylvania Evening Post*
1827	*Freedom's Journal,* first African American Newspaper
1828	*Cherokee Phoenix,* first Native American newspaper
1833	The *New York Sun,* first Penny Press daily
1846	Associated Press wire news service begins operation; rotary presses introduced
1861	Civil War begins, expanding newspaper readership
1878	New Journalism movement originated by Joseph Pulitzer
1895	William Randolph Hearst pushed "yellow journalism"
1920s	Chain consolidation marks decline in the number of metropolitan daily newspapers
1926	Network radio competes for advertising revenue
1948	Television competes as visual news vehicle
1972	Watergate scandal inspires new era of investigative reporting
1982	*USA Today* national daily launched
1998	Newspaper sites proliferate on Internet

The question of editorial **independence** and criticism of authority was raised explicitly in 1733 when Peter Zenger published a newspaper openly critical of the British governor of New York. The governor jailed Zenger for criminal **libel.** Despite British legal precedent to the contrary, Zenger's lawyer Andrew Hamilton argued that the truth of a published piece was a defense against libel. Appealing to the American jury not to rely on British law and precedent, Hamilton won the libel case, which established the important principle that true statements are not libelous.

Diurnos, direct ancestors of daily newspapers, gave daily reports and tended to be more focused on domestic events.

Independence in media usually refers to freedom from governmental control, not from owners or advertisers.

Libel is a harmful or untruthful criticism by media that intends to damage someone.

The First Amendment. The British authorities in America were operating within a European tradition, which still required newspapers to be licensed and approved by government. In the Zenger case and others that followed colonial authorities tried to control the press, particularly as calls for revolution grew. The authorities tried to apply a Stamp Tax to colonial newspapers, taxing each sheet of print and each advertisement. Publishers mocked and resisted the tax. It also provoked the Stamp Tax Congress in 1765, which proclaimed, "No taxation without representation." This is usually considered the beginning of the American independence movement.

Such efforts at controlling the press by British authorities left colonists, particularly journalists and printers like Benjamin Franklin, convinced that freedom of speech and a free press were essential for the kind of democracy they hoped to build. Even radical statements, such as calling for the overthrow of a government perceived to be unjust, had to be permitted. In 1754, for example, Franklin published the first American editorial cartoon in his *Pennsylvania Gazette.* It showed a snake chopped into eight pieces. The caption, "Join or Die," urged the colonies to unite against the British.

Political press refers to media that are clearly engaged in political comment or struggle.

Zenger and Franklin, among others, helped establish a **political press** that was very important in building support for the American Revolution and in defining the role of a free press in subsequent American democracy. Newspapers proliferated in the years before the Revolution. Most were partisan, although some tried to be neutral. Key documents and ideas, including the Declaration of Independence (1776), were published in the newspapers. In 1785, during the debates over the Constitution, James Madison, Alexander Hamilton, and John Jay first published the *Federalist Papers* in newspapers as press handouts (Altschull, 1984).

Newspapers were an important part of the revolutionary movement, although resource shortages during the American Revolution caused many to close. In 1783 the first daily newspaper in the United States, the *Pennsylvania Evening Post and Daily Advertiser,* was begun. At the Constitutional Congress, widespread agreement on the need to protect freedom of speech and of the press resulted in the **First Amendment** to the Constitution.

First Amendment to the U.S. Constitution protects freedom of speech and press.

Newspapers in the 1800s

Partisan refers to media with clear support for one particular political party, or certain leaders and ideas.

After the American Revolution, the politicization of many newspapers and magazines continued. They took on more **partisan** leanings and were often openly involved in political campaigns, like the abolition of slavery. But the press did not stay primarily political. Advertising and commercial interests began to be important as well. Benjamin Franklin was a successful publisher in large part because he was a clever writer of advertising copy.

By 1800 most large cities had at least one daily, but circulations were limited. Readers had to be literate *and* relatively wealthy: One issue cost as much as a pint of whiskey, around five cents.

Minority Press Voices

Newspapers were one of the forces that drew people into thinking about themselves as Americans, forming an "imagined community" of people who had access to the same information and identified with each other (Anderson, 1983). However, real differences existed among Americans, and not all were allowed to belong to that community. Newspapers also began to be the voices of different, excluded audiences. African American and Native American newspapers were published.

Native American Press. The first Native American newspaper, the *Cherokee Phoenix,* was established in 1828 by the Cherokee nation. This paper was written partly in the alphabet that Sequoyah, a Cherokee, invented and partly in English. This paper was begun in New Echota, the Cherokee capitol near what is now Calhoun, Georgia. Elias Boudinot was among the founders of the *Cherokee Phoenix.* Boudinot, a college-educated Cherokee school teacher, hoped that the paper would improve both the living conditions and the image of Native Americans.

In 1829 the Georgia legislature took away all the legal rights of Native Americans, including the right to freedom of speech. In 1832 the editor of the paper resigned in protest. Its publication became erratic and finally was suspended in 1834. It was not until ten years later that a new Cherokee nation newspaper was firmly established.

African American Press. The first African American newspaper, *Freedom's Journal,* was established in 1827 in New York City with Reverend Samuel G. Cornish as editor and John B. Russwurm as proprietor. The newspaper had strong ties to the abolitionist press. The goal of this paper was to encourage racial unity and the progress of African Americans in the north.

Another important African American paper, *The Northern Star* (later shortened to *The North Star*), was edited by Frederick Douglass, an escaped slave. It began publication on November 1, 1847. *The Ram's Horn,* a newspaper launched before *North Star,* introduced *The North Star* with a prospectus that read as follows:

> Frederick Douglass proposes to publish in Rochester, New York, a weekly antislavery paper with the above title. The objective of *The North Star* will be to attack slavery in all its forms and aspects; advocate universal emancipation; exact the standard of public morality; promote the moral and intellectual improvement of the colored people; and . . . hasten the day of freedom to our three million enslaved fellow-countrymen.

LEADING STAR. Frederick Douglass used *The North Star* to push for abolition of slavery.

The North Star later merged with the *Liberty Party Paper* in Syracuse, New York, and was renamed *Frederick Douglass' Paper.*

The Penny Press and the Rise of Mass Newspapers

The early 1800s saw the invention of iron presses to replace wooden presses in England and of the steam-powered press in Germany. Two-sided printing by cylinders came in 1814. By 1830 a press could print 4000 double impressions per hour. These technological innovations permitted lower-cost papers aimed at a broader audience. At the same time, social conditions favorable for the creation of the mass audience and mass newspapers were building. More people were learning to read via the expanding public education system, wages were increasing, more people were moving to the cities, and an urban middle class was growing. These groups created the nucleus of a mass audience.

However, many people still could not read or afford newspapers. This was particularly true among the waves of immigrants who arrived here from 1840 on into the early 1900s. One response was to create and sell cheaper newspapers. In both the United States and Britain, the 1800s brought forth the **Penny Press.**

Penny Press were daily newspapers after 1830 that sold for one cent and were aimed at a mass audience.

Benjamin Day launched the first low-cost daily mass newspaper, the *New York Sun,* in 1833. It sold for a penny—the first Penny Press. To offer his paper at that price, Day had to rely on advertising as well as sales. This kind of daily was one of the first media to create a truly mass audience, big enough to attract advertisers and justify their investment. Day was able to target a new, wider audience that could read but could not afford earlier newspapers. To stay in business despite the lower price, he reached out further into the urban audience, using newsboys to sell papers in greater volume.

1. What were the first newspapers?
2. What case established the precedent for freedom of the press in colonial America?
3. Who developed the minority press?
4. What was the partisan press?
5. What was the Penny Press? What led to it?

Costs decreased further in 1846 with the advent of the rotary press (which placed type on a rotating cylinder). This combination of factors spawned the modern daily newspaper and changed the newspaper business. Audience interests and purchasing power, along with production and delivery technologies, are still crucial to how newspapers continue to evolve (Sloan, Stovall, & Startt, 1993).

News gathering was also improved by the deployment of the telegraph in 1844. By the time of the Mexican–-American war during 1846–1848, telegraph technology enabled newspapers to get news of the war almost instantly—after it arrived by ship from the front in Mexico City.

Wire services are news services that supply a variety of newspapers, named originally for their use of the telegraph and its wires.

In 1846, to share the costs of covering stories, several New York newspapers formed the New York Associated Press news service, which expanded with the ability to send stories over the telegraph, thus becoming the first "wire" service. This and other regional wire services joined in 1892 to become what is now called the Associated Press (AP). AP competed domestically with the United Press Service (UP), later known as United Press International (UPI), and internationally with the British wire service Reuters and the French service Agence France Presse (AFP). These **wire services** helped newspapers lower their costs, add more general-interest material, and appeal to a wider audience.

ONLY A PENNY.
The *New York Sun* was the first low-cost daily mass newspaper, first published in 1833.

THE  SUN.

NUMBER 1.] NEW YORK, TUESDAY, SEPTEMBER 3, 1833. [PRICE ONE PENNY.

PUBLISHED DAILY,

AN IRISH CAPTAIN.

Following the Frontier. Newspapers expanded westward with the American population, following the frontier into the midwest in the 1830s and farther west around the time of the Civil War. During this period, several writers who later became famous for their books and short stories, including Mark Twain, Steven Crane, and Ambrose Bierce, made their names as newspaper journalists. Twain, for example, followed the frontier westward and worked in Hannibal, Missouri, in 1847; in St. Louis in 1853; in Virginia City, Nevada, in 1862; and in San Francisco in 1864.

As cheaper presses also moved west, newspapers proliferated and diversified. The second half of the 1800s saw over 130 Spanish-language newspapers started in the Southwest (Huntzicker, 1993). As we have seen, Native Americans published several newspapers, some of which were suppressed by state authorities to limit sympathy for the Native Americans' claims to retain their lands. Frontier newspapers were often blunt and antagonistic. Many chastised eastern liberals for sympathizing with the "Indians." Editors were opinionated. Jane Grey Swisshelm, for example, criticized the politicians of St. Cloud, Minnesota. They then destroyed her press—but made her reputation, as she rebuilt her press and exposed the mob who had destroyed it (Huntzicker, 1993).

Reaching a Wider Audience. The Penny Press, or mass audience daily, aimed its content at a wider general audience. It set patterns that still mark newspaper content: sensational coverage of crime, police news, scandal, and disasters; features about prominent or notorious personalities; social events such as weddings, deaths, and parties; shipping and commercial news; stock and money prices; and advertising. The metropolitan press covered the events leading up to the Civil War, and not surprisingly northern and southern papers often saw things very differently. Several northern papers had a major influence on the positions and strategy of the northern states. Frederick Douglass pushed hard for the abolition of slavery with *The North Star.* The *New York Tribune* under Horace Greeley championed the abolition of slavery, too, whereas the *New York Times* was somewhat more neutral.

PRESS HERO. Joseph Pulitzer pioneered the new journalism, which was sensational but news-oriented, and focused on scoops, headlines, and pictures.

The Civil War (1861–1865) helped expand newspaper readership because people wanted to know what was going on at the front as quickly as possible. That interest—fueled by reports telegraphed from the front—reinforced the newspaper focus on yesterday's events and headlines.

Newspapers of this era added an appealing new visual element—the news photograph. Earlier, Civil War photographer Matthew Brady popularized photographic images, but these could not be reproduced in newspapers or magazines without first converting them to engravings, a time-consuming process that marred the aesthetics of the pictures. It wasn't until 1880 that a process for integrating photos and text on the same page was developed and the first newspaper photos appeared (Carlebach, 1997).

The New Journalism and Newspaper Expansion. Newspapers plunged into the post–Civil War industrial expansion. Newspapers flourished in the cities where industries grew and people flocked to get jobs. Along with other industries, newspapers saw a chance to grow, and they more aggressively pursued advertising and newspaper sales. **Muckraking** characterized this period, as crusading newspapers turned their attention to the "muck" of scandals and corruption across the country in government and industry cartels. (For more on muckraking, see Chapter 3.) There was some danger that the press would be widely corrupted by city bosses eager to pay for favorable coverage. This temptation has seriously undermined the development of the press in a number of countries. Although political bosses and groups like the Tweed Ring in New York bought off some newspapers, others doggedly pursued anti-corruption stories. The rise to prominence of the *New York Times* was partly the result of its successful campaign against the Tweed Ring. (See the Media Watch box.)

Muckraking is journalism that investigates scandal, "raking up the muck" of dirty or controversial details.

This focus on investigative journalism led to an era called "The New Journalism," in which several newspapers crusaded for various causes, also building on the antislavery crusade before and during the Civil War.

Toward the end of the 1800s, newspapers began reaching even broader audiences. As European immigration increased, many immigrants published foreign-language newspapers. By 1880 there were 800 newspapers in German, Italian,

MEDIA WATCH

The Tweed Ring and the Dangers of the Advertising Bottom Line

After the Civil War, as American industrial growth took off rapidly in the north, corrupt political bosses dominated many cities. They raked off money from industry for favors and used the money to stifle opposition. In New York in the 1860s, these bosses were the dominant politicians of Tammany Hall. The ring leader was William Marcy Tweed, so the group was also known as the Tweed Ring. The Tweed Ring used city advertising money to buy the complicity of most of the city's newspapers—or at least their silence about the Ring's corruption and theft. Front pages would feature an eight-column story about the mayor's speech. Although the story was run as news, its publication would be billed to the city as advertising. This was a form of bribery to silence the press, a kind of corruption that has warped the press in many countries.

In 1870, the *New York Times* decided to launch a campaign against the Tweed Ring and its corruption and theft from the city treasury. The *Herald* newspaper and *Harper's Weekly* magazine joined ranks with the *Times*. *Harper's* role was made famous by the editorial cartoons of Thomas Nast, which made strong visual statements against the Tweed Ring. The other papers had been bought off and stayed silent. The ring retaliated financially against the *Times*, the *Herald* and *Harper's*, going so far as to remove Harper's Brothers books from the public schools. The campaign eventually brought down the ring. Subsequent investigations showed that 89 papers had received patronage, and 27 died when this source of money was cut off (Smythe, 1993).

Scandinavian, Polish, and Spanish. Some of them, such as the Polish press in Chicago and the Yiddish (Jewish) press in New York, had fairly large circulation and were politically important (Sloan, Stovall, & Startt, 1993). In the largest cities of the day, including New York, St. Louis, and Cleveland, large-circulation papers published by Joseph Pulitzer and Edward Scripps pursued a mass audience directly with sensational stories on sex, murder, scandal, popularized science and medicine, and other human-interest events. For example, Pulitzer hired Elizabeth Cochrane, known as Nelly Bly, who became famous by feigning insanity to investigate the notorious Blackwell Island insane asylum. Her stories on poor conditions and abuse of patients prompted official investigations and improvements (Everett, 1993).

Pulitzer vs. Hearst: The Rise of Yellow Journalism

Joseph Pulitzer. Hungarian immigrant Joseph Pulitzer managed to force his way into the American middle class with his intelligence. He came to the United States in 1868 to join the Army and later ended up in journalism. In 1878 he managed to pull together enough money to merge two struggling St. Louis newspapers into one, which he called the *St. Louis Post-Dispatch.* It was here that he originated the

new journalism that he later took to New York and used with the *New York World.* The journalism of the 1880s and 1890s was considered new because it was more lively, brash, self-conscious, impetuous, and sensational. It concentrated more on news, increasingly defined as the latest events of the day, and devoted less space to editorials and essay columns. **Scoops** were more important. So were gossip, big headlines, action pictures, and popular crusades (Everett, 1993).

New journalism relied on investigative reporting, big headlines, crusading for causes, and sensational stories.

Scoop is an exclusive that beats other newspapers in covering a story.

While at the *Post-Dispatch,* Pulitzer established himself as a nonpartisan social critic by conducting a series of crusades against corruption and complacency. This paper was very successful and profitable because it focused on news that seemed relevant and accessible to a very broad audience.

In 1883 Pulitzer bought the *New York World,* with the intention of publishing a newspaper for the underdogs (e.g., European immigrants) in New York City. Within only four months Pulitzer had managed to double circulation to 40,000, and within two years he had the highest circulation in New York City. He did that with a combination of new journalism and aggressive promotion and sales. In 1892 Pulitzer established the *Evening World.* The combined circulation of the two papers rose to 374,000, surpassing that of any other two papers in the United States. The *World* became the paper that others imitated. Pulitzer was a first-rate innovator and a giant of this period.

William Randolph Hearst. William Randolph Hearst was the son of the wealthy George Hearst. William Hearst was always interested in the newspaper business. After being expelled from Harvard University, Hearst asked his father if he could run the San Francisco *Examiner,* which the elder Hearst had acquired and was

MEDIA WATCH

Citizen Hearst and the Spanish–American War

On February 15, 1898, the AP correspondent in Havana cabled bulletins reporting that the battleship *Maine* had exploded and that hundreds of American sailors had been killed in the harbor. This was a pivotal point both in the Pulitzer/Hearst conflict and in the history of American news reporting. Although both Hearst and Pulitzer reported this as a Spanish attack, many historians say the explosion was probably accidental

This was the news that William Randolph Hearst, editor of the sensationalist *New York Journal,* had been waiting for. He already had reporters and illustrators in Cuba covering the insurrection against Spanish rule. Hearst had to convince these reporters and illustrators continually that there was actually a war to report. His illustrator, Frederic Remington, had cabled, "Everything is quiet. There is no trouble here. There will be no war." Hearst had responded, "Please remain. You furnish the pictures and I'll furnish the war." When the *Maine* blew up, Hearst and Pulitzer were able to use their ability to incite public opinion to urge Congress into a declaration of war on Spain two months later (Everett, 1993).

Hearst spent $3000 a day on the coverage of the Spanish–American war, for a total of about $500,000 for the year. Pulitzer spent a bit less, and the *Herald,* the *Sun,* and the AP spent about $250,000 each. The coverage catapulted Hearst's *Journal* ahead of his competitors. His promotion of the war was perhaps the high (or low) point of "yellow journalism."

using for political reasons. When his father refused, William moved to New York City and got a job on the *World.*

George Hearst finally relented and gave William control of the *Examiner,* because after he was elected to the Senate in 1887, he could no longer run it himself. William Hearst took over the San Francisco paper when he was not yet 24. He was determined to become the Pulitzer of the West. He called his paper "the Monarch of the Dailies" and claimed it offered "the most elaborate local news, the freshest social news, the latest and most original sensations" (*San Francisco Examiner,* 12 March 1887). He used the sensational, populist style that Pulitzer had pioneered and spent his father's money freely. By 1890 the *Examiner* was turning a profit.

In 1895, upon the death of his mother, Hearst inherited his family's fortune of $7.5 million. He decided to return to New York City to buy the ailing *New York Journal* for a mere $180,000. Pulitzer's reign in New York City quickly declined with the arrival of Hearst. The newcomer had not only the determination to take on Pulitzer, but also the financial resources as well. Hearst's first tactic was to hire Pulitzer's best staff people away from him with higher salaries. Hearst relied on sensationalism even more than Pulitzer and drove new journalism, which had emphasized news, to a new extreme called yellow journalism.

Yellow journalism was sensationalistic use of photos and headlines, focusing on personality, scandal and human interest stories.

Yellow Journalism. There followed a dramatic war between Hearst's *Morning Journal* and Pulitzer's *World.* One of the chief weapons was a journalistic style that came to be called **yellow journalism**. This style emphasized sensational photos and story selections, large headlines, an overemphasis on personality and human-interest stories, and sometimes even hoaxes and fake interviews. One of the results was Hearst's spectacular coverage of the 1898 explosion of the U.S. battleship *Maine* in the Havana harbor, which Hearst blamed on the Spanish, although the cause of the explosion is unknown to this day. Many historians credit Hearst's coverage with helping to push the United States into war with Spain over Cuba and the Philippines (Sloan, Stovall, & Startt, 1993).

YELLOW.
Early comic strip character called the Yellow Kid lent his name to an epoch of U.S. journalism history.

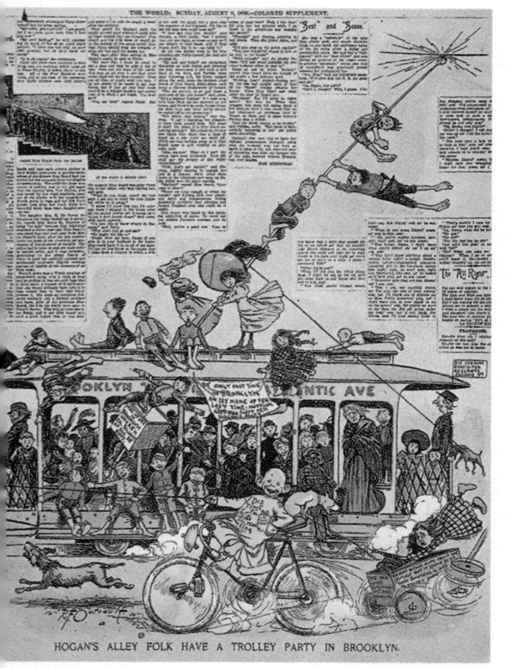

HOGAN'S ALLEY FOLK HAVE A TROLLEY PARTY IN BROOKLYN.

Yellow journalism was thus an extension of the new journalism phenomenon but lacked its soul. It got its name from a cartoon character, the "Yellow Kid." This one-toothed child in the comic strip wore a ridiculous nightshirt drawn in yellow ink. The cartoonist was hired away from Pulitzer by Hearst, but Pulitzer doggedly continued to run the strip with another artist! Thus both Hearst and Pulitzer had different versions of the "Yellow Kid" running at the same time. The episode characterized the rivalry between Pulitzer and Hearst, and gave the name to yellow journalism.

Many newspaper readers longed for a more serious newspaper, and in 1896 Adolph Ochs bought the *New York Times* and proceeded to fill this niche. Ochs was able to turn the nearly dead paper into an exceptional twentieth-century newspaper of record. He resisted sensationalism in photos, extravagant typefaces, fake stories, and stunts, which many readers were tired of. He aimed at a new, increasingly middle-class audience, stressing impartiality and independence. He made sure that advertising was clearly distinguishable from stories, unlike others who made money by allowing ads to masquerade as legitimate stories. He also lowered prices.

Yellow journalism may have gotten out of hand, but both Hearst and Pulitzer contributed substantially to journalism. Pulitzer was the innovator who developed new journalism and encouraged many who had never read a newspaper to read the *New York World.* He made most of his contributions in those 12 years before the arrival of Hearst, who imitated and exaggerated many of Pulitzer's innovations. Hearst, however, encouraged higher salaries, by-lines, and other recognition for professional journalists.

Yet, yellow journalism was more than just a result of the competition between these two men. This form of journalism can also be attributed to the fact that the 1880s and 1890s were a time when papers were no longer read only by the elite, but also by the general population. With this shift in the marketplace came a shift in the sources of income from circulation to advertising. The newspaper that survived was the one that sold its ads and subscriptions at the greatest profit, and these sales depended on the size of the audience that the paper was reaching. In other words, the lowering of journalistic quality was a result of change in the marketplace; Hearst and Pulitzer were simply responding to the change.

STOP & REVIEW

1. **What role did sensationalism play in newspapers?**
2. **What was the role of the newspapers up to and during the Civil War?**
3. **What was the "new journalism"?**
4. **What was yellow journalism?**
5. **What roles did Pulitzer and Hearst play in newspaper development?**

Newspapers Peak and Decline after 1900

Newspapers peaked as a mass medium between 1890 and 1920. Cheaper paper prices, faster printing technologies (such as the linotype in 1890), and a more prosperous reading public accelerated the growth of this medium toward the end of the century. Advertising flooded in, securing economic conditions for expansion. The Scripps family founded papers in Detroit, Cleveland, St. Louis, and Cincinnati. Under Edward W. Scripps, the group continued to expand in the 1890s and created the modern newspaper chain, based in daily newspapers in medium-sized cities. Hearst in California also started putting a chain of newspapers together. Later, in the early 1900s, Harry Chandler founded the Times–Mirror chain, and Frank Gannett founded the Gannett chain. The Scripps-Howard, Times-Mirror, and Gannett chains still survive.

Newspapers expanded much faster than the population or even the economy as a whole. The U.S. population tripled between 1850 and 1900 to almost 76 million people. Newspaper circulation increased 20-fold, from 758,000 in 1850 to 15.1 million in 1900 (McKearns, 1993).

Newspapers also proliferated in numbers. In 1899 New York had 29 dailies. Boston, Philadelphia, Cleveland, Chicago, and San Francisco had a combined total of 137. There were 1967 English-language dailies in 1900 and 2200 in 1910 (McKearns, 1993).

In 1900, 562 American cities had competing dailies, compared to less than 40 such cities by 1990 (McKearns, 1993). In 1900, many cities had 3 or 4 papers representing different ownership groups. Although newspaper readership and circulation had expanded, the number of newspapers increased much faster. By 1910 the newspaper industry had grown larger than its resources—advertising and circulation—could support.

As newspapers grew and expanded, there were not enough qualified journalists to go around. Newspaper formats also began to standardize, decreasing diversity and making it harder for papers to compete via differentiation.

A **Monopoly** is a market dominated by a single firm.

Oligopoly is when a few firms dominate a market.

Inevitably, merger and consolidation began to trim the numbers back. Hundreds of mergers occurred each year between 1890 and 1920, usually stronger papers acquiring weaker ones to get their circulation and advertising base. The merger and acquisition trend got to the point where antitrust regulators became concerned about **monopolies** or **oligopolies** emerging. This was of even greater concern in the news services that supplied the newspapers with much of their material, where Associated Press, United Press, and the International News Service completely controlled the market.

Consolidation refers to a reduction in the number of media outlets and a concentration of the ownership of media among fewer owners.

After 1900 other media—motion pictures, magazines, and phonographs—also began to compete with newspapers for the public's attention and money, furthering the impetus toward newspaper **consolidation.** By 1927, commercial radio networks would also join the competition.

Segmentation is the trend toward targeting specialized audiences in the newspaper, magazine, radio, and other media industries.

Tabloids are sensationalist and feature bold headlines, shocking photos, focused on divorce, murder, and crime.

Like other media, newspapers began to experiment with product differentiation into market **segments. Tabloids,** such as the *New York World* (1901), took further the sensationalist trend that had characterized many dailies around 1900. They featured bold headlines and shocking photos and focused on divorce, murder, and other crime—things that did often preoccupy city dwellers trying to make sense of their rapidly changing world. African American papers also shifted to a more urban focus as their audiences migrated north to work in burgeoning factories. They continued to grow during and after World War II, as an African American working-class and middle-class audience developed. The immigrant ethnic press, which often still published in Polish, Italian, and so on, began to decline as its readers became assimilated into American society and as they and their children began to read mostly in English.

The ethnic press played a significant role in helping immigrants become assimilated into the American population. Rather than promoting separate identities and politics, most of these papers prepared immigrants to support the U.S. government and to be active as citizens of their new country. The number of ethnic immigrant papers peaked in 1914 at 1300 journals and 140 dailies. These were published in 36 different languages, but 40 percent were published in German. This number declined when America went to war with Germany in World War I. The ethnic press continued to enjoy varying degrees of popularity and circulation depending on the extent of the immigrant population.

In the 1920s, newspapers began to consolidate into ever larger chains and groups. The main new group owners were businessmen like Frank Munsey, who bought, sold, killed, and consolidated papers to maximize profits. The largest owners were Hearst and the Scripps-Howard chain. In this era, Hearst and Scripps both closed over 15 papers each. The chain phenomenon continued into the 1930s, as Gannett, Ridder, and others joined the chain ownership trend. By the end of the decade, six chains controlled about a quarter of newspaper circulation (Folkerts & Teeter, 1994).

World War I (1914–1918), President Roosevelt's New Deal to end the Great Depression (1929–1939), and World War II (1939–1945) often focused news gathering and newspapers on the relationship between the newspaper medium and government. Newspapers crusaded both for and against these government interventions. For example, sensational newspaper coverage of the 1915 German sinking of the British ocean liner *Lusitania,* which killed 128 U.S. citizens, aroused sentiment in the public in favor of entering World War I against Germany.

The government created internal bureaus to evaluate press coverage first of the New Deal and then of World War II. The government also created offices to disseminate news, such as the Office of War Information, which set a number of precedents for post-war public relations, and, during World War II, to censor news and make sure that no military secrets leaked out through the newspapers. For example, the *Chicago Tribune*'s report that the Navy had advance warning of the Battle of Midway might have revealed the success of U.S. code-breaking operations (Folkerts & Teeter, 1994) and was censored.

Newspapers tried to set themselves apart from radio, which exploded in the late 1920s and could offer "headlines" much more current than those of newspapers. One technique the newspapers employed was news analysis and interpretation, with the rise of well-known commentators such as columnist Walter Lippmann. Through news analysis, papers could deal with complex government programs and economic crises, reporting various points of view in and out of government. Another technique devised in response to radio was in-depth and investigative reporting.

News competition took another turn with the growth of television in the late 1940s. Newspaper publishing expenses also continued to rise, especially the cost of raw materials like paper and ink. Television ate further into the advertising base that newspapers had once dominated. However, local dailies continued to be important social and political institutions, so although newspapers continued to consolidate, at least one daily survived in nearly all small towns, and competition survived in a few larger cities.

Newspaper chains steadily grew in dominance, as the number of dailies declined. By 1980, the 20 largest chains owned 404 dailies, controlling nearly half of daily newspaper circulation. Gannett, Knight-Ridder and Scripps-Howard continued to be major forces, especially in small and medium-sized markets, where one of them often owned the only daily newspaper in town, as the number of dailies continued to decrease. By 1993, chains owned over 60 percent of newspapers, controlling more than 70 percent of circulation (McKearns, 1993).

Later, printing costs actually went down somewhat with technological change, so new print competitors emerged. Suburban newspapers followed the middle class away from city centers into the suburbs. These papers were often owned by chains. By 1992 the largest chain, Gannett, owned 99 dailies (of 1700 nationwide). City and regional magazines competed for news and advertising. Weekly shopping newspapers popped up almost everywhere and cut into a major staple of newspaper income, the classified ad (Marsh, 1993).

Newspaper circulation plateaued at around 60 million readers in the 1960s and tended to stay there throughout the 1980s, and during the 1990s it declined 10 percent, despite the gradual increase in the U.S. population. Newspapers particularly worried that younger readers were not acquiring the newspaper habit, but rather were sticking with electronic media even when they passed such milestones as having children and buying houses, where people tend to start reading local newspapers.

One local newspaper response was to focus on community news, issues, and services. Larger newspapers often accentuated the trend toward investigative reporting and critical analysis. After the 1960s, with the civil rights movement, the Vietnam War, and the emergence of advocacy movements championing the rights of other ethnic minorities, women, and gays, some crusading papers found themselves in conflict with some of the older, middle-class readers who were a crucial part of their circulation.

Investigative Reporting and Watergate

Employment in the news media developed as a profession as the media took on more of the characteristics of big business. College training and organizations of working journalists became popular. The most important change in professional journalism was the change in the media's relationship with the government in the late 1960s and 1970s.

The media historically played the role of supporter of the government until the advent of the Vietnam War (1966–1976) and the Watergate scandal with President Nixon (1972–1974). It was at this time that the media began to see themselves as "watchdogs" and critics of the government and other institutions.

Since 1954, the United States had gradually intervened in the war between communist North Vietnam and their allies, the Vietcong, and anticommunist South Vietnam, supporting the latter despite its inability to rally popular support. Despite the introduction of U.S. troops and despite U.S. bombing of the north, the war went against the south, and American casualties mounted. Initial media coverage, following the general inclination of news media to support the U.S. cold war against the Soviet Union and China, tended to favor U.S. intervention. Amid antiwar protests across the U.S., media reports turned critical of the U.S. government effort, showing a bloody, unwinnable conflict. That set both print and television news media in conflict with government authorities (Braestrup, 1977).

Watergate was a notorious political scandal, in which Republican Party operatives burglarized Democratic Party headquarters in the Washington, D.C. Watergate complex in 1972, looking for documents that might damage Democratic Party candidates. The cover-up that followed was exposed by Carl Bernstein and Bob Woodward, two investigative reporters working for the *Washington Post.* Through determination and excellent investigative reporting, Bernstein and Woodward were able to uncover and report to the nation the foul play within the administration. These revelations ultimately led to the resignation of the President of the United States, Richard Nixon. What was originally a clumsy break-in led to a story that dramatically changed American politics and the people's view of the government—and the press's role in national politics (Bernstein & Woodward, 1974).

Since Watergate, many observers agree that investigative reporting has given way to scandal-mongering in the style of the Bill Clinton–Monica Lewinsky sex scandal (see page 119). Newspaper coverage resembles television news more and more, emphasizing color photography, eye-catching graphics, and shorter stories with less "serious news." The introduction of *USA Today* in 1982 set the stage for this change, and now all major newspapers have adopted elements of its colorful style. *USA Today* was created by the Gannett chain to fill a perceived niche for a new nonelite national newspaper, in contrast to the *New York Times* or *Wall Street Journal,* which serve political and business elites across the country.

1. When did newspapers begin to have to compete with other mass audience media?
2. When did newspapers peak in impact as mass media?
3. Why did newspapers begin to consolidate?
4. Why did newspaper chains form?
5. Which were the major chains?
6. What was the impact of Watergate on American journalism?

USA Today also took advantage of a new system of newspaper distribution via satellite that makes it possible to distribute newspapers on a national basis. Other national news publications, such as the *New York Times* and the *Wall Street Journal,* also publish their daily editions via satellite so that they can be delivered to doorsteps everywhere in the country, further eroding local newspaper sales. And all three have joined the hundreds of newspapers that are now accessible over the World Wide Web, a new source of competition for local dailies.

Industry consolidation has continued, with newspaper chains making more acquisitions. In 1992, rules against owning newspapers and other types of media outlets (e.g., radio and TV) in the same markets were eliminated. This opened the newspaper merger and acquisition game to a new breed of multimedia conglomerates, such as Rupert Murdoch's News Corp. The net effect of the continuing shakeout has been a loss of another 250 daily newspapers since the Watergate era. As newspapers fold and merge, few cities are left with competing publications, and many of those have competition only by virtue of joint operating agreements (see page 118) that merge business and printing operations, while attempting to maintain a semblance of editorial independence. And newspaper readership has once again begun a slow decline (*Source:* Newspaper Association of America).

Still, as the newspaper industry enters a new century, there is cause for optimism. Advertising revenues, as much as good journalism, are the life's blood of the newspaper business, and the proceeds from advertising are showing impressive growth. Ad sales by daily newspapers now top $40 billion a year, five times what they were in the journalistic halcyon days of Watergate (*Source:* Newspaper Association of America, U.S. Department of Commerce).

TRENDS IN NEWSPAPER TECHNOLOGY

Advances in basic publishing technology were reviewed in Chapter 3. Here we will consider only those innovations that made a unique contribution to the development of the newspaper industry. In this context, an important characteristic that distinguishes newspapers from books and magazines is the short time in which newspapers must be produced and distributed. Speed is of the essence in all phases of gathering, publishing, and disseminating the news. Thus improvements in transportation technology are a part of the story, which includes the horse-drawn trolley giving way to the train and later to the automobile and the airplane.

Technology in Newsgathering

Before the advent of the telegraph, the speed at which news was gathered was also determined by the speed of transportation systems, from the clipper ship to the pony express. The telegraph revolutionized news gathering with the advent of the first *news wire,* the Associated Press, in 1846. News then traveled between major cities in a matter of minutes rather than a matter of days, and newspapers could also better afford to cover events in distant locations by picking up the reports that were shared among all subscribers to this earliest of "on-line" service. A generation later, the telephone also improved the speed and accuracy of newspaper writing, even though some late-nineteenth-century reporters disdained it as a "lazy" way to avoid honest footwork (Sloan, Stovall, & Startt, 1993).

Until 1922, however, only the words could travel by telegraph wire, not the pictures. In that year the first *wire photo* was transmitted, on the occasion of the election of a new Pope in Rome. By breaking Pope Pius XI's picture down into a fine grid of black and white dots, it was possible to transmit it by wire from the Vatican, one picture dot at a time.

Today, all the modern means of electronic communication are found in the newsroom. Reporters scan radio, TV, and cable channels such as CNN, once again prompting grumbles about "laziness" from the old-timers. The high-tech reporter can also monitor police communication frequencies electronically and can get tips and confirm stories via e-mail. The Internet is the latest addition to the reporter's news-gathering arsenal. By monitoring Internet news sites, *chat rooms, listservs,* and *newsgroups* (see Chapter 9), reporters can turn up leads, track down rumors, and do an increasing amount of their background research inside the computer. Reporters are also using computers to compile and sift through mountains of raw data for stories about discrimination and consumer issues—a technique known as *computer-assisted reporting (CAR),* (Ciotta, 1998).

Technology in Newspaper Production

In Chapter 3 we saw how innovations such as the *rotary press, linotype,* and *phototypesetting* greatly increased the number of pages that could be printed in a few hours' time. Newspaper editions grew from a few pages to hundreds of pages, and circulation mounted into the hundreds of thousands as a result.

Teletypesetting was a significant improvement when it was introduced in the 1950s. Stories could be typeset once by a highly skilled typesetter employed by a wire service, punched out onto paper tape by the local newspaper, and then automatically fed into their own automated typesetting machines, to produce a near-perfect copy of the original story.

Later, in the late 1960s and the early 1970s, data contained on the paper tapes were stored in computer memory, paving the way for the computerization of print production, discussed in the previous chapter. Now, reporters compose and edit their stories on a computer, and the pages of the newspaper are also composed and the originals mastered inside the computer system. If and when high-speed computer printers come into use, the newspaper will be analog only at the point that the ink meets the paper.

TECHNOLOGY **TRENDS**

The Fax Gazette: Back to the Future of Newspapers

Newsletters and gazettes were initially written by bankers or trading companies for a select group of clients who could afford to pay for specific information that interested them. Similarly, one of the earliest news services, Reuters, of the United Kingdom, originally focused on supplying financial and economic news to both private clients and newspapers before it evolved into a broader news service.

The fax machine has permitted enterprising new "print" media to be sent instantaneously to the fax machines or computers of select groups of subscribers. They can cover any topic, from stocks to sports medicine to telecommunications equipment markets in Asia. These gazettes can be sent out daily, weekly, monthly, or irregularly.

To some degree, this is just a new, faster, and perhaps even cheaper means of delivering newsletters, but it has also opened new possibilities for distributing pieces that are more visual, more creatively formatted, and less regular. This is particularly the case now that the creators of such newsletters can send them directly from their computers to a regular distribution list of receivers. The computer automatically dials the list and sends the newsletter to the receiver fax over the telephone. This method also offers new possibilities for delivery in places or situations where telephone lines offer better access than conventional transportation, and where the Internet is not yet a factor.

PRODUZA MAIS GASTANDO MENOS ENERGIA ELÉCTRICA HÁ SOLUÇÕES AO SEU ALCANCE

mediaFAX

Maputo * terça-feira 04.08.92 * Nº 52/92

ZENHA, Lda.
FÁBRICA DE MOLDURAS, ESPELHOS E UTILIDADES DECORATIVAS
VIDROS, CRISTAIS
CONTACTE-NOS
Av.Eduardo Mondlane, 2711
Tlf.42 85 74
Maputo

De segunda a sexta, um diário no seu fax * Propriedade e edição: mediacoop - jornalistas associados, scrl
Editor: Carlos Cardoso * Sede: Av.Mártires da Machava, nº 1002
C.P. 73 * Tls 49 09 06, 74 39 52, 490909(ext. 208), 491154(ext. 208) * Faxes 49 00 63 / 49 09 06 * Tlx 6 - 233 * Maputo * Moçambique
Assinaturas mensais – ordinária: 50.000,00 MT * institucional: 150.000,00 MT ou 50 USD * de apoio: 300.000,00 MT ou 100 USD

CHISSANO - DHLAKAMA ADIADO 24 HORAS

1-52/92 (Roma) O "frente a frente" entre Joaquim Chissano e Afonso Dhlakama foi adiado por 24 horas devido a razões organizativas, segundo Mário Raffaelli, coordenador da mediação italiana nas conversações de paz em Roma.

Num contacto com o "mediaFax, Raffaelli disse que a cimeira terá o seu início às 11 horas de quarta-feira na Vila Maddamme, um edifício que pertence ao Ministério italiano dos Estrangeiros, não se sabendo ainda se se mantem a ideia inicial de a conferência ser aberta pelo Ministro dos Negócios Estrangeiros da Itália.

A semana passada, o Chefe da diplomacia italiana pediu a demissão tendo sido substituido por Emílio Colombo, que sábado passado tomou posse.

Chissano chega a Roma hoje, depois de ter pernoitado em Paris e Mugabe era esperado na noite de ontem, devendo coordenar com a mediação italiana a preparação da cimeira.

Afonso Dhlakama já se encontra na capital italiana depois de ter viajado do Malawi para Nairobi, a bordo do jacto executivo de Tiny Rowlands, o empresário da Lonrho que também deverá estar presente em Roma.

De acordo com a fonte da mediação, hoje mesmo terão lugar encontros informais entre os dois líderes "para criar um clima favorável" ao êxito da cimeira de amanhã.

A cimeira atraíu a Roma, em tempos de férias de verão, um numeroso grupo de jornalistas europeus, nomedamente de Portugal, o país onde a cimeira está a despertar mais interesse.

A imprensa italiana que pouco tem dado a conhecer sobre o processo de paz que decorre no seu próprio país, desperta lentamente da letargía em que anda, começando a publicar algo sobre o acontecimento.

Desde que está em Roma, há quase um mês, o enviado do "mediaFAX" viu pela primeira vez algo publicado sobre o processo de paz no último domingo quando o "Il Manifesto", de Roma, anunciou em artigo de interior que Chissano se ia encontrar com Dhlakama em Roma.

Citando Mário Raffaelli e Armando Guebuza, a notícia fazia menção ao facto de ser a primeira vez que o estadista moçambicano ia ter um encontro com o Chefe do movimento armado e lembrava que há dois anos que negociadores do Governo e da Renamo tentam alcançar um acordo geral de paz.

Fora esse artigo, os "media" italianos relegam Moçambique e duma maneira geral os países africanos ao último dos planos possíveis, dando destaque exagerado, pelo contrário, a notícias sobre Jugoslávia, os países do Médio Oriente, os da Europa do Leste, para não falar do Iraque de Saddam Hussein, que é matéria de primeira página.

PESSOAL DA RENAMO AUMENTA EM MAPUTO

2-52/92 (Maputo) A Renamo solicitou à Comissão Mista de Verificação do Acordo Parcial de Roma(COMIVE) autorização para o aumento do número do seu pessoal de quatro para oito representantes, soube o "mediaFAX" de fontes próximas da COMIVE.

O argumento defendido pelos rebeldes para tal aumento prende-se com o facto de as delegações do Governo e da Renamo, em negociações em Roma, terem recomendado o funcionamento efectivo dos postos de observação da implementação do acordo sobre os corredores da Beira e Limpopo.

" Neste momento só temos uma pessoa fora de Maputo, está no posto de observação de Chimoio. O nosso número não chega para fazermos a cobertura a todos os postos onde devemos estar", explicou ao "mediaFAX", Anselmo Vítor, representante político dos rebeldes junto da COMIVE.

Para além do pessoal a juntar-se à equipa que funciona

Para a elaboração de estudos e projectos contacte a MACOL a sua consultora
Av. 24 de Julho, 2293 / 1º andar * Tel. 421526/8 * Fax 421511 * Telex 6-731 * C.P. 4150 * Maputo

mediaFAX,

NEWS FAX.
Mozambique, just north of South Africa, is the poorest country on earth. Its first independent newspaper is a fax gazette, sent directly to the fax machines of its largely elite subscribers.

Satellite delivery of copy to printing plants has also become commonplace. Newspaper copy, complete with photo layouts, can be sent by satellite from central editorial offices to remote printing plants in distant cities. Today, all the main national U.S. newspapers—including the *New York Times,* the *Wall Street Journal, USA Today*—are printed in several different locations to make local delivery possible almost anywhere in the country.

Technology in Newspaper Distribution

But why bother with that last step of printing the paper? Why not just distribute the digital version of the paper directly to the reader's computer over a computer network? Today's Internet newspapers are by no means the first attempt at electronic newspaper delivery. In the 1930s, there were attempts to apply *facsimile* transmission to the newspaper distribution problem. The newspaper was "faxed" to a special radio receiver on the breakfast table (Shefrin, 1993). However, this mode of distribution did not catch on until a new generation of cheap, digital facsimile machines became widely adopted in the 1980s.

Videotex services delivered text and graphics through telephone networks.

In Chapter 8 we will see how an early form of computer media, **videotex,** was used to transmit news to the home. A number of unsuccessful attempts were made by the newspaper industry in the early 1980s to establish consumer videotex services, including Viewtron, Keyfax, and Gateway, in the United States. All three used telephone lines but relied on custom-built computer terminals that used the home television set as the display device. By 1986 all of these services had been discontinued, having fallen victim to a variety of technical and marketing problems, notably expensive and unreliable terminals and agonizingly slow graphics displays. Because they used TV sets as display devices, the fledgling services also had to compete with popular television entertainment (Morse, 1985).

News videotex lived on, though, in the form of consumer on-line services such as Prodigy, CompuServe, and later America Online (AOL). News, weather, and sports continued to be staples of these services, which began to flourish as the personal computer replaced the television set as the receiver. For a while, the various new on-line services attempted to make exclusive deals with major newspapers that would give them unique content to attract new on-line service subscribers; certain newspapers, for instance, were available only on AOL.

Nevertheless, the future of electronic distribution seems to be more widespread,

THE DAILY ME. **New portal sites such as Excite.com, shown here, tailor news and information to each user. In effect, they become personal newspapers.**

nonexclusive distribution over the World Wide Web (or WWW) on the Internet. There are now hundreds of newspapers on the Web, many with complete versions of their daily editions, which the reader's computer can access directly from the publishers' own WWW host sites, or *home pages.* Some news services exist only on-line, such as CNET and Wired News. In Chapter 8, we will see that these new electronic papers often have many features that their print ancestors lack, including access to archives of past articles, audio and video extensions to print stories, e-mail to the editor, and even interactive crossword puzzles and on-line forums. Some provide running "news tickers" that deliver breaking news directly to interactive insets on the computer screen.

Personalized newspapers, containing only the information that our computer "knows" we are interested in, are another widely anticipated development. Our on-line newspaper could be programmed to send us only those stories that fit a profile of our interests. But why be limited to what our local newspaper reporters can turn up for us? Popular Internet search engines, such as Yahoo!, those Web sites that let us type in keywords to help us search for information all over the Web, could co-opt this surveillance function, making themselves over into *portals* that sift through information for us and welcome us with "what's new" each time we log on to the Internet.

Nicholas Negroponte, of the Media Lab at the Massachusetts Institute of Technology, saw portals coming years ago. He called the concept of a personalized newspaper the "daily me" (Negroponte, 1995). Now that the daily me is a reality, Media Lab researchers are at work on further improvements for the newspaper of tomorrow. One might be dubbed "the daily us," since it enlists the search habits of friends, colleagues, and subject matter experts to help the reader locate relevant information. Another innovation would automatically add locally meaningful annotations to national news stories (e.g., hurricane hits land, *drops 12 inches of rain in your back yard*). They are also working on ways of navigating through the information glut by representing information in the form of three-dimensional imagery (http://nif.www.media.mit.edu/abs.html). The barriers to reading electronic newspapers while curled up on the sofa or sitting in a beach chair may also soon be removed by the development of flexible plastic computer displays that can be seen even in bright sunlight. Still no word on a "newspaper of the future" that will help with pet training, however.

Best of all, the Web newspapers are often free to the reader. Free, that is, once the reader buys a computer and begins making payments to an Internet service provider.

Technology in Newspaper Advertising

Electronic commerce is the use of the Internet, to buy and sell goods or services.

In Chapter 11 we will see how technology is transforming newspaper display advertising, making it more interactive and multimedia. Here we will briefly consider the impact of technology on the backbone of newspaper advertising, the classified ads. The Internet could eventually spell doom for classified newspaper advertising, as more and more businesses and private parties bypass it to post ads on their own Web pages. The advanced search capabilities of Internet browsers make it easy to search out job postings, deals for collectibles, pedigreed puppies, or potential life partners—and not just locally, but globally. With the further development of **electronic commerce,** it will be possible to complete the entire transaction on-line and to "shop" electronically by viewing pictures of used cars and old mattresses, and then actually purchasing them on-line. Of course, newspapers will put their own classifieds on-line, but it is not clear how newspapers will compete with free listings placed there directly by the advertisers themselves.

STOP & REVIEW

1. **What are the main recent trends in newspaper production technologies?**
2. **What are the main recent trends in newspaper delivery technologies?**
3. **How are newspapers using the Internet?**
4. **How will computers and telecommunications affect the newspaper of the future?**
5. **How will the Internet affect newspaper advertising?**

NEWSPAPER INDUSTRY ORGANIZATION

Newspaper Economics

In general, newspapers have to fight harder now for advertising and sales. The declining circulation of many traditional dailies, which lowers their revenues, has reinforced the wave of consolidation. Though other newspapers are doing well in circulation, all are challenged to compete for advertising. Newspapers still lead in overall advertising revenues, but their relative share has declined over the last 30 years.

In advertising, newspapers continue to enjoy certain advantages. They can carry local supermarket ads, including coupons, as well as more extensive ads for automobiles, say, and electronics, for local dealers. But for other kinds of advertising, like basic advertising of national brands or of goods aimed at certain market segments, such as young adults, newspapers suffer in competition with the electronic media.

The Newspaper Publishing Industry

Many types of newspapers are published in the United States. Although the overall number of daily newspapers has been steadily declining, some of the technological trends we noted earlier are increasing the numbers of certain kinds of newspapers. There are actually more newspapers with national reach now, utilizing satellite delivery and local printing, as well as increasing numbers of local and specialized weeklies published via desktop technologies (Hynds, 1980).

Dailies. Newspapers published at least five days a week are termed dailies. As described below, dailies are either national, metropolitan, or suburban. Their numbers have steadily declined, from a high of 2200 in 1910 to 1509 in 1997. Daily newspaper circulation dropped to slightly less than 57 million in 1998 (Editor & Publisher, 1998).

National Daily Newspapers. The circulation of national newspapers has actually grown (see Figure 4.1). Since the 1980s, several metropolitan newspapers have created national daily editions, using satellite delivery of material for printing in multiple locations. The *Wall Street Journal,* with the largest circulation, is considered a specialized business paper but has a broad general readership as well. The *New York Times* has headline news, news interpretation, and a focus media and business.

USA Today is a new national newspaper that did not start as a metropolitan daily. In 1982 the Gannett Group created *USA Today* as a national daily newspaper. Using a graphics-oriented format, it carries shorter news items, more entertainment, more sports, and more items from various states and regions.

As Figure 4.1 shows, the national dailies tended to grow slightly from 1992 to 1997, whereas most of the regional dailies declined slightly. One major regional daily, the *Los Angeles Times,* actually has a circulation almost the same size as that of the *New York Times* (around 1,100,000 in 1998), but it has less national cov-

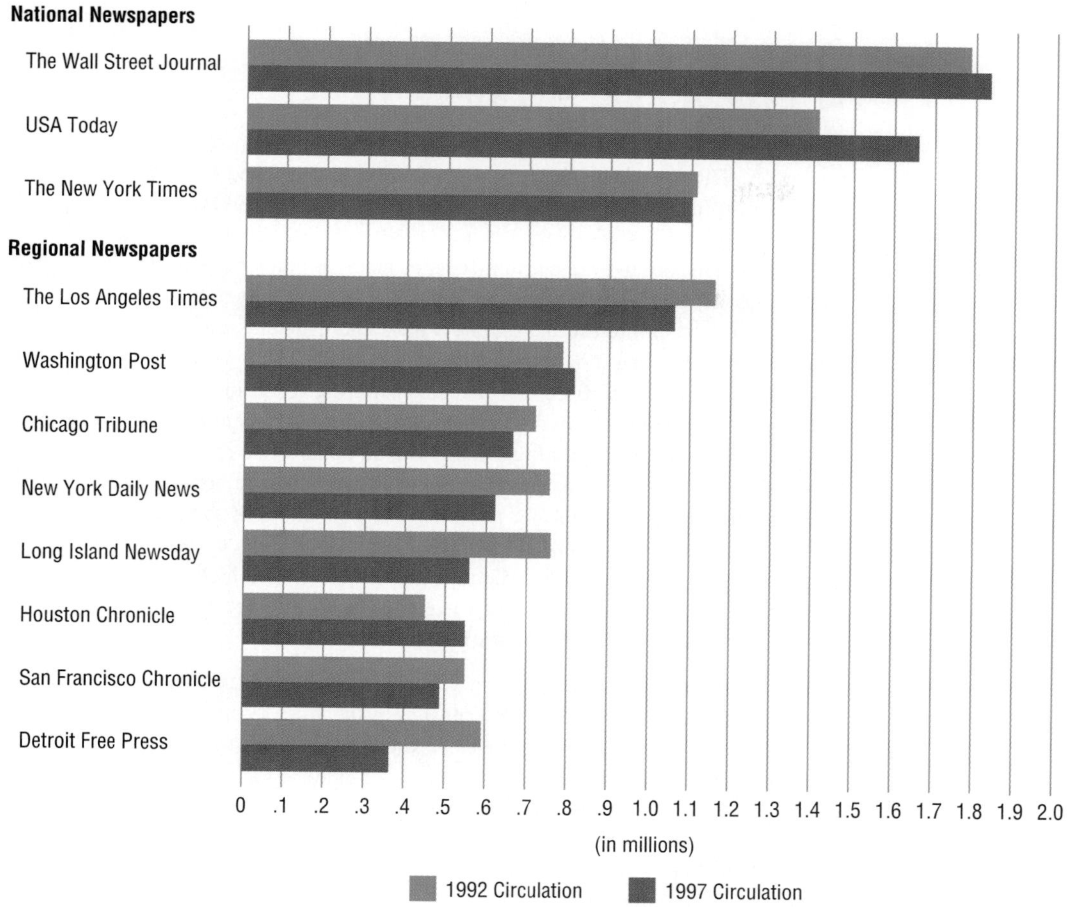

Source: Gale Directory of Publications and Broadcast Media, 1993, 1998.

FIGURE 4.1
Circulation of national newspapers 1992 and 1997.

erage and impact. The *Los Angeles Times* circulates primarily in California and the west, whereas the *New York Times* increasingly circulates nationally.

Large Metropolitan and Suburban Dailies. Compared with the national dailies, such as the *New York Times,* some of the larger metropolitan daily newspapers, such as the *Chicago Tribune, Detroit Free Press,* and *Long Island Newsday,* have shown significant declines in circulation (see Figure 4.1), and many closures and consolidations have resulted. However, a few metropolitan dailies, like *The Washington Post* and *Houston Chronicle,* have grown. A typical scenario is that one of two competing papers gains most of the circulation, advertising revenues, and classified ad business, sending the other paper into a downward spiral, ending in closure or merger with its competitor.

For example, the *El Paso Herald-Post* closed on October 11, 1998, after seeing its circulation decline from over 31,000 in 1986 to around 18,000 in 1998. Despite an effort to save money via a joint operating agreement with the Gannett-owned *El Paso Times,* the Scripps-owned paper was losing too much money. As a result, the last Texas city to have two competing newspapers will only have one daily newspaper. However, once a single newspaper dominates a city, it tends to be

MEDIA WATCH

Television and McPaper

Newspapers have had to compete with a continually increasing number of new media. Television seduced audiences for entertainment and news starting in the 1950s, followed by cable TV all-news channels in the 1980s. *USA Today,* the Gannett Group's relatively new (1982) national newspaper, seems designed to compete with television. It relies more on graphics, with its color photos, color weather maps, and icon-oriented charts. It puts more emphasis on human-interest and feature stories and generally runs much shorter stories than the other national newspapers.

Some critics have accused *USA Today* of imitating television too much and thereby losing what is distinctive about newspapers: greater depth, more analysis, more news, less entertainment. Some go so far as to call *USA Today* "McPaper"—that is, the newspaper equivalent of fast food, attractively packaged and seemingly tasty, but not necessarily as nourishing as some of the alternatives. Proponents say that *USA Today* uses graphics and concise stories to communicate news and information essentials quickly to a broader audience. Now, newspapers also have to compete with Internet news sources and *USA Today* is there at www.usatoday.com.

WWW

For Further Research:

Things like newspaper circulation are constantly changing. Learn how to keep abreast of media changes by using the WWW and InfoTrac to find current circulation figures for the top 10–25 daily newspapers. If you are using InfoTrac College Edition, try the following search terms: Newspapers-Circulation. Try the same key words using a WWW search engine. In 1998, an InfoTrac search found the following article, which gave circulation for the daily and Sunday editions of the top 25 newspapers.

"Daily Circulation Builds As Sunday Softens Slightly," Mark Fitzgerald. *Editor & Publisher,* May 9, 1998, v131 n19 p10(1)

sustainably profitable. Newspapers the size of the *El Paso Times* or the *Salt Lake Tribune* have often done very well.

Many former local daily newspaper readers have shifted to national dailies, national news weeklies, national newsmagazines, or television and radio. This decline is also related to the relative decline of many large cities, such as Detroit, as centers of industry. In the last several decades, suburban areas have increasingly become centers of industry, business, and entertainment, not just "bedroom" communities. Many people no longer commute to a large city's downtown or even go there to shop, to eat, or for entertainment. Consequently, suburban newspapers have risen in importance and circulation. The numbers of these newspapers have grown by over 50 percent since 1985. One such paper, *Newsday,* of Long Island, New York, is now among the top ten American newspapers in circulation. Small-town dailies are also gaining in numbers and circulation as many small towns continue to grow in economic importance. In response, many traditional metropolitan dailies have added suburban sections and may even publish regional editions, such as the San Fernando Valley and Orange County editions of *The Los Angeles Times.*

Weeklies. Most weeklies used to cover small-town or rural areas that were too small to support a daily. Many still do. With the growth of the suburbs, weeklies have started. About a third of weekly papers now cover the suburbs, and that number is growing rapidly.

Other forms of weekly papers are also growing. Most major cities, many medium-sized cities, and some new suburban areas now have entertainment-oriented weeklies that are given away at music stores, bookstores, and other locations, like the *Boston Phoenix* or *Austin Chronicle.* These weeklies cover dining out, movies, live concerts, and local events. Some areas also have political weeklies, and yet others have ethnic or minority group–oriented weeklies that focus on news and events within their particular community.

Wire Services and Other Newspaper Sources. No discussion of the newspaper industry structure would be complete without mentioning the many news service organizations that contribute to newspaper content. With the exception of the largest metropolitan dailies, surprisingly few of the words that appear in the local newspaper are actually written locally. Most national and international stories are taken directly from the newswires, with at most the first few paragraphs rewritten to put a unique local angle on the news. Most stories further back in the front section are lifted whole from wire service accounts.

Earlier we learned that the Associated Press was the first wire service in America—today it is still the leading national newswire. For international news, the AP competes with Agence France-Presse, Reuters, and the Interfax News Agency (covering Russia and other countries formerly part of the Soviet Union). However, there are dozens of other news services, including those run by major newspaper chains, such as Gannett, or major metropolitan newspapers, such as the Los Angeles Times–Washington Post News Service, through which stories written by their own reporters are distributed to other newspapers that subscribe to the service. There are a myriad of other news services not directly affiliated with newspapers that gather news and write stories about specialized topics such as finance (e.g., the Bloomberg News Service). And, if we count all the newspapers that distribute stories to other publications via their Web pages, there are literally hundreds, not dozens, of news services today. News services once relied on dedicated networks of wires and clanking electromechanical printers, but now just about anyone with a Web page can be a news service—*if* they can write good copy.

If we dig further back in the newspaper, we come to the national columnists on the editorial page, the comics, and the crossword puzzles that are the product of another type of organization, the newspaper *syndicators.* The King Features

Syndicate, a subsidiary of the Hearst Corporation, is the largest. Syndicators employ the cartoonists and the editorial writers or make distribution arrangements with the writers' "home" newspaper organizations. They then resell the funnies and commentaries to other newspapers on a contractual basis.

Newsletters, House Organs, and Micropublishing. Newsletters tend to serve purposes and audiences that are even more specialized and segmented than those of magazines, because they are even cheaper to produce. There are expensive business newsletters aimed at every imaginable branch of industry. There are in-house newsletters aimed at employees, union members, and supervisors. Innumerable club and fan newsletters exist for everyone from those who recreate the Civil War on weekends to those who cannot believe that Elvis is really dead.

NEWSPAPER CONTENT GENRES

Newspaper Sections and Contents

Most newspapers contain several distinct sections that serve different audiences: national news, international news, editorial and commentary, local news, sports, business, lifestyles, entertainment, comics, and classified advertising. Most newspapers even have Sunday supplements that are technically magazines.

Newspapers vary a great deal in the sections they emphasize. National newspapers focus on international news, national news, editorials/commentaries, and business news, with some lifestyle and entertainment news of a general nature. Metropolitan dailies usually lighten the news sections, focus more on local and regional news, and add more on lifestyles, entertainment, sports, and comics, with more localized ads for such businesses as supermarkets and auto dealers. Some newspapers go further and specialize

ALL THE NEWS THAT'S FIT TO PRINT . . . ON THE WEB. The *New York Times* now publishes its full daily edition on the World Wide Web. It has features—such as comic strips, archives, and computer-related stories—not found in the print version.

The New York Times
ON THE WEB

The New York Times
EXPECT THE WORLD®

NYC Weather
52° F

SATURDAY, APRIL 3, 1999 | Site Updated 2:40 PM

QUICK NEWS
PAGE ONE PLUS
International
National/N.Y.
Politics
Business
Technology
Science/Health
Sports
Weather
Opinion
Arts/Living
Automobiles
Books
Diversions
Job Market
Real Estate
Travel
SITE INDEX

FOR LISTINGS, VISIT NEWYORKtoday
- Movies
- Restaurants
- Theater
- Music
- Shopping
- Yellow Pages

The New York Times on the Web Learning Network
FOR STUDENTS, TEACHERS & PARENTS

Text Version

Archives
Classifieds
Forums
Marketplace
Services

Help
Site Tour

Home Delivery
-Order Online
-Service

NATO PLANS TO PUT TROOPS IN ALBANIA TO HELP WITH KOSOVO REFUGEE RELIEF

NATO said on Saturday that it was planning to send a force of 6,000 to 8,000 troops to Albania to provide security and emergency relief for the masses of Kosovo Albanians who have been driven from neighboring Yugoslavia by Serb forces. Go to Article
·ISSUE IN DEPTH: The Conflict in Kosovo

The Allies' War by Consensus Is Limiting Military Strategy

The need for consensus has left an unmistakable imprint on the alliance's military strategy, causing it to take a gradual approach to the bombing campaign. Go to Article
·Clinton Says No Target Is Off-Limits

Refugees Flee One Nightmare, Find Themselves in Another

Hounded from their homes and herded by police cars and tanks into columns that snake through the valleys of southern Kosovo, the flood of refugees leaving the Serbian province surged by nearly 54,000 people Friday. Go to Article
·SLIDE SHOW: Food Grows Scarce as Flood of Refugees Continues
·Germany Says it Is Willing to Accept Some Kosovo Refugees

NATIONAL

TECHNOLOGY

FIND A BOOK AT barnesandnoble.com
Search By
Go

IN ARTS/LIVING
Film Index
▶GO

MARKETS	
Dow	9832.51
Nasdaq	2493.37
S&P 500	1293.72
Russell 2000	398.74
NYSE	604.99

SEARCH THE SITE
Search
Tips

GET STOCK QUOTES
Go
Look Up Symbol

How To Drug a Five-Ton Elephant 2:34 p.m. EST

INTERNATIONAL
Guadalajara Journal: Daylight Savings, the Worst of Times

DOONESBURY © 1999 G. B. Trudeau. Reprinted with permission by the Universal Press Syndicate. All rights reserved.

in one or two kinds of material, as do localized weeklies that focus almost exclusively on local events. Other local papers also concentrate primarily on shopping, classified ads, and entertainment. Some daily and weekly newspapers highlight crime and other sensational stories. Notable specialized weeklies include sensationalist tabloids, such as the *National Enquirer,* but also include the *Sporting News,* and numerous local shopping papers, which are nothing but classified ads.

There is a trend in the late 1990s to cover technology news separately. For example, in 1998 the *New York Times* introduced a new weekly section called "Circuits" to focus on coverage of the Internet. The *Times* had previously (in 1996) created an on-line section called *CyberTimes,* which often includes material written excusively for the on-line edition.

AUDIENCES FOR NEWSPAPERS

A mass audience still exists for major metropolitan, national, and regional dailies. There is also a considerable audience for weekly newspapers, such as local entertainment- or shopping-oriented weeklies.

Almost three-fifths of adults still read newspapers daily (58.7 percent), as of 1997. That compares favorably to those who watch prime-time TV daily (42.4 percent), listen to morning drive time radio daily (25.4 percent), or watch prime-time cable TV daily (10.4 percent) (Scarborough Research Corporation, 1998). Readers over age 35 read newspapers daily more (61.2 percent) than those age 18–34 (45.6 percent). Men read daily slightly more (62.4 percent) than women (55.2 percent). Readership is highest among those over age fifty-five (71.0 percent) (Scarborough Research Corporation, 1998).

People tend to read quickly and selectively, spending less than 20 minutes on a 30-page newspaper. That is one reason why some newspapers, such as *USA Today,* are taking a more graphics-oriented and visual approach to designing their papers—it facilitates the kind of skimming and selective reading that most readers actually do. Many readers look only at certain sections that are of particular interest to them. Many also read national, suburban, or local newspapers instead of the classic metropolitan dailies. Even among newspaper readers, most consider television to be their main news source, although better-educated audiences tend to rely more on newspapers and less on television (Newspaper Association of America, 1998).

1. **What are the main national daily newspapers?**
2. **Why are the national newspapers growing?**
3. **Why are major metropolitan dailies declining?**
4. **What are the main sections and contents of newspapers?**
5. **How are newspapers adapting to competition from other media?**

Newspapers perform important functions for elite audiences. Some newspapers that focus on government policy, such as the *New York Times,* pride themselves on having an influential readership and on sometimes shaping policy debates with their articles. The *Wall Street Journal* focuses on reaching the business elite but aims at government policy makers, too. The *Christian Science Monitor* offers internationally oriented news. *The Los Angeles Times,* especially its *Calendar* section, serves the film, music, and television industries.

NEWSPAPER POLICY AND ETHICS ISSUES

Newspaper Consolidation, Chains, and Shakeout

Local market monopoly in the newspaper industry is a market served by only a single daily newspaper.

More and more cities are served by only one newspaper. These **local market monopolies** have both political and economic effects. Politically, the one newspaper is likely to reflect a single editorial perspective, although other local media may reflect other viewpoints. Economically, the choices available to both advertisers and consumers are reduced so that subscription and advertising rates may increase.

Concentration of ownership occurs when media are owned by a small number of individuals or corporations.

Nationally, major newspaper group owners have steadily acquired more newspapers. These groups can share materials and reduce costs in ways that keep marginally profitable newspapers afloat. However, this increasing **concentration of ownership** in fewer hands may also threaten to reduce the diversity of opinion represented in newspapers across the United States. Newspaper chains such as Gannett exercise national reach with their opinions and ideas. Many newspaper groups also own other media, including radio and television stations, cable television systems, and magazines, which potentially further reduces diversity of opinion in the media. In the 1980s, the Reagan administration relaxed previous restrictions on cross-ownership, in the belief that the role of government should be reduced so that competition could thrive. This tendency accelerated. An overall merger mania resulted in the consolidation and concentration of ownership in a number of industries, but particularly in the media.

Joint operation agreements occur when competing newspapers share facilities, costs, administrative structure, and advertising, while maintaining editorial independence.

Joint operation agreements are one solution to the problem of excessive concentration. When competing newspapers cannot survive economically, they negotiate an agreement with each other to share facilities, production costs, administrative structure, and advertising, while attempting to maintain editorial independence. Only about 40 cities now have competing daily newspapers and 15 of those maintain two newspapers only through joint operating agreements.

In Detroit, for example, the liberal *Detroit Free Press* and the more conservative *Detroit News* now have a joint operating agreement. They share facilities, although they try to keep their writers separate—sometimes physically, more often just in terms of organizational chart. The two newspapers produce separate editions on weekdays and combined editions on weekends. During elections the separate editorial pages in the combined Sunday edition sometimes endorse different candidates with opposite editorial rationales. Still, some fear that the overall diversity of opinion between the two may well decrease.

1. Is there still a mass audience for newspapers?
2. Who reads newspapers?
3. What are the trends among newspaper readers?
4. Why are some people concerned about consolidation in the newspaper industry?
5. How and why do local market monopolies in daily newspapers develop?

Freedom of Speech and the First Amendment

Newspapers have been far more protected in freedom of speech than electronic media such as radio and television. There have been few attempts in the United States to limit freedom of speech or of the press, especially in political terms as opposed to "moral" issues (pornography or obscene language).

For example, during the 1950s, the anticommunist campaign of Senator Joseph McCarthy resulted in several authors being blacklisted, which prevented them from publishing books or writing for Hollywood films and television, but McCarthy steered away from directly attacking the print press, especially newspapers, over issues such as how they covered communism.

Libel

However, press freedom is not absolute. Neither the publication of material that constitutes **libel,** or defamation, nor the invasion of privacy is protected by the First Amendment. *Libel* and *slander* refer, respectively, to printing, and to saying, untrue things about private citizens that might damage their reputations. Laws against libel are supposed to protect the reputations, welfare, and dignity of private citizens. Public figures, such as media professionals, celebrities, and public officials, are not generally protected against libel, on the theory that they have chosen to act in the public sphere, not to remain "private" citizens. This is because U.S. legal policy balances libel concerns against the watchdog role of the press, which is to expose corruption or incompetence on the part of officials or public figures.

Libel is an untruthful criticism by media that intends to damage someone.

Privacy of Newsmakers

Journalists often have to make ethical decisions about how far to pursue a story and how to treat the subjects of their stories. These dilemmas raise the issue of privacy. For instance, should the names of crime victims be published (Meyer, 1987)?

Press coverage of the scandal about President Clinton's sexual relationship with White House intern Monica Lewinsky raised crucial issues about how the private lives of public figures should be treated. Many in the press felt that Clinton's private sexual behavior and subsequent lack of candor, if not outright deception, about it were legitimate public issues that justified—and even demanded—extensive coverage. Others, particularly those whose views were solicited in public-opinion polls, felt that even a figure as prominent as a U.S. President deserved freedom from public scrutiny on what seemed, to them, an essentially private matter. Although the reporters were within their rights—even within their ethical bounds—the public ultimately decides whether to pay attention or not, and the saturation coverage of the scandal led many to wish that other pressing issues would get more press coverage instead.

SCANDALOUS REPORTING? Unrelenting news coverage of the Monica Lewinsky scandal made press critics wonder whether mainstream journalists had adopted the sleazy tactics of tabloid journalism.

Reporting and Content

Investigative reporting became a hallmark of the newspaper profession in the 1960s and 1970s with Vietnam and Watergate. Today, however, true investigative reporting is a novelty rather than the norm. Few journalists search out stories but rather wait for the stories to come to them. Famed Watergate reporter Carl Bernstein criticized American journalists, on this point, in an interview about the Clinton and Lewinsky affair. He felt that, unlike reporting of the Watergate scandal,

MEDIA ETHICS

The Ethics of "Tabloidization"

Until recently, tabloid newspapers such as *The National Enquirer* and *The Star* were the places where a reader might expect to find stories about famous people accused of cheating on their spouses or other wrong-doing, aliens, overweight celebrities, diet fads, and sensational crimes. More recently, tabloid editors have been heard to lament that supposedly mainstream print newspapers and magazines, such as *People, Newsweek,* and even the *New York Times,* are crowding in on the tabloid's turf.

In 1991, the *New York Times* broke at least one traditional taboo by printing many details, including the name of the victim, in stories about a Kennedy descendant, William Kennedy Smith, accused of rape. Since then, most newspapers have carried steadily increasing numbers of sensational stories, such as accounts of the investigation of the murder of child model JonBenet Ramsey, and stories of scandals, such as and Monica Lewinsky's relationship with President Bill Clinton.

The sexual scandal linking President Clinton and Monica Lewinsky represented one peak of this trend. Should the President be treated like any other celebrity, increasingly a target for minute scrutiny of his or her private life? Until quite recently, the press stayed away from reporting potentially sensational aspects of the private lives of political and other public figures, even when they knew of scandalous details. Do public figures deserve privacy? What will be the effects of denying them privacy? Will talented people shy away from public life? The line between the ethics of tabloid journalism and regular or mainstream journalism seems to be eroding. How will this affect public life? How will it affect the image and credibility of the print media themselves?

Another issue arises when mainstream media follow the tabloid practice of rushing details about those suspected of a crime into media coverage. The quick accusation of participation in the Atlanta Olympic Park bombing raised against Richard Jewell, which then had to be retracted, can be contested in terms of libel, if the accusation is proved untrue.

For Further Research: WWW

Issues like newspaper coverage and libel evolve and change. Learn how to follow current developments on such issues by using the WWW and InfoTrac College Edition to find current cases of newspapers accused of libel to see if standards are changing. If you are using InfoTrac College Edition, try the following search terms: Newspapers-Libel. Try the same key words using a WWW search engine.

"Scribe Sues Paper for Defamation," David Noack. *Editor & Publisher,* May 9, 1998, v131 n19 p14(1).

"Selleck decries lack of restraint." (Actor Tom Selleck tells Associated Press Managing Editors conference freedom of the press endangered by irresponsibility of media), Kelvin Childs.

"Jewell sues Atlanta papers; former Olympic Park bombing suspect charges *Atlanta Journal and Constitution,* nine reporters with libel," (Richard Jewell, Atlanta, GA) Stacy Jones. *Editor & Publisher,* Feb. 8, 1997, v130 n6 p12(1).

the press was doing an inadequate job of actually investigating the story. Instead, they were waiting to report what was given to them. Many in journalism agree and believe that investigative reporting, an offshoot of muckraking, is no longer fulfilling its "watchdog" role for the American public. Or it may be that cutting-edge investigative journalism is migrating to the Web, such as the *Drudge Report* (see the Media Impact box on page 122).

Accuracy and Truthfulness

Another key aspect of ethics in journalism is accuracy and truthfulness, especially in the use of sources. When a quote is presented in a newspaper, it is assumed to be a literal quote from a real person. Several reporters for major newspapers, including a *Chicago Tribune* reporter and a *Boston Globe* columnist, were fired in the late 1990s for making up quotes or fabricating sources.

A thornier problem is material attributed to a source that turns out to be a composite of several real people. When sources prefer (or even demand) to remain anonymous, one controversial solution is to combine the quotes of several real people into a composite source, or "person," that is not recognizable and won't get the real sources into trouble with their employers or institutions. For example, during the Watergate scandal, Woodward and Bernstein often quoted a source inside the Nixon administration called "Deep Throat." They insisted that "he" was a real, though anonymous, person, but others suspected he was a composite of several different sources.

Material in both news reports and columns that is not attributed to someone specific is assumed to be the original writing of the author. Using someone else's material, either verbatim or closely paraphrased, without giving credit is **plagiarism.** Another *Boston Globe* columnist was fired for plagiarizing comic George Carlin.

Plagiarism is using the exact language or a very close paraphrase of another writer or speaker without citing them as the source.

Finally, with both quoted remarks and facts or events, journalistic ethics has been assumed to require very careful checking for accuracy. The usual practice is to verify quotes with the sources and to double-check all facts by requiring that two independent sources confirm them. This practice is more consistently honored at major newspapers than at tabloids, however. Accuracy is even more of a question with some news sites on the Web.

Coverage of Sex and Scandal

Newspapers increasingly have to decide in how much detail to report the sexual affairs and other sensational or scandalous issues. This is related to issues about privacy. Do those covered in the news have a right to keep intimate details private? The decision reflects a judgment about what is important news that the public really needs to know and what is sensational detail that some of the public may want, whereas others do not. Mainstream newspapers have traditionally tried to stay away from sensational details. However, the turn-of-the-century "yellow press" and the current behavior of tabloid newspapers show that newspapers are often not above pursuing scandal for sex or other controversial bits of news that will sell extra papers.

For example, newspapers found themselves faced with increasingly explicit descriptions of sexual behavior between President Clinton and Monica Lewinsky being released by the investigative team of independent counsel Kenneth Starr. Newspapers feared that they were being used in a politicized attack on the President, as details about the sexual aspects were leaked by the investigation. Several major news organizations, such as *Newsweek,* sat on stories for several days, trying to sort out the issues, decide what level of detail was appropriate, check facts, and verify sources. In at least two cases, independent news gatherers who were uninhibited by ethical concerns, like Matt Drudge (see the Media Impact box), caught wind of the story, published details on the Internet, and forced the major organizations, including *Newsweek,* to release their reports.

When the complete Starr Report on the Clinton–Lewinsky scandal was published in 1998, newspapers faced a heightened dilemma about the appropriate level

IMPACT

MEDIA

Matt Drudge Shakes Up the Press

For a young man in his early thirties, equipped only with a cheap computer, assorted radios, TVs, and phones, and working as a one-man operation out of a $600-a-month apartment in Hollywood, Matt Drudge shook up the American journalistic and political establishments in 1998 to a remarkable degree. The first news about President Clinton having had sex with White House intern Monica Lewinsky came over the *Drudge Report* on the Internet. The e-mailed report, entitled "Newsweek Kills Story on White House Intern Blockbuster Report: 23-Year-Old Former White House Intern, Sex Relationship with President **World Exclusive**" hit his mailing list of 90,000 subscribers and was posted to his Web site. Drudge also broke a new report about Clinton groping another White House volunteer, Kathleen Willey. Both stories were being investigated by *Newsweek,* which was sitting on them to verify their accuracy.

The traditional news media, including *Newsweek* and the main national newspapers, recognize a responsibility to be very careful about putting out such stories, but Matt Drudge has no qualms. He is far readier to rush something out, with less double-checking, than the main news media. Though some consider that a serious journalistic flaw, Drudge is unrepentant. First, he thinks journalism has been overblown and needs to be simplified. Second, he thinks that the major news media have a dangerous monopoly on news—that reporting needs to be deconcentrated and opened up. But Drudge never had the benefit of any education in journalism so perhaps he is unaware of some ethical issues.

Unlike newspapers, which require a complex structure of professionals and a major economic base, a reporter on the Internet can get news out at essentially the cost of his own time and his news-gathering tools. In the case of Mr. Drudge, these tools are Internet news groups, chat rooms, and Web sites; broadcast, cable, and satellite television channels ranging from local news to C-Span (one of his favorites); and radio talk shows. Speed is one of his strong points. Newspaper reports are usually too slow for him, although, as his early release on the *Newsweek* investigation of Clinton, Lewinsky, and Willey shows, he often depends on leaks and gossip from major print media to get his information.

Drudge may herald a new wave of very small news operations that use the low cost of "publishing" on the Internet to reach a wide audience at low cost (see also Chapter 3 on the magazines *Slate* and *Salon*). Drudge says, "We've got this great new medium where people can publish what they hear and what they know and what they can see. A lot of people are uncomfortable with that . . ." (McClintick, 1998). Drudge's style of operation threatens the conventional news media's very reason for being. However, Drudge's critics say it's not just his grassroots style of Internet journalism that worries them but Drudge's lack of journalistic ethics and caution.

WWW

Drudge's style does raise some major ethical issues:

- Accuracy. He rushed out a report about spousal abuse by White House aid Sidney Blumenthal, which he later had to retract as inaccurate and apologize for.
- Fact checking, multiple-sourcing. To get the story about Blumenthal out fast, Drudge decided not to wait for fact checking and confirmation by at least two independent sources—the journalistic standard.
- Objectivity. Drudge is openly conservative and he receives financial support from conservative groups. Most journalists avoid direct financial support by advocacy groups to maintain neutrality, but Drudge scoffs that journalistic objectivity is a myth.

of detail on sex. (The report contained a level of detail about sexual encounters that could be considered obscene.) However, the full report was also available on the Internet at various Web sites, where millions accessed the report. At that point, most major newspapers gave in and published the complete report or major excerpts. However, many readers complained that they couldn't allow their children to read the newspaper the day the report was published, because the printed report was so detailed as to be obscene.

Journalism Education

Do journalists need to be specifically trained or educated in journalism? Newspapers vary somewhat in their opinions on this issue, but most newspapers, particularly in medium-sized and small markets, seek the benefits of a journalism education when hiring reporters, editors, and copywriters.

Journalism education does teach skills that are highly useful: how to write various kinds of stories, edit, copy-edit, compose a page, write editorials, and write features. Furthermore, most journalism programs provide laboratory newspapers, internships, or other experiences where student journalists can practice what they have learned in class. However, students need to work very hard on two key things: learning to write very well, and gaining some in-depth expertise in an area important for journalistic coverage. If a journalism graduate doesn't know as much or write as well as applicants who hold some other kind of liberal arts degree, the journalism degree itself will not guarantee him or her a job.

Besides teaching writing and technical skills, journalism programs make student journalists think about ethics in the media. There is not always an obvious "right answer" to ethical dilemmas, and it helps a great deal to have thought about possible ethical issues before they pop up on the job.

Newspapers, Gatekeeping, and "Information Glut"

Some news readers are responding positively to the way the Internet permits them to expand radically the information available to them, as well as focusing and personalizing their news. However, many others continue to prize and pay for the classic editing and gatekeeping functions that a good newspaper provides. As *The New Yorker* magazine noted, "Newspapers are not just yesterday's news; the good ones are carefully prepared buffets, cooked up by skilled editors who sift the news and present it in a way that makes each edition unique. Computers, for all their strengths, are very poor at replicating human judgment and intuition, and those qualities are what editing newspapers is all about." Mark Willes, chairman of the Times Mirror Company and publisher of the *Los Angeles Times,* said, "As we have this continued proliferation of news and information sources, we all need editors, and that is one of the things that newspapers provide . . . . The Internet is the epitome of an unedited information glut." (quoted in *The New Yorker,* "Demolition Man," Nov. 17, 1997, page 89)

Nicholas Negroponte of the MIT Media Lab predicts that one way of dealing with information glut will be advanced versions of the M.I.T. "newspaper of the future" idea. One possible approach is already developing: intelligent agents, software programs for the Internet that will develop a profile of what you like to read, listen to, or watch and then interact with information providers on the Internet, such as newspapers, magazines, and television Web sites, to find things that you might like.

PROFILE

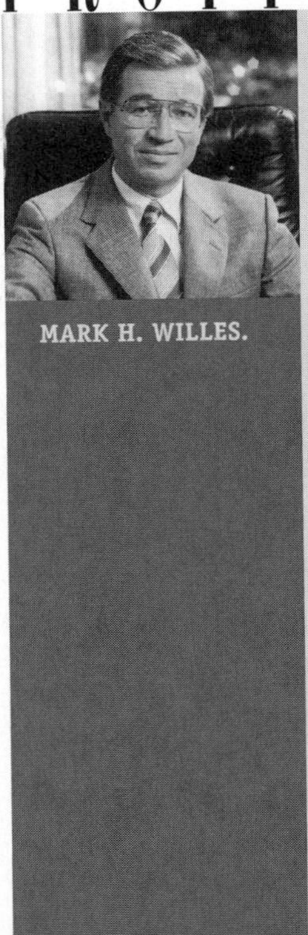
MARK H. WILLES.

Breaking Down Walls

Name: Mark H. Willes

Current Job: Times Mirror Company chairman, president and CEO; publisher of the chain's flagship newspaper, *The Los Angeles Times.* Debuted in journalism in 1995 as the Times Mirror chairman.

Age: 56

Previous Job: Vice Chairman of General Mills.

Style: Known as a cost-cutting executive.

Most Notable Achievements: Improved Times Mirror's foundering stock price, increased circulation at *Los Angeles Times.* An expanded business section brought in a 16 percent increase in advertising revenue in 1997—including $8 million in new advertising. The stock price increased form $22 a share in 1995 to $57 in 1997.

Most Dubious Achievements: Shut down *New York Newsday* (its New York City edition) and Baltimore's *Evening Sun,* cutting nearly 2000 jobs. Reorganized the *Los Angeles Times* so that each section of the paper has an advertising executive working with its editor to increase the commercial viability of the newspaper. Once suggested that stories that are more emotional, more personal, and less critical might appeal more to women readers. Apologized immediately.

Inspiration: Thinks that newspapers are a very viable business in the Information Age if they are run right. Thinks that the traditional "wall" between business and editorial staffs and functions at newspapers hurts them as businesses.

Challenges: Has expressed the view that newspapers tend to be too negative. Decreasing the "wall" between business and editorial functions of newspapers could decrease editorial and reporting independence and quality.

Promising as it seems, this sort of automated profiling and selection from Internet information still does not duplicate the editing function of a good newspaper. These editors do several things that really require human intuition and creativity. First, they perform a **gatekeeping** function: They tell you what various experts think you ought to know. Thus you avoid the frustration of reading only more of what you already know. Second, newspapers and magazines can make intelligent suggestions about new things that you may be interested in, *beyond* what you already know. This helps you avoid the claustrophobic narrowness of interests implied by Negroponte's idea of a "Daily Me."

Gatekeepers decide what will appear in the media.

1. What are the policy implication of concentration of newspaper ownership?
2. What role can newspapers play in relieving the "information glut"?
3. What First Amendment issues affect print media?
4. What are the current issues in privacy and accuracy for the press?

By definition, however, gatekeepers do in fact keep things out—things that sometimes the reader may want to know. This may be due to a simple lack of space, or the editor or other gatekeeper may have a political or economic agenda for keeping information out of readers' hands. Can newspapers be trusted to report truthfully on or even investigate wrong-doing by their own corporate parents? The merging of editorial and advertising functions at the *Los Angeles Times* (see Profile box) raises important questions about the sanctity of the gatekeeping function.

SUMMARY AND REVIEW

WHAT ESTABLISHED THE PRECEDENTS FOR PRESS FREEDOM IN COLONIAL AMERICA?

The colonial press was often critical of British governors. In a key case in 1733, Peter Zenger published a newspaper critical of the British governor of New York. Zenger was jailed for criminal libel. Despite British legal precedent to the contrary, Zenger's lawyer successfully argued that the truth of a published piece was a defense against libel.

WHO DEVELOPED THE POLITICAL PRESS THAT SUPPORTED THE AMERICAN REVOLUTION?

Zenger was instrumental. James Franklin of the independent *New England Courant* was jailed and forbidden to publish without prior approval. Benjamin Franklin moved to Philadelphia and started the successful and independent *Pennsylvania Gazette.* Most newspapers at the time were partisan, supporting either the independence movement or the British Crown. A number of key documents and ideas were published in the newspapers, including the Declaration of Independence.

WHAT WAS THE PENNY PRESS? WHAT LED TO IT?

By 1800 most large cities had at least one daily, but circulations were limited to the literate and relatively wealthy. By 1830 new technological inventions made possible lower-cost papers aimed at a broader audience. More people were learning to read, public education was expanding, wages were increasing, and more people were gathering in cities. Benjamin Day launched the first low-cost daily, the *New York Sun,* in 1833. It sold for only a penny.

WHAT WAS THE ROLE OF PRINT MEDIA IN THE CIVIL WAR? HOW DID THE WAR AFFECT THE MEDIA?

Newspapers affected the issues debate that led up to the Civil War. African American leader Frederick Douglass pushed hard for the abolition of slavery with *The North Star.* The newspapers covered the Civil War, with great disagreement apparent between northern and southern papers. Several northern papers had a major influence on the positions and strategy of the northern states. Illustration became a prominent tool of journalism during the war. Circulation grew.

WHAT WAS MUCKRAKING?

Muckraking characterized the post–Civil War period, when crusading newspapers turned their attention to exposing scandals and corruption in government and among industry cartels.

WHAT ROLE DID SENSATIONALISM PLAY IN NEWSPAPERS?

After the Civil War, the "new journalism" used sensational coverage of crime, police news, scandals, disasters, and celebrities and included features about prominent personalities and social events such as weddings, deaths, and parties. Sensationalism peaked in the "yellow journalism" of William Randolph Hearst and others at the end of the 1800s.

WHEN DID NEWSPAPERS PEAK AS MASS AUDIENCE MEDIA?

The efficiency of newspaper printing increased rapidly and probably peaked in about 1900, which coincided with the peak of the newspapers' impact as mass media. The newspaper industry had grown larger than its advertising and circulation could support. In addition, motion pictures and the phonograph also began to vie for people's attention and money. By 1927, radio would be a competitor as well.

WHAT ARE THE MAIN RECENT TRENDS IN NEWSPAPER DELIVERY TECHNOLOGIES?

Newspapers were often delivered directly in cities and in bulk along railroads and shipping lines. In the 1990s, delivery by electronic mail and the World Wide Web were becoming alternatives for "newspaper" delivery.

WHAT ARE THE MAIN NATIONAL DAILY NEWSPAPERS? WHY ARE THEY GROWING?

The *Wall Street Journal* is a specialized business paper with a broad general readership. The *New York Times* specializes in interpretation of the news and focuses on media and business. *USA Today* carries shorter news items and more entertainment. National dailies have responded to a public interest in national and international news and have been able to reach national audiences at an affordable price by using new technology for satellite delivery to primary plants.

WHY ARE MAJOR METROPOLITAN DAILIES DECLINING?

The larger metropolitan daily newspapers are losing readers to national dailies, national news weeklies, national newsmagazines, and television and radio. Their decline is also related to the decline of many cities as centers of industry. Suburban newspapers, small-town dailies, and weeklies are growing.

WHAT ARE THE MAIN SECTIONS AND CONTENTS OF NEWSPAPERS?

The national newspapers stress international news, national news, editorials/commentaries, and business, with some lifestyle and entertainment news. Metropolitan dailies usually focus more on local and regional news, and add more local lifestyles, entertainment, sports, and comics. Many weeklies focus almost exclusively on local events, shopping, and entertainment.

IS THERE STILL A MASS AUDIENCE FOR NEWSPAPERS?

Roughly three-fifths of all American adults still read newspapers.

IS THERE A TREND TOWARD CONSOLIDATION AND CONCENTRATION OF OWNERSHIP IN NEWSPAPERS?

The number of daily newspapers has been steadily declining since 1910, as ownership becomes more heavily concentrated in several large chains, such as Gannett and Scripps-Howard.

WHY ARE THERE CONCERNS ABOUT CONSOLIDATION IN THE NEWSPAPER INDUSTRY?

A number of formerly competitive newspapers have entered into joint operation agreements to share facilities, costs, administrative structure, and advertising, while attempting to maintain editorial independence. However, the lack of competition and the nature of the joint operation may well reduce independence and diversity in editorial points of view. Chain ownership may similarly reduce local independence and standardize editorial and reporting approaches across the country.

WHAT ARE THE MAIN POLICY ISSUES FOR NEWSPAPERS?

Freedom of press for newspapers has been limited at times by concerns about libel, pornography, and obscene speech, but within the media and courts, freedom of speech has usually been the dominant principle.

WHAT ARE THE MAIN ETHICAL ISSUES FOR NEWSPAPERS?

The main ethical issue for newspapers currently revolves around how to treat subjects of stories and, to some degree, sources for stories. Although newspapers usually respect the privacy of people who are not public figures, the issue is a subject of some discussion today. Accuracy and truthfulness in reporting and independence from commercial pressures are also key ethical principles.

Electronic Resources

For up-to-the-minute URLs about *Newspapers,* access the MEDIA NOW site on the World Wide Web at:

http://communication.wadsworth.com/

CHAPTER 5

Radio and Recorded Music

WHAT'S AHEAD

Recorded sound and radio have evolved together since the 1920s, along with changes in popular music styles and in recording technology. This chapter discusses how the organizational and musical forms of the radio and recording industries, their content, and policy issues related to them have changed over the last century. Now the two face an uncertain future together, as recording and broadcasting media converge on the Internet and other digital media, and as the industry reorganizes in response to deregulation.

WWW

Access the MEDIA NOW site on the World Wide Web at:
http://communication.wadsworth.com/
Choose "Chapter 5" from the selection box to access electronic information and other sites relevant to this chapter.

CRUISING AND PLAYING THE DIGITAL RADIO: LOVERS' LANE, 2009

Hello everybody. This is Dick Clark. For everybody out there on Lovers' Lane in East Podunk tonight, here's Chuck Berry with "No Particular Place to Go" from 1964.

What's Dick Clark doing on? And how did he know where we were? Anyway, I thought he was . . . .

You nerd, that's a digital voice simulation from the American Bandstand Direct Broadcast Satellite, and your mom's radio is synthesizing the local tag from information in her navigation system. And, Stanley, how about a little romantic music tonight, hmmm?

Oh. Uh, right. Right! Radio, cancel "cruising," search "love."

SEARCHING, LOVE . . . INTERRUPTING, TRAFFIC REPORT WNWZ, AM 1210 . . . Big accident downtown tonight, stay tuned for our WNWZ traffic satellite.

Why don't you just turn that darn thing off!

I can't! That's my mom's morning drive subroutine kicking in. It automatically switches to accident reports along her route, even if the radio isn't on.

Fiery tractor-trailer accident at the concert hall ramp tonight. Everybody, better watch out.

Yipes! Now my parents are going to find out we didn't even go to the opera! Take me home right away! And wipe the memory on your mom's navigation system, IF you even know how. Your mom's radio is a lot smarter than YOU are!

I couldn't help overhearing you kids. If you just double-click the memory button on my screen and then . . .

Chapter Outline

A Brief History of Audio Media
Wireless Radio Telegraphy
Early Sound Broadcasting
The Rise of Radio Networks
The Fall of the Radio Networks
The Boom in Recorded Music
The Rise of FM Radio and Specialized Formats
Trends in Audio Technology
Audio Recording
The Basics of Radio Transmission and Reception
Forms and Genres
Radio Music Genres
Music Genres and Radio Formats
Industry Organization
Record Companies
Radio Stations
Audiences for Audio Media
Policy and Ethical Issues
Radio Licensing and Regulation
Radio Ownership and Control Rules
Networks and Program Control
The First Amendment and Freedom of Speech
Intellectual Property in Recordings and Radio
Summary and Review

A BRIEF HISTORY OF AUDIO MEDIA

Human beings have been entertaining and informing one another with sound for a long time. Well before there was a written language, people sang songs and told stories. There has been a lot of speculation about what is the oldest profession, but entertaining people with songs and stories might just be it. Records and radio stand on the shoulders of a long tradition that has included shamans, village storytellers, poets, wandering minstrels, and court jesters. Even today's rock drum rhythms have their roots in sacred drumming used in ancient African religious ceremonies (Hart, 1990).

Long before sound recordings and radio, there was a substantial music industry in Europe and in the United States based on live performances, written song lyrics, and printed sheet music. Music was popularized as performers traveled from village to village, taking their music with them. With the advent of printing, music traveled even more easily as **sheet music.** Some of the earliest printed materials were lyrics and musical notations. Today, people still buy music written for voice, piano, guitar, and numerous other instruments. Many still want to play the music they like at home.

Sheet music is print reproduction of song lyrics and musical notation for people to perform.

Tin Pan Alley. In the late 1800s, the music-writing industry for popular music that came to be known as "Tin Pan Alley" emerged. It originated with New York music and lyric writers who wrote sheet music for the popular singers and musicians of the day. For example, "She's Only a Bird in a Gilded Cage," a very popular song around 1900, was sold as sheet music to people who wanted to perform it at home. Back then, specific songs were not as closely identified with a certain performer as they are now. The composer and lyricist had a more central role and were more widely recognized apart from the performer. Thus people flocked to buy the latest sheet music of well-known composers or lyricists, such as Scott Joplin, rather than waiting until a performer made the music popular.

The Victrola. Recorded music came some time before radio. During the later 1800s and early 1900s, various attempts were made to reproduce music for the public. Inventors created mechanical devices, such as music boxes and **nickelodeons,** that would play or reproduce music. Player pianos, for example, used a roll of paper or fabric with holes to dictate when piano keys would strike.

Nickelodeon is a phonograph or player piano operated by inserting a coin, originally a nickel.

RADIO AND RECORDED MUSIC TIME LINE

1877	Edison introduces the speaking phonograph
1888	Hertz transmits and receives first radio waves
1896	Marconi develops radio transmitter, goes into business
1906	Fessenden makes first sound broadcast; De Forest adapts vacuum tubes for radio receivers
1912	Radio Act
1918	Two million phonographs sold
1920	Frank Conrad starts first radio station, KDKA in Pittsburgh
1922	AT&T starts commercial, "toll broadcasting" on WEAF
1926	RCA starts NBC Radio Network; AT&T pulls out of broadcasting
1927	Federal Radio Commission (FRC) started, fixes AM band at 535–1605 kHz
1927	Advertising support becomes dominant in radio
1933	Armstrong develops FM radio
1934	Federal Communications Commission started
1938	Chain Broadcasting hearings
1941	at FCC
1947	Radio networks begin to lose ground to TV; magnetic audiotape developed by 3M
1948	33⅓ rpm and 45 rpm record formats introduced; DJ era of radio begins
1955	Rise of top 40 radio
1956	High fidelity and stereo enhance popularity of 33⅓ rpm LPs
1962	Cassette tapes introduced
1970	FM stations increase, go stereo, target segmented audience
1982	Compact disc recording format introduced
1996	Telecommunications Act sets off station merger frenzy
1998	Music sites proliferate on Internet

The first **acoustic** recording technology was developed in 1877 by Thomas Edison. He produced a prototype—a "phono-graph"—that played back the nursery rhyme "Mary Had a Little Lamb" from a rotating cylinder. In 1882 Emile Berliner created the gramophone, which used flat disks that were soon called "records," instead of cylinders. Edison and Berliner competed fiercely to set up a record industry (Everett, 1993). Edison imagined using the device to record dictation or to act as a telephone answering machine, but musical entertainment quickly became the main use.

Acoustic is sound that is not electronically amplified.

The phonograph, or record player, was a major breakthrough. In 1890, an entrepreneur named Lippincott started putting coin-operated phonographs in **penny arcades** to play records upon request. The more durable records quickly replaced the fragile cylinders. The Victor Talking Machine Company introduced the home **Victrola** in 1906. People became accustomed to listening to recorded music in their homes, using a piece of furniture that supplied entertainment. The phonograph quickly became a mass medium. By the end of World War I (1904–1918), over 2 million players were being made and sold annually by over 200 manufacturers. Record sales soared from 23 million in 1914 to 107 million in 1919.

Penny arcades were commercial entertainment areas with coin-operated sound and film nickelodeons and other amusements.

Victrola was the trade name for an early phonograph that became a common name.

NOW HEAR THIS. The phonograph, pioneered in 1887 by Thomas Edison, was already gaining popularity in the 1890s. (The big horn was the loudspeaker.)

Early Recorded Music. The penny arcade and home Victrola introduced more people to new kinds of music and helped increase the availability of music more rapidly than ever before. The notion of "popular music" caught on, as writers and composers began to discover what kinds of music most appealed to a mass audience. Records moved from early pop favorites, which tended to be sentimental and melodramatic ("She's only a bird in a guilded cage, such a beautiful sight to see . . .") to the jaunty beat of ragtime, such as the music played by Scott Joplin.

Wireless Radio Telegraphy

Guglielmo Marconi, a young Italian nobleman, successfully created a "wireless telegraph" using radio waves to carry messages in Morse code using long and short bursts of radio noise. This technique was the first practical use of radio, a major step in its development. In the 1890s, Marconi tried to promote wireless telegraphy for business and military use in his native Italy, but the government was not interested. Marconi was more successful in England, obtaining **patents** there in 1896 and in the United States in 1904, where he employed his business flair to dominate the early use of the wireless radio telegraph for two-way communications. This kind of radio was first used to coordinate ocean shipping between countries, where telegraph wires obviously could not reach. The Marconi Wireless Telegraph Company set up a series of shore radio stations to receive and retransmit telegraph signals across the ocean or from ships at sea. His company also manufactured and operated the equipment to send and receive radio telegraph messages. By 1913, Marconi dominated radio in Europe and the United States.

The wireless telegraph played a pivotal role in the *Titanic* disaster (see Media Impact), which attracted public attention to the fledgling technology. So much so, that the U.S. Congress took note and placed radio licensing under the supervision of the Department of Commerce in the Radio Act of 1912. Thus began an 85-year trend toward increasing regulation of the airwaves.

Patent is a written document that secures to an inventor for a number of years the exclusive right to make, use, or sell an invention.

During World War I, radio was used primarily as an over-the-air telegraph. Radio was a medium for business, shipping, and military long-distance communications. The U.S. Navy accelerated advances in radio technology by putting a stop to patent disputes between Marconi and other early inventors and standardizing the technologies.

After the war, Marconi tried to buy U.S. patents to consolidate a U.S.–European communications monopoly, but the U.S. government opposed foreign control of a technology that was clearly crucial for military uses. The Navy still held temporary control over radio technology and assets and proposed to make radio a government operation—an option that was also opposed by many Americans. A negotiated settlement forced the Marconi Wireless Telegraph Company to sell its American assets to General Electric (GE). In conjunction with American Telephone & Telegraph (AT&T) and Westinghouse, GE set up a new company, Radio Corporation of America (RCA), which they jointly owned, to develop the radio business. GE, RCA, and AT&T also set up a **patent pool** in 1920 so that they could all manufacture complete radio equipment. None of them owned the necessary patents to make completely functioning radio transmitters or receivers without such a pool (Streeter, 1996).

Patent pool was several companies sharing technologies that had been awarded government protection via a formal patent.

IMPACT MEDIA

Radio and the Sinking of the *Titanic*

The *Titanic* was a large, new, British ocean liner that struck an iceberg and sank suddenly in the North Atlantic in 1912. It sent a radio distress call, tapped out in Morse code over the Marconi wireless system, which was relayed to the Marconi radio operators in New York. Legend has it that they included the future director of RCA, David Sarnoff. Not only was radio crucial to the efforts to save as many passengers as possible, but it became central to reporting news about the disaster, which had riveted people on both sides of the Atlantic. Newspapers got their information from the radio, and many people, particularly young David Sarnoff, were impressed with this new medium's news potential. This type of radio communication was typical of the first 20 years of the medium's development.

SOS.
Distress signals from the Titanic called public attention to radio communication.

Early Sound Broadcasting

Even before World War I, several new technological developments made it clear that radio could go beyond the short bursts of radio noise required for two-way radio transmission in telegraph codes. In 1906, Lee De Forest created the vacuum tube, which permitted radio transmission and reception of sound, voice, and music.

Inventors and hobbyists soon began broadcasting sound. First, Reginald Fessenden, a Canadian, tried some experimental broadcasts of voices over radio waves. His transmission of music and singing in 1906 were the first successes, but the first regular broadcasts of sound on radio were started in 1912 by Charles Herrold, but he stopped during World War I. Then De Forest broadcast the election returns in 1916 (Sterling & Kittross, 1990). However, despite these early demonstrations of sound broadcasting, none of the main companies involved in radio at that time saw broadcasting to individual home receivers as a viable potential business.

Things began to change after the Navy returned radio patent controls and technology to civilian hands in 1919–1920. Frank Conrad, a Westinghouse engineer, began broadcasting regularly from a transmitter connected to his Pittsburgh factory in 1920. His programs attracted interest and then newspaper coverage. A Pittsburgh department

STOP & REVIEW

1. **What kind of music industry existed before radio? Before the phonograph?**
2. **What companies dominated two-way radio or wireless telegraphy? What was it used for?**
3. **What were the key technical developments that allowed for radio broadcasting?**

store decided to sell radios to pick up Conrad's broadcasts. Then Westinghouse realized that regular radio broadcasts could help sell radios, so they opened station KDKA in Pittsburgh in 1920. Unhampered by competing signals, KDKA could be heard in many parts of the United States and Canada. This encouraged people to start buying radio receivers—100,000 in 1922 and over 500,000 in 1923 (Sterling & Kittross, 1990).

It did not take people long to think of other things to do with radio. Stores started radio stations just to promote their own goods. Electronics companies, such as the RCA Radio Group, set up more broadcast stations so there would be something on the air to make people want to buy radios. Newspapers saw a news medium, and schools and churches saw educational potential. To avoid **frequency interference** among all the broadcasters rushing into the new medium, the Commerce Department was asked to supervise the new form of radio broadcasting. It issued hundreds of licenses in 1923.

Frequency interference takes place when two broadcasts are on the same frequency so that they interfere with one another.

Paying for Radio—The Road to Advertising. The vision of radio that determined its future came from AT&T's station WEAF, started in 1922 in New York. On the basis of its experience with the telephone, AT&T saw that radio could carry others' programs for a fee just like long distance telephony. This idea evolved into letting various manufacturers sponsor programs to advertise their goods, which further

MEDIA IMPACT

David Sarnoff and the Radio Music Box

In 1916 David Sarnoff, then commercial manager of American Marconi, wrote a prophetic memo to his boss. He proposed "a plan of development which would make radio a 'household utility' in the same sense as the piano or phonograph. The idea is to bring music into the house by wireless. . . . The Receiver can be designed in the form of a simple 'Radio Music Box' and arranged for several different wavelengths, which should be changeable with the throwing of a single switch or pressing of a single button." Sarnoff's memo was ignored, but he anticipated perfectly the physical form that radio would take within ten years, and later, as head of RCA, he had a chance to help make this vision of radio and a similar vision of television a reality.

At first, Sarnoff opposed the idea of commercial radio and proposed that listeners pay a tax on new radios that would help pay for programming, an arrangement not unlike the system later used by the BBC in Great Britain. Later Sarnoff made his peace with commercial radio and television and helped propel RCA's main network, NBC, into leadership for a number of years in both radio and television. Sarnoff had started as a telegraph operator for Marconi and then rose through the ranks to run RCA through its formative years, until 1969.

MR. RADIO.
David Sarnoff at work as a radio operator for American Marconi in 1912.

evolved into advertisers paying to have their ads carried on programs. WEAF broadcast the first "commercial" (a term derived from AT&T's accounting jargon) in 1922. AT&T originally called this **toll broadcasting,** reflecting a parallel with long-distance, or "toll," telephone calls. It also became the first broadcast network, after AT&T used its phone lines to link several of its stations. Advertisers immediately responded to the opportunity, and toll broadcasting grew quickly. AT&T began to dream of having a monopoly in this new medium and created a network of stations with WEAF as flagship. However, the U.S. government and other major electronics companies opposed AT&T's having a major role in both broadcasting and telephony (Sterling & Kitross, 1990).

Toll broadcasting was charging someone to carry a radio program or advertisement, parallel to long-distance or "toll" telephone calls.

The other early broadcasters were far from certain what to do with radio or how to pay for it. For a while, RCA and the Radio Group still saw their station KJZ as a means of promoting the sale of radios. They toyed with the idea of collecting a license fee from listeners to pay for the programming and having radio manufacturers collectively pay for programming to sell radios. They did not want to see an AT&T monopoly in radio, however, and negotiations produced an agreement in 1926 by which AT&T got out of radio and sold its network to RCA (to keep its telephone monopoly) and agreed to be a neutral transmission connection for other networks. This solution reinforced a policy pattern, which lasted until the 1990s, in which telephone companies were not involved in creating the content of communication, only transmitting it.

Advertisers were very eager to use radio to promote products. Radio offered them direct access to the home, coupled with an attractive leisure activity. In 1927 Edgar Felix, an advertising consultant, said, "What a glorious opportunity for the advertising man to spread his sales propaganda. Here was a countless audience, sympathetic, pleasure-seeking, enthusiastic, curious, interested, approachable in the privacy of their own homes." To increase the size of the audience for their ads, advertisers used music, comedy, and other entertainment. They steered their advertising toward entertainment programs, which pushed stations that way, too (Streeter, 1996). Both regulators (such as Secretary of Commerce Herbert Hoover) and the radio industry worried in the 1920s that audiences would reject radio if it carried too much advertising. However, people were so enthusiastic about the new medium that they accepted the ads without much objection, and a commercial advertising–based model was firmly entrenched by 1927 (Barnouw, 1966).

Radio Act of 1912 was the initial government regulation for licensing of transmitters.

Frequency allocation is granting exclusive right to use a radio frequency in a specific area, usually done by government agencies.

The initial government regulation, the **Radio Act of 1912,** called for licensing of transmitters by the Secretary of Commerce but was not very specific in granting powers. Secretary Herbert Hoover hoped that industry self-regulation would be adequate and held a series of national radio conferences, which were not very effective. The courts questioned Hoover's right to enforce the **frequency allocations** he assigned, so new stations started using frequencies at will, resulting in substantial frequency interference between stations.

The **Radio Act of 1927** created the Federal Radio Commission (FRC). It defined the broadcast band, standardized frequency designations, and limited the number of stations operating at night, when AM signals carry farther. The FRC and most of its rules were absorbed into the more comprehensive Federal Communications Commission (FCC) created by the Communications Act of 1934.

Radio Act of 1927 created a Federal Radio Commission, defined the broadcast band, standardized frequency designations, and limited the number of stations operating at night, when AM signals carry farther.

The Rise of Radio Networks

Networks are groups of stations that centralize the production and distribution of programming and ads.

RCA set up its radio **network,** the National Broadcasting Corporation (NBC), in 1926. Networking, or linking stations together, to share expensive programming costs made each station cheaper to operate. After buying out AT&T's radio network, RCA had enough stations for two separate networks—NBC Red and NBC Blue. NBC "Red" was the main NBC network; while the other network was eventually "spun off" under FCC pressure in 1943. It became the American Broadcasting Corporation (ABC).

Competition came quickly from the Columbia Broadcasting System (CBS), which had been acquired in 1928 by the Paley family, owners of a cigar company who had seen the potential in advertising on radio. CBS moved quickly to put together a network to rival NBC. Both NBC and CBS networks had their own stations, called owned-and-operated stations, or **O&O's,** but both began to attract a number of affiliated stations as well. By 1937, NBC had 111 affiliates and CBS had 105 (Sterling & Kittross, 1990).

O&O's are local stations owned and operated by corporations that also own networks.

The radio networks were put together by strong-willed leaders who saw great potential in the new medium. Both Sarnoff at RCA/NBC and William Paley at CBS were sons of Russian immigrants. Both were fascinated, even obsessed, with radio. Whereas Sarnoff started at the bottom as a radio-telegraph operator, Paley started at the top, having seen the value of radio in advertising the cigars made by his family's company. He had experimented with radio ads in 1925–1926, and was so impressed with the results that he wanted in. He took over the struggling CBS network in 1928 and turned it around by focusing on both entertainment and news.

Overall, by 1927 several factors had solidified the commercial model that radio was following in America.

- National commercial networks had developed.
- The Radio Act of 1927 had reduced radio frequency overlap and interference.
- The Act had assigned licenses for frequencies, letting listeners know exactly which channels stations were on.
- Stations had developed the technical ability to deliver clear, strong signals.
- Advertising was becoming the dominant means of paying for radio.
- A critical mass of households with radios had created an audience attractive to advertisers.
- Advertisers had become interested in reaching this critical mass through networks and local stations.

Economies of scale result in reduced per-unit costs when large numbers of copies are manufactured.

Network Programming. Networks took advantage of **economies of scale.** By producing top-quality, high-cost programs in their center, or "flagship," stations and sharing the programs with their O&O stations and many affiliates, they spread the costs of production around, lowering the cost for each station. Networks also created national advertising markets by giving a national advertiser the chance to be carried simultaneously on stations that covered the entire country.

MEDIA WATCH

BBC, License Fees, and the Road Not Taken

In 1922–1923, the British sent a commission to the United States to study radio development. They observed a rush toward a radio industry dominated by musical entertainment and paid for by advertising. The British commission saw that as an enormous waste of the medium's cultural and educational potential. On returning home, they recommended a very different formula: a public radio monopoly oriented toward education and culture, financed by a license fee paid by listeners, and overseen by a board intended to keep it independent of both government and private interests, such as advertisers. This system, which became known as the British Broadcasting Corporation (BBC), is still highly regarded for cultural and educational broadcasting, although many find some of the programming dry and stuffy. It represents an alternative considered, but not chosen, by the United States in the 1920s.

Early network radio programming in the late 1920s and 1930s was focused in large part on music (at least a quarter of the schedule), but it also included news, comedy, variety shows, soap operas, detective dramas, suspense, and action adventures. Thus many of the kinds of programming that we now associate with television were developed on radio.

Radio, in turn, was inspired by genres in the 1920s and 1930s from a variety of pop culture sources. Most obvious were popular musical performances, such as jazz, swing, and blues. Many performers came in from vaudeville, particularly comics Fred Allen, George Burns, and Gracie Allen. Ideas and dramatic formulas for radio soap operas were derived from melodramatic serial novels like those of Dickens. Comic books lent heroes such as Superman and Green Lantern to radio adventure shows. Pulp fiction westerns (Zane Grey) fed into radio westerns (*Gunsmoke*).

Radio had an immediate impact on recorded music. During the 1920s and 1930s, a time known as the Jazz Age, records often featured show tunes taken from the new talking movies (see Chapter 6). However, the advent of radio caused the record business to stall and almost collapse. When people could first hear music at no cost on the radio, they stopped buying records. In 1924, as radio was taking off, record and phonograph sales dropped by almost half. Later, however, people began to want to have their own copy of what they had heard on the radio. In fact, the recording industry began to rely on radio to make people aware of artists whose recordings they could purchase. This independent relationship continues to keep both the recording industry and the radio industry healthy.

Because recording technology had not achieved very high fidelity, music was primarily broadcast live. Networks introduced the most popular groups and orchestras to the entire country. Radio stimulated a demand for a variety of musical genres, ranging from classical to country and western. Musical entertainment and escape was a particularly welcome relief during the often grim days of the Great Depression from 1929 to 1939 (MacDonald, 1979).

Big Band Music and the World War II Generation. The most popular music in the 1930s and 1940s was the "big band" sound. Developed from jazz, it was the pop music of its day. Unlike jazz, big band music emphasized not improvisation but popular tunes and songs. Band leaders such as Glenn Miller and Tommy Dorsey put together orchestras that introduced a number of the singers, such as Frank Sinatra and Doris Day, who continued to lead pop music into the 1950s. The young people who fought in World War II and worked in the factories at home thought of big band as their music in much the same way that young people today identify with different strains of rock, rap, hip-hop, alternative, or heavy metal. Because people's musical tastes tend to fix on what they like when they are young, a few radio stations today still play music for the big band generation. But music also recycles; big band music even enjoyed revived popularity among many young people in the late 1990s. Dance clubs played "big band"; new "swing" groups,

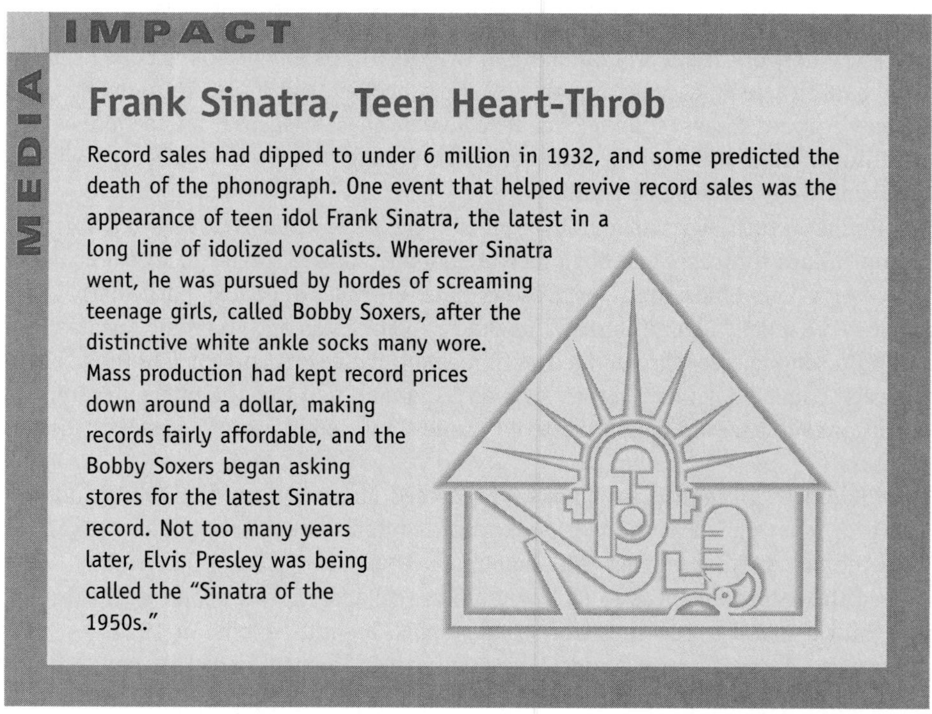

MEDIA IMPACT

Frank Sinatra, Teen Heart-Throb

Record sales had dipped to under 6 million in 1932, and some predicted the death of the phonograph. One event that helped revive record sales was the appearance of teen idol Frank Sinatra, the latest in a long line of idolized vocalists. Wherever Sinatra went, he was pursued by hordes of screaming teenage girls, called Bobby Soxers, after the distinctive white ankle socks many wore. Mass production had kept record prices down around a dollar, making records fairly affordable, and the Bobby Soxers began asking stores for the latest Sinatra record. Not too many years later, Elvis Presley was being called the "Sinatra of the 1950s."

such as the Cherry Poppin' Daddies, played on the radio; and many high schools had jazz bands that played "big band" era songs.

There was concern that the radio networks were getting too big and powerful and were abusing their power in one-sided dealings with their affiliated stations and with the on-air talent. The FCC's 1941 **Chain Broadcasting** ruling prohibited the networks from forcing programming on affiliates and put them out of the talent booking business.

Chain broadcasting refers to radio networks and their control over talent and affiliated stations.

Network radio remained strong through World War II, which in many ways represented a peak in the importance of radio compared to other media. Money spent on radio ads doubled from 1939 to 1945, surpassing expenditures on newspaper ads in 1943. Radio was the paramount information medium of the war, both domestically and internationally. Many of the networks' most famous newspeople, who subsequently started television network news, rose to prominence during the war. Internationally, the use of radio for propaganda frightened many people and stimulated a long series of investigations into the power of mass media over their audiences.

Edward R. Murrow broadcast memorable live reports from London during World War II, dramatically covering the German bombing of London and other battlefields. His reports conveyed vivid, realistic, and often highly moving word pictures. He emerged as one of the most credible and admired newsmen in the well-respected CBS news organization. He preferred to stay in the newsroom, rather than getting into administration, and he survived a career shift to television news better than many other radio newspeople (Whetmore, 1981).

The Fall of the Radio Networks

Radio networks did well through 1947, about the same time that film theater attendance peaked (1946), but as television quickly rose in prominence, becoming the main national source of mass entertainment, network radio began to slip. The number of network affiliates dropped from 97 percent of all AM stations in 1947 to 50 percent in 1955, while network revenue dropped even more.

Radio remained profitable, but the advertising shifted from a national to a local focus and began to rely on cheaper, more localized formats, such as music, news, and talk. Radio's success began to depend on the talent of each station's own announcers and on their ability to find the right music mix for their local market.

1. **Who formed the main radio networks?**
2. **How did advertising come to support radio economics?**
3. **What kind of regulation was necessary for radio to prosper?**
4. **What kinds of programming characterized radio networks during their heyday?**
5. **When and why did the original radio networks decline?**
6. **How did radio broadcasting and the recording industry affect each other in their early days?**
7. **What were the main music genres in the 1920s and 1930s?**

The Boom in Recorded Music

After World War II, several technological innovations revitalized the recording industry. In 1947, the Minnesota Mining and Manufacturing company (3M) introduced magnetic tape, a recording technology borrowed from Germany that improved sound fidelity, reduced costs, and made editing easier than was the case with records. This enabled the recorded music industry to produce the music of

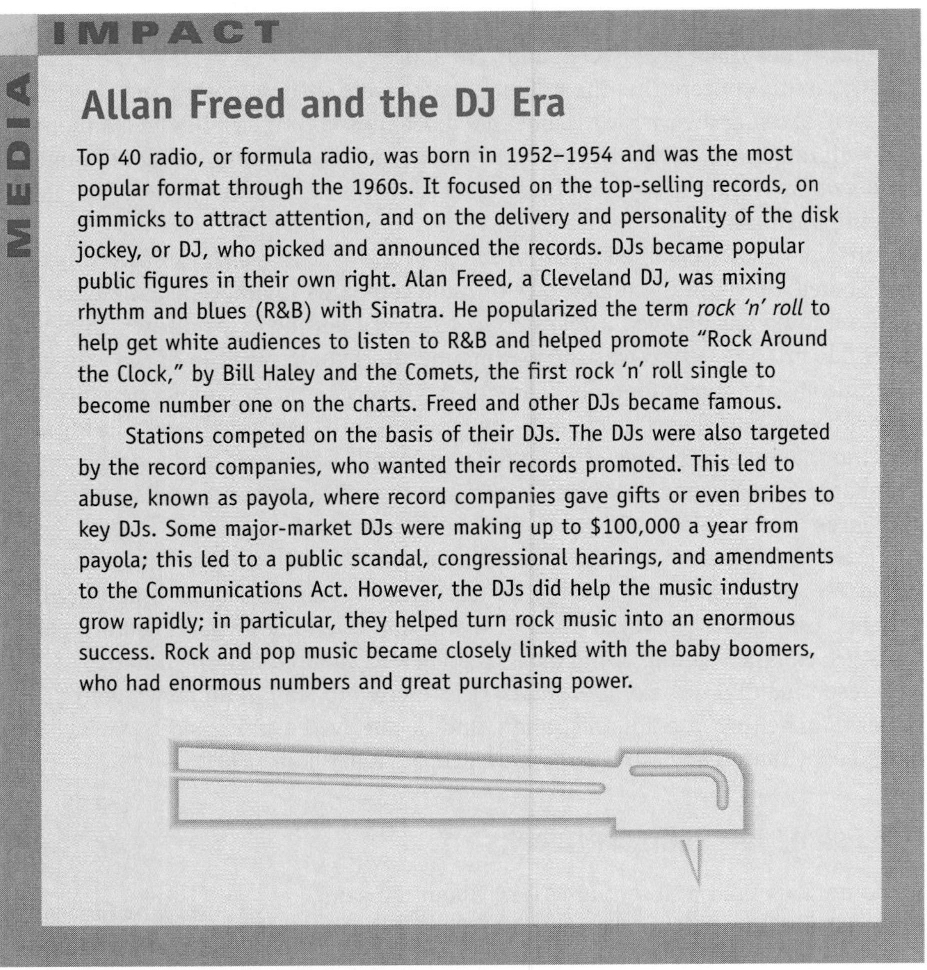

MEDIA IMPACT

Allan Freed and the DJ Era

Top 40 radio, or formula radio, was born in 1952–1954 and was the most popular format through the 1960s. It focused on the top-selling records, on gimmicks to attract attention, and on the delivery and personality of the disk jockey, or DJ, who picked and announced the records. DJs became popular public figures in their own right. Alan Freed, a Cleveland DJ, was mixing rhythm and blues (R&B) with Sinatra. He popularized the term *rock 'n' roll* to help get white audiences to listen to R&B and helped promote "Rock Around the Clock," by Bill Haley and the Comets, the first rock 'n' roll single to become number one on the charts. Freed and other DJs became famous.

Stations competed on the basis of their DJs. The DJs were also targeted by the record companies, who wanted their records promoted. This led to abuse, known as payola, where record companies gave gifts or even bribes to key DJs. Some major-market DJs were making up to $100,000 a year from payola; this led to a public scandal, congressional hearings, and amendments to the Communications Act. However, the DJs did help the music industry grow rapidly; in particular, they helped turn rock music into an enormous success. Rock and pop music became closely linked with the baby boomers, who had enormous numbers and great purchasing power.

more artists inexpensively and with better quality. (See page 144 for more information.) In 1948 and 1949, Columbia introduced the large 33⅓ rpm long-playing record (see page 144), and RCA introduced the smaller 45 rpm record (rpm stands for revolutions per minute). After a short battle over standards, the 33⅓ rpm LP with more music capacity prevailed for albums, whereas the faster-spinning but smaller-capacity 45 rpm "singles" dominated releases of single songs (Sterling & Kittross, 1990).

These record standards affected radio, too. The 45 rpm singles were well suited for DJ-oriented hit radio, that focused on single hit songs that people then bought in 45 rpm format for less than an album would cost. The *fidelity*, or sound quality, of 45 rpm singles was adequate for AM (amplitude modulation) radio but did not sound as good on FM (frequency modulation), where greater hiss and crackle, and a more limited sound frequency range, made the limits of 45 rpm single records apparent. The 33⅓ rpm format had better fidelity, which sounded better on FM.

The conflict between the 33⅓ and 45 rpm record formats was another one of the many consumer electronics format wars, in which different means of playing music or video vied for the allegiance of consumers. Together, these two new formats both drove out the earlier 78 rpm records, which were large but held only one or two songs at lower fidelity. Another format option, the eight-track cartridge tape was introduced in the 1960s as a popular means of playing recorded music. Audiocassette tapes were introduced about the same time, triumphing by the 1970s over the bulkier, less flexible eight-track tapes and the earlier reel-to-reel home tape recorders, as well. Cassette tapes were smaller and offered the advantage of recording as well as playback. In most cases, the format wars resulted from rival companies creating different standards in an attempt to gain complete control over the development of the technology. If one company's standard triumphed, it dominated the initial sales, and other manufacturers would have to pay a **royalty** to use the technology, if it was patented.

Royalty is a fee required to use another person's intellectual property.

Several technological changes also benefited the record industry. The new recording techniques enabled small, independent labels or recording companies to develop new artists and new audiences who had not been covered or served by network radio. For example, Chess Records in Chicago carried a number of blues and rhythm-and-blues artists who were played only on what were called "black" or "colored" stations back then.

Genres are types or formats of media content, such as classical music and country and western.

As a number of mass entertainment forms, or **genres,** shifted from radio to television, radio began to look for new sources of programming, which usually meant records or tapes of recorded music, to connect more directly with the musical tastes of their local audience. Radio stations began to connect with the new **labels** to create new genres of music and new musical **radio formats.** Radio came to depend more on the recording industry and to serve as a promotional device to make the public aware of new music and help the recording industry sell records. The recording industry concentrated on getting more airplay for its records by promoting them to radio stations. The relationship got a little too close when record labels bribed **disk jockeys (DJs)** to play their records, a practice known as **payola** (see Media Impact). The Top 40 format became popular (see the Genres section for more information).

Labels of record companies are particular names for a group of recordings that usually follows a consistent line of music.

Radio format is a programming approach, often linked to music genres, news, or talk, focused on a particular audience.

Disc jockey is a radio station announcer who plays records and often emphasizes delivery and personality.

Payola occurred when record companies gave gifts or even bribes to key DJs to get their records played.

The Rise of FM Radio and Specialized Formats

One development that revived radio's success with the audience was the growth of FM radio in the 1960s. FM has higher-fidelity sound, but a shorter range—essentially only within the line of sight of the radio transmitter. But that also allows for more stations in each market by reducing interference with stations in nearby markets that use the same frequency. Both FM and 33⅓ rpm records moved into stereo sound (two separate, coordinated channels of music) in the 1960s. The longer play of 33⅓ rpm records also affected FM. Longer songs could be played, which began to influence the kinds of songs that groups could record. By the mid- to late 1960s, many popular groups were recording songs much longer than the once-typical single length of 2–3 minutes. Sometimes those songs were squeezed onto a 45 rpm record, but most fans of such groups just began to buy the album that the hit song was on.

FM was first introduced in the 1930s but languished until the 1960s, because few radios could receive FM and few homes had high fidelity sound systems that could take advantage of FM's improved sound quality. Most of the FM stations simulcast the same material broadcast on AM, and FM stations were owned by the same people or groups as AM stations. FM began to develop faster after the FCC limited AM/FM simulcasting in 1963, forcing FM station owners to develop new formats to compete with the existing AM stations.

After the late 1960s, changes in the radio industry and its audience led to the eventual development of FM radio as a successful commercial medium. Radio continued to grow, along with the boom in pop music. AM licenses were becoming difficult and expensive to obtain, whereas licenses for FM stations were much easier to get.

Segmentation occurs when media focus on more specific, smaller audiences with more specialized programs and formats.

What emerged was a tendency to narrowcast—that is, to focus on **segmented** audiences with more specific formulas and formats, not just top 40. Even the radio networks themselves splintered. The ABC radio network split into contemporary, informational, entertainment, and FM services in 1968.

GUITAR HERO.
The Jimi Hendrix Experience was one of the bands that launched album-oriented FM radio in the 1960s.

Specialized FM radio formats continued to succeed. Some of these formats, such as classical, jazz, or album-oriented rock, took advantage of the musical quality of FM's higher fidelity. Much of the audience was also interested in greater sound quality, because high-fidelity and stereo systems were becoming much more popular. The move of many FM stations into stereo broadcasting had a decisive appeal for discerning listeners (Jones, 1992). FM came to dominate the radio industry. In 1993, FM stations drew 77 percent of the audience.

In 1982, a new round in the recording format wars began with the introduction of compact disc recording. This marked the beginning of a wave of digital innovation that would eventually change many aspects of both the recording and radio industries. Audiophiles were not very impressed with the shiny new discs at first, finding its sound rather harsh and brittle. But the recordings were more compact and relatively immune to picking up dust and scratches compared to LP phonograph records.

The New Network Radio Era. Though radio was characterized almost completely by local operations in the 1970s and 1980s, some of the forms of network radio began to re-emerge in the 1990s. In some cases, this resulted from stations buying into centrally produced program formats distributed via satellite. In other cases, it occurred because some large radio ownership groups began to own or produce content and act like the radio networks of old.

Syndication is rental or licensing of media products by their producers to other media companies for broadcast or distribution.

To meet the demand for interesting music, news, and talk programs, a number of outlets began to produce **syndicated** programs; one example is "shock jock" Howard Stern, whose controversial talk-radio show started in New York. Because the show attracted a large audience, Stern's parent station group began to offer it over satellite distribution to other stations. Rush Limbaugh also developed a network of stations that carried his syndicated program. Other companies offer complete radio formats, such as "The Arrow's" classic rock format on syndicated distribution; the only local elements in some of these stations are advertising and weather.

The early 1980s saw a boom in financial speculation in radio and television stations, because their values had been rising rapidly. Then several years of meager earnings drove most speculators out. Changes in FCC regulations in the 1996 Telecommunications Act permitted ownership groups to acquire many more stations and grow much larger. The new regulations essentially lifted national caps on how many stations a group could own but limited ownership slightly within a specific radio market, depending on the size of the market. In fact, even large ownership groups began to merge. CBS merged with Group W (Westinghouse) and Infinity to form a large and powerful group, but several other groups were larger, such as Capstar Broadcasting Partners, Jacor Communications, and Clear Channel Communications (see page 157).

Over 4400 stations changed hands in 1996 and 1997. Over 700 individual local owners sold their stations to groups. In a number of towns, 80 to 90 percent of radio ad revenues are now controlled by stations belonging to only two to three groups (*USA Today,* June 7, 1998, 1a-2a).

In 1990 over 50 percent of all radio stations lost money, but the late 1990s saw an increase in radio earnings. With the huge merger wave that began in 1996, merged and reorganized stations have been losing money again as competition among large groups shakes out. But the long-term prospects are good for most stations. Radio ads have been priced very low for years, so radio has become attractive to advertisers, particularly those pursuing specific audience segments.

Radio stations, particularly in FM, have continued to change formats to follow the evolution of both music genres and audience interests. The industry tries hard to target specific audience segments with unique, nonoverlapping formats, but the musical development of artists draws the audience across a changing pattern of formats. For example, Sarah McLachlen first appeared in "alternative" format stations. Later, though, she appeared on the air in a number of different FM radio formats: hot adult contemporary, "alternative," adult alternative, rock, and contemporary hits. (For more on formats and audiences, see pages 151–155 and pages 158–160.)

By the late 1990s, CDs had pushed vinyl record albums off the record store racks. Their true potential as a digital medium was unleashed as users began playing music through CD drives built into personal computers and—to the consternation of the recording industry—downloading digital music files from the Internet where they could be (illegally) copied for free. Legal CD distribution also began to move to the Internet, in the form of numerous on-line music stores that provided net surfers with the opportunity to buy recordings at Web sites for delivery through the mail. Radio stations also began to join the digital trend with hundreds of radio stations also putting their broadcasts or signals onto the Internet, using technologies such as RealAudio.

1. What led to the disk jockey era in AM radio?
2. When did FM radio begin to increase in importance? Why?
3. How did FM radio and 1960s–1970s music genres affect each other?
4. How did radio formats develop in the 1980s and 1990s?
5. What kinds of radio networks exist now?
6. Why did radio station ownership concentrate in the 1990s?

TRENDS IN AUDIO TECHNOLOGY

Audio Recording

Analog transmission uses continuously varying signals corresponding to the sounds originated by the source.

The first music recordings were purely **analog.** With Thomas Edison's phonograph of 1877, sound waves were recorded in the form of indentations on spinning cylinders covered with malleable tinfoil. A vibrating membrane transferred the sound pressure waves to a metal needle that deformed the soft foil. For playback, the indentations on the cylinder's surface pushed back against the needle and the membrane to reproduce the original sound. In the first phonographs, the sound was amplified mechanically through a horn similar to a trumpet, the classic emblem of the era's "Victrola." Listeners turned the cylinders by a hand crank or a hand-wound clockwork mechanism.

The cylinders, with their fragile coatings, were replaced by the durable flat disks (first invented in 1882 by Emile Berliner) of the gramophone in the first decade of the twentieth century (Brinkley, 1997), and the hand cranks gave way to electric motors. The plastic discs were reproduced in the thousands by pressing a metal *master recording* of the grooves into cylinders of heated plastic. In later electronic equipment, movements of the stylus, or "needle," generated an electric current that was amplified and sent to the speakers. The current activated an *electromagnet* (see Technology Demystified) attached to a vibrating membrane inside the speakers that reproduced the original sound waves. In the recording studio, the vibrating mechanical membrane was replaced by electronic *microphones*, similar to those in telephone hand sets, that convert sound waves to electric currents.

Early records spun around at a rate of 78 *revolutions per minute* (rpm) and had one or two songs per side. The high rpm's gave reasonable sound quality but limited the length of the material. Compilations of songs were literally multipage "albums" in those days; Beethoven's Ninth Symphony came as a collection of several 78 rpm disks inserted in paper sleeves and bound together in a cardboard-covered album.

In 1948 two new recording formats were introduced. The 33⅓ rpm *long-playing* (*LP*) records held 23 minutes of music per side, enough to squeeze the *Ninth* into a two-record set. The *45 rpm* records—the small records with the big holes in the middle for "singles"—held one 3-minute song to a side. Both new formats used better needles and amplification to achieve improved sound that was referred to in the 1950s as *high fidelity.*

Electromagnetic recording rearranges the magnetic fields of metallic particles in the tape according to the electrical current produced by a microphone.

Another new recording medium, **magnetic tape,** came along at the same time through a design borrowed from World War II Germany by 3M Corporation. The flexible plastic tape passed over a *recording head,* an electromagnet that imparted a *residual magnetic field* to tiny magnetic particles stuck to the surface of the tape (see Figure 5.1). The strength of the magnetic field varied with the intensity of the sound waves that hit the microphone at a particular moment. When played back, the tape ran over another electromagnet, the *read head,* which responded to the magnetic patterns stored on the tape by sending an electric current to the speakers. The first tape machines held large reels of quarter-inch tape and chewed up over a foot of it every second to achieve acceptable sound quality.

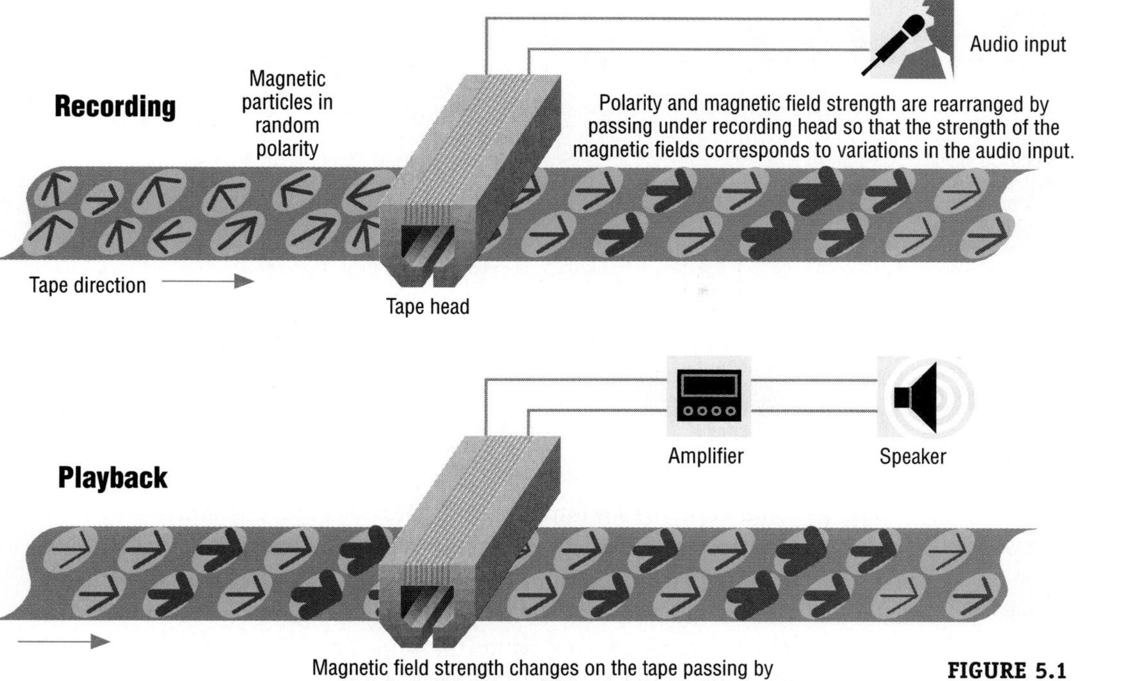
Recording
Magnetic particles in random polarity
Audio input
Polarity and magnetic field strength are rearranged by passing under recording head so that the strength of the magnetic fields corresponds to variations in the audio input.
Tape direction
Tape head
Playback
Amplifier
Speaker
Magnetic field strength changes on the tape passing by the playback head, creating a weak current that reproduces the original audio input.

FIGURE 5.1
How audio recording on magnetic tape works.

Today's *cassette tapes* originated in 1962, after improvements in recording technology made it possible to switch to a narrower tape format that could run at slower speeds.

The listening experience improved dramatically in 1956, when the first stereo recordings came out. Stereo tricks us into hearing the musicians as though they were sitting in different chairs in front of us, whereas the previous *monaural* recordings made it seem that all the sounds were coming from the same point, as the speaker on a cheap television set does. Stereo adds the illusion of depth to the music, in other words. All that was required was to separate the music into two separate sources, or *tracks,* and replay them in such a way that they were received in different ears. Of course, listeners had to "double" their high-fi systems, too, adding an amplifier and an extra speaker and buying a new stereo record player or tape machine.

Compact discs (CDs) are digitally encoded recordings that are played back by lasers.

Compact discs (CDs) arrived as the first digital consumer recording format in 1982. As we saw in Chapter 1, CD recorders convert sound waves into the 1s and 0s of computer data. A powerful laser beam burns the pattern of 1s and 0s (in the form of tiny pits) into the mold for the master recording, which is used to stamp out plastic discs by the millions. During playback, another laser shines on the surface of the disc, but the light is scattered when it hits the pits, turning the laser's reflection off for a brief moment. This pattern of "lights on" and "lights off" regenerates the computer data and, eventually, the original sound (Benson & Whitaker, 1990.) CDs faithfully reproduce the entire range of sound frequencies audible to the human ear and are less vulnerable to dust and scratches.

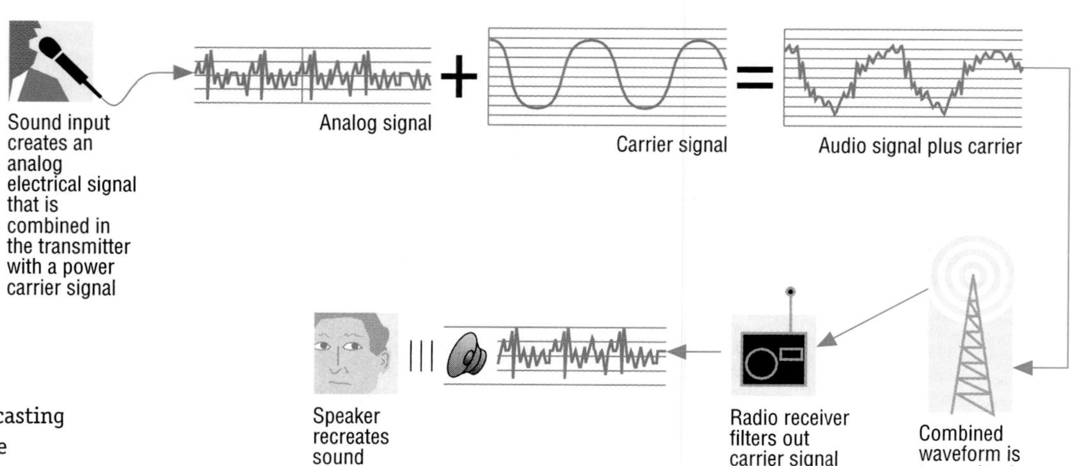
Sound input creates an analog electrical signal that is combined in the transmitter with a power carrier signal
Analog signal
Carrier signal
Audio signal plus carrier
Speaker recreates sound
Radio receiver filters out carrier signal
Combined waveform is transmitted

FIGURE 5.2
How AM radio broadcasting uses radio waves. The announcer's voice is converted to electricity by the microphone. This electrical signal is then combined with a powerful, high-frequency carrier signal and transmitted to the home receiver. The receiver filters out the carrier and recreates the original electrical analog signal, which the loudspeaker converts back to sound energy.

Digital audiotape (DAT), introduced in 1987, has succeeded primarily as a professional recording technology. It combines digitally encoded sound with magnetic tape recording techniques and so offers the advantage of letting the user make his or her own recordings. DAT was literally too good for consumers. The recording industry withdrew support for the standard out of fear that consumers would be able to make their own crystal-clear "pirate" versions of popular records. The record companies prefer consumer technologies that use *digital compression* so that only the first copy, not copies of a copy, sound right.

Music recording technology and computer media are now converging rapidly. The latest recordable CDs (CD-R) and *digital versatile discs* (DVDs; see Chapter 8) are equally at home in the CD bays of personal computers and conventional stereo systems. But files of music data can also be stored on the computer's hard drive or new, high-capacity computer disks (Chapter 8). Another new wrinkle was introduced in 1998 with the Rio personal digital stereo player. It stores CD-quality music downloaded from the Internet on a personal playback device.

The Basics of Radio Transmission and Reception

Radio waves are composed of electromagnetic energy and rise and fall in regular cycles.

Frequency is the number of cycles that waves complete in a set amount of time.

Hertz (Hz) is a measure of the frequency of a radio wave in cycles per second.

About the same time that Edison invented the record player, physicists James Clerk Maxwell and Helmholtz Hertz were conducting their own experiments with electromagnets, studying a new phenomenon known as **radio waves.** Like the waves that we make in our bathtubs when we drop the soap, radio waves rise and fall in regular cycles. The number of cycles that the waves complete in a second is their **frequency** and is measured in **Hertz (Hz).** Radio waves have much higher frequencies than waves in a bathtub and do not require a transmission medium, such as water, to propagate. Radio waves can travel much farther than bathtub waves because the electromagnetic energy they use can be detected at a distance. They are propagated primarily by "line of sight" to distant receiving antennas that are within direct view of the transmitter, but also by electrical conduction through the earth itself or by reflection off an electrically charged layer of the atmosphere, the ionosphere (see Figure 5.2).

Marconi was the first to develop a practical system of radio communication in 1896. At this point, the transmitters could only turn radio energy on and off, so telegraph codes could be transmitted and received, but sound, which required the transmission of continuous waves, could not.

Lee De Forest solved several problems of radio signal generation, detection, and amplification by inventing the **vacuum tube** in 1906. The vacuum tube permitted a weak signal to be both amplified and precisely modulated by controlling the flow of electrical charges inside a small glass enclosure. In 1906, Fessenden made the first radio "broadcast" using a telephone as a microphone. Early radio stations used a variety of frequencies for radio broadcasting, until they were standardized by the *Federal Radio Commission* in 1927. The AM radio band was long fixed at 535–1605 kHz (the k is a symbol for 1000), then extended to 1705 kHz in 1988.

Vacuum tubes can amplify and precisely modulate a weak signal by controlling the flow of electrical charges inside the tube.

AM or **amplitude modulation** refers to the fact that the sound information is carried in the height, or amplitude, of the radio wave.

FM or **frequency modulation** means that the sound information is carried in variations in the frequency of the radio wave.

Digital audio broadcasting is the transmission of radio signals in digital format.

AM is short for **amplitude modulation,** which means that the sound information is carried in variations in the height, or amplitude, of the radio wave. In an AM radio system, the electric current that comes out of a microphone or an electronic recording device is combined with a high-frequency electromagnetic carrier wave that corresponds to the frequency of a particular radio channel. For example, the carrier wave is 540,000 Hz if you have your radio tuned to 540 on the AM dial. The combined wave is amplified and fed into a *radio transmitter,* which is essentially a giant electromagnet. The combined electromagnetic wave induces a weak electric current inside your radio antenna. Then the carrier frequency is removed, and the original audio is recovered (Head, Sterling, & Schofield, 1994).

In 1933 Ed Armstrong, an RCA engineer, developed **FM,** or **frequency modulation,** radio. Though Armstrong argued convincingly and RCA gave him the initial funding, RCA management, including his friend David Sarnoff, delayed FM's introduction. At that point, in the 1930s and 1940s, RCA management was far more interested in developing television, which RCA saw as having more immediate profit potential.

In FM radio, the sound information is carried by variations in the frequency of the radio wave around the central carrier frequency, which is 101,700,000 Hz if you are tuned to FM101.7, for example. Compared to AM, FM has a greater frequency range and less static, so stereo broadcasting was begun in the FM band. AM stereo is in service, but it is much less widely used. Because FM signals can travel only in the line of sight, FM is limited to about a 30-mile range—much less than AM stations that, "on a good night," can be heard hundreds of miles away.

Digital audio broadcasting (DAB) is coming next. It transmits audio that has been converted to computer data, as in a CD recording, to special digital receivers. This will increase the quality of the sound and make radio signals much less susceptible to fading. The digital signal will also include information about the source and content of the music so that we will be able to set our radios to "seek heavy metal" if we so desire. The digital signals will also pack additional channels of information, such as news updates and alerts about travel and weather conditions. DAB has been on the air since 1997 in Europe, but U.S. broadcasters are delaying its introduction until a system that will

INTERNET RECORDINGS. Many computer savvy music fans now download the latest recordings from Internet sites, such as this one operated by mp3.com.

TECHNOLOGY *DEMYSTIFIED*

Experiments with Electromagnetism

Many people remember the day in grade school when the teacher came in with a battery, a length of wire, iron filings, and some rusty nails and said, "Class, today we are going to learn about electromagnetism." That memory is the key to understanding many modern communication systems, so let's refresh it for you.

Your teacher, let's call her Ms. Kotter, wound the wire tightly around one of the iron nails and connected the ends of the wire to the battery. Then she was able to pick up the other nails with the one wrapped in wire. This demonstrated the basic principle of *electromagnetism:* A flowing electric current generates a magnetic field.

Next, Ms. Kotter disconnected the wire and showed you that the magnetized nail could no longer pick up other nails. That proved that the electric current flowing through the wire was what made the nail into a magnet. This is what happens inside your stereo speakers, where an electromagnet tugs back and forth at an iron disc attached to a flexible membrane that beats the air in time to your music.

Although that nail could no longer pick up other nails, it could still pick up the iron filings, something it could not do before. This demonstrated that the nail had a weak residual *magnetic field,* just like the tiny metallic particles on the surface of an audiotape have after they pass under the recording head.

Then Ms. Kotter sprinkled some of the iron filings on a piece of cardboard, reconnected the electromagnet to the battery, and showed you that she could move the filings around the surface of the cardboard by passing the magnet underneath it. This proved that electromagnetic fields act at a distance, just as a radio transmitter affects the antenna on your radio from miles away.

If Ms. Kotter was a very good teacher—and if your school's science budget was up to it—she went one step further. She hooked up the coil of wire to a meter that measured electric current and moved a magnet back and forth through the middle of the coil. As the magnet moved, the needle on the meter twitched, showing that a changing magnetic field induced an electric current in the wire. This is what happens inside your radio antenna and also in the playback head of your tape recorder, converting a magnetic field back to electricity.

transmit the digital signals over existing radio frequencies—without disrupting the existing analog transmissions on the same channel—can be perfected. But radio manufacturers are not waiting to introduce new digital "car PCs" that replace the radio with an integrated CD, radio, mobile radio, and computer navigation system.

The broadcasters are going to have to hurry up if they want to remain the leading source of live sound in the twenty-first century. Many cable television systems have multiple channels of digital audio (see Chapter 7). Satellites have been transmitting audio programming to networks of radio stations for over 20 years, and the new Direct Broadcast Satellite (DBS) TV services also carry dozens of channels of CD-quality digital audio. The next step is to transmit music via satellite directly to compact mobile receivers with wafer-shaped antennas less than two inches across, bypassing earthbound radio stations entirely.

However, it could also be that the future of audio is on the Internet. Hundreds of radio stations now feed their programming to the World Wide Web through sites such as Broadcast.com, and there are many "internet only" channels that offer specialized musical fare ("continuous Nine Inch Nails") or live sportcasts that cannot be found on the air in most locales. Users can also pick their own music from thousands of CDs stored on the Web (Ramstad, 1998) and download it to their portable digital Rio player. Or they can listen to sample cuts from the latest album and even order the CD itself on-line from one of the many electronic music stores that have set up shop on the Internet. Once secure on-line commercial transactions become commonplace—and the concerns of music copyright holders are satisfied—it will be possible to download the music directly to your own (recordable) compact disk or DVD and avoid the music store altogether. And plans are afoot to broadcast the Internet to mobile users as well. The sound quality of live Internet audio is close to that of AM radio, and it keeps improving all the time. Near CD-quality stereo can even be had, if you have a fast enough network connection to download huge audio files in a timely manner.

1. How did phonograph formats change, from Victrola to long play?
2. How do CDs play back music?
3. How does magnetic recording on tape work?
4. What are radio waves?
5. What is the main technical difference between AM and FM radio transmission?
6. How does digital satellite radio broadcasting work?

FORMS AND GENRES

Even before radio, or the phonograph era, popular music was developing out of ethnic and historical traditions into genres that are still present. The roots of American popular music can be traced to several earlier **traditions.** The main ones, arguably, are English, Irish, and Scottish ballads and hymns, such as the Irish dance music still played by the Chieftains; a variety of African vocal music, rhythm, and percussion traditions, such as that done by King Sunny Ade or Ladysmith Black Mambazo; Polish polkas; and German and Austrian waltzes.

Musical traditions are genres passed along from one generation to another.

In the United States, many of these blended into various traditional strains that preceded recording and radio. African American gospel is common as church music and is performed by groups such as Sweet Honey in the Rock. White gospel is sung in churches and in country-western recordings; an example is "Rock of Ages." Appalachian folk songs, such as Emmylou Harris's "Precious Memories," are also still found recorded by country artists. Delta blues songs, such as Robert Johnson's "Crossroads," have been recorded by blues artists such as Eric Clapton. Cajun music is performed and recorded by groups such as Buckwheat Zydeco. Mexican border *rancheras* (love songs) are recorded by artists such as Linda Ronstadt ("Canciones de mi padre").

However, the early hits of the phonograph era were John Philip Sousa marches and **ragtime,** such as that performed by Scott Joplin, along with pop and light songs. Jazz, such as New Orleans dixieland, became popular in the 1920s and 1930s, along with show tunes taken from the new talking movies; Al Jolson's songs from *The Jazz Singer* are an example. **Blues** developed as a music popular among many African Americans but did not cross over much at that time, although blues artists such as John Lee Hooker have become popular since the 1960s (Dominick, 1993).

Ragtime is an early form of jazz most frequently played on the piano.

Blues is an African American musical tradition based primarily on guitar and distinctive plaintive lyrics.

Radio Music Genres

The most popular music formats of the network radio era were big band jazz (the best-known was that of Tommy Dorsey), light classical music, and movie and show tunes. But some important developments in musical genres were happening

MEDIA IMPACT

Teen Idols and Rock 'n' Roll

Although the idea may seem crazy to current teenagers, one of the original teen idols was Frank Sinatra. Sinatra was the top singer in America by 1943.

In the 1950s, music genre specifics had changed a lot from Frank Sinatra's high point. Country and R&B both affected rockabilly, which produced early rock 'n' roll by Elvis Presley, Buddy Holly, and others. Sam Phillips, founder of Sun Records, Elvis's original label, said, "What I need is a white boy who can sing colored." [sic] And he might have added "and country, too." Phillips found his man in Elvis, who sounded white, soulful, and country all at once. Rock 'n' roll was also influenced by commercial white pop music and jazz.

A few years later, in the 1960s, some of the main teen idols were the Beatles and the Rolling Stones, British rockers who were borrowing a lot, including whole songs, from American R&B (such as Chuck Berry's "Roll Over Beethoven") and blues (such as Robert Johnson's "Crossroads"). Another of the early British blues rockers, Eric Clapton, emerged as one of the main stars of the 1990s, though he was not exactly a teen idol anymore. By 1998, music genres and radio station formats had diverged and specialized to the point where teen idols, such as the youthful Hansen brothers, and rock stars in their 50s, such as Clapton, both had big audiences.

on regional networks. For example, a network of southern stations carried the Grand Ole Opry and bluegrass music, such as the Carter Family. These radio formats built on some of the main regional American music traditions mentioned above, such as southern **gospel,** blues, and **bluegrass.** New genres took off in the 1920s and 1930s; one was swing, played by big bands such as Glen Miller and Count Basie. Western "cowboy" music was recorded by traditional artists and movie singing cowboys, such as Gene Autry. "Western swing," a blend of these two genres, is still played by groups such as Asleep at the Wheel.

Gospel originated as southern Protestant religious music, with distinctive but related African American and white forms.

Bluegrass developed from English, Scottish, and Irish roots with similar instrumentation and ballad forms.

Although these genres of music were not played much on national network radio, they were recorded and played on various local and regional stations, and some spread across the country. For example, a blend of bluegrass, gospel, western, and western swing eventually became known as country and western, or country, led by singers such as Hank Williams. It was most popular in the rural south, southwest, and west, but it also followed southern migrants north as they looked for jobs in the industrial midwest and east. Later country singers such as Patsy Cline and Roy Acuff recorded in Nashville but were played in Detroit.

The blues followed African American migrants from the south to Chicago and New York, where a harder, electric blues developed in the 1940s and 1950s that greatly affected rock 'n' roll. For example, rock bands in the 1960s, such as Cream, did versions of Chicago blues songs by Muddy Waters, Robert Johnson, and Howlin' Wolf. African American blues and gospel were blended with elements of pop music into new genres such as rhythm and blues (R&B), which in turn gave rise to soul, including Motown groups such as the Supremes and the Temptations, and later into funk by groups such as Parliament.

Network radio in the 1930s and 1940s also created a number of program genres besides music. Situation comedy series were among the early successes of radio networks. In the early 1930s, for instance, the top network show was *Amos 'n' Andy*. This comedy show, peopled by white actors represented as African Americans, would probably be considered racist now but was very popular then with both black and white audiences. Radio also featured news, drama, sports, quiz shows, soap opera, science fiction, action-adventure, and superhero sagas. In the 1950s, most of these genres moved to television to take advantage of adding visuals, but they were hugely popular in the 1930s and 1940s on network radio. Movies such as *The Shadow* still mine radio serials for plot ideas.

Singers who had started with big bands, such as Frank Sinatra and Doris Day, recorded pop songs that appealed to a wide age group. These songs were ideally suited to network radio, which was still trying to appeal to a broad general audience. The formula began to fail, however, when much of the prime-time radio entertainment audience shifted to television and stations began to leave the networks as management tried to think of ways to attract a more local audience.

STOP IN THE NAME OF LOVE! Motown groups such as the Supremes dominated top 40 radio in the 1960s before the "British invasion."

Music Genres and Radio Formats

In the 1950s, after most stations had dropped away from radio networks, they began to target more segmented audiences with particular formats: programming strategies organized around a playlist of music and focused on a particular genre or audience. The most popular formats were initially middle-of-the-road (MOR), which preserved elements of the old network general-audience formula; rhythm and blues; hold-overs from the Big Band era such as Doris Day and Rosemary Clooney; and country and western.

Top 40. Contemporary hit radio (CHR), or **top 40** was probably invented by Todd Storz in 1949. He wondered why radio could not be more like a jukebox, playing the hit songs that people really wanted to hear the most over and over. Top 40 was the dominant radio format from the 1950s until the early 1970s. In the early 1960s, Bill Drake at KHJ in Los Angeles refined the format into playing only top single records. Casey Kasem varied the formula by doing popularity "countdowns." He also created one of the earliest popular syndicated radio programming services, *American Top 40*. Hundreds of stations around the world still carry his top 40 countdown programs to over 8 million listeners each week.

Top 40 is a radio format that plays only top single records, the top 40 on record sales charts.

In the late 1950s and early 1960s, most of the young audience was listening to the same overall mix of rock 'n' roll, pop, and some R&B, such as The Isley Brothers. In the early 1960s, pop singers like Frankie Avalon gradually gave way on top 40 to 1960s pop groups, such as the Beach Boys (who lifted several tunes and guitar riffs from Chuck Berry), and Motown groups such as the Supremes and the Temptations. Rock was still somewhat unified by top 40 stations until the late 1960s, with Motown, English groups such as the Beatles and the Rolling Stones, and heavy rockers such as Led Zeppelin and Jimi Hendrix all being played on the same "rock" stations (Limmer, 1981).

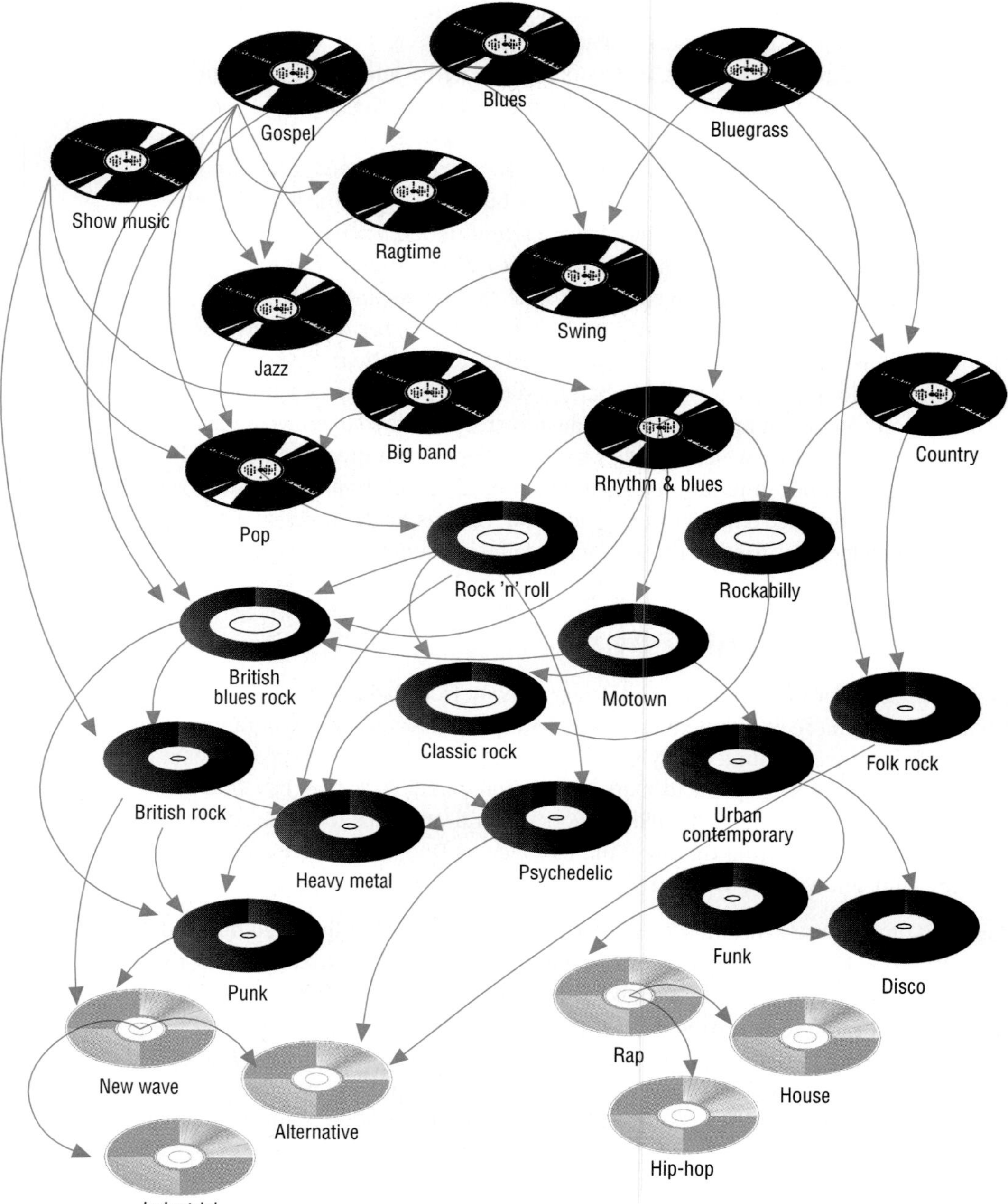

FIGURE 5.3
This chart shows some of the roots of rock music and how it has split into a number of branches over time.

FM and Audience Segmentation. Top 40 declined greatly after 1970, when FM radio stations began to diversify into distinct rock formats, such as album-oriented rock (AOR) or oldies. FM stations began to proliferate and look for ways to differentiate themselves and find more unique and loyal audiences in targeted FM formats: album-oriented rock (Bruce Springsteen), top 40 (Michael Jackson), rock oldies (The Big Bopper), heavy metal (Deep Purple), and adult contemporary (Linda Ronstadt). Other music forms and genres also showed up in FM radio formats:

blues (Robert Cray), R&B (Funkadelic), jazz (Chick Corea), big band (Glenn Miller), gospel, classical, and country and western (Tammy Wynette).

Rock grew from diverse roots and began to fragment or diversify again into a number of branches (see Figure 5.3). Some groups went further back toward their origins. Eric Clapton played blues early in his career and again in the 1990s. Some went the other way, including former blues singer Rod Stewart, who became the 1970s archetype of the pop/rock star. In the 1970s, what had been considered "rock" split into commercial or top 40 (Fleetwood Mac), psychedelic (the Grateful Dead), punk (the Sex Pistols, the Dead Kennedys), disco (KC & the Sunshine Band), country rock (the Eagles), folk rock (Richard Thompson), new wave (Elvis Costello, Duran Duran), heavy metal (Kiss), glam rock (David Bowie), and so on. The 1980s and 1990s added blues rock (George Thoroughgood), grunge rock (Nirvana and Hole), techno (the Information Society), alternative (R.E.M.), industrial (Nine Inch Nails), new age (Enya, John Tesh), ska (The Specials), reggae (Bob Marley, UB 40), rap (Will Smith), gangsta rap (Ice T), and hip-hop (Usher). By the 1990s, dozens of subgenres had descended from 1960s rock, pop, and soul roots. Bands began to describe themselves in terms as specific as "gothic progressive experimental" (Entranced, from Omaha, in 1998). And as they had first done the 1960s, radio stations began to adopt combinations of these new branches of music and others as formats.

GENRE MUTATION. Music genres continue to evolve over time. Take, for example, Marilyn Manson, the "king" of alternative industrial glamour celebrity-rock.

Part of this proliferation was due to the continuing formation of smaller labels and radio stations that gave expression to music subcultures. The increase in labels and stations was in turn the result of technological developments that lowered the price of recording tapes, records, and CDs and the cost of starting radio stations. Record labels could and did focus on very specific kinds of music and audiences. The ability to produce recordings on a desktop computer and distribute them on the Internet without a label or radio airplay further pushes genre mutations.

Proliferation of Genres and Formats. By the 1980s, FM dominated the music-oriented radio formats. More FM licenses were available, because of their shorter geographic reach, which made it logical for a larger number of FM stations to pursue more segmented audiences with increasingly specific formats. Some of the main FM formats are as follows:

Adult contemporary—a mix of oldies and softer rock hits (Celine Dion, the Backstreet Boys)

Top 40 or contemporary hit radio (CHR)—mostly current hits, usually mixing pop (Mariah Carey), alternative (Alanis Morrisette), rock (Metallica), and rap/hip-hop (Will Smith, the Beastie Boys)

Adult hits—a mix of rock (Aerosmith), pop (Barenaked Ladies), and alternative (Matchbox 20)

Country—increasingly subdivided into traditional country (Dolly Parton), contemporary/urban country (Dixie Chicks, Lee Ann Womack), and rock/country blends (Shania Twain)

Modern rock—rock album cuts (often corresponding to music videos) by current groups (Oasis, Everclear), split into hard rock (Hole, Korn), industrial (Marilyn Manson), and other branches

MEDIA IMPACT

As Alternative Becomes Dominant

Music genres and radio formats evolve quickly. Outsider music becomes insider success very quickly. Alternative music was once really that, a less popular, less commercial alternative to other forms of rock and pop. However, success moves music rapidly toward the mainstream. Groups such as Nirvana started as critical outsiders, proposing an alternative form of rock, but radio quickly moved them to the inside as the audience responded. Nirvana singer and leader Curt Cobain's suicide was the latest in a long series of examples of how such rapid success can overwhelm an artist.

Now alternative has become one of the two or three most popular forms of music and, as is also the pattern, has split into a number of fragments. Just on radio, alternative music gets played on a number of formats: "alternative," adult alternative, modern rock, hot adult contemporary, hit alternative, album-oriented rock, and contemporary. Alanis Morrisette's 1998 album *Supposed Former Infatuation Junkie,* debuted on nearly all those formats. Morrisette herself has gone from being "alternative" on a couple of early albums to the biggest female rock star of the late 1990s. Alternative rock standby the Dave Matthews Band crossed over from alternative to active rock playlists. Early alternative rock bands such as Smashing Pumpkins, Soundgarden, and Stone Temple Pilots came to be widely played on a variety of rock and contemporary formats.

For Further Research:

If you want to learn more about how the radio industry categorizes and uses contemporary music in its formats, and if you are using InfoTrac College Edition, try a search on topics such as Radio-Formats. A search on those terms produced the following article, among others:

Broadcasting & Cable, May 20, 1996 v126 n22 p51(2). "Alternative rock in the mainstream; number of radio stations carrying the format multiplies." Donna Petrozzello.

Classic rock—1960s (the Rolling Stones), 1970s (the Cars) and, on some stations, 1980s rock (R.E.M.)

Soft adult contemporary—a mix of softer current songs (such as Celine Dion or Mariah Carey) and oldies (such as Elton John); often mixed with talk forms, news, and weather, particularly on drive-time shows aimed at commuters

1. What were the main original traditions in popular music?
2. How have radio formats changed after the decline of radio networks?
3. What is top 40? How has it changed?
4. How has rock music evolved? What were its roots? How has its audience segmented since the 1960s?
5. How have radio formats evolved since 1970?
6. What are the top formats now on FM? On AM?

Oldies—1950s and 1960s rock (the Beatles), pop (Elvis), and soul (Martha and the Vandellas)

Alternative rock—originally a more "authentic" alternative to rock, metal, and pop; increasingly the mainstream of current "rock" (Alanis Morrisette, the Dave Matthews Band, Third Eye Blind)

Urban contemporary–R&B—African American music, rap (Will Smith, Puff Daddy), R&B (Luther Vandross, Cypress Hill), dance music (Tina Turner, Taana Gardner), sometimes with Hispanic sounds

Latin—subdivided both by origin (Mexican—Pepe Aguilar; Caribbean/tropical/salsa—Frankie Negron, The Music Club) and by music genre (dance music—Salsa; traditional—Mexican love songs; Latin pop—Enrique Iglesias; Latin rock—Los Fabulosos Cadillacs)

Music was not the only game on radio. As stations specialized, news, talk, weather, and sports information grew in importance. Many AM stations tend to emphasize news, talk, and sports, where music quality matters less. However, a number of FM stations also feature a mixture of talk, call-ins, music, news headlines, and weather aimed at a broad audience during morning and afternoon commuting hours (drive time). Morning shows on major stations increasingly reflect this more "talky" drive-time format. Major syndicated talk shows, such as those featuring Rush Limbaugh, Howard Stern, and Dr. Laura Schlesinger, are also carried on major AM and FM stations.

Because of AM's broader signal reach, many stations center on smaller towns and rural areas where population is less dense and where a broad-based middle-of-the-road, country/western, or oldies format makes the most sense. And AM increasingly caters to minority groups, such as Latinos, as the dominant formats move to FM.

SHOCK JOCK. Howard Stern sparked the revival of network radio with his off-color commentary. However, in radio industry lexicon, Howard is merely an "announcer."

Nearly all of these formats are for commercial radio. Several noncommercial patterns have also developed on the FM stations using frequencies reserved for noncommercial alternatives. These include

Classical music—baroque classical (Bach) up through modern "serious" music (Phillip Glass)

Experimental rock and folk—mostly found on college stations

Jazz—both current (Herbie Hancock) and traditional (Louis Armstrong) found on both commercial and noncommercial stations

A number of stations, both AM and FM, currently run the national **PBS** morning and evening news and public affairs programs *Morning Edition* and *All Things Considered.* A very few do primarily local news and public affairs.

PBS is the Public Broadcasting Service, which offers news and other programming to radio stations.

INDUSTRY ORGANIZATION

The key elements of the recording industry are the **talent** (the singers and musicians), the recording studios and technical producers, the recording companies and their various labels, the distributors, and the retailers. Also important to musicians' success are their songwriters, managers, and arrangers. They all hope to get a contract from a record company to make money.

Talent in media refers to the newspeople, actors, and singers in front of the microphones and cameras.

Groups form at a local level. There are tens of thousands of aspiring local groups and singers throughout the United States. For example, the college club scene in Athens, Georgia, produced the B-52s and R.E.M., among other groups; East Lansing, Michigan, produced the Verve Pipe; and Burlington, Vermont, spawned Phish. Such acts perform locally, try to get concert or dance bookings out of town, become better known, and make a recording to circulate to record companies. A number achieve regional status as traveling acts that circulate in a state or region. A few are discovered and make it big, but most break up, whereupon the more talented musicians form new groups and move on. Talent scouts from record companies are always looking around college towns and concert circuits for new acts, but competition is fierce.

Record Companies

Recording companies bring promising acts into the recording studio, where engineers and arrangers capture their music on tape for an album or single. Thus recording companies are the main gatekeepers of the music business; they decide who gets recorded. Falling equipment costs now enable groups to buy their own recording equipment and make their own tapes, but the recording companies still decide who gets distributed and promoted nationally on the radio, in concerts, and record stores. But the Internet now provides an independent distribution route for unknown bands.

Some of the major recording companies have a number of separate labels, each with a separate image and intended market segment. Sony Records has the Columbia and Epic labels; Time-Warner has Reprise, Elektra, and Atlantic; RCA has Arista and Ariola; Polygram has Mercury, Deutsche Grammophon, and A&M; Thorn/EMI has EMI, and Manhattan; and MCA has Motown and Geffen. Recorded music is very much an international industry. Sony is a Japanese company, and RCA is owned by the German firm Bertelsmann, Polygram by the Dutch Company Philips, and MCA by Seagram of Canada (who bought it from Matsushita of Japan). Some who watch the recording industry wonder whether foreign owners will pursue kinds of musical content different from domestic owners.

Recording companies decide which albums and songs to promote via radio, billboards, newspaper ads, and magazine ads. An important part of the promotion of the most promising groups with national potential is making a music video for MTV, VH-1, or other music-oriented cable channels. Since MTV came on the scene in 1981, it has had great influence on which records become popular and even what gets played on radio stations. MTV was originally focused on heavy metal but has since diversified to offer more rap, alternative, and other genres. MTV has over 50 million subscribers and reaches the whole country—a new national network for music. It is now difficult to have a radio hit without having a music video.

The record companies distribute recordings in a variety of ways. Rack jobbers supply the recordings seen in sale racks at large retail stores like Wal-Mart. Other kinds of distributors sell to retail music stores that specialize in recordings and related videos. Increasingly, this retail business is dominated by big chain record stores, including Sam Goody, Musicland, and Tower, and by huge general retailers such as Wal-Mart. The power of such retailers was apparent when, in 1997, Wal-Mart refused to carry certain recordings that it considered offensive; its action had major effects on sales by those artists, such as Marilyn Manson.

Record clubs such as Columbia and BMG sell CDs and cassettes directly through the mail on a large scale. These clubs are all big enough to deal directly with the record companies. Specific recordings are also pitched via TV commercials for direct-mail ordering. And a growing number of people buy albums through Internet stores, such as CD-Now or Amazon.com.

Radio Stations

Radio stations vary greatly in the size and complexity of their staff. The manager oversees planning, audience development, ratings, and sales. The program director supervises the air sound, playlists, DJs, and announcers. There is usually a music director who plans the **playlists.** Producers are usually required for anything more complex than simple announcing, such as talk shows and drive-time shows. Most stations also have a news director. Commercial stations have a sales manager and an advertising sales staff. Because almost 75 percent of radio advertising is local, the advertising sales staff is crucial for selling local advertising, as well as working with national advertisers who might want to sell national spot ads in the local market. And someone has to keep the station on the air, so there has to be an engineer on duty.

Playlists are the songs picked to fit the radio station's format and target audience.

Increasing numbers of stations use outside programming services for both music and talk shows. Many stations buy complete, packaged music services designed by outside experts who look at the prospective audience, consider the format options, and evaluate what has worked in similar markets. This approach has reduced the DJ's autonomy considerably since the more freewheeling days of the 1950s and 1960s, when DJs often picked their own records to play. Now, even the local announcer is being cut out, as local ads, weather, and song announcements are recorded at an ownership group's central production facility and shipped to stations to be played or are relayed directly via satellite. And as station groups acquire multiple stations in each market, they often economize by consolidating their management and sales staffs.

Most radio stations are privately owned and operated on a commercial basis, which creates considerable uniformity of approach. However, radio does offer a fairly diverse set of stations. There are also many noncommercial stations—owned by universities, schools, cities, and foundations—in radio. Many of these have a noncommercial programming line that lets them offer diverse cultural, entertainment, and information programs. In particular, college radio stations and PBS radio member stations may offer noncommercial alternatives.

Radio stations were once owned by many kinds of individuals and groups, but are rapidly consolidating into a few large radio groups. The largest **group owners** of radio stations are Clear Channel Communications (454 stations), Capstar Broadcasting Partners (299), Infinity (160), Chancellor Media (106), Cox Radio (59), Heftal Broadcasting (39), ABC (29), Susquehanna Radio (21), and Emmis Broadcasting (13). Most of these groups were not among the top ten 5 years ago but rather achieved this status after ownership deregulation (*USA Today,* June 7, 1998; *Media Week,* Oct. 12, 1998). Since the 1996 Telecommunications Act deregulated ownership, concentration of station ownership in the hands of new, nonlocal groups has increased dramatically.

Group owners own a number of broadcast stations but do not always provide them with common programming, as a network would.

Some of the traditional networks still carry news and other national programming for all or most of their **affiliate** stations. Although most radio advertising is local, there is still interest in national ad coverage, which encourages some network-level advertising. Some large groups, such as Infinity, have limited-content networks for their owned-and-operated stations, even though not all their stations have the same format. For example, all Infinity stations carry Infinity's syndicated

Affiliates in broadcasting are stations that contract to use the programming of and share advertising/financing with a network.

Syndicators rent or license radio programs to other media companies for broadcast.

Howard Stern show, and Infinity also syndicates the show to other stations in other markets. There are 20 to 25 main **syndicators,** such as Mediamerica, New York, which has Patrick Buchanan and Rush Limbaugh.

A variety of radio programming services are also available. Full program-service companies, such as Bonneville, provide completely automated formats, such as easy listening music. Bonneville also created the disco format in the 1970s. Full-service automation is popular because of the wave of mergers sweeping the radio industry. Locally programmed automation systems are also becoming cheaper; for example, a fully programmable system that handles up to 300 CDs, as well as tape machines for commercial and announcement inserts, costs under $10,000.

The noncommercial National Public Radio and American Public Radio systems supply national news, features, syndicated music, and other programs to public stations around the country. Their main national news shows, *Morning Edition* and *All Things Considered,* are very popular among radio news audiences. Other, smaller networks, such as the Pacifica network based in California, have survived and even grown.

STOP & REVIEW

1. **How do singers, groups, and writers get connected with recording companies?**
2. **What are record labels?**
3. **How are records distributed and sold?**
4. **How are radio station affiliates related to networks?**
5. **How have radio networks developed since the 1950s?**
6. **What kinds of radio services are syndicated?**

AUDIENCES FOR AUDIO MEDIA

Music audiences seem to show a steady trend toward segmentation, even fragmentation. In the 1950s, most young people listened to the same pop and rock music, although there were already separately defined audiences for rhythm and blues and country and western. In the 1960s, many young people thought of themselves as a broad cultural movement, unified in large part by rock music, but that unity broke down in the 1970s.

The 1970s and 1980s saw a fragmentation of the youth audience into a variety of subcultures. Disco (such as that recorded by Men at Work) started with the gay subculture to become the main 1970s dance music. Punk rock, such as that performed by the Sex Pistols and the Clash, started in the 1970s as an expression of extreme alienation from both adult culture and most existing rock music. Industrial and techno/rave music in the 1990s, like that of Nine Inch Nails and Marilyn Manson, may be linked to the technologically sophisticated descendants of punk sensibility, the cyberpunks, or to "dark alternative" or Gothic subculture.

Although their tastes may be fragmented, people still buy a lot of recordings. Listening to recordings is increasing steadily. Spending on recordings went up roughly 10 percent per year in the 1980s and 3 to 4 percent per year in the 1990s. Overall, spending on musical recordings has risen considerably, from an average of about $25 per person in 1985 to roughly $56 in 1998. Over two-thirds of Americans buy music in CD format, just under a third on cassette, and almost none on vinyl records.

Two-thirds of Americans age 12 and over still listen to radio at least briefly each day, and nearly all (96 percent) listen at least once a week (Petrozello, 1996),

TABLE 5.1 Radio Formats and Audiences

Format	Number of Stations	Typical Content	Target Audience Sex	Target Audience Age
Country	2,491	The Judds	Male/female	35–55
News/talk	1,111	Rush Limbaugh	Mostly male	25–55
Adult contemporary	902	Celine Dion	Male/female	25–45
Oldies	755	Beach Boys	Male/female	25–45
Adult standards	551	Eric Clapton	Male/female	25–45
Spanish	474	Shakira	Male/female	25–55
Religion	404	Dr. Dobson	Male/female	35–55
Contemporary hit radio	358	Spice Girls	Mostly female	12–55
Soft adult contemporary	346	Elton John	Male/female	25–55
Rock	262	Pantera	Mostly male	18–35
Adult hits, hot adult contemporary	260	Sarah McLaughlin	Male/female	25–45
Southern gospel	255	Sweet Honey	Male/female	25–55
Classic rock	240	Led Zeppelin	Mostly male	25–45
Sports	220	College football	Mostly male	18–55
Black gospel	208	Mighty Gospel Tones	Male/female	35–55
Classic hits	172	Beatles	Male/female	25–45
Urban, R&B	169	Puff Daddy	Male/female	25–45
Contemporary Christian	159	Amy Grant	Male/female	25–55
New, modern rock	137	R.E.M.	Male/female	18–35
Modern adult contemporary	134	Indigo Girls	Male/female	25–45
Alternative rock	94	Matchbox 20	Male/female	18–35
Jazz	75	Miles Davis	Mostly male	35–55
Variety	50	varied	Male/female	25–55
Easy listening	49	Michael Bolton	Male/female	25–55
Classical, fine arts	44	Pavarotti	Male/female	35–55

Source: Broadcasting & Cable, 126(6) (February 5, 1996), 41.

but listenership has been steadily declining. Average listenership in 1998 was 22 hours per week per person, down slightly from 23 hours in 1994. Only about 20 percent listen to radio networks; most listen to local programs, although the audiences for certain kinds of syndicated or network programs, such as talk by Rush Limbaugh, Dr. Laura Schlesinger, Howard Stern, and others, are growing. People listen at home (45 percent), at work (25 percent), and at other locations. Radio listening behind the wheel is rising: 68 percent of people 12 or over listen to radio in a car at least once a week (Merli, 1998).

Radio formats have fragmented along with music genres. The number of stations playing the formats listed in Table 5.1 is a rough indication of their popularity. The formats listed in Table 5.1 have fairly distinct listening audiences. The focus on youth cultures is due to the fact that teenagers and young adults are both the heaviest buyers of recorded music and the main listeners to music formats on radio.

1. **How are audiences for radio changing?**
2. **How are radio audiences related to music cultures and subcultures?**
3. **Is radio listening going up or down?**
4. **What are the target audiences for some of the main radio formats?**

MEDIA IMPACT

Is Radio Listening on the Wane?

Americans, from children to the elderly, have a constantly increasing array of media choices. Where does a traditional medium like radio fit in? Some long-term research indicates a very gradual decline in radio listening, as other media, including many ways of listening to music, news, and talk, encroach on its audience.

However, radio also seems to adapt very well to changing circumstances. People tune in radio stations over the Internet and listen while they surf the net. In fact, in the late 1990s, radio stations were rushing to get their "broadcasts" on the Internet. People are also spending more time in cars and, despite the availability of CD and cassette players in most cars, are also spending more time listening to radio as they drive.

Imagine yourself a radio program director. Want to know what the latest trends are? Learn how to keep abreast of the radio audience by using the World Wide Web to find current audience habits on radio. If you are using InfoTrac College Edition, try the following search terms: Radio-Audience. Try the same keywords using a World Wide Web search engine. In 1998, such a search found the following article, which gave estimates of the total radio audience:

Broadcasting & Cable, July 15, 1996 v126 n30 p34(1) "Radio's national audience at 210 million." (Statistical Research Inc. report) (Brief Article) Donna Petrozzello.

Another article noted that cars are now the main place where people listen to the radio:

Broadcasting & Cable, Jan 5, 1998 v128 n1 p40(1) "Listening while driving most popular." (Research Director Inc.) (Radio) John Merli.

POLICY AND ETHICAL ISSUES

The radio and recording industries are faced with a variety of policy and ethical issues.

Radio Licensing and Regulation

Initially, government officials, such as the 1920s Secretary of Commerce Herbert Hoover, hoped that industry self-regulation would be adequate to allocate radio frequencies and avoid frequency interference between stations, but chaos was the result. The Federal Radio Commission, established by the Radio Act of 1927, standardized frequency designations and procedures. Most of its rules were absorbed into the more comprehensive Federal Communications Commission (FCC) created by the Communications Act of 1934.

The FCC adopted more systematic procedures for granting radio licenses. However, the FCC's "public interest" standard for reviewing and renewing licenses has proven too vague to provide a basis for denying license renewal to misbehaving broadcasters. The FCC had enough power to compel compliance with the rules on transmitter power, height, and frequency use that it imposed to avoid frequency interference. The FCC created rules about ownership, concentration and cross-ownership, obscenity and indecency in radio content, and the role of networks and affiliates.

What gives the government the right to regulate broadcasting? Aside from simply preventing frequency interference, the basic rationale is that the communications spectrum is a scarce resource that should be run in the public interest. The licensing process is the mechanism through which the government exercises that guidance.

Radio Ownership and Control Rules

The Telecommunications Act of 1996 further refined a number of FCC rules about ownership, competition, and frequency allocation. Previous policies limited ownership first to a maximum of 5 TV stations, 5 AM stations, and 5 FM stations. That limit was later raised to 12 TV stations, 12 AM stations, and 12 FM stations. The Telecommunications Act of 1996 eliminated the national limits altogether.

Until 1992, one owner could not have more than one newspaper, one AM/FM combination, or one television station per city or market. Cross-ownership of radio, television, and newspapers was deregulated in 1992, and cross-ownership with cable TV was deregulated in 1996. Under the 1996 act, local ownership caps increase with market size from a total of 5 stations in a market with 14 or fewer commercial stations to 8 stations among 45 or more stations. The local caps remain in place to prevent group owners from monopolizing local markets.

Ownership and Diversity. The changes in ownership rules in 1996 initiated a striking **concentration of ownership** that may threaten diversity of content. Fewer owners are local residents, who presumably directly reflect local interests. Fewer owners are minorities. Minority ownership dropped from 312 stations in 1995 to 284 in 1997, especially on the FM dial, where frequencies are more desirable and more sought after (Irving, 1998).

Concentration of ownership occurs when media are owned by a small number of individuals, government agencies, or corporations.

Fewer stations are programmed locally because, as we have seen, group owners often supply programming from a central source. For example, one of the major groups, Capstar, programs for all of its southern stations from one central facility in Austin, Texas, even providing voicing for local weather and ads. The local stations are automated and play just the pre-recorded programming.

The counterargument is that concentrated ownership may actually provide more format diversity. When one group owns 6 to 8 stations in a market, they will target each one at a different interest group. For example, Capstar bought six stations in Waco, Texas. Three of them had very similar country formats. Capstar changed one to album-oriented rock and targeted the others at different country audience segments.

After people realized that few noncommercial stations had emerged from the initial scramble for AM licenses in the 1920s and 1930s, some FM frequencies were reserved for noncommercial and educational use. Frequencies are reserved in each market, typically at the lower end of the FM band. This provision has made both experimental college stations and independent foundation stations possible, and it laid the basis for the current Public Broadcasting Service and National Public Radio. This element of diversity remains unaffected by the consolidation of commercial ownership that is under way.

1. What was changed by the Communications Act of 1934?
2. What is the Federal Communications Commission (FCC)?
3. Why does the concentration of radio ownership cause concern?
4. What are the rules on concentration of radio ownership?

Networks and Program Control

Other rules limit radio and television network control over content creation and production. In 1938 the FCC initiated hearings about chain broadcasting to examine the control of radio networks over talent and affiliated stations. The resulting 1941 rules gave radio affiliates more autonomy, allowed them to refuse to carry programs without fear of retaliation, and put networks out of the talent-booking business.

With the decline of network radio in the United States, the question of network control became much less pressing. Although networks, programming services, news services, and syndicated programs all have some power over programming on a number of stations, the overall picture is fairly diverse.

However, the rise in group ownership may lead to new abuses. The old Chain Broadcasting rules protect affiliates, not owned-and-operated stations. Now that hundreds of stations are owned and controlled by the same groups, they could use their market power to manipulate talent or control the fortunes of popular music acts.

The First Amendment and Freedom of Speech

Freedom of speech protects political speech, defines and sets limits on indecent or obscene speech.

Freedom of speech continues to be a focus for both radio broadcasting and the recording industry. The recording industry has traditionally been lightly scrutinized. It has been considered analogous to publishing in that it doesn't involve use of a scarce public resource, such as the airwaves; it has a large degree of competition; and exposure to recorded music is, in principle, entirely voluntary.

Obscene speech depicts sexual conduct in a way that appeals to prurient interests in a manner that is "patently offensive" to community standards, and lacks serious artistic, political, or scientific value.

Obscenity and Indecency. The recording industry exercised a certain degree of self-censorship up through the 1960s. Groups that used **obscene** language or graphic sexual references were usually excluded from the major labels. This situation changed greatly in the late 1960s, as many of the major rock groups carried by major labels began to use more graphic language and explicit themes. This trend continued until challenged by groups of parents and others concerned about exposure to recordings that contain violence, sexist and racist imagery, and graphic language. In 1989, Tipper Gore, wife of then Senator Albert Gore, led a group that pushed in congressional hearings for warning labels about explicit or graphic lyrics on record and CD covers. A number of record labels now place such warnings on their covers, but the effectiveness of these warnings has been questioned. Some think the warnings simply attract more attention.

Radio has been more closely scrutinized under the rationale that the airwaves are a scarce resource to be used in the public interest. The FCC has maintained a series of standards restricting obscene or indecent speech. Up through the 1970s, certain words could not be used, and broadcasters were held responsible even for call-in programs to make sure that prohibited language was not broadcast. Comic George Carlin developed a comedy routine in that era about the "Seven Dirty Words You Can't Say on Radio." Those prohibitions were challenged in court (see Chapter 14), but the FCC still restricts speech that is considered **indecent**—that is,

Indecent speech is graphic language that pertains to sexual or excretory functions.

that uses graphic language pertaining to sexual or excretory functions. The FCC prohibits such language during daytime and evening prime time but has created late-night spots that are a "safe harbor" for more explicit kinds of speech. Despite the prohibition, "shock jocks" such as Howard Stern routinely violate the rule, are fined, and consider paying the fine as a cost of doing business.

STOP & REVIEW

1. What came out of the Chain Broadcasting hearings?
2. What are the limits on freedom of speech in radio broadcasts?
3. What are the limits on freedom of speech in recordings?
4. What is a copyright?

Intellectual Property in Recordings and Radio

Reuse of copyrighted music, syndicated talk shows, and other intellectual property has been a major issue for both radio and recordings. When artists record a piece of music written by someone else, whether for direct sale as a recording or for broadcast on the radio, they have to obtain permission and usually pay a royalty, a fee charged for use of the writers' intellectual property. Some well-known court cases have been fought over whether an artist used another's basic melody. This problem has been accentuated with the rise, in rap music and multimedia, of *sampling,* where artists record and reuse bits, or samples, of existing works. Courts are trying to decide how much has to be sampled to require getting permission and payment of royalties.

Distribution of music over the Internet raises another thorny copyright and intellectual property problem. Virtually flawless digital recordings can be transmitted over the Internet for recording on a hard drive, digital tape, disc, or recordable CD. Technical solutions are being sought to prevent illegal copying and transmission, while permitting the legal sale of music over the Internet.

Also complex is the **licensing** of recorded music for play over the radio. Copyright law requires payment for performance of work copyrighted by an artist, including the playing of a recording over the radio. Two main music-licensing groups—the American Society of Composers, Authors and Publishers (ASCAP) and Broadcast Music Incorporated (BMI)—serve as intermediaries between recording artists and radio stations. Radio stations get licenses for the music listed by the music-licensing group in return for a fee, usually 1 to 2 percent of the station's gross income. ASCAP or BMI then pays the copyright holders, according to how often each song is played.

Licensing is an agreement granting permission to use a copyrighted or trademarked work, for an agreed-on fee.

SUMMARY AND REVIEW

WHAT KIND OF MUSIC INDUSTRY EXISTED BEFORE THE PHONOGRAPH?

Music was performed live for audiences. It was also printed as sheet music and sold for home performance. The phonograph made casual listening easier and increased the sizes of audiences for music.

HOW DID RADIO CHANGE THE MUSIC INDUSTRY?

It further increased the reach of musical performances. It also increased the size of the audience to a truly mass audience and emphasized performers over composers. It created national audiences for music but also permitted regional genres—such as country and western and blues—to evolve.

WHAT WERE THE KEY DEVELOPMENTS THAT LED TO RADIO BROADCASTING?

Marconi pioneered radio as a form of two-way communication. The development of the vacuum tube by De Forest was crucial. It permitted continuous sound-wave transmission and reception, beyond the on/off transmission that had sufficed for transmission of coded messages in wireless telegraph systems. Other crucial developments included better microphones, amplifiers, and tuners and more powerful transmitters.

HOW DID RADIO BROADCASTING AFFECT THE RECORDING INDUSTRY?

At first, the sales of the recording industry fell off, as people moved to purchase radios instead. Over the long run, the recording industry came to rely on radio to make people aware of artists and recordings that they could purchase.

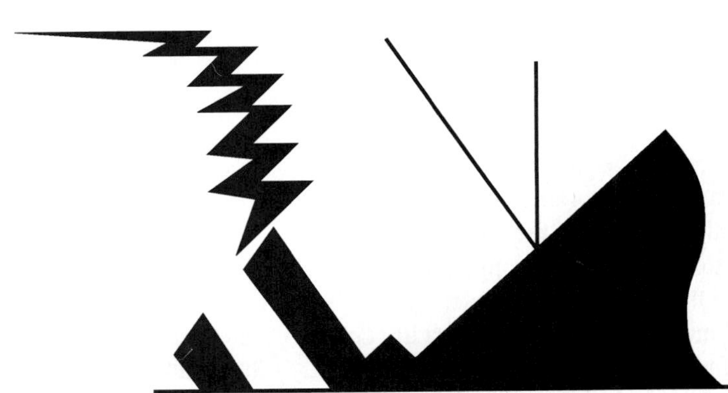

WHAT WAS TOLL BROADCASTING, AND HOW DID IT AFFECT ADVERTISING ON RADIO?

Toll broadcasting was an early form of advertising developed by AT&T. Companies paid to have messages and advertising carried by AT&T's radio network, rather like the toll paid to carry a message over the telephone. The term *commercial,* often used to describe an advertisement, comes from AT&T's accounting terminology.

WHAT WERE THE MAIN MUSIC GENRES IN THE 1920S AND 1930S?

The most popular, particularly on the national radio networks, was probably big band jazz. Country, blues, classical, Broadway tunes, and gospel were also popular.

WHO FORMED THE MAIN RADIO NETWORKS?

The main radio networks were put together by David Sarnoff at RCA/NBC and William Paley at CBS.

WHAT KINDS OF PROGRAMMING CHARACTERIZED RADIO NETWORKS DURING THEIR HIGH POINT?

Network radio relied largely on music but carried news, sports, comedy, variety shows, soap operas, dramas, suspense, and action adventures as well. Many of those genres moved to television after 1948.

WHEN AND WHY DID RADIO NETWORKS DECLINE?

After television coverage and audiences began to grow, around 1948, network radio began to lose much of its audience to television. Some of the types of entertainment it had relied on worked better for the mass audience with a visual component on television. Radio came to rely more on music, which could be programmed locally by disk jockeys playing records.

WHEN DID FM RADIO BEGIN TO INCREASE IN IMPORTANCE? AND WHY?

FM radio began to increase as more receivers became available in the 1960s. It also prospered as FM stereo became widely available and appreciation of with music quality increased among the audience.

WHAT KINDS OF RADIO NETWORKS EXIST NOW?

Some of the traditional networks continued, although some, like ABC, created more specialized subnetworks. New networks were being created by new ownership groups, such as Infinity, around popular syndicated shows, such as Howard Stern's. National Public Radio also emerged as a significant new news and public affairs programming service, linking most of the nation's noncommercial, or public, radio stations.

HOW DID PHONOGRAPH FORMATS CHANGE, FROM VICTROLA TO LONG PLAY?

The original Victrola played music off cylinders. A needle picked up vibrations from grooves in the surface. The music was not electronically amplified. The next phonographs used flat records. Later ones added electronic amplification of the sound. Speeds were reduced from 78 rpm to 45 or 33⅓ rpm, and records were made larger so that they could play more music, longer. Finally, stereo sound was introduced.

HOW DO COMPACT DISCS WORK?

Whereas phonographs reproduce analog sound from grooves in records, CDs reproduce sound digitally, from 1s and 0s recorded as pits on the CD surface. The digital signal is then reconverted to analog form and sent as electrical impulses to the amplifier and then to the speakers.

HOW DOES MAGNETIC RECORDING ON TAPE WORK?

The tape passes over a recording head, an electromagnet, that rearranges the magnetic fields on the tape according to an electric current produced by a microphone. When playing back, the tape runs over another electromagnetic head, which responds to the patterns stored on the tape and generates another modulated current that is sent to a loudspeaker.

WHAT ARE THE MAIN TECHNICAL DIFFERENCES BETWEEN AM AND FM RADIO TRANSMISSION?

AM refers to amplitude modulation. The sound information is carried in variations in the height, or amplitude, of the radio wave. FM stands for frequency modulation. The sound information is carried in variations in the frequency the of radio wave. In general, AM signals carry farther than FM, which travels strictly in the line of sight, so there is more potential for frequency interference among AM stations. Therefore, fewer AM licenses can be granted in the same cities. FM has higher-fidelity sound characteristics than AM (a greater frequency range, cleaner sound, and less static), so stereo broadcasting was begun in FM.

WHAT WERE THE MAIN ORIGINAL TRADITIONS IN POPULAR MUSIC?

Blues is an African American musical tradition based primarily on guitar and distinctive plaintive lyrics. Gospel originated as southern Protestant religious music, with distinctive but related African American and white forms. Appalachian music developed from English, Scottish, and Irish roots with similar instrumentation and ballad forms.

WHAT ARE RADIO FORMATS?

A format is a particular radio programming strategy oriented around a playlist of music and focused on a particular genre or audience.

HOW HAVE RADIO FORMATS CHANGED SINCE THE DECLINE OF RADIO NETWORKS?

Radio programming became decentralized as local stations pulled away from networks. Stations began to decide on their own formats, responding to local audiences and local competition from other stations. As more stations entered the market, formats tended to become more narrowly focused on segmented audiences.

WHAT IS THE TOP 40 FORMAT?

Top 40 is characterized by playing only top single records, usually the top 40 on record sales charts.

HOW HAVE RADIO FORMATS EVOLVED SINCE 1970?

Radio formats have tended to reflect the evolution of pop and rock music since 1970. They have followed the segmentation of the audience, and fragmentation of the music genre. This trend has been accentuated by a steadily increasing number of FM stations, which have had to specialize to find audiences.

WHAT ARE THE TOP FORMATS NOW ON FM? ON AM?

On FM, the main formats are adult contemporary; album-oriented rock (AOR); alternative; classic rock; contemporary country; classical music; and urban contemporary, usually focused on African American music, rap, hip-hop, dance, and Hispanic. Several patterns developed on the FM stations reserved for noncommercial alternatives:

classical music; experimental or alternative rock and folk, found largely on college stations; jazz, found on both commercial and noncommercial stations; and news and public affairs. AM stations tend to emphasize news, call-in talk shows, and talk and sports. AM stations also tend to serve smaller towns and rural areas, where the population is less dense and where a - broad-based, middle-of-the-road, country and western, or oldies format makes more sense.

HOW HAVE ROCK MUSIC AUDIENCES CHANGED SINCE THE 1960S?

They have segmented, fragmenting into smaller groups.

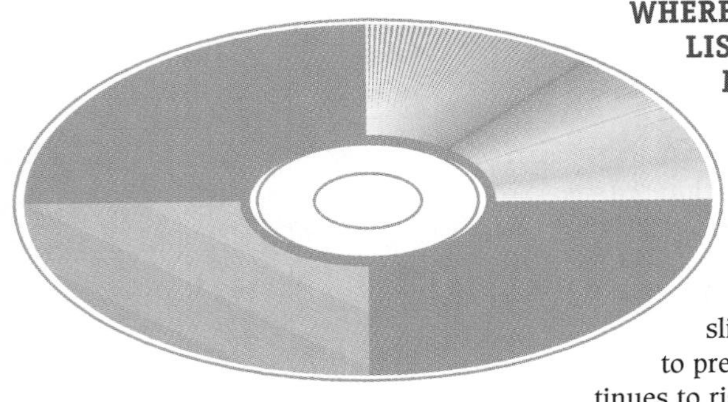

WHERE DO PEOPLE LISTEN TO RADIO MOST?

People listen to radio at home, in their cars, and at work, but overall radio listenership continues to decline slightly, while listening to pre-recorded music continues to rise.

WHAT ARE THE KEY ASPECTS OF RECORDING AND RADIO INDUSTRY ORGANIZATION?

They include the talent (the singers and musicians), the recording studios and technical producers, the recording company, the distributors, and retailers.

WHAT ARE RECORD LABELS?

Labels of record companies are particular names for a group of recordings, which usually represent a consistent type of music. One company may own several diverse labels.

HOW ARE RECORDS DISTRIBUTED AND SOLD?

Record companies decide which albums and songs to promote through radio, billboards, newspaper ads, magazine ads, and music videos. The record companies distribute recordings in a variety of ways, including rack jobbers, retail music stores, big chain stores, and record clubs.

HOW ARE RADIO STATION AFFILIATES RELATED TO NETWORKS?

Affiliates in broadcasting are stations that contract to use the programming of a network and to share advertising and advertising revenues with it. Networks also have owned-and-operated stations (O&Os). Group owners own a number of broadcast stations but do not necessarily provide them with common programming, as a network would.

WHAT WAS CHANGED BY THE COMMUNICATIONS ACT OF 1934?

The Communications Act of 1934 defined the broadcast band, standardized frequency designations, and created a more powerful regulatory body, the Federal Communications Commission (FCC). The FCC devised more systematic procedures for granting radio licenses and rules on transmitter power, height, and frequency use. The FCC imposed rules about ownership, concentration and cross-ownership; obscenity and indecency in radio content; and the role of networks and affiliates.

WHAT WAS CHANGED BY THE TELECOMMUNICATIONS ACT OF 1996?

The Telecommunications Act of 1996 changed FCC rules about station ownership limits. It eliminates previous station ownership limits. For radio, there are no national limits, and local ownership caps increase with market size from a total of 5 stations in a market with 14 or fewer commercial stations to 8 stations among 45 or more stations. This resulted in considerably increased concentration of ownership, which raises issues about content diversity, localism, and minority ownership.

WHAT CAME OUT OF THE CHAIN BROADCASTING HEARINGS?

Chain broadcasting refers to radio networks and their control over talent and over affiliated stations. After the Chain Broadcasting hearings, held between 1938 and 1941, the FCC ended network control over affiliates' program selections.

WHAT ARE THE LIMITS ON FREEDOM OF SPEECH IN RADIO BROADCASTS?

Up through the 1960s, certain obscene

words could not be used, and broadcasters were responsible for ensuring that they were not used. Those prohibitions were successfully challenged in court, but the FCC still restricts speech that is indecent. The FCC prohibits such language except during late-night spots that are a "safe harbor" for more explicit speech.

WHAT ARE THE LIMITS ON FREEDOM OF SPEECH IN RECORDINGS?

The record industry had some self-censorship up through the 1960s. But major rock groups carried by major labels began to use more graphic language and explicit themes. Congressional hearings in 1989 resulted in warning labels on record and CD covers, but their effectiveness has been questionable.

Electronic Resources

For up-to-the-minute URLs about *Radio and Recorded Music,* access the MEDIA NOW site on the World Wide Web at:

http://communication.wadsworth.com/

CHAPTER 6

Film and Video

WHAT'S AHEAD

This chapter looks at the development of the film industry from silent films in black and white to computerized animation and special effects. It examines the major film forms, or genres; technological changes; studio and industry organization; film audiences; and the issues of content ratings, conglomeration, and control.

Access the MEDIA NOW site on the World Wide Web at:
http://communication.wadsworth.com/
Choose "Chapter 6" from the selection box to access electronic information and other sites relevant to this chapter.

SNIDDLER'S GULCH, WYOMING, 2010

Hi Fred. I haven't seen you since that History of NAFTA class in high school. Weren't you headed off to California to get into making movies?

I was, but I hated the smog, so I came back here and got my UCLA film school degree over the Web.

Sounds cool. I'd hate the smog too. But how did you learn to use cameras, direct people, and all that film stuff?

A lot of movies don't use cameras or real people anymore. You'd be amazed with what you can do with computers now. You can do all the scenery, music, and special effects. You can even rent the rights to use computer simulations of famous actors.

You mean, like Marilyn Monroe?

Yep. Some of the dead ones are even pretty cheap. For my senior film, I had Rudolf Valentino play Hamlet. It takes a while to make the acting interesting, but heck, you can do it yourself and even still live here in good old Sniddler's Gulch.

Really! How are you gonna work in films from here, though?

You've just got to find a good agent. I've got one named Ralphie in Newark. He specializes in virtual actors and on-line directors like me. He says the biggest problem is that I can't "do lunch" with studio types if I stay here.

Chapter Outline

A Brief History of Film
The Rise of Stars and the Studio System, 1919–1927
Revolutionary Talking Pictures
The Movie Industry During the Studio Era
Film and Television, 1948–1960
Studio Changes and Independent Filmmakers
Films on Cable and Video
Trends in Film Technology
Technology of Movie Sound
Improving Film Visual Technology
Film Special Effects
Computer Revolution in Film
Movie Theater Technology
Film Genres
Silent Films Set the Patterns
Film Genres That Exploit Sound
Later Films Expand the Variety of Genres
Industry Organization
The Film Industry
Independent Filmmakers
Film Distribution
Consolidation and Change in Film Industry Ownership
Audiences for Film
Policy, Social, and Ethical Issues
Violence, Sex, Profanity and Film Ratings
Vertical and Horizontal Integration
Film Piracy
Film Preservation
Summary and Review

Motion pictures are the technical means for taking a series of photographs at a constant speed to portray motion.

A BRIEF HISTORY OF FILM

The early years of film were marked by experimentation with content and forms, major technological innovations, and disputes over who could use, control, and benefit from the inventions. The first challenge was to capture motion on film.

Can horses fly? This seemingly silly question inspired a key development in the evolution of motion pictures. In 1877 Leland Stanford, a California railroad millionaire (and founder of Stanford University) bet $25,000 that a galloping horse actually lifts all four hooves off the ground at the same time. The hooves flew too fast to settle this by merely looking at the horse with the naked eye and the best still photographs of the day were also ambiguous. It looked like galloping horses always kept at least the tip of one hoof on the ground.

Photographer Eadweard Muybridge came up with a conclusive means to settle the bet. He made a series of still pictures of a galloping horse, mounted them on a rotating cylinder and then gave the cylinder a spin. To the stationary viewer gazing at a fixed point on the spinning cylinder, the picture of the horse seemed to "move," but more slowly than in real life. At last it could be seen that at a certain point in each stride, all four hooves left the ground at the same time (Brockway, Chadwick, & Hall, 1997). Muybridge took advantage of a quirk of the human vision system, *persistence of vision,* which leaves a brief afterimage on our retinas. The next trick was turn it into a useful way of recording and showing events in motion.

Thomas Edison and his assistants, Thomas Dickson and Fred Ott, invented the first functional **motion picture** camera in 1888, filming 15 seconds of Fred Ott sneezing. Edison and Dickson also invented the kinetoscope projector. But many others, including the French Lumiére brothers, were working on the challenge, too.

The pace of competition was quick. The first successful premieres by the Lumiéres and Edison were in 1896. By 1900, there were 600 Nickelodeons in New York City.

For a while, most films simply showed short (10–25 minutes) black and white, silent depictions of actual events—a kind of reportage of events in motion, such as horse races. By 1903 some films were developing more of a story line and plot. *The Great Train Robbery,* made

FILM AND VIDEO TIME LINE

1888 Edison develops motion picture camera
1900 – 1909 Edison and Biograph compete
1900 Nickelodeon era
1903 *The Great Train Robbery*
1915 *Birth of a Nation* first feature film
1919 Golden age of silent films begins
1927 *The Jazz Singer* is first "talkie"
1930 Almost all films talk
1939 *Gone with the Wind*
1941 *Citizen Kane*
1946 Peak of film box office—90 million attend weekly
1948 Start of television cutting into film theater audience; major studios have to divest their theater chains
1960 Films become more sexy (*Goldfinger,* 1964) and violent (*The Wild Bunch,* 1969)
1968 MPAA movie ratings introduced
1977 *Star Wars* highlights focus on big-budget blockbusters
1980 VCRs introduced
1982 *E.T.* box office and video champ
1995 *Toy Story* first completely computer-generated film

by William S. Porter in 1903, was the first **story film,** or **movie,** and was very popular. At first, audiences ducked when the outlaw's gun fired.

Story films, or **movies,** introduced the idea of telling a story, usually fictional, with a plot and characters.

Edison wanted to create a standard by licensing his technology, but he found himself competing with the somewhat superior Biograph camera and projector technologies, run by the American Biograph and Mutoscope Company. This first battle ended in 1909 with an agreement between Edison and Biograph to pool **patents** under the Motion Picture Patents Company (MPPC) to establish a single motion picture standard using the best technologies available.

Patents secure for an inventor the exclusive right to make, use, or sell an invention for a certain number of years.

The MPPC collected a fee from every film and distributed it to the inventors on the basis of the number of patents each held. Although the MPPC tried to control the new film industry, independent producers started to use bootleg equipment and moved their base of operations far away from New York, where the MPPC companies were based. The independent producers chose Hollywood, California, for its good weather and ready availability of space for studios. The industry became centered in Hollywood after 1915, and the old MPPC companies based in New York lost their control.

Films began to use larger screens for better image quality. That made more complex action sequences possible. Filmmakers put dialog into titles on screen to make the narration more complex. In 1915, film director D. W. Griffith took a major step forward in film form and technique with the controversial Civil War drama, *Birth of a Nation.* Griffith used well-produced outdoor battle scenes, close-ups, and cuts between different simultaneous sequences of action, such as the threat to an imperiled heroine and the rescuers riding to save her, to increase dramatic tension. It was also the first full-length **feature film.** (Films over 1½ hours long became known as feature films.) It was the most popular film in the United States for over 20 years. However, the film, set during and after the Civil War, features Ku Klux Klan members as its heroes and was used by the Klan as a

Feature films are longer story films, usually over 1½ hours.

recruiting film. Although the film was revolutionary in form, it was racist in content, reflecting Griffith's own upbringing.

Silent films conveyed plot with expressions, actions, and subtitles, before sound technology.

In this **silent film** era, from 1903 to 1927, film storytelling developed considerably. Films were black and white and they were silent, but these very limitations forced them to be creative, using the actors' expressions and gestures, as well as music and subtitles, to tell the story. It also made the audience use their imaginations. The music for the film was live at first, usually performed by an organist, who played music written for the film but could also improvise. Films frequently borrowed or adapted plots from novels. Movies became longer, as audiences came to expect the medium to tell more complex stories (Knight, 1979).

Hollywood has had several "booms" or "golden ages" of prosperity, artistic success, and widespread cultural impact. These have been followed by "busts" when the film industry lost parts of its audience to newer media technologies. The first golden age was the age of silent film.

The Rise of Stars and the Studio System, 1919–1927

Film studios are production companies that have achieved considerable stability or success over time, often by relying on the same directors and actors.

From their new base in California, several major **film studios** developed a strong industrial production capability, producing movies almost on an assembly line. Studios developed their own complete teams of actors, writers, directors, technicians, and equipment that enabled them to produce large numbers of successful feature films. Short subjects were also popular, especially serials—stories told in a series of 15- to 20-minute episodes, each with a cliff-hanger ending, over several weeks. One silent era serial favorite was *The Perils of Pauline,* which literally left our heroine hanging over a cliff waiting to be rescued by our hero the next week.

The **star system** was the film studios' use of stars' popularity to promote their movies.

As more movies were produced, film studios discovered that certain actors and actresses had such appeal that they could attract viewers no matter what the movie was about. The idea of the movie **star** was born. Fan interest in stars was seen as an excellent way to draw audiences to new movies. The dashing and romantic Rudolph Valentino (*The Sheik*), Lillian Gish, Mary Pickford ("America's sweetheart"), and Charlie Chaplin (funny and sympathetic in *The Tramp*) became such attractions that their names appeared above the name of the film on theater marquees. The importance of the star actor or actress was linked to the rise of the studio system. The major movie studios grew by developing a stable of actors, writers, and directors who worked for them on a contract basis over a period of years.

Although silent, early movies were visually powerful enough to create both adoration and controversy. Some movies in the 1920s shocked much of the audience with sexual themes, partial nudity, and depiction of a fast urban life, as in "The Jazz Age," where both men and women "partied" hard. Stardom also made the private lives of the stars more visible, and some of their lives were scandalous to many viewers. In a notorious case, silent film comedian Fatty Arbuckle was accused, wrongly, as it turned out, in 1922 of brutally raping and murdering an aspiring actress. In response to this and other incidents, the industry decided to impose self-censorship before it was censored by the government or others, such as the Catholic Legion of Decency, which threatened a boycott of films. In 1922, the studios created the Motion Picture Producers and Distributors of America, which became known as the Hays Office after its head, Republican National Committee chairman and Presbyterian Church elder Will Hays. The Hays Office created voluntary content guidelines, the Motion Picture Code. The Catholic Church, B'nai Brith, Elks, Masons, and National Education Association all pushed for more mandatory adherence, and their efforts led to a Production Code that forbade scenes that gave a positive portrayal or image of "crime, wrong-doing, evil, or sin." A large number of words and slang phrases, such as calling a woman an "alley cat," were forbidden. Hays soothed public complaints but imposed a tough internal censorship that bridled the creativity of industry writers, directors, and actors (Knight, 1979).

FILM LEGENDS.
Stars were important to the success of the film medium. Douglas Fairbanks and Mary Pickford (bottom Row) were so big that they started their own studio, United Artists (with Charlie Chaplin and D. W. Griffith).

Revolutionary Talking Pictures

Attempts were made almost from the beginning of film to make the moving pictures talk. Edison thought pictures would be necessary to get people to listen to sound recordings. Edison's talented assistant Thomas Dickson experimented with movie sound before 1895. Most early systems relied on a record player coordinated with the film (Ellis, 1990). The studios were initially reluctant to invest in sound technology, as were the movie houses. Eventually, however, one of the then small studios, Warner Brothers, made the commitment to develop sound technology and, with the help of AT&T's Western Electric company, created short talking film clips called *The Vitaphone Preludes.* The fourth "Vitaphone" film was a breakthrough: *The Jazz Singer* in 1927. It featured two sections of recorded music and included singing that was synchronized with the film so that the singer's lips moved when they were supposed to. Earlier attempts at "talking pictures" had featured music, but *The Jazz Singer* also had a little bit of dialog, which fascinated the audience.

"**Talkies**" effectively ended the golden age of silent movies. That crisis for actors and studios used to making silent films was captured well in the musical classic *Singing in the Rain* (1952). Although audiences were very excited by the new potential of filmed voice and music, some artists could not adjust. Acting had to become less overstated and stylized, now that plot could be carried by dialog and not just expression and gesture. The actors' vocal quality became critical. Studios suddenly had to become skilled in the use of sound effects and music. Some actresses and actors, such as the sultry Greta Garbo, made a smooth transition, but many did not have the vocal quality or more subtle acting skills to survive the shift. Talkies required an influx of new talent, such as James Cagney, Spencer Tracy, Clark Gable, and Fred Astaire, who came largely from vaudeville and Broadway.

Talkies were films with synchronized soundtracks, which emphasized dialog, singing, and music.

The possibility of dialog created new kinds of possibilities for both drama and humor. However, the need to use fixed microphones made the first talkies much more static and less visually adventurous than the best silent films. Still, the audience preference for talking pictures was clear. Because audiences liked talkies, they made more money, so by 1933 nearly all films were talkies. In 1930, 22 percent of theaters still showed silent films, by 1933 almost none did.

Movies emphasized their new attraction, sound, by creating a series of extravagantly produced musicals, with lavish visuals, dancing, and singing. Movies such as those of Ginger Rogers and Fred Astaire epitomized the elegant escapism of the new talking, singing, and dancing movies. The pure fantasy of *The Wizard of Oz* (1939) is another enduring example of brilliant 1930s escapism. Most of the American audience sought a refuge from the harsh economic times of the Great Depression (1929–1939), which threw many people out of work. Hollywood responded with a number of imaginatively escapist films to help people forget their troubles. The other main genres of the 1930s were adventure serials, comedies, suspense stories, mysteries, and crime dramas. (For more on movie genres, see page 187.)

The cultural impact of movies in America in the 1930s was extraordinary. Most people went to the movies at least weekly, sometimes more often. They got weekly news information from newsreels, such as Fox's *Movietone News* and *March of Time* newsreels, which provided much of the information people had about the rest of the world, including the buildup to World War II (1939–1945). They waited from week to week to see what would happen next to Flash Gordon or other heroes of the serials that played before the feature. Most of all, they lost themselves for a time in the feature length stories told by the stars. The Depression kept some people away (revenues did sag at first after the economic crash of 1929), but most people tried hard to find the money for the movies.

The combination of massive movie attendance, controversial themes and images of sex and gangsters, and concentrated studio power continued to cause many people to worry about the movies' effect on society, particularly on young people. The Hays Office continued to exercise close scrutiny over film content. A special exception was required to let Clark Gable say, "Frankly, my dear, I don't give a damn" in *Gone with the Wind* (1939).

The Movie Industry During the Studio Era

A **merger** is the economic joining of two or more previously unrelated companies.

Movies made a lot of money. As profits went up and movies became a profitable business, a **merger** wave took place. The Great Depression killed off many small producers and nearly 5000 independent movie theaters (Gomery, 1991). Their misfortune actually strengthened the economic situation and control of a few big studios, and it concentrated production decision in the hands of a very few studio executives.

Vertical integration is the concentration of ownership that occurs when companies with the same owner handle different aspects of a business, such as film production and distribution.

By 1930, a fairly stable pattern of studio organization emerged. There were five major studios: Paramount, Loew's/MGM, Warner Brothers, Fox, and RKO. These studios owned their own distribution chains of movie theaters. Control over production, distribution and exhibition enabled studios to make sure that their movies were distributed and played widely, but it constituted a form of **vertical integration** that would ultimately draw the attention of federal regulators concerned about the concentration of power in the studios.

All five of the major studios shared several key characteristics. They integrated film production and theatrical distribution. They owned extensive production facilities. They relied on teams of stars and directors who made several movies together for them. They developed both prestigious feature films and **B-movies,** which were cheaper and not so prestigious but made consistent profits. However, each studio also had its own distinctive style.

B-movies are cheaply and quickly made genre films.

- Paramount was the most profitable and powerful studio, with over 1000 theaters. It adopted a conservative strategy, and relied on proven directors such as Cecil B. DeMille (known for extravagant epics such as *The Ten Commandments*) and stars like crooner Bing Crosby and comedian Bob Hope.
- Loew's/MGM had impressive facilities: 27 sound stages on 168 acres. It sought prestige with new Technicolor musicals, but it also made a lot of money with B-movies such as the *Tarzan* adventures.
- Twentieth Century–Fox combined two studios, developed new stars such as Tyrone Power and Betty Grable and also made money with documentaries including *March of Time* and *Movietone* newsreels.
- Warner Brothers went from marginal status in the 1930s to number three by 1949 by promoting talking pictures, then comedies, genre films such as Errol Flynn's *The Adventures of Robin Hood* (1938), and cartoons starring Bugs Bunny, Elmer Fudd, and Daffy Duck.

MEDIA WATCH

Orson Welles's *Citizen Kane*

In the 1940s American movies matured. They began to tell stories that were more complex, less escapist, and frequently darker and less optimistic. The classic film of the period was *Citizen Kane,* directed by Orson Welles in 1941, which offers a fictionalized account of the life of William Randolph Hearst, the newspaper baron well known for sensationalism and excess (see Chapter 4). Like *Birth of a Nation, Citizen Kane* achieved innovation in several areas. In plot, the story works backward as a reporter pieces the tale together. The film uses sound effects, echoes, and music to enhance the storytelling. In technique, Welles put together dozens of new effects that he and others had developed, including zooms, radical changes of perspective through extreme close-ups, lighting effects, the use of shadows, and unusual camera angles. *Citizen Kane* was a critical success but a public relations disaster, as the result of a highly publicized controversy in which William Randolph Hearst, the unnamed subject of the film, attempted to prevent its release by buying up all the prints.

BEST FILM, EVER?
Orson Welles's *Citizen Kane* popularized a number of filmmaking techniques, including new camera angles and types of shots.

- RKO, Radio-Keith-Orpheum, produced some quality films, notably *King Kong* (1933), Fred Astaire and Ginger Rogers musicals, and *Citizen Kane* (1941), but got most of its money from its movie houses and from cheaper, more predictably profitable B-movies.

The minor Hollywood studios of the 1930s and 1940s included several that are now major players: Universal, Columbia, and United Artists. During the studio era, these studios struggled because they did not control their own distribution and exhibition networks. They made most of their money with B-movies.

- Universal Pictures' only real successes in the 1930s and 1940s were low-budget productions such as Abbot and Costello comedies, *Flash Gordon* serials, *Woody the Woodpecker* cartoons, and horror movies(e.g., *Dracula,* 1930).
- Columbia Pictures was a small, independent producer that rose to make classic Frank Capra movies, such as *It Happened One Night* (1934), but made more money from "B" westerns with Gene Autry and Three Stooges shorts.
- United Artists was founded by silent era stars—Mary Pickford, Douglas Fairbanks, and Charlie Chaplin, along with D. W. Griffith—who wanted a distributor for their productions. It prospered most in the 1920s when these founders were still creating movies.

Another two studios were even smaller, Monogram and Republic. Republic was famous for a time as a producer of action serials, whose cliff-hangers and action sequences have been liberally borrowed by the likes of Steven Spielberg in his *Indiana Jones* movies and George Lucas in *Star Wars.* Republic was also the first home of cowboy hero John Wayne.

MEDIA WATCH

Beyond Disney: Chuck Jones's Animation at Warner Brothers

For classic animation from the 1930s and 1940s, most people tend to think first of the Walt Disney studio, which produced such famous animated films as *Snow White* and *Cinderella*. However, many think that some of the best and most original animation came from Chuck Jones at the Warner Brothers Studio. At first, in the 1930s, Warner tried to imitate Disney, with somewhat bland, innocent characters such as Porky Pig in *Loonie Tunes*. By the 1940s, though, Chuck Jones, Tex Avery, and others at Warner began to create a more original product—more irreverent, more topical, more brash in tone, and with a more adventurous, nonrealistic visual style. It flowered in the 1950s in several cartoons that are considered among the best ever made. One of Chuck Jones's most famous cartoons, *One Froggy Evening* (1955), produced the singing bullfrog, with straw boater hat and vaudeville cane, who is now the symbol for the Warner (WB) Television Network. Another of his most famous cartoons, *What's Opera, Doc?* (1957), a visually and aurally outrageous takeoff on Wagnerian opera, has Bugs Bunny in opera singer drag playing Brünnhilde while Elmer Fudd in armor sings "Kill the Wabbit" to the tune of the "Ride of the Valkyries."

See http://www.chuckjones.com/history/ WWW

The studio system, the big five with their distribution and theater chains, the little three, and the even littler two peaked after World War II in 1946–1948. The war ended the economic limits imposed by the Great Depression on movie production and movie going, enabling the whole system to make more money. Right after World War II, there was an even brighter, if brief, bubble of prosperity for the film industry, as returning soldiers and sailors joined the masses of people attending the movies weekly. The year 1946 was the peak of audience exposure and financial success for **theatrical films** in the United States. Around 90 million Americans went to the movies every week to see hits like *It's a Wonderful Life.* In 1947, the U.S. film industry **grossed** $1.7 billion, a figure that sank to $900 million by 1962, reflecting competition from a new medium (Mast & Kawin, 1996).

Theatrical films are those released for distribution in movie theaters.

Gross refers to the overall revenue of films from box office distribution before expenses are deducted.

STOP & REVIEW

1. **What innovations did D. W. Griffith introduce into silent films?**
2. **What was the studio system?**
3. **Which were the main studios?**
4. **What changed with talking pictures?**

Film and Television, 1948–1960

By 1948, the film industry faced significant competition from a new technology: television. Film attendance also declined as returning World War II veterans started families and moved to the newly established suburbs, far away from downtown movie theaters (Gomery, 1991). Hollywood first responded with drive-in movies and later, in the 1960s, shifted to new movie houses in suburban shopping centers.

The film industry initially fought the potential threat of television by not releasing new movies for broadcast on television. In fact, films made after 1948 had clauses in their contracts prohibiting release to television. Despite these efforts, however, television quickly cut into Hollywood's theatrical **box office receipts.**

Box office receipts are the money made from selling tickets to movies in theaters, not counting video, television, etc.

Separating Production and Distribution. The film industry suffered a severe, concurrent blow to its theater-based revenues. The government had become concerned with the **concentration of power** and vertical integration in the Hollywood system, where studios both produced movies and controlled their distribution. In 1948, the government ordered studios to get out of at least one aspect of film business: production, distribution, or exhibition. Studios challenged the decision, but it was confirmed by the Supreme Court (*United States vs. Paramount Pictures,* 1948).

Concentration of power occurs when media are owned or controlled by a small number of individuals or companies.

The biggest four—MGM, Warner, Paramount, and Fox—struggled to readjust after agreeing to sell off their theater chains. Paramount and United Artists sold off their exhibition chains. MGM/Loew's struggled for almost a decade in the courts to avoid separating the company's Loews theater chain from its MGM studio. They finally split in 1959, and MGM shakily emerged as a separate studio entity.

Ironically, this forced divestiture of theatrical distribution took place at a point when studios were losing their dominance, just as box office receipts dropped and many theaters closed. Almost every small town went through the shock described in *The Last Picture Show* (1971), as thousands of small-town theaters disappeared.

The film industry began to realize that if they couldn't beat television, maybe they had better join it. Smaller studios such as Republic and RKO started selling movies to television in the early 1950s. So did Warner Brothers when it changed hands in 1956. In fact, until the late 1960s, Warner's main source of profit was from distributing films to television (Gomery, 1991).

Disney started producing programs specifically for television: *Disneyland* for ABC (1954–1957), followed by *Mickey Mouse Club* (1955–1959). Other studios followed. The first regular studio-produced series was a western, *Cheyenne* (1955–1956). Warner Brothers and Paramount both made much of their money in the 1950s and 1960s by producing series for television. The networks began to order most of their programs from studios or other outside producers since it was then cheaper to buy programming from companies that were already geared up to create it (Sterling & Kittross, 1990). Later, television networks were forced to buy most of their programs from the studios because of government rules that limited how much network programming the network itself could create or own. Those rules on financial syndication were designed to diversify the sources of television production. They were certainly a boon to Hollywood studio producers.

By 1961 the film boycott of television was over as "Saturday Night at the Movies" (NBC) topped the ratings. Television networks have been using movies strategically ever since to compete with each other. Airing movies became an even more important way for UHF and independent stations—even many PBS stations—to compete with network programs.

SPECTACLE. **Big-budget, big-screen historical epics such as *Ben Hur* were Hollywood's answer to competition from television in the 1950s.**

Technological Innovation to Compete with TV. As audiences got used to television, they began to demand something different from movies. Part of the film industry response was in technological innovation. Although Technicolor had been invented in 1917, it spread slowly with films such as *Gone with the Wind* (1939) and Disney cartoons. Other suppliers of color technology, such as Eastman Kodak, also entered the market. By the early 1960s, nearly all films were in color.

Another relatively successful technological innovation aimed at competing with TV was wide-screen film. CinemaScope had been developed in the 1920s, but it took hold only under encouragement from the head of the Fox studio in the early 1950s. Studios finally embraced the new *widescreen* idea, but outfitting theaters proved expensive and took quite a long time.

Hollywood also tried to compete with TV by mounting lavish, big-budget spectacles such as *Ben Hur* (1959). However, extravaganza movies could also backfire, as did Fox's *Cleopatra,* which cost $30 million in 1963 and didn't come close to breaking even. This attempt to bet on movies that might become blockbusters while trying to avoid high-budget disasters continues to be a daily reality for Hollywood. For example, until *Titanic* (1997) became the all-time box-office hit, grossing over a billion dollars by 1998, many in Hollywood saw its director, James Cameron, as the author of an over-budget disaster.

In the 1960s, Hollywood also capitalized on the fact that it could include more controversial material than TV could. This included sex in movies such as the

James Bond thriller *Goldfinger* (1964) or social issues, such as racial prejudice, in films like *Guess Who's Coming to Dinner* (1967).

By the 1960s the power of the movie studios was declining. Independent producers gained more of a role in producing movies, film studios began to spend much of their time producing series for television, and the studio system, as it had flourished in its golden era, died.

Studio Changes and Independent Filmmakers

Although movie studios suffered in the 1950s, only RKO actually went out of business. Most changed hands. Most struggled through a cycle of lean years with few hits and fat years when a hit saved the day; *The Godfather* (1972), for example, made Paramount an unprecedented $1,000,000 a day for its first month.

Columbia and United Artists in some ways fared better than the larger studios by not having to adjust to the loss of theater businesses. Warner and Columbia Pictures made television series. Universal was acquired by MCA and also went into television production. United Artists capitalized on distributing movies, such as John Huston's *The African Queen* (1951), for talented independent producers. Disney moved into the studio ranks with animation and its Buena Vista production and distribution company, which produced family fare epitomized by *Mary Poppins* (1964).

As independent producers gained more power, several things happened to American movies. Audiences changed, becoming younger, more cosmopolitan, and more interested in sensation and social observation. The values and current interests of teenagers and college students began to dominate films (Mast & Kawin, 1996).

New directors pushed into Hollywood from outside the studios and the star system, some from 1960s underground films, some straight from film school, some from TV commercials. They transformed traditional Hollywood genres, often by increasing the use of sex, violence, and social controversy. Directors Woody Allen (*Annie Hall,* 1976) and Francis Ford Coppola (*The Godfather,* 1972) tended to create much more offbeat, personal films, some of which turned out to be major commercial successes.

In the 1960s, films became more political and topical. Some films explored current issues, such as the Vietnam War. For instance, although *M*A*S*H* (1970) was set in Korea, it was filled with the antiwar sentiment many Americans harbored about Vietnam. Films such as *Taxi Driver* (1976) explored the underside of city life, while *The Graduate* (1967) explored the angst of growing up in the suburbs. Films reexamined American myths, including cowboys and the West in the hyperviolent *The Wild Bunch* (1969) and the hard-bitten detective in *Chinatown* (1974).

By the 1960s, American society was undergoing a rebellion against the repressive Victorian-era morality that had inspired the Hays Office. The Hays Office itself closed down in 1945, although the code technically remained in force until 1966. Meanwhile, local censors were handcuffed by free speech rulings from the U.S. Supreme Court. Movie producers continually pushed the limits of what was acceptable, which led to new calls from concerned parents that raised the specter of government censorship. Instead, the industry again opted for self-regulation, this time in the form of content ratings administered by the Motion Picture Association of America (see page 195).

Even as films seemed to turn inward to focus on American culture in the 1960s and 1970s, they were still selling very well abroad. The studios had joined together as the Motion Picture Export Association of America (MPEAA) in the 1930s and had taken control of much of the international film distribution business. Exports were one of the things that continued to keep Hollywood profitable throughout the 1950s and 1960s.

In the 1970s–1990s, filmmakers such as Steven Spielberg (*ET, Back to the Future, Schindler's List*) rediscovered that film has a visual intensity well beyond that of television, especially in the darkened movie house with a big screen. Thus action sequences, striking landscapes, and special effects became competitive advantages for movies. As more sophisticated sound systems emerged, intense sound also characterized the movie theater experience.

Films on Cable and Video

By the late 1970s and early 1980s, the film industry began to take increasing advantage of cable TV and rented videotapes as new distribution channels. Cable TV boomed as a source of viewing alternatives to network television, particularly after the launch of nationwide service by Home Box Office (HBO) in 1975 (see Chapter 7). Channels such as HBO relied almost exclusively on feature films for their content. Even the new satellite-based cable superstations WGN, and WTBS—WOR, used quite a few old films. This helped the film industry regain some of the audience and revenue that it had lost to television in the 1950s and 1960s.

Videocassette recorders (VCRs) also became more widespread in American homes throughout the 1980s. The use of VCRs diffused very quickly. Prices dipped to under $100 by the late 1990s, and over 80 percent of American homes acquired a VCR. People used VCRs to record and replay favorite shows off television or cable and to view movies rented from video stores.

Initially the movie industry was nervous about VCRs, fearing that illegal copying or piracy would keep people from paying for either a movie ticket or a video rental. The Motion Picture Association of America (MPAA) initially tried to suppress the diffusion of the technology, fearing massive piracy. When that attempt failed, the MPAA put a great deal of energy into demanding the enforcement of laws against illegal video copying of movies, both in the United States and abroad. As the law enforcement crackdown began to reduce piracy, and as more people started renting legitimate copies from a rapidly expanding set of video rental outlets, the MPAA studio producers began to realize that video was more of a gold mine than a threat.

The video rental business started with small independent rental shops, who bought video stock from distributors. It later consolidated decisively, with independents shrinking, with some supermarkets and other stores renting videos as a sideline, and with massive video rental chains, like Blockbuster and Hollywood Video, taking most of the business.

The spread of video rentals ultimately contributed both to the blockbuster phenomenon and to audience segmentation. Even today, many people rush to the video store to get the latest hit movie. (This makes it possible to stage media events to promote movies, such as the midnight rentals and sales of *Titanic* touted as a sales event by many stores for the early hours of the first day it was available in video.) By contrast, other people walk straight by "top renters" to find Japanese animation, old cowboy movies, old *Star Trek* episodes, or whatever else captures their attention. One result is that a lot of B-movies now go straight to video, where loyal fans are waiting for yet another teenage beach sex comedy or yet another crazed android from the future.

Independent stations, usually on UHF, also began to show more old movies and reruns of hit series from syndication services. All these choices benefitted the film industry.

In general, the film industry began to produce for more narrowly focused audiences. After the "mass" audience had moved to television, film had to aim at more specific groups. For **first-run distribution** to movie theaters, most films were increasingly targeted at a specific audience, the 18–25 year olds who still went out to film theaters.

STOP & REVIEW

1. **Why did studios want to own their own distributors and movie theater chains?**
2. **Why did federal regulators force the studios to divest themselves of their movie theater chains in 1948?**
3. **How did Hollywood and its films change to compete with television?**
4. **When did the studio system decline? Why did it decline?**
5. **What impact have independent filmmakers had?**
6. **What effect have new distribution technologies, such as video and cable, had on the film industry?**

First-run distribution for films is to movie theaters, usually followed by video, cable TV, TV, etc.

On the other hand, one or two blockbuster movies such as *The Godfather* (1972) could ensure a studio's financial health for years by reaching a wide audience. Thus, audience segmentation works against Hollywood's continuing urge to create blockbuster movies that aim beyond segments to capture as much of the mass audience as possible to create maximum profits.

Star Wars (1977) is usually pointed to as the turning point in a return to spectacular, big-budget blockbuster filmmaking. Films hurried to take advantage of the latest special effects, often raising costs. The star system also returned with a vengeance, which also raised film costs as stars such as Arnold Schwarzenegger could get over $10 million for a film. The *Titanic* phenomenon in 1997–1998 showed just what a single blockbuster could do.

By the 1970s, "made-for-TV" movies became increasingly common. These could be turned into TV or cable TV series if they were popular, as was *Buffy the Vampire Slayer* (1997). Made-for-TV movies often did surprisingly well against other movies and series. Some even got eventual theatrical release, such as *Gettysburg* (1993), which was made for Turner Network Television. By the 1990s, audiences and revenues for cable channels were such that "made-for-cable" movies became relatively common on channels such as HBO and TNT, surpassing the number of "made-for-TV" movies.

Of course, as we all know, the history of film does not end with George Lucas. By the late 1990s, the movie industry was again transformed by new technology and market forces. Home video has become a driving force with revenues from video store rentals and direct sales of videos (known as *sell through*) outstripping box office

TITANIC HIT. ***Titanic*** **became the all-time box office draw in 1998, reviving Hollywood's faith in big-budget pictures.**

PROFILE

STAR WARRIORS. George Lucas rose to fame with his *Star Wars* film series.

George Lucas

Occupation: Screenwriter, film director, producer, and media entrepreneur.

Born: May 14, 1944, in Modesto, California

Education: University of Southern California's film school.

Big Break: He met Francis Ford Coppola through a scholarship sponsored by Warner Brothers Studio. They formed American Zoetrope, a film company that let Lucas direct *THX 1136* (1971). This gave him enough momentum to make *American Graffiti* (1973), which cost under $1 million, made over $50 million, and made Lucas a millionaire.

Big Achievement: Probably his masterwork was his next film, *Star Wars* (1977), which he wrote and directed for his new company, Lucasfilm Ltd.

Inspirations: To write and visualize *Star Wars,* he tried to make an archetypal hero story. He studied fairy tales, ancient mythology, and the myth studies of Joseph Campbell. He also borrowed liberally from other mythic action films, World War II movies about aircraft carriers and fighters, westerns, Errol Flynn's swashbuckling sword fights, Buck Rogers and Flash Gordon movie serials, and comic books.

Next Moves: Lucas made a *Star Wars* trilogy that also included *The Empire Strikes Back* (1980) and *Return of the Jedi* (1983). The first installment of the second trilogy, *The Phantom Menace,* debuted in 1999.

Expansions: He expanded Lucasfilm into post-production facilities and multimedia research. He went into other companies and technologies. Industrial Light and Magic was formed in the 1970s to do cutting-edge special effects. Skywalker Sound is a state-of-the-art recording studio that does post-production for filmmakers and mixing for the music industry. LucasArts did research and development to create games on CD-ROM.

receipts two-to-one. Large video rental chains even demanded a share of the profits from filmmakers. The cost of producing major films skyrocketed as producers raced to outdo each other with spectacular computer-generated special effects. In hopes of spreading those costs over larger and larger audiences, the industry began to internationalize both with respect to its ownership—which now included foreign investors such as Sony Corporation and Rupert Murdoch—and with respect to its audiences. Movie-making at the major studios began to gravitate more toward genres (e.g., science fiction, action adventure) that could "translate" across cultures. But outside of the major studios, there was a revival in independent filmmaking, as computer technology drove down the cost of "small films" and offered the prospect of a renaissance in filmmaking apart from the financial pressures of the blockbuster mentality that gripped Hollywood.

TRENDS IN FILM TECHNOLOGY

Eadweard Muybridge's first motion picture of a galloping horse used a rather unwieldy recording system—the horse's hooves triggered trip wires on 700 still cameras to yield a mere 60 seconds of action. Muybridge's visit to American inventor Thomas Edison in 1888 inspired the first movie camera, the kinetograph.

It was actually a close relative to Edison's phonograph (see Chapter 5), invented a decade earlier, in that the pictures were recorded a frame at a time on a hand-turned revolving cylinder with a light-sensitive surface. Soon the cylindrical photographic plates gave way to strips of the newly invented Kodak film. Edison's 1892 kinetoscope was the first playback mechanism for the masses—but for only one viewer at a time. The Lumiére brothers originated the movie projector in 1895 by shining a light through the strip of picture transparencies, unspooling them at the same speed at which they were taken, and enlarging them with an optical lens. If the frames were changed fast enough (20 frames per second was about right), the viewer of the projection had the sense of natural, continuous motion. This was because the afterimage of each frame persisted in the viewer's vision system just long enough for the next frame to appear.

Apart from some advances in film processing and developing, basic motion picture technology did not change much over the next 25 years. As movies got longer, it became necessary to replace the hand cranked projector with an electric motor. This was the era of *silent films,* when the actors' words appeared printed on the screen, not spoken, and theme music was played by a live organist in the theater.

Technology of Movie Sound

Edison created the first talking movie in 1913 but as we noted earlier, the first full-length *talkie,* or movie with sound, was *The Jazz Singer,* released in 1927. *The Jazz Singer*'s sound was supplied by AT&T Bell Labs scientists, who devised a way to record the sound on film and synchronize it on the film with the pictures—a major improvement over earlier efforts to coordinate record players with films. A photoreceptor picked up variations in the light shining through the sound track of the film and reproduced them as weak electric currents. AT&T used amplifier and loudspeaker technology available from its telephone network to amplify the weak electrical impulses into full sound. The same basic principles are still used today, although additional sound tracks have been added over the years—first for stereo, then for multichannel *surround sound.*

Improving Film Visual Technology

Early inventors also improved the visual aspects of the film. First, the film exposure rate was speeded up slightly, from 18 or 22 frames per second in early films to 24 frames per second. This eliminated the jerkiness that was apparent to some viewers. It is also what makes actors in early films look like they are moving at high speed all the time when the film is played on modern 24-frame-per-second projectors. The old scenes are essentially being played back in "fast forward" relative to the original speed at which they were photographed.

Film also got wider, growing from 8 mm to 16 mm to 35 mm and later to 70 mm (that's the width of each frame of film, in millimeters; 1 mm is about 1/25 of an inch). This expanded the field of vision for the filmgoer in the interest of imparting a better sense of reality. Widescreen CinemaScope was embraced in the early 1950s by all studios except Paramount, which had its own VistaVision system. The *widescreen* process that eventually took over was Panavision, which is still used extensively (Gomery, 1991).

Color had been present in some of the earliest films, around 1910, but color scenes had to be painstakingly tinted by hand, frame by frame, on each print. Color films did not become widely available until the *CinemaScope* process of color photography debuted in 1939. Another color process, Technicolor, was introduced in 1922, but the owners of Technicolor had a tight monopoly that restricted its spread until a 1950 **consent decree,** following a U.S. government antitrust suit. Other suppliers of color technology, such as Eastman Kodak, also entered the market, and most films were in color by the 1960s.

A **consent decree** is an agreement by the subject of an antitrust suit to change practices without formally admitting guilt.

Film Special Effects

Special effects are another essential piece of film technology. Early audiences were easy to fool with simple stop action effects. If you showed them a magician climbing into a box and closing the lid, stopped the camera long enough for the magician to exit and then restarted the film to show an empty box, early moviegoers were convinced that the magician had magically escaped. Later, the actors were filmed against the backdrop of another film projected from behind to give the impression that actors in the studio were really paddling a boat in the rapids or engaging in other dangerous stunts. And many a model train and toy boat were sacrificed before a close-up lens to simulate real-life cataclysms.

Modern special effects are often traced back to the 1933 classic *King Kong,* although most of the special-effects wizardry in that film had appeared in earlier films. The big ape was actually an 18-inch furry doll with movable limbs that were painstakingly moved one frame at a time. When Kong grabbed our heroine Fay Wray, she was filmed in the clutches of a life-sized mock-up of a giant gorilla's arm. *King Kong* was the first film to use a technique called *front projection.* When Fay appeared struggling on the top of the Empire State Building, a building model was shot with a miniature movie screen on its roof, onto which pictures of the real Fay struggling were projected. *King Kong* also relied heavily on the already-familiar *rear projection,* in which live actors were filmed against a neutral backdrop and then *composited* with a background shot of, say, a charging dinosaur. The background was *matted,* or blacked out, in the areas where the actors would appear so that the two images could be superimposed. Stop action, compositing, matting, and scale models are still the staples of many special-effects sequences today (Bannon, 1998; Brosnon, 1974).

Computer Revolution in Film

As in the rest of the media, the computer is taking over in special effects. *Star Wars* (1977) used computer-driven cameras to construct multilayered space battles. One of the first noteworthy uses of **computer animation** was in a 16-minute segment of the 1982 Disney film *Tron,* which took place inside a computer-generated virtual world. In 1995, Pixar Animation's *Toy Story* became the first full-length computer-animated film (see Technology Trends). In other words, all the images were generated inside a computer. No one had to draw each

Computer animation is the use of computers rather than hand drawing and coloring in film animation.

TECHNOLOGY ***TRENDS***

Steve Jobs's Virtual Film Studio

Pixar Animation Studios is the first virtual movie studio, making animated feature films the new way, with computers. Pixar emerged from both the Disney training school for animators and the special-effects revolution kicked off by George Lucas' *Star Wars* films. In 1984, Disney animator John Lasseter joined Lucas' special-effects group, which became Pixar. In 1986, Apple Computer founder Steve Jobs, anticipating a computer revolution in animation, bought Pixar. He wanted to make stories that children would talk about, and he wanted to transform the way in which the stories were told. Chief animator Lasseter got things rolling by making several award-winning short animated films: *Luxo, Jr.* (1986) and *Tin Toy* (1988).

Jobs wants Pixar to be "the next Disney—not replace Disney—but be the next Disney" (*Business Week,* Nov. 23, 1998, p. 142). In the meantime, Disney has been crucial to Pixar's takeoff. Disney released Pixar's first feature film, *Toy Story,* in 1995, as part of a three-movie deal that splits profits between Pixar and Disney and throws Disney's marketing and distribution muscle behind Pixar's films. However, Disney is gearing up to do its own completely computer-animated films soon. So before long, the two will be competing.

Pixar is carving out its own style, with technology-driven animation that allows more movement, more lifelike backgrounds, and more lifelife textures. Still, this is animation, and *Toy Story* succeeded in part because of a unique stylization that looked three-dimensional but still cartoon-like. Films must also tell good stories at a rapid production pace. Jobs plans to do one movie a year, roughly comparable to Disney's pace. The costs are one-third lower because one-third fewer animators are required. Characters, backgrounds, and the like can also be modified and recycled within the computer for future films. In 1998, Disney-Pixar released the animated feature film *A Bug's Life,* which was an immediate box office hit.

FOUR-LEGGED INSECTS.
The lavish animation of *A Bug's Life* (1998) was a giant step forward in computer animation.

For Further Research:
If you are interested in following developments in computer animation, try both the World Wide Web and InfoTrac College Edition, if you are using the InfoTrac College Edition. A search for topic words "computer animation" produced a number of technical articles such as "Disney Gets Animated Over Pixar," *U.S. News and World Report,* March 10, 1997, v.122 n9 p. 58.

frame, or cell, of animation as in all previous animated movies. Increasingly, computer-generated monsters and sets are filling in for scale models.

Sometimes computer images stand in for real actors in dangerous action sequences, such as the "people" falling off the *Titanic* (1997) as it slipped beneath the waves. The waves were computer-generated, too. Computer effects are also what made it possible for Forrest Gump (1996) to be inserted into an otherwise real historical film clip to shake hands with President John F. Kennedy. It is only a matter of time before we will see the first computer-generated movie star. If their heirs' financial interests can be satisfied, we may see new movies with deceased stars such as Marilyn Monroe and James Dean (Rose, 1998).

Special effects are glitzy, but the real computer revolution in Hollywood is taking place behind the scenes, during the *post-production* process when films get their finishing touches. Film editing used to involve unspooling miles of raw film footage and manually cutting and splicing to make a master copy. Now the filmed sequences are transferred to computer media where they can be accessed at random and spliced with the touch of a button—a process known as *nonlinear editing.* Not only is this faster, but it also allows the editor to be more creative in playing "what if" when sequencing the raw footage, adding the sound track, and making adjustments in the framing and lighting of the original images. Even celluloid film itself could become obsolete with the advent of digital cameras that record high-quality images directly in digital formats and store them on computer disc—no chemical film processing required.

1. Who developed the basics of film camera and projector technology?

2. How does movie sound work?

3. How was movie image quality improved?

4. How have special effects in film developed?

Computers have become involved in nearly all aspects of movie making. "Desktop" filmmaking is fast becoming a reality. Small groups of talented people can produce an entire film on personal computers with off-the-shelf software without any actors, directors, cameras, sets, or key grips. Digital filmmaking lowers costs, opening the film industry to student filmmakers and diverse artistic visions. The Internet is beginning to serve as a distribution mechanism for the digital filmmakers, removing the last "analog" stop in film production and perhaps also the last financial barrier to the solo film artist-auteur (Marriott, 1999). In fact, we already have virtual film studios, such as Pixar Animation Studios, run by Steve Jobs, cofounder of Apple Computers.

Movie Theater Technology

What will the movie theater of the future be like? The odds are that it will be a lot like today's, although the screen could be a giant computer screen showing films beamed in directly by satellite. There is something about the movie experience as a social event that has allowed the medium to thrive in the face of onslaughts from TV, cable, home video, and perhaps even the Internet. Or maybe it's the smell of the popcorn! Movies have always tried to stay a step ahead of the competition by offering an aesthetic experience that cannot be duplicated by its competitors, so look for bigger screens and ever more sophisticated sound systems. One example of things to come may be the increasing popularity of *IMAX* movies, where 70 mm film is used with very large screens and surround sound to give a much more realistic experience. Many people almost get airsick when a biplane in the classic IMAX film *To Fly* dives over the rim of the Grand Canyon.

But don't look for the "feelies," "stinkies," or "tasties" that science fiction writers and movie technology gurus have predicted since the 1930s. The sensory modalities of touch, smell, and taste are now better understood, and computer interfaces are being developed to stimulate each one artificially. However, this will probably occur in computer-based *virtual reality* immersion environments that will require users to wear helmets and special body suits with sensor arrays, as depicted in *The Lawnmower Man* (1992), for example. This is the antithesis of the shared environment that makes moviegoing a social event. Back in the early 1950s, *3D* (three-dimensional) movies fizzled for three important reasons that may stand in the way of these other sensory enhancements: They made many movie patrons nauseated and the 3D glasses got in the way if you tried to smootch your sweetie. They also looked silly.

Still, 3D movies are one innovation that is likely to appear at some point, only without the cardboard glasses and the airsickness bags. Laser light has potential for creating lifelike, moving three-dimensional images. Pass the virtual popcorn, please.

Although the movie theater may never die, it is undeniable that movies are increasingly viewed in the home. In the next chapter, we will examine the key technology breakthroughs in video tape that led to the advent of the home video cassette recorder in 1975. However, VCRs are being supplanted by a new technology, the digital versatile disc (DVD), that will mark the convergence of the computer and home movie viewing. The DVD uses the same basic recording technology as the familiar music CD (see Chapter 5), only it has far greater storage capacity—enough to store an entire feature film. It offers the benefits of higher quality video and more compact players that can be fully integrated into other digital multimedia systems, including the home computer.

FILM GENRES

Early filmmakers drew on novels, paintings and illustrations, vaudeville, circuses, and other forms of entertainment as models, yet they also created a number of classic types, or **genres,** that still greatly affect film and other media. Current films, television series, made-for-TV movies, miniseries, and even new forms of video and multimedia production often follow classic film formulas. Genre formulas use characteristic narratives, images, settings, characters, plot themes, music, and effects. In a horror film, for example, people expect to see riveting and frightening images, hear creepy music, see scary characters, experience a tense plot, and watch vulnerable characters be threatened. Writers and producers are always looking for new angles, but they must still meet certain kinds of audience expectations. Genres help a great deal in marketing movies to audiences. Think of walking into a video rental store, where you think in terms of genre categories. Do I want to browse the aisles for action, comedy, or science fiction?

Genres are types or formats of media content.

Westerns, science fiction, mysteries, horror, and situation comedies are all popular film genres. Film critics, scholars, and fans enjoy arguing about whether a certain film represents this or that genre. For instance, is *Star Wars* (1977) really science fiction, or is it a western dressed in science fiction costumes? Or to name other genres Lucas drew from, is it a war movie or a swashbuckling pirate movie? (See Profile.) The real point of genre categories is to help us understand how the formulas work, alone or in combinations, and what effect the shows have on their viewers.

TABLE 6.1 Silent-Film Genres

- Westerns, such as *The Great Train Robbery* (1903)
- War movies, with battles and character conflicts, such as *Birth of a Nation* (1915)
- Horror, including the original Dracula, *Nosferatu* (1922)
- Romances, love stories such as *The Sheik* (1921)
- Physical comedies, with car crashes and pratfalls (such as the Keystone Cops shorts) or facial expression and body language (such as Charlie Chaplin and Buster Keaton films)
- Historical costume dramas, with fictionalized plots, such as D. W. Griffith's *Intolerance* (1916)
- Documentaries, such as *Nanook of the North* (1921)
- Action/adventure, such as Douglas Fairbanks' *Thief of Baghdad* (1921)
- Melodramas, such as *The Perils of Pauline* (1914)

Silent Films Set the Patterns

Silent films established some classic genre formulas that are still followed today. Because producers of silent films had to rely on visuals, with only brief written dialog shown on title slides inserted in the film, they were oriented toward action and lavish sets. However, the genres they relied on are alive and well today; witness physical comedy (the *Home Alone* movies) and historical costume dramas (*Titanic*). Table 6.1 describes the main silent-film genres.

Film Genres That Exploit Sound

When "talkies" came in, new genres (such as musicals, with singing and dancing) emphasized the advantages of the new medium. A series of films by the elegant dancing team Ginger Rogers and Fred Astaire, starting with *Flying Down to Rio* in 1933, put music and motion together.

Comedies became more verbal, with jokes and sophisticated bantering added to their basic repertoire of slapstick and sight gags. Several comedy subgenres were created. The zany comedies of the Marx Brothers, such as *Night at the Opera* (1935), poked fun at authority. Screwball comedies, such as *It Happened One Night* (1934), featured Clark Gable, Katharine Hepburn, Cary Grant, and other big stars in elegantly set and clever but silly stories.

Sound, dramatic visuals, and action were combined in increasingly complex formulas that often addressed concerns of the day (or at least of the decade). Crime stories, such as *Little Caesar* (1930), reflected a real-life increase in organized crime that grew with the prohibition of alcohol. Another was *The Maltese Falcon*—the classic detective film. Directed by John Huston, it featured Humphrey Bogart, who went on to star in several other classic 1940s films, including *Casablanca* (1942). A key genre variation on these detective films was the *film noir,* "the dark film," which tended to be more skeptical, even cynical, and had antiheroes instead of the simpler heroes of earlier films. Classics of this genre include *Double Indemnity* (1944), *Out of the Past* (1947), and *Gun Crazy* (1952).

TABLE 6.2 Early Sound Film Genres

- Crime dramas, with cops, gangsters, and violence, such as *Little Caesar* (1930)
- Animation, such as *Snow White and the Seven Dwarfs* (1937)
- Screwball comedies, with glamour and light humor, such as *It Happened One Night* (1934)
- Character studies, such as *Citizen Kane* (1941)
- Detective movies, with complex heroes, such as *The Maltese Falcon* (1941)
- Suspense, such as Fritz Long's *M* (1931)
- Monster movies, such as *King Kong* (1933)
- Horror movies, such as *Dracula* (1931)
- Musicals, such as *Flying Down to Rio* (1933)
- War films, such as *Wings* (1931)
- Film noir, "dark," skeptical films, such as *Double Indemnity* (1944)
- Serials, such as *Buck Rogers*

Suspense and mystery stories, such as Alfred Hitchcock's *The 39 Steps* (1935), constitute another major genre of Hollywood films. Historical epics were another specialty. The most successful film of the 1930s was *Gone with the Wind* (1939), set in the South during the Civil War, with a melodrama-like cast of archetypal characters: the swaggering, handsome hero Rhett and the strong-willed heroine Scarlett.

After the Japanese attack on Pearl Harbor in 1941 and the German declaration of war on the United States, World War II films such as *Bataan* (1943) were popular as a facet of American patriotism (Gomery, 1991). The war was such a pivotal experience for so many Americans that war films persisted long after World War II was over, with movies like *The Great Escape* and *The Longest Day* still being made in the 1960s. By the late 1960s, the growing negative public reaction to the Vietnam War changed the nature of war films to a more critical view.

The Western as a genre peaked in the 1940s and 1950s. It reflected a largely positive view of American culture. The West became a focus for exploring the American myth and American character. The director John Ford, for example, created a number of classic westerns. They gradually changed from the optimistic view exemplified by *She Wore a Yellow Ribbon* (1949) to films such as *The Man Who Shot Liberty Valance* (1962), which emphasized the hypocrisy of the U.S. myth of the West, and *Cheyenne Autumn* (1964), which began to consider the perspective of Native Americans as "good guys," with a different slant on the American conquest of the West.

Table 6.2 lists the main early sound film genres that took shape in the 1930s and 1940s.

1. **What were some of the main silent film genres?**
2. **How did sound change what could be done in movie content?**
3. **What genres came in with talking films?**
4. **What film genres were prominent in the 1930s and 1940s?**
5. **What film genres changed or developed in the 1960s?**

Later Films Expand the Variety of Genres

The earlier genres lay the foundation of movie-making formulas. These are still present, but an explosion of new film genres began in the 1950s and continues today as filmmakers experiment with new ways to attract audiences—

TABLE 6.3 Recently Evolved Film Genres

- Youth rebellion movies, such as *The Wild One* (1954)
- Spy stories, with gadgets and action, such as James Bond in *Goldfinger* (1964)
- Romantic comedies, with varying degrees of sex, such as *Pillow Talk* (1959)
- Science fiction, such as *Forbidden Planet* (1956) and *Terminator* (1984)
- Slasher movies, such as *Friday the Thirteenth* (1980) and *I Know What You Did Last Summer* (1997)
- Rock music movies, such as *A Hard Day's Night* (1964) and *Spice World* (1998)
- "Black" movies, such as *Superfly* (1972)
- Spanish-language movies, such as *El Mariachi* (1992)
- Coming-of-age movies, in which teenagers discover things about themselves, such as *The Breakfast Club* (1985)
- Antiwar movies, such as *Apocalypse Now* (1979)
- Sword and sorcery movies, with magic and muscles, such as *Conan, the Barbarian* (1982)
- Disaster movies, such as *The Towering Inferno* (1974)

and to put TV viewers back into the empty movie houses. Table 6.3 lists several more recently evolved film genres.

The lists in the foregoing tables may seem long, but it is good to realize that there are a lot of variations on genres. New genres proliferate in search of audience segments. However, the basic ones, with the kinds of genre categories that you find in video stores, continue to dominate, particularly as Hollywood continues to play with basic genres with new technological tricks for this year's blockbusters. In particular, filmmakers focus on a core of classic genres to reach very broad audiences both in the United States and abroad. In recent years, U.S. blockbusters at home and abroad have come from those genres in which American big budgets and special effects can be used to best advantage: action-adventure, crime, horror, drama, and science fiction. The biggest blockbusters, such as *Star Wars,* tend to creatively combine elements from a number of genres to reach the audiences to which all those elements appeal.

INDUSTRY ORGANIZATION

The Film Industry

Today, the film industry is a high-volume mixture of large and small players. There are eight major producers: the old-time studios—Columbia, Fox, MGM, Paramount, Universal, and Warner Brothers—along with Buena Vista (Disney) and Tri-Star (Sony). Each produces 15 to 25 movies per year, or about half of the roughly 500 feature films released annually by Hollywood (www.MPAA.org, 1999). At the height of Hollywood's fame in 1946, the major studios each produced 40 to 50 movies each year. The major Hollywood studios currently invest an average of about $53 million per film, plus high *overhead* to keep the studio organizations running, so the stakes are very high and the pressure to produce big hits is enormous.

Independent Filmmakers

There is also an extensive, much less formal network of **independent filmmakers.** These "indies" usually produce films for much less than the **major studios,** often only a few million dollars. A classic pattern is that new filmmakers eke out a hodgepodge of financing for their first film. If their film succeeds, they might get studio backing for subsequent films. For example, Michigan State student filmmaker Sam Raimi borrowed money from friends to make *Evil Dead* (1983), which succeeded well enough in the horror film market for him to get more money for *Evil Dead II* (1987) and major studio financing for *Darkman* (1990). Likewise, Spike Lee made *She's Gotta Have It* (1986) for $200,000, but after that film made $7 million, Columbia produced his next, *School Daze* (1988).

Independent filmmakers ("indies") usually produce fewer films than the majors and at much less cost—often a few million dollars.

Major film producers are the larger studios, each of which produces 15–25 movies per year.

The system for independent filmmakers is slowly getting more organized. People willing to back films now scout major film schools and short-film festivals to see what new filmmakers look promising, perhaps to invest limited funds in a first film. Once new filmmakers have their first feature film, there are a variety of festivals where they can try to get their work seen. There are both national festivals, such as the Sundance Festival in Park City, Utah, and regional festivals, including South by Southwest, in Austin, Texas.

Independent filmmakers and smaller production houses have grown in power since the 1960s (they now account for about half of the movies that are distributed) but they have a shaky existence, often doing only as well as their latest films. Independent studios Carolco, which produced the *Terminator* movies, and Orion, which had *Dances with Wolves* (1990) and others, hovered on the brink of bankruptcy in 1992 until they were bought by Ted Turner.

Film Distribution

The major studios are increasingly part of industry conglomerates. They still control most film distribution, as they have since the 1920s. If a studio produces a film, then that studio handles its distribution to theaters and video, cable TV, and overseas releases. Anyone who makes an independent film must still turn to a film studio or some other distribution company to make those connections and get the film distributed to the various outlets. That gives the studios a stake in many of the independent films that they distribute, but it also gives them more control than independent filmmakers think is healthy.

However, maneuvers around studios to arrange distribution of a film are also possible. Cable and video release rights, which are often arranged before production, can help finance nonstudio productions by known independent producers. Steven Soderbergh financed his innovative independent film *sex, lies and videotape* (1989) primarily by selling the video rights to RCA/Columbia Home Video (Mast & Kawin, 1996).

In general, there are many more film distribution options now than in the heyday of studio control. The archetypal distribution for a major film might be theatrical distribution, then international theatrical distribution, pay per view, pay cable, videocassette rentals and sales, network exhibition, basic cable networks, and finally syndication. Increasingly, all the domestic steps have an international

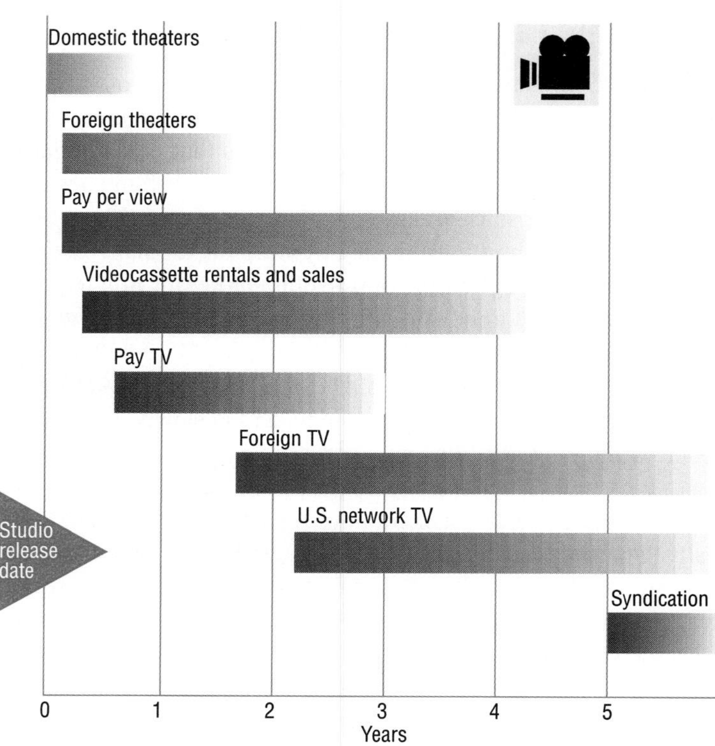

FIGURE 6.1
Films are now released in a series of "windows" to a variety of media.

Windows are times in the film release sequence for showing films in theaters, on pay per view, and so on.

parallel (see Figure 6.1). Films are distributed to a series of **windows,** or times linked to specific channels, such as theaters, video, and cable. There may be some variation in the exact order, depending on whether basic cable networks outbid a broadcast network for rights, for instance. Many films are not seen as being worth the *promotional costs* for theatrical release and go straight to video stores and cable. A quick walk through any video rental store or channel surfing through late-night cable will unearth many teenage beach comedies and low-budget horror films that never make it to the theaters but still turn a profit in the more complex film distribution business centered on "direct to video."

Home Video. Americans spent over $16.9 billion in total on home video in 1998. This trend has produced an enormous industry, although some people wonder whether the current video rental and sales boom will decline considerably as cable television increases in terms of the number of film-oriented channels, pay-per-view, and movies-on-demand options.

In the production aspect of the video business, the ten largest film studios account for over two-thirds of videocassette sales. In between studios and local rental shops are a group of distributors, including CBS/Fox Video, RCA/Columbia Home Pictures, Vestron, Tri-Star, Orion, and dozens of others. The retail side of video is the most complex and changeable. It is dominated by chains, such as Blockbuster Video, that have become big players, as Blockbuster's participation in the 1994 Viacom takeover of Paramount Studios shows. However, Viacom has since decided that video rental is not a core business for it and has spun Blockbuster off again as a separate company. Other retailers, particularly supermarkets and convenience stores, now have racks of videos for sale next to the paperback books and records. And home video sales are fast becoming a staple of on-line commerce on the Internet.

OUTDRAWING THE THEATER. Home video rentals have replaced movie theaters for the over-25 set.

Consolidation and Change in Film Industry Ownership

The film industry has recently been characterized by (1) combination or integration with television networks, (2) consolidation of studio ownership, (3) foreign ownership, and (4) integration in international operations.

Twentieth Century–Fox provides the best example of the integration of film studios with television networks. Rupert Murdoch's News Corp. bought Fox's film and TV production studio, along with TV stations formerly owned by Metromedia, to launch the very successful Fox Network. Viacom similarly bought Paramount to use it as a platform to start the UPN TV network in 1993. Time Warner also used its Warner Studio to launch its own television network (WB TV). Rupert Murdoch is using Fox as part of yet another strategy, the creation of an integrated global television system. Murdoch uses Fox film and television to produce content for its satellite TV channels in Europe (British Sky Broadcasting, Sky Europe), Asia (Star TV), and Latin America (Sky Latin America).

Disney took another route to film-TV integration by merging with ABC/CapCities in 1995, bringing Buena Vista's production of movies, prime-time TV shows, and cartoons to ABC's existing television network and the group's three cable channels (which include ESPN).

MGM has exemplified and suffered the ups and downs of studio ownership consolidation. It acquired UA (United Artists) in 1981, to re-enter the film production business, but failed. The MGM film library was sold to Ted Turner and the production facilities to TV producer Lorimar, then to Warner, then to Columbia. MGM-UA was sold to Crédit Lyonnais, a French bank, which has failed to revitalize it.

Columbia Pictures Entertainment was purchased by Sony, of Japan, which also owns Tri-Star. Despite people's fears of foreign control over content, Sony has hired Hollywood production managers, and both Columbia and Tri-Star have behaved like other production studios. Universal was similarly sold to Matsushita in 1990, but its new owner made little money, struggled to manage a foreign production system, and resold Universal to Seagram of Canada in 1997.

Murdoch is the most ambitious in creating a globally integrated operation. But all of the film studios are heavily involved in exporting films and television programs. Some, such as Disney, have explored satellite channels or other direct operations in various parts of the world.

1. **What are the main film studios or production companies now?**
2. **How do independent filmmakers differ from studios?**
3. **What is currently the typical distribution cycle of a film?**
4. **What has been the effect of home video on the movie industry?**
5. **What has been the effect of film studio integration with television networks?**
6. **What has been the impact of the foreign purchase of film studios?**

AUDIENCES FOR FILM

The main audiences for film are no longer in the movie houses. Films are now viewed primarily on television, cable, or video. The average amount of time spent watching films on video has increased dramatically in the last decade. Over four-fifths of American homes have a VCR. Over three-fifths of Americans rent videotapes at least occasionally. Young adults, especially those with young families, are among the heaviest renters, and children's videos are the most popular genre (McCourt, 1998). The average household spends over $170 per year renting and buying videocassettes. Film viewing at theaters is now most common among people aged 15 to 24, a third of whom go to movies at least once a month, compared to a fifth of all adults. Although smaller proportions of young adults are attending movies than in previous years, the number of young adults is growing as a baby "boomlet" swells, so movie-makers will continue to be swayed by young audiences.

However, films are often still made to maximize the box office earnings of the initial theatrical distribution. The initial box office is what gives a film its "buzz," its momentum. Thus studios still often make movies for people who go out to the movies. Table 6.4 shows that the top earning movies are typically crowd-pleasing blockbusters. This makes the typical movie theater goer, who is younger and more tolerant of sex and violence, disproportionately influential in decisions about what kinds of movies are made.

Movie theater attendance is gradually coming back as a mainstream activity. The number of movies admissions per year dropped precipitously from over 3 billion in 1950 to 920 million in 1970. It has since climbed back to 1.3 billion in 1997 (www.mpaa.org/useconomicreview/1997).

TABLE 6.4 Top 10 Domestic Movie Earners of All Time

Films that constitute the United States and Canada elite 10, as calculated by Variety.
(Listings are as follows: film, releasing company, year of original release, director, and gross domestic box office receipts. This last list updated on June 23, 1998.)

Film	Company	Year	Director	Box Office Gross (in millions)
Titanic	Paramount	1997	James Cameron	1,010
Star Wars	Fox	1977	George Lucas	460
E.T.—The Extra-Terrestrial	Universal	1981	Steven Spielberg	400
Jurassic Park	Universal	1993	Steven Spielberg	357
Forrest Gump	Paramount	1994	Robert Zemeckis	329
The Lion King	Buena Vista	1994	Roger Allens, Rob Minkoff	313
Return of the Jedi	Fox	1983	Richard Marquand	309
Independence Day	Fox	1996	Roland Emmerich	306
The Empire Strikes Back	Fox	1980	Irvin Kershner	290
Home Alone	Fox	1990	Chris Columbus	286

Source: http://www.variety.com/numbers/domestic.asp

Most films are increasingly targeted at specific audiences: action-adventure such as the *Die Hard* movies for young men, romantic "date" movies such as *You've Got Mail* (1998) for young couples, coming-of-age movies such as *The Breakfast Club* (1985) for teen-agers.

1. How have film audiences changed in the last two decades?

2. What has been the impact on film production of a younger audience?

3. How are films targeted now?

POLICY, SOCIAL, AND ETHICAL ISSUES

The film industries are embroiled in a number of policy issues that have affected how they conduct business and the kinds of content they create.

Violence, Sex, Profanity, and Film Ratings

For years, one of the most powerful forces in the entertainment industry has been the Motion Picture Association of America (**MPAA**). The MPAA, composed of the major film studios, has been a major player in American culture and politics.

MPAA (Motion Picture Association of America) is a sales and lobby organization that represents the major film studios.

After years of debate and what seemed to be an increase in the number of movies with profanity, explicit sex, and violence in the 1960s, the Motion Picture Association of America instituted a rating system in 1968 to give people an idea of what they might encounter in a film. With some further modifications over the years, the **MPAA rating** categories are now as follows:

MPAA ratings is a movie rating system instituted in 1968.

G—For all ages; no sex or nudity, minimal violence

PG—Parental guidance suggested; some portions perhaps not suitable for young children, mild profanity, non-"excessive" violence, only a glimpse of nudity

PG 13—Parents strongly cautioned to give guidance to children under 13; some material may be inappropriate for young children

R—Restricted; those under 17 must be accompanied by parent or guardian; may contain very rough violence, nudity, or lovemaking

NC-17—No one under 17 admitted; formerly rated X; generally reserved for films that are openly pornographic, although some mainstream films receive it

Many people have debated the appropriateness and utility of these ratings. Some argue that as a form of industry *self-censorship,* they violate freedom of speech for filmmakers. Others argue that, as with music lyric advisories, the ratings simply excite the interest of younger viewers. Many observe that the restrictions imposed on teen-agers by R and NC-17 ratings are not enforced by theaters, whose managers are aware that teens are the main moviegoers. The ratings system also allowed filmmakers to continue to produce films with sexually explicit and violent content, because they can argue that audiences are alerted to avoid such material. Almost two-thirds of all movies are released with an R rating (MPAA 1997 figures). However, many parents have expressed appreciation for the ratings, which do give them something to work with in guiding children's viewing.

Since the MPAA ratings have been in place for years, it is interesting to see whether they provide a useful precedent, or model, for rating other kinds of media.

Specifically, lawmakers in Congress have mandated a ratings system for television programs as part of the Telecommunications Act of 1996.

The MPAA president, Jack Valenti, has been a highly effective lobbyist in Washington for years. In 1993, for example, he argued against any kind of restrictions on violence in film or television programming (MPAA members also produce much of American television network programming). He lost this debate but has since tried to model the new television ratings system on the existing film ratings, rather than using ratings that separately examine sex, violence, and language for each program.

Vertical and Horizontal Integration

Horizontal integration is concentrating ownership by acquiring companies that are all in the same business, such as television stations.

With the continuing trend toward concentration, vertical integration and **horizontal integration** among diverse branches of the entertainment industries are becoming a major policy issue. Most major film studios are now part of larger conglomerates. Some of those, such as Disney, Time Warner, and Fox, cover nearly all aspects of media production, distribution, and exhibition. For example, Disney, Time Warner, and Fox now produce both film and television, which they can distribute through their own television networks and over their own cable channels, which, in the case of Time Warner, can also be carried over its own cable operators across the United States. By controlling both production and distribution, it is vertically integrated in both film and television. By controlling several forms of distribution, broadcast television, cable channels, and cable systems, it is horizontally integrated.

1. Why were film ratings developed?
2. What are the pros and cons of ratings?
3. Have vertical and horizontal integration in the film industry affected content diversity?
4. What copyright and piracy problems does the film industry face?
5. What is the Motion Picture Association of America (MPAA)? What does it do?

This raises two key issues. One is the potential abuse of market power. If Time Warner cable systems or its new WB Television network discriminates in favor of Warner productions, that may keep other potential producers from getting access to markets for their products. Fear of this kind of abuse of market power prompted the United States, in 1948, to force film studios to divest themselves of their theatrical distribution and exhibition chains, in order to give nonstudio producers more access to distribution for their films.

Syndication is rental or licensing of media products by their producers to other media companies for broadcast, distribution, or exhibition.

The most important aspect of this deregulatory trend for the film industry was the decision to eliminate the so-called financial-syndication rules. These rules declared that television networks could have a financial interest in, or control **syndication** rights over, only a small fraction of what they showed on television. Now that these rules have been eliminated, there is a tendency for broadcasters to merge with film studios in order to gain more revenue from both production and distribution of films and television programs. The acquisition of Disney by ABC, the acquisition of Turner and his MGM film library by Time Warner, and the use of both Paramount and Warner studios as the base platforms for new television networks are evidence of this new concentrated pattern.

Film Piracy

Illegal use of copyrighted intellectual property has been a serious issue for the film industry. Estimates of financial losses to studios and other film copyright holders resulting from illegal copying or piracy are in the hundreds of billions of dollars, both in the United States and abroad.

YOU HAVE BEEN WARNED. This message from the FBI is a visible reminder of the intellectual property rights of film copyright holders.

Films have been relatively easy for many people to copy ever since videotape technology came into wide use in the 1980s. Given its potential for abuse, the MPAA fought the manufacture and sale of VCRs for consumer use, anticipating that they would make piracy easier. Its attempts to block the technology were unsuccessful, so the MPAA has switched strategy.

The film industry hopes to discourage illegal film copying on videotape at the consumer level. Consumers may make, for their own use, a videotape copy of a film that is being broadcast or cable-cast. However, they may not sell or rent that copy to anyone else. A consumer may not make a copy of a videotape playing from one VCR onto another. That deprives the film copyright holder of possible future revenue if the consumer should want to see the movie again. This is why all videotaped films have an FBI warning against illegal copying at the beginning of the tape.

The big issue in piracy is illegal copying by people who intend to sell or rent the illegal copy. That is what really defrauds copyright holders of rentals or sales that they might otherwise have from potential consumers who rent or buy the illegal copy instead of the legal one. Only legal copies provide royalties to the copyright holders, compensating them for the expense and work that went into the movie. Thus the film industry, via the MPAA, has pushed law enforcement officials both in the United States and abroad to enforce copyright laws by pursuing large-scale, commercially oriented pirates. Those who are illegally copying tapes on a large industrial scale are the ones targeted by enforcement efforts.

The MPAA has had remarkable success in getting most governments to crack down on film piracy. The U.S. government has helped apply pressure on other governments to enforce the existing international copyright agreements. Nearly all governments have signed the Berne Copyright Convention, which covers video piracy.

New issues arise in protecting intellectual property that exists in digital form since it is easier to pirate digital material because a computer can be used as the main copying tool. That is now likely to become true of movies as well, now that entire films can be placed on a digital versatile disk that can be played by a computer or a digital TV receiver. Many factories worldwide already pirate CDs and CD-ROMs, which are very similar, so as DVD becomes a major consumer medium, we can expect to see pirated movies on DVD disks also. The enforcement and policy problem is not really different, however. It still involves getting effective enforcement of laws against large-scale commercial pirates.

Filmmakers are trying to push their own "high tech" solution to enforcing digital copyright with the DIVX standard for DVD players. DIVX users purchase specially encoded DVD recordings from local video stores, but after a predetermined number of days, the picture is scrambled. The user then has to pay more to purchase further viewing rights.

Film Preservation

Although scholars now widely recognize film as a major art form in its own right—the modern-day equivalent to great novels or paintings by the masters—the sad fact of the matter is that our film heritage is literally crumbling to dust all around us. The biggest problem is that the nitrate film stock that was in use until the early

ETHICS

MEDIA

Do Filmmakers Need to Think about Social Impacts? Should Viewers Edit Movies?

In a movie about Los Angeles, *Grand Canyon,* one of the main characters is a filmmaker who makes very violent movies. One day he is shot in a mugging attempt and is suddenly caught up in remorse. Has he contributed to the wave of violence that just engulfed him, too? As he recovers—and realizes that violent films are his livelihood—he is suddenly struck again by the need for artistic freedom, which includes expressing the violence in our culture.

While this character is a satire of filmmakers, it raises a real issue. Should filmmakers take responsibility for the social effects of their movies? Or is their role to create art and let the chips fall where they may? The prevailing trend in America is toward unrestricted artistic freedom divorced from social considerations. But religious critics and social philosophers, present and past, such as Walter Benjamin, have argued that the artist is not absolved from responsibility to contribute positively to society. Artists should either raise people's consciousness about issues or, at the very least, refrain from contributing to social harm.

As Chapter 12 discusses, even the researchers do not always agree on how deep or pervasive the effects of violence or sex in movies really are. Yet headlines constantly remind us that some people do tend to imitate specific acts of violence or reckless behavior that they have seen on screen. If even a few mimic an unusual act of violence that a filmmaker dreams up, should that filmmaker feel any responsibility? What if larger numbers of people don't directly imitate the act but come to see it as more normal or acceptable?

Industry spokespeople usually make two counterarguments: first, that individual viewers are not as vulnerable to film messages as is commonly supposed; and second, that individuals and families have a responsibility to make their own decisions about what to watch and what to make of it. For the mainstream of society, making responsible choices is probably the right answer. But how far should they go? People always make choices about what to see. The first author's family doesn't watch horror, violent suspense, or slasher films because they give most of us nightmares—a good disincentive. But what if people could edit out the scenes they don't want to see, in order to see the rest of the film? Airlines and television already edit films to get rid of scenes, images, or language that they anticipate might bother a number of viewers.

As films become available in digital form, on formats like digital versatile disk (DVD), technologies are rising that might let people edit out scenes for themselves, according to various criteria. "Content customization" software is likely to be able to let people specify a level of sexuality, violence, and/or profanity that they don't wish to exceed. The software would screen a "content map" created to summarize the images, actions, and language in various scenes, or even frames of the film. The viewer would then see a somewhat crudely edited, but customized, version of the film adjusted to his or her own sensibilities.

Copyright authorities fear that such customization on the fly might violate the filmmaker's copyright control of the material. Filmmakers themselves are becoming upset that someone would effectively re-edit, even mutilate, their film. They fear a loss of artistic integrity. There are precedents. When some groups wanted to show edited versions of *Schindler's List* to eliminate nudity, Steven Spielberg refused, saying that the nudity in the film showed an exercise of power over helpless women in concentration camps and had little to do with sex. Such differences in point of view may be irreconcilable. Technology may help make the conflict over who gets the final word on movie content much more pervasive, as people suddenly have to make many more personal choices about exactly what to watch and as control over movie content shifts from directors to viewers.

1950s is chemically unstable. First the image fades, and then the film stock itself gets sticky and finally turns to dust—sometimes even exploding in the vaults through spontaneous combustion. Already, most of the film from the silent era has been irretrievably lost, and the film classics of the '30s are in danger. The solution is to transfer the films to "safety stock" with a shelf life of 200–300 years, but there is a backlog of over 100 million feet of film that will take 15 years to copy at the present rate—by which time many precious film moments will be lost forever.

But recent movies have their own special problem: colors fade after as little as five years in storage. You can see this as you watch older films on TV—all the colors seem dull or brown. There is no obvious solution here, although copying to digital storage media may eventually save the day. However, the color films must first be "separated" into red, green, and blue color masters, a very expensive process indeed (American Film Institute, www.afi.org).

You may have heard of film colorization—a process by which computers create colors for old films—but that can only be a last resort. That approach is anathema to film historians since they feel it has been used to despoil (some of them prefer the term "mutilate") black and white film classics such as *It's a Wonderful Life.* The fact that film colorizers such as Ted Turner are able to claim a copyright and turn a profit on the new color works only further infuriates film preservationists who decry the commercialization of masterpieces of classic film.

However, digital technology should eventually end one of the most serious affronts to cinematic artistry—the practice of "panning and scanning" films for television. Movies are basically "too wide" for the television screen, so the broadcaster either has to put black bands at the top and bottom of the picture (known as letterboxing) or move the TV camera back and forth across the movie image, focusing on only one part of it at a time. The new digital High Definition Television (HDTV, see Chapter 7) systems should put an end to that, since they offer wider screens that match the movie image.

SUMMARY AND REVIEW

WHO INVENTED THE MOTION PICTURE CAMERA?

Thomas Edison, in 1888, although others competed by 1900.

FOR WHAT INNOVATIONS IN SILENT FILMS IS D. W. GRIFFITH RESPONSIBLE?

D. W. Griffith pioneered in using a large screen, well-produced outdoor battle scenes, moving shots, and close-ups. His 1915 *Birth of a Nation* was the first feature film.

WHAT WAS THE STAR SYSTEM?

Rudolph Valentino, Lillian Gish, and Charlie Chaplin were such attractions that their names appeared above the name of the film on movie marquees. The studios rose on the basis of this star system, using the stars' popularity to promote their movies.

WHAT WAS THE STUDIO SYSTEM?

The studio system consisted of production companies that employed the complete set of facilities and people required to make and distribute movies. The major movie studios grew by developing a stable of actors, writers, and directors who worked for them over a period of years.

WHICH WERE THE MAIN STUDIOS?

The main Hollywood studios were United Artists, Paramount, MGM (Metro Goldwyn Mayer), Fox, Warner Brothers, Universal, Columbia, and RKO.

WHAT CHANGED WITH TALKING PICTURES?

Talking pictures created a sudden change, starting with *The Jazz Singer* in 1927. Acting became less overstated and stylized. The actors' voices and the use of sound effects, as well as music, became important. Talkies required an influx of new talent, which came mostly from vaudeville and Broadway.

WHAT WERE THE MAIN FILM GENRES OF THE 1930S AND 1940S?

In the 1930s, movies emphasized their new attraction, sound, by creating a series of extravagantly produced musicals, with dancing and singing. The other main genres of the 1930s were comedies, crime dramas, suspense, mysteries, and historical epics.

WHEN DID THEATRICAL FILM ATTENDANCE BEGIN TO DECLINE?

Theatrical film attendance and the revenue of studios at the box office began to decline after 1946, as television viewing made strong, steady inroads into film theater attendance.

HOW DID HOLLYWOOD AND ITS FILMS CHANGE AFTER THE ADVENT OF TELEVISION?

The film industry initially fought television by not releasing any new movies to be shown on television. The film industry was closely tied to theatrical chains, and television quickly cut into their revenues. However, as small theaters closed all over America in the 1950s, the film industry began to realize that it couldn't beat television. Disney started producing programs for television in 1954, and other studios followed. By 1961 the film boycott of television was over.

WHEN DID THE STUDIO SYSTEM DECLINE?

By the 1960s, the power of the movie studios was declining. Independent producers gained more of a role in producing movies, and film studios began to spend much of their time producing TV series.

WHO INVENTED THE MOVIE CAMERA AND PROJECTOR?

Thomas Edison invented most of the major components of the camera, while the Lumiére brothers in France discovered the principle of projecting light through the transparent film strips.

HOW IS SOUND PLACED ON MOVIE FILM?

Bell Labs scientists discovered a way to use a photoreceptor on the film to create light variations corresponding to sound waves, which could be reproduced as an electrical current, then amplified for the speakers.

HOW HAS FILM BEEN IMPROVED?

By increasing the number of frames or images per second, making the image wider, and adding color.

HOW HAVE FILM SPECIAL EFFECTS CHANGED?

Mechanical models, as in the classic 1933 *King Kong,* have been made more sophisticated and ultimately replaced by computer-generated images. Superimposition of images and the use of background matts have also been made more sophisticated by computers.

HOW DO INDEPENDENT FILMMAKERS DIFFER FROM STUDIOS?

The major film producers are the old-time studios—Columbia, Fox, MGM, Paramount, Universal, and Warner Brothers—along with Buena Vista (Disney) and Tri-Star (Sony). Each produces 15–25 movies per year. Independent filmmakers, or "indies," usually produce fewer films and for much less money than the majors—often a few million dollars.

WHAT IS CURRENTLY THE TYPICAL DISTRIBUTION CYCLE OF A FILM?

Typical distribution for a major film might now be theatrical distribution, international theatrical distribution, pay per view, pay cable, videocassette sales, network exhibition, basic cable networks, and finally syndication. It is increasingly common for all the domestic steps to have an international parallel. There may be some variations as when basic cable networks outbid a broadcast network for rights, for instance. Many films seen as not being worth the promotional costs for theatrical release go straight to video stores and cable.

WHAT IS THE MOTION PICTURE ASSOCIATION OF AMERICA (MPAA)? WHAT DOES IT DO?

The MPAA is a sales and lobby organization that represents the major film studios.

WHAT WERE SOME OF THE MAIN SILENT-FILM GENRES?

The silent-film genres included westerns, war movies, science fiction, romances, physical comedies, and historical costume dramas.

WHAT WERE SOME OF THE MAIN GENRES OF THE STUDIO ERA?

The studio era produced films representing the genres that evolved during the silent-film era and added musicals, dramas, melodramas, verbal comedies, film noir, and detective movies.

WHAT PROGRAMMING GENRES CAME TO TELEVISION FROM HOLLYWOOD?

The film industry has fed most of its formulas into television in one way or another: action-adventure movies, westerns, detective dramas, war stories, and cartoons (developed into series forms).

WHO WATCHES THE MOST FILM IN THEATERS? ON VCRS?

Young people under 25 years of age watch the most films in theaters. VCR viewing is highest among those in their middle years and those with young families.

WHY WERE FILM RATINGS DEVELOPED? WHAT ARE THEIR PROS AND CONS?

After years of debate and what seemed to be an increase in movies with explicit language, sex, and violence in the 1980s, the MPAA instituted a ratings system to give people an idea of what they might encounter in a film. Many parents and church groups have expressed gratitude that the ratings give them something to work with in guiding children's viewing. Some critics argue that as a form of industry self-censorship, ratings violate freedom of speech for filmmakers. Others argue that the ratings simply draw the interest of younger viewers. The restrictions on teen-age viewing of films rated R and NC-17 are often not enforced by theaters, because teens are the main moviegoers.

WHAT ARE THE ISSUES ON FILM PIRACY AND COPYRIGHT?

Piracy, or illegal copying of film, increased since the use of VCRs became widspread, and has cost the industry hundreds of billions of dollars in revenue. The Motion Picture Association of America pushes for enforcement of copyright laws to curb piracy. New digital technologies, such as digital versatile disk (DVD), threaten to increase copying again via computers.

WWW Electronic Resources

For up-to-the-minute URLs about *Film and Video,* access the MEDIA NOW site on the World Wide Web at:

http://communication.wadsworth.com/

CHAPTER 7

Television and Cable

WHAT'S AHEAD

This chapter looks at the development of television, beginning with broadcast networks, its subsequent fragmentation into a number of "narrowcast" cable channels, and how that has affected the major genres of programming. It examines the development of television technologies and their impact on TV audiences and industry organization. It also looks at some major policy and ethical issues in television: ownership concentration, diversity of content and ideas, free speech, and fairness.

Access the MEDIA NOW site on the World Wide Web at:
http://communication.wadsworth.com/
Choose "Chapter 7" from the selection box to access electronic information and other sites relevant to this chapter.

DORMITORY TV LOUNGE. UNIVERSITY OF IOWA, 2010

Hey Joe, Jennifer. What are you guys watching?

It's this cool new show called *Friends* about some people just out of college who work in New York and hang out together in a restaurant.

Huh. Sounds like the one I was going to watch, called *Buddies,* but I think that one is set in Seattle. Gloria, que pasa? What are you going to watch?

Oh, It's this great new show called *Amigos.* It's in like San Antonio or someplace. It's kinda fun. They hang out in a *taqueria* and talk a lot, kinda slide back and forth between Spanish and English, just like I like to do.

Well, we do have four big-screen TVs in here. But you know what? Let's try something and just watch 'em all in different windows on the same TV.

Well, OK. Might be fun, but what about the sound?

If it bugs us, we can always put on headphones.

This is spooky. The dialogue is the same. Hey Gloria, what are they saying in *Amigos*? I don't do Spanish so well.

It *is* spooky. The dialog is the same in Spanish, too. In fact, I think the actors are the same. Look at that Latino dude there . . . looks almost just like the Anglo dude in New York.

You know, I think the New York and Seattle dudes are the same, too, except the guy in Seattle has a plaid shirt on.

Wow! I wonder what those Hollywood types will think of next.

Chapter Outline

A Brief History of Television, Cable, and Satellite TV
From Radio Networks to Television Networks
Diversifying the Television "Vast Wasteland"
Network Television Faces Competition in the 1980s–1990s
Trends in Television Technology
Television Transmission and Reception
Cable TV
New Multichannel Technologies
Home Video
Digital Television
TV Genres
From Radio and Film to Television
How TV Genres Developed
Genres and Forms in Multichannel Programming
Industry Organization
The Television Industry
Cable Industry Structure
Network Ownership and Group Station Owners
Cable Ownership and Control
Audiences for Television
Audiences for Multichannel Media
Policy and Ethical Issues
Ownership Rules
Owner Interference with TV News
Violence Warnings and Controls
Diversity and Minority Ownership
Fairness Doctrine
The Need to Visualize TV News
Summary and Review

NTSC (National Television Systems Committee) developed the U.S. television standard in 1941.

A BRIEF HISTORY OF TELEVISION, CABLE, AND SATELLITE TV

Even as radio was developing as a major broadcast medium in the late 1920s, and film was experimenting with "talkies," some people were thinking about "radio with pictures" as a next step. The audience loved film's visuals as much it did radio in the 1920s–1940s. So why not combine the two?

In the 1920s and 1930s, television developed technologically in a series of steps. In 1922, 21-year-old Philo Farnsworth, allegedly by pondering the rows in the plowed fields of his native Idaho, came up with the idea of an "image dissector," scanning an image in a series of lines. Working with a group of engineers at RCA, Vladimir Zworykin invented the iconoscope tube in 1923. Both of these pioneers had come up with the essential technology for a television camera—an electronic scanning system. Another independent inventor, Allen Dumont, had developed the essential technology for a receiver picture tube.

In the next decade, television was moving ahead around the world. The first British broadcast occurred in 1935. The first U.S. broadcast was the Columbia–Yale baseball game in 1939. The final standards for U.S. television were worked out by a government-mandated compromise among manufacturers, the **National Television Systems Committee (NTSC)**. The 1941 NTSC black-and-white television standards are still in use (Udelson, 1982).

World War II (1939–1945) put television on hold in the United States. Some experimental stations stayed on the air, while hundreds of license applications were pending. Broadcasters, advertisers and investors were uncertain about whether the technology was ready. In the late 1940s, improved cameras and technology for connecting stations into networks reduced some of the uncertainty, and stations started to rush onto the air in 1948 (Sterling & Kittross, 1994).

However, it looked as though the existing FCC technical standards did not allow for nearly enough stations to cover the United States while preventing interference from overlapping stations, so the FCC imposed a freeze on new station applications from 1948 to 1952. The 108 stations approved before the freeze continued operations,

TELEVISION MILESTONES TIME LINE

1923	Zworykin invents iconoscope tube
1927	Farmsworth applies for TV patent
1948	TV takes off
1948 – 1952	TV station license freeze spurs cable TV
1954	Disney studio makes *Disneyland* for ABC
1960	Kennedy–Nixon debates on TV
1961	Newton Minnow calls TV a "vast wasteland"
1965	Color television broadcasting increases
1967	Carnegie Commission on Educational TV; Congress passes Public Broadcasting Act
1968	TV coverage of Vietnam Tet Offensive
1972	FCC allows urban cable systems
1975	HBO goes national via satellite
1979 – 1984	Cable TV franchise wars in large cities; rise of TCI, Time Warner, and other cable multiple system operators
1987	Fox television network debuts
1994	U.S. DBS systems launched
1994 – 1995	Time Warner starts WB television network; Viacom, owners of Paramount and Universal, starts UPN network
1996	Telecomm Act permits vertical integration of nets, studios, cable
1998	AT&T buys TCI—cable-telephone convergence

and the number of sets in homes rose dramatically from 250,000 in 1948 to 17 million in 1952. Television fever was particularly contagious along the East Coast, for many cities in the Midwest and West were not covered yet. The spread of television in America was one of the fastest *diffusions of an innovation* (see Chapter 2) in the history of consumer electronics.

The 1952 FCC rules, known as the *Sixth Report and Order,* clarified the **VHF** (very high frequency) television band (channels 2–13) and opened the **UHF** (ultra high frequency) band (channels 14–83, later reduced to 14–69). The VHF allocations gave no more than three to four licenses to any city, which effectively limited the number of national television networks to three until much later, after UHF and cable TV developed. At first, only VHF stations prospered, because they could broadcast a better signal over a greater distance than UHF stations could.

VHF stands for very high frequency television in channels 2 to 13.

UHF stands for ultra high frequency channels 14 to 69.

The birth of cable TV was one consequence of TV fever. It started as a community antenna television service (CATV) in 1948, bringing television to remote small cities and towns that did not get clear broadcast signals. Broadcast television was supportive of cable TV at first when it just helped extend the reach of local stations to areas that were physically blocked from good reception, but broadcasters soon began to worry that cable TV would become an economic threat.

From Radio Networks to Television Networks

Television **networks** grew up after 1948, when AT&T's new coaxial cable technology for connecting stations into networks made technical networking possible. Three television networks grew out of the three radio networks—NBC, CBS, and ABC—discussed in Chapter 6. A fourth, the Dumont Network had no radio connections; this short-lived attempt to start a fourth network lasted from 1944 to 1955.

Networks are groups of stations that centralize the production and distribution of programming and ads.

MEDIA WATCH

Born on a Mountaintop—Community Antenna TV

In the summer of 1948 the citizens of Mahanoy, Pennsylvania, were feeling left out of a new media trend that was sweeping the nation—television. Mahanoy was situated some 60 miles from the nearest television stations in Philadelphia, and the Allegheny Mountains blocked signals from even the tallest rooftop antennas. Perhaps the unhappiest man in Mahanoy was John Walson, the local appliance dealer and an employee of the power company. He sold television sets that, unfortunately, produced only blasts of static. To demonstrate television to potential customers, he had to take them to the top of a nearby mountain. Soon tiring of these treks, Walson connected the mountaintop antenna to his appliance shop in the valley below, stringing together eight homes along the way. To keep a forest of TV antennas from sprouting in the Alleghenies, Walson developed the concept of using one antenna to service numerous homes. At about the same time, the same idea occurred to Ed Parsons, a radio station employee in Astoria, Washington, and the cable television industry was born.

The NBC and CBS television networks were developed from strong radio networks, whereas ABC came from a weaker, secondary radio network spun off by NBC after a court order in 1943. While RCA dominated the technology of television through its patents, its network, NBC, could not dominate programming or the audience. William Paley at CBS focused on programming, paying high salaries to attract stars away from NBC. As the television networks began to develop distinct characters, CBS and NBC together dominated both the ratings and the race to gain affiliated stations. In fact, ABC was rumored to be close to bankruptcy more than once. In 1954 only 40 of 354 stations were primarily affiliated with ABC.

TV PIONEER. **One of the pioneers of television was Vladimir Zworykin, shown here demonstrating an early television receiver.**

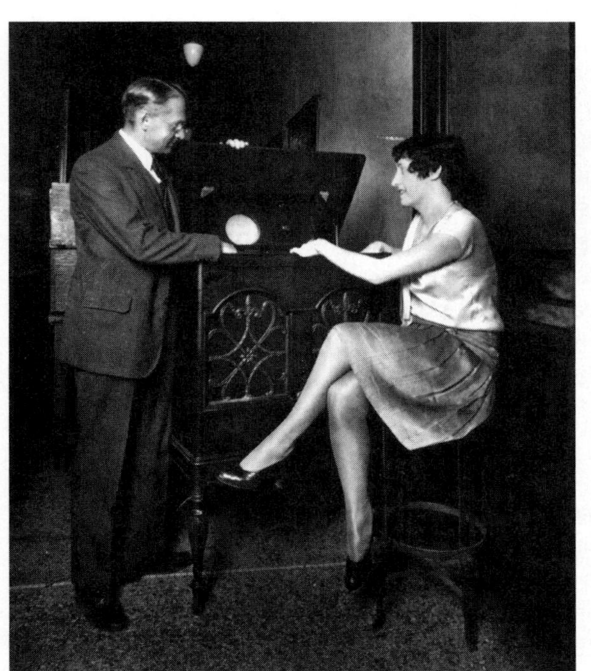

The early developers of network television came largely from radio (Whetmore, 1981) and theater, less from film in Hollywood, at least at first. Television producers worked hard to create a separate identity for television. They often had training in New York style news, entertainment, and show business, and they wanted to create something new, not just to reflect the style of Hollywood.

Many of the programs that television originally featured came directly from radio. Those included westerns such as *Gunsmoke* (1955–1975), soap operas such as *The Guiding Light,* and comedies such as *The Jack Benny Show* (1950–1977). The TV **variety show** evolved in part from radio variety shows, but its roots also reached further back to **vaudeville.**

As we noted in Chapter 6, the Hollywood film industry initially saw television only as a competitor. At first, Hollywood refused to let television broadcast feature films made after 1948. Nevertheless, television made such deep inroads into the weekly film-going audience in the 1950s that movie theaters closed by the thousands across America. By the early 1950s, some film studios, such as Warner Brothers and Disney, shifted their strategy to "if you can't beat 'em, join 'em" and began to produce programs for television. By the 1960s, film studios were spending much of their time producing series for television.

Variety shows combine a number of elements such as comedy, music, games, interviews, and amateur try-outs.

Early TV Programming. Comedy dominated television programming through the late 1940s and 1950s. Comedy star Milton Berle, "Uncle Milty," was NBC's chief attraction. Berle was the forerunner of TV stand-up comedy. He stood on the stage and told jokes. He also wore outrageous outfits, often dressing in drag. He was the kind of new entertainment phenomenon that drove people to buy televisions. Bob Hope and others followed in Berle's footsteps. Comedy combined with music on NBC to form variety shows, such as *Your Show of Shows* (1950–1954) with Sid Caesar and Imogene Coca. One of the driving forces in creating new directions in programming at NBC was Sylvester "Pat" Weaver, father of actress Sigourney Weaver. He introduced periodic specials and magazine programs such as *Today* and *Tonight,* which dominated their time slots on television for many years (MacDonald, 1994).

Vaudeville was a stage show of mixed specialty acts, such as songs, dances, skits, comedy, and acrobatics.

CBS also had its own stand-up comics, such as George Burns and Gracie Allen, but CBS moved in a different direction by introducing **situation comedies,** such as Jackie Gleason's *Honeymooners,* still considered a classic of the genre. Sitcoms proved to be an economical and appealing comedy format over the long run. CBS sitcoms developed with *I Love Lucy* (1951–1959) and *The Dick Van Dyke Show* (1961–1966). CBS also introduced westerns, which had been popular on radio,

Situation comedies feature a group of characters in a comic situation dealing with new tensions or issues each episode.

MEDIA WATCH

TV—From New York to Hollywood

Until 1956 most television was done live from New York. Many think of the 1950s as television's "Golden Age," primarily because of the concentration at that time on original drama. This was partially due to the early television audience—an affluent, educated, urban group who liked live drama. But also, videotape recording was not available yet, so programs had to be live. Programs such as *Studio One* and *Kraft Television Theater* featured such top playwrights as Rod Serling and Gore Vidal, along with Broadway acting stars.

However, by 1957 nearly all entertainment production had moved to the West Coast to take advantage of the Hollywood talent pool. Network news and soap opera production stayed in New York. The networks produced the news, and the soaps were produced either by the networks or by advertising agencies or soap company sponsors for the networks. Other programs, including sitcoms, action adventures, made-for-TV movies, and dramas, were increasingly produced by film studios or independent television producers in Los Angeles for network use.

Television also started using Hollywood feature films. In 1961, NBC introduced *Saturday Night at the Movies* to use movies that were often cheaper and better made than network series. As the supply of post-1948 feature films began to dwindle, NBC and others began to produce "made-for-television" movies. Heavy use of movies on network television continued into the mid-1970s, when both pay channels and superstations on cable TV began to drain off much of the supply of movies on television and much of the audience for such features.

IMPACT

MEDIA

Murrow, McCarthy, Blacklists, and Politics on TV

Edward R. Murrow of CBS News had become famous for his radio news coverage from London during World War II. His fame grew after a series of controversial and pointed documentaries and reports on his regular news show, *See It Now.* Although others had criticized McCarthy, Murrow felt strongly that the news media were not standing up to McCarthy. In 1954, on *See It Now,* he used footage of McCarthy's own press conferences to expose the excesses of the anticommunist crusade, which had destroyed the careers and lives of many people on the basis of little evidence.

Others corroborated his contention that McCarthy's charges and lists were often unfounded, and the Senate ended up censuring (reprimanding) him. To many, these events demonstrated the growing power of television news in the 1950s.

MCCARTHYISM. Joseph McCarthy campaigned against communism in Senate subcommittee investigations and at press conferences.

such as *Gunsmoke* (1955–1975). CBS addressed itself to the rural and small-town nature of much of the television audience in the 1960s with entries such as *The Andy Griffith Show* (1960–1968) and *The Beverly Hillbillies* (1962–1971).

ABC began to bridge the gap with Hollywood by ordering the first television series produced by a film studio, *Disneyland* (1954–1961), followed a year later by the children's program *The Mickey Mouse Club* (1955–1959) and then a studio-produced western, *Cheyenne* (1955–1963). ABC aimed many of its programs, such as the Disney shows, the teenage dance program *American Bandstand* (1957–1987), and the western *Maverick* (1957–1962), at a younger audience and also worked on creating a niche in sports. In the late 1950s, ABC introduced more action-adventure with *77 Sunset Strip* (1958–1964), *The Rifleman* (1958–1963), and *The Untouchables* (1959–1963); these kinds of programs moved ABC into a more competitive audience position.

Television news was very popular in the early years, but it confronted an ugly political crisis early in the 1950s. Trading on the Cold War rivalry with the Soviet Union that began in 1948, several American politicians were crusading to expel from media and government any people they thought were sympathetic to the Soviet Union or to communism, its political philosophy. This crusade led to the "blacklisting" of a number of writers and performers who were suspected of being sympathetic to left-wing causes. Those blacklisted often lost their media jobs; some even committed suicide. Senator Joseph McCarthy (Republican, Wisconsin), chair of a Senate subcommittee on investigations, staged a number of public witch hunts. *McCarthyism* became a catchphrase for politically motivated persecution.

Unfortunately, most of the Hollywood and television managers went along with the blacklisting and even created their own in-house lists.

TV in the 1960s—A Vast Wasteland? Television continued to develop as a force in American society. In 1960, 65 million people watched the presidential campaign debates between John F. Kennedy and Richard Nixon, one of a series of encounters between television and politics. Those who listened to the debates on radio were more likely to think Nixon had won than those who watched on television, where Kennedy was visually appealing but Nixon had jowls and a "five o'clock shadow." Television (in 1963) showed Kennedy's funeral to a shocked nation, along with the murder of his alleged assassin. And it brought into millions of homes the civil rights movement in the South, the Vietnam War, and the domestic protest marches against the war.

Television developed technically in the 1960s, too. Screens gradually got bigger. Color broadcasting, which originated in 1953, became increasingly common by 1965, adding to television's visual impact (Barnouw, 1990). Prices declined, so some families began to have multiple sets.

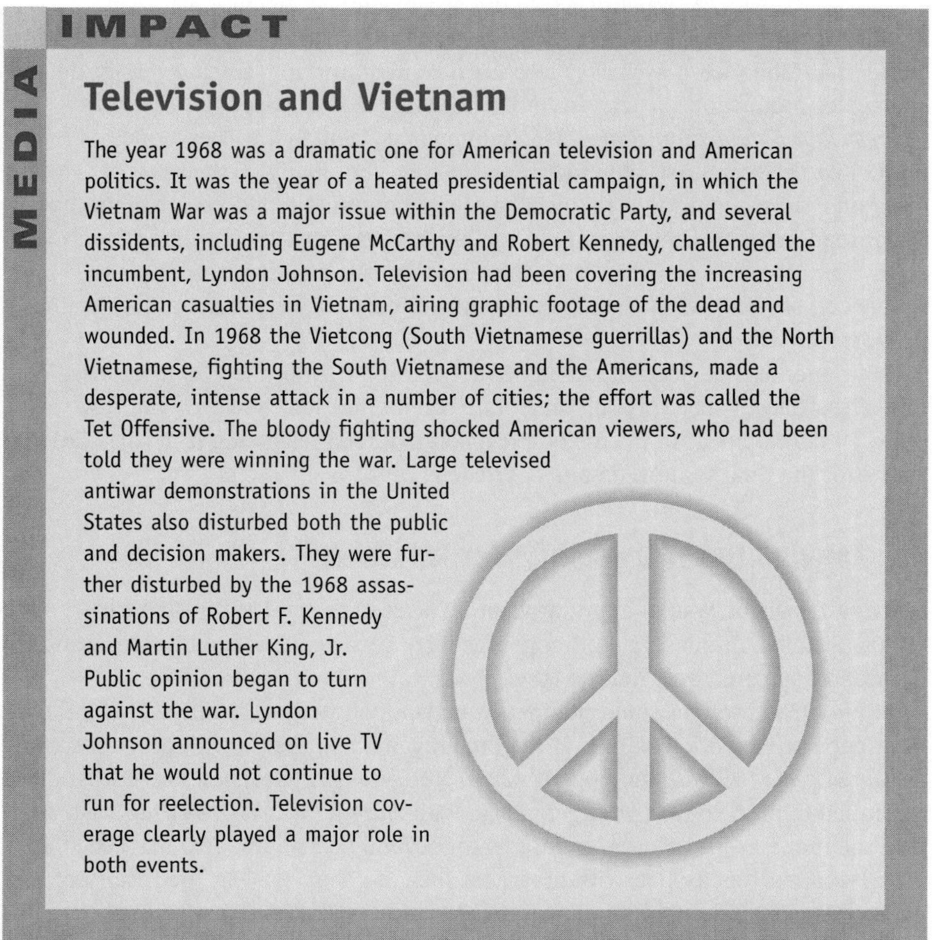

MEDIA IMPACT

Television and Vietnam

The year 1968 was a dramatic one for American television and American politics. It was the year of a heated presidential campaign, in which the Vietnam War was a major issue within the Democratic Party, and several dissidents, including Eugene McCarthy and Robert Kennedy, challenged the incumbent, Lyndon Johnson. Television had been covering the increasing American casualties in Vietnam, airing graphic footage of the dead and wounded. In 1968 the Vietcong (South Vietnamese guerrillas) and the North Vietnamese, fighting the South Vietnamese and the Americans, made a desperate, intense attack in a number of cities; the effort was called the Tet Offensive. The bloody fighting shocked American viewers, who had been told they were winning the war. Large televised antiwar demonstrations in the United States also disturbed both the public and decision makers. They were further disturbed by the 1968 assassinations of Robert F. Kennedy and Martin Luther King, Jr. Public opinion began to turn against the war. Lyndon Johnson announced on live TV that he would not continue to run for reelection. Television coverage clearly played a major role in both events.

In the 1960s and 1970s, some television variety shows (such as *The Smothers Brothers,* 1967–1975), sitcoms, and dramas began to reflect a more critical point of view about social issues. The series *M*A*S*H* (1972–1983), about the struggle of doctors working in a field hospital in the Korean War, was viewed by many as an indirect critique of the Vietnam War (1965-1973). Norman Lear's *All in the Family* (1971–1983) mixed humor with satire about racial bigotry, Vietnam, and the Nixon administration (1968–1974). However, many of the most popular 1970s programs, such as *The Brady Bunch* (1969–1974), were light entertainment (MacDonald, 1994).

STOP & REVIEW

1. **What innovations did Farnsworth and Zworykin introduce?**
2. **Why did the FCC freeze television licenses from 1948 to 1952?**
3. **What is the NTSC standard? How was it developed?**
4. **Where did the television networks come from?**
5. **What were the main television genres of the 1950s?**
6. **How did television affect society in the 1960s?**

The networks were popular and powerful in the 1960s, but some critics and regulators wondered why television wasn't more diverse, more educational, and more culturally rich. The Federal Communications Commission (FCC) Chairman in 1961, Newton Minnow, called American television a "vast wasteland" of mediocre, uninformative programs (Sterling & Kittross, 1990). Critics complained that network programming tended to be similar and repetitive (see the accompanying Media Watch box). Federal regulators feared that the three commercial networks had too much power over television content and moved to diversify the sources of production for television. In 1970, the FCC imposed the *Financial Interest and Syndication Rules,* widely known as **"Fin-Syn."** These rules prohibited the broadcast networks from making very many of their own programs, from acquiring a financial share of programs produced for them that they broadcast, and from sharing in the profits generated by a program's reruns or "syndication." These rules were a boon to outside producers, such as the Hollywood studios, which had been producing most of the programming for the networks anyway.

Fin-Syn or Financial interest in Syndication Rules by FCC kept networks from producing or owning most of their programming to increase diversity.

But another FCC action favored the networks. In 1966, the FCC took jurisdiction over cable TV as a form of "interstate communication by wire," and froze cable TV development in the major television markets, relegating it to rural CATV status for the time being (Parsons & Frieden, 1998).

Diversifying the Television "Vast Wasteland"

Network television was in many ways at its peak in the late 1960s and early 1970s. Sitcoms, dramas, and other genres were very popular as audience **ratings** hit peaks that could only decline later.

Ratings are audience surveys that show what proportions of all households with a television are watching a specific show.

The 1970s brought some changes in network strategy. CBS tended to be the most popular network. It aimed at the broad, general audience with programs such as *The Beverly Hillbillies* and *Green Acres.* NBC stressed television movies. ABC continued to pitch toward younger people with *Happy Days* (1974–1984), which held the number-one position in ratings for several years. ABC also succeeded in the new miniseries format, with programs such as *Roots* (1977), the history of an African American family brought over to America as slaves. Over 140 million

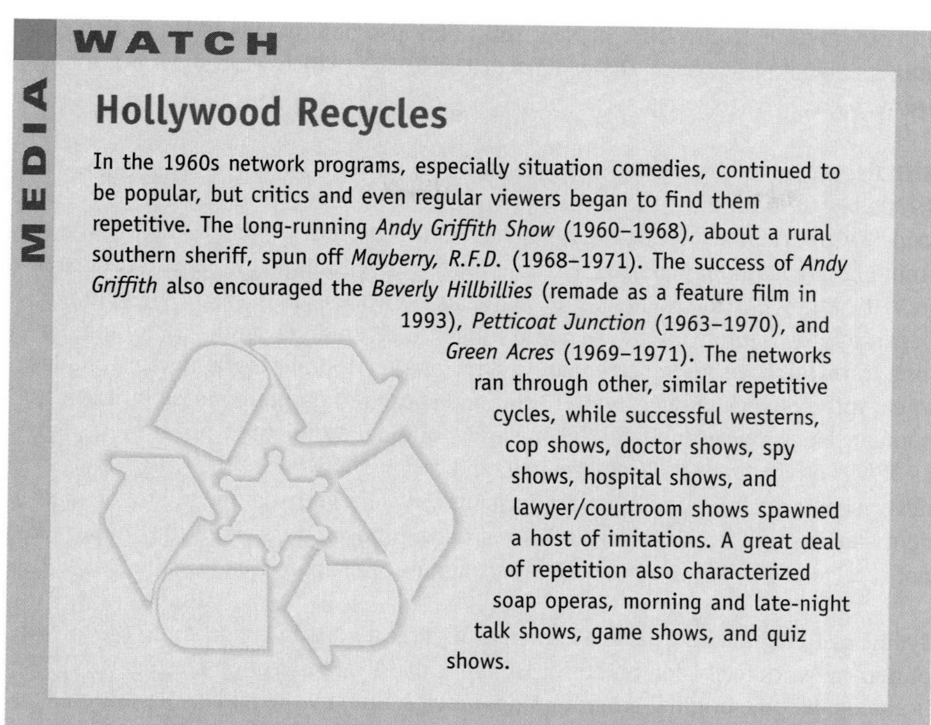

MEDIA WATCH

Hollywood Recycles

In the 1960s network programs, especially situation comedies, continued to be popular, but critics and even regular viewers began to find them repetitive. The long-running *Andy Griffith Show* (1960–1968), about a rural southern sheriff, spun off *Mayberry, R.F.D.* (1968–1971). The success of *Andy Griffith* also encouraged the *Beverly Hillbillies* (remade as a feature film in 1993), *Petticoat Junction* (1963–1970), and *Green Acres* (1969–1971). The networks ran through other, similar repetitive cycles, while successful westerns, cop shows, doctor shows, spy shows, hospital shows, and lawyer/courtroom shows spawned a host of imitations. A great deal of repetition also characterized soap operas, morning and late-night talk shows, game shows, and quiz shows.

Americans saw at least part of *Roots,* making it one of the major television successes of the 1970s. Several of its episodes are still among the ten programs with the largest audience in the history of American television.

The 1970s represented the peak of audience viewing for network television. Cable TV, UHF, and even PBS began to erode the networks' audience by the late 1970s and 1980s. Even though the audience ratings for the networks were high, many in the audience were beginning to look for alternatives.

Public Television. But many were looking for alternatives to the "vast wasteland" of network TV. The concept of noncommercial educational television dates back to the 1950s. Part of the reason for the 1948–1952 FCC freeze on licenses was to reserve frequencies and licenses for educational TV. Universities and others experimented with various forms of educational television, but the programming tended to be low-budget and not very compelling. Nothing had taken off at a visible, national level.

The inspiration for the current era of public television began with a report by the Carnegie Commission on Educational Television in 1967 that recommended the creation of a funding agency, the Corporation for Public Broadcasting (CPB). Congress enacted the Public Broadcasting Act in 1967. It established the CPB, followed in 1969 by the Public Broadcasting Service (PBS), which distributed programs to public stations. Major PBS stations, such as WGBH-Boston, emerged as program producers. *Sesame Street* (1969), came from Children's Television Workshop; public affairs programs by Bill Moyers

SYNDICATED VANNA. Longtime syndication hit *Wheel of Fortune* is licensed directly to local TV stations.

and others came from WNET in New York. PBS also bought successful British programs, including *Upstairs, Downstairs* (1974–1975), which were shown in the *Masterpiece Theatre* series.

UHF Television. In another effort to diversify television, the FCC in the 1960s and 1970s began to promote the development of UHF stations (channels 14–69). The cable TV freeze in 1966, for example, was aimed at protecting small UHF stations from big city stations imported by cable. Their limited range and power, compared to VHF stations, made them less attractive as network affiliates, so UHF stations began to grow largely as **independents.** Most UHF stations stagnated for quite a long time, but their audience began to grow as they found programming formulas to eat into network popularity. UHF stations started to program more old movies, popular television reruns, and, increasingly, original **syndicated programs,** such as *Wheel of Fortune* (1983–). Original syndication shows were those that had never been broadcast on network television but were licensed directly to independent stations and even network affiliates during those hours when they either did not receive or did not use network programming (Eastman, Head, & Klein, 1989).

Independents are those stations not affiliated with a network.

Syndicated programs are rented or licensed by their producers to other companies for broadcast, distribution, or exhibition.

Syndicated Programming as an Alternative. Syndication was important to the growth of non-network television on both UHF and cable TV. Syndication started with licensing of some original programming, movies, and, by the mid-1950s, reruns (programs that had finished their first runs on network television). Programs were licensed or syndicated not by the networks, but by their original producers or by middleman groups that bought rights to programs from producers, packaged them, and then sold the rights to stations. The original producers were typically Hollywood studios or independent producers, such as MTM (Mary Tyler Moore Productions).

Syndication on network affiliates got a boost in 1970 when the FCC limited network programming of prime time to three of the four hours between 7 and 11 P.M., the Prime Time Access Rule. This was supposed to open up more broadcast time for local production, but nearly all network affiliates used syndicated national programming instead. This demand, plus the growth in the 1980s of basic cable networks that relied heavily on reruns and other syndicated material, increased the amount of first-run or original syndication from 25 new shows in 1980 to 96 in 1986 (Sterling & Kittross, 1990).

The Rise of Cable TV. Cable created other alternatives to network TV. By 1970, cable operators were expanding to small cities and towns that received only the three broadcast networks of the day—ABC, CBS, and NBC—to respond to a perceived audience interest in more program options. To accomplish this, they imported **distant signals,** usually those of independent television stations from nearby major television markets.

Distant signals are cable channels imported from major television markets.

Until 1972, cable operators were kept out of the largest television markets by the FCC to nurture local UHF stations. The FCC feared that imported distant signals would undermine independent UHF stations. In addition, if the distant signals carried the same programs as the local TV channels, the latter's ratings might suffer. Broadcasters also felt that it was unfair for cable operators to retransmit their programs at a profit without compensating them.

Without original programming, however, cable TV did not appeal to enough suburbanites and city dwellers to justify the expense of building cable systems in their neighborhoods. By the late 1960s, many urban residents already had access to UHF and other broadcast signals that expanded their viewing options beyond network television. Without access to large urban audiences, there was no way to justify the development of original programming for cable.

One solution to the programming problem was to offer movies and live sporting events on special channels. Cable subscribers were required to pay an additional monthly fee for these channels—a service that became known as **pay TV.** In the early years, local cable operators picked their own movies and fed them into unused channels on their systems, but the potential for new national movie channels existed.

Pay TV is the practice of charging cable customers an extra monthly fee to receive a specific channel, usually movies or sports.

A **superstation** is a distant signal that is distributed nationally via satellite.

Basic cable includes the local channels, distant stations, and satellite signals that cable operators offer for a basic monthly fee.

HBO and the Rise of the Cable Networks. In 1972 the FCC mandated that each new cable TV system have at least 20 channels as they lifted the freeze on urban cable systems. This created an opportunity for cable-originated programming to fill the (then) unused channels and to spread costs over a larger audience.

Home Box Office (HBO) was the first to capitalize on this opportunity. In 1975 HBO created the first national cable network by beaming a championship prize fight between Joe Frazier and Muhammed Ali to a national audience via satellite. HBO followed up with a regular schedule of "first-run" movies that had not yet appeared on television. HBO proved popular, and pay television revenues lifted cable out of the doldrums.

Also in 1975, a young television station owner in Atlanta named Ted Turner put WTBS on satellite. This spawned the idea of a **superstation,** distributing a local television station nationally via satellite. Turner profited by selling advertising at premium rates to advertisers who wanted to reach a national audience. Because the superstation derived considerable revenue from its advertising, Turner could charge cable operators much less than HBO could. Cable operators included the superstation as part of the basic monthly charge for service, a practice that popularized the term **basic cable.** WGN from Chicago and WOR (later WWOR) from New York also appeared via satellite in short order.

Networks that were available only on cable also began to appear. The first were the Christian Broadcasting Network (CBN, later known as The Family Channel), the Cable Satellite Public Affairs Network (C-SPAN), and the Entertainment and Sports Network (ESPN). By 1982 there were three dozen satellite networks available on cable. In 1980 Turner launched a second network, the Cable News Network (CNN), which became a staple of cable channel lineups everywhere. These channels amplified the appeal of basic cable service, giving rise to a new concept in TV programming—*narrowcasting,* or devoting an entire channel to one particular genre or audience segment.

Now that cable had some programming of its own, it had something to offer in urban areas. Large companies that

GOOD BET.
Black Entertainment Television (BET) was one of the first national basic cable channels. BET has developed such original programming as the movie *Race to Freedom: The Underground Railroad,* featuring Courtney Vance and Janet Bailey.

Multiple system operators (MSOs) are cable companies that operate systems in two or more communities.

Local origination is cable programming created within the community by the cable operator.

Public access is cable programming created by community residents and organizations without the involvement of the cable operator.

Must Carry Rules required cable TV systems to carry local broadcast television channels on their systems.

owned numerous cable systems, **multiple system operators (MSOs)**, such as Time Warner and Tele-Communications, Inc. (TCI), bid for the right to wire the cities. At this time, municipal authorities typically awarded a single, exclusive cable franchise after a competitive-bidding process. The cities added to the franchising frenzy by setting requirements for many "extras," such as **local origination** and **public access** channels on which local residents and government bodies could show their own programs. Public access led to the development of both local programs and some alternative networks, such as Deep Dish Television, which air programs on a series of public access channels across the U.S.

As cable TV began to prosper and extend its subscribership deeply into suburbs and cities, the television networks and the FCC again became concerned about the competition hurting broadcast television. Not everyone could subscribe to cable, so the FCC did not want "free" TV seriously damaged. The FCC required cable systems to carry all local television channels, both VHF and UHF, on their systems, a provision known as **Must Carry Rules.** This was a particular boon to UHF stations, because their signals on cable were now as clear and strong as those of VHF stations.

MSOs—The Rise of Tele-Communications, Inc. and Time Warner. By the end of the franchising competition, TCI had assumed a preeminent role in the cable industry. Under the leadership of John Malone, TCI won the confidence of Wall Street investors and mounted an acquisition campaign that made TCI the largest cable company of all. Malone also invested in programming services, beginning with Black Entertainment Television (BET) in 1979. Over the years, TCI and its spinoff, Liberty Media, obtained financial interests in a dozen cable networks, including Ted Turner's. Other cable industry giants also grew rapidly, including Continental (later acquired by telephone giant US West and renamed Media One), Comcast, and American Television and Communications (ATC) (later part of the Time Warner conglomerate). Time Warner bought up a number of systems and is now the other dominant MSO, alongside TCI.

In 1984, as part of a general deregulatory trend under the Reagan administration, the FCC removed cable rate regulation. As a result, cable operators increased their prices and revenues, and the value of cable systems skyrocketed in the late 1980s. The new urban cable systems, most with 50 or more channels, opened new slots for yet more cable networks. Furthermore, rate deregulation meant that cable operators could readily generate the money to pay for them. The lure of programming and profits also attracted some new competitors eager to cash in on the multichannel gold rush. The 1984 Cable Act also forced cable operators to share programming channels with other new wireless technologies, which stimulated development of satellite reception directly in the home.

TVRO (television receive only) is a backyard satellite receiver that lets individual homes receive the same channels that are intended for cable systems.

TVRO, SMATV, and DBS: Backyard Cable. By 1983, a complete **television receive-only (TVRO)** "dish" installation 6–8 feet across could be had for only a few thousand dollars. These devices enabled owners to receive HBO, WTBS, MTV, and dozens of other cable channels completely free of charge. Many rural residents installed their own backyard systems. This actually benefited the cable industry, because it extended the audience for advertising-supported cable channels to areas that were beyond cable's reach. Soon owners of large apartment buildings and condominium complexes began installing their own dishes as well, creating

satellite master antenna television (SMATV) systems that were, in effect, mini-cable systems. These systems cut both the cable operators and the cable networks out of the profits and led the cable networks to begin scrambling their programs prior to satellite transmission.

SMATV (satellite master antenna television) is a TVRO system serving an entire apartment building or housing complex from a central satellite antenna.

Direct broadcast satellite (DBS) systems are another effort to cash in on satellite-delivered entertainment. DBS systems differ from the TVRO model in that subscribers are required to pay a fee for the programming. The signals are scrambled so that only authorized subscribers can receive them. However, it wasn't until 1995 that DBS operators, led by DirecTV and Primestar, successfully entered the U.S. market with a full range of programming options, new digital transmission technology, and easy-to-install "pizza-sized" satellite dishes.

DBS (direct broadcast satellite) is a satellite service that is sold directly to home subscribers.

Home Video. The spread of **videocassette recorders (VCRs)** and video stores in the 1980s also posed a potential threat to both television and cable TV. It was feared that home video would wipe out the demand for pay-TV channels and lure people away from network programs. As it turned out, many pay-cable subscribers continued their subscriptions and merely added home video to their existing entertainment options. However, the home video trend did coincide with a leveling off of pay-TV subscriptions and with a decline in network viewing.

VCRs (videocassette recorders) are home videotape machines.

Network Television Faces the Competition in the 1980s–1990s

By the early 1980s, network television was pressed by competition from cable TV, independent UHF television stations, and rented videotapes (see Figure 7.1). All

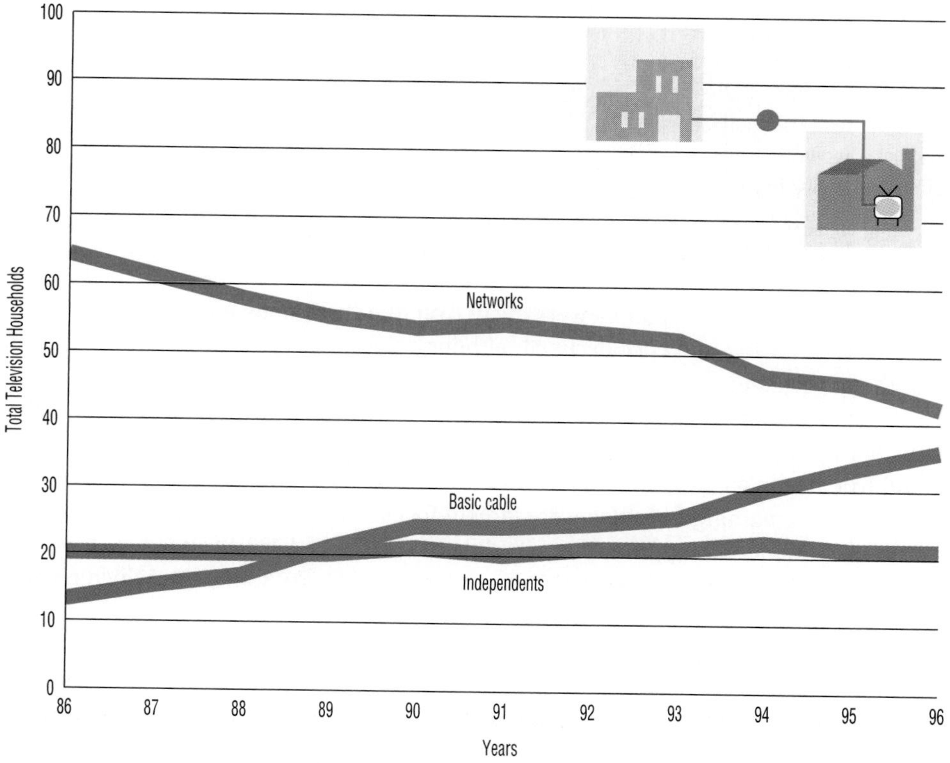

FIGURE 7.1
Network TV (CBS, NBC, ABC, Fox) has steadily lost part of its total audience to basic cable TV channels.

MEDIA ETHICS

Corporate Takeovers and News Emphasis

Steven Brill, of *Brill's Content* (November 1998), notes a conflict of interest for corporate managers trying to improve the economic performance of media companies for stockholders. To rein in costs of television operations, they have to cut back on programming expenses, which is often most visible in their newscasts, which usually lost money but were valued for their prestige. This has been accentuated by takeovers of television networks by larger corporations. News managers with their eye on the corporate bottom line took over from the original managers, who saw themselves as media and newspeople first and as business people second. This pattern is visible in what happened at all three major networks in the 1980s.

- In 1985, ABC was bought for $3.5 billion by Capital Cities. Under Cap Cities' management, ABC was under heavy pressure to cut costs and make its news operations profitable. By 1987, about 300 news staffers—one-fifth of all the employees there—had lost their jobs (Auletta, 1991). Cap Cities, in turn, sold out to Disney in 1996.
- In 1985, Loews, led by Larry Tisch, gradually acquired control of CBS. Although Loews was theoretically an entertainment company, with bases in movie theaters and experience in the film studio business, it was very profit-oriented. Tisch cut 215 news jobs almost immediately, a move that resulted in a publicly visible and damaging fight between him and his news division (Auletta, 1991). CBS was later purchased by Westinghouse in 1996.
- In 1985–1986, GE, led by Jack Welch, gradually acquired NBC. Welch was famous for cutting costs and improving stock prices of companies. His manager for NBC. Bob Wright, called network news "a dinosaur" and cut over 350 news jobs by 1990 (Auletta, 1991, p. 226).

There is a lingering controversy about whether such measures saved newscasts by reducing their financial losses or whether they irreparably damaged the television network news form.

For Further Research:

If you want to find out more about broadcast journalism and how it is evolving, you can try such Web sites as the Poynter Institute's Broadcast Journalism Bibliography, http://www.poynter.org/research/biblio/ bib_bj.htm. Using the InfoTrac College Edition, a search on "television news-economic aspects" produced several items, including this updated view on the issue by an insider:

WWW

Vital Speeches, Jan 1, 1998 v64 n6 p168(4) "The state of television news: in the business to make money." (Speech by Sam Donaldson, television news personality) (Transcript)

these choices began to pull viewers away from the three networks. The network television viewing audience declined, although the networks continued to get most of the advertising.

The response of the three main television networks was to offer less original network programming and to concentrate more on a steady evening flow of tried and true formulas, or genres, that yielded a consistent response. Critics charged that those remaining formulas were largely focused on sex and violence. For instance, the network prime-time schedule in the fall of 1983 included such programs as *The A-Team* (1983–1987) and *Magnum, P.I.* (1980–1988), which relied on action, violence, and sex appeal.

The networks did try some new formulas (Gitlin, 1985). They brought in evening soap operas, such as *Dallas* (1978–1991), which succeeded very well in the 1980s. The networks also began to target African American audiences, who tended to be somewhat more loyal network viewers, with programs such as *The Cosby Show* (1984–1992) and with increasing numbers of strong black characters in dramas such as *Hill Street Blues* (1981–1987) and *Miami Vice* (1985–1989).

Network programming, particularly its news programs, also changed in the 1980s and 1990s as a result of changes in network ownership. The big three networks passed into the hands of managers who were not, first and foremost, "broadcasters" but rather businessmen who felt a primary responsibility to stockholders rather than to an ideal of journalism. After acquiring CBS in 1985, for example, Larry Tisch focused network efforts more on the financial bottom line. One of the things he did was to reduce expenditures on the news division by cutting staff, facilities, and overseas bureaus (Auletta, 1991).

STUPID PET TRICKS. ***America's Funniest Home Videos*** **was one of many "reality programs" to hit the airwaves in the 1990s.**

To find lower cost, more profitable program genres in the 1990s, the networks began to increase their repertoire of talk shows and "reality" programs, such as *Rescue 911* (1991–1995) and *Cops* (1989–). Shows such as *America's Funniest Home Videos* (1990–) were popular and were much cheaper to produce because they relied substantially on "found" footage, such as home videos or, in the case of *Cops,* police footage, store surveillance cameras, and the like.

However, situation comedies staged a major comeback later in the 1990s with shows that were oriented to younger audiences. The networks feared the loss of the profitable, younger demographic group to MTV and other cable channels, so they fought back with shows such as *Friends* (1994–). In fact, a number of sitcoms were aimed at a fairly broad age range, such as *Home Improvement* (1991–), *Roseanne* (1988–), and *Frasier* (1993–). Dramas such as *ER* (1994–) also continued to be popular with a wide audience; thus classic network genre also found itself renewed.

New Television Networks Enter the Fray. Ironically, just as audiences for network television were declining, attempts to start additional national networks were made for the first time since the 1950s. Several crucial things had changed: Cable made UHF stations into more viable potential network affiliates, the strategy of focusing channels on specific audience segments appealed to advertisers, and regulatory changes permitted television program producers, such as film studios, and television networks to combine.

In 1987 Rupert Murdoch started the Fox television network, using the Fox film studio as a program production base. Ironically, although cable TV was eating away at network audiences, cable was one reason for Fox's success. Most of the affiliates that Fox attracted were formerly independent UHF stations. These stations were interested in gaining network affiliation, which was still more profitable than being independent. Cable eliminated the old UHF disadvantage of limited signal reach and quality by bringing UHF Fox local affiliates to a wide range of homes with acceptable picture quality. Fox also benefited from a network writers' strike in 1988 that resulted in more reruns on the other networks. But most important, it pursued a targeted television strategy by pursuing younger audience segments with shows such as *Beverly Hills 90210* (1990–) and the more sexually

PROFILE

MEDIA BARON. Rupert Murdoch, as chairman of the News Corporation, is one of the most powerful media magnates in the world.

World Media Baron

Name: Rupert Murdoch

Born: Melbourne, Australia, 1931

Education: Worcester College, Oxford

Position: Chairman, News Corporation

Style: Wants to rule the world, or at least the media parts.

Most Notable Achievements: Owns the fifth-largest media group in the world, with $11 billion in revenues in 1997, and the one with the widest worldwide reach in television. Founded Fox Television Network.

Most Dubious Achievements: In order to try to get Chinese permission for his Star TV satellite channels to cover China, was willing to cancel the BBC news in 1994 after it offended the Chinese leadership. In 1997, launched ChinaByte which provides highly censored Internet access and content for millions of Chinese.

How He Got Started: He worked for the London *Daily Express* and then returned home to take over his father's newspapers, the *Sunday Mail* and *The News,* in Adelaid, Australia.

His Inspiration: Murdoch is one of the original believers in synergy among different forms of media. He took the first step by using an American film studio to launch an American television network. He envisioned a worldwide media empire where film studios, television, newspapers, and on-line ventures help feed each other.

How He Got to the Top: He built a newspaper empire in Australia, specializing in tabloids. He then expanded to Great Britain, where he bought the tabloid *News of the World* of London and followed in America with the tabloids *Star* and *New York Post.* He eventually moved into more respectable newspapers, such as *The Times* of London. In 1985 he became an American citizen and acquired Twentieth Century–Fox Film Corporation. He also bought several American television stations, consolidating them into a new television network, Fox, Inc. In 1990 Murdoch inaugurated British Sky Broadcasting. In 1993 he purchased Star TV, a pan-Asian television service based in Hong Kong. Both were part of his plan to build a global television network.

Where Does He Go from Here? He wants to cover even more of the world with his television networks, especially in Asia (Star TV), Latin America (Sky Latin America), and - Europe (Sky Broadcasting). He also is venturing into the Internet with services such as ChinaByte.

explicit *Melrose Place* (1992–). Fox also pursued more urban and racially diverse audiences than the big three networks with programs such as *In Living Color* (1990–1994). Fox pushed the limits of middle class sensibility with such programs as *The Simpsons* (1989–). However, these programs and Fox's strategy evolved. By the late 1990s, *The Simpsons* had incorporated more clearly prosocial and family-friendly messages and had become one of the major "family programs" on television.

In 1994–1995, two more new television networks were started. Time Warner started WB, using its film studio as a program production base. Viacom, owner of Paramount Communications, used both the Paramount and Universal studios as a base to start UPN, the United Paramount Network. They were joined in 1998 by yet two more, PaxTV and USA. None of these networks offered full schedules of programming, even in evening prime time. Like Fox, both WB and UPN worked with independent stations, often on UHF, to get them to use as much of the network's programming as possible. Both were working hard to get coverage in as many major markets as possible and to spread into medium and small markets as well.

Broadcasting Consolidation. The crucial regulatory change in the 1990s for both new and old networks was the decision to tolerate more vertical and horizontal integration between program producers and program distributors—that is, broadcasters. First, the financial syndication (Fin-Syn) rules, which prohibited networks from owning most of their own programs, were removed. That change was intended to help the traditional networks become more profitable again, which it did. Networks started purchasing or producing more of their own programs. One of the feared outcomes also seemed to be coming true: Networks were favoring their own productions over those of independent producers even if the latter were better, because the economic return from a program a network owns is much higher than the return from one that it doesn't own. Removing the Fin-Syn rules also encouraged other film and production studio owners to dream of having their own networks to broadcast their own shows, including Fox, WB, and UPN.

Second, rules about concentration of ownership were relaxed so that companies like Disney that produced large programs could buy large television networks like ABC. The Telecommunications Act of 1996 also freed networks to acquire more owned and operated stations, further expanding their ability to profit from their own programming through advertising sales.

But the biggest issue for network television today is staying profitable. Cable TV networks now outdraw the broadcast networks in prime time and increasingly pull away the most profitable segments of the audience. Meanwhile, programming costs for prime time hits are skyrocketing to the point that even top shows, such as *ER,* are no longer making profits. In a last gasp effort to keep a broad national audience, the networks are paying ruinous sums for broadcast rights to sporting events. But as ABC network president Pat Fili-Krushel admits, "The network economic model is no longer good." And at NBC, they ponder the unthinkable—turning themselves into a pay channel (Roberts, 1999).

1. How did cable spread throughout the United States?
2. What laws and regulations shaped cable TV?
3. Which technologies were critical to cable's early growth?
4. What contributions did John Walson, Ted Turner, and John Malone make to the development of the cable industry?
5. How have cable and video affected television programming?
6. What enabled a fourth network, Fox, finally to succeed? What enabled WB and UPN to start?

TRENDS IN TELEVISION TECHNOLOGY

Television Transmission and Reception

Picture Tube. The key to understanding the technology of television is in a personal anecdote from the childhood of your textbook's second author, whose father fancied himself an amateur television repairman. During one Saturday afternoon repair session, a puff of smoke (and several of the "seven dirty words" we learned about in Chapter 5) came out of the back of the set as the entire picture collapsed into a single twinkling point of light. The sound played on, so the young Dr. LaRose was able to discern that the changes in the light's intensity corresponded to scene changes in the TV program. The light faded almost to complete black when the camera cut away to a commercial, then flashed intense blue-white when the pitch for "Speedy AlkaSeltzer" came on.

With a slip of the screwdriver, Dad had accidentally damaged the circuits that steered the point of light back and forth and up and down across the screen. This unmasked the "magic" of television: The entire television picture was merely a single point of light that heretofore had moved so fast that it tricked the eye into seeing a full-screen, continuously moving picture. It was almost as disconcerting as finding out the truth about Santa Claus.

A **picture tube** fires an electron gun at dots on the inside of the TV screen. These dots glow with varying intensity to create an image.

The light was produced by a continuous beam of charged particles that were being shot from an electron gun at the rear of the **picture tube.** When they hit the inner surface of the tube, they stimulated a special substance coating the tube to give off a glow. The more electrons hitting the surface at a given instant, the brighter the glow. Recalling our experiments with electromagnets described in Chapter 5, we can appreciate that a moving electric charge and magnetic fields interact with one another. Dear old dad had disabled a set of electromagnets encircling the neck of the picture tube that directed the beam back and forth across the screen 525 times to create each full-screen picture, one line at a time—a feat that it duplicated 30 times a second.

This simplified account describes the picture tube system that Bell Labs researcher Allen Dumont announced to the world in 1927. The first television broadcast in the United States didn't happen until 1939, though, when a handful of viewers in the New York area saw a Yale–Columbia baseball game on tiny 2-inch screens. The basic transmission rules were set in 1941 by the *National Television Systems Committee*, which lent its name to the NTSC standard of 525-lines-per-frame and 30-frames-per-second analog television transmission still used today in the United States and much of the Far East. The only significant modification of the standard over the years was the introduction of color television in 1953. The color tubes worked by firing three electron guns simultaneously—one each for red, green, and blue—at corresponding color dots on the screen. The eye blends these primary colors to make various hues (Benson & Whittaker, 1990).

Television Transmission. How are the electron guns activated? The television broadcast signal works in much the same way as *AM radio* (see Chapter 5), except that variations in the amplitude of the high-frequency carrier correspond to the light and dark values of the picture instead of to the loud and soft portions of the audio. The amplitude changes are separated from the carrier inside the TV set and then fed into the electron gun (see Figure 7.2). TV sound is added by a separate FM radio signal carried in the upper part of the television channel.

Frequency bands are parts of the electromagnetic spectrum authorized for a particular purpose.

Hertz is a measure of the frequency for the signal, in cycles per second.

Television is transmitted in two **frequency bands,** *VHF (very high frequency)* and *UHF (ultra high frequency),* in which each channel is allocated a range of frequencies, or bandwidth, of 6 MHz. The M is a symbol for 1 million, and Hz is the abbreviation for **hertz,** a measure of the frequency of the signal, in cycles per second. There are 12 VHF channels, channels 2 to 13, in the frequencies 54–72, 76–88, and 174–216 MHz. FM radio is sandwiched in between TV channels 6 and 7 at 88–108 MHz. You can verify this if there is a channel 6 on the air in your

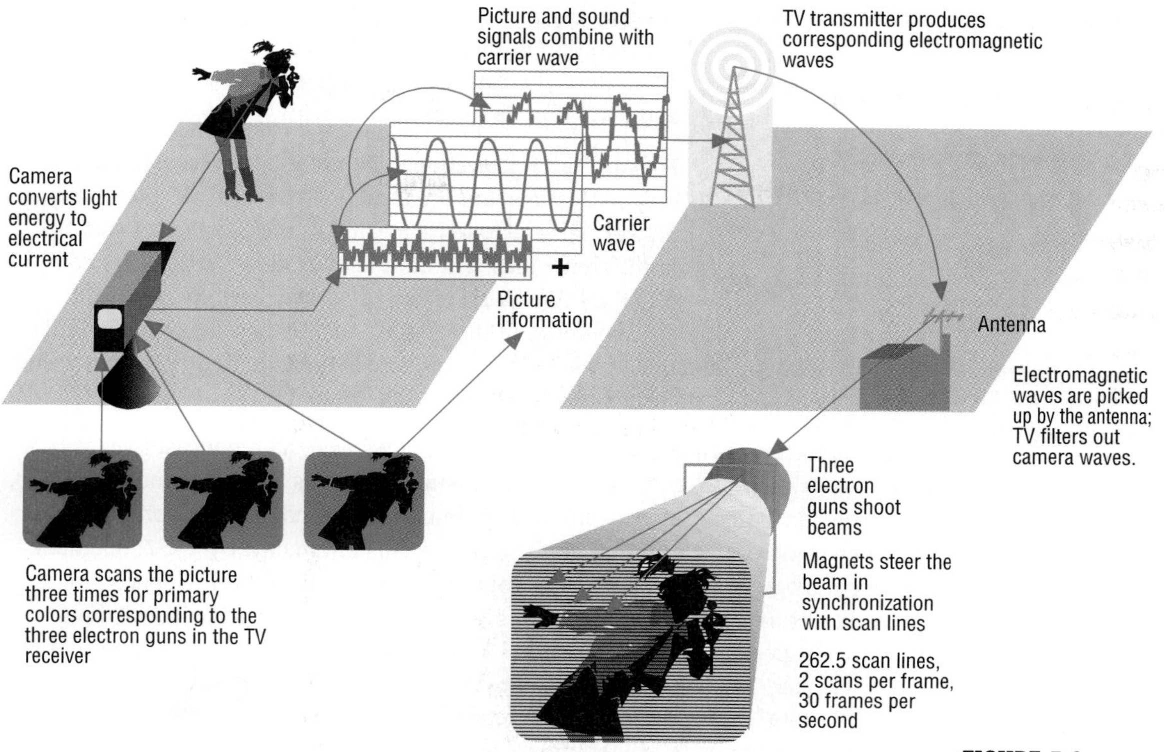
Picture and sound signals combine with carrier wave
TV transmitter produces corresponding electromagnetic waves
Camera converts light energy to electrical current
Carrier wave
+
Picture information
Antenna
Electromagnetic waves are picked up by the antenna; TV filters out camera waves.
Three electron guns shoot beams
Magnets steer the beam in synchronization with scan lines
262.5 scan lines, 2 scans per frame, 30 frames per second
Camera scans the picture three times for primary colors corresponding to the three electron guns in the TV receiver
Phosphorescent picture tube lights up when electrons hit it

FIGURE 7.2
A broadcast television signal goes from the camera to the transmitter, through the air to an antenna, to the TV set.

area. You can pick up its audio on some FM radio sets by cranking the tuner way down to the low end. There are 56 UHF channels, channels 14 to 69, between 470–806 MHz, but channel 37 is reserved for radio astronomers and can't be used for television (Benson & Whitaker, 1990.)

TV Cameras. This takes us back to the studio. Here, the key element is the camera tube. It was the center of an early 1920s **patent** dispute between the independent inventor Philo Farnsworth and Vladimir Zworykin at RCA. Farnsworth and Zworykin both developed the essential technology for a television camera—an electronic **scanning** system. After a long series of patent suits, Farnsworth was compensated $1 million for his claims by RCA. The camera tube transforms light into an electric charge, which is scanned by an electron beam following a back-and-forth, up-and-down pattern identical to that used in the picture tube. The beam causes a discharge of energy corresponding to the intensity of each point of light. These variations in the amplitude of the voltage modulate the picture carrier.

Patent secures to an inventor for a number of years the exclusive right to make, use, license, or sell an invention.

Scanning is the method that makes TV pictures out of a series of 525 separate picture lines.

At least that is the "Americanized" version of the invention of television, for, as with many other important inventions, several countries lay claim to it. We should definitely not slight the contributions of British inventor John Logie Baird, who in the 1920s came up with a television system that used mechanical scanning. He also made the first trans-Atlantic television transmission and the first video recordings—using 78 rpm records! Baird also put the British Broadcasting Corporation on the air with the world's first public TV broadcasts in 1935. And French and

1. Who developed the basics of television camera technology?
2. How does a television camera work?
3. How does a television picture tube work?
4. What is scanning?

German engineers made significant improvements in color broadcasting in the 1960s, although they had the unfortunate effect of creating separate television standards, SECAM and PAL, that are incompatible with America's NTSC.

Network Interconnection. The preceding discussion covers only local television broadcasts. A nationwide television network also requires a means of interconnecting stations in different cities. The first television networks were completed by AT&T, using *coaxial cable,* back in 1948 and **microwave** transmitters). Beginning in the 1970s, satellite became the standard means of relaying signals to network affiliates across the land and for transmitting feeds of local news and sporting events back to the networks.

Microwave is a high-capacity system that transmits information between relay towers on highly focused beams of high-frequency radio waves.

Audiotape is magnetic tape used for recording audio.

Digital means computer readable.

Video Production Trends. The early television shows were all broadcast live for lack of a practical way to record and edit them. **Audiotape** was around in the late 1940s, but television transmissions contained so much more visual information than audio that they could not be captured on the tape systems of the day. By 1957, magnetic tape technology had improved to the point where it was useful for television, and the networks saw the obvious advantages it would offer for production, making editing and special effects much easier. And reruns permitted new sales and profits. Today, virtually everything is on tape except for coverage of breaking news events.

The **digital** film production techniques that we discussed in Chapter 6 have also been adopted by television. Film and video production techniques are converging as a result. *Nonlinear editing* has had a particularly important impact on television, because it speeds up the post-production process dramatically. Digital graphics, special effects, and computer animation are also becoming common on the home screen.

Another implication of digital video is that television editing, character generation, special effects, and animation can be done on desktop computers and computer workstations which are becoming less expensive and more powerful all the time. Miniaturized solid-state cameras and other production components have also dropped in price, putting the technology of professional-quality video editing within the reach of the home video enthusiast.

Cable TV

Coaxial cable is the high-capacity wire used for cable television transmission.

Early cable systems placed TV signals on the same type of cable that AT&T used in the first national TV networks. **Coaxial cable** had a single long wire running down its axis and a second conductor that was wrapped around it like a long metal tube. This arrangement kept unwanted signals from entering the cable and also prevented the cable signals from leaking out and interfering with other communications. (For more on cable technology, see Chapter 9.)

The channel capacity of cable systems improved over the years, with the development of cable amplifiers that handled higher and higher frequencies. By the late 1980s, systems carrying 50 channels were common, and some had over 70 channels. Coaxial cable technology was reaching its limits, though. Cable operators turned to **fiber optic cable** to transport signals from their head ends to their sub-

Fiber optic cable systems use light instead of electricity to communicate.

scribers' neighborhoods. If extended all the way to the home TV set, fiber could theoretically expand the channel options to hundreds instead of mere dozens.

However, the coaxial cable that comes into the living room is the most expensive of all to replace, and optical interfaces for individual television sets are still prohibitively expensive. Successful experiments with digital transmission techniques now make it possible to push coaxial cable to new limits by providing a **compressed** video signal. Five or ten channels can now be placed in the same space once required for a single channel. In 1998, TCI and Time Warner began to upgrade their systems to hundreds of channels via the new digital cable technology.

Digital compression reduces the number of computer bits that have to be transmitted.

New Multichannel Technologies

The advantages of digital compression also impressed some of cable's competitors. In 1995 a new generation of direct broadcast satellite (DBS) services appeared. The new DBS systems use digital channel compression to provide more programming and use more powerful satellites so the receivers need only measure one or two feet across. There is also a growing array of earth-based wireless cable systems. Wireless cable has been around since the late 1960s, when conventional broadcast channels were scrambled and offered as pay-TV services. Later systems offered up to 16 channels using the Multichannel Multipoint Distribution Service (MMDS) to broadcast in frequencies outside of the normal television band. Now, another block of frequencies has been set aside for a service that has been dubbed "cellularvision" since it combines the technology of television and cellular telephony. These systems offer hundreds of channels of digitally compressed, high-quality video in urban areas where DBS operators have made few inroads against cable. Cellularvision also has the capacity to make the two-way wrist TV from the old Dick Tracy comic strips a reality.

Home Video

For home video taping, another breakthrough was required. Early video recorders required huge reels of 2-inch tape, climate-controlled environments, and delicate handling by trained technicians, all of which made them unsuitable for the living room. The key development was **helical scanning.** It stores video tracks on a slant (imagine cutting up tape and pasting it slantwise), so the length of the tape could shrink to manageable proportions. Today's Video Home System (VHS) players rely on this technique (Benson & Whitaker, 1990).

Helical scanning stores video frames at a slant, like cutting up tape and stacking it slantwise.

But a compromise still had to be made to make home taping possible: There was still too much information to record movies at practical tape speeds. The solution was to degrade the quality of the picture, effectively reducing the number of horizontal "lines" in the picture. Home video viewers notice this compromise as graininess or blurring of bright reflections.

Digital Television

The aim of **high-definition television (HDTV)** is to improve the quality of video and make it suitable for projection on large-screen home theater systems by dou-

High-definition television (HDTV) uses more scan lines to provide a clearer and more detailed television picture.

YOUR NEXT TV. Broadcasters hope that the introduction of high-definition TV service in the United States in 1998 will spark new interest in over-the-air television.

bling the number of vertical scan lines and widening the picture to match movie theater screens. Initial plans for HDTV service involved an analog system developed in Japan, but these were dropped in favor of an all-digital system in 1994.

Digital television cameras sample pictures by cutting them up into thousands of elements (pixels) and assigning a binary number to each point.

Just as audio CD technology samples sound waves and turns those samples into digital information, **digital television** systems sample pictures by cutting them up into thousands of picture elements (pixels) and digitally encoding the result. However, television pictures are more complex than audio and require a great deal more capacity, or *bandwidth,* to transmit, even after taking advantage of *digital compression.* And the extra lines and width of the HDTV picture more than double the bandwidth required by the conventional NTSC signal.

Part of the digital signal can be sandwiched into unused portions of the NTSC signal, but that's not enough. To provide the extra capacity, the FCC gave broadcasters a second frequency in the UHF band. The "simulcasting" of digital TV and conventional analog signals began in 1998. In 2006, broadcasters are supposed to turn in their analog licenses. That's the year that the FCC hopes all broadcasts will be in digital format—and you will have bought a new HDTV receiver (Gruley, 1997).

However, each television station faces millions of dollars in expenditures to convert to the new technology. The sets and pancake make-up that look fine on analog TV will have to be upgraded and all the old reruns reformatted. Broadcasters are therefore reluctant to take the plunge. And consumers may balk at the cost of HDTV receivers—several thousand dollars initially—and may not agree that the improvement in picture quality is worth the price.

Indeed, the future of digital TV could be "low-definition" digital transmissions over the *Internet* that bypass the local TV station altogether and place no demands on the communications spectrum. Today's live Internet video transmissions are grainy and jerky, even when reduced to a few inches across, with a quarter of the resolution of today's TV pictures. Furthermore, they are limited by the speed of home connections to the Internet. Although live video over the Internet is still poor, acceptable quality video can be downloaded over the Internet and replayed on the computer screen. Still, the Internet shows viewers all over the world pictures and video that no broadcaster or cable channel would carry. Improvements in the speed of home Internet connections promised by cable and telephone companies will make broadcast quality video possible on the World Wide Web in the future.

In fact, the evolving convergence of television and computers has sparked a battle between the television and computer industries over the way pictures are displayed. Television executives favor continuing the *interfaced scanning* approach, in which the 525 vertical picture lines are divided into two interwoven sets of 262.5 lines. "Computer types" want the *progressive scanning* method, which treats each frame as a single set of 525 lines but causes flickering on some older TV sets.

Computer–TV convergence could take any of several different forms. For example, new multimedia computers can insert conventional television pictures on the screen, and some computers now have tuners that can pick up local TV broadcasts. One system of "surfing the Web," Microsoft's WebTV, used the television screen as the display device and let users navigate with a hand-held control that resembles a TV remote control. Eventually, the TV signal itself could be used to transmit Web pages related to program content, such as player statistics during sportscasts (Bank, 1997). Another new approach is to put a computer on top of your cable TV set. These *set-top boxes* convert digital cable channels for display on your analog set, as well as provide high-speed Internet access, electronic shopping, and advanced interactive services, and allow you to play computer games.

1. **What is the essential breakthrough that made home video possible?**
2. **How are cable television pictures transmitted to the home?**
3. **What new technologies are emerging as competitive threats to cable TV?**
4. **What is high-definition television (HDTV)?**

TV GENRES

From Radio and Film to Television

Television was affected most in its beginnings by radio. A number of **genres,** and even specific programs, came straight from network radio programming to television in the 1940s. Several genres that had worked well on radio clearly worked even better visually. For example, although comedy has an important verbal element, it can be enlarged with such visuals as gestures, expression, actions, and props. Action–adventure succeeded remarkably well on radio in diverse forms or subgenres, such as cowboy, detective, spy, science fiction, thrillers, and superheroes. All of these clearly worked better with visuals and moved to television.

> **Genres** are types or formats of media content.

The main radio genres that came over to television are listed in Table 7.1 The film industry has also fed many of its movies and most of its formulas into television in one way or another. Most of the visual techniques of movies were

TABLE 7.1 Television Genres That Came from Radio

Variety

- Shows, such as *The Ed Sullivan Show* (1948–1971), which gave the Beatles their first U.S. television exposure

Comedy

- Comedy shows dominated by a single comic, such as Red Skelton (1951–1971)
- Ensemble comedies with a group of comics, such as Sid Caesar's *Your Show of Shows* (1950–1954) and *Saturday Night Live* (1979–)
- Situation comedies revolving around an ongoing plot, such as *The Honeymooners* (1955–1956) and *I Love Lucy* (1951–1957)

Drama

- Soap operas—daily melodramas sponsored largely by laundry and house-cleaning products—such as *The Guiding Light* (1952–) and *General Hospital* (1963–)
- Miscellaneous dramas, such as *Kraft Television Theater* (1947–1958), *The Waltons* (1972–1981), and *Touched by an Angel* (1994–)
- Medical programs—dramas centered on doctors, such as *Marcus Welby, M.D.* (1969–1976), or on hospitals, such as *ER* (1994–)
- Legal dramas—dramas centered on lawyers and courtrooms, such as *Perry Mason* (1957–1974) and *L.A. Law* (1986–1994)
- Western dramas, such as *Gunsmoke* (1955–1975) and *Dr. Quinn, Medicine Woman* (1992–1998)

Action–Adventure

- Mysteries, such as *Alfred Hitchcock Presents* (1955–1986)
- Science fiction, such as *Star Trek: Deep Space Nine* (1993–)
- Detective series, such as *Dragnet* (1951–1959, 1967–1970) and *NYPD Blue* (1993–)
- Superhero series, such as *Adventures of Superman* (1951–1957)

Sports

- Sports presentations, such as ABC's *Monday Night Football* (1970–)

Game Shows

- Game shows now use visuals as well as dialog, such as *Wheel of Fortune* (1983–)
- Quiz shows now use visuals as well as a question-and-answer format, such as *Jeopardy* (1983–)

Children's

- Educational programs, such as *Sesame Street* (1969–)
- Entertainment such as *Mickey Mouse Club* (1955–1957)

News and Public Affairs

- News—many newspeople moved form radio to television
- Public affairs programs, such as Edward R. Murrow's *See It Now* (1952–1955) and CBS' *60 Minutes* (1968–)
- Talk shows, both morning and evening, such as *Today* (1952–) and *The Tonight Show* (1962–)
- Documentaries, such as CBS' *Harvest of Shame* (1960), which exposed migrant workers' living conditions
- Reality programs, which first brought real-life stories to the studio, such as *Queen for a Day* (1955–1965) and *Jerry Springer* (1992–), but now chase it down or recreate it, such as *Rescue 911* (1989–)

adaptable to television, if they looked good on the smaller screen. Some of the genres of film that relied on sweeping visuals, detailed visuals, or really large-scale action shots had to be adapted to fit television. For example, historical costume drama, which has to emphasize close-ups, faces, and personalities, rather than large battles, outdoor visuals, and so on. Although this kind of adaptation is possible, American television has more often concentrated on film genres that are

TABLE 7.2 Television Genres That Came from Film

- News—film newsreels also affected the visual style of TV news
- Musicals—despite some efforts, musicals never did well on TV, with the exception of *The Monkees* (1966–1968).
- Animation—cartoons, developed into series forms, from *The Flintstones* (1960–1966) to *The Simpsons* (1989–)

easier to adapt, such as animation. The main film genres that came over to television are listed in Table 7.2.

How TV Genres Developed

During the 1960s and 1970s, television made dramas and situation comedies out of the kinds of dramatic situations that people were more familiar with: courtrooms, hospitals, and police stations. Building on genre roots in radio and film adventure stories, a general action–adventure genre developed with a number of predictable formulas involving chases and good guy/bad guy characterizations, but subtypes focusing on cops, spies, and cowboys also diversified into separate subgenres. Similarly, a general sitcom format has diversified into various TV subgenres that have evolved over time, addressing topics or themes of the moment.

Still, one sitcom, *Seinfeld* (1990–1998), was notable for being about "nothing"—for not having a specific hook or major theme. It did not have a focus on family issues (*Roseanne,* 1988–1997), on gender images (*Home Improvement,* 1991–1999), or on a specific genre reference such as science fiction "aliens" in *Third Rock from the Sun* (1996–). Still, *Seinfeld* became the highest-rated and most profitable show on American television for its last several years. Clearly, the classic network television genre, the general sitcom, still has considerable life in it.

There are several enduring tensions about the creation of programs and genres for television. One is as old as television: the question of formula versus novelty. Genres have evolved precisely to give producers reasonably predictable formulas for creating shows that audiences will recognize, enjoy, and feel comfortable with. Certainly different people with very different expectations sit down to see the latest NBC sitcom versus the latest MTV rap video or the breaking news on CNN. However, television history also demonstrates that hit programs also need to innovate within their formula, or at least go back to a variation that most people have forgotten. Most seasons bring an innovative show or two that other programs then imitate. The innovators tend to draw a much bigger audience than the imitators, although sometimes an imitator figures how to do the new formula better. Generations of critics and viewers have railed at Hollywood for being too imitative, but innovation is risky, so recycling and imitation never go away.

The other major current tension is between the major networks enduring urge to find mass audience hits, such as *Seinfeld,* as opposed to programs aimed at niches or market segments, such as children, early teens, or mature adults. Mass audience hits make much more money for the network, but they are swimming against the tide of audience segmentation and channel narrowcasting. Although *Seinfeld* was a big hit in 1998, its audience ratings would have been considered only a modest success in 1978; since then much of the audience has moved to cable and more focused genres, profitable niche programming.

Genres and Forms in Multichannel Programming

Narrowcasting targets media channels to specific segments of the audience.

Perhaps cable television's most important contribution to programming is the concept of **narrowcasting,** the creation of channels dedicated to particular interests or segmented groups of viewers. An analogy can be drawn to the magazine industry, where a wide array of magazines dedicated to special interests have supplanted general-interest publications such as *Life* and *The Saturday Evening Post.* Likewise, specialized cable channels such as HBO (movies), ESPN (sports), and MTV (music) are winning more and more viewers from general-interest broadcast TV networks (see Table 7.3).

Narrowcasting probably would not have been possible without cable. For one thing, there are too few TV channel allocations available in any given area for entire channels to be dedicated to specific types of content. Advertising sales are predicated on reaching the widest possible audience, so it does not make sense to broadcast programs that appeal only to a small fraction of all the potential viewers. Advertising-supported basic cable networks are subject to the same advertising economics, but they also derive part of their income from subscription fees and can spread the program origination costs over thousands of cable systems, making it worthwhile to target programs to relatively small audiences.

Cable channels can also be profitable while reaching small audiences if they have an inexpensive source of programming. Although many cable channels have original programming, the staple of most networks is "used" material (old movies or classic TV shows), free material (music videos provided by record companies), or material that is inexpensive to produce (weather forecasts) compared with prime-time entertainment programming.

Genre channels feature programs of a certain type, such as movies or sports events.

Genre Channels. Most cable networks represent the extension of programming genres found on broadcast television to channel-length format. The earliest cable networks represented some of the most popular categories of programming, such as news. We will call these **genre channels,** because almost everything that appears on them is of the same genre of programming. A second wave of networks went after subgenres, such as business news. As programmers groped for ideas for hundreds of channels, virtually every type of program or program segment that has ever appeared on television has acquired its own channel. And genre channels themselves are beginning to diversify. For example, by 1998 the "news" category includes channels dedicated to world news (CNN, FOX news, MSNBC), regional news (Northwest Cable News), local news (NY1 News), repeated-on-the-half-hour news (Headline News), sports news (ESPNEWS, CNNSI), weather news (The Weather Channel), entertainment news (E! Entertainment Television), business news (CNBC), international news (CNN International, BBC), and news programs from around the world (SCOLA).

Not all of the cable genres imitated commercial television. One network, the Discovery Channel, amplified the nature and history programming found on public

TABLE 7.3 Cable Television Channels

Genre Channels	
Genre	**Examples**
Education	Knowledge TV
Movies	American Movie Classics, Cinemax, Home Box Office, Showtime
Music	MTV, Country Music Television, VH-1
News	Cable News Network, CNN Headline News, CNN International, SCOLA, The Weather Channel, Fox News
Government meetings	C-SPAN, C-SPAN II
Religious	The Inspirational Network
Sports	ESPN, Fox Sports Channel, ESPN2
Shopping	Home Shopping Network, QVC Network
Cartoons	The Cartoon Network
Science fiction	The Sci-Fi Channel
Stand-up comedy and sitcoms	The Comedy Channel
Courtroom coverage	Court-TV

Demographic and Lifestyle Channels	
Genre	**Examples**
Women	Lifetime
Children	Nickelodeon, The Disney Channel
Families	The Family Channel
African Americans	Black Entertainment Television
Hispanics	Galavision
Country	The Nashville Network

General Audience Channels	
Genre	**Examples**
Superstations	WTBS, WGN, WWOR
Cable-originated	USA Network, Turner Network Television, FX

Source: Ultimate TV—www.ultimatetv.com/tv/us/cable

broadcasting to channel form. Knowledge TV features another PBS specialty, the telecourse. One of the most popular cable genres, the disk jockey format of music video channels (MTV, VH-1, Country Music Television), was copied from radio.

Some cable genres, such as community programming, local city government broadcasts, and home shopping channels, are relatively new and original. They have only distant relatives in regularly scheduled broadcast programming. Program-length commercials were long forbidden on broadcast TV, so the shopping networks were truly cable originals. The same is true of adult channels that feature movies deemed "too sexy" for broadcast television.

Channels with Target Audiences. Other channels—called **demographic channels**—are built around groups of people rather than program genres. Programming is assembled from several genres to appeal to members of the target group. One of the first basic cable networks, Black Entertainment Television, is a prime example. Its programming includes sitcoms, music videos, black college sports, news, and public affairs programming for African American viewers. Women (Lifetime), children (Nickelodeon), Hispanics (Univision and Galavision) are among the other target audiences catered to by dedicated channels.

Demographic channels are designed to appeal to audiences with shared demographic characteristics.

Other cable channels targeted to groups of people might better be described as **lifestyle channels;** their programs are aimed at people who share a common interest or way of life, regardless of their demographic characteristics. There are channels for families with children (The Family Channel), golfers (The Golf Channel), and people who think of themselves as "country" (Nashville Network).

Lifestyle channels are targeted to audiences with certain common interests.

General-Audience Channels. Other cable channels maintain a balance of programming intended to attract a broad **general audience** throughout the day. In effect, these channels translate the broadcast television programming strategy to cable.

General-audience channels contain a variety of program types for a wide audience.

1. What film genres contributed to television genres?
2. What radio programs and genres moved over to television?
3. What kinds of genres has television developed on its own?
4. Name four types of cable programming and give an example of each.
5. What are some of the Cable TV genre channels?

The superstations best embody this approach, because they are TV stations in their local areas. These stations include WTBS (Channel 17 in Atlanta), WGN (Chicago's Channel 9), WWOR (Channel 9 from New Jersey), KTLA (Channel 5 from Los Angeles), and WPIX (New York's Channel 11). In addition to the usual diet of old movies and television reruns found on independent television stations everywhere, most superstations are the "home stations" of professional baseball, basketball, and hockey teams. There are also general-audience channels, such as USA Network and Turner Network Television (TNT), that are not superstations but whose programming imitates the independent television station mix.

Even with 175 national channels already in operation, cable programmers haven't begun to run out of program ideas to make into channels. The extra channel space opened up by the new digital cable systems has unleashed a torrent of new programming ideas. Where will they get 500 channels' worth of programs? One answer is to cater to more and more specialized genres and audience groups, as do the Fox Family Channel's spin-offs, the Boyz Network and the Girlz Network. In the music video category, there is a wide range of channels that reflect various musical genres, beginning with the major strains of popular music (rap, heavy metal) and extending to the more esoteric forms (e.g., BET's gospel, HipHop, and World Music). Movie channels, such as HBO and Encore, have "multiplexed" several satellite feeds, which schedule current movies at staggered starting times, just like the multiplex movie theaters at the local shopping mall. Another approach is to dedicate channels to specific movie genres (action–adventure, love stories, mystery, westerns, movies in Spanish). Dozens of the new channels will be devoted to **pay-per-view** programs, including live sporting events and the 30 (or 50 or 200) movie titles that are the "top renters" in home video stores (National Cable Television Association, www.ncta.com). If movies don't appeal to you, new lifestyle channels built around personal interests from classic war planes (Discovery Wings) to outdoor life (Outdoor Channel) are appearing.

Pay-per-view is when cable subscribers order a specific program and pay a separate fee just to receive that one show.

INDUSTRY ORGANIZATION

The television industry is organized differently at several levels: production, distribution, and station or network broadcast or exhibition.

The Television Industry

Television Production and Distribution. Most production is done nationally by film studios, independent producers, and broadcast or cable networks. The most dramatic recent change is the rapid increase of programming produced by networks for themselves. This is particularly true for those television or cable networks that are owned by film studios or conglomerate groups, which include production studios, such as Fox, ABC (Disney), WB (Warner Brothers) Time Warner, UPN (Universal-Paramount) and Turner Network Television (Time Warner).

Local news production increased considerably in the 1980s, from around an hour to two hours or more per day for the typical station. Local news is profitable, because it is popular, it is increasingly affordable to produce (given declining equipment costs), and the advertising revenue goes to the local station—it is not shared with the network or a program syndicator (Gitlin, 1985).

Stations also show an increasing amount of syndicated programming. These are either reruns of programs previously aired on networks or "new" programs produced by independent production companies, usually talk shows such as *Geraldo* and *Oprah,* game shows such as *Wheel of Fortune* and *Jeopardy,* or "reality" programs such as *Rescue 911.* These programs are distributed through syndicators, which are usually separate specialized companies that may be part of larger companies, such as Hearst Entertainment Distribution, or independent companies, such as Western International Syndication. Stations simply pay for the programs ("cash"), pay a reduced price and show some advertisements or commercial spots arranged by the syndicator ("cash plus barter"), or pay nothing but give the syndicator more commercial minutes to sell to national advertisers ("barter"). Independent stations rely heavily on syndication, and network affiliates increasingly drop network programming in favor of syndicated programs that they think will draw bigger audiences.

Networks supply a great deal of programming to their **O&Os** (network-owned-and-operated stations) and to their affiliates. The networks have traditionally produced news programs, sports events, some talk shows, some soap operas, documentaries, and a few series, but until recently, most entertainment programs were purchased by networks from film studios or independent producers. That changed with the abolition of rules on syndication by Congress in 1993 that permit networks to produce or own the programs they show.

O&Os are stations owned and operated by networks.

TV Programming Strategy. Network television programming is subdivided and shaped by time of day and by the types of people who watch at a given time.

- Early morning: "Breakfast shows" such as *Good Morning America* target a broad range of adults.
- Late morning–early afternoon: soap operas and talk shows, such as *Jerry Springer,* target housewives, older people, an students who might be home then.
- After school: Cartoons, young adult comedies, and lighter sitcoms target children and adolescents.
- Early evening: News, local and national, plus syndicated game shows for general adult audiences.
- Prime time: Sitcoms, dramas, and feature films for a broad general audience of adults, adolescents, and children.
- After prime time: Talk shows such as *David Letterman,* comedy, and music aimed at younger adults and adolescents.

- Late night: Old movies and syndicated series aimed at insomniacs and young adults.

Local stations' programming strategy is similarly guided by time of day, except that they care most about when to schedule local news, especially for early and late evening. They also have to decide whether to pre-empt network programming at certain times and substitute syndicated programming instead—something that is increasingly common.

Television Advertisers. In 1996 advertising revenue was $42.5 billion, which is still a lot of money, even if cable TV and other new media technologies are beginning to cut into television's advertising base. Advertising money still goes disproportionately to network television (24 percent) compared to newspapers (22 percent) or radio (7 percent). Cable TV advertising was 3.5 percent ($6.03 billion) in 1996 and growing rapidly ($6.85 billion in 1997) (Alsop, 1998; Cable Television Advertising Bureau, 1998).

The advertising money comes at three levels: national advertisers, national spot or regional advertisers, and local advertisers.

- National advertisers sell general-consumption items, such as soft drinks or cars, so their ads should reach a broad national audience. They usually buy advertising time on national television networks.
- National spot or regional advertisers usually sell things with a more regionalized or localized appeal, such as surfboards or snow tires. They usually buy spots in specific regions on both network affiliates and independent stations.
- Local advertisers, such as automobile dealers and supermarkets, sell a variety of things to local customers. They usually buy ads on local stations, either network affiliates or independents. These kinds of ads can be placed in network programming in those spots not occupied by network-arranged ads or during locally programmed news and syndicated programs.

Affiliate stations take programming and advertising from a network.

The Networks. For many years, television networks were limited to owning five VHF stations (O&Os), which they tried to locate in the biggest markets for maximum revenue. In order to achieve national coverage, they sought **affiliate stations** in other markets. The network ownership limits have now been lifted, but most network stations are still affiliates. Stations sometimes change affiliation to ally with a network that they believe offers stronger programming. Such changes were rare for a long time, but stations seemed to become more willing to change affiliation in the 1990s.

A network has a more complex operation than does a station. One division usually manages the owned-and-operated stations, another deals with affiliate relations, and another handles the technical operations of network program delivery. The networks' sales staff works with national ads and advertising agencies. In programming, the network staff works with producers and studios or production companies to develop entertainment programs, news operation, and sports.

Many television stations are owned by groups. In management, advertising sales, and equipment, station owners benefit from the economies of scale of multiple station ownership. In the beginning, the major owners were the three networks. The networks still own and operate stations in the largest U.S. markets, and these stations are a major source of revenue for the networks. Since the 1996 Telecommunications Act deregulated station ownership, the networks have been increasing the number of stations they own.

AFFILIATE PROGRAMMING. Local affiliates of major TV networks also produce their own programming—notably, local news shows.

The Affiliates. At the local level, most commercial television stations have an administrative or managerial structure, a sales force to sell local advertising, engineering or technical staff for studio and transmitter operations, a news operation, and a production staff for news and other original programming. Stations also usually have contracts out for network affiliation (unless they are independent), research and ratings services, programming consultants, and legal services. The affiliation contracts specify compensation fees—paid by the networks to compensate stations for advertising slots they "lose" to network TV ads.

The Independents. Independent stations buy most of their programming from syndication services and sell nearly all of their advertising in the local, regional, or national spot markets. Thus they actually need more complex programming operations than network affiliates, who take most of their programming from the networks. They also may need a larger advertising sales force, again because they do not have a network to provide national advertising. Independents are usually UHF channels; most of the VHF channels have network affiliations. Network affiliates are more profitable, although independents' profitability has improved in the last 10 years. Still, as we noted earlier, when the Fox network recruited affiliates in the late 1980s, followed by WB, UPN, Pax, and USA in the 1990s, largely out of the ranks of independent UHF stations, the stations were happy to sign up. Affiliation improved their financial prospects and, to some degree at least, simplified their programming task.

Public TV. Public television has grown into a tangle of local and regional stations linked by the Public Broadcasting Service (PBS). The Corporation for Public Broadcasting still has a strong role in funding, but increasingly, producers depend on a mix of funding from CPB, PBS member station contributions, **corporate underwriting** or sponsorship, public contributions, and foreign network cosponsorship. In return for their financial support via underwriting, contributing corporations and foundations are acknowledged in a short announcement on air that is not quite a commercial but that expresses appreciation for their support and describes what they do. At the local level, PBS stations are increasingly dependent on local institutional sponsors, such as universities, and particularly on direct viewer support, which is one reason why PBS stations always seem to be soliciting viewer membership pledges for contributions.

Corporate underwriting on PBS television stations is financial support of programs in return for a mention of the underwriter on the air.

1. How are television stations organized?
2. What are the main differences between network affiliates and independent stations?
3. Why did many independent stations join the Fox Network?
4. What role does corporate underwriting play in PBS?
5. Where do PBS programs come from?

PBS programming tends to be developed by the larger PBS member stations, such as WGBH in Boston, which initiate proposals and put together packages of support. Programming for PBS has been made more competitive by the fact that several cable TV channels, including the Discovery Channel and the Arts & Entertainment Network, now compete with PBS for audiences with programming very similar to what has characterized PBS: documentaries, highbrow drama, and nature programs. PBS, in turn, occasionally runs former commercial network programs, such as *The Lawrence Welk Show* and *The Avengers,* that might also be found on a cable superstation or an independent commercial station, because those programs appeal to the adult part of its audience. The most exclusive PBS programming now tends to be its educational programs for children, like *Sesame Street,* which enjoys broad support among parents (Children's Television Workshop, www.ctw.org).

Cable Industry Structure

On the surface, cable television appears to be a highly localized medium—a result of the practice of granting cable franchises at the municipal level. In some 13,000 individual communities, each system picks up broadcast and satellite signals and relays them to subscribers in its franchise area. The monthly subscription fees are used to pay cable networks for the right to carry their programming. These fees range from a few cents per subscriber per month for C-SPAN to several dollars per month for pay TV channels such as HBO. The local cable operator is responsible for maintenance of the system, billing, marketing, and customer service. Many systems sell advertising slots on basic channels to advertisers in their communities. Home shopping channels pay cable operators a commission on the sales generated in their franchise areas.

TABLE 7.4 The Top Five Multiple System Operators (MSOs)

Rank		Subscribers (in millions)
1	AT&T/Tele-Communications, Inc. (TCI)	11.3
2	Time Warner Cable	10.5
3	Comcast	5.4
4	Media One	5.1
5	Cox Communications, Inc.	3.7

Source: Cablevision Magazine Top 100 MSO's, April 26, 1999. http://www.cvmag.com/database/db_topco.htm

Multiple System Operators (MSOs). Most systems are owned by cable multiple system operators (MSOs), the largest of which control hundreds of systems and serve millions of subscribers across many states (see Table 7.4). The largest cable MSO is TCI, with 15.7 million subscribing households. Next is Time Warner with 12.6 million. TCI, Time Warner and the others who round out the "Top Six" (MediaOne, Comcast, Cox, and Cablevision Systems) account for well over 60 percent of all subscribers (National Cable Television Association, 1998). Large MSOs use their market power to negotiate substantial discounts on programming fees and equipment purchases. They also set corporate-wide policy on local programming and pricing and marketing strategies, and they decide about which cable networks are carried on local systems.

Basic Cable Networks. Over 175 basic cable TV networks are now delivered via satellite. The basic networks derive their revenues from two sources: advertising and **affiliate fees.** The affiliate fees are paid by cable operators, usually on a per-subscriber basis. Many basic networks also make local advertising spots available. There are cable system interconnects that link cable operators in a given metropolitan area for advertising sales. The largest cable networks—Cable News Network (CNN), ESPN, and USA Network—are found on virtually all cable systems, whereas other networks appeal to highly specialized niches.

Affiliate fees are monthly per-subscriber fees that cable networks charge to local cable operators for the right to carry their programs.

Many cable operators now interconnect their networks with the Internet. High-speed connection to the Internet using cable's very high bandwidth capacity is proving to be a major part of cable TV's package of services to customers in many areas. @Home is the leading Internet cable service.

Pay-TV Networks. Home Box Office is still by far the largest pay-TV network. The other leading networks are Showtime, The Disney Channel, Cinemax, The Movie Channel, and Encore. Pay-TV networks generally derive their revenues from affiliate fees. Because these networks have only this one way to raise revenues, the affiliate fees are substantially higher than for basic services; they sometimes reach several dollars per month per subscriber.

Not all pay networks carry video programming. There are video game channels, such as The Nintendo Channel. A dozen audio services represent a wide variety of musical genres, some offering compact disc–quality digital audio. Text-based services specialize in program listings and news headlines.

Pay-per-View Networks. Pay-per-view (PPV) programming is also delivered by satellite and is financed by affiliate fees predicated on the number of subscribers who order each pay-per-view selection. The leading pay-per-view networks are Request and Viewer's Choice. The main program categories for PPV have been sports, especially boxing and professional wrestling; recent films; and adult programs, especially for travelers in motels. Revenues were more than $600 million in 1996, about 45 percent of that from special events like boxing (Parsons & Frieden, 1998). More emphasis is being placed on newly released feature films now that high-capacity digital cable systems can offer more choice to potential customers.

Cable Franchise Authorities. In most states, cable is regulated at the municipal or county level. New Jersey and Connecticut opted for statewide regulation. Local regulation is usually delegated to a city employee who is advised by a local cable commission. These commissions monitor the performance of their cable companies when local franchises come up for renewal.

Direct Broadcast Satellite Networks. Direct Broadcast Satellite (DBS) companies such as DirecTV pick up satellite feeds from cable television networks, and they also originate their own programming that is not available on cable. They transmit channels on their own high-powered satellites directly to their customers, who pay subscription fees to the DBS operator, an arrangement that eliminates the local cable system's role as "middle person." With all-digital systems, the DBS networks have more channel capacity than cable, much of which is used for pay per view. Missing from DBS lineups are local TV stations that are not carried on satellite.

Network Ownership and Group Station Owners

Here's who owns the major TV networks:

- NBC is owned by General Electric, which also has interests in aerospace, financial services, appliances, home video, and TV production. It had seven TV stations and bought more in 1995, including three owned-and-operated stations, but it sold off its radio and record operations in the early 1990s.
- ABC/CapCities merged with Disney in 1995, bringing theme parks and production of movies, prime-time TV shows, and cartoons to a group that had a television network, 3 cable channels (including ESPN), video production, 10 television stations, and 21 radio stations.
- Fox Broadcasting Corporation is owned by Rupert Murdoch's News Corp., along with Twentieth Century Fox film and TV production studio; TV stations formerly owned by Metromedia; satellite TV channels in Europe, Asia, and Latin America; and print media in Australia, Britain, and the United States.
- UPN is a TV network started in 1993 by television station owner Chris Craft and Viacom, which had acquired Paramount movie and TV studios, Blockbuster video stores, MTV and Nickelodeon cable channels, and Simon & Schuster publishing.
- WB TV is a TV network started by Time Warner, which owns Warner Brothers studio, Warner Music, and Home Box Office, a number of cable systems, Time Inc. magazines (including *Time, People,* and *Fortune*), and a major interest in Turner Broadcasting, which includes CNN, TNT, the Cartoon Network, and the MGM film and cartoon library.

B.C.
Before cable TV, antennas filled the skies.

Thus, most television networks have ownership connections with film studios or other major sources of content. However, CBS/Westinghouse and NBC/General Electric are concentrating on acquiring more broadcast distribution stations.

Cable Ownership and Control

Perhaps no other segment of the communications industry has been so profoundly shaped by efforts to regulate ownership interests as cable. Its survival as an independent industry relied on regulations that, until the early 1990s at least, prevented local telephone companies from buying cable systems or providing television services in their territories. As soon as these restrictions were relaxed, the telephone industry quickly made its move, in some cases acquiring interests in cable companies and in other cases announcing plans to build their own cable networks. Broadcast television networks and, to a lesser extent, large broadcast and publishing group owners were kept from dominating the cable industry through other ownership restrictions, but these restrictions were lifted, too.

Protected from outside domination, cable gave birth to giants of its own. Throughout the 1980s, the largest cable companies became very aggressive in acquiring new properties. Many companies prominent in the early history of cable, including Teleprompter (and its successor, Group W), Storer Cable, and United Cable, disappeared entirely. By 1992, the 15 largest cable MSOs controlled over half the cable subscribers in the United States and attracted the attention of Congress and antitrust regulators.

As TCI became more **horizontally integrated** by acquiring other cable MSOs, it also became more **vertically integrated** by obtaining interests in cable programming networks. TCI owned interests in the Discovery Channel and Turner Broadcasting and spun off a subsidiary, Liberty Media, that holds substantial interests in several other networks. Turner played his own vertical integration game by acquiring the MGM Studios film library and later purchasing two small Hollywood studios that could make new programs for Turner's networks. A parallel development was the merger of Time, Inc. (owner of HBO and the second-largest MSO) with Warner (another large MSO with interests in publishing and music) into a new multimedia conglomerate, Time Warner.

Horizontal integration is concentrating ownership by acquiring companies that are all in the same business.

Vertical integration is concentrating ownership by acquiring companies that are in related businesses.

The next step in vertical integration was typified by U.S. West's investment in Time Warner. Other cable-telco combinations include BellSouth's investments in Prime Cable and QVC Networks (owner of cable shopping channels), Nynex's investment in Viacom, and Southwestern Bell's alliance with Cox Cable. In 1994 a "megamerger" involving TCI and Bell Atlantic fell through in the wake of new cable rate regulations, but this only paved the way for new vertical alliances, such as an agreement between TCI and computer software giant Microsoft to launch an interactive computer channel.

As transnational firms jockey for strategic position in the Information Age, they seek all of the "pieces" necessary to put multimedia telecommunications networks into the home and the workplace. A good example is AT&T's 1998 acquisition of TCI to give AT&T access to homes for local telephony and Internet access, integrated with cable and other services. The pieces include telephony, retail distribution (local cable systems and video stores), wholesale distribution (cable networks), and software production (publishers and movie studios). The final piece is the hardware to bring digital signals into the home and provide users with an interactive interface. This makes further alliances involving consumer electronics and computer firms a distinct possibility.

1. How is the cable industry organized?
2. What is meant by horizontal and vertical integration in the cable television industry?
3. How is cable programming different from that of broadcast TV?
4. What is the impact of cable on broadcast TV?
5. How is cable regulated?

AUDIENCES FOR TELEVISION

Americans are extremely well equipped for television viewing. Almost all U.S. households have at least one television (98.3 percent), and almost all of those are color sets (98 percent). Around two-thirds of U.S. households have two or more television sets, more than two-thirds have remote controls (to facilitate **channel surfing**), and around 82 percent have videocassette recorders.

Channel surfing uses remote controls to browse briefly through a number of channels, viewing short bits of each.

Share of the audience is the proportion of those actually watching at that moment, *not* of the whole potential audience.

By the late 1990s, about as many people still watched network television as watched cable TV or independent stations. However, both cable and independents have steadily cut further and further into network television's **share** of the audience, which went from 90 percent of the prime-time audience in 1979 to under 50 percent in 1999. In the 1997–1998 season, according to Nielsen Media Research, the four major networks, including Fox, had 57 percent of the total television audience. The historical "big three" networks, without Fox, had less than 50 percent, an all-time low point for network television (NCTA, 1998).

Television viewing in general is highest among families with children, among older people, among women, and among African Americans. It is lower among better-educated and higher-income viewers. Families with "basic" cable watch more total television that those with just over-the-air television, and those with pay cable watch substantially more yet, and those with home video watch even more on top of that. Network audiences tend to be largest compared to cable among urban, minority, and lower-income viewers (National Cable Television Association, 1998).

Even before cable TV broke the audience into smaller segments, the television audience was already differentiating in terms of who watched what. In general, news is less popular than drama, suspense, mystery, sitcoms, variety shows, and feature films, among younger viewers and teen-agers. Still, television has long been most people's main source of news (Robinson & Godbey, 1995), although it has been declining recently. Sitcoms and movies appeal most to younger viewers, whereas variety and news appeal most to older viewers. Sports appeal more to men, drama and soap operas more to women (Livingstone, 1998).

Network television audiences tend to be older. Fox and ABC have both played to, and attracted, younger viewers. CBS has sometimes appealed to younger viewers, sometimes to an older core audience.

The demographics of network TV viewers has become a controversial topic. In 1998, there was an unprecedented decline in network viewership in one of the audience segments most coveted by advertisers, young males. The networks were so outraged by the numbers from Nielsen Media Research that they vowed to back a competing rating service that presumably would give them the numbers they needed. The networks were much more sanguine about another demographic viewing trend—the tendency of white audiences to watch only shows with white actors while African American audiences tend to watch only shows with black characters—a trend encouraged by clustering shows with African American performers together in blocks. The response of network executives to this "ghettoization" of television was simply that they were business people, not social reformers (Sterngold, 1998).

Audiences for Multichannel Media

In about 67 percent of American homes, broadcast television has to compete with cable TV (Alsop, 1997) and another 10 percent have direct broadcast satellite TV services. All but 3 percent of American homes—homes located largely in remote rural areas—are passed by a cable network. Nearly all cable households (96 percent) have 30 or more channels, and most (57 percent) have 54 or more. About two-thirds of cable subscribers also subscribe to pay channels (National Cable Television Association, 1998).

Who does not have cable? Older households, especially those without children, and low-income homes are relatively unlikely to have cable. Most nonsubscribers say that they cannot afford cable, that cable is not worth its cost, that they do not watch enough TV to justify a subscription, or that their viewing needs are met by broadcast television (Cable Television Advertising Bureau, 1988).

Ratings for individual cable programs are minuscule by broadcast TV standards. A "hit" cable program may attract only 2 or 3 percent of all cable television households—about an eighth of the audience for a "hit" prime-time broadcast television series. However, viewing accumulated across all cable channels is significant, and over half (54 percent) of all viewing in cable households is accounted for by cable networks. Cable homes watch over 25 percent more television overall than noncable households (Cable Television Advertising Bureau, 1998).

1. What are some popular prime-time television genres?
2. Is the network television audience growing or declining? Why?
3. What effect has cable television had on the audiences for broadcast television networks like ABC, CBS, and NBC?
4. Who is least likely to have cable?

POLICY AND ETHICAL ISSUES

Ownership Rules

Initially, in order to limit the power of any single group over the diversity of content, ownership groups were limited to 5 television, 5 FM, and 5 AM stations. Opponents in the 1980s argued that media are diverse *because of* competition, including that from cable TV, and the limits were relaxed to 12 TV, 12 AM, and 12 FM stations, with a national television coverage limit of 25 percent of homes. The 1996 Telecommunications Act eliminated the limit of 12 TV stations and raised the national television coverage limit to 35 percent. In individual markets, no company can own more than one TV station.

Even before the round of mergers, acquisitions, and alliances between cable and telephone companies in the 1990s, there were concerns about excessive vertical and horizontal integration and the impact of competitiveness in the cable television industry. Congress and the FCC have intervened in the ownership issue at various times, first to protect cable from being bought up by broadcasters and telephone companies and later to prevent the mature cable television industry itself from devouring newer systems, such as satellite TV and wireless cable.

Why restrict ownership? Excessive horizontal integration, which might result if major MSOs kept acquiring more and more cable subscribers, can lead to anticompetitive practices. For example, TCI reportedly uses its market power as the largest cable operator to negotiate special low rates for basic and pay programming services. Other cable operators then have to pay higher rates, which they pass along to the consumer and which eventually undermine the profits of the other cable companies, in turn making them more vulnerable to being acquired, themselves, by TCI. The networks that TCI carries on its systems are almost assured of success, whereas the others are severely handicapped. In one notorious case, the cable giant threatened to remove a channel from its system, thereby dramatically lowering the value of the network, and then one of TCI's affiliated companies turned around and bought the network at a bargain price. At some point in the future, such maneuvering could give TCI and a few other multimedia giants a virtual veto power over new programming concepts.

Vertical integration—such as occurs when cable MSOs acquire interests in movie studios, programming networks, and DBS companies as well as their core business in home distribution—also has pitfalls for the consumer, particularly when some of the businesses are regulated and others are not. There is a temptation to **cross-subsidize** the unregulated parts (movie studios and cable networks) with inflated rates paid by customers of the regulated entities (local cable systems) and their customers. The addition of telephone service to the picture with AT&T's acquisition of TCI raises issues reminiscent of the halcyon days of the old AT&T monopoly, when it was accused of draining profits out of its local telephone operations and of using profits from its local phone companies to subsidize competition in the long-distance market. Instead of the competition between cable and telephone companies that Congress hopes to foster, the outcome may be a single telecommunications monopoly encompassing voice, data, and video communications. This could lead to higher rates, poorer service, and less diversity in the points of view presented to the consumer.

Cross-subsidize applies revenues from a profitable area to a less profitable one.

However, there are also some arguments in favor of less competition and more concentrated ownership. For example, the combination of telephone and cable companies might save the consumer money by making it possible to construct a single fiber optics–based information superhighway to the home. If telephone and cable companies compete, consumers might have to pay for two superhighway systems instead of one. As information technologies converge with mass media and assume ever more importance in the world economy, there is also a question of maintaining America's competitive position. Further vertical and horizontal integration might be desirable to create companies large enough and diversified enough to compete successfully on the world stage.

Owner Interference with TV News

The potential for corporate interference with news coverage by media owners is increasing, because media owners are now more frequently diversified corporations with nonmedia interests. When journalists in a company's media holdings criticize actions by other parts of the company's diverse operations, there is a rational reaction to try to mute the criticism. The top decision makers of diversified conglomerates are less likely to have backgrounds that train them in news values and ethics. They are more likely to think about the overall profits and image of the corporation and are less likely to hold news autonomy and objectivity sacred. Thus they are tempted both to censor negative news about other parts of the company and to use news programs to promote other parts of the company, in the name of synergy.

Journalists are faced with the same ethical dilemmas. They may have to decide what to do when an order comes from above about how to cover a story. They must work in a climate of *self-censorship,* in which they simply come to know that it isn't a good idea to prepare a critical story about another company within the same conglomerate. The following, which concerns ABC and Disney, illustrates internal censorship.

> "Jim Hightower, the witty, folksy former Agriculture Commissioner from Texas, whose radio show was broadcast in 150 markets, used to boast to 2 million listeners. Then ABC merged with Disney and Cap Cities. Hightower related to his listeners Disney's practice of replacing its full-time workers at Disneyland with contract labor, recruited from a homeless shelter. He also attacked ABC TV for bending down and kissing the toes of Philip Morris. Gradually, ABC stopped trying to sign up new stations for the show and in a matter of months canceled the show without notice. ABC insisted the show was not producing sufficient advertising revenue. Hightower countered that the show would have been very profitable if it had been permitted to accept $250,000 worth of union ads. But ABC would not accept those ads because they constituted 'advocacy.'" (Institute for Alternative Journalism, 1997, http://www.fourthestate.com/synergy.html).

Similar temptation either to reduce criticism or to expand positive coverage can arise with companies that are major advertisers on a station or network. As a young consumer affairs reporter, it can be difficult to file a hard-hitting story about the unfair sales practices of a company that is one of your station's main advertisers.

Violence Warnings and Controls

People have been concerned since the early 1950s over the question of sex, violence, and graphic language on television. There have been debates and considerable research about the amount and effects of these elements, an issue discussed in greater detail in Chapter 12. Pressure for wholesome children's programming finally resulted in the passage of the Children's Television Act in 1990. The act mandated that TV broadcasters serve educational and informational needs of

VIOLENCE WARNING.
Parental advisories such as these are voluntary ratings supplied by the networks to help parents control children's viewing. They also help to stave off criticism about excessive violence on television.

TVY—All Children
TVY7—Directed to Older Children
TVG—General Audience
TVPG—Parental Guidance Suggested
TV14—Parents Strongly Cautioned
TVM—Mature Audiences Only

children as a condition of having their FCC licenses renewed. However, no precise definition of what constituted educational content was provided, and the FCC was uncomfortable treading on the sacred ground of the constitutional free speech rights of broadcasters, writing rules general enough to allow *Teenage Mutant Ninja Turtles* to be counted as educational. After years of quibbling over what was "educational" and what was "specifically designed for children," a quantitive standard of 3 hours per week of children's programming was set (Kunkel, 1998).

A second facet of the children and television controversy is to limit content of a violent or sexual nature, because it may harm impressionable young minds. Here again regulatory efforts run up against the First Amendment and its protections of free speech, so industry self-regulation has been the inevitable outcome of the periodic controversies over TV sex and violence. Unfortunately, self-regulation has not been effective in the eyes of child and family advocates, and television continues to be an exceptionally violent and sexual place. For their part, broadcasters insist that it is up to the parents to control their own children.

The latest attempt to resolve this conundrum involves a mixture of high-tech and voluntary content ratings patterned on those long used by the film industry (Chapter 6). The Telecommunications Act of 1996 requires that new television sets sold in the United States include a "V-chip" that enables viewers, particularly parents, to block programming, via an electronically encoded system. The industry is required to develop a ratings system for "violence, sex and other indecent materials and to agree voluntarily to broadcast signals containing such ratings." Industry leaders agreed in a 1996 summit meeting with President Clinton to produce this ratings system and implemented it in 1998, but not without continuing controversy. Parents complained that the rating system provided too little useful information, was confusing, and that NBC did not go along with this rating system.

Diversity and Minority Ownership

Another key issue is how to promote diversity of points of view in television and film. During the 1980s, the Reagan administration policymakers at the FCC, particularly Chairman Mark Fowler, argued that the increase in alternative channels created a more truly open marketplace of ideas and eliminated the problem of diversity. They argued that instead of relatively few networks dominating scarce channels, multiple channels almost automatically promoted multiple points of view. Others are less optimistic, particularly given the early 1990s trends toward cross-ownership and integration among producers, cable TV companies, and telephone companies.

This all seems to make sense until one actually gets down to cases. One measure of diversity is TV station ownership by females and minorities, and the fact is that they are drastically underrepresented in the ranks of TV station owners and board memberships (Irving, 1998). Minorities are also underrepresented on television. According to data compiled by the Screen Actors Guild, African, Hispanic, Asian, and Native Americans appear in only 20 percent of all roles in movies and television, although they constitute 27 percent of the U.S. population. And, as we saw earlier, most of the minority actors are limited to roles in racially segregated programs that are shown in blocks of programs targeted primarily to minorities (Wynter, 1998). This same pattern is reflected in the so-called target marketing of harmful products such as malt liquor and cigarettes to minorities. Thus we see the dirty underbelly of audience segmentation—it may be becoming a euphemism for audience segregation.

Fairness Doctrine

One of the more contentious examples of Reagan administration deregulation, based on assumptions about increased options with multichannel technologies, came with the 1987 withdrawal of the Fairness Doctrine. That doctrine had put stations on notice that the FCC expected them to devote time to controversial issues of public importance and to provide opportunities for the expression of opposing views when only one side had been aired. Most attention centered on the second part, the **right of reply.** Although broadcasters were given substantial leeway in defining what was controversial and in deciding what constituted equal time, the networks and individual stations still felt that the Fairness Doctrine actually had a **chilling effect**—that is, it inhibited stations from airing controversial programs. That led many conservatives, in particular, to oppose the doctrine, especially because syndicated programs by conservative pundits such as Rush Limbaugh

Right of reply gives time to present opposing views on broadcast stations when only one side has been aired.

Chilling effect is when fairness rules inhibit stations from airing controversial programs.

MEDIA ETHICS

What Do You Do When the Truck Doesn't Blow Up?

One of the most notorious cases of simulating a news event for the purpose of getting good visuals for a news story came in 1992 on *Dateline NBC.* The producers simulated a truck explosion by purposely igniting leaking fuel when it failed to blow up on its own, to illustrate a story on design flaws that led General Motors trucks to explode under certain circumstances.

How would you handle the issue if you were the journalist? The Gannett Newseum in Arlington Virginia lets visitors say how they would react to the following situation:

"You're a producer of a network newsmagazine. You've learned about a teenager who died in a fiery crash. A design defect in his pickup is suspected. Telling his story might save lives. But after repeated attempts, you can't get one of these trucks to explode. It isn't good TV without riveting video."

"What do you do?" (Each possible answer is followed by the percentage selecting it.)

A. "Scrap the story. The truck won't blow up. Maybe it's safe." (28 percent)

B. "Rig the pickup to explode. The story is important. Video is crucial." (14 percent)

C. "Rig the explosion video, but admit that it's a 'simulation.'" (56 percent)

The preferred current ethical practice is the third option. Simulation or re-enactments would be carefully labeled.

If you want to find other examples of how television journalists face ethical dilemmas, you can search the World Wide Web on sites such as www.askjeeves.com, which permit more complex questions. Or if you are using the InfoTrac College Edition, search under the keywords "television news-moral and ethical aspects."

Source: "Ethics: How Would You Handle the Dilemmas That Journalists Face?" *Brill's Content,* November 1998, p. 42.

1. Why have the cross-ownership rules on radio and television stations been relaxed?
2. What are the current rules?
3. Why are content ratings being enacted for television? What are their pros and cons?
4. Has the increasing diversity of television and cable channels eliminated the need for regulation of content?
5. What was the Fairness Doctrine? Who opposes it?

were among those that some stations felt reluctant to air when replies had to be allowed. A proposal in 1993 to renew the Fairness Doctrine raised this debate again, but it has not been reinstated.

The Need to Visualize TV News

Broadcast news is often guided by the need to find stories that have a dramatic visual element that makes for good television. That can lead to two ethical dilemmas. One is the temptation to ignore or downplay an important story because it doesn't have any good images to go with it. That effect can be subtle. It is easy to cover one story briefly because there are no attached visuals, while dwelling more on another because it has exciting imagery.

A related ethical dilemma is the occasional impulse among television journalists to stage or create visuals for a story. The Society for Professional Journalists Code (see Media Ethics, Chapter 14) urges journalists to "Avoid misleading reenactments or staged news events. If reenactment is necessary to tell a story, label it." (http://spj.org/ethics/, 1998)

SUMMARY AND REVIEW

WHO INVENTED THE BASIC TELEVISION CAMERA AND PICTURE TUBE TECHNOLOGIES?

In 1922, Philo Farnsworth, an independent inventor, and Vladimir Zworykin, of RCA, both invented the essential technology for scanning an image into lines—a TV camera. Allen Dumont invented the picture tube.

WHAT IS THE NTSC STANDARD? HOW WAS IT DEVELOPED?

The 1941 NTSC black-and-white television standards are still in use, particularly 525 lines per frame and 30 frames per second. These standards for television were worked out by a government-mandated compromise committee, the National Television Systems Committee (NTSC).

WHY DID THE FCC FREEZE TELEVISION LICENSES FROM 1948 UNTIL 1952?

Television stations started to rush onto the air in 1948. However, the existing FCC technical standards did not allow for nearly enough stations to cover the United States or to prevent signal interference.

HOW DID CABLE SPREAD THROUGHOUT THE UNITED STATES?

Cable television started as a shared community antenna service for rural communities in 1948. It expanded into suburban areas beginning in 1972 and reached the largest cities only in the early 1980s. Today, cable is accessible to about 98 percent of all U.S. households, and over 67 percent of those homes subscribe.

WHICH TECHNOLOGIES WERE CRITICAL TO CABLE'S EARLY GROWTH?

Coaxial cable made it possible to transmit dozens of channels to homes in a cable franchise area. Satellite transmission made many distant signals, superstations, and other new channels available throughout the country.

HOW DID HOLLYWOOD REACT TO TELEVISION?

The film industry initially fought television by not releasing any new movies to be shown on television. However, the film industry began to realize that it couldn't beat television. Disney started producing programs for television in 1954, and other studios followed. By 1961 the film boycott of television was over.

WHAT CONTRIBUTIONS DID JOHN WALSON, TED TURNER, AND JOHN MALONE MAKE TO THE CABLE INDUSTRY?

John Walson created the first cable television system in Mahanoy, Pennsylvania, in 1948. Ted Turner established the first basic cable network, WTCG (later, WTBS), in 1975. John Malone is responsible for the emergence of TCI as the world's largest cable television operator.

WHAT ENABLED A FOURTH NETWORK, FOX, TO SUCCEED?

In 1987, Rupert Murdoch started the Fox television network. Cable TV helped Fox, since most Fox affiliates were independent UHF stations, which cable brought to most homes with perfect picture quality. Fox also pursued a targeted television strategy by pursuing younger viewers and more urban and racially diverse audience segments.

HOW DOES A TELEVISION CAMERA WORK?

The camera tube breaks light down into scanning lines, which can be scanned by an electron beam. The beam causes a discharge of energy that turns into electrical voltage variations. The lines of resolution (525 for NTSC) are the lines per frame scanned by the electron beam and later reproduced by the picture tube in the receiver.

HOW DOES A TELEVISION PICTURE TUBE WORK?

A picture tube, or cathode ray tube, fires an electron gun at dots on the inside of the screen; the dots glow with varying intensity to create an image.

WHAT IS THE DIFFERENCE BETWEEN VHF AND UHF?

VHF uses the very high frequency band and UHF uses ultra high frequencies. Both require 6 MHz in channel width. There are a maximum of twelve VHF channels. There are currently 56 UHF channels.

HOW ARE CABLE TELEVISION PICTURES TRANSMITTED TO THE HOME?

The cable operator's head end picks up channels from satellite, microwave, broadcast, and local studio sources, which are then transmitted over a coaxial cable network to the home.

WHAT NEW TECHNOLOGIES ARE EMERGING AS COMPETITIVE THREATS TO CABLE TV?

DBS, MMDS, and cellular television systems have equal access to cable programming.

HOW ARE TELEVISION STATIONS ORGANIZED?

Most commercial television stations have an administrative or managerial structure, a sales force to sell local advertising, engineering or technical staff for studio and transmitter operations, a news operation, and a production staff for news and other programming.

WHAT ARE THE MAIN SOURCES OF PROGRAMMING FOR NETWORKS AND THEIR AFFILIATES?

Networks supply a great deal of programming to their O&Os (network owned-and-operated stations) or affiliates. The networks themselves produce news shows, sports events, some talk shows, some soap operas, documentaries, and, increasingly, their own series. Formerly, "Fin-Syn" regulations required most entertainment programs to be purchased by networks from film studio production units or from independent producers.

WHERE DO PBS PROGRAMS COME FROM?

PBS programming tends to be developed by the larger PBS affiliate stations, such as WGBH in Boston. They initiate proposals and put together packages of support from Corporation for Public Broadcasting foundations, corporate underwriters, etc.

HOW IS THE CABLE INDUSTRY ORGANIZED?

Most local cable systems are owned by multiple system operators (MSOs) and purchase their programming from the various basic, pay, and pay-per-view networks, predicated on monthly per-subscriber affiliate fees. The local systems also sell advertising on basic cable channels. Some MSOs own interests in programming services as well as in the local systems that distribute them to the public. Regulatory oversight is provided by local cable franchise authorities and the FCC.

WHAT IS MEANT BY HORIZONTAL AND VERTICAL INTEGRATION IN THE CABLE TELEVISION INDUSTRY?

Horizontal integration happens when large MSOs such as TCI and Time Warner acquire interests in other cable operators who also own local distribution networks. Vertical integration happens when cable MSOs acquire interests in related businesses, such as cable programming networks. Both vertical and horizontal integration raise the potential threat of monopolistic practices that may harm the consumer.

HOW IS CABLE PROGRAMMING DIFFERENT FROM THAT OF BROADCAST TV?

Most cable channels are built around the concept of narrowcasting to specialized audiences, predicated either on a common genre of programming or on the demographic characteristics or lifestyles of their viewers. However, some general-audience cable channels emulate the broadcast TV model. Music videos are among the more novel cable programming forms to emerge.

WHAT IS THE IMPACT OF CABLE ON BROADCAST TV?

The proportion of viewers who tune in to prime-time broadcasts from ABC, CBS, and NBC has declined dramatically in recent years. Cable households are heavy viewers of television, and over half of viewing in cable households is now devoted to channels available only on cable.

WHAT PROGRAMMING GENRES CAME TO TELEVISION FROM RADIO?

Variety shows, comedians, ensemble comedies, situation comedies, soap operas, dramas, western dramas, mysteries, science fiction, talk shows, sports, news and public affairs, documentaries, and game shows.

WHAT PROGRAMMING GENRES CAME TO TELEVISION FROM FILM?

Action-adventure movies, and cartoons (developed into series forms).

WHAT WERE THE MAIN TELEVISION GENRES THAT EVOLVED IN THE 1950S AND 1960S?

Comedy, music, variety shows, periodic specials, magazine programs, news, situation comedies, westerns, sports and action adventure. In the 1960s and 1970s, some television variety shows, sitcoms, and dramas began to have a more critical and social point of view.

IS THE NETWORK TELEVISION AUDIENCE GROWING OR DECLINING? WHY?

The network audience has been declining steadily. Cable TV, and independent stations have cut into network television's share of the audience, which went from 90 percent of the prime-time audience in 1979 to under 50 percent in 1999.

WHY DOES CABLE HAVE NARROWCASTING INSTEAD OF BROADCASTING?

Narrowcast channels are those devoted to special interests or audience groups, made possible by the large number of channels available on cable TV systems. Since cable networks derive all or part of their revenues from subscriptions, as well as from advertising sales, it is also economically feasible to offer narrowcast channels that appeal to only relatively small audiences.

HOW DO CABLE SUBSCRIBERS AND NONSUBSCRIBERS DIFFER?

Almost all American homes have cable service available, but only two-thirds subscribe. Nonsubscribers tend to have low household incomes or are older residents, often without children.

WHY HAVE THE CROSS-OWNERSHIP RULES ON RADIO AND TELEVISION STATIONS BEEN RELAXED?

Initially, ownership groups were limited to five television stations and five FM and five AM radio stations. The goal was to limit the power of any single group over content so as to increase diversity. Opponents argued that media were diverse because of competition and that ownership rules could safely be relaxed. The 1996 Telecommunications Act eliminated most of the limits.

HOW IS CABLE REGULATED?

Regulation of cable TV is now shared between the FCC and local franchise authorities.

WHY WERE TELEVISION AND CABLE CONTENT RATINGS DEVELOPED?

Pressure for action built after years of hearings did not produce effective industry self-regulation. The Telecommunications Act of 1996 required the television industry to develop a ratings system for violence, sex, and "other indecent materials," and to broadcast signals containing those ratings. New television sets sold in the United States must include a V-chip to enable viewers to block programming based on that electronically encoded system.

Electronic Resources

For up-to-the-minute URLs about *Television and Cable,* access the MEDIA NOW site on the World Wide Web at:

http://communication.wadsworth.com/

CHAPTER 8

Computer Media and the Internet

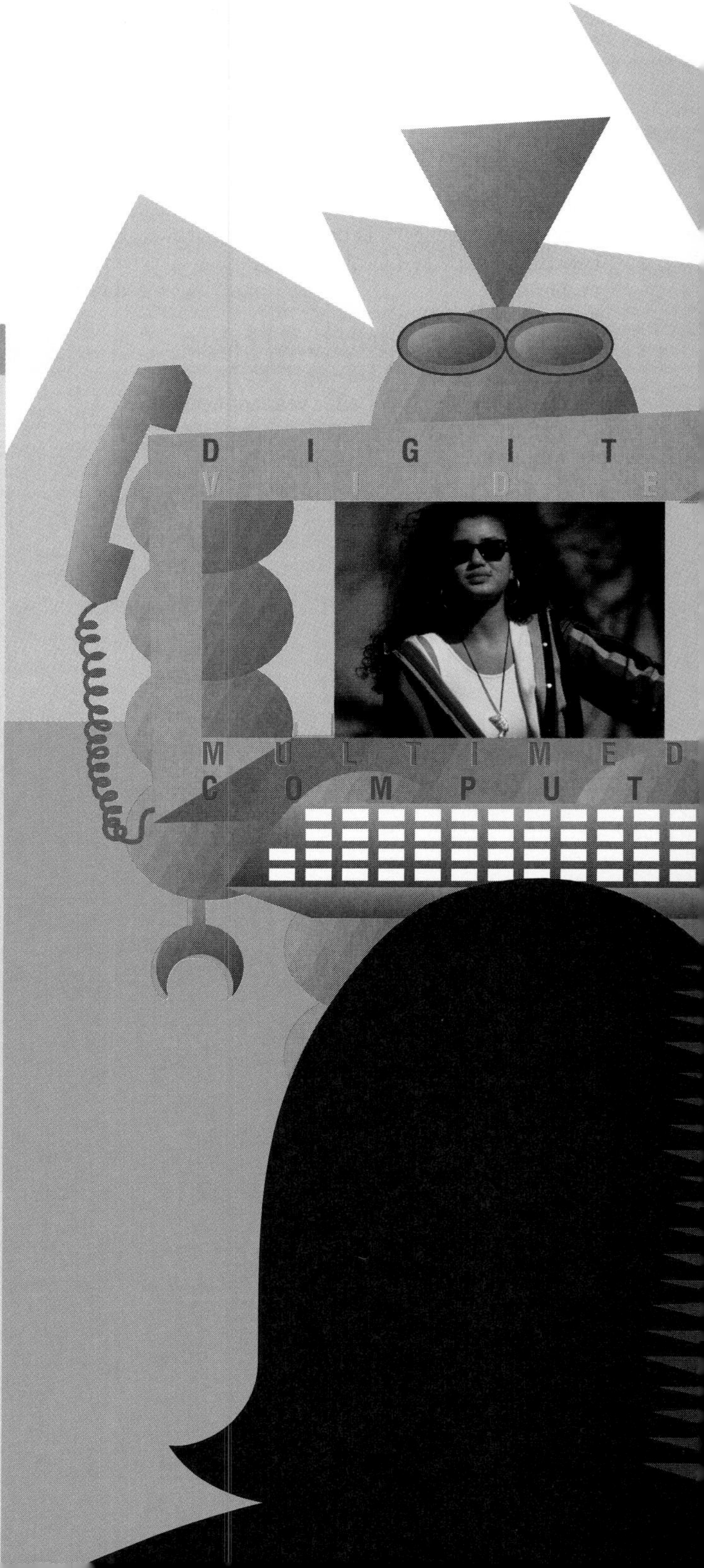

WHAT'S AHEAD

It is not possible to study the mass media these days without considering computer media. This chapter traces the history of computers from their early origins in the nineteenth century down to the latest developments on the World Wide Web.

WWW

Access the MEDIA NOW site on the World Wide Web at: **http://communication.wadsworth.com/** Choose "Chapter 8" from the selection box to access electronic information and other sites relevant to this chapter.

HAPPY (VIRTUAL) BIRTHDAY

Voice call coming through from Ali, madam.

Excellent! I'll take it in the study.

Happy birthday, Mom! Did you get my present?

Yes! I'm glad someone remembered. Where are we today?

Let me show you!

Okay. DeeVee, give me widescreen color video. Now, what am I looking at?

This week I'm in San Francisco, and you're looking at the sunset in Golden Gate Park.

Spectacular! And I see you're wearing that pendant I sent you for your birthday.

Oh yes, it's so perfect, I wear it to all my client meetings now.

I'm glad to see you getting some wear out of it. It cost me plenty! Heard from your father lately?

Oh, all the time. Why just yesterday he . . .

Never mind, I hear all I want to through the lawyers. Dear, when will I get to see you?

Well, next week I'll be in Paris. I'll call you from there.

No, I mean really see you.

Oh, Mom, you know I can't . . .

Please. I'll buy the plane ticket. I'd do anything if I could just really see you, just once.

Mom, I . . . I . . . I . . . I . . . I . . . I . . . I . . . I . . . I . . .

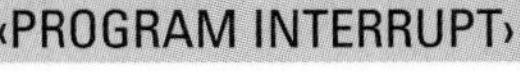

Sorry, madam, but the Net just informed me that ALI the Artificial Lifelike Intelligence is not programmed for the function you have requested. Shall I reset?

(Sigh.) Okay, take it from the top. And make her look less like the ex-husband this time, OK?

Happy birthday, Mom! Did you get my present?

Chapter Outline

A Brief History of Computer Media
The Dawn of the Computer Age
Preparing for Doomsday: The First Computer Networks
The Rise of the Personal Computer
The Birth of On-Line Services
Shifting Fortunes, Shifting Technology in Personal Computing
The Evolution of the World Wide Web
Trends in Computer Media Technology
Trends in Computer Media Hardware
Computer Media Software Trends
Future Directions in Computer Media
Web Technology Trends
Computer Media Genres
Internet Functions, Internet Protocols
What's on the Web?
Computer Software Genres
Using Computer Media
Structure of the Computer Media Industry
Computer Hardware Industry
Computer Software Industry
Content Providers
Who Runs the Internet?
Policy, Social, and Ethical Issues
Ownership and Control
Internet Governance
Censorship
Antisocial Behavior
Encryption
User Privacy
Intellectual Property
Summary and Review

A BRIEF HISTORY OF COMPUTER MEDIA

Were it not for the cancellation of a research grant, the **computer** could have been invented in the nineteenth century. In 1822 Charles Babbage, professor of mathematics at Cambridge University in England, created the *difference engine,* a mechanical calculator that could automatically produce mathematical tables. Babbage's "grantsmanship" was not equal to his mathematical genius, however, and his funding from the English government ran out in 1833 (Evans, 1981; Wulforst, 1982).

Computers are electronic data processing machines.

The earliest ancestor of the Internet arrived at about the same time across the Atlantic, in the form of Samuel F. B. Morse's *telegraph* network, in 1844. Chapter 4 described how the Associated Press *newspaper wire service* got its start in 1846, making it the first electronic information service and also the earliest precursor of today's World Wide Web. Stock market "tickers" and "racing wires," which telegraphed the results of horse races, are other early examples of information services.

The Dawn of the Computer Age

But for the lack of a glass of whiskey, the computer might never have been developed to this day. Many people—including the federal judge who decided a pivotal computer patent case in 1972—credit the invention of the first electronic computer to John Vincent Atanasoff. Although he never assembled a complete working system, he produced models of computer memory and data processing units at Iowa State University in 1939. The story goes that Atanasoff drew the inspiration for his invention indirectly from the desire to have a bourbon and soda in a southern Illinois bar. Iowa was a "dry" state back then, and he had to drive almost 200 miles for his drink, which gave him plenty of time to think about inventing the computer!

More sobering inspiration came from the hostilities of World War II (1939–45). Starting in 1943, the British secret service used the first working all-electronic digital computer (named *Colossus*) to crack Nazi secret codes. The quest to calculate artillery aiming tables more efficiently led to the creation of the first general-purpose computer, the *electronic numerical integrator and calculator (ENIAC),* at the University of Pennsylvania in 1946. Materials shortages prevented ENIAC from being

COMPUTER TIME LINE

1822	Babbage invents the computer
1844	Morse's telegraph, data network forerunner
1846	Associated Press, first information service
1939	Atanasoff designs first modern computer
1943	Colossus computer cracks Nazi codes
1946	ENIAC goes into operation
1951	UNIVAC first commercial computer
1956	IBM consent decree
1964	Octopus, first local area network (LAN)
1965	BASIC computer language
1969	ARPANET established
1972	Pong, first video game
1972	Alto, first with mouse and graphical user interface
1975	Altair, first personal computer
1979	Prestel, first videotex system
1984	Apple Macintosh, first graphical PC
1991	Internet opens to commercial users; HTML developed, the World Wide Web is born
1996	Telecommunications Act and Communications Decency Act passed
1998	Microsoft antitrust case filed

finished in time to make a contribution to World War II. ENIAC helped start the Cold War, though, by completing calculations for the first hydrogen bomb.

In 1951, ENIAC's inventors, J. Presper Eckert and John Mauchly, went on to create UNIVAC, the first commercial computer. But by 1956, the computer industry was dominated by the company that became almost synonymous with computing, *International Business Machines,* or *IBM.* To resolve an antitrust suit filed against IBM by the U.S. Justice Department, the company agreed in a 1956 consent decree to keep computer manufacturing and computer services—the processing of computer applications for its customers—in separate subsidiaries. This basic structural separation between hardware and information services is still reflected in computer media today, even though the consent decree was nullified in 1996.

Preparing for Doomsday: The First Computer Networks

The first data communications network was also an instrument of war: the SAGE air defense system first developed in the early 1960s. Its display unit was the inspiration for the "doomsday television" that is the backdrop for *Dr. Strangelove* (1964) and dozens of other apocalyptic movies from the Cold War era on which the movements of fleets of bombers and flights of missiles were projected onto a room-sized map of the world. The first telephone **modems** were deployed at this time to feed *digitized* bomber counts into the *analog* phone lines that interconnected the system. One of the first civilian examples of a data communication network was the American Airlines SABRE airline reservation system in 1966. It connects—it is still in use today—airline ticket counters and travel agents across the country to a central computer, providing central control of airline reservations and ticketing. The first **local area network (LAN)** was the 1964 Octopus network at the Atomic Energy Commission's Livermore Laboratory. It extended high-speed data

Modems convert digital data to analog signals for transmission over analog networks, such as the public telephone network.

Local area networks (LANs) are high-speed computer networks that link computers within a department, a building, or a campus of buildings.

communication to entire office buildings or campuses of buildings. In 1966, there began experiments with a **wide area network (WAN)** that would allow researchers to continue developing nuclear weapons even if the rest of civilization were wiped out in a nuclear war. *ARPANET,* as the *Advanced Research and Projects Network,* became known, was first operational in 1969 and was the forerunner of today's Internet.

Wide area networks connect distant users to centralized computer systems.

The Rise of the Personal Computer

Meanwhile, IBM's success with room-sized *mainframe* computers was bolstered by the spread of networks linking them to display screens at remote locations. But IBM was so wedded to its huge mainframe computers that it missed the shift to smaller ones. In the early 1960s, Digital Equipment Corporation developed low-cost "mini" computers about the size of an office desk standing on end for specialized purposes such as manufacturing production control and scientific computing. By the time IBM came out with its own desk-sized computers, they were about to be eclipsed by the even smaller **personal computer** that could sit on a desktop.

Personal computers are computers for individual users.

The *Alto* computer, developed in a research lab by the Xerox Corporation in 1972–1974, was the first desktop personal computer as we think of it today. It was a personal workstation that boasted a mouse, its own advanced programming language, a "friendly" user interface, and a high-speed network called Ethernet. The Alto was a research project that never made it to market, however, as the Xerox Corporation focused attention on copy machines instead of computers.

The first commercially available personal computer, the *Altair,* was announced in the January 1975 issue of *Popular Electronics.* However, the first specimen was literally "lost in the mail" on the way to its photography session at the magazine. An empty metal box filled in for it on the magazine cover. Despite the excitement, however, the "real" Altair was not very impressive. All it could do was play a simple-minded game in which the user imitated the patterns of flashing lights on its control panel (Freiberger & Swaine, 1984; Young, 1988).

Nonetheless, the Altair inspired the development of the computer medium as we know it today. A young computer hacker from Seattle by the name of William Gates developed an advanced computer programming language for the new machine, BASIC. Gates had dropped out of Harvard and founded *Microsoft Corporation.* The Altair also prompted young electronics enthusiasts Steve Jobs and Stephen Wozniak to build their own computer in a spare bedroom at Steve's mother's house. The second iteration of their design, the *Apple II,* included such amenities as a keyboard, a built-in power supply, and a color monitor (all lacking in the first Apple) and was an immediate success upon its introduction in 1977. Computers had entered the home. With the **floppy disc drive,** the Apple II added a convenient way to read and store computer programs that in turn spawned an explosion in software development. In 1979, the first electronic spreadsheet program, *VisiCalc,* made it possible for the personal computer to complete complex financial calculations, a feature that stimulated wider adoption of the Apple IIb by business people and consumers alike.

Floppy disc drives store computer data on a flexible ("floppy") plastic disc coated with a magnetized film.

And then there was Pong, the first computer video game, invented in 1972. A form of electronic ping-pong, it was a wildly popular arcade game. It came out in a home version in 1974 and was most home players' first introduction to the world of video games, albeit on a dedicated home player unit. People started using their personal computers to play games, too. In fact, this soon emerged as the most popular home computer application (Calica & Newson, 1996).

The Birth of On-Line Services

Another development that paved the way for the information superhighway was **videotex.** This medium grew out of early experiments with computerized information services conducted by the British Post Office in 1974 (Bouman & Christofferson, 1992). Following the wide area network model pioneered by SAGE and SABRE, videotex used telephone lines to connect remote terminals to central computers. Initially, these systems used home television sets to display the text and graphics (hence the "video" part of the name). The British experiments led in 1979 to the world's first commercial videotex service, Prestel, later to CompuServe and ultimately, to *America Online.*

Videotex is the delivery of textual information over telephone networks.

Shifting Fortunes, Shifting Technology in Personal Computing

IBM finally made its big move into personal computers in 1981, and its *Personal Computer (PC)* soon outstripped the Apple computer. Ironically, IBM sowed the seeds of its own downfall in the personal computer market—as well as that of Apple. Instead of relying on its own proprietary computer chips and software, as it had in the mainframe business, IBM turned to Intel Corporation for the chips and to Microsoft for the basic *disk operating system (DOS)* software. But Intel and Microsoft also sold their products to companies competing with IBM and Apple. Soon machines featuring Intel hardware and Microsoft software dominated the personal computer industry.

Another step forward came in 1984 when Apple's *Macintosh* computer first put high-resolution graphics and multimedia capabilities in a personal computer. In 1987, Apple Computer made another lasting contribution before entering a 10-year decline. It began distributing copies of a remarkable new program, *hypercard,* with each new Macintosh. Hypercard popularized the **hypertext** concept, the "linking" function that makes it possible to navigate between files of computer text and graphics by "mouse clicking" on keywords or icons. This later became the navigation metaphor for the World Wide Web (Calica & Newsom, 1996).

Hypercard and popular painting and presentation software also stimulated interest in the graphics capabilities of personal computers because high-resolution, full-color graphics were available by the late 1980s. Unfortunately, it was hard to move graphics between computers; the floppy discs of the day could not hold the large graphics files, and high-speed computer networks were still in their infancy. A higher-capacity alternative was in the wings, however, in the form of *compact disc* players for home music systems, which used the same digital format that computers required. By 1988 compact disc players were available for computers, launching another two new media forms, the **compact disc read-only memory (CD-ROM)** and the **multimedia** computer (Calica & Newsom, 1996).

Hypertext links pages of computer text and graphics so that users can navigate by clicking on keywords or icons.

CD-ROM (compact disc read-only memory) drives hold discs that store large amounts of computer data and work, similar to compact disc music players.

Multimedia systems integrate text, audio, and video and let users select the presentation mode.

The Evolution of the World Wide Web

The marriage of videotex, hypertext, computer graphics, CD-ROM, and the advanced data processing and graphics capabilities of personal computers created the environment in which the **World Wide Web** was born. The further evolution of ARPANET, from a weapon of war in the 1960s to a medium of commerce in the 1990s, was also important. Over the years, use of this network gradually spread from nuclear weapons researchers to other users at major universities, and it was renamed the *Internet* and put under the management of the National Science Foundation (NSF) in 1986. In 1991 the Internet was opened to commercial users, and the NSF started withdrawing its financial support. In 1991 the CERN laboratory in Switzerland established the **hypertext markup language (HTML)** which was the basis for the development of the World Wide Web (CERN, 1998; Network Solutions, 1998). The Web, as it is known for short, proved to be the "golden application" that has propelled home computer ownership to new heights.

The **World Wide Web** (or Web) is the multimedia portion of the Internet.

Hypertext markup language (HTML) is the programming language used to create pages on the Web.

Now the Web is rapidly converging with conventional communications media forms. It is recognized as a burgeoning new medium for advertising, even as its increasingly popular electronic commerce sites undermine the role of conventional mass media advertising by making it possible to attract customers and complete purchase transactions without leaving the Web environment. Established mass media outlets are rushing out Web versions of their product and investing in successful Internet properties, such as NBC's purchase of the Snap Internet search engine in 1998. Other efforts, such as Microsoft Corporation's Web TV service, aim to integrate Web content with the conventional media consumption experience. Cable TV systems offering Internet service and telephone companies that complete calls over the Internet are further evidence of the convergence trend.

TRENDS IN COMPUTER MEDIA TECHNOLOGY

Trends in Computer Media Hardware

Computer Generations. The evolution of computer technology is often discussed in terms of several "generations," which are defined in terms of the types of components used in their *central processing units,* where all the data processing and computations take place. First-generation computers, such as the 1946 model ENIAC, used old-fashioned *vacuum tubes.* The second generation replaced these with *transistors* in the 1960s and the third generation used integrated circuits that placed thousands of transistors on a single computer "chip" no bigger than a thumbnail in the 1970s. All of today's personal computers are part of the fourth generation. They use *very large scale integrated (VLSI)* chips that can hold millions of components each. Large mainframe computers exemplify the fifth generation. The latest mainframes use *parallel processing* units capable of working simultaneously on a single computing problem (Evans, 1981; Wulforst, 1982). This approach is beginning to work its way into the Internet, where the servers that store and distribute information over the World Wide Web are moving to parallel processing to increase their speed.

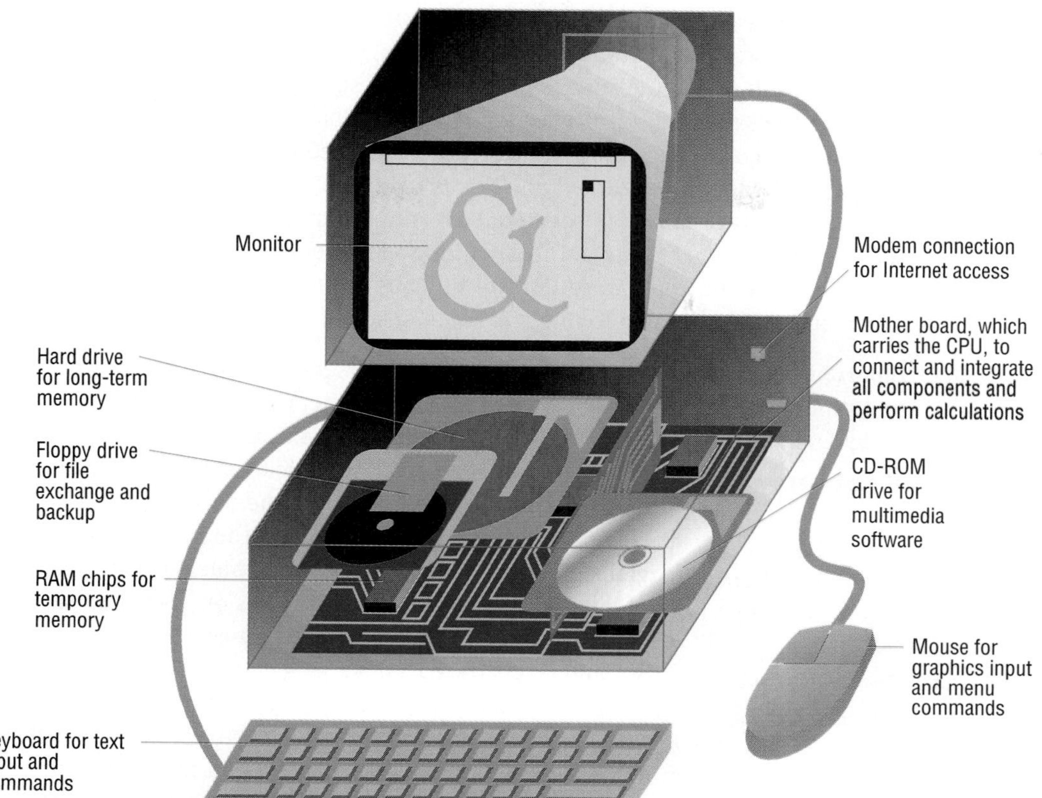

FIGURE 8.1
Personal computer systems include the central processing unit (CPU), the monitor, input devices (keyboard and mouse), and data storage (hard disc and floppy disc).

Short-Term Memory. Computers need *short-term memory* so that they can "remember" the results of their tasks and store their instruction programs temporarily for ready access. Early computers used large matrices of tiny doughnut-shaped magnets for this, but they couldn't be made small enough to keep up with the increasing volume and speed of data processing. Transistors and integrated memory circuits solved the problem by storing the 1s and 0s of computer data in the form of electrical voltages. They act something like a matrix of tiny rechargeable batteries. The processing unit charges up the "battery" when it wants to store a 1 and discharges it when it wants a 0 (see Figure 8.1). Today, many personal computers hold tens of millions of bytes in their temporary, or *random access memory (RAM),* units. Each **byte** consists of eight of the tiny "batteries," each representing a single binary computer digit, or **bit.**

A **byte** is (usually) eight computer bits. Each byte can represent a single numerical digit or letter of the alphabet.

Long-Term Memory. *Long-term memory* saves computer programs and data for long-term storage. Early computers relied on magnetic tape systems, very much like conventional audio tapes (see Chapter 6), that store information in tiny globs of magnetic material on the surface of a spool of plastic tape. (Tape drives are still used to back up computer network servers.) However, the computer had to "fast-forward" the tape to just the right point before it could "play" each piece of data, which slowed things down considerably. Modern *hard disc drives* also store data in

Bits, short for *b*inary dig*its,* are the basic 1s and 0s of computer data.

tiny globs of magnetic material, but on the surface of a rigid, rapidly spinning, small, flat disk. The *recording head* that "reads" the spinning disk moves quickly back and forth across the surface to where the desired piece of data resides. *Floppy discs* use the same basic principles but have a flexible plastic disc. Another type of permanent storage holds the basic instructions needed to start, or "boot up," the computer when it is first turned on. This is *read-only memory (ROM),* a form of permanent storage that uses solid-state circuits. Compact disc read-only memory (CD-ROM) is another important form of long-term memory. Like music compact discs, the data are stored in patterns of tiny pits on the surface of a plastic disc, which are read back by reflecting a beam of laser light off the surface.

Input/Output. Paper tapes and punch cards and magnetic storage media were used to communicate data to and from the earliest computers. Keyboard input and *cathode ray tube (CRT)* output did not become common until the 1960s. A computer's CRT operates much as a television tube does (see Chapter 7). An electron "gun" at the back of the tube shoots a stream of electrons at the front of the screen, lighting up globs of luminescent material on its inner surface. The point of light moves so quickly that it fools our eyes into seeing a continuous image. However, each frame of the computer screen is constructed from a single top-to-bottom scan of the picture tube, instead of by interlacing two scans to make one frame, as the television does, a fact that now complicates the convergence of computers and television.

Aside from the keyboard, the *mouse* is the most familiar input device. It originated in pioneering work at the Stanford Research Institute in 1968, but was first introduced to the general computer public in 1983 on board the Apple Lisa, forerunner to the Macintosh. Spurred by continuing efforts to make personal computers more user-friendly, a wide variety of input options became available, including joysticks, trackballs, pressure-sensitive tablets, touch-sensitive screens, and optical scanners such as those found in supermarket checkout lanes.

STOP & REVIEW

1. **What were the contributions of Charles Babbage, John Vincent Atanasoff, Grace Murray Hopper, and Eckert and Mauchly to the early development of the computer?**
2. **How did the personal computer come about?**
3. **What are the origins of the Internet and the World Wide Web?**
4. **What are the important components of computer systems and how do they function?**
5. **Compare the relative merits of the network computer and the multimedia computer.**

Computer Media Software Trends

The First Programs. Back in 1946, in order to tell ENIAC to shift from calculating artillery shell trajectories to, say, work on the design of the hydrogen bomb, technicians had to move electrical cords and mechanical switches by hand. There was no **software.** EDSAC, a 1949 British computer, was the first that could store its own programs in electronic memory and, without stopping, change the operation it was performing, such as switching from doing multiplication to extracting square roots.

Software consists of the programs and codes that instruct computers what to do.

Computer Languages. Early computer software was written exclusively in *machine language:* coded instructions, consisting entirely of 1s and 0s, that drove the binary circuits inside the computer. FORTRAN, released by IBM in 1955, allowed programmers to use recognizable words, such as "RUN" and "GO TO" and was the first *high-level language.* COBOL, the first language designed to approximate plain English, was developed by Navy Commodore (later, Rear Admiral) Grace Murray

PROFILE

"MOTHER OF THE COMPUTER." Grace Hopper played a key role in the early development of the computer and spent her later life lecturing about the future of computing.

Mother of the Computer

Name: Grace Murray Hopper

Education: A B.A. in math and physics from Vassar and a Ph.D. from Yale in 1934.

Position: Rear admiral, U.S. Navy

Style: Admiral's uniform, long silver braid done up in a bun.

Greatest Achievement: She wrote COBOL, the first "user-friendly" computer software to use plain English in its commands; it is still in use today. She also has the unique distinction of being the only woman ever to have a warship in the U.S. Navy named after her, the destroyer *U.S.S. Hopper.*

Most Dubious Achievement: Grace found the first computer "bug"—a moth that climbed into the Mark II computer.

Her Inspiration: Grace inherited a love of mathematics from her mother and came from a family with a strong military tradition.

Entry Level: Her first job was a teaching position in math at her alma mater. She joined the Navy as a lieutenant in 1943.

How She Got to the Top: Lt. Hopper was assigned to an early computing project at Harvard University funded by the U.S. Navy. There she took charge of programming two computers, the Mark I and Mark II. She later wrote the first program that automatically compiled computer commands into machine code, and she wrote programs for UNIVAC in the early 1950s. COBOL came out in 1959. She devoted her later life to traveling the world lecturing about the future of computing.

In Memoriam: Grace passed away in 1992 at the age of 86.

Source: http://www.sdsc.edu/Hopper/hopper_links.html

Hopper in 1959. *BASIC (beginner's all-purpose symbolic instruction code),* introduced in 1965, is used in many personal computer programs and video games. It was a version of BASIC for the Altair personal computer that gave William Gates and Microsoft their start. Advanced programming methods use pictures and symbols, rather than words, to issue commands and are known as *graphical user interfaces (GUIs).* Although popularized by Apple Computer, GUIs originated with Xerox's Alto computer back in 1972–1974.

Web Software. As noted earlier, *hypercard* and *hypertext markup language (HTML)* were key software developments leading to the World Wide Web. Another important milestone was the popularization of **browser** software, such as Netscape, that converted the HTML commands into attractive interactive displays on personal computers. The future of Internet software lies in the further development of the *Java* programming language. Java makes it possible for all types of personal computers to download and run short files of computer code, called applets, that run locally on the user's computer.

Browsers are the computer programs that display information found on the Web.

Future Directions in Computer Media

Data Networks. Computer communication over the Internet has become so important that it may drive the future evolution of the computer. Computer network technology trends are treated in depth in Chapter 9, but suffice it to say that the

TECHNOLOGY *TRENDS*

Computers Read My Mind, Caressed My Flesh!

No, this is not a headline from a supermarket tabloid but rather a concise summary of some of the latest developments in computer interface design. Even before voice-controlled interfaces and virtual reality helmets are fully developed, computer designers are looking forward to faster and more realistic interfaces.

Controlling computers by thought alone is not so far-fetched as it may seem. Some of the electrical activity of the brain is detectable on the surface of the skull and can be picked up by an electroencephalograph, or EEG. An operator can produce distinctive EEG patterns by thinking about peculiar phrases, such as *tangerine pillow,* and get the computer to respond to the distinctive patterns.

In some respects this is nothing new. Back in the 1960s, psychologists were training subjects to focus their brain waves on certain frequencies and had fun running electric trains and other electrical devices under brain-wave control (the more intense the subject's brain waves, the faster the train went). Still, we are a long way from thinking the word *save* and having the computer save a file. Furthermore, some of the most interesting brain functions, such as learning and pleasure and pain sensations, take place deep in the brain and cannot readily be distinguished in the EEG. Serious research on brain implants—computer interfaces or even entire computers that would be surgically implanted inside the brain—is under way (Fixmer, 1998).

Computers that feel and touch? That is in the realm of possibility, too. Touch-sensitive screens have been around for years, but new interfaces are capable both of responding to the pressure of touch and of reproducing tactile sensations at the other end of the interface. Thus you could place the palm of your hand on the interface and give someone a massage at the other end of the network. Run your finger in a circle, and they get tickled. Today the body glove responds with digital outputs when we move it. Tomorrow, the body glove could move around us in response to digital input.

Fixmer, R (August 11, 1998). The melding of mind with machine may be the next phase of evolution. The *New York Times,* cyberTimes edition.

general goal is to put multimedia connections capable of millions of bits per second in every home and work cubicle. Personal computers with internal *digital subscriber line (DSL)* modems that operate on phone networks may eventually become the standard. But, as we shall see, cable television, satellite, and even broadcast television companies are in the race as well. Meanwhile, get ready to throw out your old style telephone modem.

The Network Computer. With all these high-speed networks coming our way, some observers are beginning to wonder just how powerful, and expensive, a personal computer really needs to be. The *network computer* is another option that would download its software on demand through high-speed network connections, perhaps using software written in the Java language. Little long-term memory would be required, and no floppy disc drive. Throw out that computer you own now, too? That is partly the premise behind the hot-selling new Apple Computer model introduced in 1998, the iMac. However, the cost of a full-blown personal computer—one that includes a floppy drive—is rapidly falling into the range of ubiquitous consumer electronics appliances such as VCRs, which counters the network computer trend.

Computers Everywhere. In the same vein, computers are in the works that will sit atop the television, allowing your TV set to interface with the Internet as well as the new digital television services. This is one piece of consumer electronics gear that has yet to acquire a catchy name or an obscure acronym. These computers are called simply *set-top boxes* (McCracken, 1997). But they will probably not be sitting on top of your current television. Rather, you will want to send that to the recycler to make way for your first *digital television* with the digital receiver built in.

Another less-is-more trend in personal computers is the *personal data assistant (PDA),* a pocket-sized information device that you can carry with you. The PDA accepts your handwritten scribbles, keeps you in constant contact by telephone, and even monitors the Internet for you. Now throw out your notebook, your pager, and your portable phone. Another minimalist vision is that computer chips will be found in a growing array of everyday objects, from microwave ovens, to couches ("No feet on the sofa, please!") to VCRs ("Please reset my clock"), complete with voice command recognition and speech-processing capabilities (Bell & Gray, 1997). The prices of the image sensors such as those found in digital cameras are also dropping, so your appliances may soon be able to see you as well as hear you. You might as well add all of your household appliances and personal possessions to the scrap heap then. And throw your wardrobe on top. "Wearable" computers are already a reality, presaging the integration of computer chips and mobile phones into articles of clothing.

The Multimedia Computer. Networking aside, perhaps the most significant trend in computer media is *multimedia,* which entails adding voice and video to personal computers (see Figure 8.2). Here is where the convergence of mass media, computers, and telecommunications systems literally hits home, now that most new personal computers come with these capabilities built in. Integrated multimedia

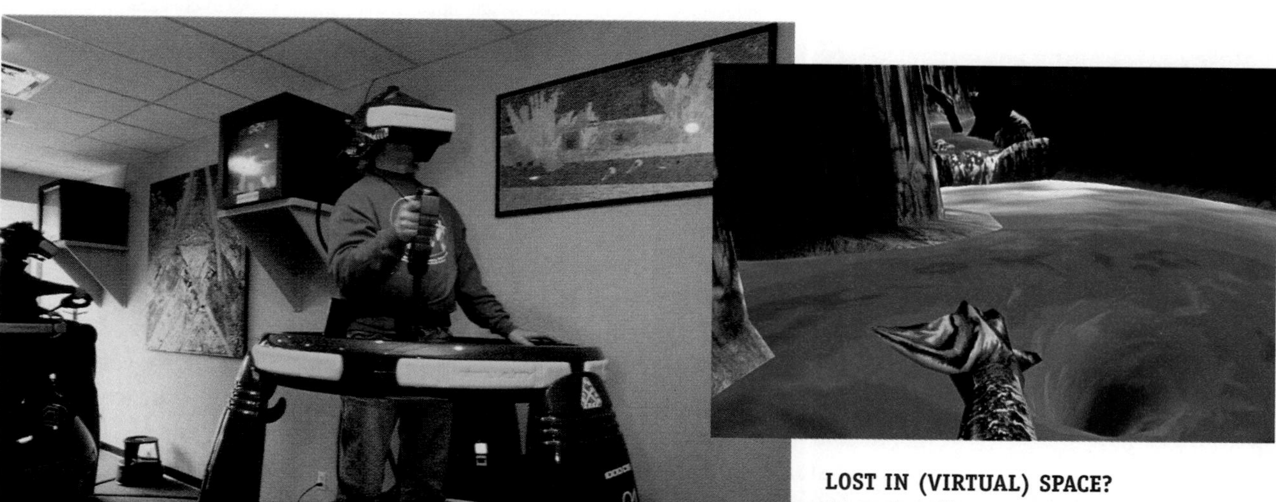

LOST IN (VIRTUAL) SPACE?
Virtual reality systems like this let the user enter a computer-generated world of his or her own.

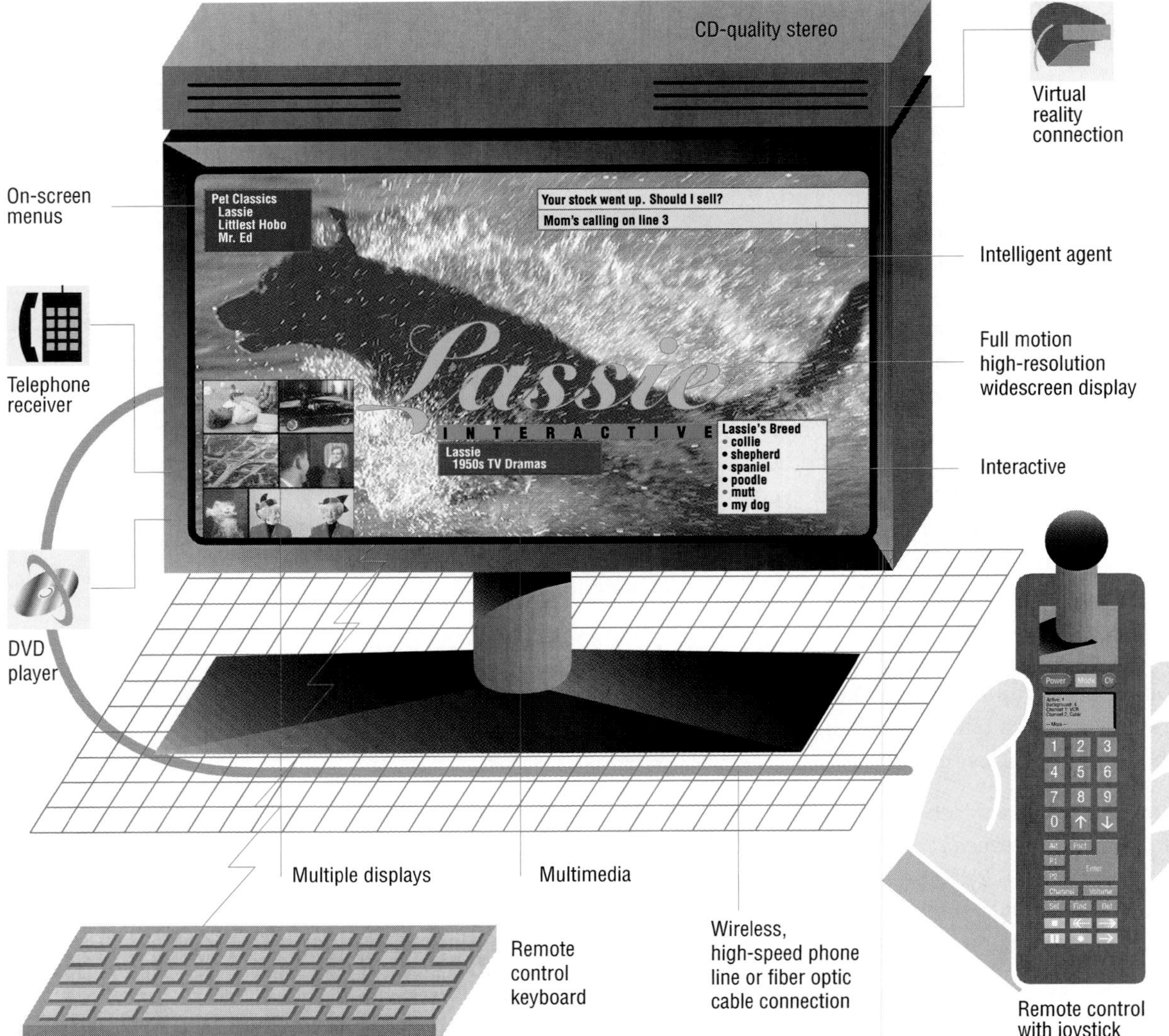

FIGURE 8.2
The multimedia computer may evolve into an all-purpose media player and information appliance.

> **Virtual reality** gives users the sense that they are "inside" a computer-generated reality.

computers are usable across a wide variety of applications that we still distinguish as "television," "telephone," "radio," and "computers." Thus you can retire your TV, radio, and telephone! **Virtual reality** systems take this one step further, immersing you in an environment of sound and vision that gives you the subjective impression of being in an alternative reality (Biocca, 1997). No more sunglasses or sun tan lotion, either!

In fact, *multimedia* developments could actually impel the personal computer in the *opposite* direction from the minimalist network computer model. Instead, personal computers might become more and more powerful, adding tens of billions of bytes of storage to handle audio and video recording, editing, and playback in the home. However, one thing we can count on is that additional computer processing power will be there if we need it. Personal computers capable of processing a billion bits of information per second are becoming a reality. According to *Moore's Law,* processing capacity in computers doubles about every 18 months (Moore, 1996).

Storing Data. With this increase in processing power, however, long-term storage technology becomes a problem again. CD-ROMs can store an entire record album, but not an entire movie. The answer is **DVDs,** or **digital versatile discs,** which pack 25 times as much information as a conventional CD. From the start, these systems were designed to handle audio and computer data and video data with equal ease; they are beginning to replace CD-ROM drives as the standard in personal computers. There go your VCR and your CD player, right in the trash.

A **DVD** (digital versatile disc) is a high-capacity digital storage medium that is the successor to CD-ROM.

Web Technology Trends

In the next chapter we will explore trends in data communications technology that affect the way we access the World Wide Web, but we should consider here some other developments that directly affect its content. With *multicast* technology, the same content can be shared among thousands of users without a dedicated feed to each and every one. Instead, content is sent to intermediate points across the Internet, where it is then "reflected," or duplicated, and sent on to end users. *Streaming* is what makes it possible to transmit audio and video over the Internet in something close to real time. Instead of sending huge media files all at once, the originating server sends a continuous stream of short files, each with a small segment of the audio or video. The same approach is used in *Internet telephony* that makes "free" calls across the Internet possible. *Push media* reverse the form of interaction usually found on the Internet in that the server automatically sends, or pushes, the content to the user instead of making the user request access to information over and over again. These sites are sometimes called *channels,* a term that emphasizes their similarity to TV broadcasts, complete with commercials and on-line "channel guides" to hundreds of such offerings. New versions of the basic *hypertext mark-up language (HTML)* that governs the display of images are spreading, including a versions with extended interactive (*DHTML,* "D" for dynamic) and user-customizable features (*XML,* "X" for extensible), another for displaying virtual reality (*VRML*), and a stripped-down version for displaying Web pages on the small screens of hand-held computers.

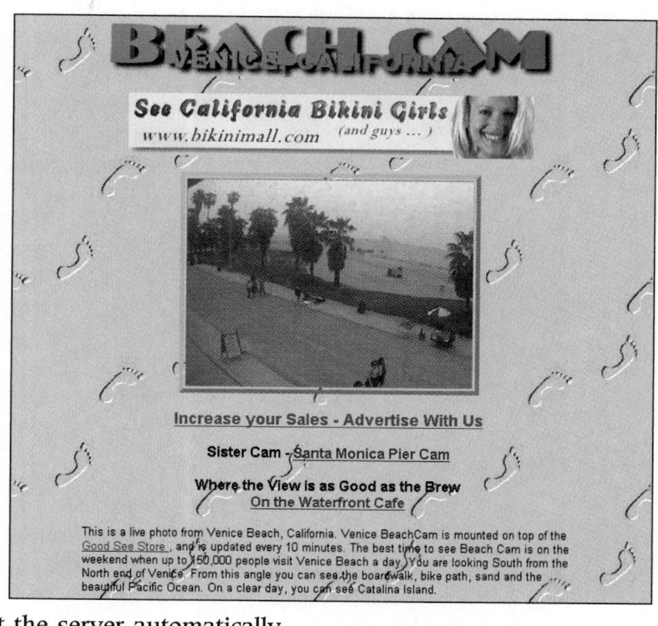

BEACH CAM
VENICE, CALIFORNIA
See California Bikini Girls
www.bikinimall.com (and guys ...)
Increase your Sales - Advertise With Us
Sister Cam - Santa Monica Pier Cam
Where the View is as Good as the Brew
On the Waterfront Cafe
This is a live photo from Venice Beach, California. Venice BeachCam is mounted on top of the Good See Store , and is updated every 10 minutes. The best time to see Beach Cam is on the weekend when up to 150,000 people visit Venice Beach a day. You are looking South from the North end of Venice. From this angle you can see the boardwalk, bike path, sand and the beautiful Pacific Ocean. On a clear day, you can see Catalina Island.

TV OF THE FUTURE? Streaming technology makes it possible to view videos over the World Wide Web.

COMPUTER MEDIA GENRES

Internet Functions, Internet Protocols

Protocols are sets of rules for computer communication that govern such functions as physical interconnection, addressing, routing, error checking, and data formatting.

TCP/IP (transmission control protocol/Internetworking protocol) is the basic protocol used by the Internet.

One way to look at the Internet is through the various patterns of communication, or **protocols,** that exist on it (December, 1996). In all, there are over 100 different protocols associated with the Internet, a family of protocols known collectively as **TCP/IP (transport control protocol/Internet protocol).** Many of these govern the

TECHNOLOGY **DEMYSTIFIED**

Make Your Own Web Page!

It's really pretty easy to be a Web page author. The first step—getting yourself connected to the Internet—is by far the most difficult. You need first a computer, then a modem, then an information service provider, then some browser software, then a lot of patience and some help from your friends. . . .

After that, it's all down hill! You can actually make a Web page with any word processing program if you are willing to learn a little hypertext markup language (HTML) and save your file as "plain text" within .html file extension.

```
‹HTML›
‹P›THIS IS MY WEB PAGE‹/P›
‹P›This is my lost dog Skippy.
‹A IMGSRC="skippy.gif"›Skippy‹/A›.‹/P›
‹P›‹A HREF="www.ibm.com">P.S. I dig
computers.‹/A›‹/P›
‹/HTML›
```

will produce the simple Web page you see here, with a link to the IBM web page at www.ibm.com. HTML tutorials are available on the Web. And you can easily copy the commands from other people's Web pages by simply clicking on View-Source on your Web browser's top line command bar and copying the instructions into your file.

But you don't have to do that. It is a lot easier to download, from the Web, free software that will automatically write those commands for you. Netscape Communicator (available at www.netscape.com) or Front Page Express (www.microsoft.com) will let you start composing the text for your Web page right away. Or look for the latest in free HTML authoring software by using "HTML tools" or "HTML authoring" in a keyword search on a Web search engine (e.g., HotBot or AltaVista). Once you have the software, just open a new blank file and start typing the tragic tale of your long-lost collie Skippy.

No Web page is complete unless it links to somewhere else on the Web. That's easy, too. Just press the link button (it usually has an icon that looks like a link in a chain—get it?) and enter the universal resource locator (URL) of the site you want to link to, say, the "Lassie Come Home" theme music (at http://www.collieworld.com/lassie.htm).

You might also want to show a picture of Skippy. That is a little more difficult. You have to get

inner workings of the network, such as rules for addressing, routing, error checking, and acknowledging messages between locations. The protocols that are readily apparent to Internet users fall into only a few major categories.

- **Electronic mail.** The Internet offers connections to e-mail users around the world and to private e-mail networks operated by large organizations. The Internet has thousands of electronic mailing lists (*listservs*) that make it possible to "broadcast" e-mail to special-interest groups. *Usenet* is an on-line news service where users post articles about topics of interest. The interests are quite varied indeed, ranging from technical computer information to bizarre sexual practices to news from exotic places around the globe.
- **File transfers.** Electronic documents and computer programs can be downloaded to your own computer with the *file transfer protocol (FTP)* program. Most documents that are published on the World Wide Web are placed there by using FTP to transfer files from the author's personal work station to a server that first stores and then distributes the information on the Web.

THIS IS MY WEB PAGE
This is my lost dog
Skippy
P.S. I dig computers

MY WEB PAGE.
Simple HTML codes format Web pages like this one on the World Wide Web.

pictures scanned into computer-readable format. Chances are your local library, college, or photocopying store can do that for you. Just be sure to get the file in .GIF or .JPG format (skippy.gif or skippy.jpg—and you *can't* just change the file extension, you actually have to reformat the file). Many of those "1-hour" photo stores also give you the option of getting your pictures on disc, although you may have to change formats. Once you have your picture of Skippy in GIF, then you click on the "insert picture" button in your HTML editing software and type in Skippy.gif where it asks for a graphics file name. Finally, rename your HTML file index.html.

Then, by hitting the "preview" button, you can see a preview of how your page will look on the web. At that point, however, your Web page is still stored locally on your computer; you still have to publish it on a Web server. How? Push the "publish" button, naturally. Just fill in ftp:// followed by the file location of the place on your Web server where you want the file to be located (you get that from your service provider). The publish feature uses the *file transfer protocol (FTP)* to transfer it there over the Internet. But so can anyone else in the world who has your URL. And in a few days or weeks, the search engines may find it, so you might hear from Skippy's new owners!

Actually, the publishing step is not so easy. If you have a commercial supplier, you might have to pay extra for the storage space on the server. You also have to make sure that your HTML file and your graphics files are in the same location on the server and that all the references to links and external files are exactly as they should be. Sometimes even minor variations in case (capital or small letters), spacing, or in those annoying little /\|~_-^& characters can be fatal.

- **Chat.** Internet users can engage in on-line dialog with other users from all over the world by typing messages back and forth inside private "rooms" that are sponsored at various locations on the net. *Internet relay chat (IRC)* is the commonly used protocol.
- **Locators.** *Domain name service (DNS)* translates lettered web addresses that people use (such as www.msu.edu) into the numerical addresses that the Internet uses (such as 35.9.7.102). Other protocols let the user locate specific users and specific files on the Internet.
- **Remote access.** *Telnet* is a means of logging into computers from remote locations for the purpose of accessing files and programs as though they were located on one's own computer. *PPP (point-to-point protocol)* and *SLIP (serial line interface protocol)* are two means of accessing local nodes on the Internet through regular phone lines.
- **Document display.** The **hypertext transfer protocol (http)** is what makes it possible to link from one location to another on the World Wide Web. The use

http (Hypertext transfer protocol) is the Internet protocol used to transfer files over the Web.

of http:// at the beginning of an address on the web identifies what follows as a location on the Web. The *hypertext mark-up language (HTML)* governs the display of Web pages on the screen. *Gopher* was an early form of document display for purely text-based documents.

What's on the Web?

URLs (uniform resource locators) are the addresses of pages of content on the Web.

The World Wide Web's content can be characterized according to the various domains that are represented in its **uniform resource locators (URLs)**. These are the jumbles of letters, "slashes," and "dots" that indicate the network addresses of content stored on web servers. An example is www-DOT-telecommunication-DOT-msu-DOT-edu-SLASH-faculty-SLASH-larose (www.telecommunication.msu.edu /faculty/larose), which will get you to the home page of one of your authors, located on a server maintained by the Telecommunication Department at Michigan State University (MSU).

Each URL has a code that indicates the type of Web page, or the "domain" to which it belongs. The ones that users in the United States are most likely to encounter are as follows:

.EDUCATION
Web sites produced by educational institutions are among the most popular on the Web.

.edu is reserved for educational users, including colleges and universities. These pages contain electronic copies of many of the paper documents that institutions of higher education publish, from sports schedules to course catalogs. Such pages provide access to the institution's library card catalogs, to interactive student services such as on-line registrations, and even to Web-based "virtual" courses.

.gov is for government agencies. At these sites you are likely to find "welcome to our agency" organizational mission statements and pictures of the men and women who run things, as well as electronic versions of the documents and brochures that the organization publishes. Some of these sites provide government services, such as allowing users to fill out applications and submit tax returns.

.org is a lot like the .gov category when it comes to content, but it is reserved for nongovernment, not-for-profit organizations, such as the Public Broadcasting Service (PBS).

.mil is set aside for military organizations, a reminder that the Internet originally evolved from a nuclear weapons research project.

.net is for *Internet service providers (ISPs)* such as UUNET. Unless the ISP is also a content provider, these sites usually just contain descriptions of network availability, rates, and special services, such as e-mail. People and organizations that rent space for their Web pages from ISPs also have .net in their addresses.

.com, short for "commercial," also has its share of "welcome to Blivet Corp." pages that list the corporate divisions and their products. But this is also the domain in which most of the "sizzle" is found. It is home to Web versions of popular print and electronic media, computer games, commercial information services, and a growing array of *electronic commerce* sites that allow Web surfers to purchase products and services through their computers. Internet service providers that double as content providers are also likely to have a .com name, as in aol.com.

These six domains are not the only ones you will find if you surf the net. Outside of the United States, domains are assigned according to country. For example, .it is for Italy, and .fr is for France. Countries with catchy domain names are gaining thousands of "virtual citizens." Tonga's .to domain lends itself to memorable constructions such as welcome.to and sell.to. Another South Pacific Island, Niue, is popular in France, where its .nu domain sounds like the French word for "nude," a domain in which French Internet users like to post pictures of themselves *au naturel* (Murphy & Hofacker, 1997). To relieve a worldwide shortage of domain names, seven new ones are coming: .firm, .store, .web, .arts, .rec, .info, and .nom (for personal web pages).

It may be premature to speak of "genres" for such a rapidly evolving medium, but some common forms have started to appear:

Entertainment sites are one genre, or perhaps we should say "infotainment," since they feature varying mixtures of information and diversion. *Multimedia* and *interactivity* are two watchwords for these sites. Even such hallowed mass media as the *New York Times* go interactive and multimedia when they reach the Web. They add new sections for the Internet crowd (such as a technology section, with articles about computer media), links to past articles, on-line forums, and multimedia extensions, including audio and video files and computer simulations. And the on-line version of the *Times* even has the cartoons and TV listings disdained by the staid printed version. The paper might well change its slogan from "All the news that's fit to print" to "All the news that fits, we print, and the rest goes on the Web." Time Warner, The Weather Channel, Disney, and publishing giant Ziff-Davis run the most popular sites in this category (MediaMetrix, 1997).

Search engines such as Yahoo and Excite! are a new media form, although obvious print precursors may be found in library card catalogs and *The Reader's Guide to Periodical Literature.* These are index sites that allow users to type in keywords to find listings of pages with related content.

Software sources include the home pages of Microsoft and Netscape, and CNET's download.com, from which the latest versions of Internet browser software can be downloaded.

Internet service providers include the home pages for full-blown on-line services such as AOL as well as companies that simply provide the connections, such as AT&T and UUNET. Where content is offered, it is usually organized around categories familiar from the newsstand, such as news, entertainment, travel, computing, health, and personal finance.

Interpersonal communication sites include e-mail services, chat rooms (such as ICQ at www.ICQ.com) and directory pages such as Switchboard and Four One One. Many sites on the World Wide Web now offer their own e-mail services, so it is no longer necessary to leave the Web to send e-mail.

Portals are a new genre that combines search engine, interpersonal communication, and information functions in an effort to become an all-purpose, customizable "launch pad" that users will visit first whenever they go on the Web. Portals greet you by name and keep track of your favorite types of content.

Electronic commerce refers to the capability of completing on-line purchases and financial transactions on the Web.

Electronic commerce sites are another new genre. They let you shop for products and complete the purchase of consumer goods and services on the Web. Amazon.com, the on-line bookstore, is perhaps the best-known example. Travel, music, and computer software and hardware are other popular categories.

Computer Software Genres

Computer software can be divided into six basic categories, with most titles now distributed on CD-ROM (NPD, 1997) or downloaded from the Internet.

Business productivity software covers the titles that are most often found on personal computers in the work environment. These include basic computer operating systems from Microsoft and Apple, Internet browser software, and so-called "productivity suites" that combine word processing, spreadsheet, graphics, and other business applications in a single package—Microsoft Office, for example.

Personal productivity software simplifies routines in our daily lives at home. Personal finance and tax titles such as *Quicken* are big sellers, and so are programs that help users compose personalized greeting cards.

Educational software is mainly targeted to children. The top sellers are "edutainment" titles that use entertaining game formats to introduce serious educational lessons in math, literature, and science.

Utilities include programs that scan for viruses on personal computers and help optimize computer performance.

Reference titles include computerized encyclopedias, atlases, and Bible studies.

Entertainment software has several subgenres. There are adventure myth games such as *Riven* and *Myst,* action–adventure games such as *Quake* and *Tomb Raider,* simulator games that give the user the look and feel of the airplane cockpit or the race driver's seat, and computerized versions of traditional board games such as *Monopoly.*

USING COMPUTER MEDIA

THE NEW MASS MEDIUM. Computers are becoming a common fixture in U.S. households.

The personal computer was adopted initially in better-educated, upper-income homes (Dutton, Rogers, & Jun, 1987) but its use has spread to about 43 percent of U.S. households (Pew Research Center, 1999). Typical home computer installations now include printers, modems, CD-ROMs, sound cards, and speakers (MediaMetrix, June, 1997).

However, computer ownership is by no means uniformly distributed. Only one-fifth of African American homes have personal computers, half the proportion of whites. Three-fourths of households earning $75,000 a year or more have computers—five times the rate of those earning under $15,000. And, the gaps are widening over time (NTIA, 1998). The gap is particularly worrisome for school children. Almost three-quarters of white students have home computers, compared to less than one-third of African American students. The disparity does not exist because African American families don't want computers; nearly twice as many African American families want one, in fact, compared to white families. Low income may be the problem: The differences between races disappear after adjusting for household income, except among households earning less than $10,000. Computer ownership is generally related to income for both whites and African Americans (Novak & Hoffman, 1998).

Over two-fifths of U.S. adults use the Internet at home, work, or school, and over 10 percent use it every day. The demographic differences between users and nonusers are disappearing as the Web goes mainstream. Nearly as many females as males now use the Web, eliminating the "gender gap" in Internet access. Web users are still younger than nonusers and also better educated—senior citizens and people with a high school education or less are among the "have-nots" (Pew Research Center, 1999). And the racial and income-related disparities in computer ownership are reflected on the Internet. Whites are three times more likely to subscribe to on-line services as African Americans and households with incomes of $75,000 a year or more are ten times as likely to subscribe as those living in poverty (NTIA, 1998).

How do people use the Internet? Electronic mail is the most prevalent activity on the Internet. The Web is also becoming a popular source for entertainment and travel information. An increasing number of users rely on the Web for the news—about two-thirds of Internet users turn to the Web for news updates on a weekly basis (Pew Research Center, 1999). Ratings for Web sites have appeared, and the most popular are those run by search engines (e.g., Yahoo!), software

MEDIA IMPACT

Who Are the "Have-Nots"?

New surveys about computer use are always coming out. Update the statistics in this chapter for yourself by searching for the latest research. Many surveys classify responses by characteristics such as ethnicity and income. List the disadvantaged groups—those who have the lowest usage. How do you explain these differences? Any full Web search engine will do, but if you have the InfoTrac College Edition, use *computer AND (usage OR user) AND survey* for a basic search on computer usage. Alternatively, use *(computer OR Internet OR Web) AND (usage OR user) AND survey* to cover all the bases, but you may get more "hits" than you can use! Add *NOT (corporate or business)* to filter out studies that deal only with business users. And limit the search to the last year if you want to restrict it still more—an especially good idea if you are using a general-purpose search engine. InfoTrac College Edition automatically limits your search to 2 years.

WWW

1. Who are the leading makers of computer hardware and software?
2. What is the difference between a content provider and an Internet service provider?
3. List the major Internet protocols and the major types of content on the Web.
4. Define the computer *have-nots*. Who are they?

companies (e.g., Netscape), internet service providers (AOL), and conventional media (Disney), which have invaded the Web (NetRatings, 1999). Surfers visit an average of over 300 different Web pages a week and spend over five hours a week on them (NetRatings, 1999).

Aside from cruising the Web, what else are home users doing with computer media? One answer seems to be "nothing." Home computers are idle for over half of the time they spend switched on. Aside from that, the most important activities seem to be "fussing with the computer": organizing files, changing screensaver patterns, and modifying settings in the operating system. Then come word processing, computer games, and computer communications, including the use of the Internet (Rigdon, 1996).

STRUCTURE OF THE COMPUTER MEDIA INDUSTRY

The computer media industry has several major sectors. Hardware manufacturers make the computers, and software publishers make the programs that run on the machines. Content providers develop content and data bases that are distributed over computer networks and in computer software. Internet service providers (ISPs), which are the companies that sell access to the Internet, are part of the communications infrastructure discussed in Chapter 9. Telephone, cable, and satellite companies are also part of that infrastructure.

Computer Hardware Industry

The hardware business breaks down into four general areas: the computers (further subdivided into *supercomputers, mainframes, minicomputers, workstations,* and *personal computers*), computer *storage devices* (such as disk drives), and the *peripherals* (such as printers and modems) that go with the computers. Thousands of firms are also engaged in the manufacture of *components* and materials that go into these products, ranging from power supplies to computer cabinets to the glue used to hold the components together. In the home computer market, Compaq, Dell, and Gateway are the leading manufacturers. The two companies that started the personal computer trend, Apple and IBM, are now bit players in the market for home computers, although IBM still dominates the mainframe computer field and produces popular lines of laptops, while Apple made a comeback with its new line of iMac computers. Sun Microsystems and Silicon Graphics are the leaders in producing the powerful *workstations* that engineers, graphic designers, and media special effects specialists rely on to deliver mainframe computing speed on their desktops. In 1998, Compaq bought Digital Equipment Corporation, long the leader of the minicomputer industry, setting the stage for a new wave of consolidation in the computer hardware industry—and also further blurring the once-clear distinctions between personal computers, workstations, and minicomputers.

Computer Software Industry

The software industry has three major segments: companies that write customized computer programs for their clients, those that sell *prepackaged software,* and those that design computer integrated systems, such as the ones used to run large, automated factories. The manufacturers of prepackaged software are the ones that provide popular application programs (word processing, electronic spreadsheets, computer games) for personal computers. Currently, this segment alone is several times the size of another well-known "software" industry, motion pictures. Microsoft dominates the personal computer end of the software industry at large, and is also the leader in many application categories, including word processing, spreadsheet, and presentation software.

Software manufacturers resemble book publishers in that many of their sales to individual users are made through retail outlets that offer a wide selection of software titles from many different publishers. Much of the software that winds up in the hands of private consumers is sold bundled together with computer hardware at the time of the initial purchase. However, sales to institutional buyers, such as large corporations, account for the lion's share of software sales. Increasingly, software companies sell their software in the form of *site licenses* that allow a specified number of computer network users to access the software simultaneously, rather than buying separate copies for each member of the organization.

A great deal of computer software is also distributed directly to the consumer as *freeware* or *shareware* over the Internet. This is software, such as the UNUX operating system, for which the authors do not claim copyright protection or whose developers lack a sophisticated distribution network and who hope that users will pay voluntarily. And then there are Internet browsers and the many special-purpose Internet "helper" programs called *plug-ins.* These are also distributed free, but they are still part of a money-making scheme. Their creators profit from the sale of other programs that are used to make new content and the specialized software that runs the information servers on the Internet.

Content Providers

Content providers are the people and organizations that create the content we see on our computer screens. Some content providers are outgrowths of software publishers. For example, Microsoft has its own on-line magazine, called *Slate.* Makers of computer games combine the roles of software publisher and content provider. Other content providers are familiar mass media organizations, including most of the leading newspapers (e.g., *New York Times),* magazines (e.g., *Time*), and television networks (e.g., ESPN). Some **internet service providers (ISPs),** such as America Online (AOL), double as content providers by gathering and packaging—and in some cases creating—information for their subscribers. But we also need to include the many sources, ranging from the National Weather Service to the author of the local elementary school lunch menu, who create the raw information that others shape into information services. In a sense, anyone who has ever posted her or his own "home page" on the World Wide Web is a content provider.

Internet service providers (ISPs) are the companies that provide connections to the Internet.

Computer media have given birth to a new breed of media producer, the multimedia design house. These firms are cropping up in clusters around the country; the SOMA (South of Market Street) District of San Francisco and Silicon Alley in New York City are two prominent ones. These are the companies that provide the "sizzle" for Web sites, the ones that come up with the visually stunning graphics and interactive features that spark the "coolest" pages on the World Wide Web.

But the less glamorous *information services* industry easily dwarfs all other content providers. This industry includes companies that create data bases that are distributed over the Internet or on CD-ROM, as well as companies that process electronic mail and financial transactions for large corporations. The leading such companies are IBM, Dun and Bradstreet, and Electronic Data Systems (Trade Point, 1995).

Who Runs the Internet?

To understand the organization of the Internet, it is important to consider its history. The Internet started as a U.S. Defense Department network, later expanded into an academic research network under the guidance of the National Science Foundation, was subsequently privatized, and is now evolving into a truly international network. Each of these stages has left its own administrative residue.

One of the most important organizational issues is the assignment of addresses and names. In 1998, an international not-for-profit organization, the Internet Corporation for Assigned Names and Numbers (ICANN) was entrusted with this task. ICANN oversees several competing private companies that replaced a single firm, Network Solutions, Inc. that previously had the job. Now ICANN decides who gets the rights to domain names and charges an annual fee for the privilege.

ISOC (the Internet Society) is a nongovernmental international membership society that promotes the orderly use and development of the Internet. It is modeled after the professional associations that college professors belong to—a throwback to the period when the Internet was primarily a research network run by major universities. The Internet Architecture Board (IAB) is the working committee within the Internet Society that makes important policy decisions about operations and future developments. Its members are, for the most part, employees of large corporations (such as IBM, AT&T, and Microsoft) that have important financial stakes in the development of the Internet. Technical matters are overseen by the Internet Engineering Task Force (IETF) through its various working-group committees (Network Solutions, 1998).

POLICY, SOCIAL, AND ETHICAL ISSUES

Ownership and Control

What if the owners of the information superhighway could take a page out of the book of John D. Rockefeller and other Industrial Age "robber barons" by using the network as a tool to extend monopoly control over other industries? Software giant Microsoft Corporation stands accused of just that. It has replaced IBM as the prime target of *antitrust* regulators. In 1998, the U.S. Justice Department filed an antitrust suit to stop Microsoft from abusing its market power by bundling its Internet browser software with its Windows operating system (which controls 90 percent of the market), a practice that was seen to be driving competing browser makers (Netscape) out of business, a form of **horizontal integration.**

Horizontal integration is concentrating ownership by acquiring companies all in the same business.

Microsoft chairman Bill Gates might respond that the Information Age is like no other, that the fast pace of technological change makes monopolies impossible—just look at the rise and fall, and the return of Apple and IBM, for example. Meanwhile, Gates is investing in an astounding array of ventures in other areas of the "convergence business," including cable television, broadcasting, photo archives, and high-speed satellite data networks, activities that raise new fears of excessive **vertical integration.** But now that AOL has acquired Netscape, Chairman Gates might also argue that AOL Chairman Steve Case is really the "new Rockefeller," not he.

Vertical integration is concentrating ownership by acquiring companies that are in related businesses.

Internet Governance

As the Internet continues its evolution from a U.S. Department of Defense research project to a global communications medium, some thorny social issues are cropping up, which in turn call into question the Internet's organizational structure. Although the Internet can be characterized as a collaborative, cooperative effort on the part of computer professionals around the world, the historical role of the U.S. government and the growing role of U.S. corporate giants cause concern. Critics fear the *corporatization* of the Internet—the increasing influence of commercial interests on

MEDIA IMPACT

Join in the Debate

Is there anything about the Internet that has you in a lather? Don't just sit there, join in! One nice thing about the Internet is that nobody can tell you are "just a student." As long as your arguments are sound (and sometimes, just passion will do), you can get a hearing and maybe find some points that will add to your discussion in class.

First, get up to date on the issues, though, so you won't seem uniformed when you chime in. The basic search engine strategy here is simple: *(Internet OR Web) AND {issue}*. You could plug in any of the topic headings from the "Policy, Social, and Ethical Issues" section as the {issue}—for example, use *(Internet OR Web) AND Censorship*. This will turn up the names of specific pieces of legislation and advocacy groups to which you can then redirect your search.

WWW

Next, find yourself a forum. DejaNews is a search engine just for newsgroups, at www.dejanews.com; its "interest finder" will suggest discussion groups to you on the basis of your keywords. Remember that you should monitor a newsgroup for a while before you join in and don't barge into groups that obviously do not share your point of view. You may find out the hard way how bad a spam attack, or abusive e-mail (called "flaming") and other mean Internet tricks, can really be.

its governance and growth—will undermine the Internet's democratic nature and make it just another means of perpetuating the economic *status quo* (McChesney, 1996). Thus some advocate putting the key administrative functions in the hands of not-for-profit organizations with international oversight, such as ICANN (see page 270).

Earlier in this chapter we joked about throwing out your computer, radio, TV, CD player, VCR, telephone, living room furniture—and even your sunglasses—to make way for the information superhighway. But the huge transfer of wealth from consumers to multinational corporations that this represents is perhaps no laughing matter. The companies that set the technical standards for this transition stand to profit immensely and could form powerful transnational monopolies that operate against the best interests of consumers around the world.

Government control is the conventional answer to the threat of corporate abuse, but such supervision is inherently difficult to impose on a medium that freely crosses international boundaries. National governments have trouble resisting the temptation to control content, either in the name of public morality or political orthodoxy (see Chapter 15). Governments also like to tax what they control, which could retard the growth of the Internet, especially as it branches out into *electronic commerce.* Thus far, the U.S. government and many other national governments around the world are resisting the urge to tax the Web and are keeping their subsidiary jurisdictions—states, counties, and towns—in line.

On the other hand, the job of running the Internet is becoming too big to entrust to volunteer labor, as is now the case. On one fateful day, the volunteers managing the Internet accidentally erased most of the addresses on the network so that most Web pages were temporarily inaccessible (Quick, 1997). A group of self-appointed volunteers monitors "spammers" who invade the various Usenet newsgroups, and the anti-spammers cancel out what they regard as "junk mail" (Richtel, 1998). In another incident, the operator of the Internet's most important address server redirected the Internet to another computer, which some saw as an attempt to "hijack" the Internet (Quick, 1998). Moreover, the Internet's current caretakers tend to be more technical than political in their orientation. This situation is certain eventually to invite the intervention of national or international political institutions.

Censorship

Perhaps the thorniest social issue is content regulation. Just about anyone can put just about anything on the Internet,—and they often do. Discussions of all imaginable varieties of sexual experience—many complete with pictures—are available. Hate someone? Chances are, your hate group has a forum somewhere on the Net.

The Internet poses some unique problems for anyone who might like to clean up these stains on the information superhighway. The number of "sources" is in the tens of millions, and no one is really in charge of network content. The users of the network are also the "publishers," but they do not have to subscribe to any code of professional journalistic ethics. And how can we regulate content on an international network that encompasses societies with widely varying notions of what is obscene or politically correct?

In the United States, the Communications Decency Act portion of the Telecommunications Act of 1996 sought to address the issue by banning indecent content. Germany imposed a sweeping ban on indecent content, prohibiting all mention of words such as *breast* and *buttocks.* China and Singapore go further, screening their Internet users from content deemed politically—not just morally—"indecent" (see Chapter 15).

The Communications Decency Act was quickly struck down by the courts as being an impermissibly vague abridgement of First Amendment freedoms on the Internet. Congress made a second try with the Child On-Line Protection Act in 1998. The new law narrowed the prohibitions to cover commercial sites only, targeted only content harmful to children, and required age verification on adult sites in hopes of passing muster with the First Amendment.

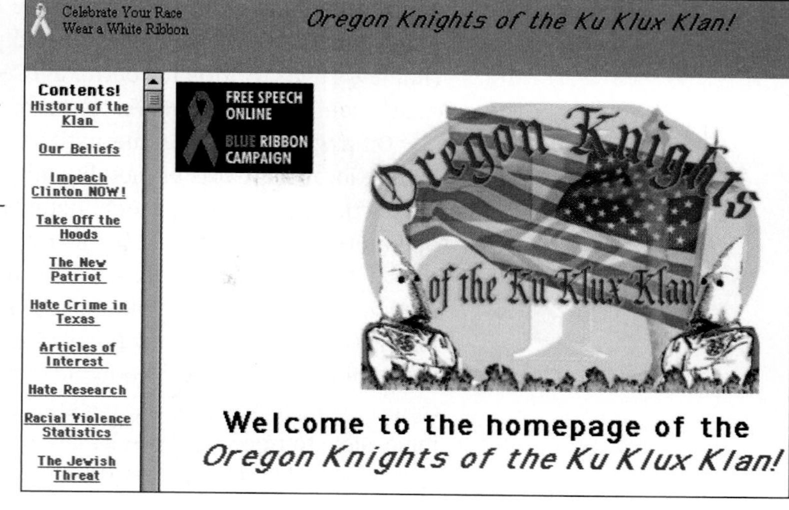

CYBERHATE.
The World Wide Web is in danger of becoming a recruiting ground for extremist hate groups such as the Ku Klux Klan.

Some favor computer programs that filter out files with naughty words or suggestive pictures. Internet Service Providers such as America Online sometimes step in to remove pages or shut down discussions that they find inconsistent with their notions of a "family" information service. But some smut always trickles through, and these efforts sometimes yield unintended results. For example, Germany's ban on the word *breast* blotted out information on breast cancer as well as *Playboy* pictorials.

The Internet community responded with a plan to enact voluntary content ratings, called the *Platform for Internet Content Selection (PICS),* which will be embedded in each file on the World Wide Web. Parents and schools would then have a relatively powerful method of screening out offensive material. But free speech advocates argue that even this would have an undue chilling effect on the free exchange of ideas on the Internet (Harmon, 1997).

If electronic censorship fails, society cannot rely on parents; only about a third of them regularly supervise their children's computer use. Outside the home, would-be censors have their hands tied by civil liberties challenges that limit the use of **filtering software** (software that automatically blocks access to adult sites) to screen out unwanted smut in libraries and schools (Tech Law Journal, 1998).

Filtering software automatically prevents Web users from visiting pornographic Web sites.

Antisocial Behavior

Another problem is the growing number of cases in which the virtual life on the Web spills over into real life, sometimes with alarming consequences. This is the old issue of mass media effects, but with a dangerous new facet. Armed with an interactive medium that integrates mass communication and personal communication, the twisted minds behind the content have the ability to reach out directly to the impressionable—or be contacted by them. Indeed, there are horror stories of child molesters contacting their prey through Internet chat rooms, marriages ruined by on-line love affairs, even murderous Internet fantasies enacted in real life. One youth was found guilty of a hate crime for sending harassing racist e-mail to Asian Americans whose names he had plucked off Internet discussion groups (Rainey, 1998). Efforts to control antisocial behavior by regulating content create a classic confrontation between free expression and public morality.

On a wider scale, the international scope of the Internet lends itself to undermining local standards of morality and legality. Law enforcement agencies have no jurisdiction across international boundaries. On-line gambling is a prime example. Operators set up Internet casinos and "bookie joints" in Third World countries or Native American reservations where such activities are legal, allowing gamblers all over the world to have a "piece of the action" and avoid paying taxes on their winnings. Currently, the money travels back and forth in wire transfers and credit card transactions, which leave no money trail for law enforcement to follow. And electronic commerce could make such illicit activities easier to engage in and almost impossible to trace. Conversely, laws enacted to shut down on-line gambling could also have a chilling effect on the growth of legitimate forms of electronic commerce (Pulley, 1998).

Encryption

Encryption means the writing of a message in a secret code.

Another barrier to policing the Internet is encryption. Illegal transactions and illicit content can be masked by the use of secret codes. **Encryption** technology is cheap, easily available, and powerful enough to frustrate all but the most ingenious code crackers in the law enforcement community.

Law enforcement officials would like you to "file" a copy of your encryption code with a federal agency so that officials would be able to decode your messages—only under court order, of course—to check for criminal or national security violations. Internet users and civil liberties groups are up in arms over the proposal, claiming that it is an unreasonable invasion of privacy by the government and makes all users vulnerable in the quite likely event that someone eventually "cracks" the secret code key. Others believe that this system will be unnecessarily costly and, ultimately, will be ineffective as sophisticated crooks apply their own secret codes to messages (Davis, 1994).

User Privacy

Another threat to privacy lies in the relative ease with which interchanges on the Internet—ranging from credit card transactions to simple visits to Web pages—can be recorded, traced back to their origin, and collated with other data. Existing means of matching consumers to computer data are already a serious privacy concern. The expanded use of the Internet could make this process ruthlessly efficient and extend the snooping to new lows, such as spying on our media habits and personal affiliations.

The unique ability of the Internet to blur the boundaries between mass communication and interpersonal communication has caused a serious privacy problem, *spamming.* Spamming occurs when direct marketers or outright con artists do mass e-mailings to the unwary user, often with names and addresses garnered from chat rooms or newsgroups operating in open cyberspace.

MEDIA ETHICS

Ethical Internet Surfing

Sometimes it may seem that the Internet has no rules, but that is not true. Most Internet providers have a code of ethics on their home page under "Acceptable Uses" or "User Policy." These are guidelines, not laws, but the penalty for disobeying them can be the heavy Internet users' equivalent of "death": termination of your account.

No harassment. Don't use the Internet to harass other users such as by sending them abusive e-mail, spam (unsolicited mass e-mail distribution), or "mail bombs" of repetitive, unwanted messages. "Trolling"—making provocative statements in newsgroups to get people to visit your Web site, for example—is also to be avoided. If your account is at a university, school authorities will take an especially dim view of sexual or racial harassment, and it may have legal or disciplinary consequences far beyond cancellation of your e-mail privileges.

No misrepresentation. Middle-aged men posing as teenagers in hopes of luring young sex partners obviously violate this guideline. But it also precludes using someone else's name to sign up for services or listservs. Of course, if you are in a multiuser game or another Internet environment where everyone has a false identity and everyone knows and agrees on the rules, this "misrepresentation" is acceptable.

No hacking. That means no using the Internet to gain unauthorized access to other people's accounts or to computers run by organizations. Also, no stealing passwords or credit card numbers. And no sabotaging other people's computers or Web pages or the Internet itself.

No lawbreaking. If you use the Internet to commit an act that would be illegal in the "real world," you also violate an important principle of proper Internet behavior—and you may make yourself liable to prosecution under the laws that cover the real-world behavior. Thus, to make explicit what should go without saying, no using the Internet to deal drugs, distribute child pornography, defraud others, violate copyright protection, or publish lies (libel) about others.

Your own provider may have additional guidelines. Universities, for example, generally have a policy that prohibits the commercial use of the Internet. Using your Web page to promote your rock band might get you into trouble, and using it to sell pirate recordings of an Aerosmith concert almost certainly will. Providers also vary in how they check for violations. Some only respond to complaints, whereas others take it upon themselves to seek out abusers by systematically sifting through e-mail and Web page text.

Internet users who use the Web to gripe about products or people may also find themselves the targets of lawsuits when their information service providers expose their identities (Johnston, 1995). Widely available Internet tools can be used to track down everything you say in Internet newsgroups. In one case, a Navy enlisted man identified himself as "gay" in an America Online profile, only to have this information turned over to the government for disciplinary purposes by AOL (Quick, 1998b).

Cookies are another privacy threat. These are tiny files that some Web sites deposit inside our computers. Usually, their function is benign: recording information about personal preferences or previous transactions that the site can use to verify our identity or customize its content to our needs. However, the cookies can also reveal personal information about us and can even be used to search out sensitive information buried elsewhere on our computer hard drives. Now cookies are being used to match information that we leave at different Web sites—including our demographic characteristics, the types of information we seek, the products we buy, and the types of diversions we enjoy—for the purpose of popping up ads that are tailored just to us (Hansell, 1998).

The *Electronic Communications Privacy Act* (1987) supposedly keeps government agencies from snooping without a court order, but that didn't protect the gay sailor. Electronic privacy invasions by parties other than government agencies are unrestricted, however, apart from the existing protections regarding the use of consumer credit information (see Chapter 14). A survey of commercial Web sites conducted by the Federal Trade Commission (FTC, 1998) found that only about 1 in 50 such sites had a comprehensive privacy protection policy. Less than a tenth of the children's sites that were surveyed notified parents when collecting information from children, an abuse that was promptly remedied with new legislation. Efforts to legislate electronic privacy face the hurdle of opposition from powerful commercial interests, although there is a movement to establish voluntary guidelines that would require Web sites to inform visitors of their privacy rights (Quick, 1998b). Crusaders against spam have to tread especially lightly around the rights of the spammers to free speech, and they may also have to settle for a voluntary compliance approach.

A **patent** is a written document that secures to an inventor for 17 years the exclusive right to make, use, or sell an invention.

A **copyright** is a legal privilege to use, sell, or license intellectual property.

Intellectual Property

Patents give inventors the exclusive rights to their inventions for 17 years, during which time they can demand royalties from others who wish to use them. The patent claim for the invention of the computer, made by Eckert and Mauchly for the ENIAC, was denied. The inventors waited too long to file, especially after allowing a *public use* by the government on the H-bomb project.

Copyrights also protect creators' rights, but for works of art and literature rather than inventions. From the software perspective, patents are superior to a mere copyright in that they protect against *reverse engineering*—copying an invention that performs the same basic functions as the inventor's but uses different underlying computer instructions. Copyright offers protection only against duplication of the underlying computer instructions and of the screen display and command sequences—the general "look and feel" of software, such as a spreadsheet program.

SHUT DOWN. Music copyright holders represented by the National Music Publisher Association (NMPA) are closing down Web sites such as this one that distribute lyrics to popular songs without paying royalties to their authors.

lyrics.ch
the international lyrics server
Find the lyrics to 114,500 songs!
Our servers have been confiscated by the police. The NMPA has brought suit against us. After some meetings with them we see good chances to go back online in April. See the Press coverage.
Meanwhile, see our Links for other lyrics pages.
Chat with Pascal and Roger (the founders of ILS) on April 8th, 1999, 8:30pm CET on Sonicnet Switzerland (That's 2:30pm New York Time)
Enter your e-mail address to get a notice as soon as we are online again.

Until 1990, computer software was considered unpatentable on the grounds that computers merely executed mathematical formulas that were the product of mental processes, rather than patentable devices. But that changed dramatically in the early 1990s.

Intellectual property rights are now on a collision course with the freewheeling culture of the Internet. Although copyright is usually discussed in terms of protecting the rights of starving artists and authors, it is also supposed to encourage the creation of new works that build on that which is already published. Now many

MEDIA IMPACT

Finding Safe Harbor in Copyright Bay

About the only thing easier than making your own Web page is violating the Copyright Act while you are creating it. It is sooooo easy to copy text, graphics, and even interactive programs from other Web pages and make them your own. But it is illegal, and many copyright owners really do care. Try scanning a picture of Mickey Mouse into your Web site, and you may well get an intimidating letter from a lawyer at Disney Corporation ordering you to cease and desist. In fact, just about *anything* you copy off another site or out of a print publication is probably a violation unless you obtain permission from the author. Sometimes the site explicitly says that you are free to use the images there as long as you credit the source, but you have to be sure that the site you copy from owns the rights to the work in the first place. Animations, video files, and sound recordings are also generally off limits.

As a student, you may feel that this inhibits your creativity and keeps you from expressing yourself on the Web. Fortunately, there is a set of relaxed, relatively clear-cut guidelines (they are only guidelines, not laws) for student projects. These Fair Use Guidelines for Educational Multimedia allow students to borrow the following items without too much danger of getting into copyright trouble:

10 percent or 1000 words, whichever is less, of printed text

10 percent or 3 minutes, whichever is less, of moving pictures

10 percent or 30 seconds, whichever is less, of sound recordings or lyrics

No more than five pictures from any one artist or photographer

There are also special rules for poetry and numerical data bases. The overall rule is that you can't reproduce any copyrighted work in its entirety.

Copies of the guidelines continually move around the Web so the best strategy to locate them is to enter "fair AND use" and "educational AND multimedia" into a full Web search engine such as HotBot.

believe that the balance is tipping too much in favor of the copyright owners. In 1998 the U.S. Congress passed the Sonny Bono Copyright Term Extension Act. It extended the period of protection to the life of the author plus 70 years and made Internet service providers liable if they knowingly carry sites that violate copyright rules. As mass media conglomerates such as Disney and Time Warner have made a splash on the Internet, they have become very aggressive in closing down sites that use images from copyrighted works they control.

Some emerging intellectual property disputes even have the potential to destroy the Web by attacking its basic functions. For example, there is an effort to protect by copyright the use of Web links, which would force Web page designers and Internet service providers to obtain permission from, and pay, the sites they link to. This would undermine the basic hypertext function of the Web (Orwall, 1997). Other publishers are trying to crack down on *framing*, the common practice of displaying someone's Web site within a border, or frame, that belongs to someone else's site (Quick, 1997).

On the other hand, there is a lot of piracy going on, because the Internet makes it ridiculously easy to copy text and graphics from one Web page to another.

1. Who does run the Internet?
2. How could digital media "robber barons" manipulate the information superhighway to their advantage?
3. What are some of the ways to keep Internet pornography away from small children?
4. What is the encryption issue about?
5. What are some of the major threats to privacy on the Internet?
6. What is the difference between a copyright and a patent?

Student Web page projects are frequent offenders, although there are some simple rules to follow (see the accompanying Media Impact). Several "technical fixes" are in the works that might protect content developers while not totally shutting off access to information and dampening creativity. One possibility is that as cheap and secure electronic commerce becomes available, it will be possible to demand payment on the spot for copyrighted content consumed off the Web. Electronic "watermarks" embedded in Web graphical images and audio files provide a way to identify illicit copies, and encryption could be used to prevent access to files on which users have not paid royalties (Wiggins, 1997).

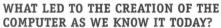

SUMMARY AND REVIEW

WHAT WERE THE EARLY ORIGINS OF COMPUTER MEDIA?

Charles Babbage created plans for the difference engine, a mechanical precursor of the modern computer, in the 1820s. Samuel Morse's telegraph was the earliest precursor of today's computer networks. Early telegraph wire services such as the Associated Press were the forerunners of information services on the Web.

WHAT LED TO THE CREATION OF THE COMPUTER AS WE KNOW IT TODAY?

The first electronic computer was designed, though not successfully built, by John Vincent Atanasoff in 1939. Data processing needs in World War II resulted in the construction of the first working digital computer, Colossus, and the first programmable computer, ENIAC, developed by Eckert and Mauchly. The SAGE system, which produced breakthroughs in computer memory, data communications, and display technologies, was also inspired by military needs.

HOW DID THE PERSONAL COMPUTER ORIGINATE?

Advances in integrated computer memory circuits made it possible to construct small-scale computers. The Altair was the first personal computer, although the Apple II was the first machine of its kind that would be recognizable to today's PC user. College dropouts Steve Jobs, Stephen Wozniak, and William Gates share the credit for key developments in personal computer hardware and software, and computer giant IBM gave personal computers their initial boost into the workplace.

WHAT ARE THE ORIGINS OF THE WORLD WIDE WEB?

Today's Internet began in 1969 as ARPANET, a computer network using the TCP/IP protocol to transmit messages between defense-related research labs. It slowly evolved to serve wider groups of academic and organizational users before being opened up to all computer users in 1991. The World Wide Web represents one of the most successful protocols used on the Internet, the hypertext transfer protocol (http). It was the culmination of developments in computer graphics, hypertext, and consumer videotex services that crystallized with the creation of the HTML language in 1991.

WHAT WERE THE IMPORTANT DEVELOPMENTS IN COMPUTER TECHNOLOGY?

Computer central processing units went through five stages of development in terms of the types of components used in their central processing units—from electronic tubes in the first computers to very large scale integrated circuits today. Advances in computer software, short-term and long-term memory, modems, local area networks, and interface devices were also critical to the development of the computer.

WHAT ARE THE IMPORTANT COMPONENTS OF A PERSONAL COMPUTER?

The computer's central processing unit is where data are processed and calculations carried out. Short-term memory holds the programs, or software, that run the computer and saves the results of the calculations on a temporary basis. Long-term memory, in the form of floppy or hard discs, makes it possible to save programs and information after the computer has been turned off. Computer interfaces, such as the cathode ray tube, keyboard, and mouse, let the user interact with the computer programs. A modem is a device that makes it possible to send programs and files of data between computers over telephone networks.

WHAT ARE SOME POSSIBLE FUTURE DIRECTIONS FOR COMPUTER MEDIA TECHNOLOGY?

One is to make personal computers simpler, perhaps yielding stripped-down "network computers" that will only be able to display material from the Web and "embedded computers" that will be found in many everyday devices such as TV sets and household appliances. The other direction is the design of more sophisticated multimedia computers that will replace all of the other communications media found in the home today. Both scenarios foretell the evolution of the Web into a multimedia network that will carry radio, TV, and phone conversations.

HOW DO PEOPLE USE COMPUTER MEDIA?

About two-fifths of U.S. homes have a personal computer. Minorities and low-income households are less likely to have computers available. About 40 percent now use the Internet at home, at school, or at work.

HOW IS THE COMPUTER MEDIA INDUSTRY ORGANIZED?

Computer hardware companies such as Compaq make the computers. Software companies such as Microsoft manufacture common computer applications, but again there are many specialized niches for particular types of software, and other companies specialize in designing custom software for specific users. Content providers are the companies that create information for the Web and multimedia applications, whereas Internet service providers make the actual physical connections to the Internet. No one entity owns or controls the Internet or the Web. They are run by a patchwork of voluntary organizations, including the Internet Corporation for Assigned Names and Numbers (ICANN) and the Internet Society.

WHAT ARE THE MAIN GENRES OF COMPUTER MEDIA?

Internet genres can be defined in terms of the major varieties of protocols that are used, which include e-mail, file transfers, chat, locators, remote access, and document display. The Web is an example of the latter. Web pages may be categorized by their domain names (such as .com and .edu) or by the nature of their content. Entertainment sites and search engines are the leading categories today, but new genres (such as portals and electronic commerce sites) are continually emerging. The Internet aside, the main types of computer software are designed to improve productivity at home or on the job. Educational, computer utility, reference, and entertainment titles are the other leading types.

WHAT SOCIAL ISSUES WILL BE IMPORTANT IN THE FUTURE DEVELOPMENT OF COMPUTER MEDIA?

Most computer media issues revolve around efforts to guide the future of the Internet. Some proposed policies are aimed at keeping the Internet open and diverse, such as by protecting individual privacy, preventing monopolization by corporate interests, and keeping it free of taxation or direct control by national governments. Others would clamp down on cyberspace by restricting pornography, encryption, and hate speech or by strictly enforcing the intellectual property rights of copyright and patent holders.

Electronic Resources

For up-to-the-minute URLs about *Computer Media and the Internet,* access the MEDIA NOW site on the World Wide Web at:

http://communication.wadsworth.com/

CHAPTER 9

Communications Infrastructure

WHAT'S AHEAD

With media convergence, ties to specific infrastructure channels are weakening now that newspaper articles, radio and TV programs, and also computer data and telephone conversations can be transmitted digitally through the same network or communications infrastructure. This chapter outlines the history of this revolutionary change in the communications infrastructure and explores the new issues it raises for us and our society.

Access the MEDIA NOW site on the World Wide Web at:
http://communication.wadsworth.com/
Choose "Chapter 9" from the selection box to access electronic information and other sites relevant to this chapter.

PARTYING DOWN ON THE INTELLIGENT NETWORK

Wow! Volume Four of Jimmy Buffett's Greatest Hits. Gotta have it!
‹Dialing 1-888-PARTIES›

Hellowww Mr. Aberthnot are you calling to check on that shipment of Jimmy Buffett's Hits Volume Three if you remember we said we would send it out to you last Tuesday and . . .

No, I'm calling for Volume Four. Saaay, how did you know it was me and that I already ordered. In fact, I don't remember placing a call to you at all!

Your DeeVee picked up your voice command and relayed it to us and of course we have Caller ID and keep a complete record of all your orders matched with your consumer behavior and I see that you have all of Jimmy's albums now AND you like your margaritas so would you like to join our margarita-of-the-month club for a 30 percent discount on alcoholic beverages in the Jimmy Buffett style starting with five gallons of the new watermelon-kiwi margarita for you and all your friends?

Wow! Gotta have it! Let me give you my . . .

No need just touch your DeeVee's fingerprint scanner and the charge will show up on your next multimedia bill. [CLICK.]

[DeeVee.] Hiya, friend! This is Jimmy Buffett! I'm changing channels for all my new friends to tell them about my fun new exercise video, "Party-hearty." Give 'er a look! One-two, shake that thang! Now take a hit of that watermelon-kiwi margarita! One-two, sit down if you're tired! One-two, it's only $36.95! . . .

Wow! Gotta have it! But who said you could change my channels, Jimmy? And close down the video links you opened to all those middle-aged guys wearing Hawaiian shirts and grass skirts and swigging margaritas in front of their DeeVees!

Chapter Outline

Historical Development of the Information Infrastructure
From Telegraph to Telephone
The Government vs. AT&T
The Video Infrastructure: Cable Television
The Government vs. Cable
The Wireless Infrastructure
The Rise of the Internet
The Government Steps Aside
Trends in Infrastructure Technology
The First Telephone
Overcoming Distance
Untangling the Wires: Advances in Transmission Technology
Getting Where You Want to Go: Switching
Becoming Digital: Trends in Digital Networks
Communicating Anywhere: Mobile Communication Trends
Infrastructure Services
Residential Services
Business Services
Using the Infrastructure
Industry Organization
Telephone Carriers
Internet Service Providers
Internet Organization
Cable Television
Mobile Carriers
Satellite Carriers
Private Networks
Equipment Manufacturers
Issues in the Infrastructure Industry
Ownership and Control
Content Control
Subsidies
Universal Service
Spectrum Allocation
Network Security
Piracy
Summary and Review

HISTORICAL DEVELOPMENT OF THE INFORMATION INFRASTRUCTURE

Most great civilizations have had an impulse to create a communications infrastructure capable of rapid-distance communication. The ancient Greeks and Romans had fire towers to carry messages from distant outposts of their vast empires. The Yoruba civilization in eastern Africa relied on a network of drummers. The Anasazi people of the ancient American Southwest had a centralized "broadcasting" system of fire signals in place in the twelfth century C.E. In Napoleon's day, a network of signal towers carried urgent dispatches across France (Holzmann & Pehrson, 1994).

From Telegraph to Telephone

Still, Samuel F. B. Morse's invention of the telegraph in 1836 was significant in that it provided the starting point for the telecommunications technology and communications infrastructure industries as they exist today. The first words that Morse sent over the first operational telegraph system in 1844, "What hath God wrought?", only slightly exaggerated the significance of the new form of communication. By 1859 telegraph lines spanned the continent, and by 1866 they connected the continents of the world via undersea cables. Historian Daniel Czitrom (1982) called the telegraph "lightning lines" to reflect both the speed of information transmission and the transforming effect of the new communication system. Businesses grew in size and scope as they found that they could use the telegraph to coordinate activities among far-flung branches. Together with the railroads, the telegraph made a national economy possible as regional companies found that they could expand to cover the entire country. The telegraph also had an important mass media function, through wire services such as the Associated Press that delivered the news of the day to every city and town.

The next step toward today's information superhighway resulted from an attempt to improve the telegraph by getting it to carry multiple messages on a single wire. The inventor, a speech teacher by the name of Alexander Graham Bell, initially called his invention the "harmonic telegraph." But while experimenting in his Boston laboratory one March day in 1876, he acciden-

COMMUNICATIONS INFRASTRUCTURE TIME LINE

1844	Telegraph service begins
1859	Telegraph goes coast-to-coast
1866	Transoceanic telegraph
1876	Bell invents the telephone
1910	AT&T buys Western Union
1913	AT&T promises Universal Service, fair competition
1915	First transcontinental phone call
1934	Communications Act regulates telecommunications
1948	First cable television system
1962	First communications satellite, first digital phone network, first pagers
1965	First digital phone switch
1969	ARPANET, forerunner of the Internet
1972	Congress opens urban markets to cable
1973	HBO becomes first channel delivered via satellite
1978	Cellular telephone service begins in United States
1979	First fiber optic network
1984	AT&T divests itself of its local operating companies
1995	DBS service in the United States, digital cellular phones
1996	Telecommunications Act opens up competition; AT&T spins off equipment manufacturing
1997	Merger mania in the telecommunications industry begins
1999	AT&T buys TCI

tally spilled some acid on his lap and called out for his assistant. "Mr. Watson, come here, I want you," he said, and the apparatus on his desk magically relayed his words over wires into the next room. Mr. Watson came running, and the telephone was born (Brooks, 1976; Cole, 1991; Temin, 1987). In Chapter 13, we will see that the early phones had a profound impact in shaping the commerce and the social life of the late nineteenth century.

Alexander Graham Bell established the Bell Telephone Company in the following year, 1877. Five years later, in 1882, the Bell System acquired Western Electric, an electrical manufacturing firm. This put into place the second cornerstone of a powerful telecommunications giant that would begin calling itself American Telephone and Telegraph, or AT&T for short. Building first on Bell's patents and later on strong-arm business tactics, AT&T dominated the telephone industry by 1910. It then made a move to monopolize the entire telecommunications infrastructure of the day by acquiring Western Union, the largest telegraph company in the United States. This was in an era when monopolies were considered a major social evil. With the threat of a suit under the 1890 *Sherman Antitrust Act* looming, AT&T canceled the Western Union deal in 1913, said it would play fair with its competitors, and promised to bring telephone service to all—the pledge of *Universal Service.*

This effort eventually expanded the reach of the telephone outward from the wealthy tradespeople and professionals who owned telephones at the turn of the century (Fischer, 1992). Soon the telephone became a lifeline to rural families and helped spur the move from the cities to the suburbs.

LIGHTNING LINES. The telegraph transformed communications in the business world in the late 1880s. Here telegraph wires span a busy New York City street.

The Government vs. AT&T

AT&T's retreat on the antitrust issue was the beginning of an era of government intervention in the telephone industry that would last most of the twentieth century. For a time it appeared that government control might become complete, following the model of state-run phone systems in Europe. All U.S. telephone and telegraph systems were put under the control of the Post Office in 1918, at the end of World War I, but the rate increases that ensued provoked a public clamor for a speedy return to private ownership only a year later.

What emerged was a privately owned monopoly regulated by the government. In return for the right to operate as the sole provider of telephone service in a specified service area, AT&T and the other surviving local phone companies agreed to open their books to regulators and accept a fixed percentage of profit on their investments while extending service to the largest possible number of users. This model became known as *rate-of-return regulation* at the state level. This arrangement shielded telephone subscribers from the predatory pricing of an unrestrained monopoly, while assuring company stockholders of a steady, if relatively modest, return on their investment.

The federal government's role was codified in the *Communications Act of 1934,* which defined AT&T's role as a *common carrier.* That is, AT&T and other local telephone companies could transport telecommunications traffic over facilities that were available on an equal basis to all paying customers, but they could not have a financial interest in the creation of the content that was carried. AT&T also had to submit regular financial reports to the new Federal Communications Commission and to file with the regulators the rates, or *tariffs,* it charged.

However, AT&T's ownership of both local and long-distance telephone companies, as well as the company that made equipment for both, continued to raise antitrust concerns, resulting in Sherman Antitrust Act (see Chapter 14) suits in 1949 and 1974. The second suit, settled in 1982, finally succeeded in breaking the Bell monopoly, forcing the *divestiture* of AT&T's local telephone companies, while allowing it to keep its long-distance and telecommunications equipment manufacturing businesses. But by the time the *modified final judgment (MFJ),* the agreement governing the divestiture, took effect two years later, in 1984, two other cracks had already opened in the AT&T monopoly. Competing companies had already won the right to provide long-distance service and to sell equipment that users could connect to AT&T's network.

The Video Infrastructure: Cable Television

HOME BOX OFFICE.
HBO played an important role in the expansion of the cable industry in the 1970s by providing an attractive alternative to network television.

In Chapter 7 we traced the early development of cable television as a community antenna service for remote communities in the 1940s and 1950s. Cable stayed close to its rural roots for over 20 years. During this time, the fortunes of the new industry rose and fell with the tides of regulation from Washington, DC. The freeze on new television stations between 1948 and 1952 spurred cable growth in the early years. But between 1966 and 1972, cable operators were kept out of the largest television markets by FCC decree in an effort to nurture new local UHF stations (channels 14–69) that were threatened by popular distant signals that cable could import from Chicago or New York (see Chapter 7).

When that ban was lifted in 1972, large companies that owned numerous cable systems, **multiple system operators (MSOs)**, engaged in a high-stakes bidding war for the right to wire America's cities for cable television. With the spread of satellite distribution of cable programming pioneered by HBO, many new channels (such as ESPN and CNN) were established, appealing to yet wider audiences. By 1985 nearly every major city in the United States had cable TV. This era was also marked by the ascendancy of Tele-Communications, Inc. (TCI) as the largest cable multiple system operator.

Multiple system operators (MSOs) are cable companies that operate in two or more communities.

The Government vs. Cable

As it spread to the cities, cable became big enough to attract the attention of regulators again. The *Cable Act of 1984* deregulated cable television rates amid concerns that municipal franchise authorities were becoming too demanding in their dealings with cable operators. However, complaints about increasing cable rates soon spurred Congress to reimpose rate regulation in the *Cable Act of 1992.* Congress also took steps to create competition for cable by abolishing exclusive franchises and by forcing channels such as ESPN to make their programming available to other distribution technologies such as satellite. The new laws continued to protect the interests of broadcasters by forcing cable companies to carry local TV stations—a policy called **must carry**—and to compensate broadcasters for the off-air programming they imported from distant cities.

Must carry is the requirement that cable operators carry all locally available broadcast TV signals.

The Wireless Infrastructure

The 1992 Cable Act breathed new life into efforts to deliver multichannel TV programming to the home without wires. HBO's first satellite dishes were 30 feet across and cost $100,000 in 1973, but a decade later a complete *television receive only (TVRO)* "dish" installation only 6 feet wide could be had for a few thousand dollars. Anyone with the appropriate equipment could receive HBO and dozens of other cable channels just for the cost of installing the receiving equipment. Many rural residents and apartment building owners took advantage of this, in effect cutting out both the cable operators and the cable networks. Because of the lost revenue, the cable channels *scrambled* (i.e., electronically disrupted the pictures) their transmissions and sold the descramblers only to bona fide cable operators.

This foiled the "free" satellite reception. However, the 1992 Cable Act opened up the descrambler sales to other distribution outlets besides the local cable operator.

Direct broadcast satellite (DBS) is a system of transmitting television signals from satellites to compact home receivers.

This paved the way for **Direct Broadcast Satellite (DBS)** systems. These differ from the TVRO model in that subscribers are required to pay a fee for the programming. They can either buy the receiving equipment separately or have its cost folded into their monthly fees. In 1995 a wave of DBS operators, led by DirecTV and Primestar, revived the U.S. satellite TV market with a full range of programming options, new digital transmission technology, and easy-to-install, "pizza-sized" satellite dishes. Although DBS could offer more channels with better reception and lower cost than cable, DBS operators were not allowed to transmit the major broadcast networks in areas where a local network affiliate could be received (Gruley, 1997). This limited the appeal of DBS relative to cable.

Another competing alternative, earth-bound *wireless cable* pay TV channels, actually antedated HBO by several years. *Subscription television (STV)* beamed movies and sporting events to homes over a UHF television channel. *Multipoint distribution systems (MDS)* used special high-frequency transmitters to reach their subscribers. Both thrived into the 1980s in urban areas that had not been reached by cable. However, as single-channel services, they did not last long after cable came to town. Later updates of wireless cable technology revived the concept by employing **digital compression** to expand capacity to dozens of channels.

Digital compression reduces the number of computer bits that have to be transmitted.

While wireless pay television sputtered, wireless telephone services enjoyed phenomenal success. *Mobile telephones* have been around since 1946, but it wasn't until **cellular radio** service was inaugurated in 1978 that the system could handle large numbers of users. To pave the way for the new wireless service, the FCC reallocated some channels that had formerly been reserved for UHF TV (channels 69–88) to mobile telephony. The cellular system also had a new design based on subdividing service areas into smaller and smaller cells that could be continually split to accommodate new users. A second generation of digital wireless phones entered service in the United States in 1995 following an auction of new frequencies conducted by the FCC. Also, these new *personal communication service (PCS)* phones were lighter and made mobile data communications far more accessible. (Harte, Levine, & Prokup, 1997). In 1998, the FCC auctioned another block of wireless frequencies for mobile interactive systems that would integrate telephony, video, and Internet access. That year also saw the debut of the first worldwide satellite telephone system, Iridium.

Cellular radio is a mobile telephone service that subdivides service areas into many small cells to maximize the number of users.

SEE THE LIGHT.
Fiber optic cables such as these are now common in telephone and cable TV networks.

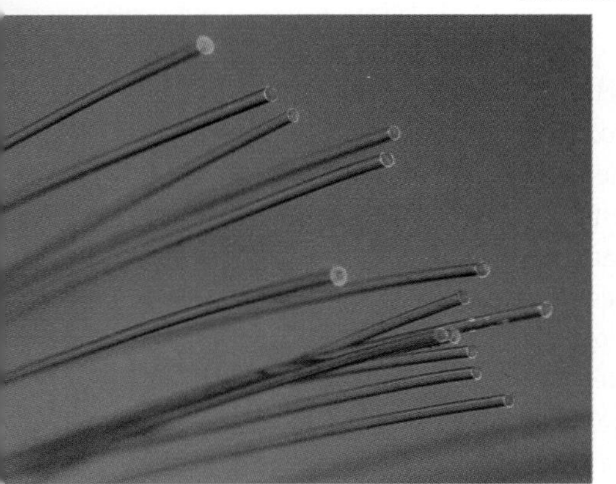

The Rise of the Internet

In Chapter 8 we saw how the Internet grew out of the 1969 Defense Department research project ARPANET into a worldwide communications medium by the early 1990s. Obviously, the evolution of the Internet went hand in hand with developments in the communications infrastructure. Only as new data transmission technologies entered the public telephone network was the Internet able to grow in scope and speed. But in the early 1990s, the Internet started to drive the infrastructure, instead of the other way around, as the growth in Internet-related data traffic outpaced the growth in conventional voice telephone services for the first time.

From an infrastructure perspective, there are two major sections of the nation's public networks that need to be upgraded for the Internet: the *backbone* or high-speed network that carries data between major nodes on the Internet and the *last mile* connection that links individual homes and businesses to those nodes. By the early 1990s, new technologies such as fiber optics were widely available from existing telecommunications carriers to meet the needs of the backbone. The last mile connection to the home was the problem. There, local telephone companies still enjoyed a monopoly on voice-grade lines but they had no incentive to adapt the conventional telephone network to deliver high-speed connections to the home user.

MEDIA IMPACT

Monitoring the Telecom Act

For Further Research:

How is the Telecommunications Act of 1996 working out? Is it creating more competition for telecommunications companies and better, cheaper, and more innovative services for all consumers, as was planned? You can check out the latest results of this grand policy experiment yourself. If you are using the InfoTrac College Edition, just enter "telecommunications act" as the keyword. A quick scan of the headlines and the abstracts of the latest articles listed will give you an idea of what the hot issues are. Try tracking them over time by making a table with the title and date of each article, along with the issue (such as long-distance competition, phone rates, or universal service) that is involved. To find out what the Telecommunications Act means for you, the consumer, just add "AND consumers" to your keywords.

WWW

On the Web, just use a full Web browser such as Hotbot (www.hotbot.com) and use "Telecommunications Act" as a keyword, limiting your search to those words in the page title only. You can find a hypertext summary compiled by the communications law firm of Blumenfeld & AMP Cohen at www.technologylaw.com/techlaw/act_summary.html. To find out about the latest efforts by the FCC to fine-tune the Act, try www.fcc.gov/telecom.html. The Benton Foundation maintains a compendium of resources related to the latest telecommunication policy issues and regulatory developments at www.benton.org. For the telephone industry point of view, visit TelecomPolicy.net (just use that as the URL).

The Government Steps Aside

The success of wireless telephones and DBS services, the promise of the Internet, and the need to modernize that last mile were some of the factors that helped to jump-start a radical reform of telecommunications infrastructure regulation in the United States. Generally, the end of the twentieth century witnessed a resurgence of faith that a competitive marketplace would heal all of society's ills, including paving the way for the Information Superhighway. The **Telecommunications Act of 1996** swept away many business restrictions and most federal rate regulation in the telecommunications industry. For example, local telephone companies became free to offer cable TV service, and long-distance and cable companies were allowed to break into the local telephone and the new Internet access businesses (Baldwin, McVoy, & Steinfield, 1996).

To get in fighting trim for the new era of competition, AT&T shed its unprofitable computer manufacturing business as well as its successful telecommunications equipment business. Thus in 1996 AT&T finally chose to do to itself what several generations of federal regulators could not force it to do: get out of the equipment manufacturing business (Keller, 1996). Following suit, telecommunications firms of all stripes immediately set about forming new alliances aimed at giving them the advantage in the newly competitive markets.

The **Telecommunications Act of 1996** is the legislation that opened the U.S. telecommunications industry to competition.

Many were disappointed to see that the immediate impact of the Telecommunications Act was not the wide-open competition that Congress had envisioned. Rather, it launched a wave of consolidation that resulted in big infrastructure companies getting even bigger. For example, two of the large regional telephone

1. What were the origins of the telephone and telegraph?
2. Why did the government want to break up AT&T?
3. What key developments marked the spread of cable TV?
4. How did mobile phones get started? Satellites? The Internet?
5. What was the impact of the Telecommunications Act of 1996?

companies that were spun off in the AT&T divestiture, Bell Atlantic and NYNEX, later combined into a single firm that controlled the communications infrastructure from Maine to Virginia. Then Southwestern Bell bought Pacific Telesis and Ameritech, reducing the number of regional phone companies from seven to only four. Upstart long-distance carrier WorldCom bought up a number of its smaller rivals and then topped itself by buying giant MCI, the nation's number two long-distance carrier (after AT&T). In 1999, AT&T completed a deal to buy cable TV giant TCI in hopes of recreating what it once had—an integrated long-distance and local telecommunications company. Meanwhile, cable operators took advantage of deregulation to raise cable TV rates. High entry costs associated with building local telecommunications networks remain a barrier to new competitors.

Still, there were some encouraging signs that competition would work eventually. *Competitive local exchange carriers* (CLECs)—including those run by cable TV systems—made some inroads against the regional phone company monopolies. *Internet service providers (ISPs)* such as UUNET also applied competitive pressure by diverting more and more of the nation's data communications into their own networks. With growing demand for *Internet telephony* (calls placed over the Internet instead of over conventional phone lines) as well as heated wireless competition, newcomers continue to challenge the local phone monopolies.

TRENDS IN INFRASTRUCTURE TECHNOLOGY

The First Telephone

An appreciation of Morse's telegraph—and all of the electronic media that followed—begins by harking back to that basic electricity experiment popular in many grade schools that we introduced previously (see Chapter 6). The teacher wraps wire around a big nail and hooks the wire up to a battery. Then she closes a switch that sends electricity flowing through the wire, and the nail instantly turns into a magnet that can pick up other nails. When she opens the switch, the current stops, and the nails clinging to the magnetized nail drop dramatically back to the table. Morse's telegraph operated on the same principle, except that the telegraph key acted like the teacher's switch, turning the flow of electricity on or off, and the magnet caused a thin strip of metal to click up and down many miles away as it became magnetized and demagnetized. The pattern of clicks followed a special code devised by Morse that spelled out all the letters of the alphabet.

Now we can take a closer look at what Alexander Graham Bell was doing that day in the lab when the acid spilled on his trousers. When he called out to Mr. Watson, the air pressure waves from his voice hit a flexible membrane. A wire was attached to the membrane, and as Bell shouted, the wire bobbed up and down in a beaker of acid, varying the electrical resistance in the circuit in response to the pressure waves in Bell's voice. This device thus incorporated the principle of the *variable resistance transmitter.* The wire was connected to an *electromagnet* in the next room, which tugged at a flexible steel reed. In response to the varying electric current, air pressure waves reached Watson's ears.

The earliest phones were attached to dedicated telegraph lines (there were no switches), connecting two points that were no more than a few miles apart (there were no means to amplify the signals). Users had to shout "Hoy! Hoy!" into the transmitter to attract the attention of the party at the other end, who then responded "Hoy! Hoy!" (Bell disdained the use of "hello" for all his years.) The alerting problem was soon solved by Watson, who invented the electromagnetic ringing device still used today, but the other limitations were the subject of continuing technological development. Many of the solutions eventually found their way into mass media systems, including motion pictures, radio, broadcast TV, cable TV, and satellite TV, and indeed were often invented in the laboratories of the telephone giant that Bell founded (Fagen, 1975).

"HOY!"
Here Alexander Graham Bell inaugurates the line between New York and Chicago in 1892.

Overcoming Distance

One of the first inventions to emerge from AT&T's research labs was a practical *repeater amplifier.* It used the *audion tube,* a 1906 invention by Lee De Forest that also was a key component for radio and television. Early long-distance callers had to compensate for electrical noise and losses by shouting into the telephone, but no one could shout all the way from New York to San Francisco! In the first transcontinental call in 1915, Bell again had the honor of uttering the first words: "Hoy! Hoy! (he still refused to say "hello") Mr. Watson? Are you there? Do you hear me?" Watson did.

Untangling the Wires—Advances in Transmission Technology

Within a decade of Bell's invention, telephone poles with up to 30 cross-arms literally darkened the skies above the largest cities. The search began for a way to put more than one telephone conversation on a pair of wires. The solution, first used in 1918, was *multiplexing.* Each telephone conversation was combined with a slightly different high-frequency signal, called a *carrier wave,* just as multiple radio programs are transmitted simultaneously, each on a different channel.

THE LAST MILE.
Conventional telephone lines such as these have insufficient capacity for today's Internet and multimedia communication.

Microwave. After World War II, radar transmitters developed to detect enemy ships and planes were adapted to communications systems. *Microwave* systems first entered the public telephone network in 1948. Thousands of individual calls were multiplexed, again using the same basic principle that allows multiple radio signals to be transmitted simultaneously on adjacent channels through the air. However, instead of broadcasting the transmissions in all directions, microwave systems use directional transmitters located atop tall buildings or towers some 20–30 miles

Coaxial cable is the high-capacity wire used for cable television transmission.

Satellite systems are microwave systems on which the relays are in Earth's orbit instead of on towers.

apart to send information in a tightly focused beam. Microwave also proved effective in carrying television signals between cities; the first coast-to-coast linkup was in 1951 (O'Neill, 1985). And cable television companies began using microwave networks to transport television signals from distant cities to their *headends.*

Coaxial Cable. Local distribution of the TV signals from the cable headend to the subscriber was accomplished by another carrier technology that emerged from the World War II battlefields, **coaxial cable** (see Figure 9.1). This was a wireline technology that improved on conventional telephone lines by using fatter wires shielded from outside interference so that they could carry more information. Coaxial cable was also used for high-capacity telephone trunks and to connect early television stations into networks.

Satellite. In 1945 science fiction writer Arthur C. Clarke recognized a revolutionary application of the new microwave technology. What if we placed the microwave transmitters in orbit around the earth so they could span the globe? Essentially, that is all **satellite systems** are. A powerful microwave transmitter, or *uplink,* on the ground beams the signal up to a receiver in space, which then retransmits the signal down to distant earth stations. Another wartime innovation, the ballistic missile, made this feat possible to imagine. The first communications satellite, Telstar I, went into orbit in 1962. History records the first words spoken on this occasion, too, but they were something less than momentous: "Will everybody please

FIGURE 9.1
The cable headend feeds broadcast, satellite, microwave, and local origination signals into a coaxial cable distribution network of trunks, feeders, and drops to individual homes.

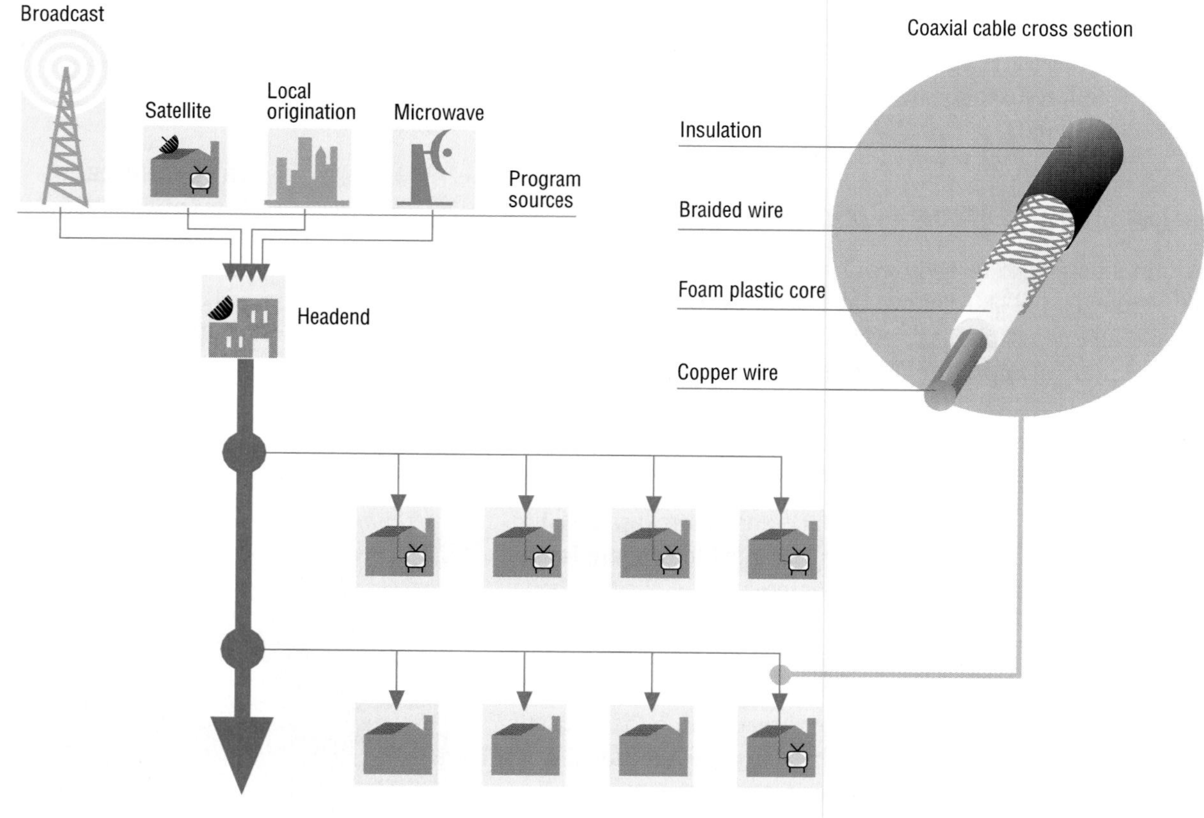

TECHNOLOGY **DEMYSTIFIED**

Satellites

In effect, satellites are antenna towers in the sky that retransmit television in two very long "hops," one from a satellite *uplink* station on the ground to the satellite and then back from the satellite—essentially, a microwave relay device launched into earth orbit—to the *downlink* connected to the cable head end. Satellites that orbit at an altitude of 22,300 miles match the rotation speed of the earth and are thus called geosynchronous satellites. This means they maintain their position in the sky so that the downlink antenna can be pointed at a fixed location.

Cable networks such as CNN and HBO feed their signals directly into their own satellite uplinks. Distant TV signals for superstations are boosted into space by picking them up off the air and retransmitting them through satellite uplinks to cable television operators (CATV) or satellite master antenna TV (SMATV) systems that serve individual buildings or housing complexes.

At the cable head end, the signals are converted from satellite frequencies and placed on local cable channels. Home satellite receivers can receive the same channels, and for a time, thousands of homes received cable channels "free" on backyard satellite dishes called television receive only (TVRO) dishes. However, cable networks now scramble their transmissions and require home satellite viewers to pay monthly fees for the descramblers. New, more powerful direct broadcast satellite (DBS) systems transmit digital programming to small rooftop antennas.

get off this line?" There were so many dignitaries listening in on the historic transmissions from space that the circuit was overloaded. During the 1970s, satellite technology made major inroads into terrestrial microwave and wireline networks, especially in international long-distance routes and cable television (Hudson, 1990). Later, satellites were more powerful, allowing a gradual shrinkage in the sizes of the receiving dishes. Digital technology expanded the capacity of satellites.

Digital Carriers. Also in 1962, an event that would eventually reshape the world of communications took place inside the AT&T central office in Skokie, Illinois. The first digital telephone call was made to Chicago. Until then, telephones still worked about the same way as they had for Alexander Graham Bell: Air pressure waves created by human vocal cords were converted to continuously varying electric currents and then changed back to air pressure waves that the ear could sense as sound. The new digital carrier system, known as a *T1,* converted the voices to a stream of discrete digital pulses for the trip between Skokie and Chicago and then reconstructed a simulated voice for the listener on the other end. By combining short digital voice samples from multiple calls, it was possible to handle up to 24 simultaneous conversations on a single circuit (Millman, 1984).

Fiber Optics. Another way to expand capacity is to use beams of light instead of pulses of electricity to transmit information, *fiber optics.* Alexander Graham Bell was granted a patent for a "photophone" in 1880, but practical application had to

TECHNOLOGY **DEMYSTIFIED**

Fiber Optics: Why You Can Hear a Pin Drop

The basic principles of fiber optic transmission are quite easy to grasp. Essentially, fiber optic systems shine a laser light into a very long glass tube. If the information we wish to transmit is in digital form, we simply turn the laser on when we want to transmit a 1 and turn it off when we want to send a 0. The light rays reflect off the sides of the tube and can be made to travel hundreds of miles without amplification or retransmission if the glass is pure enough. At the other end of the glass tube, the light shines onto a detector that converts light to electric current, and the original sequence of digital electrical pulses is recovered. The signal can be regenerated for retransmission, switched into another circuit, or converted back into the human voice. By the way, these are not *Star Wars* lasers but tiny solid-state devices that fit into a package about the size of your thumb and would not put out enough light to singe your eyebrows, let alone burn through the hull of a space cruiser.

The main advantages of fiber optic systems are speed and quality. Fiber optic systems can transmit data at rates of billions of bits per second, compared to conventional phone systems and tens of millions of bits per second for coaxial cable systems. Because the data are transmitted as light waves instead of electrical pulses, they are immune to the electrical interference that causes static and distortion in electronic systems. That is why you literally can "hear a pin drop" over a fiber optic telephone network.

await the invention of the *laser* at Bell Labs in 1958. Lasers provide a powerful beam of pure light well suited to communication by light waves. The first commercial system was installed in 1979, and within a decade fiber optics were in wide use in long-distance networks and had started to make their way into local telephone networks and corporate data communications networks. Cable companies are banking on **fiber optic systems** as they build their own version of the information superhighway.

Fiber optic systems use light instead of electricity to communicate.

Getting Where You Want to Go: Switching

Manual Switching. Switching equipment is the other key component of the infrastructure. Millions of telephone operators would be needed to handle today's telephone traffic if calls were still manually patched together with electrical plugs as they were in the early days. Instead, today there are far fewer than the 150,000 operators employed in the 1920s before automatic switching was instituted.

Automatic Switching. The early automatic switches were close relatives of the jukebox. Mechanical arms rotated and jiggled up and down in response to the numbers dialed, touching tiny electrical contacts that were connected to subscribers' telephone wires. By 1946 automatic switches—and telephone company supervisors—kept the entire Bell System running despite a nationwide telephone operators' strike (Schindler, 1982). Beginning in 1951, even long distance calls could be dialed automatically from the home. Large organizations today now find it profitable to install their own switches, called *private branch exchanges (PBXs). Key systems* are an economical alternative for smaller companies.

WOMEN'S WORK?
Early telephone switchboard operators completed calls manually under close supervision and in difficult working conditions.

Digital Switching. In 1965, AT&T first crossed the telephone switch with a computer to produce the first *digital switch.* Now, all the giant clattering electromagnetic switches and swarms of technicians that once filled the gigantic vaults of telephone central exchanges have been replaced by refrigerator-sized electronic switches humming quietly to themselves in the dark (Millman, 1984).

Intelligent Networks. Computer-driven switches also gave rise to the *intelligent network.* Back in the earliest days of the telephone, all of the actions necessary to establish and terminate a telephone call (*signaling,* in telephone jargon) passed through the same physical connection that the voices did. In contrast, the intelligent networks of today use a separate high-speed data network for these functions. This network "checks ahead" to see whether your party is on the line before attempting to ring their phone, so you no longer have to hang on the line for a minute or more while intermediate connections are established. This makes possible services such as *caller ID,* which connects the intelligent network to a digital display on the subscriber's telephone and the *follow me* services that automatically redirect calls to your new location.

Cable Converters. Cable television and satellite services have their own switching problem, but it is a far simpler one than that just described. All they have to do is turn their service on and off at each location and make sure that subscribers get the channels they paid for but can't view the rest. A crude but effective switching solution was used for the first 25 years: The cable company would send an installer to rip out your wires if it wanted to shut your service off—or if you failed to pay your cable bill.

Things became more complicated with the addition of pay channels such as HBO and, later, programming options that could be purchased by the month or even by the event. Too many installers in too many trucks were rolling around. The solution was *addressable converters* that turned themselves off and on in response to digital codes broadcast through the system. Each converter has its own unique address, so the pay channels can be turned on and off without sending the cable guy. The first such system was introduced in Columbus, Ohio, in 1973. As we discussed in Chapter 8, the cable converter is getting a make-over into a new style set top box, which will decode TV signals transmitted in digital formats and integrate conventional TV with related Web content.

Becoming Digital: Trends in Digital Networks

Modems. The easiest way to send data between computers is to turn on a tiny electrical voltage to represent a 1 and to turn off the voltage to represent a 0. This is

MEDIA WATCH

The Fight of the (Next) Century: Cable Telephone or Telco TV?

The battle of the century is going on right in your living room. It is a contest to determine who will bring the interactive broadband (i.e., high capacity) network of the future to your home. To get in the ring, each contender will have to spend hundreds of billions of dollars and "bet the business" to see who wins. It promises to be a knock-down fight, and the referee has left the ring. The Telecommunications Act of 1996 lifted almost all of the restrictions that kept communications infrastructure industries from invading each other's turf.

But *you* stand to be the big winner—or the big loser—since you, the consumer, will wind up paying for it all. The outcome of the fight will also do much to determine the entertainment and information services that you and your descendants will have available in your home well into the next century. And we can't stand on the sidelines for fear that other countries with better infrastructures might knock us out of the ring of international economic competition.

The Contenders

The Baby Bells are the sluggish heavyweights in this contest. They have ten times the financial resources of the cable industry. Technically, the telcos have the advantage of operating a network that is well on the way to going all-digital and all-fiber. The copper telephone wires coming into your home, which cannot carry a lot of video, are their major weakness. The new *digital subscriber line* (DSL) technology may meet the need for Internet access and even provide video on demand. Beyond that, the telcos must extend the fiber network to each home, and that could cost half a trillion dollars. They see easier profits in the long-distance telephone business and have been slow to answer the bell in the broadband contest.

The cable companies have a broadband video network and are rapidly adding fiber optic transmission technology to their networks but are still paying off the debt from their last big expansion in the 1980s. Their big weakness is a lack of two-way capability for telephone service and Internet access. For now, they are sticking with pushing cable modems that offer World Wide Web access now and the potential for Internet-based telephone service in the future.

Opening Rounds

Both combatants have made some exploratory jabs at the competition, but there has also been some stumbling around the ring. Telephone companies such as Ameritech are building their own cable systems, whereas others are buying cable operators outright; witness Southwestern Bell's acquisition of Continental Cablevision. However, they have been slow to roll out new technology such as DSL. Cable has been pushing its cable modems to ride the wave of interest in surfing the Web. But its first attempt at integrating cable and telecommunications, Time Warner's Full Service Network in Orlando, Florida, was a costly failure.

Other Contenders

AT&T's entry into the cellular telephone business and its acquisition of cable giant TCI will get it back into the local telephone business and enable it to get a video signal into the home. Satellites are another possibility. Direct broadcast satellite video systems are here—complete with Internet connections—as are satellite-based mobile telephones. The FCC is encouraging "cellular video" technology that would make it possible to carry voice and data transmission, video teleconferences, and hundreds of channels of video programming to the home over the air via earth-bound transmitters. Electrical power utilities are a long shot, too, because they already have a fiber optic network in your neighborhood to carry monitoring and control information so they can jump in the ring quickly.

what computers do when they are talking to themselves through their internal circuitry. Unfortunately, telephone systems reject electrical pulses like these for the benefit of owners of old-fashioned rotary dial phones that use strings of electrical pulses to dial numbers. The solution to the problem of connecting computers to the phone line was the development of the **modem,** or MOdulator-DEModulator. To transmit data, modems use the same sound frequencies that we use to talk. For example, to send a 1, the modem transmits a high-pitched tone for a short amount of time. To send a 0, it transmits a lower-frequency tone. Subsequent developments in modem technology have revolved around ingenious ways to represent more than one data bit each time the signal changes. The "speed limit" on computer modems has doubled every few years. By 1997 conventional modems could send data over a standard phone line at 52,000 bits (although the ads say 56,000), or about six single-spaced pages of text, per second.

Modems convert digital data to analog signals for transmission over analog networks such as the public telephone network.

Digital Cable. Fortunately, modems are not limited to telephone lines. *Cable modems* now carry data to Internet users right alongside HBO and CNN, at speeds ranging up to an astonishing 10 million bits per second—or about 1000 single-spaced pages of text per second. However, cable systems need extensive modifications before they can transmit data both to and from the home, which has limited the spread of this technology. To convert to digital, cable operators usually have to replace their coaxial cable backbone networks with fiber optics, replace all their one-way amplifiers with two-way units, and add costly set top boxes to decode the digital signals in the home. They can also digitize incoming TV signals at their headends by representing the color and brightness information of each dot, or pixel, on the screen as a string of 1s and 0s, and then transmit the data stream using the same basic techniques as modems. They use *digital compression* to expand their channel capacity, squeezing five or six channels into the space of one by removing redundant information (e.g., background scenes that do not change between frames) from the digital signal. (The same basic digitization and compression techniques are also used to broadcast data over the air, in PCS and DBS networks as well as new digital television and radio services.)

Digital Subscriber Line. Now telephone companies are pushing **digital subscriber line (DSL)** technology as their entry into the race to rewire America. DSL uses existing telephone wiring and can provide video as well as data and voice transmission, at speeds of millions of bits per second, on standard telephone lines. Unlike conventional modems, DSL requires a change in the connections inside the telephone company's central office and, sometimes, extensive modifications in the local telephone network as well (Fleming & McLaughlin, 1993). Despite slow deployment, some computer makers are putting DSL modems in new computers to take advantage of the ubiquity of telephone lines.

Digital subscriber line (DSL) is a high-speed digital phone service that can transmit audio, video, and computer data over conventional phone lines.

ISDN. Another approach is to modify the telephone network so that it can accept digital pulses in their purest form, without changing them into sound. This is the approach that digital carrier lines such as the T1 use. *Digital carrier* technology reaches the home in the form of *integrated services digital network (ISDN)* lines. This is twice as fast as conventional phone lines (and faster than most Web sites can send information), but these lines are limited to 128,000 bits per second

TECHNOLOGY ***TRENDS***

Keep Track of Your Internet Options

For Further Research:

A constant stream of new Internet access options is becoming available: 28.8K, 33.6K and 56K phone modems , ISDN, T1, cable modems, digital subscriber line, wireless Internet, and satellite. But which can you actually get where you live and what can you afford? Finding out is not always easy. A good place to start is with the list of Internet service providers in your area, from www.thelist.com. At a glance you will find the providers that serve your area code, along with the types of dial-up services they offer. You can click on the names of the providers to get price information.

But thelist relies on companies to volunteer information, and what you see is not always up-to-date or accurate, so it still pays to check around on the latest services and rates once you narrow the field a little. Thelist also caters to "conventional" ISPs who use the public telephone network to provide access. To turn up other options, type in "internet AND" along with the appropriate keyword, such as "wireless," "cable," "satellite," "cellular," etc. Use geographical terms related to your locale ("East Lansing" "Ingham County" "Michigan") to limit the search.

Digital subscriber line and Integrated Services Digital Network are perhaps the hardest to track down, because their access is dictated at the level of the local telephone exchange, not necessarily by city, county, or state. You might try searching the Web site of your local telephone company and looking for the names of departments or contact persons associated with these products. But those who try to call telco customer service lines are usually frustrated—the service reps are not yet trained to handle those inquiries in most cases. Perseverance is the key.

(getting slow by today's standards), require a visit from an engineer to install, and sometimes have per-minute usage fees attached to them.

Packet switching breaks up digital information into individually addressed chunks, or packets, so that many users can share a single channel.

Packet Networks. The most important innovation of the ARPANET project was a means of transmitting data over long distances in a way that did not require dedicated connections between users as normal telephone calls do. This approach, known as **packet switching**, divides data streams into chunks, or packets, of data and mixes the data from many different users together into a shared, high-speed transmission channel, rather than dedicating a channel to each pair of users. Each chunk of data carries an address in it so that the packets can be reassembled at the receiving end (see Chapter 1). This approach is used in the TCP/IP Internet protocol (see Chapter 8) and also in high-speed data networks that organizations run for themselves: **local area networks (LANs)**. The *messages* are switched rather than the *circuits* as in current phone networks. This means that many users can share a single high-capacity circuit, such as a digital carrier or fiber optic line. Packet switching is now being applied to voice telephone calls, too. Calls are digitized (see Chapter 1) and then divided into packets. Such calls may be terminated to conventional phone lines (making it possible to replace conventional telephone switches with packet switching), but they can also be completed entirely between computers connected to the Internet.

Local area networks (LANs) are high-speed computer networks that link computers within a department, a building, or a campus of buildings.

Internet 2 is the "next generation" Internet.

Internet 2. A major upgrade for the Internet, **Internet 2** (University Consortium for Advanced Internet Development, 1998), is currently under development. It involves significant upgrades of the transmission capacity of the Internet backbone network, as well as the development of new types of communication schemes, or *protocols,* that will speed the flow of data across the network and reduce congestion. Internet 2 will support transmission speeds of billions of bits per second and make it easier to synchronize audio and video feeds with text and graphics files. Internet 2 thus has the potential to bring about the complete integration of all of today's diverse communications infrastructure networks.

Communicating Anywhere: Mobile Communication Trends

A very different solution to the "last mile" problem is to eliminate wires entirely, relying on the airwaves to transmit all types of information. The airwaves are already crowded with radio and television transmissions—and huge portions of the communications spectrum are reserved for government uses, primarily military—so the key to wireless solutions is to make more frequencies available or to use the ones we have more efficiently.

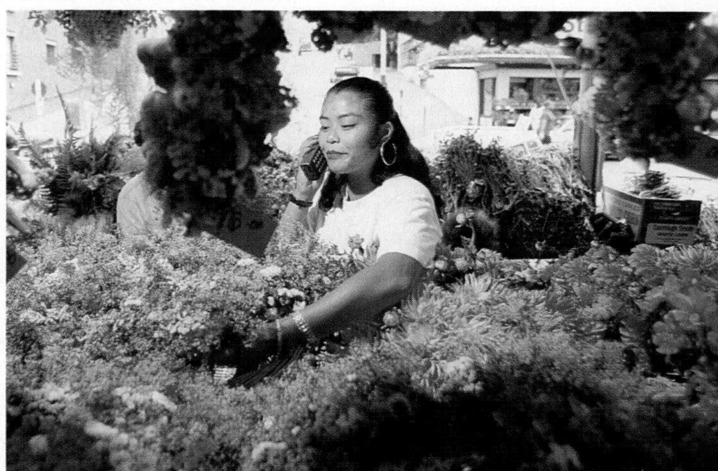

CALL ANYWHERE, ANYTIME. Cellular phones allow individuals to be in constant communication with others, wherever they may go.

Mobile Telephone. The original mobile telephone service operated from a single central antenna in each metropolitan area and had a total capacity of only 46 simultaneous conversations. This meant that the 47th caller did not receive a dial tone, which happened often. The result was years-long waiting lists for new mobile telephones.

Pagers. *Paging services* were introduced in 1962 to relieve some of the pent-up demand. Pagers are actually small radio receivers that monitor a single radio channel "piggybacked" on top of a local FM radio station signal or a satellite frequency for a unique numerical code that is their signal to "go off."

Cellular Radio. Pagers still could not keep up with the growing need for mobile communications, however, and this need led to the introduction of *cellular radio* in the United States in 1978. Cellular radio takes its name from the practice of dividing large service areas into clusters of small zones, or cells, each only a few miles across. Because the transmitters located in each cell are relatively weak, it is possible to reuse the same communication frequencies for other users in different parts of the same city. As the user moves from one cell to the next, the call is *handed off* to the next antenna in the network and automatically reassigned to a new channel. The latest *PCS* phones work a lot like cellular radio, except that the cells surrounding each transmitter are much smaller—only a few hundred yards across. They also use *digital transmission,* which means that several users can share the same frequency, and this further expands network capacity (Harte, Levine, & Prokup, 1997).

LEO Satellites. Earth-based mobile communications systems are now being challenged by a new generation of satellites that fly in *low earth orbit (LEO).* The lower orbits mean that the users' receivers can be small and portable and that they can use a small whip antenna instead of a dish. However, low-flying satellites constantly change their position relative to the surface of the earth, so dozens of satellites are needed to ensure adequate coverage (Cole, 1997). The Motorola Corporation's Iridium network, launched in 1998, uses this approach. Other new communications satellites fly in somewhat higher orbits and are called middle earth orbit (MEO) systems. Another new satellite technology consists of GPS (geopositioning satellite) systems that help find lost boaters, drivers, and hikers by comparing the signals they receive from three or more satellites turning overhead.

INFRASTRUCTURE SERVICES

Just as in the other communications media industries that we have studied, there are also basic types, or *genres,* of services offered by infrastructure companies. One common way of categorizing them is to distinguish between residential services for the home user and business services for organizations.

Residential Services

Basic telephone service has the acronym *POTS,* which stands for *plain old telephone service.* The basic POTS functions—dial tone, transmission, and switching—have changed little since the 1880s. The spread of computerized switching equipment in recent decades has added a number of options, including touch tone dialing and custom calling services such as call waiting, speed dialing, three-way calling, and call forwarding.

Custom local area signaling services (CLASS) represent the transition to the *intelligent network.* These services include *caller ID,* automatic redial, a second-number option (one line that answers two different numbers, sometimes also known as the "teen line"), and the ability to screen automatically so that some calls ring through and others don't. The intelligent network also improves response to emergency calls by automatically looking up the address associated with the number: enhanced 911 (Briere, 1993).

Voice mail is a lot like an answering machine, but the recording device is in the telephone company's central office. Voice mail has additional features, such as the ability to take a message while the line is busy and to "broadcast" voice mail messages to multiple recipients.

Although many home users rely on the their telephone lines and modems to connect them to the Internet, there is a growing array of service options for the "netizens" among us. Telephone companies offer *integrated services digital network (ISDN)* lines (see page 295) that more than double the top speed of the fastest modems by using a digital connection between the user and the telephone company's central office. Another option is to buy a second line and use a new type of modem that can send data on both lines at once, in effect doubling the speed. The latest must-have innovation coming on the scene is the *digital subscriber line (DSL)* with transmission speeds from 1.5 to 20 million bits per second.

These digital services are designed to compete with the *cable modem* services that many cable operators now offer, which also have data speeds of millions of bits per second. Satellite companies such as DirectTV are also offering Internet access, although regular phone lines have to be used for the return link that the user must have to place the request for information that is downloaded through the one-way satellite circuit.

For video, the main infrastructure option available to the home user is still cable television, although direct broadcast satellite (DBS) services offer comparable prices, often with superior transmission quality and more options. The telephone companies' new digital subscriber line (DSL) services are able to transmit video as well.

Business Services

Businesses have access to a wide range of service options that are unfamiliar to residential users. For starters, business phone lines are priced differently from consumer lines. Businesses pay higher monthly charges and are usually charged a few cents for each local phone call. *Centrex* (short for *centr*al *ex*change service) is a special service for organizational users who do not own their own telephone switches. The telephone company reserves a block of lines in its central office for a corporate office location. Calls made within this group do not incur the per-call charges that normally apply to business lines.

Leased lines differ from regular telephone lines in that they are dedicated to the user—they never get a busy signal. They are also priced on the basis of a flat monthly charge. By aggregating large volumes of traffic on such dedicated lines, corporations can realize significant savings. *Virtual private networks* are the latest wrinkle. Instead of physically connecting locations with pieces of wire, they use intelligent network switching (see page 293) to reserve capacity on public networks for large customers. By taking advantage of these options, large corporate customers can make long-distance calls for a small fraction of what residential users pay.

CAN YOU SEE US, DALLAS? Teleconferencing systems are becoming a common business tool.

Public Data Networks. Organizations also have many more data communications options. *Digital data services (DDS)* are special lines that are able to accept data directly in digital format at speeds up to 1.5 million bits per second without converting to analog form through a modem. To achieve the highest data transmission speeds, users install digital carrier systems such as the *T1,* which has a capacity equivalent to that of 24 phone lines. The next step up is the *T3;* it sends data at 45 million bits per second. Even faster digital carriers, capable of speeds of billions of bits per second, are available on fiber optic networks that make up the backbone of today's Internet.

Video teleconferencing is becoming common on private corporate networks that use high-capacity satellite, microwave, or fiber optic systems. A growing number of videoconferences go through the public network on digital carriers, and organizations also utilize high-speed dial-up lines (ISDN lines are popular) that let them add locations that are not on their private networks on an as-needed basis. Videoconferences require specialized network interface devices, called *codecs* (short for coder-decoder), that digitize and compress video to reduce transmission costs, using techniques similar to the advanced HDTV systems.

Not all of the video in the workplace is in the form of live videoconferences, however. Many corporations maintain, for creating **business video,** extensive in-house production facilities that rival those of broadcast television studios. Most of the business videos produced by these studios are educational, ranging from orientation tapes for new employees or new products to full-length courses on management practices or technical topics.

Business video programs are created by organizations for their employees and customers.

USING THE INFRASTRUCTURE

In its earliest years, the telephone spread first to the wealthiest classes of society (Fischer, 1992). The vision of universal telephone service is still not quite a reality, although about 94 percent of U.S. homes now have phones (NTIA, 1998). The average telephone user today is on the phone about 20–30 minutes each day. Women (especially those who list their occupation as "homemaker"), minorities, and young singles are the heaviest phone users. Males and people over age 75 are the lightest users (LaRose, 1999). Telephone penetration among minority households is much lower than average; it is only about 85 percent among African American homes and among homes with household incomes less than $10,000 (NTIA, 1998). Personal credit problems with long-distance companies drive many low-income users off the telephone network (Mueller & Schement, 1995). Among those homes that do subscribe to phone service, more and more have two or more phone lines to handle Internet access and facsimile (Landler, 1995). About 20 percent of the U.S. population has a cellular phone (Hardy, 1996).

Cable coverage television is close to ubiquitous: About 97 percent of all homes have cable passing by their doors (CableLabs, 1997), although only 68 percent of those subscribe (Cabletelevision Advertising Bureau, 1997). Economically disadvantaged households are unlikely to have cable television, although there is also a small group of wealthy homes that are apparently too busy to need cable. Only about half the homes with annual incomes of $20,000 or less subscribe to cable. Penetration soars to 82 percent in homes making over $60,000 per year (Cabletelevision Advertising Bureau, 1997). Senior citizens are also relatively unlikely to have cable (LaRose & Atkin, 1988).

INDUSTRY ORGANIZATION

The organization of the infrastructure industry is a relatively complex one, largely because of regulatory restrictions that limited the types of businesses that infrastructure companies could enter. Industry organization is also changing rapidly in the wake of the Telecommunications Act of 1996, as infrastructure companies combine in an effort to become what was once prohibited: a one-stop source for all our telecommunication needs. We need at least a rudimentary grasp of industry structure to understand the barriers—and opportunities—that present themselves as these formerly disparate entities converge. Industry structure also informs our choices as consumers and informed citizens.

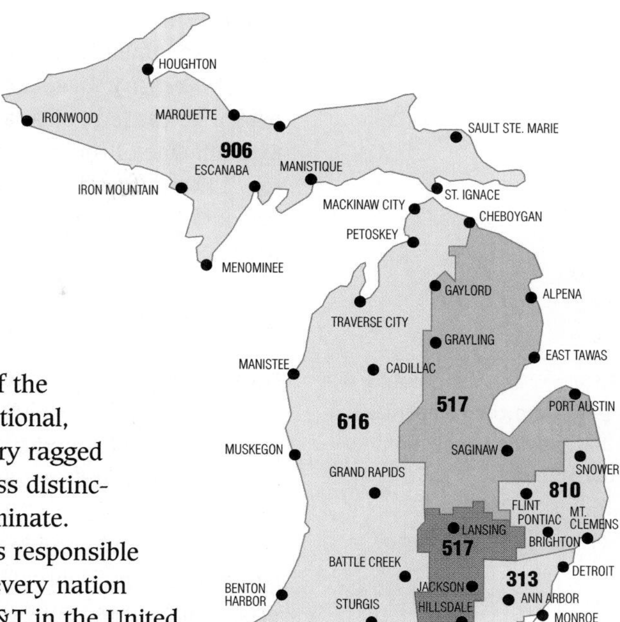

FIGURE 9.2
The boundaries between local and long-distance service are set by local access and transport area (LATA) zones. Area codes, such as 517 in Michigan, often have multiple LATAs, such as one centered on Lansing (shown in brown) and another in Saginaw (in gold), so that calls between them, within the area code, are long-distance.

Telephone Carriers

Companies that provide telephone service can be roughly divided into three distinct categories based on the scope of the calls they have been traditionally allowed to carry: international, long-distance, and local. The distinctions are becoming very ragged indeed, because this is precisely the type of line of business distinction that the Telecommunications Act was designed to eliminate.

International record carriers (IRCs) are the companies responsible for carrying long-distance calls between countries. Once, every nation had a single international long-distance carrier; it was AT&T in the United States. Now MCI and Sprint compete with AT&T for international traffic, and many other countries have also instituted competition in international long distance.

Interexchange carriers (IXCs, in telephone industry jargon) have the exclusive right to carry *domestic* long-distance telephone calls. In this context, long-distance calls include not only those that are made between area codes (such as between Grand Rapids, area code 616, and Detroit, area code 313) but also within area codes that cross *local access and transport area (LATA)* boundaries. These boundaries were set up at the time of the AT&T divestiture to demark local and long-distance calls. For example, the 517 area code in Michigan includes two LATAs, one serving the capital city of Lansing and one covering Saginaw (see Figure 9.2).

Calls from Lansing to Saginaw are inter-LATA calls and thus can be handled by an interexchange carrier such as AT&T, but ironically *not* by Ameritech, the local phone company that serves both cities. Under the Telecommunications Act of 1996, Ameritech cannot offer long-distance service to its local customers until it promises to open up its own local exchange business to competition. Why? Because Ameritech would have a natural (but unfair) advantage in signing up long-distance customers in its own local service areas. AT&T, MCI (now a part of WorldCom), and Sprint account for most of the U.S. long-distance market. The remaining slice of the long-distance market "pie" is divided among hundreds of smaller long-distance companies, including a growing number that complete calls over the Internet instead of using conventional phone networks.

Local telephone service is the domain of the *local exchange carriers (LECs)*. The 1984 AT&T divestiture collapsed the 22 different local operating companies it owned into seven **regional Bell operating companies (RBOCs)**, which have since merged down to four: Bell Atlantic, US West, Southwestern Bell and BellSouth. In addition, about 1300 *independent* local telephone companies survive that were

Regional Bell operating companies (RBOCs) are the local telephone operating companies of which AT&T divested itself in 1984.

never affiliated with the Bell system. The largest of these, however, GTE Corporation, also joined forces with Bell Atlantic in yet another titanic merger deal.

Competitive local exchange carriers (CLECs) compete with the incumbent local exchange carriers, such as Bell Atlantic, which are descendants of the old Bell System. One of the main thrusts of the 1996 Telecom Act was to make it possible for CLECs such as Metropolitan Fiber Systems (since bought by WorldCom) and Teleport (now owned by AT&T) to provide competition in the local loop, where the RBOCs still had monopolies.

Internet Service Providers

Internet service providers (ISPs) are the companies that provide connections to the Internet.

Internet service providers (ISPs) are some of the newest players in the information infrastructure; they are the ones that connect you to the Internet. Some companies, such as America Online, provide their own content as well as connections to the Internet and so combine the roles of ISP and content provider (see Chapter 8). Others, such as UUNET (another subsidiary of WorldCom), are purely ISPs in that they simply provide the basic access, either leasing and reselling high-speed connections from telecommunications carriers such as MCI or building their own private networks. But they do not produce their own content to any significant degree. The major long-distance carriers also offer ISP services. Currently there are about 10,000 ISPs in all (thedirectory, 1998), and many are small local operations.

PROFILE

CONVERGENCE COWBOY. Bernard Ebbers took advantage of telecommunications deregulation to turn a small phone company into one of the world's largest telecommunications carriers.

The Convergence Cowboy

Name: Bernard J. Ebbers

Born: Edmonton, Alberta, in 1941

Education: Graduate of Mississippi College, Jackson, Mississippi

Position: Chairman, Worldcom

Style: Aggressive deal maker, enjoys running a cattle ranch and teaching Sunday school in his spare time between deals.

Greatest Achievement: Climaxed a string of acquisition deals by taking over MCI communications in 1998, the world's record business acquisition at the time.

Most Dubious Achievement: Once nursed an ambition to become a professional basketball player.

Inspiration: Telephone deregulation.

Entry Level: His first job was delivering milk. Launched his entrepreneurial career in 1974 by buying a motel that grew into a string of Best Westerns.

How He Got to the Top: He started a small long-distance phone company in 1983 and expanded by rolling up a string of 40 acquisitions of progressively larger competitors. Just prior to the MCI deal, he attracted national attention by buying Metropolitan Fiber Systems, a leading CLEC that itself had snapped up UUNET, the leading Internet ISP. Then he bought the networking operations from two other Internet heavyweights, AOL and CompuServe.

Where Does He Go from Here? He wants to be *your* local and long-distance phone company and your Internet provider, too. Now he's looking for international markets to conquer, but first he has to prove that he can lead MCI to financial success.

Sources: Fennel, T. (1997). The last man standing. *Maclean's*, November 24, p. 100. Meyer, M. (1997). Who is this guy? *Newsweek*, October 13, p. 52.

Internet Organization

The Internet itself is a very special case. We saw in the last chapter that it is run as a not-for-profit, cooperative enterprise involving its users and several major regional data network consortia. From an infrastructure perspective, the Internet is made up of high-speed digital carrier lines that are leased by these regional networks from Interexchange carriers, notably MCI. At the local level, the ISPs lease or own high-speed digital carrier lines that connect their local users to the Internet. The end users themselves use dial-up lines from their local phone company or leased line connections to get to these access points.

Cable Television

On the surface, cable television appears to be a highly localized medium, because there are municipal cable franchises in some 13,000 communities. However, most cable systems are actually owned by huge cable *multiple system operators (MSOs),* which control hundreds of systems and serve millions of subscribers across many states. The largest MSOs are Time Warner and TCI (now known as AT&T Broadband and Internet Services). AT&T, and the other members of the Top Five (Media One, Comcast, and Cablevision Systems) account for almost 60 percent of all subscribers. The MSOs negotiate with channels such as HBO and CNN to carry their programs on the MSOs' local systems.

Mobile Carriers

Mobile communication carriers include various paging and radio telephone services, but cellular radio is the biggest. The largest cellular radio carrier in the United States is McCaw Cellular, which was acquired by AT&T in 1994. In 1995 the FCC auctioned off a new block of mobile telephone frequencies for the new digital personal communication service and expanded the number of licensees from two to five in each market in order to increase competition. Now mobile phones are becoming popular enough—and cheap enough—to replace the wireline phone network and provide some competition in the local exchange.

Satellite Carriers

Satellite carriers are also poised to enter new markets. Most of the satellite transmissions today are video, primarily the national feeds of broadcast and cable networks. Direct broadcast satellite (DBS) firms are in a separate category. The largest ones serving the United States are DirecTV (they bought the number two DBS company, Primestar in 1999) and Echostar. *INTELSAT* and INMARSAT are two international consortia; the former specializes in transmissions to fixed ground stations, and the latter provides mobile service. Comsat is the U.S. representative in both consortia. Both are about to be thrown into competition with a number of new companies in the race to cover the globe with instant telephone and Internet access delivered by satellite, notably the Iridium network launched by the Motorola Corporation in 1998.

Private Networks

Private networks are privately owned telecommunications networks.

Private networks owned and operated by private organizations are another important component of the information infrastructure. Private networks link up all the information technology in the organization. For example, General Motors operates what is perhaps the world's largest private network to connect its many factories and office buildings around the world. Corporate networks often include transmission links and network control centers that are owned and operated by the company, as well as lines leased from telecommunications carriers. Many large organizations are also installing their own private versions of the Internet, called *intranets.* These networks take advantage of cheap and familiar Internet technologies but restrict data access to the company's employees to protect their private data. Another take-off on Internet technology is the extranet, which links large organizations to networks of customers and suppliers. Many large organizations may have their own in-house telecommunications departments that employ hundreds of people, whereas others *outsource* their information systems to systems integrators such as Electronic Data Systems (EDS). EDS or its competitors run the corporate networks on a contractual basis so that the company does not have to incur the expense of staffing its own telecommunications department (Spohn, 1997).

Another key component of the private infrastructure is the local area network (LAN), high-speed data networks that cover a relatively confined area—the size, say, of a large office building or a campus of buildings (see Figure 9.3). College students who use on-campus computer labs to access the Internet are usually connected through such networks. These are important because multiple users can share computer programs and peripheral equipment (such as laser printers), and files can be shared, which enables users to work collaboratively on group projects and to access common databases and the Internet. It also saves the expense of buying each and every employee a laser printer and a personal copy of Microsoft Word.

STOP & REVIEW

1. **How were each of the limitations of the first telephones overcome?**
2. **How are cable television pictures transmitted to the home?**
3. **What are important current trends in computer networks?**
4. **Define and distinguish the following terms: IXC, LEC, CLEC, RBOC, IRC, ISP.**
5. **How is the cable TV industry organized?**
6. **What is the difference between a private network and an LAN?**

Equipment Manufacturers

The final set of players in the vast game of multimedia convergence are the manufacturers of equipment that constitute the infrastructure. The telecommunications equipment manufacturing industry can be broken down into three major categories: network (primarily switching and carrier systems used by network operators), transmission (such as fiber, microwave, satellite, and mobile), and user equipment. The latter is commonly called *customer premise equipment (CPE)* and includes consumer telephone sets as well as the switching equipment owned by corporate users. Many telecommunications manufacturers are highly specialized, concentrating on only one or two of these categories and even filling specialized niches within the major industry segments. Lucent Technologies, a spinoff of AT&T, is the overall leader in this industry.

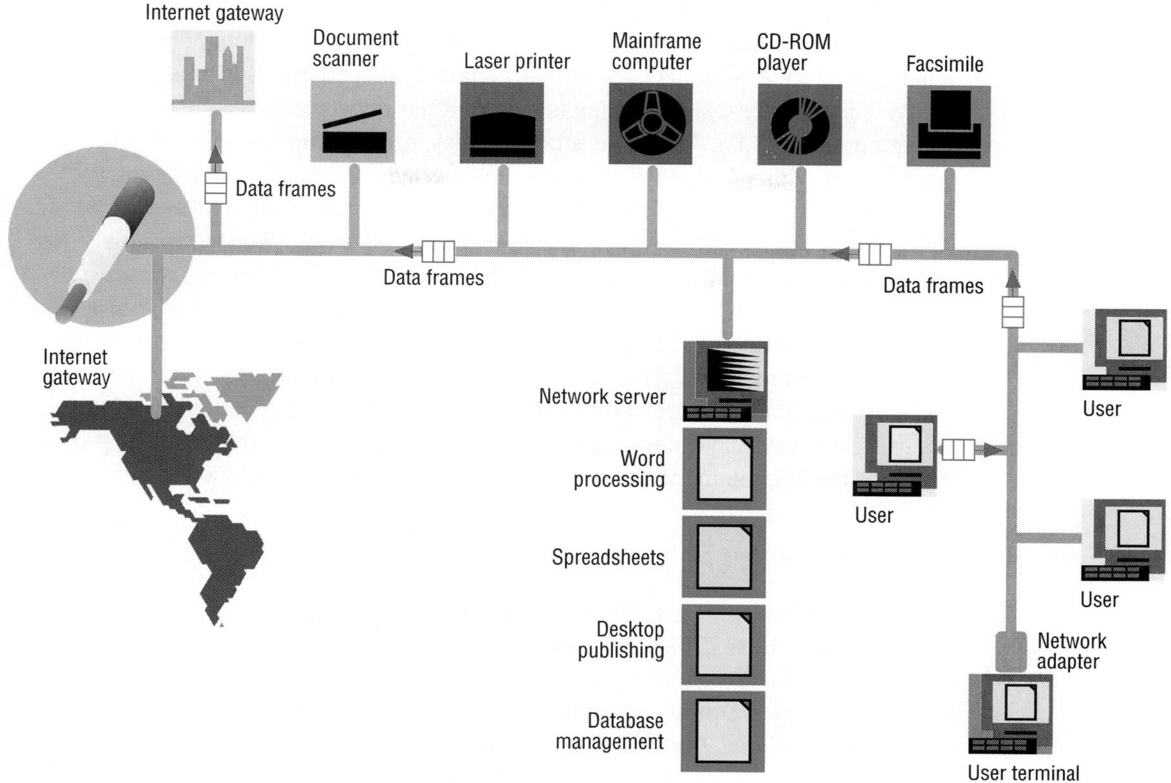

FIGURE 9.3
Local area networks allow multiple users to share peripheral devices such as printers and to access software stored on a shared file server.

ISSUES IN THE INFRASTRUCTURE INDUSTRY

The main issues confronting society regarding the infrastructure industry are ownership and control, subsidies, universal service, spectrum allocation, and network security.

Ownership and Control

The Telecommunications Act of 1996 was intended to resolve ownership and control issues by undoing a tangle of ownership rules and line-of-business restrictions and opening all segments of the infrastructure industry to competition. However, we have seen that the promise of competition is still largely unfulfilled and the principal result has been huge mergers and business alliances that cut across not only geographical boundaries but also the institutional boundaries of yesterday's telecommunications, computer, mass media, and information industries. The hope is that industry structure will remain fluid in response to the newly deregulated environment and to continuing technological change.

The regional Bell operating companies (RBOCs, such as Bell Atlantic and Southwestern Bell) are usually cast as the villains on the ownership issue, because they still maintain a virtual monopoly over local telephone service. The Telecom Act dangled the "carrot" of entry into the long-distance arena over the heads of the RBOCs, if they would agree to open up their local telephone monopolies by leasing portions of their local network infrastructure to competitors. But thus far, they have successfully resisted attempts to open their networks by challenging the Telecommunications Act in the courts (Cauley, 1996). Another issue is whether RBOCs and cable companies can offer advanced data services (such as Internet access) without sharing their networks with competitors, such as America Online.

Even if meaningful competition comes about, there is always the danger that the competition will focus on big-spending corporate infrastructure users, leaving the needs of residential subscribers unmet and perhaps further raising home telephone rates. Although competition in the long-distance market has actually lowered rates overall, *local* telephone rates have risen, to the detriment of poor and elderly telephone subscribers who make few long-distance calls (Cole, 1991). Meanwhile, cable TV rates continue to rise, forcing Congress to revisit the provision of the Telecommunications Act that calls for cable deregulation.

Content Control

Should infrastructure providers also be allowed to control content? There is a potential for abuse if they do, particularly if the infrastructure provider—a local telephone or cable company, for example—holds a virtual monopoly. We discussed this issue in previous chapters in terms of preserving diversity, but there is another facet to the debate: The infrastructure provider could charge favorable rates to its own in-house content provider, driving competitors out of business.

For a long time, U.S. regulators tried to keep the content and the networks separated. The 1934 Communications Act prohibited infrastructure companies from owning a financial interest in content, defining them instead as *common carriers,* who were mandated to sell their services on an equal basis to all comers. This distinction began to erode with the growth of the cable industry, where there are strong financial ties between content providers such as CNN and network providers such as Time Warner Cable. In the 1996 Telecommunications Act, the common carrier principle was set aside, on the assumption that competing infrastructure networks would arise.

Meanwhile, in the cable industry, debate rages on about the status of *must carry* rules that dictate that cable companies have to carry all of the locally available broadcast stations on their systems. Cable operators complain that this includes many seldom-watched local channels that subscribers would prefer to replace with national satellite channels. They see the must carry rules as an infringement on their rights to free speech. Broadcasters counter that without *must carry,* many TV stations would go off the air, reducing the diversity of opinion available to the consumer. In the latest round in this battle, the Supreme Court sided with the broadcasters (Gruley & Roichaux,1997).

Subsidies

Competition also raises the subsidization issue. In an unregulated environment, there is the potential for companies to compete unfairly by using revenues siphoned from businesses in which they enjoy a virtual monopoly to subsidize other businesses where they want to drive out the competition. For example, regional Bell operating companies (RBOCs) could bankroll their entry into the long-distance market with revenues from their monopoly in local service and (temporarily) offer incredibly cheap long-distance calls until they demolished the competition. Before it was broken up in 1984, AT&T had diverted revenues from long-distance operations to subsidize local telephone service with the regulators' blessing. Now consumers and business users have ended up footing that bill, in the form of the *access fees* that are built into our long-distance phone bills. The fees flow back to the local carriers, in the form of a four-cent-per-minute charge added to every long-distance call.

However, there is one group that does not have to pay the access fees, Internet access providers such as UUNET, which need large numbers of telephone lines so that their subscribers can dial into their high-speed Internet access lines. Some argue that this unfairly burdens people without computers—including the poor and the elderly—in essence, forcing them to pay part of the phone bill for the Internet users. Some policy makers want a *modem tax* that would equalize the burden, but others fear that this would only drive low-income homes—and many libraries and schools—off the Internet.

The growing numbers of people who place long-distance telephone calls over the *packet-switched* Internet instead of through conventional circuit-switched telephone networks also rip through a complex fabric of subsidies. Domestic long-distance calls placed on the Internet cost only a few cents per minute, a fraction of the rate on conventional networks, because they evade state and local telephone taxes. As Internet data, they are transformed in the eyes of the Federal Communications Commission from "basic" telecommunication services that incur access fees to support universal service programs (see the next section) to "enhanced" information services that have no such obligations. They are also exempt from local taxes because of a freeze imposed by Congress on taxes on Internet commerce. Finally, the companies that carry the long-distance Internet calls do not have to pay, to local telephone companies, fees that are meant to subsidize local networks, as we discussed in the preceding paragraph.

International long-distance phone calls placed on the Internet can be an even bigger bargain than domestic long-distance calls, cutting costs from dollars per minute to pennies per minute. Here, the trick is to evade the special charges that various countries impose on international phone calls. Once again, the Internet calls do not "count" as phone calls and so get around the charges—at least for now.

Universal Service

This brings us to another vexing infrastructure issue: How to ensure affordable access for all? This debate goes back to the *universal service* doctrine that shaped the regulation of the telephone industry for so many years. Telephone access is a necessity in low-income households, a reality recognized by the public assistance system, which includes telephone service among the basic utilities covered by welfare payments. The low monthly rate offered through *lifeline service* is another option to assist low-income households. However, the rise in local telephone rates since the AT&T divestiture continues to limit telephone penetration in low-income households, and many potential subscribers also have credit problems that prevent them from obtaining telephone service (Mueller & Schement, 1995). And how will universal access be ensured in an environment in which several competing companies offer local telephone service? Won't they naturally cater to businesses and well-off consumers who promise the greatest profits? The Telecommunications Act of 1996 pledges to maintain the concept of universal service. However, mechanisms for subsidizing universal service—such as all telecommunications companies paying into a common fund—have yet to be finalized (Benton Foundation, 1996). Meanwhile, universal service is declining, especially in rural areas where phone companies now refuse to connect remote homes (Volgelstein, 1997).

The spread of the Internet also raises the question of expanding the definition of universal service beyond basic telephone service to data communications, computers, and information services. In 1998, the Schools and Libraries Corporation was established by the FCC to grant discounts of up to 90 percent to libraries and schools for Internet access technologies such as T1 lines. But neither initiative solves the problems of maintenance and training, nor do they extend access to the homes of the disadvantaged. And the funds for all universal service schemes are ultimately passed back to the consumer, further exacerbating the problem of affordable access.

Spectrum Allocation

Historically, communication frequencies were regulated by the government and licensed to communications companies. It was viewed as necessary for the government to regulate the allocation of this scarce and precious resource. However, recent advances in technology, such as digitization and channel compression, and changes in attitudes toward the proper role of government have undermined this position. The tendency now is for the government to hold spectrum auctions and sell frequencies to the highest bidders. For example, the frequencies for the new personal communication service systems were handled this way (Noam, 1996).

Because less government bureaucracy is needed to monitor the new system, the proceeds from the sales go into the public treasury, and theoretically this should reduce the tax burden for all. However, private ownership of communication frequencies can also mean less government influence in ensuring important social goals such as equitable access and diversity of opinion. The application of the new policy has also been uneven. When broadcasters were authorized new channels for digital television service, they received the frequencies at no charge and with few "strings" attached.

Network Security

An information society is inherently dependent on the functioning of its communications infrastructure. Lately, however, some serious cracks have appeared as a result of network overloads, technical bugs, and outright mischief.

In areas with high concentrations of Internet users, it is now difficult to get a dial tone on the telephone. When many people simultaneously take long "surfing safaris" on the Web, they tie up circuits for hours, and there are not enough lines or telephone switches to go around. The situation is exacerbated by Internet access providers who fail to provide sufficient access lines for their customers. When lucky users do get through, they tend to want to keep the connection open for hours, which means busy signals for other phone subscribers (Kim, 1996). The Internet's backbone network is also overworked. One of its founders, Robert Metcalfe, predicts a "gigalapse" in which the entire network will become so overloaded that it will crash (Levy, 1996).

Computer glitches are familiar to Internet users. But they also affect the intelligent telephone network, which is itself a giant computer of sorts. In one incident, all long-distance calls in and out of Washington, DC, were blocked for several hours by a computer malfunction. The "year 2000 problem," or Y2K bug, graphically demonstrates the potential for infrastructure problems to disrupt daily life. Billions were spent to keep planes from crashing and the lights from going out on January 1, 2000 by stopping computers from thinking that it was the year 1900, instead of the year 2000. (Computer dates were allocated only two digits in computer software to save data storage space.)

Deliberate sabotage is another danger. Information technologies have given rise to their own unique forms of criminal behavior (Mandell, 1990; Sieber, 1986). A graduate student at Cornell, Robert Morris, brought down research computers all over the country by injecting a self-replicating, self-propagating virus program into the Internet. Another scenario for future "info wars" against the information infrastructure could include terrorist attacks with computer viruses that might bring down the electrical power grid or key national defense systems.

Piracy

Theft of service is a $10-million-a-year problem for cable television, and it costs cellular radio companies in excess of $1 billion each year. Telephone hackers use "blue boxes" that defeat the inner workings of telephone switching systems and allow telephone calls to be placed free. Stephen Wozniac and Steve Jobs, founders of Apple Computer, gained their first experience with consumer electronics by selling blue boxes to their classmates at the University of California. Now the most popular scams involve the theft of telephone credit card account numbers and the sale, on the black market, of cellular radios with authorization codes that duplicate those of legal users.

For every security threat, there is a security countermeasure, but at what cost? Each new password and personal identification code is a further burden on the network user. Technological fixes such as fingerprint scanners and retinal scanners would add to consumer costs and raise privacy concerns. But then again, theft of service is also an expense borne by the user: Infrastructure providers just pass on the losses to their customers. The most cost-effective fix is network monitoring, but that destroys privacy and chills freedom of expression by allowing network providers to listen in on communications.

STOP & REVIEW

1. **What are the major types of consumer and business telephone services?**
2. **What are the demographics of people without telephones and cable TV?**
3. **Why are phone calls completed over the Internet so cheap?**
4. **How is universal service implemented in the United States?**
5. **How secure are the infrastructure networks we rely on?**

SUMMARY AND REVIEW

WHAT WERE THE EARLY ORIGINS OF TODAY'S INFORMATION INFRASTRUCTURE?

Morse's telegraph and Bell's telephone were the first electronic communications networks. The telegraph spawned newspaper wire services that were forerunners of computer information services today.

WHAT ROLE DID AT&T PLAY?

Bell founded the company that was to become American Telephone and Telegraph (AT&T). AT&T's effort to monopolize the infrastructure by buying the Western Union Telegraph Company in 1910 led to government regulation that shaped the entire infrastructure industry for decades. Important interventions included the Communications Act of 1934 and the modified final judgment (MFJ) that forced AT&T to divest itself of the companies (regional Bell operating companies, RBOCs) that provided local telephone service, while retaining its long-distance network. These policies established the basic structure of the telephone industry today.

HOW DID CABLE SPREAD THROUGHOUT THE UNITED STATES?

Cable television started as a shared antenna service for rural communities in 1948. A freeze on new TV stations between 1948 and 1952 gave cable an early boost. Between 1966 and 1972, the FCC kept cable out of large TV markets to protect broadcasters. Cable operators expanded into suburban areas beginning in 1972 and reached the largest cities only in the early 1980s. The Cable Act of 1984 left cable largely unregulated.

HOW DID THE WIRELESS INFRASTRUCTURE DEVELOP?

Although mobile telephone service dates back to 1946, early systems were plagued by insufficient capacity. Paging services originated in the early 1960s to meet some of the demand for mobile communication. In 1978 cellular radio service was introduced in the United States, expanding the capacity of mobile telephone networks. Early wireless pay TV services were rivals to cable, but modern direct broadcast satellite (DBS) systems provide more serious competition.

WHAT IS THE SIGNIFICANCE OF THE TELECOMMUNICATIONS ACT OF 1996?

The aim of the Telecommunications Act was to remove most of the regulations that apply to telecommunications infrastructure industries and replace regulation with competition. However, the immediate impact of the act was to trigger a wave of consolidation within the industry while local telephone companies continued to resist competition.

HOW WERE THE TECHNICAL LIMITATIONS OF THE FIRST TELEPHONES OVERCOME?

The first phones were very limited in their range, connectivity, and ease of use. Amplifiers and carrier systems overcame the limitations of distance and untangled the maze of wires that darkened the skies over major cities. The capacity of telephone networks has continually improved with coaxial cable, microwave, satellite, and fiber optic transmission systems. Meanwhile, advances in switching technology gradually reduced the labor-intensiveness of the telephone network and made it possible for telephone subscribers to dial numbers anywhere in the world automatically. Digital communication first came to the telephone in 1962, making possible further improvements in capacity and transmission quality and ultimately leading to such "intelligent network" services as caller ID.

HOW DO CABLE TELEVISION PICTURES GET TO THE HOME?

The cable operator's headend picks up transmissions from satellite, microwave, broadcast, and local studio sources. The channels are combined electronically and transmitted to the home over a coaxial cable network. A set-top converter is used to recover the channels and play them on the home television receiver. Pay TV signals may be scrambled so that only homes that pay an additional monthly fee may receive them. New addressable cable systems make it possible to authorize electronically the reception of entire pay channels or specific programs, a type of distribution called pay-per-view.

WHAT ARE THE IMPORTANT TECHNICAL TRENDS IN DIGITAL NETWORKS?

The modems that convert computer digits to analog data for transmission have reached their limit. New cable television modems and digital subscriber line services transmit millions of bits of information per second from the home. Packet switching provides a modern alternative to conventional telephone switches that integrates data, audio, and video on the Internet.

WHAT ROLE MIGHT WIRELESS COMMUNICATIONS PLAY IN THE FUTURE?

Digitization has also meant vast improvements in the capacity and quality of wireless networks for mobile communications. New satellites with low earth orbits and the opening of new frequencies for terrestrial communication make wireless technologies possible contenders in the battle to build the information superhighway.

WHO RUNS THE INTERNET?

The high-capacity backbone that interconnects major Internet nodes is operated by interexchange carriers, and local connections to those nodes are handled by information service providers (ISPs) and local telephone companies. ISPs provide basic internet connections and sometimes also provide content (as in the case of America Online), but most content providers are independent.

WHAT ARE THE BASIC INFRASTRUCTURE SERVICES?

Infrastructure services are broadly categorized into residential and business services and also by the type of information they carry—text, audio, or video. Business users have a number of options available that may be unfamiliar to home users, including private telephone switches (PBXs) and organizational discounts on groups of telephone lines (Centrex) as well as high-speed digital connections, such as T1 lines.

HOW DO PEOPLE USE THE TELECOMMUNICATIONS INFRASTRUCTURE?

Telephones are found in nearly all U.S. homes. Over two-thirds have cable television connections. Infrastructure access is not equally available to all. Low-income and minority households are less likely than others to have phones, cable, or Internet connections.

WHY IS THERE A TREND TOWARD FOSTERING MORE COMPETITION IN THE INFRASTRUCTURE INDUSTRY?

Policy makers hope that competition will mean lower prices and more advanced and faster services for the telecommunications consumer. They believe that competition is the best way to create the so-called information superhighway and preserve the universal service principle.

WHAT IMPORTANT CHALLENGES DOES THE TELECOMMUNICATIONS INFRASTRUCTURE POSE FOR SOCIETY?

Society must also decide how to allocate scarce resources, such as the communications spectrum, to competing interests. And the growing reliance on the information infrastructure for all manner of commercial and public purposes makes society increasingly vulnerable to technical disruption of infrastructure providers.

HOW IS THE TELEPHONE INDUSTRY ORGANIZED?

Telephone companies are classified according to the scope of the calls they are permitted to carry. Local exchange carriers (LECs) can carry local calls, whereas interexchange carriers (IXCs) carry domestic long-distance calls, and international record carriers (IRCs) carry international calls. Local access and transport areas (LATAs), established under the terms of the AT&T divestiture, distinguish local and long-distance calls. Competitive local exchange carriers (CLECs) are a new type of telephone carrier permitted to carry local telephone calls in competition with an established local exchange carrier. Many large corporations also maintain their own private telephone networks.

Electronic Resources

For up-to-the-minute URLs about *Communications Infrastructure,* access the MEDIA NOW site on the World Wide Web at:

http://communication.wadsworth.com/

CHAPTER 10

Public Relations

THIS CHAPTER IS BY **DON BATES,**
MANAGING DIRECTOR, MARKETING AND NEW MEDIA, MEDIA DISTRIBUTION SERVICES, NEW YORK, NY.
MR. BATES ALSO TEACHES AT THE NEW SCHOOL UNIVERSITY, AND AT THE NEW YORK INSTITUTE OF TECHNOLOGY.

WHAT'S AHEAD

This chapter describes the practice of public relations, the organized effort to gain favorable action on behalf of one or more goals or objectives. In this chapter, we trace the origins of the public relations profession, examine the current structure of the industry, and describe the technological trends that are transforming the public relations industry within the information society.

WWW

Access the MEDIA NOW site on the World Wide Web at:
http://communication.wadsworth.com/
Choose "Chapter 10" from the selection box to access electronic information and other sites relevant to this chapter.

CONVERSATION WITH THE PERSONAL RE-EDITOR (PR)

Why don't people like me? I want them to like me.

Candidly, sir, it's hard to like anyone as rich, powerful, and ruthless as you are. You need the Personal Re-editor!

If you weren't a computer, I'd fire you for saying that!

Let's start right there. I'm going to put my Nasty Filter™! on all of your electronic communications. From now on, whenever you yell "You're fired," it will come out *"We're not communicating effectively."*

You @!!!#% computer, I'm going to kick your keyboard down the stairs for being so impertinent!

"You're a nice computer, please tell me more!" See how it works. You sound more likable already!

Oh, all right, as long as I don't have to listen to my own twaddle. What about my yellow fangs? My own children cringe when I smile.

I'm going to completely re-edit your video image. No more fangs, no more steely glare, no more snarl.

So how's this going to help me slip the AT&T deal by Congress? They're the last piece. Then I'll own everything, everything, I tell you!

I'll synthesize a flattering DeeVee biography out of your new image and send it as electronic mail to every registered voter. The news media will get a likable interactive news release that they can interview themselves. Viewers will be able to send a personalized video call to their senators demanding that they okay the deal.

But what if they still don't like me?

Don't worry, sir, the bio will remind everyone that you own controlling interests in several consumer credit databases and tactfully mention their outstanding credit card balances. If you just give people a chance to like you, they will, sir, believe me, they will!

How much will my lawyers charge for this?

"Isn't this unethical?" No sir, computers don't have any ethics!

Chapter Outline

History of Public Relations
Hail, Caesar!
The Origins of Modern Public Relations
The American Way
Public Relations in the Age of the Robber Barons
PR Pioneers
Public Relations Matures
The Rise of Public Relations Ethics
Trends in Public Relations Technology
New Mass media—TV Leads the Way
Videoconferencing
Satellite Broadcasting
Video News Releases
Personal Computer
On-Line News and Information
Advanced Telephony
The Internet—A New Dimension for Public Relations
Forms of Public Relations
The Publics of Public Relations
Good vs. Bad PR: A Commentary
Elements of Successful Public Relations
Industry Demographics
The Public Relations Profession
Public Relations Issues
Private Interests vs. the Public Interest
Professional Ethics
Professional Development
Use of Research and Evaluation
Public Relations and Society
Summary and Review

HISTORY OF PUBLIC RELATIONS

Edward Bernays, whom many have considered the founder of modern public relations, wrote, "The three main elements of public relations are practically as old as society: informing people, persuading people, or integrating people with people. Of course, the means and methods of accomplishing these ends have changed as society has changed. In a technologically advanced society, like that of today, ideas are communicated by newspaper, magazine, film, radio, television, and other methods" (Bernays, 1961, p. 12).

For Bernays and other historians of the practice, public relations has always gone hand in hand with civilization; in their eyes, much of recorded history can be reinterpreted as the practice of public relations. Whereas primitive societies were ruled almost exclusively through fear and intimidation, more advanced cultures learned to depend on discussion and debate. As rulers sought to build consensus, persuasion became less and less grounded in force and more and more grounded in words. With the invention of writing, public relations began to take shape.

Whether they were promoting their image as warriors or kings, leaders of ancient civilizations such as Sumeria, Babylonia, Assyria, and Persia used poems and other writings to promote their prowess in battle and politics. In Egypt much of the art and architecture (statues, temples, tombs) was used to impress on the public the greatness of priests, nobles, and scribes.

In ancient Israel, the Bible and other religious texts became a powerful means in history for molding the public mind. With the growth of the Hellenic world, the word, both written and spoken, exploded as a force for social integration. The Athens marketplace became a center of public discussion concerning the conduct of business and public life. Oratory flourished, and the public interest became a central concern of philosophical speculation.

Hail, Caesar!

In ancient Rome, the force of public relations was evident in phrases such as *vox populi, vox Dei* ("the voice of the people is the voice of God") and *res publicae* ("public affairs"), which means "republic." Julius Caesar carefully prepared the Romans for his crossing of the Rubicon in

PUBLIC RELATIONS TIME LINE

49 B.C.E.	Julius Caesar promotes himself in "Caesar's Gallic Wars"
1600	Catholic church's Congregatio de Propaganda Fide established
1792	French establish world's first propaganda ministry
1871	P. T. Barnum's "Greatest Show on Earth" formed
1900	Publicity Bureau of Boston established
1904	Ivy Lee becomes public relations counselor
1913	Ludlow Massacre establishes value of corporate public relations
1920	The press release is invented
1929	Bernays stages Torches of Freedom march to promote smoking
1948	Public Relations Society of America founded
1980	Birth of video public relations
1989	*Exxon Valdez* public relations disaster
1998	Council of Public Relations Firms founded

49 B.C.E. by sending reports such as "Caesar's Gallic Wars" (52 B.C.E.) on his epic achievements as governor of Gaul. Most historians agree that he also wrote his Commentaries as propaganda for himself.

Recognizing the power of news to mold public opinion, Caesar published a daily paper called *Acta Diurna* ("daily acts" or "daily records") that continued for 400 years. Besides notices of births, deaths, and marriages, it contained government decrees and accounts of fires and severe weather.

When Christianity emerged at the height of Roman influence, the teachings of Jesus and his apostles took center stage in the battle for religious dominance in the public mind. Once the Christian church took shape, Bernays explains, it relied on eloquent speeches and letters, such as Paul's epistle to the Romans, to win converts and guide the faithful.

The Origins of Modern Public Relations

Public relations continued to develop even during medieval times, using the "new media" of that day, such as the Bayeaux Tapestry, a woven wall hanging that extolled the Norman Conquest of England in 1066. It was not until the Renaissance and Reformation that the foundation of the modern world arose—and with it the underpinnings of the kind of public relations that has become vital to the management of public and private institutions. Great documents of liberty crystallized the power of public opinion. For example, the Magna Carta—the thirteenth century English charter of rights and liberties—was the inspiration for the U.S. Constitution.

The word *propaganda* was originated by the Catholic Church. In the seventeenth century, it set up its *Congregatio de Propaganda Fide,* the "congregation for propagating the faith." In doing so, it explicitly acknowledged the need for a third party to facilitate communication between the government and the people (Bernays, 1961). With the spread of new knowledge in new forms—such as translations in the fifteenth century of the *Bible* from Latin into everyday languages,

Public opinion is the aggregate view of the general population.

Propaganda is the intentional influence of attitudes and opinions.

mass-printed books, and newspapers—came an explosion of **public opinion.** When the French Revolution arrived, the stage was set. In their Declaration of the Rights of Man and Citizens (1789), the leaders of the French Revolution proclaimed the right of citizens to express and communicate thought freely.

In 1792 the National Assembly of France created the first **propaganda** ministry. It was part of the Ministry of the Interior and it was called the *Bureau d'Esprit,* or "Bureau of the Spirit." It subsidized editors and sent agents to various parts of the country to win public support for the French Revolution.

The American Way

England's rebellious American colonies produced a host of public relations experts who used oratory, newspapers, meetings, committees, pamphlets, and correspondence to win people to their cause. Included among them were Benjamin Franklin, John Peter Zenger, Samuel Adams, Alexander Hamilton, James Madison, and John Jay. Adams has been called the great press agent of the American Revolution for fashioning the machinery of political change. Hamilton, Madison, and Jay are credited with winning ratification of the Constitution by publishing letters they had written to the press in 1787–1788. Today, these letters are known as the *Federalist Papers.*

In the same light, the other great documents produced by the founders of the United States—the Declaration of Independence, the Constitution, and the Bill of Rights—may all be seen as masterworks of public relations. These documents, so essential to the notion of tying one's destiny to the public interest, also helped establish the United States as the breeding ground for pursuing **public relations** as a business as well as a profession that represented the diverse interests of democracy and free enterprise.

Public relations are organized activities intended to favorably influence the opinions and behavior of the public.

Many American legends are the result of public relations campaigns. For example, the legend of Daniel Boone was created by a landowner to promote settlement in Kentucky. Davy Crockett's exploits were largely created by his press agent, Matthew St. Clair, in an effort to woo votes away from President Andrew Jackson. The master of all nineteenth century press agents was Phineas T. Barnum. Showman par excellence, Barnum created a wave of publicity stunts and coverage that made his circus, "The Greatest Show on Earth," an irresistible draw in every city and town it visited after its inception in 1871. Press agentry was so successful that it became an essential undertaking for companies that depended on the public's attention. Indeed, the success of Barnum and his colleagues in manipulating the press was so great that, to this day, the media still harbor skepticism toward anything that suggests commercial promotion.

Public Relations in the Age of the Robber Barons

It was in the last two decades of the nineteenth century and the early years of the twentieth century that public relations bloomed in the fullest sense. This was the era of America's wild and woolly development as the center of capitalist enterprise, when industry, the railroads, and utilities exploded across the face of the nation.

The hard-bitten attitudes of businessmen toward the public were epitomized in 1892 by the cold-blooded methods of Henry Clay Frick to crush a labor union in the Carnegie-Frick Steel Companies plant in Homestead, Pennsylvania. The employees' strike was ultimately broken and the union destroyed by the use of the Pennsylvania State militia. Brute force might have won that battle, but the employees would eventually win the war of public opinion. Much of public relations history is woven into this unending struggle between employer and employee, though today, fortunately, the war is waged with public relations professionals, not private police or armed guards (Cutlip, Center, & Broom, 1985).

Corporations quickly learned the value of combating hostility and courting public favor through professional public relations. Corporations also learned the value of **publicity** in attracting customers. Companies across America established **press bureaus** to manage the dissemination and coverage of news favorable to themselves and unfavorable to their competitors. The "battle of the currents" between Westinghouse (advocates of alternating-current power transmission systems) and Thomas A. Edison's General Electric (direct current) is one of the earliest examples of how public relations was first conducted in the United States by powerful economic interests. Using former newspapermen as their publicists, the companies fought each other tooth and nail for media attention, political influence, and marketing advantage.

Vol. 2.] "GO AHEAD!!" [No. 3.
THE CROCKETT ALMANAC
1841.
Tussel with a Bear. See page 9.
Containing Adventures, Exploits, Sprees & Scrapes in the West, & Life and Manners in the Backwoods.
Nashville, Tennessee. Published by Ben Harding.

BORN ON A MOUNTAINTOP. An early public relations success in the Untied States was Davy Crockett, many of whose feats were inventions of his press agent, Matthew St. Clair.

Trade associations also caught the public relations fever in the late 1800s. The Association of American Railroads claims it was the first organization to use the term *public relations,* in 1897 in the *Year Book of Railway Literature.*

In the 1900s, public relations came of age with the evolution from individual press agents and publicists to counseling firms that offered the services of experts in the field. The nation's first publicity firm, The Publicity Bureau, was founded in Boston in 1900 by George V. S. Michaelis, Herbert Small, and Thomas O. Marvin. In 1906 the bureau came into prominence when it was hired by the nation's railroads to oppose adverse regulatory legislation that was then in Congress. The firm failed in its efforts, but soon thereafter most railroads established their own public relations departments.

Publicity is the key function of public relations directed to obtaining free, favorable media coverage.

Press bureau is the office of an organization charged with disseminating information to the media.

PR Pioneers

Ivy Ledbetter Lee. Lee was perhaps the most famous of the early public relations practitioners, and with good reason. Lee helped develop many of the techniques and principles that practitioners follow today. He believed in open communications with the media, and he was candid and frank in his approach to the press. He understood that good corporate performance was the basis of good publicity. Many believe that his major contribution was to humanize wealthy businessmen and to cast big business in a more positive light.

Lee, a former Wall Street reporter, became a public relations counselor with George Parker in 1904, although he didn't use the term *public relations* until more than a decade later. He believed that business had to tell its story honestly, accurately, and openly in order to win public understanding and support. Some of his most famous clients were the Pennsylvania Railroad and the Rockefeller family.

On their behalf, he developed a publicity policy of "the public be informed"—in contrast to the infamous statement of financier William Vanderbilt, "the public be damned." When he sent news releases and other statements to the press, Lee included a copy of his Declaration of Principles, which read in part,

> This is not a secret press bureau. All our work is done in the open. We aim to supply news. This is not an advertising agency; if you think any of our matter properly ought to go to your business office, do not use it. Our matter is accurate. Further details on any subject treated will be supplied promptly, and any editor will be assisted most cheerfully in verifying directly any statement of fact. In brief, our plan is, frankly and openly, on behalf of the business concerns and public institutions, to supply to the press and public of the United States prompt and accurate information concerning subjects which it is of value and interest to the public to know about.

Some of Lee's most important work was for the Rockefeller family, which he began to assist in 1914. In that year John D. Rockefeller, Jr., asked for his advice in handling the so-called Ludlow Massacre that began in 1913 in southern Colorado when some 9000 people went on strike. In April 1914, an accidental shot led to a battle in which several of the miners, two women, and 11 children were killed.

With the Rockefeller name being pilloried across the land, Lee told the younger Rockefeller to practice a policy of openness. He had Rockefeller visit mining camps after the strike was over to see for himself the conditions under which miners worked. He also advised John D. Rockefeller, Sr., who was attacked by muckrakers as an arrogant capitalist, to let the public know about his charitable contributions, which, until then, he had kept secret.

In the end, Lee died in disgrace for putting his considerable skills to work in getting the Soviet Union recognized in the United States in the 1930s and for assisting the Interessen Gemeinschaft Farben Industrie, a Dye Trust that was eventually taken over by the Nazis. The Germans didn't take Lee's advice, which was to be open and honest, but the damage was done. Lee was covered in the press as "Hitler Press Agent" (Hiebert, 1966).

Edward L. Bernays. Bernays and his associate and wife, Doris Fleischman, were among those who competed with Lee for prominence during this time. Bernays is credited with coining the term **public relations counsel** in the first book on the subject, *Crystallizing Public Opinion,* originally published in 1923. In 1928, he published *Propaganda* and in 1952 his textbook *Public Relations.*

> A **public relations counsel** is a person who provides professional public relations advice.

In his practice and in his many books, Bernays saw public relations as an *art applied to a science*—the art of communications applied to social science. He and his colleagues went well beyond publicity in their roles as consultants to business, government, and not-for-profit enterprises.

In 1917, during World War I, the Committee on Public Information, also known as the **Creel Committee** after the name of its chairman, former newspaper reporter George Creel, was organized to help sell war bonds and generally to promote the war effort. Bernays was among those who lent his talents to the war's publicity front. World War II had the Office of War Information, which organized

> The **Creel Committee** built public support for U.S. involvement in World War I.

one of the largest public relations campaigns in history to muster support for America's entry into the war. Between world conflicts, the Roosevelt administration relied heavily on public relations techniques to promote its New Deal legislation.

Bernays actually became a full-fledged public relations counselor in 1919 when he established his own *counseling firm* with his wife. Over the years, they represented hundreds of clients in all major fields of business. They also worked with not-for-profit organizations such as the National Association for the Advancement of Colored People (NAACP).

BULLET THEORY.
World War I showed the power of public relations in getting citizens involved in the war effort.

One of Bernays' most famous and quintessential campaigns was the 1929 Torches of Freedom March in which he had ten carefully chosen women walk down Fifth Avenue smoking cigarettes. The women were advancing feminism while setting the stage for a surge in smoking by women. What the public and the press didn't know was that he was employed by the American Tobacco Company, raising an ethical issue that still confronts the public relations profession today.

Bernays also helped establish beer as "the beverage of moderation" and created innumerable **front groups,** such as the Trucking Information Bureau and Better Living Through Increased Highway Transportation, to pursue private interests with the support and assistance of the general public.

Recently, two books have been published that view Bernays as the father or master of *spin,* the art of intentionally manipulating public opinion in support of one's products, services, ideas, or issues without regard for truth or reality. These books are *PR!: A Social History of Spin,* by Stuart Ewen (1996), and *The Father of Spin: Edward L. Bernays and the Birth of Public Relations,* by Larry Tye (1998). Ewen says spin "obliterates the distinction between persuasion and deception."

Despite this criticism, Bernays remains a dominant figure in the field of public relations for his books and his tireless efforts to educate generations of PR practitioners, as well as institutions representing business, government, and not-for-profit enterprise, in the value of public relations as a tool of management and human relations.

A **front group** works on behalf of another organization whose direct involvement might be controversial.

Arthur W. Page. Page was another pioneer. He integrated public relations throughout AT&T and the Bell system when he was the regulated company's first public relations vice president in 1927. Page was a pace-setter, building AT&T's reputation as a *good corporate citizen.* He promulgated five principles of successful corporate public relations that are as valid today as they were more than 50 years ago:

1. To make sure management thoughtfully analyzes its overall relation to the public.

2. To create a system for informing all employees about the company's general policies and practices.

3. To create a system giving contact employees (those having direct dealings with the public) the knowledge needed to be reasonable and polite to the public.
4. To create a system drawing employee and public questions and criticism back up through the organization to management.
5. To ensure frankness in telling the public about the company's actions. (Seitel, 1997)

Public Relations Matures

A **press release** summarizes news and information in a form that is preferred by the media.

The **press release** was invented in the 1920s. It is written in the form of a news story but presents only the point of view of the organization (or public relations firm) that produces it. Newspaper reporters often use information from press releases to help them write their own stories. It is said that Ohio Bell Telephone discovered that if it handed out "canned" news in this form, newspaper reporters would stop going to telephone rate hearings (Bleifuss, 1994).

With the post–World War II economic boom, which turned the United States into the wealthiest country on earth, public relations prospered as never before. New and old institutions of business, government, and not-for-profit enterprise had seen what public relations had done for the war effort, and they wanted to tap its evolving power for purposes of publicizing their products and services for the burgeoning consumer markets, both at home and abroad.

Public relations agencies are for-profit consulting firms staffed by public relations professionals.

By the late 1960s, public relations had matured into a full-blown professional enterprise, comprising, in the United States, several hundred **public relations agencies,** large and small, and more than 100,000 individual practitioners whose ranks have mushroomed to double that number as the new millennium dawns. Along the way, the PR "legends" and "stars" of yesteryear were replaced by a new breed of highly skilled executives whose names and front-page exploits became far less important as a measure of success than their day-to-day accomplishments as professional public relations communicators.

As a group, PR practitioners grew more alike in their education, knowledge, and practices. On the job, they became the promotional voice for thousands of public and private interests, performing a wide variety of communications functions aimed at swaying the views of customers, employees, stockholders, taxpayers, investors, and legislators.

PR practitioners also devoted increasing amounts of time and effort to more sophisticated issues such as improving the relations of their clients with their employees, customers, or investors. At the highest levels, they are involved in **crisis communications** and what has become known as **reputation management.** Public relations specialists are now an integral part of top management, often reporting directly to the president or CEO of the institutions they serve.

Crisis communications are designed to ameliorate the public relations impact of crises.

Reputation management involves managing an institution's public image.

The Rise of Public Relations Ethics

The contributions of early pioneers such as Bernays, Lee, and Page did much to inject a spirit of professionalism into the practice of public relations. They were firmly opposed to Barnum's credo, "There's a sucker born every minute." Throughout history, however, critics have charged that public relations too often manipulates the public interest for private gain, using the press, special events, and other activities merely to sell more products or to create an image that masks or sugarcoats an otherwise problematic reputation.

At the macro level, critics such as Marvin Olasky (1987) say that public relations in the late nineteenth and early twentieth centuries worked to restrict economic competition. At the micro level, some critics, particularly in the media, think that what public relations people do every day is frivolous, concocted, inaccurate, superficial, and even dangerous to liberty and freedom.

The **Public Relations Society of America (PRSA)** is the main professional organization in public relations.

Are these criticisms valid? In some instances, yes. In one notable case, a Hollywood publicist concocted a story about a fictitious "best-dressed" contest to promote to movie stardom the career of an unknown by the name of Rita Hayworth, who later became a famous movie star of the 1940s and 1950s. In another incident that wound up before the Supreme Court, railroad publicists created phony organizations to criticize the rival trucking industry.

Incidents such as these led to the formation of the **Public Relations Society of America (PRSA)** in 1948 and to the promulgation by that organization in 1950 of a *Code of Professional Standards* (see page 341) and in 1959 of a *Declaration of Principles,* both of which have been strengthened over the years to reflect shifts and changes in moral and social values. Since these voluntary guidelines were introduced, more than 200 colleges and universities have begun offering undergraduate and graduate degrees in public relations.

1. **What were the contributions of Edward Bernays and Ivy Lee to the development of modern public relations?**
2. **What have been some of the greatest public relations successes in American history?**
3. **What is propaganda?**
4. **What are some social criticisms of public relations?**

TRENDS IN PUBLIC RELATIONS TECHNOLOGY

Throughout most of the history of public relations, practitioners depended on a pen or pencil and a printing press to do their jobs. All they needed was a means to write down their thoughts and a way to distribute what they had written to their target audiences. With the invention of electricity, technology in the larger sense became more important. Mass media and mass communication became the norm in public relations activities. Radio and television emerged as powerful new carriers of the public relations message. The telephone, electric typewriter, and photocopier also became essential public relations tools. But perhaps the most significant technological advances of all have been television and the personal computer.

New Mass Media—TV Leads the Way

Only in the last 20 years or so has television been truly harnessed as a new technology for public relations purposes. Using in-house and commercial facilities for production and distribution, public relations practitioners in companies, government agencies, and not-for-profit organizations began in the 1970s to create their own broadcast-quality television programs and products.

The most popular applications came in the form of promotional videos, video news releases (press releases distributed in video form), and videoconferencing (teleconference with moving images). Public relations practitioners saw a vast opportunity in the exploding public addiction to television and film. Television brought them closer to their audiences and gave them increasing control over the content and delivery of communications.

Videoconferencing

Videoconferencing has become especially effective, because it enables large audiences at different sites to see each other and listen and talk by phone. Today, many large corporations have their own in-house television networks that broadcast internally produced meetings, employee relations programs, news conferences, and special events. These networks are also used to inform, train, and motivate sales staff, executive management, and others. Similar facilities can be rented through major hotel chains and private videoconferencing suppliers.

An early example of high-powered videoconferencing for PR purposes occurred in 1982, when Johnson & Johnson used the technology to reach hundreds of reporters in 30 cities with breaking news and information about the Tylenol product-tampering scare. Coca-Cola also used videoconferencing to stage an international celebration of its 100th anniversary with a live, two-day satellite broadcast linking its U.S. event site in Atlanta with simultaneous events in London, Sydney, Tokyo, Nairobi, and Rio de Janeiro as part of a spectacular global party.

Satellite Broadcasting

With the development of satellites to transmit television and radio programming domestically and around the world, *satellite broadcasting* has become an important public relations tool that continues to grow in popularity for certain applications.

A **satellite media tour** is a press briefing broadcast via satellite.

Satellite media tours (SMTs) are the primary application for public relations professionals who need to work with the media long-distance. With an SMT, a celebrity or company spokesperson spends a few hours in a broadcast studio being interviewed by reporters who are receiving the video and sound in their own respective studios. Interviewers may broadcast the session live, edit it into a larger news or talk show, or tape it for later use. A good spokesperson can handle 10–20 interviews in 2–4 hours. As part of the SMT, videotape of a product or service can be transmitted to interested stations.

SMTs are typically used when the spokesperson can't or doesn't want to travel to many remote locations for press interviews. Thus they are very convenient for CEOs, movie stars, and rock musicians, whose intensely busy schedules and lifestyles make it difficult, if not impossible, for them to travel freely. For example, to promote Energizer Battery's "Toy Line," a toll-free number where viewers can write for a free brochure, *Toys with Play Power: A Grown-Ups' Guide to Great*

Kids' Stuff, the company held an SMT in advance of the hectic holiday gift-buying season. The SMT featured Joanne and Stephanie Oppenheim, co-founders of a consumer research organization that bears their name and provides independent reviews of the best products for children. The two experts answered questions, talked about toy trends, and offered advice on the best multi-cultural and gender-free toys, toys for kids with special needs, and tips for shopping for toys. The SMT resulted in 27 telecasts, including major stations and markets across the country.

Video News Releases

A **video news release (VNR)** is a video version of a traditional printed press release.

Video news releases (VNRs) are one of the newest and hottest public relations tools. Developed from television and VCR technology, these are the equivalent of print news releases, except that they are written and designed to be seen and heard, not read. They have become an especially important tool for public relations professionals who want to reach large audiences via television. They enjoy great credibility because they are used as part of TV news broadcasts. Since the advent of VNRs, the number of firms making them has grown into the hundreds and the number of videos into the thousands.

Although they can be expensive to produce, the free coverage that VNRs receive as publicity material is often extensive, so they are usually well worth the expense, especially compared to what an organization would have to pay in paid advertising to gain comparable on-air time and attention. Stations generally edit them to suit their needs. Typically, they are 90 seconds to 2 minutes in length and feature separate video and voice tracks. They are also packaged with 3–5 minutes of additional, unedited "b-roll" (outtake) footage, along with printed scripts known as "slates," to facilitate editing.

DWJ Television and its sister company, PCS Broadcast Services, teamed up to produce a VNR to promote a new packaging innovation called the "Clean-Top" carrier as an alternative to the traditional six-pack beverage ring carrier, which has been implicated in the deaths by entanglement of birds and other animals. Sponsored by Forma-Pack, the manufacturer of the new carrier, which features a ringless design, the VNR incorporated interviews with Roger Powers, president of Keep America Beautiful, and Forma-Pack's CEO, Peter Sust, as well as footage depicting the plight of "Ed the Duck," who got entangled in a ring-top carrier. To support the video news release, which was distributed by satellite during and after "Earth Week," DWJ and PCS sent samples of the "Clean-Top" carrier to stations, accompanied by a letter promoting different angles for the story. The VNR garnered 102 telecasts with an audience of more than 8 million viewers.

Unedited b-roll packages are also a form of VNR. They are distributed to TV stations in much the same way as video releases. On the heels of their historic race for the home run record, for example, Mark "Big Mac" McGwire and Sammy Sosa appeared in national McDonald's commercials featuring the company's flagship sandwich, the Big Mac. On behalf of Golin/Harris, McDonald's corporate PR firm, West Glen Communications, a national video production company, recorded outtakes of the McGwire-Sosa "shoot" for a b-roll package that was fed via satellite on October 14 and 15, 1998, the same week the commercials began airing. Within two days of the feed, West Glen had placed the footage on more than 100

MEDIA WATCH

Tips for Effective Video News Releases

- The narrator or "reporter" is heard, not seen, because stations prefer to show their own reporters on air, usually holding a microphone with the station's logo.
- The unseen narrator or reporter is recorded on only one of the videotape's two soundtracks so that stations can have their on-air reporters renarrate the track without losing other essential sound. When a release is delivered via satellite, versions with and without a narrator may be fed.
- Titles identifying spokespersons, experts, and others who speak in the video or on-air are left for stations to do in their own graphic style. The information for titles may be put on a printed transcript accompanying the tape or in the opening titles of the satellite feed.
- A suggested "lead-in" or script for a station's on-air reporter or anchor may also be put in the transcript or opening titles, as well as an "anchor graphic" (the picture seen over the shoulder of an anchor introducing the story in the videotape).
- To facilitate editing by stations, the printed transcript may include precise timings for each scene in the release or in accompanying additional footage.
- Raw footage is included so that stations can have additional video to work with when and if they edit the release.

Example: Neutrogena Soap

The main body of the video news release concentrates on debunking the myth that expensive lotions and moisturizers can keep skin from aging. A third-party spokesperson—a noted dermatologist—states that the best way to take care of facial skin is to wash with warm water and a milk soap like Neutrogena. The product is mentioned only once, and then in passing. While the announcer talks about expensive products that do not really work, the video shows cosmetics counters in department stores. It shows the doctor examining a patient's skin and, while he is talking, a woman is washing her face. While the Neutrogena packaging is not seen at any point, the soap being used is the clear, amber-colored bar that has become synonymous with the product.

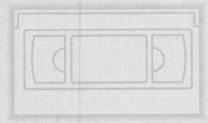

television stations nationwide, including network affiliates in such top markets as New York, Los Angeles, Chicago, Dallas/Ft. Worth, Detroit, and Atlanta. National hits included CBS's "Up to the Minute" and "E! News Daily" on E! Entertainment TV.

Despite their widespread use, video news releases have generated a great deal of controversy, usually initiated by newspaper and magazine articles expressing shock that some television news stories are actually produced by public relations people. Public relations people, on the other hand, argue that a video release can supply visuals and an in-depth approach to a subject beyond the reach of rushed daily news shows. Despite this difference of opinion, there is general agreement that the people who produce video news releases should do them professionally, identifying their sources, and that stations receiving them should judge their suitability for broadcast on the basis of whether they represent their subjects objectively.

Personal Computer

Today, all public relations firms or departments have personal computers, often linked by internal and external networks. Whereas only a few years ago press lists were manually typed on envelopes and labels, or imprinted from metal Addressograph plates, they are now routinely maintained on computer. Documents that once took hours to produce can now be put together in a matter of minutes. Similarly, the labeling and mailing can be handled within a few hours instead of days.

More recently, computers have become the gateway to a booming array of online and in-house databases that put valuable research and information at the PR practitioner's fingertips in seconds. The most common applications are word processing, time and activity reports, accounting and billing, telecommunications, issues tracking, financial planning and budgeting, media list development and management, and project management and scheduling. Until recently, public relations professionals depended on general software such as Lotus 1-2-3 or Microsoft Word for these applications. Today, however, a growing number of service companies are offering PR-specific products, most of them related to the dominant task in most public relations operations: publicity and media relations. Most come with or are associated with a database of media information, such as the names, addresses, phone and fax numbers for members of Congress, securities analysts, and thousands of reporters and editors around the world.

One company, Media Distribution Services (MDS), has a database of more than 200,000 print and broadcast media in the Untied States, plus all daily newspapers worldwide. The lists are classified by editorial interests and audience characteristics and are updated each day by electronic mail. Such software is used to create media lists, conduct basic media research, run media mailing labels, and send faxes and e-mail messages to editors and reporters.

Besides media management software, public relations practitioners can buy print labels or computer disks of preselected media from media mailing list suppliers. They can also take advantage of **broadcast fax services** which can distribute a handful or hundreds of faxes to the press in minutes. And they can use **public relations news services** which send news releases directly to major newspapers and other outlets. These "wire services," such as PR Newswire and Business Wire, are particularly valuable for timely dissemination of business transactions of publicly traded companies.

Broadcast fax services send faxes of news and information to the media.

Public relations news services electronically disseminate PR news to the media.

Other software analyzes press clippings and news coverage. These services analyze a customer's publicity for *message content,* audience exposure, competitive share, geographical distribution, return on investment, positive versus negative impressions, and other factors. They can evaluate the effectiveness of media campaigns.

For tracking and billing time and expenses, other software packages have been adapted to the needs of public relations practitioners. These products record and invoice time, purchases, and out-of-pocket expenses. They automatically generate financial reports and profitability analyses.

Similarly sophisticated software encompasses a wide range of communication applications (see Table 10.1) associated with public policy management. These systems can be organized in a hierarchical form, resembling a family tree or file

TABLE 10.1 Functions of PR Management Software

Managing Contributions	Tracking Issues
Grants	Legislative
Matching gifts	Regulatory
In-kind gifts	Judicial
Monitoring "Players"	**Managing Events**
Coalitions	Meetings
Political action committees	Conferences
Political allies	Seminars
Managing Media	**Handling Administration**
Mailing lists	Word processing
Contacts	Financial analysis
Interviews	Record keeping

cabinet approach to information, or as a relational database in which data are stored in cross-referenced tables for easier search-and-find capabilities. For example, a large public university facing tough financial cuts in state allocations year after year needed to convey to state legislators the significant benefits that it brought to each district throughout the state. From a grassroots organizing perspective, this meant matching students, alumni, faculty, staff, donors, and other beneficiaries, such as vendors, to their respective legislative districts so that the former could explain how the cuts affected their interests. By utilizing data-matching software provided by Legislative Demographic Services, the university was able to link thousands of university- affiliated people to state districts, producing an array of computer-generated reports that detailed the impact the university had on each of the state's districts. Those reports, in turn, were produced as statistical tables and, more important, visual maps. The picture the university was able to paint convinced legislators to curtail planned budget cuts because it was clear what the cuts would do to constituents "back home."

On-Line News and Information

On-line databases are Internet sources of news and research provided by for-profit and nonprofit organizations.

Along with the growth in computers has come a growth in **on-line databases** through which public relations practitioners can improve their ability to research subjects, monitor media coverage almost instantly, and retrieve important information in a timely fashion. Among the many services available are Bloomberg, NEXIS-LEXIS, CompuServe, Dow Jones News Service, Associated Press, and FIND. They are accessed by phone and computer. For broadcast media, companies such as Video Monitoring Service offer "clips" from on-air audio and video. As the evaluation of public relations results grows in importance, these and related services will become increasingly important. And as their prices drop, they will become more and more accessible to larger numbers of practitioners.

Many organizations are developing their own internally generated information services. The White House, for example, maintains a bibliographic file of remarks made by the president in all of his speeches. The public utilities industry keeps a database of information on rate and regulatory issues that affect its members. These databases are a ready source of assistance for staff, researchers, writers, reporters, and others. They make it easier to use information efficiently and effectively and can include everything from simple mailing lists to detailed analyses of issues.

Advanced Telephony

New interactive technologies give public relations professionals some new tools of the trade. New media such as electronic mail, fax, and interactive television, and some not-so-new media such as the telephone, are starting to supplant the conventional mass media as the essential communication links in modern democracy.

Some interesting examples emerged from the 1992 U.S. presidential campaign. Democratic presidential hopeful Jerry Brown abandoned traditional fund-raising efforts in favor of a grassroots campaign supported by pledges made through calls to an 800 number. He also eschewed conventional campaign spots, producing program-length infomercials for cable TV instead. Billionaire independent candidate Ross Perot adopted some of the same tactics in 1992, although he used the 800-number calls more as a type of electronic referendum to validate the legitimacy of his candidacy. He also used closed-circuit satellite teleconferences to reach out to his supporters. Perot proposed a scenario wherein, when he was elected, citizens would engage in an electronic dialog with him using dial-in telephone polls. (A side note on Jerry Brown: Although he lost in his bid for the presidency, he continued in politics and, in the summer of 1998, was elected mayor of Oakland, California.)

Special-interest groups soon turned to high-tech methods. In the first month of the new congressional session that followed the 1992 election, the volume of telephone calls to the Capitol doubled, reaching over 4 million per month. One flood of calls, apparently triggered by revelations that Justice Department nominee Zoe Baird had hired an undocumented alien as a babysitter, was credited with torpedoing her nomination.

Another torrent of voter feedback was unleashed by the National Rifle Association (NRA) in a bid to preserve the right to keep and bear automatic assault weapons. NRA members placed calls to a 900 number, which automatically generated a letter to Congress in the caller's name.

Another tactic is the "patch through." Political consultants scan computerized mailing lists for probable supporters of a cause. Computers automatically identify and place calls to likely prospects; then live operators explain the issue and offer to patch the caller through directly to his or her congressional representative or to the White House.

At the U.S. Chamber of Commerce, a computerized dialing system places calls to members when an issue of vital importance is before Congress. The members then press 1 to send a mailgram, press 2 for voice mail, or press 3 for electronic mail (Engleberg, 1993; Houston, 1993; Kelly, 1992).

Some politicians have turned to their own high-tech methods to stem the flow of electronic public relations. Congressional staffers retaliated for one unwanted flood of communications by sending junk faxes that jammed the offending special-interest group's fax machines. The Clinton administration installed an interactive voice mail system that allows callers to "vote" on the president's economic plan before recording a brief message for the president. You can also access the White House Web site (www.whitehouse.gov) and obtain the texts of his latest speeches.

The Internet—A New Dimension for Public Relations

Even though it is only just beginning to grow as a communications technology, the public relations field has been quick to take advantage of the Internet for communications purposes although independent public relations firms trail corporate PR departments in this regard (Dilenschneider Group, 1996). The reason is simple. PR people want to establish beachheads of contact with the people already on the Internet and with the rest who eventually will follow.

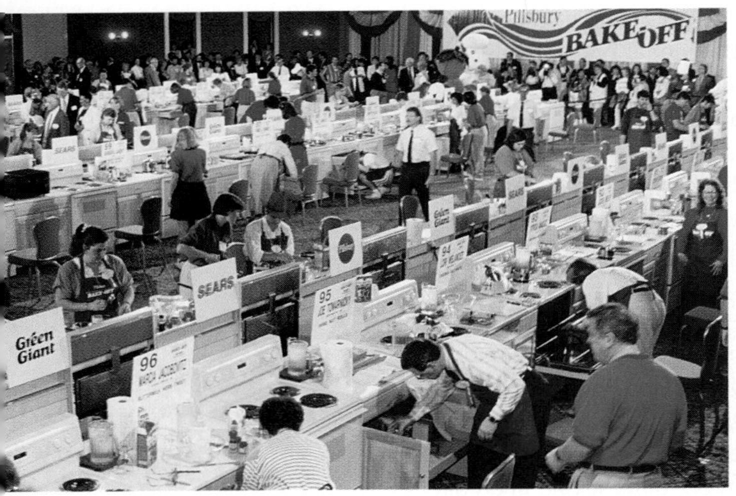

PR EVENT.
Staging special events, such as Pillsbury's annual Bake-Off® cooking contest, is an example of one form of public relations: the special event. (Photo courtesy of the Pillsbury Company)

For example, Fannie Mae, the Washington, DC-based mortgage financing company, has created an award-winning *intranet* site (see Chapter 8) to provide employees with access to all of the information in the company's computers. Called "Home Site," it allows the 3700 employees to check company stock information and read news clips. Individual divisions can use it to communicate with the entire company.

Although many intranet sites are static, Fannie Mae's includes an interactive Space Age site, where employees can submit ideas about the company or any of its products, add to other people's ideas, and participate in brainteasers. According to the company, the site attracts about 2000 individual sessions daily. The company is thinking about adding a "concierge" service that employees could use for such mundane but important concerns as ordering flowers or finding a dog sitter.

In general, however, corporate public relations practitioners have been moving cautiously in unleashing the full power of the Internet for PR purposes. Currently, their primary use of the Internet has been monitoring what others are saying about them, and stories related to them, in the news and other commentary that runs on-line every day. A handful also monitor "rogue" or unauthorized sites critical of corporations, such as mcspotlight.org and flamingfords.com (see Media Watch, page 330 for more on these sites). Some 40 percent regularly use the Internet to monitor competition, but only 17 percent go on-line to contact investors, 15 percent to confront a crisis, and 2 percent to communicate with legislators and government officials. Work they do with the press is usually handled in one-to-one e-mail messages rather than mass e-mailings of news releases or other information. They also monitor the Internet for copyright violations.

Electronic press kits are CD-ROM or Internet versions of printed press kits.

A **Web cast** is a real-time PR event or press briefing broadcast over the Internet.

In addition, public relations practitioners have been using the Internet for a variety of communications that have been designed especially for electronic and digital transmission. Some of the most obvious are the creation, maintenance, and hot linking of Web sites for the press, investors, and consumers; e-mail newsletters; on-line annual reports with video and sound; and **electronic press kits.** The latter include photos, fact sheets, audio, and video that can be distributed on a CD-ROM or downloaded from the Internet by editors and reporters as necessary. The same material can be used for an interactive **Web cast,** a new Internet public relations tool that combines video, audio, and text to enable people to observe real-time PR events interactively as they are happening or immediately thereafter.

Some corporations are using the Internet for electronic news centers. A good example is Bell Atlantic (www.bell-atl.com), whose site makes it easy for the press to access company news announcements and staff contacts. And leading public relations firms are establishing Web sites that can be uploaded at a moment's notice to provide information, in a crisis, to target audiences. Such companies minimize or eliminate the time delay that would occur if they had to wait for the print and broadcast media to contact them, or for e-mail, fax, or mail to reach their publics. For example, if a car manufacturer suddenly had to recall many of its vehicles, it would launch its own version of the story as rapidly as possible through a prepared Web site. These crisis-preventive Web sites are also intended to control rumors and showcase a company's forthrightness in communicating quickly.

PR practitioners are also beginning to use the Internet to contact new media, which include a growing array of *electronic magazines* such as *Salon,* which are available only on the Internet, and *on-line editions* of traditional print and broadcast media. They are part of the new universe of *cyberspace media.* And PR practitioners are taking advantage of Internet "talk soup" opportunities such as *Usenet new groups* and *list servers* to get their company's or clients' messages out. In the political arena, the Internet can be used for such things as sending "stooges" into *chat rooms* to skew discussion, and for turning visitor registrations into fund-raising mailing lists (see Chapter 8).

The Internet is clearly a valuable tool for public relations purposes, but it also has its limitations. Veteran public relations practitioners with strong backgrounds in technology have been advising colleagues to view the Internet—at least for the foreseeable future—as a complement to, not a replacement for, traditional public relations practices. As Jim Horton, whose Web site (www.online-pr.com) features a wealth of Internet public relations resources, has written, "The Internet is far from the Holy Grail of communications that some people [would] have us believe, although its significance as a public relations tool will continue to grow in the years to come."

Still, the many on-line news sources on the Internet add to the number of media outlets that expand the venues for public relations material. Whereas practitioners once directed their publicity at a few tightly controlled local and national media outlets, they suddenly had scores of additional channels to work with, providing many more opportunities for their clients to be seen and heard. PR spokespersons also have more opportunities to appear on news and talk shows, whether on satellite-delivered national channels or local channels and leased-access channels.

Thus, for public relations the explosion of nontraditional outlets means greater opportunities for publicity and promotion. It also means complications. Whereas in the past practitioners only had to concentrate on a few well-established venues, they now have to consider hundreds, if not thousands. They have to be more sophisticated in knowing when and how to use technology more efficiently and effectively in order to avoid problems such as over-communicating (going to too many people with too many messages) and adding unnecessary time and expense to the process. Cost-benefit ratios become more critical in communications decisions.

STOP & REVIEW

1. **When are video news releases more effective than printed ones?**
2. **How have new electronic media outlets such as the Internet changed the practice of public relations?**
3. **What are some of the functions that personal computers perform in modern public relations agencies?**
4. **What are some of the high-tech approaches that are used to influence political opinion?**

FORMS OF PUBLIC RELATIONS

Definitions of the term *public relations* abound. Following are the two most commonly found in the industry:

MEDIA WATCH

Cyber Crisis—A New Public Relations Worry

There is also another, more sinister side to the Internet, as has been pointed out by public relations counselor Don Middleberg, president of Middleberg Associates, a New York public relations firm. Writing in *PR Tactics* (November 1996), he says, "Despite all the excitement created by the Internet, there is an emerging dark side. It is small now, but growing. We are talking about a new type of crisis, one that communicators must be concerned about and prepared for." He calls it a *Cyber crisis.*

"In our new media age," he adds, "it is possible for almost anyone to single-handedly wreak havoc, create controversy, or mar the image of your company by using the great equalizer—the Internet. A lone, disgruntled employee (or a small group of Internet savvy people) can rapidly disseminate his/her message as loudly and effectively as a multi-billion dollar company."

Recently, Ford Motor Co. found itself in the midst of an Internet attack by a group of cyber citizens demanding the recall of 26 million cars and trucks that it claimed were dangerous. The Association of Flaming Ford Owners (AFFO) posted a Web site (www.flamingfords.com) describing an alleged fire hazard. The group also sent out a mass e-mail to 8500 domain managers, promoting the site and asking them to add links back to the "Flaming Ford" site.

McDonald's is also experiencing a cyber crisis. The McInformation Network is an activist group dedicated to "breaking the chains of censorship by multinational companies." The group created the anti-McDonald's Web site McSpotlight (www.mcspotlight.org) to provide the press and public with information on the "McLibel" trial, a libel suit that has been under way since 1990 when McDonald's sued two people who published, on the Internet, a fact sheet entitled "What's Wrong with McDonald's."

To prepare for and handle an Internet crisis, Middleberg advises PR representatives to know the basics: Surf the Web, join "listservs," and linger in news groups that talk about the company and its areas of interest. More specifically, he offers the following advice:

- Research and assess the situation.
- Do not ignore or underestimate the problem. It is essential to treat an Internet attack like a true media crisis. Respond.

"Public relations is the management function that identifies, establishes, and maintains mutually beneficial relationships between an organization and the various publics on whom its success or failure depends." (Cutlip, Center, & Broom, 1985)

"Public relations helps our complex, pluralistic society to reach decisions and functions more effectively by contributing to mutual understanding among groups and institutions. It serves to bring private and public policies into harmony." (Public Relations Society of America)

In more practical terms, "on the job," the public relations unit, whether one person or many people, has a wide range of responsibilities. Here are a few of the most important:

- Advises and counsels the organization on communications questions affecting its publics.

MEDIA WATCH

Continued from previous page

- Try to reach the source or individual who is attacking your company on the Internet and establish a dialog.
- Communicate your side of the story to that source with the intent of clearing up misunderstandings, misleading information, or inaccuracies.
- Listen. Is there common ground?
- Be ready to respond immediately, preferably on your own Web page and to the on-line media, as well as through traditional media outlets.

Cases where libel may be involved present more problems, he notes. "Lawyers will want to take action, but this may not be the best way to handle the situation. Because there have been few precedents and rulings concerning libel and the Internet, it is unlikely that your company will win such a suit. In addition, the case will likely be expensive and may very well draw unwanted media attention to the crisis." Middleberg concludes, "In this new media age, public relations practitioners must not only be ready to use the benefits of the Internet, but also be positioned to help clients deal with crises on the information superhighway."

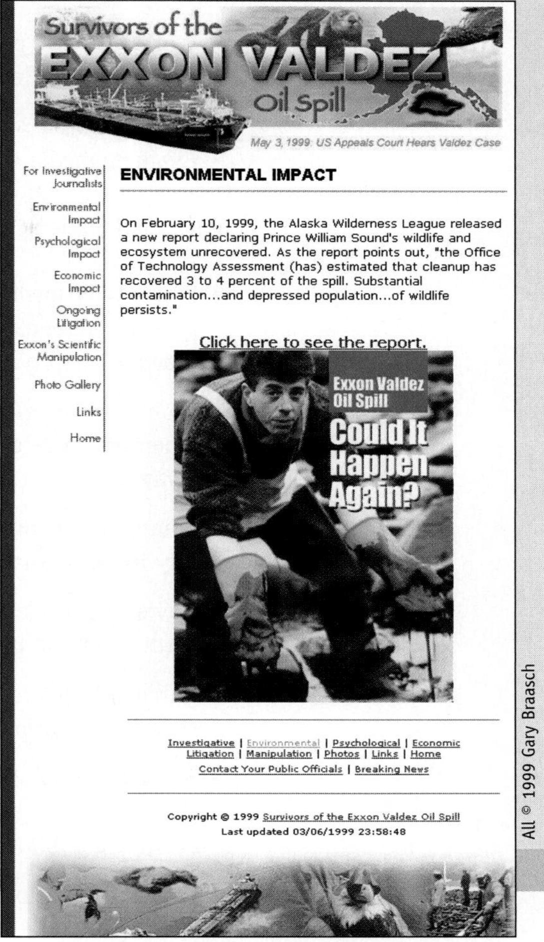

All © 1999 Gary Braasch

PR NIGHTMARE.
Public relations professionals worry that the Internet perpetuates negative images long after a disaster. The *Exxon Valdez* oil spill took place in 1989, but it is still a focal point of sites on the Web.

- Serves as an early-warning system on emerging issues related to the organization's success.
- Provides technical support for other management functions with an emphasis on publicity, promotion, and media relations.
- Acts as a gatekeeper between the company or organization and its publics, most conspicuously with representatives of the press, legislators, and government officials.

Among the many functions that PR practitioners perform, publicity and **media relations** are arguably the most important. Upwards of 70 percent of the average practitioner's week is devoted to working with the press to encourage news and feature coverage of their employer's or clients' interests. This involves the full range of media relations assignments:

Media relations focuses on establishing and maintaining good relations with the media.

- Strategize, plan, and coordinate media relations and publicity.

- Prepare and disseminate news releases, press kits, and press alerts.
- Call, write, fax, and e-mail editors and reporters.
- Work with any public relations services required to assist them in their endeavors—for example, print, mail, fax, e-mail, and "wire" information to the press.
- Evaluate media relations and publicity results.

Public relations is usually organized into several key categories:

- Publicity or media relations—Gaining press coverage through news releases, press conferences, and other materials. Upwards of 70 percent of what PR practitioners do is concentrated in this area.
- Promotion or selling—Developing and disseminating print and audiovisual materials, arranging exhibits and displays, and providing promotional give-aways.
- Community relations—Working with community groups and other key community interests that can influence public attitudes and public policies.
- Government relations—Assisting or influencing state, local, or federal government action on problems involving legislation, regulation, and related activity.
- Public information—Developing and disseminating print and audiovisual materials whose purpose is to inform, educate, and assist.
- Special events—Planning and managing internal and external events such as ground breakings, ribbon-cutting ceremonies, tours, and open houses aimed at attracting public attention.
- Employee relations—Assisting management in informing staff at all levels about personnel policies and practices, labor relations, contracts, benefits, and other issues that involve the health and welfare of the labor force.
- Issues management—Identifying and helping to manage the big issues that affect institutional success, such as air and water pollution (the environment), foreign competition, ethnic diversity, and plant closings or relocations.
- Lobbying—Working with legislators and their legislative aides to influence the content and course of legislative action that affects institutional practices, through contributions to political action committees (PACs), campaign contributions, and other direct assistance not included as part of more conventional government relations efforts.

How much time and money an organization puts into each of these functions depends on the level of need. Employers and clients with big issues and big problems tend to do more. Organizations with less of a need might devote most of their energy to one or two areas. Over time, however, every organization makes use of all these functions, except perhaps for lobbying, which smaller, less visible enterprises often do not engage in. There are also distinctions based on purpose. Government agencies, for example, tend to favor public information because of their public service orientation. Not-for-profit organizations might also lean toward public information, in addition to public relations activities that support fund raising.

The Publics of Public Relations

Public relations activities are addressed to one or more of the many publics that can influence an organization's success: customers, employees, shareholders, donors, the press, and so on (see Table 10.2).

When public relations practitioners refer to "publics," they mean the audiences they communicate with as part of their daily work. Depending on the needs and interests of the institutions or clients they represent, a particular list of publics could be pretty extensive. For example, the typical multinational corporation has to deal with customers, banks, legislators, regulators, unions, employees, stockholders, investors, competitors, suppliers, community neighbors, trade associations, and the press in order to conduct its business. In contrast, the average nonprofit organization might only have to deal with a few publics besides the press, for example, employees, donors, legislators, and volunteers. Table 10.3 shows the key PR publics for most for-profit institutions. Normally, the publics are targeted with a mix of PR tools and techniques, many of which are used in conjunction with related, but independently developed marketing, advertising, and human resources initiatives.

Although *ink,* as press coverage is often called by PR practitioners and those in the media, helps a company or organization to be seen and heard by the public and key audiences, its ultimate value should be more tangible. Viewed strategically, it should help a company or organization with bottom-line issues. That is, it should sell products, attract investment, and lure new employees, while building community and legislative support and improving management.

TABLE 10.2 The Many Publics in Public Relations

For Businesses
Shareholders
Customers/consumers
Employees
Suppliers
Financial institutions
Legislators
Community activists
Print/broadcast media

For Not-for-Profit Enterprises
Contributors/donors
Clients/consumers
Volunteers
Employees
Members
Suppliers
Legislators
Community activists
Print/broadcast media

For Government Agencies
Taxpayers/voters
Legislators
Related government agencies
Employees
Community activists
Print/broadcast media

Good vs. Bad PR: A Commentary

Good public relations has many benefits: improved credibility and accountability, stronger public identity, more favorable press coverage, greater sensitivity to public needs, improved employee morale, larger market share, increased sales, and better internal management. Bad public relations can exist as well, often because the people in charge of the function do their jobs poorly or because the company or organization operated outside the bounds of the public interest.

TABLE 10.3 Key PR Publics and PR Tools Used to Reach Them

PR publics	PR communications (examples)
Customers/clients:	Special events, newsletters, billing inserts
Employees/managers:	Newsletters, employee videos, company Web sites
Stockholders/investors:	Earnings releases, annual reports, annual meeting
Legislators/regulators:	Letters, research reports, personal contacts
Print/broadcast media:	News releases, press conferences, press interviews

PROFILE

PERSONAL TOUCH. "When all is said and done, it is how you connect with people on a human, personal level that will ensure your success."

The Personal Touch

Name: Terrie Williams

Education: Graduated *cum laude* from Brandeis University in 1975 with a degree in psychology and sociology; holds a Master of Science in social work from Columbia University

Current Job: President of the Terrie Williams Agency

Previous Position: Developed the PR department of Essence Communications, Inc. (ECI), the multimillion-dollar publishing, marketing, and entertainment company.

Style: Believes in connecting to people on a human, personal level in business.

Most Notable Achievements: Launching the Terrie Williams Agency in 1988 with superstar Eddie Murphy and jazz legend Miles Davis as its first clients, and expanding that client base to include many other of the well-known entertainment, sports, political, and corporate figures and organizations in the United States and abroad. Adopting her son Rocky, whom she met through a high school mentoring program. Publishing her best-selling book, *The Personal Touch: What You Really Need to Succeed in Today's Fast-Paced Business World.* She was the first woman of color to be honored with the New York Women in Communications Matrix Award in Public Relations.

How She Got to the Top: It started as simply as reading an article on PR, followed by taking a PR course. Not long after she met Miles Davis and Eddie Murphy, she opened her firm. She emphasizes the importance of attending professional meetings and serving as a mentor to others.

Where Does She Go from Here? She wants to write more books and to motivate more people to realize their potential, and most important, to impact the lives of young people.

BAD PR.
The 1989 *Exxon Valdez* oil spill is a classic example of how bad publicity can hurt major corporations.

Perhaps management allowed the production of faulty products, permitted pollution of the firm's surroundings, or illegally manipulated the price of the company's stock. Public relations might help to soften the fallout from such an event (negative press coverage, public outrage, regulatory punishment), but only a change in management policy or practice will truly make a difference. If one cliché dominates public relations thinking, it is this: "You can't make a silk purse out of a sow's ear."

An example of poor PR was Exxon's handling of the 1989 disaster in which one of its tankers, the *Exxon Valdez,* ran aground near Valdez, Alaska, and spilled 250 million gallons of crude oil. It was the largest spill ever in North America, affecting more than 1200 miles of water, damaging some 600 miles of coastline, and killing as many as 4000 Alaskan sea otters along with thousands of sea birds and other precious wildlife. In the aftermath, Exxon's chairman, Lawrence Rawl, decided not to visit the site, an action that was interpreted by area residents and the public at large as arrogance of the first order. He also didn't comment on the event for a full week, and the company established its media center in New York, not in Valdez where the action was.

MEDIA IMPACT

A Year in the Life of a Public Relations Campaign

Suppose an electrical power utility decides to implement a community-wide program to help clean up local waterways, with the goals of educating the public about environmental pollution, improving the quality and safety of waterside recreation, getting local legislators and the press to view the utility as a good corporate citizen, and persuading more customers to look kindly on its services and rates. Public relations would have the primary responsibility for keeping the cleanup in the public eye, taking reasonable advantage of the situation to get credit where credit is due for the utility. The utility's public relations unit might plan the following:

- A press conference to announce the launch of the program, combined with delivery and follow-up of press kits that include news releases, project descriptions, resource lists, and cleanup priorities.
- Speeches that the CEO and other top executives would give throughout the year to local business and community groups.
- Posters, flyers, and other prepackaged information to recruit volunteers from local schools, churches, and community groups and to excite and motivate employees about the benefits of the program and their role in making it successful.
- Public service announcements for use in free air time on local television and radio stations.
- Paid ads and advertorials promoting the utility's role in launching the cleanup effort and promoting the utility as a good corporate citizen that runs a well-managed business but whose primary concern is serving the public interest and all of its customers equally.
- Kickoff special events such as cleanup parties, a parade through town, meetings of public officials, and an essay or art competition.
- A press and information bureau to track cleanup activities and report the results to the community via news updates, awards, and other forms of recognition.

In the end, Exxon got pilloried in the press for its handling of the crisis, and public sentiment turned decidedly against the company. After all was said and done, the disaster had cost the company more than $2.5 billion in cleanup costs, legal judgments, and other expenses. The *Valdez* story has also become a textbook "classic" of how *not* to handle public relations in an emergency (Seitel, 1997).

Elements of Successful Public Relations

The practice of public relations is based on *research and evaluation,* including public opinion polls, readership surveys, mail questionnaires, telephone interviews, focus groups, and literature searches. Of necessity, then, good public relations begins with a serious assessment of public attitudes. Without adequate background on the people you are trying to reach and how they think, it is next to impossible to communicate effectively. More specifically, without research and evaluation, you cannot design programs that will change or modify the views of your target audiences.

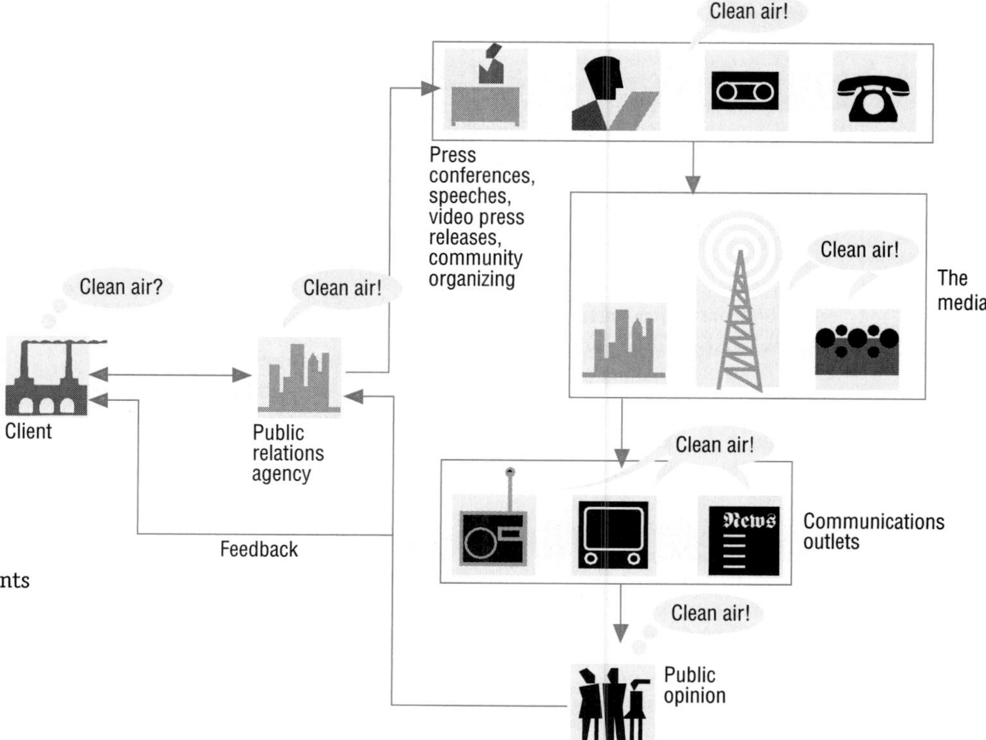

FIGURE 10.1
Public relations agencies organize communication events such as press conferences, speeches, and telemarketing campaigns to alert communications media organizations to important issues so that the subsequent media coverage will sway public opinion in favor of the client. Opinion polls and direct responses from the public provide feedback to the client and the agency.

Second, public relations is a planned effort, not a hit-or-miss proposition (see Figure 10.1). Planned means managed. *Managed* means based on overall organizational objectives, not just the public relations unit's views. Planned effort begins with a written action plan for a year or more ahead that allows for changes and contingencies along the way. This plan must have the approval of top management. It schedules needed publications and communications, such as a monthly newsletter, the annual report, and speeches and presentations for special events. More important, the plan sets up a timetable and strategies aimed at achieving overall goals for the program.

Third, public relations has the goal of public support. The public might support a for-profit organization by purchasing products, investing in stock, or voting for or against specific trade regulations. Public support for a not-for-profit organization might take the form of donations of money or material, volunteer assistance, or paid memberships. For a government agency, it might mean legislative influence, taxpayer cooperation, or public participation.

Over time, the public relations unit makes use of most of the print, electronic, and face-to-face communications available in our society. These are the tools and techniques (see Table 10.4) that help organizations to reach their publics. They are the vehicles that carry information back and forth between private and public interests.

It is also important to realize what public relations is not. To do public relations, practitioners often make use of the full range of mass communications—advertising, marketing, opinion research, print media, electronic media—but these enterprises have their own principles and practices, and the people involved are experts in their own right with their own stock of knowledge and experience. What these experts do and how they do it are different from what public relations practitioners do. Understanding these differences helps keep the public relations function in perspective and helps avoid management and client misunderstandings about what to expect from its application and what to pay for the services involved.

INDUSTRY DEMOGRAPHICS

Although *public relations* is the preferred generic term in most corporations, the overall function is also known by other designations that might appear in an organization chart or in the titles of practitioners. Among the most popular are *public affairs, corporate communications,* and *corporate relations.* In specific industries such as public utilities, you might find the term *consumer affairs* or *community relations;* in not-for-profit and government organizations, *public information* or *marketing communications.* In addition, the overall function might be subdivided further to reflect specific jobs, such as investor relations, financial relations, and media relations.

Today, all leading corporations have public relations departments of one sort or another. The same goes for major not-for-profit organizations such as colleges, hospitals, and national charities. And government has similar operations, though here they are called public affairs offices or public information offices.

To assist these entities, there are some 4000 independent public relations firms, most with a handful of people, but scores with 50 or more. The largest firms have more than 1000 employees worldwide. The Top 10 agencies for 1997 are shown in the *Jack O'Dwyer's Newsletter* annual ranking of firms (see Table 10.5).

There are also commercial wire services, such as PR Newswire and Business Wire, that disseminate prepackaged news releases to news outlets nationwide. Unlike the traditional wire services such as AP, which are financed by subscrip-

TABLE 10.4 Public Relations Activities

Annual reports
Brochures, flyers, circulars
Press kits
Press conferences
News releases
Editorials
Speeches
Feature articles
Video news releases
Satellite broadcast media
Tours
Videoconferences
Teleconferences
Exhibits and displays
Photographs
Videotapes and films
Audiotapes and compact discs
Advertorial programming
Paid advertisements
Public service advertisements
Legislative testimony
Sports sponsorships
Event sponsorships
Plant tours and open houses
Technical seminars
Public demonstrations
Slide shows
Speakers' bureaus
Opinion polls and surveys
VIP visits
Novelties
Meetings and conventions

TABLE 10.5 Top Ten Public Relations Firms

Firm	1997 Income	Employees	Web Site
Burson Marstellar	$264 million	2100	www.bm.com
Shandwick	$159 million	1750	www.shandwick.com
Porter Novelli International	$148 million	1300	www.porternovelli.com
Fleishman-Hillard	$135 million	1100	www.fleishman.com
Edelman PR Worldwide	$134 million	1300	www.edelman.com
Ketchum PR Worldwide	$ 97 million	800	www.ketchum.com
Manning, Selvage & Lee	$ 64 million	450	www.mslpr.com
GCI Group	$ 62 million	650	www.gcigroup.com
BSMG Worldwide	$ 62 million	550	www.bsmg.com
Weber PR Worldwide	$ 61 million	550	www.weberpr.com

Press clipping services "clip" newspaper stories.

Broadcast transcription services transcribe radio and television coverage.

tion fees from their subscribers, commercial wire services charge hundreds of dollars to PR practitioners who use them. The PR field also has companies such as Media Distribution Services (MDS) and Bacon's, both of which offer printing, mailing and fax services devoted to reaching the press in the United States and abroad. Finally, there are **press clipping services** such as Luce and Burrelle's, and **broadcast transcription services** such as Video Monitoring Service (VMS), which charge PR practitioners for monitoring coverage of their clients or employers.

Some 200,000 people work full time in public relations. Aside from their job titles, public relations professionals are also characterized in terms of the organizations they belong to and the publications they read. Although the Public Relations Society of America has dominated the public relations industry for most of its history, competing organizations have formed to serve particular specialties or power groups within the profession.

Chief among these groups are the International Association of Business Communicators (IABC), the National Investor Relations Institute (NIRI), and Women in Communications Incorporated (WICI). There are also several invitation-only organizations for senior practitioners, such as the PR Wisemen, the Arthur Page Society, and Women Executives in Public Relations (WEPR). In 1998, the Council of Public Relations Firms was established to represent the business and professional interests of the PR agencies in the United States.

There has been a comparable growth in professional societies worldwide. Besides the European-based International Public Relations Association (IPRA), which acts as a kind of clearinghouse for practitioners outside the United States, there are membership associations along the lines of the PRSA in the majority of democratic countries. All are devoted to improving the practice of public relations in the public interest.

The growing power and professionalism of public relations are also reflected in the development, over the past 30 years, of several respected publications that cover the field. Besides weekly newsletters such as *Jack O'Dwyer's Newsletter, Bulldog Reporter, PR News,* and *prreporter,* there are magazines such as *PR Strategist* and *Communication World,* newspapers such as *PR Tactics* and *PR Week* (launched in November 1998), and research journals such as *Public Relations Review* and *Public Relations Quarterly.* Newsletters such as *Interactive Public Relations Report* and *Interactive PR & Marketing News* have come into being to serve the interests of the growing ranks of new media and technology specialists.

For most of the history of modern public relations, those doing the day-to-day work came from the ranks of newspaper reporters and editors. Today, the field attracts individuals from a wider variety of backgrounds, virtually all of them college graduates with degrees (both undergraduate and graduate) in the liberal arts, large numbers of whom studied journalism, marketing, mass communication, and English. Several thousand have majored in public relations at one of more than 200 colleges and universities offering such programs.

The management ranks in public relations are still overwhelmingly male-dominated. The situation is changing, of course, though perhaps more slowly than in other pursuits such as accounting, human resources, and business management generally. Public relations is also overwhelmingly white in its racial composition, although efforts are under way to attract nonwhite practitioners to the field. Within PRSA, committees and task forces are working on the challenge.

Salaries in public relations begin around $18,000–$25,000 and can rise as high as $200,000–$400,000 or more in the largest corporations and public relations firms, according to studies by the organizations such as PRSA and publications such as *prreporter,* a weekly newsletter. Currently, the average salary is probably $50,000–$100,000.

According to *prreporter's* most recent study (October 1998), the overall median (or middle) salary has risen to $63,400, up $3000 from 1997. The median PR salary in corporations was $76,000, whereas the median for PR practitioners in PR firms, ad agencies, and consulting organizations was $70,000. For self-employed counselors, the median was $60,000.

Beginning practitioners in public relations usually start in the area of publicity and media relations, writing and editing news releases, contacting reporters and editors, and generating press coverage. Seasoned practitioners are more involved in planning and management. When they do write, it is most often speeches, proposals, and presentations. When they work with the media, it usually involves broader editorial issues and higher-level contacts.

In addition to their education and experience, practitioners are supported by active PRSA and IABC programs of continuing education and accreditation. To become accredited, practitioners must pass rigorous oral and written examinations. Half of those who take the PRSA test fail.

The public relations field is growing and will continue to grow as society becomes more complex and as larger numbers of individuals and organizations seek public support for their endeavors. The influence of public relations will also expand, as larger numbers of practitioners become part of traditional top-management teams, applying their communications skills and knowledge across all management functions.

PUBLIC RELATIONS ISSUES

Issues affecting public relations include the conflict between private and public interest, professional ethics, professional development, and the use of research and evaluation.

Private Interests vs. the Public Interest

Publicity is an appropriate pursuit of private as well as public institutions in a free society. Just like individual citizens, corporate entities have the right to speak on their own behalf and to promote their interests under the law, both criminal and civil.

This doesn't mean that the media are passive instruments in the process. They, too, are largely corporate, profit-making enterprises, but they work within the framework of their own standards of conduct. As the Code of Ethics of Sigma Delta Chi, the Society of Professional Journalists, explains, "The public's right to know of events of public importance and interest is the overriding mission of the mass media. The purpose of distributing news and enlightened opinion is to serve the general welfare." The Code also states, "Freedom of the press is to be guarded as an inalienable right of people in a free society. It carries with it the freedom and the responsibility to discuss, question and challenge actions and utterances of our government and of our public and private institutions," which means, among other things, that journalists should not accept press releases at face value without checking their facts and asking counterbalancing opinions (see Chapter 14).

Thus, there is a natural tension between the media and institutions of business, government, and not-for-profit enterprise. This tension can be seen and heard daily in the press when corporations are charged with corruption, environmental pollution, undue political influence, and restraint of trade—in sum, with using their money, power, or influence in ways that compromise or undermine the public interest. In recent years, the agenda of issues has expanded to include critical social issues, such as racism in a prominent example involving the Texaco Corporation.

On November 4, 1996, the *New York Times* published a story accusing senior company officials of "belittling the company's minority employees with racial epithets," such as "black jelly beans," in private meetings. Most damaging for the company, some of these conversations had been recorded clandestinely by a disgruntled senior coordinator of personnel services, who shared them with lawyers who eventually brought a $520 million lawsuit against Texaco on behalf of 1500 black employees. Within hours of the first story, the American media exploded with a frenzy of damning coverage. Texaco became the corporate scapegoat as the nation's news and magazine editorials corroborated the company's guilt. The cost to Texaco was $176 million to settle the discrimination lawsuit. It also initiated a corporation-wide effort to eliminate racism in the workplace.

Relations between the media and society's institutions aren't always adversarial, however. Every day, the press gives large amounts of favorable coverage to numerous aspects of institutional enterprise—strong company earnings, successful government initiatives, noteworthy charitable events. Much of the background for these and related stories, particularly in the business press, comes from PR representatives who send news releases and **pitch letters** to editors and reporters suggesting angles that they and their publications or stations might take. PR representatives also make countless phone calls to the media. When necessary, they organize press briefings, press luncheons, and other "contacts" to stay in touch with editors and reporters for offensive as well as defensive purposes.

Pitch letters are designed to interest editors and reporters in covering a topic from a given perspective or "angle."

In general, the issue for the media and society's institutions when it comes to media relations and publicity boils down to one word—*fairness.* The media has an obligation to cover institutions as objectively as possible. The institutions, in turn, have an obligation to operate in the public interest. For PR practitioners, the challenge is to promote their clients and employers aggressively without distorting the truth.

MEDIA ETHICS

From the *PRSA Code of Professional Standards for the Practice of Public Relations*

- A member shall conduct his or her professional life in accord with the public interest.
- A member shall exemplify high standards of honesty and integrity while carrying out dual obligations to a client or employer and to the democratic process.
- A member shall deal fairly with the public, with past or present clients or employers, and with fellow practitioners, giving due respect to the ideal of free inquiry and to the opinions of others.
- A member shall adhere to the highest standards of accuracy and truth, avoiding extravagant claims or unfair comparisons and giving credit for ideas and words borrowed from others.
- A member shall not knowingly disseminate false or misleading information and shall act promptly to correct erroneous communications for which he or she is responsible.
- A member shall not engage in any practice which has the purpose of corrupting the integrity of channels of communications or the processes of government.
- A member shall not guarantee the achievement of specified results beyond the member's direct control.

Professional Ethics

Public relations exists in the context of a constant struggle with the companion issues of credibility and accountability. Every day practitioners must ask themselves and those they work for, directly and indirectly, whether what they are doing and saying is believable and whether what they earn and spend is in keeping with the best interests of the publics they serve. The answers affect what and how practitioners write, speak, plan, and program their activities. The answers also influence results. Not to be credible and accountable is a surefire recipe for failure.

Allied to credibility and accountability is the issue of ethics—the ethics of personal behavior as well as the ethics of public relations strategies and messages. Practitioners must continually ask themselves whether what they do to generate public attention is within the bounds of reasonableness, good taste, and truth. They must make a concerted effort to eliminate public relations initiatives that are false and misleading. This is especially difficult for practitioners hired as promotional mouthpieces rather than as communications strategists.

Both the PRSA and the IABC have codes of ethics and standards to help focus the responsibility of practitioners (see the Media Ethics box). In addition to its code of ethics, the PRSA has a Board of Ethics and Professional Standards with procedures for handling breaches of the code. Violations can lead to expulsion from membership. Unethical behavior often also leads to public censure when the circumstances of the infraction become known.

Professional Development

Other issues for practitioners involve professional development and personal growth. Clearly, there is a need for practitioners to become more sophisticated about how to use new technology for communications purposes. They also have to learn more about the basics of business, how it is structured, and how it is managed. Since most practitioners enter the field after studying liberal arts or after having worked in journalism and publishing, they have little knowledge of how corporations and small businesses operate. To communicate profit and loss issues for their clients, they need to get up to speed as quickly as possible. There is also a great concern in the field about maintaining the high standards in writing and thinking that have been the foundation of the practice's success over the years. Senior practitioners, in particular, complain about how difficult it is to find employees who are strong, journalistically oriented writers.

There has also been tremendous growth in the numbers of local, national, and international public relations conferences, seminars, and workshops sponsored by professional associations, universities, and for-profit enterprises. These meetings cover everything from the basics of public relations to trends and issues driving the management of organizational communications. And the PRSA has developed an **accreditation program** to judge an individual practitioner's understanding and knowledge. It also has a *fellows program* to recognize long-term involvement in, and major contributions to, the practice of public relations.

An **accreditation program** is a voluntary certification program.

Although the accreditation and fellows programs have no legal status, they are viewed as measures of professional integrity and success. In this sense, they open doors to jobs, promotions, and industry leadership. More generally, they underscore the public relations field's interest in improving the value of what practitioners do as communicators in the information society.

Use of Research and Evaluation

A general criticism often leveled against the industry is that practitioners need to conduct more research and increase their evaluation of the impact and effectiveness of their PR efforts. Although both activities are included in the traditional public relations planning process, PR research and evaluation are still used scantily in helping to define the goals of programs and activities and later in measuring their effectiveness.

Part of the reason for the limited use of research and evaluation is money. Most public relations budgets allocate little money for anything beyond the essentials. These budgets focus largely on how-to, not why-to, thinking. To move forward in this area, practitioners need to integrate research and evaluation into their plans and budgets. They also need to educate top management on the value of research and development in designing and delivering more effective messages and programs.

Environmental monitoring tracks and weighs the environment in which a given institution operates.

Audits are formal assessments of the internal and external forces affecting an organization.

In addition to providing clearer direction for programs, research helps build the theory and practice of public relations, linking the field to other mass communication functions in the process. Major research techniques in public relations include **environmental monitoring** (assessing the corporate climate), **audits** (evaluating an organization's standing with its publics), and **readability studies** (analyzing a publication's effectiveness).

Readability studies assess how well publications achieve their goals.

In the absence of research and evaluation, public relations effectiveness is compromised and the practitioner's credibility and accountability suffer. Unless you know where you are going and have some expectation of results, you will never really know whether you have succeeded. And unless you can point to hard data substantiating the impact of your programs, the client or employer will always be suspicious of promises and recommendations.

Public Relations and Society

More broadly, public relations practitioners are faced with two sets of issues: those related to the public interest and those related to how and why they practice their particular art of communication. They have to worry about what the public wants as much as what their employers want. Consequently, they live with a divided sense of self. They are both makers of messages and messengers. But most practitioners seem to relish their role despite its inherent difficulties. They understand the importance of the role that public relations plays in society, and they are willing to tolerate criticism in order to accomplish their goal.

In a speech before the Arthur W. Page Society titled "The Truth Is in the Consequence," public relations pioneer Allen Center (1983) addressed the implications of the changing role of public relations in society:

> There is no longer a serious question about the essentiality of the public relations function, or the expertise with which it is carried out most of the time. . . . At no period in my lifetime have the basic abilities to monitor and interpret information, to respond effectively, to relate public opinion to an organization's affairs, and to communicate persuasively been of more critical importance in the successful management of all kinds of enterprises. Similarly, at no time in my life has there been a greater need to use these abilities in ways that can help produce empathy, compromise, reconciliation, dialogue, and understanding rather than contention, controversy, animosity, prejudice, or misunderstanding. . . . Work to change and to improve things for the future within the framework of a free, open, democratic, and competitive society—on the payroll. You can't change much of anything by brooding, or getting into a big argument, or being fired, or sitting on the sidelines. You have to stay in the game.

1. What are some of the important elements of ethical behavior in public relations?
2. What is the role of evaluation in public relations?
3. Why is professional development especially important in the public relations field?
4. What are some techniques for evaluating public relations?

SUMMARY AND REVIEW

HOW DID PUBLIC RELATIONS DEVELOP?

In a sense, public relations is as old as history itself. The rulers of ancient empires, political propagandists, and the propagators of the world's great religions were among the first to use public relations techniques. In this light, the Federalist Papers, the Bill of Rights, and the popularization of frontier heroes such as Daniel Boone and Davy Crockett may be seen as examples of successful public relations campaigns. Modern public relations evolved in the late nineteenth century as large corporations sought to defend their interests in the arena of public opinion. The first independent public relations counsel was established in the early 1900s. Ivy Lee was an early practitioner who worked to improve the image of the industrialists of the late nineteenth century. Edward Bernays is widely regarded as the originator of the current professional practice. Mass-persuasion propaganda campaigns during both world wars were also influential in expanding the scope and effectiveness of public relations.

HOW ARE CHANGES IN COMMUNICATIONS MEDIA ALTERING PUBLIC RELATIONS?

Expansion in the number of media outlets, especially in newspaper publishing and cable television, has expanded the opportunities for public relations professionals to present their message to the public. Video news releases were developed to help place public relations stories in television newscasts. Satellite networks and videoconferences afford new opportunities to deliver highly targeted press briefings. Electronic mail, mass calling, and facsimile are also being applied in modern public relations practice.

Meanwhile, the internal operations of public relations organizations are being transformed by the adoption of personal computers to automate many routine public relations tasks and to gain access to relational databases and on-line information services that offer public relations information. Public relations techniques used in political campaigns are also taking advantage of advances in computer and telecommunications technology, giving politicians new opportunities to circumvent mass media channels and state their case directly to the public.

WHAT ARE THE KEY ELEMENTS OF SUCCESSFUL PUBLIC RELATIONS?

Public relations campaigns succeed to the extent that they promote mutual understanding between the organization that sponsors the campaigns and one or more of the publics on which the organization depends to achieve its goals. Successful public relations campaigns are based on research and evaluation of public attitudes, employ careful planning, have the goal of winning public support in some tangible way, and use communications media to achieve their ends. Public relations campaigns thus rely on the successful execution of related advertising, marketing, opinion research, and media campaigns, but the public relations function is distinct from all of these.

WHAT ARE SOME OF THE TECHNIQUES USED IN PUBLIC RELATIONS?

The techniques used to reach the public depend on the nature of the public relations message and on the nature of the public or publics to which they are addressed. For businesses, the important audiences include shareholders, customers, employees, suppliers, the financial community, community activists, legislators, and the media. Annual reports, press releases, speeches, teleconferences, news conferences, "advertorials," and public tours are some of the techniques commonly used on behalf of corporate public relations clients. Not-for-profit groups and government agencies must address many of the same publics, and they also must reach volunteers and members of the general public. In their public relations campaigns, they rely more on unpaid forms of promotion, such as public service announcements and door-to-door canvassing by volunteers.

HOW IS THE PUBLIC RELATIONS INDUSTRY ORGANIZED?

Most large organizations have their own public relations departments, although they go by various names, including public affairs and public information. There are also thousands of independent public relations firms that supplement corporate PR departments or perform these services for smaller firms. Public relations may also be categorized in terms of functions, including media relations, promotion, community relations, government relations, public information, special events, employee relations, issues management, and lobbying. Public relations professionals are often members of such organizations as the Public Relations Society of America and the International Public Relations Association.

WHAT ARE SOME CRITICISMS OF PUBLIC RELATIONS?

Critics contend that public relations is an organized attempt to mislead the public and to represent the interests of large corporations at the expense of the public good. In the past, public relations campaigns have stooped to such tactics as concocting fictitious news events and creating phony organizations to promote their causes. Now public relations professionals subscribe to the Public Relations Society of America's code of ethics to avoid such abuses.

WHAT ARE THE STANDARDS FOR ETHICAL CONDUCT IN PUBLIC RELATIONS?

Continuing growth and change in the practice of public relations require continuing attention to the issue of ethical conduct. Public relations professionals face conflict between the interests of their clients and standards of conduct defined by the Public Relations Society of America's Code of Professional Standards. These standards require practitioners to maintain high standards of honesty and fair play and always to operate in the public interest while serving the interests, and maintaining the confidence, of their employers.

WHAT DOES IT MEAN TO BE A PUBLIC RELATIONS PROFESSIONAL?

Today's public relations professionals hold college degrees in fields such as liberal arts, journalism, marketing, mass communication, and English. Also, more than 100 colleges offer programs in the field of public relations. Practitioners seek accreditation from professional societies such as the Public Relations Society of America and follow the society's ethical standards. They keep up-to-date by reading professional publications aimed at the public relations field. They also participate in continuing education programs to develop their abilities throughout their careers.

WHAT IS THE ROLE OF RESEARCH AND EVALUATION IN PUBLIC RELATIONS?

Research helps public relations practitioners improve the effectiveness of their activities, and evaluation helps them determine how effective they have been. Environmental monitoring, audits, readability studies, and evaluation activities such as soliciting feedback from public relations clients and publics are examples of research and evaluation methods. The role of research and evaluation must expand if public relations professionals are to maintain a high degree of credibility and accountability for their actions.

Electronic Resources

For up-to-the-minute URLs about *Public Relations,* access the MEDIA NOW site on the World Wide Web at:

http://communication.wadsworth.com/

CHAPTER 11

Advertising

THIS CHAPTER WAS WRITTEN BY **DANIEL A. STOUT, PH.D**, ASSOCIATE PROFESSOR OF COMMUNICATIONS AT BRIGHAM YOUNG UNIVERSITY. HE HAS PUBLISHED NUMEROUS ARTICLES ON ADVERTISING AND IS CO-EDITOR OF THE BOOK, *RELIGION AND MASS MEDIA: AUDIENCES AND ADAPTATIONS.*

WHAT'S AHEAD

In this chapter, we examine advertising from the perspective of the information society, paying particular attention to strategy, technology, and audience. A brief history of advertising is followed by a discussion of industry structure and advertising agencies. At the end of the chapter, a number of ethical issues are identified.

Access the MEDIA NOW site on the World Wide Web at:
http://communication.wadsworth.com/
Choose "Chapter 11" from the selection box to access electronic information and other sites relevant to this chapter.

AND NOW FOR A WORD FROM OUR SPONSOR . . .

DeeVee, pause. Snack time! Let's see what's in the fridge tonight!

Drink me, I'm calorie free!

Finish me quick, before my expiration date!

Yeesh. Refrigerator, reduce light level below threshold for the barker chips . . . mmmm, good sandwich . . . DeeVee, resume *Casablanca,* Interactive Movie Classics.

> NOW! New improved jumbo extra fresh and fluffy . . .

. . . AND resume automatic commercial filtering . . .

> We'll alwaysh have Parish, shweetheart . . . eshpecially NOW with dishcount European vacation packagesh from . . .

. . . AND embedded product promotion filtering . . . say, I am planning a trip to Philadelphia, come to think of it . . .

> <Reservation Channel> Fly Keystone Airlines, with the lowest rates and best movie selection to Philadelphia! Order now and receive a complimentary hoagie with your choice of toppings!

DeeVee, run the deception checker on the ad copy, then get me a flight on Tuesday afternoon . . . no exit seats . . . show *The Maltese Falcon* at my seat . . . and hold the mayo!

> <Done. Incoming voice call.>

Identify caller.

> <877-356-7654>

I don't recognize it, screen with Pest ID.

> <Information Superhighway Telemarketing>

Hang up!

> <Answer this call and win a free trip to Philadelphia!>

HANG UP!

> <Answer this call and they'll give you a dollar.>

GO AWAY!

> <Answer this call and they'll give you TWO dollars.>

Hmmmmm. Let me know if they hit twenty dollars. Meanwhile, back to the movie . . .

> We'll alwaysh have Philadelphia, shweetheart . . .

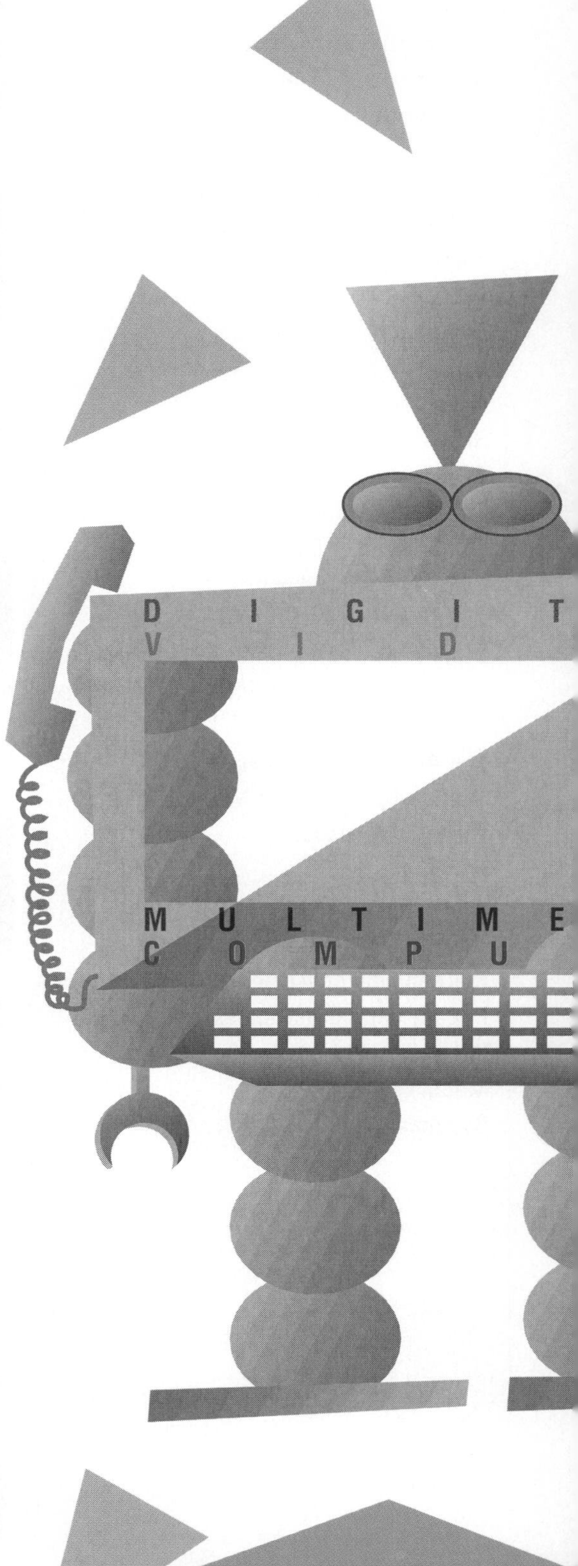

Chapter Outline

A Brief History of Advertising
Advertising in America
The Rise of the Advertising Profession
Hard Sell vs. Soft Sell
The Era of Integrated Marketing Communication (IMC)
Trends in Advertising Technology
Advertising Industry Organization
Advertisers
Inside the Advertising Agency
Advertising Media
Research
Advertising Genres
One-Voice Marketing
Use of Popular Culture
Relationship Marketing
Direct Marketing
Other Forms of Advertising Communication
The Key to Success: Understanding Consumer Needs
The Advertising Audience
The Media Evaluation Model
Advertising Issues
Ethics
Promotion of "Consumption Values"
Advertising and Children
Stereotyping of Women and Minorities
Privacy and Intrusiveness
Deception and "Puffery"
Media Literacy
Summary and Review

A BRIEF HISTORY OF ADVERTISING

Although the goal of **advertising** has always been to inform and persuade, it is undergoing dramatic changes as a form of communication. Advertising messages are more frequent, ubiquitous, and personal; they are carried by a wider range of communication technologies than in years past. This section describes some of the economic, cultural, and technological events that ushered in the era of sophisticated contemporary advertising.

It is often thought of as a twentieth-century phenomenon, but some form of advertising has existed for centuries. Since the time when people began living in small groups and villages, attempts have been made to persuade large groups to purchase or trade goods. Some archaeologists, for example, must have been disappointed when their translations of ancient Greek and Egyptian stone tablets revealed solicitations to stay at particular inns for the night or listed goods for sale! Signage on the walls of ancient cities of Greece and Rome also marketed tangible goods such as food and wine.

Another ancient form of advertising was the *town crier,* who told the citizenry about the "good deal" to be found "just around the corner." Unlike signs, which contained only information regarding the merchant, the criers also informed the citizens of the news of the day. Because the crier, or his agent, was compensated for his assistance in getting the advertising message out in the context of the news, there are interesting parallels with the newspaper of today (Applegate, 1993; Roche, 1993; Schramm, 1988).

With the introduction of the printing press in Europe in 1455, and later the industrial revolution, businesses accessed ever-larger markets for their goods. The printing press also spawned a new form of advertising, the *handbill.* The advantage of handbills over signs and town criers was that the message could be copied efficiently and distributed to many people in a relatively short time, and the content could be expanded to include as much description as was thought necessary to promote the transaction. Flyers and hand-distributed leaflets are still much in use today, particularly by local retailers and candidates for political office. Printing also enabled the first newspaper advertisements, which began around 1625.

Advertising is communication that is paid for and is usually persuasive in nature.

ADVERTISING INDUSTRY TIME LINE

1625	First ad in an English newspaper	1914	FTC established
1704	First classified ads	1926	First radio network
1833	Penny Press originated	1948	First TV network
1849	First ad sales agent	1960s	First 30- and 60-second TV commercials
1871	First formal ad agency	1980	Era of creativity begins
1887	Magazine advertising	1990s	Era of integrated marketing
1895	Image ads introduced	2000	Internet advertising flourishes

Advertising in America

The earliest newspaper ads in America were in the form of **classified ads** published in the Boston *News-Letter* in 1704 (Sandage, Fryburger, & Rotzoll, 1989). An example of advertising from the colonial period is the following ad, which appeared in Benjamin Franklin's newspaper, the *Pennsylvania Gazette.*

> To be SOLD A Plantation containing 300 acres of good Land, 30 cleared, 10 or 12 Meadows and in good English Grass, a house and barn lying in Nantmel Township, upon French Creek, about 30 miles from Philadelphia, Enquire of Simon Merideith.

Classified ads are brief newspaper advertisements, usually one column wide.

Franklin expanded the space devoted to advertising and was the first to apply creative writing skill to advertising copy. He was also the first to include illustrations alongside the copy.

Colonial advertising reveals a great deal about the freedom advertisers had to make a wide range of claims about their products. An advertisement in the December 9, 1778, issue of the *Pennsylvania Packet,* for example, extols the medical and dental expertise of "Dr. Baker," who could perform teeth transplants or graft natural teeth onto "the old stumps." The ad also promises that Dr. Baker's stay "will be very short." Obviously, Dr. Baker needed to leave town before his deception was discovered.

In the nineteenth century, economic forces were at work that would eventually give the average citizen the ability not only to read about but also to purchase the "new," "revolutionary" products. The **Industrial Revolution** in America, which brought about mass production by the end of the eighteenth century, played an integral part in the rise of modern advertising. Later, the technological convergence of electricity, internal combustion engines, and steam power led the United States to a situation where more products were being manufactured than could be consumed. This created a need for sophisticated, persuasive messages that stood out in a competitive environment. Some say this period marked the emergence of **consumer culture,** in which, according to Featherstone (1990), increased acquisition of products was promoted to maintain profits and provide important symbols of status and success. In other words, advertising at this time made a transition from simply explaining where hats were available for sale, for example, to attempting to persuade consumers of the importance of buying more hats to look

The **Industrial Revolution** produced a situation in which more products are manufactured than can be consumed.

In a **consumer culture,** social status is largely defined by the acquisition of goods and services.

good and achieve status (Ewen, 1976; Leiss, Kline, & Jhally, 1990). By 1895, "image advertising," or the attempt to sell the prestige as well as the function of products was fairly common.

Benjamin Day's *New York Sun* originated the concept of the mass circulation newspaper, or penny press, in 1833. From that point on, we see advertising emerging both as a form of persuasive communication, bought and paid for by the advertiser, and later as an economic engine with the potential to support the media enterprise financially. Another important influence in the penny press era was Robert Bonner, whose *New York Ledger* printed large display advertisements in the 1850s, breaking the bounds of the newspaper column format. However, the continuing reluctance of many newspapers to carry display ads left the door open to the first magazine advertising in the 1860s.

EARLY PRINT ADVERTISING. Advertising increased toward the end of the eighteenth century as more products were mass produced and more people became potential consumers. This ad for Cook's Virginia tobacco appeared around 1720.

The Rise of the Advertising Profession

In examining the history of advertising, it is also necessary to acknowledge the work done by its practitioners. These include **media representatives, advertisers,** and **advertising agencies.** The earliest advertising professionals were essentially advertising agents, who wholesaled advertising space on behalf of publishers. The best-known advertising agent from this era was Volney B. Palmer, who started in the advertising business in 1842 and coined the phrase *advertising agency* in 1849. Palmer represented some 1300 newspapers and originated the *commission* system, under which publishers paid a fee on completion of an advertising sale. Palmer also offered a wider range of services than other agents. He not only sold advertising space but also produced the ads, delivered them to the publishers, and verified their placement.

Media representatives work on behalf of media outlets to help sell advertising.

Advertising agencies are independent organizations that create promotional campaigns on behalf of advertisers.

In 1865 George P. Rowell, considered to be the founder of the advertising agency as we know it today, began contracting with local newspapers for a set amount of space and then brokered the space to clients. This made Rowell something of an independent "middleperson" who had to cater to both publishers and advertising clients. Rowell published an influential newspaper advertising directory, *Rowell's American Newspaper Dictionary,* in 1869 and advised his clients on which newspaper to select for their needs.

Another advertising pioneer of the nineteenth century was Francis Wayland Ayer, founder of the firm N. W. Ayer & Son (F.W. was the "son"). Ayer's most important contribution was to change the role of the advertising agency by making it the servant of the advertiser, rather than the publisher. In 1875 he originated the *open contract plus commission* system, under which he contracted with the advertiser to mount an advertising campaign in exchange for a commission on the advertising sales, but the fee was paid by the advertiser rather than by the publisher. Under this arrangement, Ayer also had the freedom to change publications, which enabled him to negotiate the best possible advertising rates for the client. Ayer was an important voice in the evolution of advertising ethics, promising to always work in the best interest of the advertiser—and refusing ads for products that he considered harmful and ads he thought were deceptive.

On the client, or advertiser, side, John Wanamaker stands out. This Philadelphia merchant discovered that he could distinguish his store from other department stores in the city by setting a fixed price on his goods—which was not the practice of the day—and by offering a money-back guarantee. He also found that when he informed the public of these policies via newspaper ads, his sales increased on the day following the announcement. This led him to increase the size and frequency of these messages and to employ someone on his staff to create the advertisements. This writer was John Powers, who in 1880 became one of the first professional **copywriters.**

Copywriters write the text of advertisements.

Wanamaker was also the first to question publicly the value of advertising. When asked to comment on how he felt about the large sums of money he was expending on newspaper advertising, he responded, "I know that half of my advertising expenditure is wasted; the problem is, I don't know which half." This comment continues to haunt the advertising profession today—although it also benefits the many advertising research companies that have used it as their own sales pitch since the turn of the century.

Political propaganda also played an important role in the evolution of modern advertising. During World War I, advertising found its voice directed away from the materialistic needs of the average citizen and toward the good of the country as a whole. This campaign—in which Albert Lasker, an advertising pioneer and managerial genius, played an important role—included activities designed to build public sentiment for the war effort as well as appeals to the home front to curtail unnecessary consumption and to "Buy War Bonds" instead.

War propaganda contributed to modern advertising by introducing persuasive techniques that emphasized zeal and emotion. Songs of World War I illustrate this. In 1917, for example, George M. Cohan wrote the popular patriotic tune "Over There" to drum up support for the war effort. Such songs contributed to the ongoing development of advertising jingles, which combine the emotional power of music with short, catchy slogans about products. Propaganda techniques also benefited the advertising industry by giving new evidence of the apparent power of commercial communication to affect public opinion. What had previously been a somewhat suspect marketing tool was seen in a more favorable light as a consequence of its success in promoting the war.

ADVERTISING AS WAR PROPAGANDA.
During World War I, advertising turned from promoting consumption of goods to getting citizens involved in the war effort by buying war bonds.

As we saw in Chapter 5, the 1920s witnessed the rise of a powerful new mass medium for advertising: the radio. Radio came of age as an advertising medium in 1926 when RCA purchased a chain of radio stations from AT&T, including WEAF in New Jersey, and established the National Broadcasting Company. The creation of the radio network concept provided national advertisers with an unprecedented means of distributing messages to prospects across the nation simultaneously (Fox, 1984). The new medium was designed to bring news, information, and entertainment to the public at large and depended exclusively on revenues received from advertisers.

The years following World War II saw the explosive expansion of television as an advertising medium, especially after the establishment of national television networks in 1948. Television quickly grew to compete with other forms of mass communication as the key creative medium for national advertisers. The combination of sight and sound gave advertisers the ability to demonstrate products to millions of viewers in a dramatic way. Soon, TV personality John Cameron Swazy was attaching watches to outboard motor rudder blades and snowplow treads in order to prove that "Timex takes a licking but keeps on ticking." Other commercials showed that Bic pens could still write after being shot through blocks of solid oak with high-powered rifles, and that Samsonite luggage was undamaged after being dropped from an airplane. Although magazine advertising was also a growing medium, television enjoyed the ability to demonstrate products.

At first, television advertisers followed the practice prevalent in the radio industry of sponsoring entire programs. By the 1960s, however, program sponsorship had given way to the purchase of advertising time in 60- or 30-second (and later 15-second) increments. In the early 1980s, cable television emerged as another new advertising medium. By 1998 the once-dominant broadcast television networks had seen their piece of the evening television audience slip to under 50 percent.

By the 1990s, the computer was beginning to have an effect on contemporary advertising. Computer databases and electronic linkages via the Internet create potentially efficient and personal ways to reach consumers. Through interactive media, advertisers are finding new ways to micro-target specific groups and provide the type of information that consumers want. This trend is explored in detail in the section on trends in advertising technology.

Hard Sell vs. Soft Sell

A defining moment in advertising occurred in 1905 when John E. Kennedy, a copywriter working in partnership with Albert Lasker at the Lord & Thomas advertising agency in New York, redefined advertising as "salesmanship in print." Before then, advertising copy was usually brief and hyperbolic, and most ads sought a mail-in response from the reader—a variety of advertising we now call **direct marketing.** Kennedy, an experienced salesperson, felt that advertising copy should offer consumers reasons why they should go out and buy the product by presenting arguments much as a live salesperson would do. This "hard-sell" approach to advertising as a mediated sales tool helped focus the creative message and introduced the "reason why" philosophy to copy preparation (Wells, Burnett, & Moriarty, 1995), a philosophy that Lasker championed throughout a long and distinguished career.

Direct marketing is a form of advertising in which an immediate response is requested from the customer.

The "soft-sell" approach was pioneered at about the same time by Stanley Resor and his copywriter, Helen Lansdowne, at the J. Walter Thompson agency. This approach tended toward an emotional rather than a rational appeal. Saturn advertising is a contemporary example of the soft-sell approach in automobile advertising. From magazine ads to TV commercials to in-store displays, messages feature Saturn buyers describing how the car reflects their values; all ads have a conversational style that is relaxed and friendly. Instead of making a glitzy sales pitch, owners are depicted at home or at work simply talking about the quality of the product and the fair price. In a typical print ad, two Saturn employees talk with pride about the Saturn corporate culture of quality and positive social values. This open, "tell it like it is" theme even filters down to the showroom floor, where salespeople take a no-dicker price approach; they answer questions but never overpower the customer. The Saturn Web site also reflects this soft-sell tone and graphics scheme.

The soft-sell approach became so prevalent by the 1980s that this period is often referred to as the **era of creativity.** That is, advertising during this time was as much about entertainment as it was about marketing. Wendy's "Where's the Beef?" campaign and the "Mikey" character in commercials for Life Cereal are considered classic 1980s examples of how advertisers incorporate entertainment formats such as television situation comedy into marketing communication.

In the **era of creativity,** advertisers emphasized entertainment as well as information.

The Era of Integrated Marketing Communication (IMC)

Although advertising has traditionally been associated with the "big five" media (television, radio, newspapers, magazines, and billboards), there are far more options today—from Internet banners to movie trailers on video cassettes. The vast number of technological options has helped create a phenomenon known as **integrated marketing communication (IMC),** which encourages the use of virtually all communication channels available to the advertiser. According to Burnett & Moriarty (1998), IMC is the "practice of unifying all marketing communication tools—from advertising to packaging—to send target audiences a consistent, persuasive message that promotes company goals."

Integrated marketing communication (IMC) assures that the use of all commercial media and messages is clear, consistent, and achieves impact.

While advertising has long been the most common form of marketing communication, it no longer dominates the way it once did. For example, in recent years the ready-to-eat cereal industry has done more sales promotion (coupons, sweepstakes, sampling, etc.) than advertising. In the era of IMC, advertising is but one of many options, and the extent to which it is used depends on the needs of the advertiser. For example, Oakley, one of the most successful manufacturers of sunglasses and sports eyewear attributed much of its success to the nontraditional medium of *stickers.* Executives learned that consumers were so eager to be associated with the prestige of the Oakley brand, that they were willing to purchase stickers and place them on their car windows, motorcycles, and other possessions. Today, companies do not restrict themselves to advertising, but instead try to find that combination of marketing public relations, sales promotions, and direct marketing that best achieves their goals.

1. How would you describe "advertising" as a form of communication?
2. What role did the Industrial Revolution play in ushering in the era of modern advertising?
3. Which advertising techniques were influenced by war propaganda?

TRENDS IN ADVERTISING TECHNOLOGY

The technology of advertising has developed side by side with the technology of mass media. We will not recount these developments here since they are covered in Chapters 3 and 7, but will instead focus on the ways in which information technologies are starting to transform conventional advertising forms.

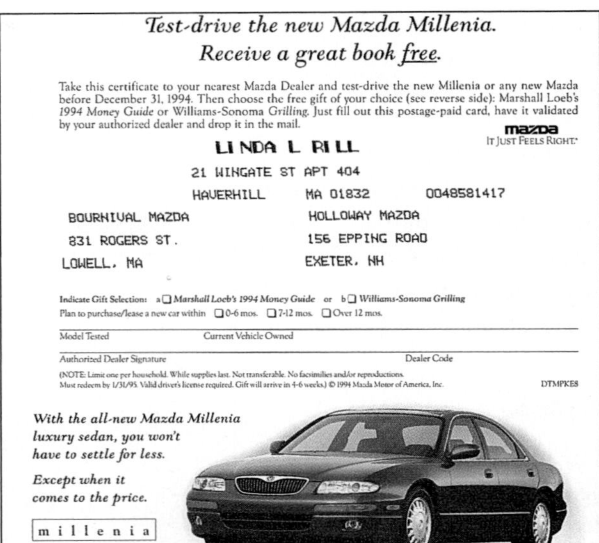

Test-drive the new Mazda Millenia.
Receive a great book free.
Take this certificate to your nearest Mazda Dealer and test-drive the new Millenia or any new Mazda before December 31, 1994. Then choose the free gift of your choice (see reverse side): Marshall Loeb's 1994 Money Guide or Williams-Sonoma Grilling. Just fill out this postage-paid card, have it validated by your authorized dealer and drop it in the mail.
mazda
It Just Feels Right.
LI NDA L RI LL
21 WINGATE ST APT 404
HAVERHILL MA 01832 0048581417
BOURNIVAL MAZDA
831 ROGERS ST.
LOWELL, MA
HOLLOWAY MAZDA
156 EPPING ROAD
EXETER, NH
Indicate Gift Selection: a ☐ Marshall Loeb's 1994 Money Guide or b ☐ Williams-Sonoma Grilling
Plan to purchase/lease a new car within ☐ 0-6 mos. ☐ 7-12 mos. ☐ Over 12 mos.
Model Tested
Current Vehicle Owned
Authorized Dealer Signature
Dealer Code
(NOTE: Limit one per household. While supplies last. Not transferable. No facsimiles and/or reproductions.
Must redeem by 1/31/95. Valid driver's license required. Gift will arrive in 4-6 weeks.) © 1994 Mazda Motor of America, Inc.
DTMPKE8
With the all-new Mazda Millenia luxury sedan, you won't have to settle for less.
Except when it comes to the price.
millenia

THIS AD'S FOR YOU! Technology now allows ads in magazines to be personalized to each subscriber, as this automobile ad from *Time* magazine illustrates.

Print media now use computer and telecommunications technologies extensively and may even claim to be the first mass media to enter the computer age. Many of these developments are behind-the-scenes advances in the creation, production, and distribution of print publications via computer platforms that do not directly affect the advertising process. One meaningful contribution of the computer to print advertising is **selective binding.** This automated technique enables the publication to build unique versions of each issue for selected groups of readers. For example, *Newsweek* has over 150 separate editions targeted by geographical location and the characteristics of recipients. This technique makes it possible for advertisers to segment audiences into smaller groups and avoid costly wasted circulation, even though the ads may be more expensive.

Another electronic trick of the trade is the ability to print information that makes reference to an individual reader. Not only do you see your name printed in the text of a mailing from a marketer such as Publishers Clearinghouse, but you can also read it in the pages of a magazine in the text of an advertisement ("Hey, Ms. Jones, have we got a computer for YOU!).

Selective binding allows publishers to create multiple versions of the same publication.

Database marketing is used when advertisers store information about consumers so that they can personalize messages.

Technological advances are creating new ways to build relationships between consumers and brands. **Database marketing,** another computer-based technique, makes this possible on a grand scale. Advertisers store information about consumers so that messages can be personalized in the future. One need not look farther than the corner grocery store for an example of the use of this technology. Customers fill out a questionnaire giving the local food store manager information (address, occupation, income, product preferences, etc.), which is stored in a database along with a scanned-in record of purchases. If a consumer regularly buys chocolate chip cookies but hasn't been to the store in recent days, the database is programmed to mail a discount coupon for the customer's favorite cookie brand. Alternatively, coupons might be issued directly at the check-out aisle.

Another example is that of Lands' End, Inc., which sells clothing and related merchandise via catalogs. The customer data file is so extensive that when an order is phoned in, the operator is able to "call up" the individual from the database and identify all the items he or she has ever purchased from the company.

The Internet also has great potential as an advertising medium. Consumers can visit Web sites, ask questions, and even make purchases. It is both an *impulse* and a *directional* technology. The impulse potential arises from the growing number of browsers or "surfers" who respond to commercial messages on a whim as they use the Net for other purposes. For example, a reader of a book review in the on-line version of the *New York Times* may impulsively decide to click on the Barnes and Noble ad to order a copy. The Net becomes a directional medium when consumers decide to purchase a particular product and then go to a company's Web site to do so.

Perhaps the most interesting aspect of the Internet, however, is its interactive nature. Whereas traditional media (such as television, magazines, and newspapers) are finite sources of information, the Internet becomes a responsive and flexible

TECHNOLOGY ***TRENDS***

Advertising Agencies of Tomorrow: How One Company Is Integrating New Media

Agencies are independent organizations that execute advertising campaigns for their clients (see p. 359). Although associated primarily with the creation of traditional advertising forms, such as TV commercials, newspaper ads, and billboards, many agencies are adjusting to the new marketing opportunities provided by the Internet. "Studeo," a new company in Provo, Utah, is a good example of how new media are altering the ways agencies do business. Companies such as Arthur Anderson, American Express, Netopia, Host Marriott, Pioneer, and TenFold are hoping that Studeo can help them better understand how to use new media to reach their marketing objectives.

"The old school agency is history," according to David Allen, CEO of Studeo. "The ability to blend traditional media with new technology has given us a leg up on other agencies that haven't figured out what to do with the Internet."

While many agencies see the Web as just another medium, Allen places it at the center of everything the agency does. "The Internet is a rich source of information and companies expect their advertising agency to know how to get consumers to their Web site," according to Allen. "Few agencies know how to do this, and even fewer know how to communicate to customers one-to-one on the Internet once they arrive."

Studeo is the result of a recent merger of a traditional advertising agency and an Internet development company. Bringing the two staffs together had its problems at first. Todd Shepherd, Studeo's president, recalls the initial tension.

"We had art directors grounded in the traditional principles of print advertising and computer programmers who spoke nothing but the language of cyberspace. While it was a little dicey at first, it wasn't long before we realized we had a powerful combination here," Shepherd says. "As our people began to work together, we realized that we had created a model for the future of the advertising agency business. We began to look at advertising as no longer static, but as an ongoing exchange with consumers through media that is interactive."

According to Allen and Shepherd, students considering a career in the agency business will have to be flexible and know how to solve problems. "Ground yourself in traditional advertising principles, but realize that there are a million ways to apply those principles," Allen says. "The Internet is an endless sea of content, and the ability to steer someone through it requires a combination of persuasive talent and technological know-how. The rules of good advertising still apply, but it takes someone who knows how to use them with new media," according to Allen. In order to cultivate this knowledge, Studeo has added a "technical services" department to the existing agency organization.

"This type of expertise," Allen asserts, "gives us the ability to apply advertising creativity in media that our agency did not previously understand."

While executives at Studeo consider the Internet to be the heart of marketing communication, not all agency professionals agree. Many hire outside companies to do Web advertising for their clients, but Shepherd believes this is a mistake. "Agencies that don't have new media in-house are missing the boat in terms of relationship marketing. The Internet is not an afterthought; it is the core of all strategies."

data source through the two-way exchange of messages. The Web site for Hallmark cards exemplifies this unique feature. A "reminder service" is available whereby customers are asked for prominent names and birthdays and are later contacted through e-mail when it's time to send that person a greeting card. According to Duncan and Moriarty (1997) these technological advances allow advertisers to communicate "with" consumers rather than the traditional method of talking "to" them, thus enabling advertisers to "grow" consumers and build strong brand relationships. (Why not do an electronic search to learn more about this topic? If you are using InfoTrac College Edition, enter the following terms: "database marketing," "relationship marketing," and "integrated marketing communication.")

The jury is still out on this new medium, however, and a number of professionals express caution. According to Michael Bloomberg, founder and CEO of Bloomberg L.P., the Internet has not yet achieved its potential as a marketing vehicle. At a recent national summit on the future of Internet advertising, he told the audience, "We are focusing more and more on becoming media we were trying to differentiate ourselves from" (MediaPost, 1998). These criticisms are primarily aimed at *banner ads,* or square computer screen inserts providing links to the larger advertisers' homepages. Much of this advertising resembles billboards and retail print layouts and hence often fails to convey the medium's inherent user-friendly features. Preliminary indications are that conventional advertising techniques have not yet proved consistently effective on the Internet (Jerram, 1997). In fact, whereas traditional advertising adheres to design principles of simplicity and brevity, new evidence indicates that larger, more complicated banner ads are more memorable (Beatty, 1998).

Use of this technology is expanding, however. Although only $39 million was spent on Internet advertising in 1995 (compared to the $32.4 billion spent on television advertising), expenditures will probably hit $3 billion in the year 2000 (Braverman, 1996). Projected growth is partly based on the medium's unique ability to build databases. When consumers visit a site, they are often asked to "register" by providing demographic information. Because a consumer profile is stored at the Web site, a wide variety of producer–consumer interactions are possible for many years to come. According to Bob Schmetterer of EURO RSCG Worldwide, "When it comes to building brand loyalty and conviction, the opportunity presented by the Internet is unparalleled" (MediaPost, 1998, p.1). Privacy is a concern, however, and advertisers must accommodate consumers and inform them about how information collected will be used in the future.

Advertisers continue to explore the convergence of interactive and multimedia technologies. This will increase the number of new strategies, such as personalized ads, ads on demand, and even instant coupons transmitted to homes via set-top printers. But **Internet TV** may be the most important technological development for advertising in the near future (Pavlik, 1998). Though in its infancy, this technology combines the benefits of on-line and multimedia with the high audience reach of television. Through the use of a set-top box, consumers can browse the World Wide Web as a part of the television viewing experience.

Internet TV allows consumers to watch television and then access on-line advertising from the same TV set.

The oldest form of advertising, the outdoor sign, is also slated for a high-tech makeover. New technology recently purchased by a number of TV sports networks imposes signage onto stadium and arena walls that do not exist outside of the television screen. In other words, this form of *virtual advertising* creates a reality for the home viewer that is decidedly different from that experienced by the fan attending the game. Virtual ads reach large audiences and can be changed quickly and efficiently. This innovation could also effectively "block out" advertisers that have ads posted in the sports venues but are not affiliated with the commercial broadcast of the event.

Although it is unlikely that these developments will spell the end of conventional advertising, marketing communication will have a new look in years to come. Two-way communication will be more common, and traditional media such as newspapers and magazines will add on-line products to their traditional channels of distribution. Today, for example, advertisers in *The Houston Chronicle* may also opt for an ad on the *Chronicle*'s Web site.

However, at least some of the new advertising technologies have created new tensions for advertising agencies, media representatives, mass media, and all other "middlepersons" that have traditionally mediated between the advertiser and the consumer. Cable home shopping channels already give marketers a direct pipeline to the consumer that eliminates the need for an advertising agency. Home shopping is rapidly evolving into a computer medium, in which consumers view digital catalogs stored on high-capacity computer storage media or receive interactive "junk mail" sent to them on computer disk. In either case the conventional mass media would also be left out of the picture.

Other advertisers are experimenting with kiosks, stand-alone computer terminals that provide in-depth product information right at the point of sale. The "intelligent shopping cart" has made its appearance, complete with a computer display that directs the consumer to product locations and special promotions throughout the supermarket. Some grocery chains are installing, over their check-out lanes, television monitors that telecast news of in-store specials and messages from brand advertisers. And the cost of computer chips that can synthesize the human voice is dropping quickly, raising the specter of the "talking cereal box" shouting advertising slogans at us as we walk down the aisle. On the other hand, digital multimedia systems should make it possible to "zap" commercials and (electronic) print ads more effectively—to filter them out automatically or even to jam the advertiser's computer network with e-mail objections in response to an especially intrusive commercial.

1. What is "database marketing," and how is it changing advertising today?
2. How might new technologies affect the practice of advertising in the future?
3. Why are marketing professionals divided in their opinions about the future impact of Internet advertising?

ADVERTISING INDUSTRY ORGANIZATION

Someone or some organization must identify the need for an advertising message—and foot the bill for the campaign that results. This initiator is the advertiser. Then the message must be created. Here the responsibility may either be retained by the *advertiser* or be subcontracted to an *advertising agency.* Next, the message must be placed in one or more of the **advertising media,** each of which has its own organizational form and structure. **Research organizations** then help all concerned evaluate and measure the target group, the message content, and the media *vehicles* under consideration. As a means of understanding the structure of the industry, readers can follow the development of an advertising campaign from the moment of its conception by an advertiser to its presentation to the public by examining Figure 11.1.

Advertising media are the communication channels that carry messages to consumers.

Research organizations compile statistics about consumers and their media habits and evaluate advertising messages.

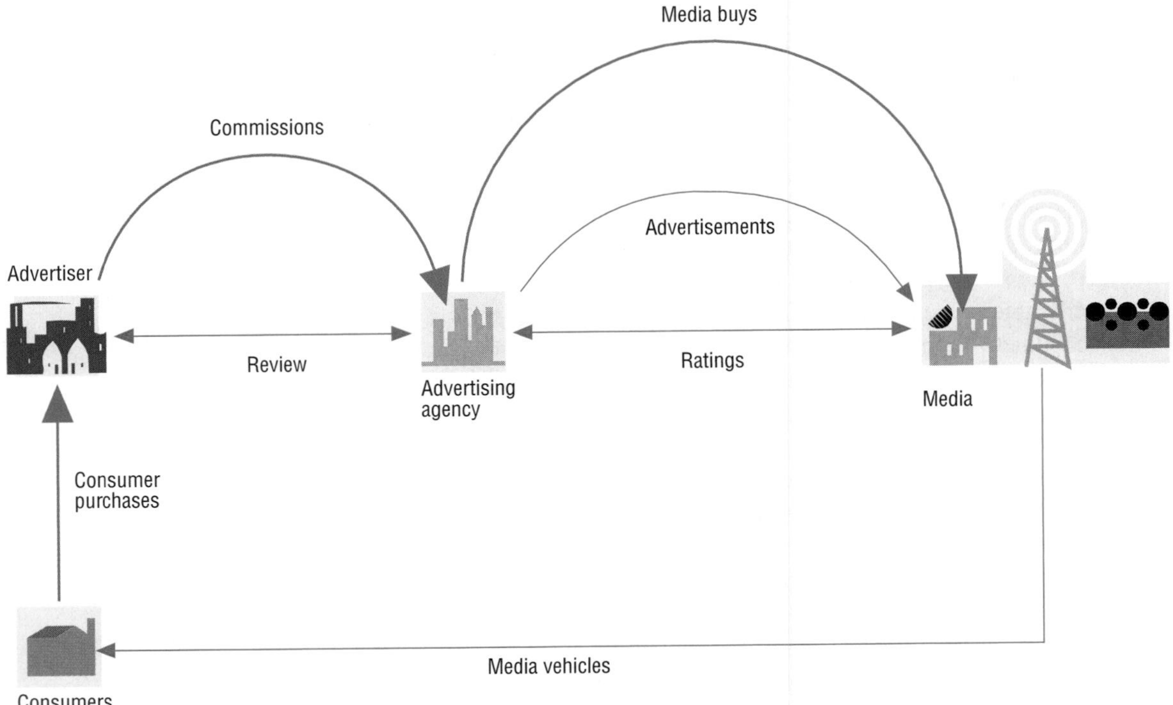

FIGURE 11.1
The advertising process depends on money (green arrows) and information (red arrows) flows among advertisers, their agencies, the media, and consumers.

Advertisers

The top categories of advertising expenditures are automotive, retail, business and consumer services, and entertainment and amusements (see Table 11.1). Leading national packaged-goods companies such as Procter & Gamble and the major automotive companies lead the list of major advertisers.

In the past, it was not unusual to find the chief executive officer involved in decisionmaking about the advertising budget. This is less common in today's age of product segmentation. To cope with the myriad duties involved in getting a brand to market, companies typically assign the advertising, budgeting, and execution responsibilities to a **marketing manager** in charge of a family of **brands,** who in turn delegates the advertising duties for a specific family of products to a **brand manager.** Although the day-to-day advertising operation is normally handled by the brand manager, ultimate approval of the advertising budget is typically handed down from the marketing manager level or higher.

Marketing managers are in charge of a family of products for an advertiser.

A product's name, design, and symbols constitute a **brand,** which distinguishes it from other products.

Brand managers are in charge of one specific product.

Advertising managers coordinate the advertiser's efforts across all of its products.

In a large company that sells a product for a national audience, the advertising process begins when the marketing manager calls for a meeting with the **advertising manager** of the firm to discuss advertising goals, deadlines, and expectations for the coming year. The creation of the advertising message is generally not performed by the company itself but instead is delegated to an advertising agency (see Figure 11.1). An advertising agency can provide an outside, objective perspective that companies can't get internally. The advertising manager invites a number of agencies to make presentations and, when one is selected, acts as a liaison between the firm and the agency.

In those cases where the company is a local retailer, the process is much simpler. Typically, the owner determines approximately how much to spend on advertising in the coming year, writes the ads, and arranges to have them placed in local newspapers, on radio stations, or in other local media. This is not to say, however, that the selection of the target for the ad or the development of the message is any less important. It is just that the process unfolds on a somewhat lesser scale than in a national program.

Local retailers also take advantage of *co-op advertising* support from national companies. For example, a department store that buys a product such as Kodak film gets an allowance for advertising. Kodak also provides print ads for retailers to use. In other words, a good share of local advertising is actually paid for by national advertisers.

TABLE 11.1 Top Ten Advertising Categories*

Category	Expenditure
Automotive	$12,873.4
Retail	10,860.7
Business and consumer services	9,031.8
Entertainment and amusements	5,889.3
Food and food products	4,194.0
Drugs and remedies	3,981.0
Cosmetics and toiletries	3,684.3
Travel, hotels, and resorts	2,836.4
Computers, office equipment	2,332.6
Direct-response companies	1,880.0

*Dollars, in millions, from top 500 agency brands. Interactive media bought on a commission basis only.

Source: Advertising Age on-line archive.

Inside the Advertising Agency

Most major companies do not want to plan and produce advertising campaigns themselves. Their business is to produce and sell a product, be it tennis shoes, soft drinks, or dog food. Therefore, a variety of advertising agencies have grown up at local, national, and international levels to plan and produce ad campaigns for them.

Agencies are independent organizations of businesspeople and talented individuals who do nothing but create and place **advertising plans** (see the Media Watch box) for their clients. As we noted earlier, one of the first advertising agents, Volney B. Palmer, came on the scene over 100 years ago. Eventually Palmer and other media brokers offered more and more services, such as designing advertisements. The top agencies of the 1990s in terms of creative excellence and financial stability are listed in Table 11.2. According to *Advertising Age* magazine, these "Agencies of the Year" consistently exhibit strategic thinking and win the best accounts because of their reputation and management stability (Cuneo & Petrecca, 1998).

The **advertising plan** is a written document outlining the objectives and strategies for a product's advertising.

Full-service agencies offer a wide range of advertising services, including research, strategy development, and media placement.

Account executives are the liaisons between the agency and the client.

Today, **full-service agencies** complete virtually all elements of an advertising campaign including research, strategic planning, and generation of creative ideas for ads. Examples of major full-service advertising agencies include Ogilvy & Mather, which produced the memorable campaign for American Express in the 1980s, and Bates USA, which produced the Wendy's campaign featuring company founder Dave Thomas. These companies employ **account executives,** who act as liaisons between the agency and the client. They mobilize and coordinate all of the agency's work on the advertising campaign.

TABLE 11.2 Advertising "Agencies of the Year" Winners for the 1990s*

Year	Agency
1997	TBWA Chiat/Day
1996	Foote, Cone & Belding, San Francisco
1995	Fallon McElligott
1994	DDB Needham Worldwide
1993	BBDO Worldwide and Deutsch
1992	Hal Riney & Partners
1991	Wieden & Kennedy

*Selection criteria based on creative excellence, management stability, financial stability, strategic thinking, and account wins/losses.

Source: Cuneo & Petrecca, 1998, p. s8.

The Creative Department. A key element in the advertising plan is the **creative strategy,** or what the advertising will say in order to achieve the objectives of the campaign. Using the research data as a foundation, copywriters and graphic designers in the creative department begin work on a creative concept or "big idea." *Concepting* is the act of saying something in a unique way but at the same time ensuring that the message is "on strategy" with what needs to be communicated for the product to sell. For example, a Marriott hotel commercial recently stressed the importance of a good night's sleep by showing a groggy, sleep-deprived

Creative strategy is a written statement about what advertising must say in order to achieve marketing objectives.

man sitting at a table in front of a large audience. When the host finishes announcing the guest speaker, the groggy man is startled, and begins to applaud enthusiastically. Then someone leans over to inform him that he has just been introduced. Because this commercial is both entertaining (presents a humorous situation) and relevant to the consumer's needs (communicates the importance of a good night's rest), it is said to have a strong creative concept.

A variety of creative professions may be involved in the ad's execution: writers, artists, art directors, musicians, graphic designers, content or subject experts, and research people. What emerges after a period of creative incubation is not a single clear-cut solution to all of the client's problems, but rather several executions, one of which will be able to survive the critical *client review* process. Once an execution gets approval from the client, the assignment is given back to the creative department for final production.

Media departments negotiate on behalf of the advertiser to buy space from media companies.

The Media Department. Meanwhile, the agency's **media department** is hard at work selecting media to carry the client's message, given the budget available. The

MEDIA WATCH

Elements of an Advertising Plan or Campaign

- The **situation analysis** explains where the company is, how it got there, and where it wants to be in the future. It identifies relevant problems that must be addressed by advertising and gives a detailed description of the consumer of the product.
- **Objectives** are those things we want the advertising campaign to achieve. Most advertising plans include both business objectives ("Increase unit sales by 25,000 during the next year") and communication objectives ("Achieve 65 percent awareness of the product within the target market"). Objectives differ according to the nature of the product, competition, consumer demand, and available budget.
- The **Target Market Profile** is a description of those individuals who would be the most likely to purchase the product. The target profile usually includes demographics (the target's age, sex, ethnicity, and income) and psychographics. Psychographics are lifestyle descriptions of the consumer's attitudes, interests, and opinions.
- The **positioning statement** is a short paragraph explaining how the company wants the consumer to perceive the product. A lot of things can be communicated (price, quality, convenience, and so on), but what is the most important thing the advertising has to convey? A recent campaign for Southwest Airlines positions the product as a friendly airline whose discounted fares offer "freedom to move about the country." The advertising is light, is humorous, and consistently conveys this theme.
- The **creative strategy** is the part of the plan that describes the specific theme and approach of the advertising. In other words, the creative strategy is a description of what the advertising will actually look like. In national campaigns, the strategy contains a *big idea* or a fresh and interesting way to make a point about the product. The big idea for Little Caesar's Pizza is an animated Caesar character in a Roman toga who utters, "Pizza, Pizza!" in all ads to communicate that you always get two pizzas for the right price.
- The **media plan** lists the communication vehicles that will carry the advertising. Should television be used? Why or why not? If Internet advertising is rejected, what are the reasons? A good media plan ensures that enough of the right people are reached at an efficient price.

PROFILE

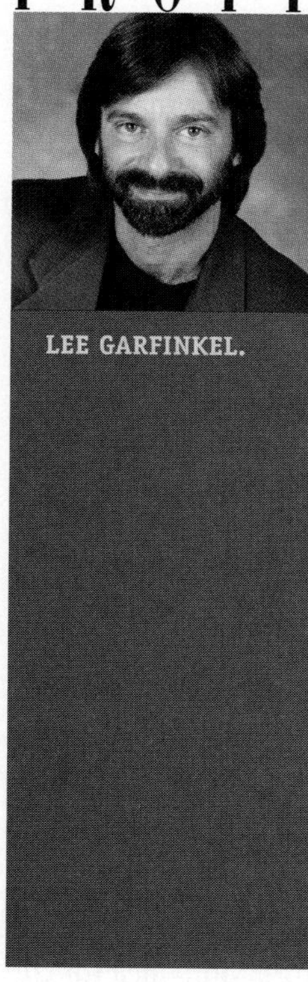
LEE GARFINKEL.

Creative Philosopher

Name: Lee Garfinkel

Early Years: Grew up in the Bronx, New York

Position: Chairman and Chief Creative Officer, Lowe & Partners/SMS

Style: An individualist who resists formulaic approaches to advertising.

Most Notable Achievements: Won awards for best car commercials four years in a row; wrote national advertising for Pepsi; and became chairman of Lowe & Partners/SMS, which is known for great creative work.

Most Dubious Achievements: Because he was a "talker," his first-grade teacher put him in the back of the room with an easel and paintbrush.

Entry Level: Two years as a stand-up comic taught him a lot about how to communicate with people.

Inspiration: A challenge from Frank Lowe, founder and chairman of the Lowe Group, to build a great advertising agency.

How He Got to the Top: His approach to advertising underpins a number of great campaigns for Sony, Sprite, Perdue, and Mercedes-Benz. First, he believes that "great" advertising both gets attention and sells products. He also believes in an approach that rejects applying rigid rules in all situations. The rules are different, he argues, for each client.

Where Does He Go from Here? Garfinkel isn't satisfied with a "great creative agency." He wants to create a great agency in general, where all departments understand the objectives and display creativity at many levels.

Sources: "What Lee Sees," *Advertising Age,* April 6, 1998, p. 18. (Advertisement for the *Wall Street Journal.*) "About the Judges," 1999 International ANDY Awards Web site. Personal interview with Michael Dragnin, Communications Director, Lowe & Partners.

account executive works constantly to keep all parties up-to-date on one another's progress. Once the creative and media recommendations are approved by the client, the *media buyer,* a specialist within the media department, initiates negotiations with media suppliers for the purchase of specific media vehicles to carry the advertising message. The initial media document and budget recommendation prepared by the media department contained only the type of media recommended, not specific newspapers, magazines, or broadcast programs. This is by design, because the media plan is normally prepared up to a year before the ad is produced.

Today, clients expect more than ever from advertising agencies, including advice on how best to use sales promotion and marketing public relations. If you are using InfoTrac College Edition, research on-line the many recent changes in advertising agency services. Enter the terms "advertising agencies," "sales promotion," and "marketing public relations."

Advertising Media

The main economic base of many American media is advertising. For commercial radio and television stations, it is by far their most important source of revenue, whereas newspapers and magazines depend on a combination of newsstand sales, subscriptions, and advertising. In selecting media, advertisers consider whom they want to reach, what kind of message or information they want to communicate, and the costs of various media.

In an advertising campaign, the media swing into action at the request of the advertising agency's media buyer. Upon notification that the media plan has been approved by the client, the ad agency's media buyer contacts the appropriate **media representative** firm to determine the current costs and availability of media vehicles under consideration. For newspapers and magazines, a rate card is provided that lists the costs of various ads according to size and frequency. For television, the media representative identifies available timeslots that meets the buyer's general criteria in terms of the number of target prospects that can be delivered at the time of day in which the buyer wishes to advertise. The "media rep" counsels with station salespeople to determine what price will be charged for commercial time in the identified programs. Finally, a package of programs is delivered by the rep to the buyer at the agency.

Media representatives are intermediaries between advertising agencies and media outlets.

The buyer examines the list of programs, their prices, and the audience delivery estimates. Advertisers try to reach the largest number of people in the target audience at the lowest possible price. The costs of various media depend on several factors: the size of the audience, the composition of the audience (age, wealth, education, and so on), and the prestige of the medium. In general, media with larger audiences can charge more for accepting and carrying advertisements. However, a smaller, more specifically focused audience can sometimes be even more valuable to an advertiser than a larger, more heterogeneous one. Comparisons among vehicles are made on a **cost per thousand (CPM)** basis—that is, on the basis of the cost of reaching a thousand members of the target audience for the ad. This efficiency comparison is determined by dividing the cost of each ad by the size of the audience it delivers, in thousands. The general goal is to try to reach the largest number of the target audience for the lowest dollar investment (Martin & Coons, 1998), but many other factors may also be considered, including the inherent characteristics of different media. Table 11.3 lists some of the strengths and weaknesses of various advertising media.

Cost per thousand (CPM) is a way of comparing advertising costs in terms of the price paid to reach 1000 members of the target audience.

The nature of the target audience also affects media selection. Often media advertisers want to reach a broad **general audience.** Some advertisers want to sell products, such as soap or soft drinks, that might interest virtually everyone in a mass audience. Other advertisers might use a general-audience medium if it has a high impact on a particular group they want to reach. For example, although a very broad audience watches prime-time network television, ads are often placed there for products aimed primarily at older people, such as denture adhesive cream. Television may reach a larger proportion of older people than any other **audience segment.** An advertiser that wants to sell athletic shoes to teenagers will pick just the television shows and radio stations that appeal selectively to teenagers.

General audience means that the audience is made up of a large group of people from all walks of life.

Audience segment is a subgroup of consumers with specialized tastes and media habits.

Advertisers also take into account the nature of the media and the kinds of ads they can carry. A television ad with the style of music video may be important in capturing the interest of young men to tell them about a new athletic shoe. Television packs a certain kind of punch that just sound on a radio station, or a still image in a magazine, may not be able to achieve. The advertiser might decide to

TABLE 11.3 Strengths and Weaknesses of Advertising Media

Medium	Strengths	Weaknesses
Newspapers	Intense coverage Flexibility Prestige Dealer or advertiser coordination	Short life Hasty reading Moderate to poor reproduction
Magazines	Market selectivity Long life High reproduction quality Prestige Extra services	Inflexible area coverage/time Inflexible to copy changes Low overall market penetration Wide distribution
Television	Mass coverage High impact Repetition Prestige Flexibility	Fleeting message Commercial wearout Lack of selectivity High cost
Radio	Audience selectivity Immediacy Flexibility Mobility	Fragmentation Transient quality of listenership Limited sensory input
Internet	Cost-efficient Personal Interactive	Loss of privacy Low reach Technical expertise required

run a few television commercials to capture attention and then remind people of the product with radio spots, billboards, magazine ads, and so on. Usually an advertiser will try to mix media to make sure that everyone in the target group is exposed to the pitch in one form or another, several times. For sports shoes, that mix might include ads on network television shows popular with young people, ads on MTV to reach those who do not watch much network television, ads on FM stations aimed at young men (which may be different from stations targeting young women), and ads in magazines about team sports, music, outdoor activities, cars, and other things of interest to young men.

After this analysis is complete, the buyer again contacts the media representatives and the negotiating process begins in earnest. At its conclusion, the media buyer informs the client about the buys via the media planner or account executive, notifies the agency's accounting department to prepare the necessary billing documents, and contacts the execution arm of the creative department (sometimes called the *traffic department*) to deliver the finished ads to the proper media organizations at the appropriate time.

Research

An integral part of the entire advertising process is research. Those involved with **marketing research** collect and analyze data about product sales and factors that affect consumer opinions about products. In the advertising agency, account

Marketing research is the collection of information about consumer opinions of products.

executives depend on research analysts and account planners to provide in-depth consumer profiles and key information about the competition. In other words, they try to get into the head of the consumer and obtain a deeper, more thorough understanding of what "drives" him or her to buy products.

Media research compiles data about media consumption for the advertising industry.

Media research experts work for the media and the media departments of the advertising agencies to give them information about patterns of exposure to the mass media. Media research encompasses:

- Target audience delivery information for radio and television broadcasts
- Circulation figures for magazines and newspapers
- Profiles of the users of consumer products
- Media usage habits
- Qualitative studies that gauge audience reactions to specific media vehicles
- Reports on annual advertising expenditure levels of the leading national brands
- *Copy tests* that evaluate the effectiveness of ads that are under development

Examples of research companies and the audience information they provide are shown in Table 11.4.

Each medium has its own audience measurement "language," but television's is perhaps the most widely used—and the most arcane. In this lexicon, a *television household* is a home with a (working) television set. There are about 90 million of these households in the United States. A *HUT* is a *household using television,* an estimate of all the households in the United States that are using television during a particular time period. A **rating** is the percentage of all television households tuned in to a particular program. Each rating point is one percentage point, representing about 900,000 households. A *share* is the percentage of HUTs watching a program: thus, it is based on only the number of homes actually watching television. It is this measure that is of greatest interest to advertisers (see Figure 11.2).

Ratings are the percentages of TV households watching particular programs.

The A. C. Nielsen Company compiles ratings and share data by distributing diaries to random samples of homes, in which family members record all the programs they watch. National TV ratings are derived from *audimeters,* electronic devices attached to the television that record each move of the television dial. *People meters* are electronic devices that record *who* is watching, as well as what is

TABLE 11.4 Research Services and the Audience Data They Provide

Medium	Company	Audience Report Content
National television	A. C. Nielsen	Ratings for programs on the national TV networks
Local television	A. C. Nielsen	Ratings for programs broadcast by local TV stations
National radio	RADAR	Ratings for network programs by local radio stations
Local radio	Arbitron	Ratings for stations broadcasting in the local market
Newspapers	Audit Bureau of Circulation	The number of newspaper copies sold
Magazines	Simmons/MRI Research	Ratings for the top magazines in the U.S.

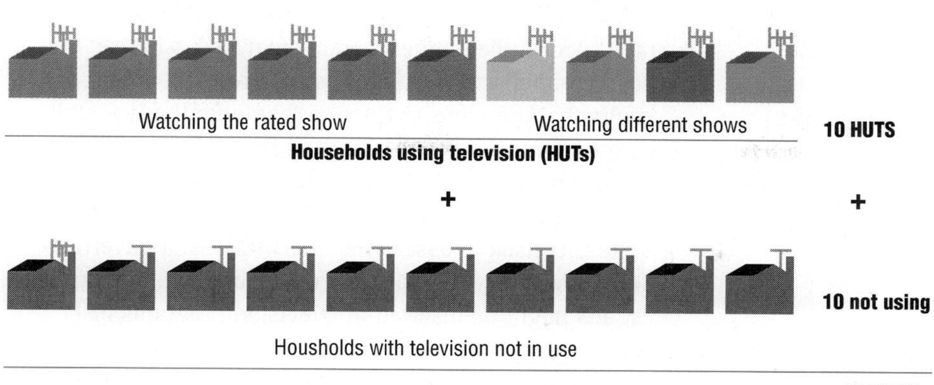

= 20 TVHH

1 household without television

Total HH = 21

$$\text{Rating} = \frac{\text{Number watching rated show}}{\text{TVHH}} = \frac{6}{20} = 30\%$$

$$\text{Share} = \frac{\text{Number watching rated show}}{\text{HUTs}} = \frac{6}{10} = 60\%$$

FIGURE 11.2
Ratings are computed by dividing the number of homes watching a show by the total number of households. Shares are computed by dividing by the number of households using a TV at a particular time.

being watched, by getting family members to push buttons periodically to indicate who is in the room. The search is now on for "passive" people meter techniques that will record individual viewing without requiring viewers to touch buttons—such as sensing their body heat or by "recognizing" their faces with digital pattern recognition devices. Advanced systems may even tell advertisers when viewers are paying attention to the TV set, when they are smiling at the program (or nodding off to sleep), or when they are paying attention to specific commercial segments.

Audience measurement studies are sufficient to tell us whether the advertising message is being exposed to a target group and roughly what numbers are involved, but it does not provide insights into how or why the advertising is able to communicate successfully. For this purpose,we need a second dimension of audience research, one that enables the advertiser to talk directly with the target group. Because this research focuses on individuals and what "drives" them, it is often referred to as *motivational research.* Examples of this form of audience research include focus groups and mall intercepts.

Focus groups are small groups of 6 to 12 people who fit the profile of the target audience. A moderator leads the group through a series of open-ended questions relating to one or more advertising issues of interest. The purpose of the session is to derive insights into how the advertising campaign may be ultimately received by the target group.

Focus groups are small group interviews intended to explore consumer reactions in depth.

Mall intercepts involve contact with members of the target group at shopping malls. This approach, while useful for gauging initial reaction to or awareness of

1. Who are the key people required to execute advertising campaigns?
2. What are the main departments within the advertising agency?
3. What is "co-op advertising"?
4. Why is "concepting" such an important term for copywriters?

an advertising campaign, provides less insight than the focus-group technique. However, the results from mall intercepts can be mathematically analyzed, whereas the focus group discussion is less structured and produces results that are more qualitative than quantitative. Mall intercepts are also a useful means for letting consumers sample products and obtaining their reactions to products.

Another form of advertising-related research, **copy testing,** is used to assess the effectiveness of advertisements while they are still under development. For example, test ads might be inserted in television programs in selected markets, and researchers might contact respondents by phone to determine if they can recall seeing the ad on the day after it appeared. More sophisticated methods allow direct comparisons of ads by doing "split runs" of magazines in which alternate versions of the same ad are sent to different households. Cable television systems can also be used in this way to provide comparisons of alternate treatments for television commercials.

Copy testing evaluates the effectiveness of advertisements.

ADVERTISING GENRES

Of course, advertising must communicate important information about products (such as price, features, channel of distribution and the like), but it also requires a creative way of stating these facts that cuts through the clutter of competing advertisements and gets the attention of consumers. As shown in Figure 11.3, all messages have an informational dimension and an emotional dimension. Because advertising has to get the attention of audience members who are usually not interested in the message, how the message is conveyed is just as important as what is said. In this section we look at advertising as a form of communication in terms of both its style and its content. First, we offer an explanation of "one-voice" marketing. Next, we explain how advertisers use symbols of popular culture. Then a discussion of relationship marketing and direct marketing is followed by a list of other forms of advertising communication. Finally, "buying motives" or consumer needs are discussed as the keys to advertising success.

One-Voice Marketing

Effective advertising campaigns reflect a consistent message, tone, and format. Often referred to as *continuity of theme,* this concept holds that advertising works best when it communicates one main idea the same way across media. As in *positioning,* the advertiser must select out of an array of possibilities (such as quality, price, and convenience) the specific way the product should be understood and must say that one thing in virtually all ads. In the 1950s, for example, Lever Brothers positioned Dove not as a soap, but as a complexion bar; it has since been associated more with cosmetics than with hand soap.

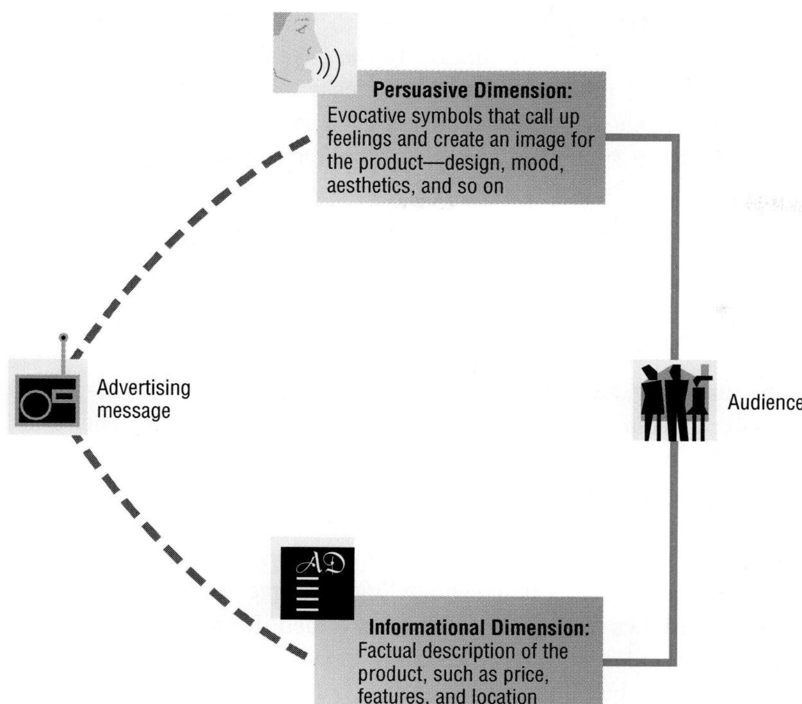

FIGURE 11.3
All communication has informational and persuasive dimensions. In order to cut through the clutter of competing messages, advertising often emphasizes the emotional as much as the informational.

Once a product position is selected, it is communicated in one voice consistently across media. For Intel, that one feature is the Pentium processor, which Intel wanted consumers to understand, does something exciting to computers in terms of speed and efficiency. To make this point, dancing computer chip workers called BunnyPeople were used in all advertising. These funky characters in fluorescent suits became an icon for the Pentium chip as Intel took them to trade shows, computer stores, and even street fairs in China. They have been featured in a variety of ads, and 450,000 BunnyPeople dolls were given away as a sales promotion (Bertrand, 1998). By featuring them in a wide range of media, this **one-voice marketing** enhanced consumer recall of the idea that something exciting is going on in your computer with Intel.

One-voice marketing assures that all commercial messages have continuity of theme.

Use of Popular Culture

One way in which advertisers align themselves with consumers is through the art and entertainment of **popular culture.** By borrowing familiar symbols in mass media from genres such as rap music, country line dancing, and apocalyptic science fiction movies, advertisers promote consumer identification with the product. Recent Nike commercials, for example, use the quick cuts and shaky camera images made popular by MTV and other forms of music video. Advertising also capitalizes on the strong emotions and values of the youth culture. In the 1960s, for example, the Coca-Cola campaign "I'd like to buy the world a Coke" featured folk music and reflected young people's concerns about achieving harmony and world peace. Ultimately, advertising turns out to be a reflection of social and

Popular culture includes art and entertainment that is widely shared by a population.

cultural norms due to a tendency to communicate in the language of the familiar. The Vietnam war provided the political context for the Coke commercial, which itself became as much a plea for friendship between peoples as it was an advertisement for a soft drink. Similarly, the Seven-Up Company used psychedelic color images in advertisements drawing on 1960s pop art styles. More recently, the popularity of African American music forms such as rap and hip-hop have emerged in advertising. One example is popular rap artist L.L. Cool J's appearance in a Gap jeans commercial. He tells consumers about the jeans to the pulsing beat of free-style rap.

Relationship Marketing

Relationship marketing is when consumers develop a strong preference for a brand through one-to-one communication.

In **relationship marketing,** advertisers and consumers communicate one-to-one through personalized media such as the Internet, direct mail, or the telephone. One of the most significant business trends to occur in the last decade, relationship marketing gets beyond the one-way channels of "mass media." Computers, for example, make personal and relevant messages possible in an interactive fashion. Companies use databases to personalize messages, with an emphasis on talking with consumers and "growing" them rather than sending out the same message to everyone.

The telephone continues to be an important instrument for relationship marketing. Credit card companies, such as American Express, often study the demographic characteristics and buying habits of each individual cardholder in order to identify specific products that "fit" specific lifestyles (such as life insurance, special hotel accommodations, luxury gift items, and the like). In order to personalize transactions and build relationships, QVC, the home shopping network, often features telephone callers discussing, on the air with the show host, their product-related experiences.

Relationship marketing is successful when brand loyalty is achieved. This is the goal of automobile dealers who create a timeline for each car purchased. Three months after the initial purchase, a letter is fired off reminding the new owner that it is time for a tune-up. As the car gets older, additional letters are sent, offering a wide variety of discount services, up to and including special offers on a new car purchase.

Direct Marketing

Although direct marketing was an aspect of most ads in the last century, more recently it has become a discipline unto itself. More and more, direct marketing techniques and advertising techniques are beginning to converge, especially as the advertising industry turns to new, more interactive forms. Many advertising agencies now have direct marketing departments, whose activities are rapidly growing in importance.

Direct marketing is a form of advertising that requests an immediate consumer response.

Direct marketing differs from conventional advertising in that it concentrates the marketer's resources on the most likely prospects, rather than sending a message to a wide audience in the hope that at least some of the prospects will receive it (Nash, 1992; Sirgy, 1998). Direct marketing also has a quality of immediacy, because recipients of the message are asked to take direct action, such as placing an order over the phone or returning a printed order blank by mail.

MEDIA WATCH

Other Forms of Marketing Communication Related to Advertising

Corporate advertising. When Saturn runs commercials claiming to be an environmentally conscious company, their goal is to use advertising to improve their image in the community. This type of advertising is intended to sell products indirectly.

Sales promotion. Some forms of advertising are designed to speed up the purchase decision. Contests, sweepstakes, coupons, and price incentives are popular sales promotions. When McDonald's gives away Big Macs every time a U.S. athlete wins a gold medal, it is engaged in a sales promotion.

Publicity. The Taster's Choice coffee soap opera commercials depicting a romance between two neighbors in an apartment building are so popular that they have generated news stories on television and in newspapers. This form of advertising isn't paid for and is highly credible.

Event marketing. Organizations also advertise by sponsoring events that people care about and participate in. Tostitos tortilla chips recently sponsored the Fiesta Bowl college football game, for example. The company name was included in virtually all advertising of the event.

Although direct marketing messages do not have the same "glitz" as mass media advertising, they do have two major advantages over other forms of advertising: (1) They can be customized to individual consumers, using personal forms of address and bits of personal information gleaned from computer databases, and (2) their effectiveness can be measured so that they can be continually fine-tuned.

Direct marketing encompasses a wide variety of communications media and marketing needs. It has long been popular with book publishers, record clubs, and magazines, but now it is coming into favor with a full range of advertisers. *Direct mail* ("junk mail") solicitations, *catalog* sales, and *telemarketing* are perhaps the most obvious forms of direct marketing activities. However, anyone who has ever called an 800 number to order the "the greatest hits of the sixties," dialed a 900 number, returned a magazine subscription form, entered a magazine contest or sweepstakes, sent in a donation to a TV telethon, or redeemed a coupon clipped from the newspaper has also responded to a direct marketing appeal. *Infomercials* are a new form of broadcast direct marketing. These are program-length, made-for-television presentations whose sole purpose is selling the featured product or service. The infomercial concept has been taken to its logical conclusion in the form of entire cable networks devoted to hawking products through 800 numbers—the *home shopping channels.*

The Internet is also emerging as a major medium for direct marketing. Consumers can purchase products directly on the Web, skipping intermediate steps of in-store shopping. Amazon.com, for example, offers instant access to more than 1.5 million book titles and purports to be "the world's largest bookstore."

The direct marketing industry relies on many of the same creative and media professions that advertising does, but it has some unique disciplines of its own as well. For example, there are firms that specialize in compiling and matching computerized telephone and mailing lists, others that specialize in assembling direct-mail packages, others that receive only 800-number calls, and others that just open return mail and complete (or "fulfill") the orders.

Research also takes on a distinctive character in direct marketing campaigns. Direct marketers are able to gauge the results of their advertising appeal, as well as the appropriateness of the media chosen, by counting the dollars in the cash register at the end of the day. This direct cause–effect measure allows the advertiser to try out various approaches and see their results immediately without resorting to the various media research services.

AT YOUR FINGERTIPS. Catalogs are available for every conceivable product.

Other Forms of Advertising Communication

Here are some additional ways in which advertising can be used to try to affect actions taken by members of the target market:

- *Give new information.* This includes announcements by advertisers regarding new products or product improvements, sweepstakes or contests, and other items of a newsworthy nature. The government-funded advertising campaign on the use of condoms to help prevent the spread of the AIDS virus is an example.
- *Reinforce a current practice.* This type of message is used primarily by advertisers that currently enjoy a dominant position in a product category and need to make consumers less receptive to competitive appeals. This is one of the most efficient uses of advertising, because it addresses the "heavy user" of the product who does not need to be convinced of its merits. In this case, the advertiser tries to increase **brand loyalty,** the propensity to make a repeat purchase of the product. A popular example of this type of ad is Coca-Cola's animated polar bears.

> **Brand loyalty** is the consumer's propensity to make repeat purchases of a specific brand of product.

- *Change a predisposition.* This approach is exemplified by the often-annoying ads that take on a competing product head-to-head. It is also the most difficult type of ad to execute successfully because it needs both to address and to change the purchasing habits of those who regularly use a competitor's product. (Furthermore, the competitor often answers with its own campaign.) Advertisers tend to be satisfied when they succeed in raising *brand awareness,* or the consumer's ability to identify the product. An example is a Red Roof Inn's campaign in which business travelers who frequent mid-priced hotels are invited to stay at a Red Roof and save the money they would have spent on amenities that they don't really want, such as mints on the pillow, a postage stamp-sized swimming pool, and a dingy bar.

The Key to Success: Understanding Consumer Needs

Whatever communication approach is used, all advertising must appeal to a **buying motive** to be successful. Table 11.5 lists 15 consumer needs, or motives, to which most advertising appeals. The copywriter selects a creative approach that is unique and addresses one of the consumer needs listed in the table. A classic case study discussed by Lisa Fortini-Campbell in her book *Hitting the Sweet Spot* (1992) is that of Jell-O, which demonstrates how consumer needs are essential to good strategy. An ad campaign based on a consumer need for lighter desserts was launched, but the only result was a continued decline in sales. Market data revealed another consumer need beneath the surface: the fun and creativity of making dessert. That is, Jell-O's core consumer was motivated more by dessert as an event to look forward to than by its lightness or heaviness. Uncovering this consumer need enabled the company to adopt a creative approach that, through a memorable song, communicated the theme line "Make Jell-O gelatin, and make some fun." The new approach helped stop the decline in the brand's market share (Fortini-Campbell, 1992).

The **buying motive** explains the consumer's desire to purchase particular products.

TABLE 11.5 "Consumer Needs"

Achievement	The need to accomplish difficult tasks.
Exhibition	The need to win the attention of others.
Dominance	The need to hold a position of influence.
Diversion	The need to have fun.
Understanding	The need to teach and instruct.
Nurturance	The need to support and care for others.
Sexuality	The need to establish sexual identity.
Security	The need to be free from threat of harm.
Independence	The need to make one's own choices.
Recognition	The need to receive notoriety.
Stimulation	The need to stimulate the senses.
Novelty	The need to do new tasks or activities.
Affiliation	The need to belong or win acceptance.
Succorance	The need to receive help and support.
Consistency	The need to achieve order.

Source: Adapted from Robert B. Settle and Pamela L. Alreck, *Why They Buy* (New York: Wiley, 1986), pp. 26–28.

THE ADVERTISING AUDIENCE

Advertising rarely succeeds without a deep, thorough understanding of consumers. In fact, audience insight is indispensable to the advertising industry. Effective campaigns begin with an identification of the psychological and cultural influences on buying behavior. This knowledge allows advertisers to group consumers into segments, or **target audiences,** on the basis of similar product needs and media use. Defining the audience for an advertising message typically starts with a profile of those individuals who would be the most likely to purchase the product. This profile can be developed by looking at current users of the product or by examining users of competitive products in the same category. There are several different approaches to segmentation.

Target audiences are groups that share the same product needs and media usage habits.

Usage-based segmentation divides consumers in terms of their amount of consumption. Usage information can be gleaned from internal sales records or from research services. A leading supplier of product usage information is Simmons Research Services, which maintains a database of consumers who report on their product consumption habits for a wide array of goods and services. From these sources the advertiser can determine the relative size of heavy-, medium-, and light-user groups, as well as their geographical distributions. Long-distance telephone ads that emphasize volume discounts for heavy telephone users are an example of advertising based on this approach.

Usage-based segmentation divides consumers according to their amount of consumption.

Demographic segmentation categorizes people on the basis of the personal and household characteristics that the U.S. Census Bureau tabulates, such as age,

Demographic segmentation is based on social or personal characteristics, such as age, sex, education, or income.

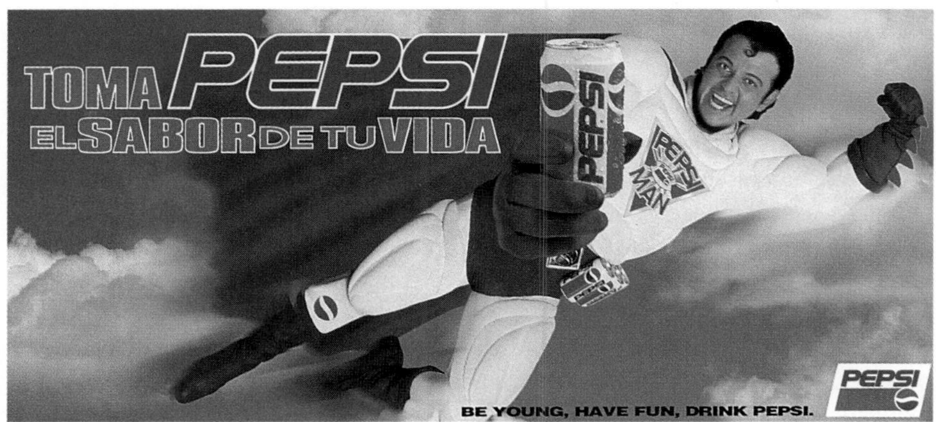

¿HABLA PEPSI? Ads targeted to specific ethnic groups are an example of demographic segmentation.

sex, ethnicity, and income. This form of segmentation is especially popular, because most of the market research and audience research reports used in the advertising industry are indexed by these categories. For most advertisers of consumer products, women between the ages of 18 and 49 are the primary target group; they make the most purchases in supermarkets and department stores.

Of all demographic variables, ethnicity and age hold the most potential for marketing. For example, if U.S. Census projections hold, the Hispanic market will be the largest ethnic group in the United States, in terms of both population and buying power, by 2010. The Census Bureau also indicates that the African American population is younger and growing faster than "non-ethnic" Americans. It is also possible that Asian Americans could be among the top three segments in terms of purchasing power by the year 2010. These are important developments for advertisers whose messages may not be keeping pace with the diversity evolving in the market. The demographic landscape is much different today, and advertising must be designed to reflect this.

Census data also reveal a growing senior market. Just as the 25–34 and 35–44 age groups have been essential to advertisers, the 50+ segment that they are becoming will be extremely important in years to come. This is likely to have dramatic effects on future marketing strategies. Given their leadership roles in business, government and other fields, seniors are often opinion leaders who influence what others buy.

Lifestyle segmentation categorizes people on the basis of their attitudes, interests, and opinions.

Lifestyle segmentation groups audiences according to their attitudes, interests, and opinions. For example, two consumers may have identical demographic characteristics—say, female, age 34, living in an urban area, with a professional occupation. However, when we also consider their attitudes, interests, and opinions, we discover that one is environmentally conscious, whereas the other has no interest in the green movement. The former recycles, is a member of the Sierra Club, and uses cloth diapers; the latter sees environmental groups as extremists and always buys disposable diapers. The former reads *Utne Reader;* while the latter enjoys *U.S. News and World Report.*

Geodemographic clustering categorizes consumers based on the demographic characteristics common to the area in which they live.

Geodemographic clustering, another version of demographic segmentation, is made possible by applying statistical analyses to census data so that advertisers can characterize people by the areas (usually postal zip codes or census tracts) where they live. The theory is that inhabitants of specific geographical enclaves share similar demographic profiles and buying habits. The PRIZM system, created by the Claritas Corporation, is one of the most widely used sources of this type of consumer data. Consumers are divided into 62 categories based on urbanization and social class. For example, at one end of the affluence scale is the "Blue Blood Estates" segment. Its members typically are 35–54, are college educated, work in executive-level occupations, earn high incomes and live in elite suburban neighborhoods. At the other end of the scale are members of the "Hard Scrabble" group, who reside in rural areas, are over 35 years of age, have not completed high school, and earn low incomes. This approach is beloved by direct marketers, because they can use it to target their mailings and phone calls.

The Media Evaluation Model

The audience for advertising is thus a predesignated target group. This process may seem simple enough, but one problem has persisted: that of "linking" the target group to the media vehicle itself (see Figure 11.4). That is, not all media channels are universally available to all members of the target audience, not all members are exposed to any particular vehicle carried on the channel, and not all of them see the ads in the vehicle, recall those ads, or are affected by them.

1. Why is Dove soap a good example of product "positioning"?
2. What is the relationship between advertising and popular culture?
3. What are some buying motives that advertisers appeal to?
4. What are four ways of segmenting advertising audiences?

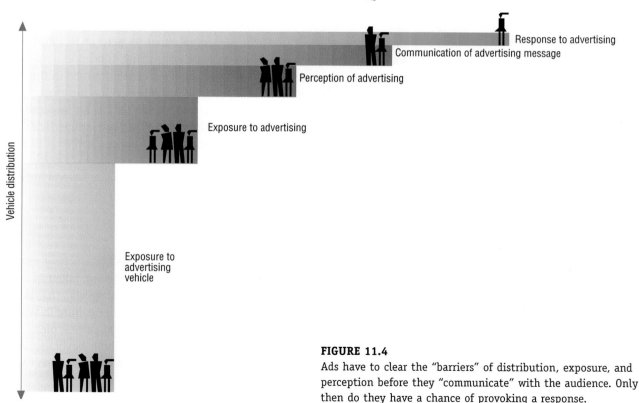

FIGURE 11.4
Ads have to clear the "barriers" of distribution, exposure, and perception before they "communicate" with the audience. Only then do they have a chance of provoking a response.

ADVERTISING ISSUES

Advertising serves a number of positive economic, social, and educational functions in society. In terms of its value to business, it can create competitive advantages; from a social perspective, it makes life easier by telling us what is available on the market. There are, however, a number of ethical issues related to advertising. Some argue, for example, that there is too much advertising and that it helps create false needs to buy particular products. Others worry about the impact it has on vulnerable audiences such as children. Additional criticism centers on issues such as stereotyping, privacy, and deception.

Ethics

Ethics is a branch of moral philosophy that studies how individuals decide what is morally acceptable behavior. In advertising, ethics is about the process of selecting one moral value over another when writing, designing, or placing advertisements. Emerson Foote, for example, resigned as chairman of McCann-Erickson, one of the world's largest and most prestigious ad agencies in protest over its willingness to create cigarette advertising (Fox, 1984). He was making a choice between the value of free expression on the one hand (tobacco companies are legal products and have a right to advertise) and the value of health concerns (mounting evidence of the link between smoking and cancer) on the other.

Advertising educators are increasingly interested in these types of issues and are more frequently including discussions of ethics in their classes. A recent survey of university professors, for example, reveals that 97 percent feel the study of ethics is an important part of a student's advertising education, and 90 percent agree that ethics is "increasingly becoming an important issue" in the professional environment (Harrison, 1990, p. 257). Another study, however, concludes that advertising students are not likely to be exposed to an in-depth or systematic study of ethics. This is because of the uneven and often superficial exposure their professors have had to the formal study of ethics (Tucker & Stout, 1998).

In this chapter, we identify a number of ethical issues and raise several questions for class discussion.

Promotion of "Consumption Values"

According to some scholars, advertising does more than just sell products; it also promotes a materialistic way of life. This view holds that advertising, taken as a whole, implies that happiness is achieved by consuming material goods. That is, the long-term impact of advertising has been to create a consumer culture in which the acquisition of goods and services is the foundation of societal values, pleasures, and goals. Examples include lifestyle advertising for alcoholic beverages, which often situates products in luxurious settings. The emphasis is as much on the wealthy lifestyle of the user as on the product itself.

Americans are the targets of an astonishing number of commercial messages. It is estimated, for example, that the average consumer is exposed to some 3000 advertisements each day (*The Future,* 1997). Debate has raged over the ultimate effect of these images. Some scholars express concern that this volume of advertising encourages "false needs" in consumers. Social critics such as Herbert Marcuse, Jean Baudrillard, and Stewart Ewen argue that advertising touches not on the real interests of consumers, but on superficial needs: envy, ego gratification, and power. They argue that when advertising trades in the core function of a product (a shoe's comfort and durability) for a lifestyle appeal (shoe as symbol of a desirable lifestyle), it promotes a "culture of consumption" in which consumers subscribe to the idea that problems can be solved quickly by simply acquiring products (Featherstone, 1991). However, other observers have questioned whether advertising creates a consumer culture or is, rather, simply a by-product of our consumer impulses. The brief format of advertising may also seem to promote the instant-solution approach to life. That is, the short dramas of 30-second commercials often show physical or social ills quickly remedied with a few pain killers or a shot of mouthwash.

Advertising and Children

Young children are thought by many parents and researchers to make up a vulnerable audience. According to Schudson (1984), vulnerable audiences are those who lack sufficient resources to make informed decisions about advertising appeals. Organizations such as Action for Children's Television (ACT) and the Center for Science in the Public Interest (CSPI) have supported policy and legislative proposals designed to help protect young audience members.

Although the effects are not fully understood, several studies confirm that (1) preschool-age children have difficulty explaining the intent of commercials, (2) children exposed to advertising make frequent requests for products to their parents, and (3) parental discussions of advertising increase children's comprehension of commercials (see the summary of research in Rajeev & Lonial, 1990).

Policy makers are particularly concerned with the issue of how well young children (of preschool age) can explain the purpose of commercials. Over the years, children have watched cartoon shows featuring "The Smurfs" and "He-man" only to find these same characters used to sell products such as pasta and toys. In an effort to help children distinguish between commercials and regular TV programs, the *Children's Television Advertising Practice Act* required that kids be informed when programs end and commercials begin. This act also placed restrictions on advertisers using program characters to sell products.

Issues that involve children's advertising continue to arise in the news. Recent controversies include the educational programming of "Channel One," which raises the question of whether advertising should be aired in public schools, and the 1996 *Telecommunications Act,* which exhorts advertisers to use the rating system developed by the television industry when designing commercials aimed at children.

These issues come down to the question of whether children are a "vulnerable" audience. That is, what are the responsibilities of advertisers if children lack the cognitive capacities to make mature consumer decisions? This question has triggered calls for increased sensitivity to young audiences, as well as new support for media literacy programs that educate children about the purpose and techniques of advertising.

The perspective of the advertising industry may be somewhat self-serving, but advertisers remind us that children have always had a desire for information about products available to them. Parental supervision also plays an important role in how children come to use advertising in everyday life. This view suggests that children also learn from advertising and that exposure to it helps prepare them to cope with the complexities of society.

If you are using InfoTrac College Edition, you can find out what recent studies have revealed about the effects of advertising aimed at children by entering the terms "advertising and children" and "media literacy."

Stereotyping of Women and Minorities

When one ignores diversity and makes sweeping generalizations about a group's values, behaviors, and beliefs, a *stereotype* is formed. Ethicists have long insisted that advertisers have an obligation to depict societal groups such as women and minorities equitably and fairly. Prior to 1980, African Americans were rarely featured in television commercials (Dates & Barloe, 1997). Although black celebrities (such as Michael Jackson, Lionel Ritchie, and Bill Cosby) began appearing in commercials by the 1980s, it remained evident that advertisers were using "black celebrities, but few black faces" (p. 93). In other words, despite the fact that African Americans are found in all professions from technical to managerial, advertising tends to reflect the stereotype that successful African Americans are usually sports or popular music stars.

How advertisers portray women has also been controversial. In an extensive review of the scholarly literature on the subject, Wood (1994) concludes that women are consistently underrepresented and are less likely to be depicted in professional occupations. Women also tend to be portrayed as taller and thinner than average, a practice that raises the question of whether advertising encourages a feeling of dissatisfaction with one's own body. Drawing on the psychological literature of modeling theory and social learning theory, a number of books on the subject have been published in the popular press. These include *Reviving Ophelia: Saving the Selves of Adolescent Girls* (Pipher, 1994), which argues that adolescent girls are immature consumers, who lack a healthy skepticism about advertising techniques that appeal to desires for sophistication and perfect body image. Pipher argues that these ads create a particular type of tension stemming from futile attempts by teenagers to achieve the "perfect image."

Industry professionals counter that advertising is a reflection of society rather than a shaper of values. Nevertheless, some advertisers have tried in recent years to make advertising more inclusive through more diverse depictions of women and minorities.

Privacy and Intrusiveness

There are two primary areas of concern about advertising as a privacy issue: (1) Fears about the misuse of personal information being collected and stored through databases and Web sites, and (2) the perceived encroachment of commercial messages into areas that many would like to see closed to advertisers (feature-length films, telephone, fax, and the like).

As we noted earlier in the chapter, relationship marketing techniques use databases to personalize messages and address specific needs of consumers. Many online businesses, for example, require the disclosure of personal information including (but not restricted to) name, address, telephone number, occupation, and income. Consumers, however, feel considerable anxiety about providing this type of data on the Web (Grainger, 1998). This apprehension stems from unanswered questions about how the information will be used and whether it will be sold to other marketers.

The ubiquitous nature of advertising has raised another type of privacy question: Are there places that should be protected from advertising? In recent years, advertising has appeared on eggs, on parking meters, and in public bathroom stalls; proposals have been made to put commercial messages on postage stamps. Space might also be the final frontier for advertising. A private company recently disclosed plans to launch a mile-long billboard into space, and NASA has considered selling ads on the hull of its rockets in order to help finance the U.S. space program (Warloumount, 1996). Consumers are often annoyed when they are powerless to separate themselves from commercialism. Telemarketers interrupt family meals, advertisers tie up fax machines, and through *Channel One* and the Internet, commercials are now aired in public schools, a domain that was previously commercial-free.

The question of how privacy issues will affect future advertising is worth considering. A number of associations of advertising professionals are considering self-regulation in order to show responsibility and respect consumers. In direct marketing, self-imposed guidelines have been created to ensure, for example, that individuals are not telephoned late at night and are informed whether information obtained will be sold to other advertisers.

Deception and "Puffery"

In order to preserve their good name, most advertisers go to great lengths to avoid deceptive advertising. However, blunders can happen, particularly when the advertising message is prepared by a third party—the advertising agency.

Just such a problem occurred in the early 1990s, when the Volvo Company was found to have "rigged" a commercial that apparently demonstrated Volvo's ability to withstand the weight of a heavy truck placed on its roof. Other vehicles were not so fortunate and suffered severe damage. However, the production company hired to film the spot had reinforced the Volvo, and weakened the other vehicles. When this fact came to light, Volvo was forced to pay a fine, and the company suffered immeasurable damage to its credibility.

Prior to industrialization in the United States, deceptive advertising rarely emerged in the courts. Under the ancient law of *caveat emptor* ("let the buyer

MEDIA ETHICS

Advertising and "Ethics"

Here are six simple rules that may help you to protect yourself against situations that will compromise your ethics, and thus your professionalism in advertising.

1. **Make your ethical decisions now.** Examine case studies of ethical dilemmas and make decisions about what your own conduct will be. It is much easier to stick to ethical decisions you have already made based on personal and professional values than it is to make those decisions in the face of pressure and financial need.
2. **Develop empathy.** Remember the old golden rule. Walk a mile in someone else's shoes and treat others as you would expect to be treated. A little bit of empathy and compassion goes a long way and increases the chances of receiving compassion and assistance when *you* need it.
3. **Take the time to think things through.** Chances are that if you feel rushed in an ethical decision, you are being railroaded into doing something unethical and unwise, something you would not do if you had more time to think it through.
4. **Identify behavior as what it really is.** Lying, cheating, and stealing by any other names are still lying, cheating, and stealing. In today's complex business environment, we have an incredible ability to sanitize issues and rationalize behavior by using less poignant terms like "white lies," "half truths," "omission," or "creative storytelling." But deception of any kind is lying; achieving success by anything but honest and ethical means is cheating; and appropriating anything that does not rightfully belong to you or your employer is stealing.
5. **Recognize that every action and decision has an ethical component.** Ethical decisions seldom emerge suddenly. They are the seemingly innocuous decisions and actions leading to the point of ethical crisis. Every decision you make has an ethical component even if it is not immediately obvious. Make sure to review the ethical ramifications of actions and decisions along the way. Project where a given decision will lead. Doing so will help you avoid many ethical crises that might otherwise "sneak up" on you.
6. **Establish a freedom fund.** With the very first check from your first job, start a savings account to which you contribute each time you are paid. Most ethical behavior is a result of feeling you simply cannot afford to behave otherwise. If you are asked to do something that violates your personal or a professional code of ethics, a freedom fund allows you to quit a job rather than compromise standards.

Source: Adapted from L. J. Wilson (1997). *Strategic program planning for effective public relations campaigns,* 2nd Ed. Dubuque, Iowa: Kendall Hunt. p. 114.

beware"), it was assumed to be the consumer's fault if he or she had been duped by a false advertising claim. With the passage of the *Federal Trade Commission Act* of 1914, however, the government began cracking down on deceptive practices in advertising. Today, the **Federal Trade Commission (FTC)** is active in regulating advertisers if (1) the message is likely to mislead the consumer, (2) the consumer is found to be acting reasonably under the circumstances, and (3) the omission, falsehood, or representation is "material" or likely to affect actual purchase decisions (Letter, 1983).

The **Federal Trade Commission (FTC)** is the major regulator of advertising thought to be deceptive.

Enforcement procedures by the FTC can include a *cease and desist order,* prohibiting further communication of the deception, and *corrective advertising,* requiring public clarification and admission of the falsehood. Exxon, for example, agreed in 1997 to place television spots explaining that Exxon Supreme 93 gasoline does not make engines cleaner, nor does it bring down maintenance costs (Overbeck, 1998). The FTC had found that the engine-cleaning additives in Exxon's premium gasoline were also included in all of its other grades, as well as in gasoline offered by many competitors.

The government, however, does not usually regulate what is called *puffery,* or exaggerated assertions in advertising that can't be proved (see the Media Ethics box). Puffery ranges from small-business claims such as, "Best pizza in the world" to national slogans such as Gillette's "The best a man can get." These statements, though seemingly harmless on the surface, raise a number of questions about truth in advertising. At which point should advertisers be required to substantiate their claims? Are particular audiences such as children more vulnerable to puffery? Is it up to the government to monitor the total range of deception in the advertising industry? Is puffery "deceptive" in the same way as falsehood?

Responding to criticisms about puffery, professionals give numerous examples of prosocial, or positive, images in advertising. Mattell Barbie commercials, for example, have been shown to reflect positive values of achievement and physical fitness through the tagline "We girls can do anything!" (Stout & Mouritsen, 1987). A more recent commercial by MasterCard not only touts the benefits of the product but indirectly emphasizes strong family relationships by stressing the idea that time with those you love is "priceless." Professionals argue that advertising reflects a wide range of cultural values, many of which are positive.

Media literacy is the ability to use advertising and other forms of media in optimal ways in everyday life.

Media Literacy

Students, educators, and professionals aren't likely to agree in their approaches to the ethical dilemmas just mentioned. However, considerable support is growing for the **media literacy** movement in the United States, which encourages the creation of educational programs designed to develop critical thinking by children as they are exposed to advertising and other media genres. Such programs already exist in Great Britain and Australia. Advocates of media literacy programs hold that although it is important to criticize producers of media messages, it is equally important to educate young people about the inner workings and strategies of the advertising industry. This, they argue, will not only create better-informed consumers but also encourage future advertising professionals to ponder important ethical issues before they begin their careers.

1. Who was Emerson Foote and what ethical decision is he often associated with?
2. What are some of the main social criticisms of advertising?
3. Why has privacy fueled such a heated debate in terms of contemporary advertising?
4. What does the Federal Trade Commission (FTC) do?
5. What is the relationship between media literacy and the impact of modern advertising?

SUMMARY AND REVIEW

WHAT WERE THE ORIGINS OF ADVERTISING?

Advertising dates back to the shop signs and town criers of ancient times. The advent of mass-circulation newspapers in nineteenth-century America gave advertising its initial boost. At first, advertising professionals worked on behalf of the media rather than the advertiser. Volney B. Palmer was the most influential advertising professional of that era. George P. Rowell, the founder of modern advertising, was the first to represent the interests of the advertiser as well as the publisher. The evolution of the modern advertising agency was completed by F. W. Ayer, who made the agency the servant of the advertiser rather than the publisher.

WHAT INFLUENCED THE DEVELOPMENT OF CONTEMPORARY ADVERTISING IN THE TWENTIETH CENTURY?

With the Industrial Revolution came a competitive environment that required advertising to be persuasive as well as informative in order to break through the clutter of competing messages. The soft sell, pioneered by Stanley Resor, emphasized the emotional appeal of the product. Advertising was pressed into service during times of war and economic crises, inspiring advertising campaigns on even grander scales. Radio, television, and computers emerged as important new advertising forms.

WHAT HAS BEEN THE IMPACT OF THE COMPUTER ON ADVERTISING?

Computers allow advertisers to build databases and store information, so personalized messages can be sent via the Internet. Database marketing helps build deeper relationships with consumers.

WHAT IS INTERACTIVE ADVERTISING?

The Internet makes it possible to order goods and services directly from home at the touch of a button. We can call up advertisements on demand, and ads are much more personalized to our unique identities and interests. Other forms of advertising might radically change the nature of the advertising industry, placing more reliance on direct marketing techniques and new channels that are not part of existing mass media systems.

HOW ARE ADVERTISING CAMPAIGNS INITIATED?

Marketing managers and brand managers who work for major advertisers budget and plan advertising strategies that will help them introduce new products or increase the sales of existing products. They work with an advertising manager to coordinate their companies' overall advertising efforts. Once a campaign is planned, they might contact one or more advertising agencies to execute the plan.

HOW ARE CAMPAIGNS ORGANIZED INSIDE AN ADVERTISING AGENCY?

The account executive is the liaison between the advertiser and the advertising agency staff. The account executive coordinates the activities of the creative department, which creates the ads, and the media department, which determines where the ads will be placed. Copywriters conceive of creative ideas and write the ads. The agency's media buyer negotiates with the media.

HOW DO ADVERTISING AGENCIES WORK WITH THE MEDIA?

The media buyer may negotiate directly with media outlets or may work through an intermediary media representative firm. Alternative advertising placements are evaluated by comparing them on a cost-per-thousand basis, although other factors related to the qualitative nature of the medium and a specific advertising vehicle may also be considered. The agency's traffic department takes charge of delivering the finished advertisements to the media.

WHAT IS THE ROLE OF RESEARCH IN THE ADVERTISING PROCESS?

Advertisers rely on market research to help them understand the target market. In the agency, account planners ensure that there is a strong connection between research findings and the final advertising message.

HOW ARE BROADCAST AUDIENCES MEASURED FOR ADVERTISING PURPOSES?

Media research companies provide two basic types of statistical measures that advertisers use to compare the programs, or vehicles, in which their ads are carried. Using television as the example, a rating indicates the percentage of all homes with televisions tuned to a particular program. A share indicates the percentage of all homes actually using television at a given time that are tuned into the program. Ratings and shares may further be classified according to demographic characteristics such as age and sex.

WHAT ARE THE DIFFERENT TYPES OF ADVERTISING?

Advertising is generally designed to achieve one of three basic goals: to provide new information (brand awareness), to reinforce a current practice (brand loyalty), or to change an existing predisposition. Advertising genres are further categorized according to the type of buying motive they appeal to. Advertisers have identified 15 needs, or buying motives, to which most messages appeal.

WHAT IS DIRECT MARKETING?

With direct marketing, the recipient of the advertising message is asked to make a direct and immediate response to the ad, such as by mailing in a printed order blank or dialing an 800 number to place an order. Telemarketing, home shopping channels, infomercials, and catalog sales are other common examples. The popularity of direct marketing is likely to increase in the future as the spread of interactive technologies such as the Internet makes it easier to place orders in direct response to advertising.

HOW ARE ADVERTISING AUDIENCES CATEGORIZED?

Although some advertisements are directed to a general audience, most are tailored to a specific market segment or target audience. These subgroups may be categorized in a variety of ways. Common approaches include product usage, demographic (social and personal) characteristics, lifestyles (predicated on attitudes, interests, and opinions), and geographical area (geodemographic clustering).

WHAT IS THE DIFFERENCE BETWEEN DECEPTION AND "PUFFERY"?

Advertisers and their agencies must constantly strive to avoid dishonest advertising practices, such as making deceptive claims. But advertisers must also consider the ethics of exaggerated claims that can't be proved (puffery).

WHAT OTHER ISSUES RELATED TO ADVERTISING ARE CAUSING CONCERN TODAY?

Advertising in the information society has triggered a number of social controversies, including the promotion of consumption values, encroachments on privacy, stereotyping, and advertising aimed at children.

Electronic Resources

For up-to-the-minute URLs about *Advertising,* access the MEDIA NOW site on the World Wide Web at:

http://communication.wadsworth.com/

CHAPTER 12

Media and the Individual

WHAT'S AHEAD

What are the effects of the thousands of hours we each spend every year with the communications media? In this chapter we investigate that issue. In the next chapter we will examine the broader implications of media consumption for society at large.

Access the MEDIA NOW site on the World Wide Web at:
http://communication.wadsworth.com/
Choose "Chapter 12" from the selection box to access electronic information and other sites relevant to this chapter.

ONE AFTERNOON, AFTER SCHOOL

Roadrunner Channel—Enter parental authorization code

[8523456]

INVALID CODE—ACCESS DENIED

Darn!

Interactive Mud Wrestling—Enter parental authorization code

[8523465]

INVALID CODE—ACCESS DENIED

Drat!

Dirty Joke Chat Room—Enter parental authorization code

[8523546]

PARENTAL CODE RECOGNIZED—PLEASE WAIT

Yessss! I knew it had to be one of her phone numbers!

Dialing Ajax Multimedia Corp. 852-3546

Uh oh . . .

So! You've been trying to crack my parental advisory code again, I see. Just for that, I'm cutting you off from everything except the Homework Helper, and if the DeeVee has to call me one more time at work, you're going to be sorry. And I'm going to have it monitor your keystrokes, so you'd better get busy, young lady!

Gee whiz, Mom, I was just trying out a new program!

Click!

[Running . . . Homework Helper keystroke emulator]

Gosh darn! Where did she come up with that new parenting software? Now I am going to have to read a book, or something.

Chapter Outline

Research on Effects of the Media
The Deductive Approach
The Inductive Approach
Quantitative vs. Qualitative Methods
Content Analysis
Experimental Research
Survey Research
Ethnographic Research
Theories of Media Effects
Media as Hypodermic Needle
The Multistep Flow
Selective Processes
Social Learning Theory
Cultivation Theory
Priming
Other Perspectives
Communications Media and Antisocial Behavior
Violence
Prejudice
Sexual Behavior
Drug Abuse
The Effects of Computer Media
Communications Media and Prosocial Behavior
Information Campaigns
Informal Education
The Effects of Advertising
The Effects of Political Communication
Summary and Review

"Media bashing" has long been a popular, if somewhat predictable, ritual. Media critics find new evidence of harmful media effects, the media refute the claims, the talk shows and editorial columns buzz, and public hearings are held. Then the media retreat behind the First Amendment protections of free speech (see Chapter 14), they promise to regulate themselves, and the debate simmers down until the next controversy arises.

The sources of concern may be seen at every flip of the dial or click of the computer mouse. The media seem to encourage violence, sex crimes, drug abuse, racism, and sexism by showing them in full color on the screen or on the page (see time line, page 385). The media also are blamed for undermining family values, religion, schools, political institutions, and cultural identities, all for the profit of big media corporations. Violent computer games and pornographic content on the Web add more fuel to an old controversy, and also raise new fears about bringing real-life child molesters, hate mongers, and criminals into the school or the home via the Internet.

Media industry executives defend themselves by pointing out that society's ills have deeper causes, such as the disintegration of the family and economic and racial oppression, that are unlikely to be much affected by an evening's entertainment. They argue that the media merely reflect society, not shape it. They see their job as making money for their investors by producing content that people like, not as acting as surrogate parents. They point to the many examples of wholesome and informative media content that they make available. They also point to flaws and inconsistencies in research studies. And finally, they emphasize that as broadcasters they have an obligation to uphold the First Amendment, which protects the rights of all to free speech.

Until 1996, pitting the First Amendment rights of the media against the health and welfare of children produced a noisy impasse in which the voices of the researchers were drowned out in the heat of the public debate. The Telecommunications Act of 1996 broke the logjam by mandating the *V-chip,* an electronic device that automatically blanks out television programming that contains violence, sex, or offensive language at the command of parents. Television and cable networks went along with the plan by embedding in their programs, for

MEDIA AND THE INDIVIDUAL TIME LINE

1898 Newspaper publisher William Randolph Hearst summons the United States to war—"Remember the Maine!"

1903 First violent film (*The Great Train Robbery,* also the first film ever)

1914 World War I propaganda efforts highlight mass media power

1915 First racist feature film (*Birth of a Nation,* also the first feature film ever)

1932 U.S. movie industry institutes voluntary censorship

1933 – 1945 Nazi propaganda machine holds Germany in thrall

1942 Systematic studies of propaganda techniques by U.S. military

1950 First swear words on U.S. television (*Arthur Godfrey Show*)

1954 U.S. Senate hearings on the effects of television violence on juvenile delinquency; Liz Taylor says "virgin" for the first time on film (*The Moon Is Blue*)

1960 Klapper concludes media have limited effects

1961 Second round of Senate hearings on TV violence. First exposure of navel on U.S. television (*Dr. Kildare*)

1965 Bandura publishes Bobo doll study

1968 National Commission on the Causes and Prevention of Violence concludes that TV violence encourages violent behavior; First interracial kiss on U.S. television (*Star Trek*)

Movie industry institutes film ratings

1972 U.S. Surgeon General releases research report on television and social behavior

1975 Under FCC pressure, broadcasters adopt the "family hour" to provide wholesome early-evening TV programming

1976 "Family hour" struck down by courts

1977 First bare (female) breasts exposed on American television (*Roots*)

1980 First beheading on American television (*Shogun*)

1986 Meese Commission report on the effects of pornography

1990 Children's Television Act mandates broadcast television programming specifically designed for children

1991 First homosexual kiss on U.S. television (*L.A. Law*)

1994 National Television Violence Study

1997 Parental advisories instituted for TV programs

1998 TVs equipped with V-chips introduced

Sources: Liebert & Sprafkin, 1988; Muto, 1997; Jensen & Graham, 1993.

the V-chip to catch, a new system of voluntary content codes. The Telecommunications Act also included the Communications Decency Act, which represented an effort to clamp down on computer smut. This provision was quickly struck down on First Amendment grounds (although later revived in a second piece of legislation in 1998, see Chapter 14), but the computer industry responded with its own voluntary rating system that injects content codes into Web pages on the Internet. At last parents and educators may have effective tools to protect children from the harmful effects that researchers have warned us about for years. They can use the electronic content codes to prevent offensive content from ever appearing on television and computer screens—provided, of course, they have the advanced television sets and computers with which the codes can be used.

RESEARCH ON EFFECTS OF THE MEDIA

Media effects are changes in knowledge, attitudes, or behaviors resulting from media exposure.

What are the effects of the communications media and how do we know about them? **Media effects** are changes in knowledge, attitude, or behavior that result from exposure to the mass media. There are two main approaches to understanding these effects.

The Deductive Approach

Independent variables are the causes of media effects.

Dependent variables are the consequences, or effects, of media exposure.

Many social scientists begin with a causal theory of media effects. Next they derive, or deduce, predictions about media effects from the theory and then test these predictions through systematic observation. The results of their research either support the theory or refute it, which leads in turn to new theoretical paradigms. Essentially, they follow the scientific method. In other words, for social scientists studying media effects via the deductive approach, mass media exposure is usually the viewed as the "cause," or **independent variable.** Exposure to media content is seen as the trigger for certain mental processes and behaviors that are the "effects." These effects—such as antisocial or prosocial behaviors—are called **dependent variables** (Wimmer & Dominick, 1997).

VIOLENCE.
Violence in society is a major concern of parents, social scientists, and policy makers, many of whom see media violence as the cause.

The Inductive Approach

Another approach used by researchers is first to observe people's interactions with media and with each other and then to induce, or infer, from these real-life situations, theories about what causes might be leading to what effects. In this approach, the observations come first and the theory comes after. Certain scholars from this school reject the notion of causality. Some researchers believe that the communications media, our culture, and every one of us all have reciprocal influence on each other and that there is no one-way flow of cause and effect. Others even question the very existence of cause and effect on philosophical grounds, arguing that it is an illusion foisted on us by a technological society (Postman, 1992). Many of these scholars refer to themselves as *critical theorists,* because they are critical of social science research theories and methods as well as of the media institutions.

Quantitative vs. Qualitative Methods

Many social scientists use quantitative methods that allow them to enumerate their findings and analyze statistical relationships between independent and dependent variables. Other scholars infer the relationships from qualitative methods, such as by studying the symbols in media content or observing behavior in natural settings.

MEDIA IMPACT

Critical Communication Theory

Paul Lazarsfeld (1941), one of the pioneers in communications research, was the first to point out the difference between what he called *administrative* research, which takes existing media institutions for granted and documents their use and effects, and *critical* research, which criticizes media institutions themselves from the perspective of the ways they serve dominant social groups. Most of the research described elsewhere in this chapter, even that which results in "criticism" of the media for excessive sex or violence, falls into the administrative research category, because it fails to critique the basic foundations of existing media institutions. Critical theorists reject these administrative approaches to communication theory and the underlying source-message-channel-receiver model (which critical theorists have redubbed the "linear model" or "transmission paradigm") on which they are based (see Chapter 2). Instead, they use theoretical approaches drawn from such fields as history, feminist studies, cultural anthropology, Marxist political economic theory, and literary criticism to examine the power relationships and hidden ideologies expressed in media content and media institutions (Chomsky & Herman, 1988). In so doing, they hope to expose and eliminate patterns of cultural oppression and domination predicated on social class, ethnicity, and gender (Grossberg, 1993; McChesney, 1993; Steeves, 1993).

Critical theorists have their own methods and their own vocabulary that further distinguish their approach. Critical theorists generally reject traditional methods of research, including quantitative content analysis, experimental research, and survey research methods, and some even reject the scientific method on which many communication studies are based. Instead, critical theorists favor interpretative and inductive methods such as semiotics (see Chapter 2), historical research, and ethnography. Rather than talking about how communication effects are limited by selective perception, some critical theorists would state that audiences are active "readers" of media "texts." They would focus on the prominence of the audience instead of on the source of the media messages (Morley, 1992). Likewise, critical theorists speak of "group mediation" (for example, Barbero, 1993) or "interpretive communities" (Lindlof, 1994), whereas social scientists use the term *multistep flow* to describe the way in which social interactions affect perceptions of the media.

All the methods used to study media effects have their own relative strengths and weaknesses that we need to understand to evaluate their contributions to the media effects debate. For example, media executives who oppose policy proposals that are based on media effects research often criticize the methods used by the researchers. Leveling these criticisms at researchers can help them block policy proposals, such as increases in wholesome children's programs, on the grounds that the research results are not valid.

Content Analysis

Content analysis quantifies the nature of the content found in the media. Researchers begin with systematic samples of media content and then apply objective definitions to classify the content. For example, if researchers want to find out whether television has become more violent over the years, they might select a representative "composite week" of prime-time programming. They would develop

Content analysis is a quantitative description of the content of the media.

objective definitions of violence, such as "sequences in which characters are depicted as targets of physical force initiated by another character." Trained observers would then classify each of the scenes in the sample of shows and compare notes to make sure that their definitions were consistent. Then the researchers would record the number of violent acts per hour and compare the results with those of previous studies (Gerbner & Gross, 1976).

These kinds of studies create detailed profiles of media content and identify trends in that content over time. However, they cannot be used as a sound basis for drawing conclusions about of the *effects* of the media. For that, we must conduct research that involves the audience, for as we shall see, the audience often perceives the media in a different way than the researchers—or the producers of the content—do. Also, because content analysis is a time-consuming task, researchers sometimes take only a limited sample (such as one week's worth of prime-time television shows) and confine themselves to the major broadcast networks. This obviously would not reflect the full range of programming. In addition, the definitions used in such studies can sometimes be problematic. For example, if a character in a situation comedy slaps another character on the back and they begin laughing, is that violence? What if a character is hurt by a hurricane instead of another person? What about the violence of a football game? verbal abuse? According to some definitions these are violent acts; according to others they are not.

A recent content analysis of television violence conducted by researchers at three major U.S. universities (Federman, 1998) overcame many of the problems that plagued past efforts, at least in the area of television violence studies. With multimillion-dollar funding provided by the cable television industry, the researchers examined content from across three entire television seasons, rather than a single composite week, and included 23 different cable television and broadcast networks. They also were very sophisticated with their definitions of violence, examining the context of violent acts—for example, whether the violent behavior was rewarded or punished—rather than simply counting the number of gunshots and body blows, as previous studies had done.

The researchers found that television continues to be very violent. In all three TV seasons they studied, three-fifths of all prime-time programs contained violence, and each violent program averaged over six violent incidents per hour. On the basis of their findings, they estimated that preschoolers who watched 2 hours of television daily would witness 10,000 violent acts each year. Moreover, much of the violence involved the types of "high-risk" portrayals that children are most likely to imitate. These include incidents in which the violence is committed by an attractive character in a realistic setting and in which there are no harmful consequences to either the perpetrator or the victim. In contrast, only one in 20 programs had antiviolence themes. Incidentally, these figures left out two types of programming that are both extremely violent and very "high-risk," according to the researchers' own definitions: professional football and news programs. The industry sponsors of the study didn't want anyone goring those sacred money-making cows! Still, the study stands as a model of content analysis research informed by theories of media effects.

TECHNOLOGY **TRENDS**

On-Line Research Methods

An interesting side effect of the blossoming interest in the Internet among communications researchers is that the Internet is now being used as a medium to conduct research. To glimpse the future of survey research, start with a full Web browser such as Hotbot, and use "(survey) and (Web or (on and line))" as the keywords. A host of survey sites with questionnaires, and others with the results of on-line surveys, will appear. As you look through the sites, ask yourself how the on-line versions compare with conventional methods, using some of the concepts we have examined in this chapter such as sampling and generalizability.

One of the staples of qualitative research, the focus group, is also undergoing an on-line makeover. Focus groups can now be convened on-line so that respondents can be drawn from a wide area, thus overcoming a severe limitation of the conventional method that required interviewees to be physically present at a specific location. Content analysis is also enhanced: Every time you look for keywords in a search engine, you are getting a computer to do content analysis for you. Similarly, the programs that monitor visits to Web sites and keep track of how you travel inside of them are computer-driven ethnographers of sorts.

Experimental Research

Experimental research studies the effects of media in carefully controlled situations that manipulate media exposure and content.

Experimental research studies the effects of media under carefully controlled conditions. Typically, a small group sees a media presentation that emphasizes the type of content under study. For example, preschool children are shown violent cartoon shows, and their responses are compared with those of preschoolers exposed to media that lack the "active ingredient"—that is, nonviolent cartoons. Although the subjects for experimental studies seldom represent society as a whole in a statistical sense, they are randomly divided between the two test groups.

The random assignment is important because it minimizes the impact of individual differences among subjects. If we did not assign randomly—if we simply asked the children to raise their hands if they want to see a Roadrunner cartoon—the aggressive children would probably volunteer, and our results would therefore reflect the nature of the children rather than any effect of the media content. The same goes for sex, age, social status, and other variables that might affect the outcome; the randomization process cancels out their effects by putting equal numbers of boys and girls, old and young, rich and poor, in each group.

Perhaps the most influential experiments in the annals of media effects studies were those conducted by Albert Bandura (1965) and his colleagues at Stanford University. They showed preschoolers a short film in which a child actor behaved aggressively toward a Bobo doll, an inflatable plastic doll the size of a small child with the image of a clown printed on the front and sand in its base so that it rocks back and forth when hit. The actor in the film, which Bandura called the model, punched the doll in the nose, hit it with a mallet, kicked it around the room, and threw rubber balls at it. This aggressive sequence was repeated twice in the film.

All of the children in the study, tots from a local nursery school, saw this part of the action. However, there were three different endings to the film, and the

TAKE THAT, BOBO.
In Bandura's classic experiment on imitation of violence, children were shown a movie (top four frames) of a model hitting a "Bobo" doll. If children saw the model rewarded for this behavior, they treated the doll similarly (middle and bottom rows).

children were randomly divided into groups that each viewed a different ending. For the children who represented the "model-rewarded condition," an adult actor appeared and rewarded the aggressor with verbal praise, soda, candy, and Cracker Jacks. In the "model-punished condition," the second actor scolded the first and spanked him. A third group of children, representing the the "no-consequences condition," saw only the opening sequence.

After the show, which the children were told was a TV program, subjects were led to a playroom equipped with a Bobo doll, a mallet, some rubber balls, and assorted other toys. As adult observers watched, many of the children in the model-rewarded and no-consequences conditions imitated the aggressive acts they had seen; those in the model-punished condition tended not to do so. However, even the children in the model-punished condition had learned how to perform the behaviors—when adults offered them candy, they started beating up the Bobo doll, too.

The researchers concluded that the punishment the children experienced vicariously in the model-punished condition inhibited their aggressive behavior. However, the most important finding of the study was that the no-consequences condition also produced a great deal of imitation. This suggested that mere exposure to television violence—whether or not the violence was visibly rewarded on screen—could spur aggressive responses in young children.

The value of such a carefully controlled design is that it rules out competing explanations for the results (such as the possibility that subjects who saw the violent films were already violent children). Only the endings of the film (also known as the experimental treatment) were varied among groups, so that any subsequent differences among them (such as the beatings the subjects inflicted on their own Bobo dolls) could be attributed to the media content in question.

However, the small and unrepresentative samples used in experimental studies, which often consist of college students in introductory classes or the small children of university professors, raise questions about **generalizability**—the degree to which the results apply to other populations and settings. In addition, the measures that are used (written responses to a questionnaire or highly structured experimental tasks) and the conditions under which the experiments are conducted do not adequately reflect the real-world situations of ultimate interest, such as behavior in an actual child's playroom or on a school playground. This is called the issue of *ecological validity.*

Generalizability is the degree to which research procedures and samples may be generalized to the real world.

The experimental treatments may also be unrealistic in that (1) they often involve much more intense sequences of the content in question than are likely to be encountered in the real world, and (2) they are often presented as disjointed segments that do not show the context of the actions portrayed. For example, in studies of the effects of pornography, brief excerpts of sex scenes from several different pornographic films are edited onto a single tape. The edited sequences have a lot more "action" than is commonly seen in the original films, which intersperse the sex scenes with some token plot and character development. Moreover, experimental subjects in such studies, often recruited from first-year college courses, may be exposed to content that they might not normally see, a circumstance that may tend to exaggerate the effects that are observed (Anderson & Meyer, 1988).

Survey Research

Survey studies are familiar to most of us, because they employ the same basic methods as public opinion polls and market surveys. For example, researchers interested in examining the effects of violent video games could administer a survey to a random sample (see the Media Ethics box) of college students at universities all over the country. Media effects are inferred by statistically relating the independent measures of media exposure ("How many violent video games have you played in the last week?") to the dependent variable of interest (such as self-reports of violent behavior). If those who play a lot of video games also engage in a lot of violence, whereas those who do not play such games are relatively nonviolent, we would say that the two variables are **correlated.**

Survey studies make generalizations about a population of people by addressing questions to a sample of that population.

Correlations are statistical measures of association between two or more variables.

Survey studies are more generalizable than experimental studies, because the samples often represent larger populations, such as all U.S. college students in our example. They can also attempt to account for a wider range of factors than just the experimental manipulation, such as peer pressure to play violent games and religious beliefs that discourage playing them.

However, survey research provides ambiguous evidence, at best, about cause and effect. In our example, it is possible that aggressive students simply like to play violent video games. In other words, violence causes the playing of video

MEDIA ETHICS

Would You Mind Answering a Few of Our Questions?

For Further Research:

Communications research is everywhere, it seems. From questionnaires in the mail, to phone calls at home, to the questionnaires your professor asks you to fill out in class, it may sometimes seem that you are being bombarded with questions about every aspect of your media behavior, your background, and your personal life. Sometimes you might just like to make it stop, but that only triggers more mailings, phone calls, and urgings to "please take the survey if you want extra credit." What gives the researchers the right to intrude?

It is important to remember that both you and society can benefit from your cooperation in research studies. Ratings, reader surveys, and cable subscriber surveys provide the feedback that the media industry needs to serve you better. The studies that your teacher and other social scientists conduct help increase our knowledge of the role that communications media play in society, or they help to inform public policy debates. Your opinions truly do count in communications research studies, so you should provide them willingly and honestly when you can.

However, not all surveys are legitimate, and not all researchers adhere to accepted ethical guidelines. This is a special problem with phone surveys. Too many times, what starts out as a survey winds up being a sales pitch. If you don't go along, the so-called "interviewer" may resort to abuse, begging, or intimidation to keep you on the line. The information you give, along with your name, address, and phone number, may be turned over to direct marketers who put you at the top of their "sucker lists." In the most blatant cases, the interviewer will suddenly turn salesperson on you while you are still on the phone.

Such "researchers" are acting unethically. According to the ethical guidelines of the American Association for Public Opinion Research, professional researchers may not lie to you or coerce you in any way. All information that can be used to identify you through your responses must be kept confidential and your name may not be disclosed for nonresearch purposes (marketing, for instance).

Many academic researchers must adhere to even stricter standards. The American Psychological Association (APA), for example, expects ethical researchers to stress that your participation is voluntary and that you may withdraw at any time. They should seek your informed consent to participate, after informing you of the nature of the study and the amount of time—or other commitment—that is expected of you. And, if you are participating in the study for extra credit in a class, an alternative activity should be available by which you could earn the same credit.

Many colleges and universities also have a *human subjects committee* that is mandated by the federal government to safeguard your rights as a research subject. Such committees review and approve research studies prior to their implementation, especially if an experimental design is used or if sensitive information (such as information about your sexual behavior) is collected. Some human subjects committees also uphold the APA guidelines and have special provisions of their own. Others may require that all projects, including interviews and surveys, be approved.

For more information on this subject consult your institution's home page and enter "human subjects guidelines" if the site has a search engine, or look through categories relating to "research" linked from the home page, or visit the American Psychological Association site, www.apa.org. WWW

games instead of the other way around. It is also possible that both violent behavior and video game playing are both caused by some unexamined third variable, such as lax parental supervision. This is the sort of situation in which experimental studies or ethnographic research (see below) might help to sort out the ambiguities.

Perhaps the most widely reputed media effects survey studies are longitudinal studies of the impact of television violence that survey the same subjects again after a number of years (an example is Huessman, 1982). The researchers asked the parents of 8-year-old children to identify the children's favorite TV programs and then asked the children's playmates to rate the children on their antisocial behavior. Then they recontacted the same families 5 and 10 years later and readministered the survey. If the youngsters who watched a lot of television are more violent as teens or adults than the ones who watched relatively little television as children, then we can conclude that childhood television exposure does indeed encourage violent behavior later in life. If some of the adults in our follow-up surveys have subsequently reduced their television viewing but remain violent people, we can rule out the competing explanation that "violent people like violent television." In other words, we can be fairly certain that violent television causes violent behavior, instead of violent behavior causing viewership of violent programs (violent people like to watch violence, in other words). In fact, that is what Huessman and his colleagues concluded, although the relationship was found only among boys.

However, very few survey studies are repeated over time; most are just "one-shot" studies that compare media exposure and behavior but ignore the *direction* of any causal relationship. In other words, they can't distinguish whether TV causes violence or whether violent people like violent TV shows, for example. Even longitudinal studies cannot account for the influence of variables the researchers leave out, such as parental supervision, that might explain both violence and television viewing. We should also note that other longitudinal studies of TV violence have found no effects (Milavsky et al., 1982). Still others have yielded rather puzzling results, including a later study by Huessman and his associates (Huessman & Eron, 1986) that showed a violence effect for girls but not for boys. Furthermore, a pattern of inconsistent findings emerged from similar studies in Poland, Finland, Israel, and Australia. This raises the issue that media effects may not be generalizable across cultures.

Ethnographic Research

Ethnography is a naturalistic way of looking at the impacts of communications media. It adapts the techniques anthropologists use to look at cultures in a holistic way. Ethnography places media in a broad context of media users' lives and cultures. For instance, an anthropologist who had studied a Brazilian village for many years, since before television was introduced there, saw changes that seemed to stem from television. He observed how villagers used television, watched it with them, and then systematically interviewed them, using both in-depth, open-ended interviews and survey questionnaires. His results showed a considerable broadening of information about the outside world over the years, a notable liberalization of attitudes about gender and racial roles, and a rise in material aspirations, along with some loss of interest in local festivals and traditional ways of doing things (Kottak, 1990).

Ethnography is a naturalistic research method in which the observer obtains detailed information from personal observation or interviews over extended periods of time.

Although ethnographers sometimes use questionnaires, ethnography is often seen as an alternative to survey research. Surveys make it possible to compare

THE SCIENCE OF SAMPLING

"How could my favorite candidate lose? All my friends voted for her!" Did you ever hear yourself say this after an election? The answer to this riddle is the key to understanding the science of survey sampling. Clearly, your circle of friends does not adequately represent the opinions of the entire electorate. How do you avoid being startled by the results of future elections? Well, you could simply ask more people outside of your inner circle, but that takes time and effort. What types of people should you ask? How many? How should you select them?

Survey sampling methods have evolved as a reaction to some classic blunders encountered in answering these very same questions. The most famous blunder of all was committed by *Literary Digest,* which had a good record of predicting the outcome of presidential elections in the 1920s and early 1930s. The magazine collected "ballots" from its readers, supplemented by mailing lists compiled from telephone subscriber records. Tens of thousands of responses were received, but in 1936 the poll picked Alf Landon, who was soundly trounced by Franklin Roosevelt. In the aftermath, researchers realized that there was an inherent bias in the telephone subscriber lists that were used. During the Depression, only about a third of all homes had phones, and these were mostly upper-income homes, where Roosevelt had little support.

By applying the science of probability sampling, researchers found that they could get more accurate results using far fewer respondents. One key is to start with a list that includes all members of the population under study. In the case of election polls, this means using voter registration lists. However, 94 percent of homes now have telephones, so the bias involved in polling by phone is a great deal less than it was in the Depression era, provided that we take care to screen out potential respondents who are unlikely to vote.

The other important point is to sample the list randomly, so that everyone on the list has an equal chance of being selected. One way to achieve this would be to cut up all of the phone books in the country, place the individual listings in a giant revolving metal drum, and start picking numbers. This would obviously be quite cumbersome and would overlook the many homes (about 30 percent) with unpublished numbers. Most survey firms therefore use a random-digit-dialing technique in which a computer generates random numbers to fill in the last two digits of the listed numbers.

If we follow these simple rules, we can get an accurate response by contacting only a few hundred respondents. For example, a sample of 400 respondents can adequately represent the entire country with only a 5 percent margin of error.

So why do polls still come out wrong, and why do different polls so often disagree? One problem is the volatility of public opinion. People can simply change their minds between polls or between the last poll and election day, and political preferences are a lot less stable than they once were. Another problem is accurately determining who the individuals likely to vote are when qualifying them for the survey. The rate of response to surveys is another problem. Americans are inundated by surveys of all types, and in some areas, fewer than a third of the households contacted agree to participate. If certain types of respondents refuse more often than others, the results of the poll may be biased.

many people through standardized questions, but they may impose a structure of meaning and specific response categories on the respondents. That approach yields standardized responses that are easier to compare, but ethnographers value letting people speak in their own words, using their own concepts and categories.

Ethnographies can yield great depth of information about a particular place at a particular time, but they do not permit much generalization. Although ethnographers try to record information so thoroughly and accurately that others would reach the same conclusions from their data, such reliability is hard to achieve. Our Brazilian anthropologist did similar studies in several other locales, but to create generalizations about the effects of television in Brazil, he had to resort to survey techniques with standardized questions and more representative samples. Moreover, ethnographers can get so close to their respondents that they sometimes influence the events they are observing, and bias results.

Thus, the different types of research methods tell us different things. Content analyses often show that the media are suffused with violence and sex, for example, but tell us nothing about the actual effects on the audience. Experimental studies often find evidence of effects, even from extremely short exposures of 15 minutes or less, but cannot assess how other factors may reduce or enhance those effects. Survey studies use larger, more representative samples than experimental research but seldom reach unambiguous conclusions about the effects of media exposure. Ethnographic research also can make important contributions to our understanding of the implications of mass media using qualitative methods but the results are sometimes too subjective and particularistic to duplicate. It is important to explore the issue with a variety of different methods.

1. What are some of the concerns about the impact of media on society that lead to "media bashing"?
2. Contrast the inductive and deductive approaches to studying the effects of the media.
3. What is a media effect?
4. What is the purpose of content analysis?
5. In what ways are experimental studies superior to survey studies? In what ways are they inferior?
6. What do ethnographers do?

THEORIES OF MEDIA EFFECTS

Besides considering what effects the media have on us, researchers have also tried to sort out exactly how the media work their way into our psyches. For example, do we absorb media content like a shot from a hypodermic needle or is the process more complicated? In the following paragraphs, we will consider several different theories of how the mass media affect us. Figure 12.1 compares them in highly abbreviated form.

Media as Hypodermic Needle

Earlier (see Chapter 4) we recounted the story of how the United States was seemingly driven into war with Spain in 1898 as a result of sensational newspaper coverage concocted by newspaper publisher William Randolph Hearst. His papers trumpeted the news of the sinking of the battleship *Maine* (the true cause of which

Theoretical model	Example	Audience response	
Hypodermic	War!	Do exactly what media say	We want war!
Multistep	This means war	Follow opinion leaders who interpret media	People are saying this means war
Selective process	It's the moral equivalent of war	Interpret their own way	War? What war?
Social learning	Let's go get 'em!	Imitate behavior shown in media	Let's play war!
Cultivation	It's war on the streets	Think real world works like TV world	It's a scary world out there
Priming	Blam!	Media trigger related thoughts	Happiness is a warm gun

FIGURE 12.1
There are a number of alternative theories about how to understand mass media effects.

The **bullet model**, or **hypodermic model**, posits powerful, direct effects of the mass media.

Persuasion is the use of convincing arguments to change people's beliefs, attitudes, or behaviors.

remains unknown to this day) and of alleged atrocities by Spanish soldiers against innocent Cuban women so loudly that the thirst for war became unquenchable.

Perhaps more than any other, this event was the genesis of the belief that the mass media were extremely powerful, capable of swaying minds with the impact of a speeding **bullet** or a **hypodermic** injection, images that led to theoretical models of the same names. The theory was bolstered by the apparent power of propaganda from World War I (1914–1918) and World War II (1939–1945) to whip entire nations into a frenzy. For example, World War I propaganda about alleged German atrocities against innocent women and children in Belgium "demonized" Germans in the eyes of the American public and helped to hasten the United States' entry into that war on the side of the British. Later, Nazi propaganda seemed to play a vital role in sparking the truly demonic Holocaust of World War II.

American propagandists eager to boost support for U.S. wartime efforts on behalf of the cause of freedom began the systematic study of the most convincing propaganda techniques. Experimental studies of **persuasion** begun during World War II focused on identifying the types of verbal arguments (one-sided vs. two-sided appeals, and fear appeals vs. reasoned arguments) that are the most convincing in various situations and with different types of people (Hovland, Lumsdane, & Sheffield, 1949).

The Multistep Flow

Survey studies of the processes of social influence conducted in the late 1940s presented a very different model from that of a hypodermic needle—a model in which a **multistep flow** of media effects was evident. That is, most people receive media effects secondhand, through the personal influence of opinion leaders (Katz & Lazarsfeld, 1955). The opinion leaders themselves are influenced by more elite media rather than everyday mass media channels. For example, as the first step, political opinion leaders might take their cues from *The New Republic,* a magazine devoted to liberal political and social commentary for an elite audience. In the second step, the opinion leaders share their opinions with members of their immediate social circles—say, the "Friday night regulars at the country club," but only after some modification and adaptation of the opinions to the norms of that circle. The members of that circle also belong to other social groupings (including their own families, co-workers, and members of other clubs to which they belong) that are influenced in turn by them, and so on. Eventually, social influence radiates outward in society to people who have never heard of *The New Republic.* But at every step in the process, the social influence is modified by the norms and conventions of each new social circle it enters. Opinions are blended with other opinions that originate from other elite sources and may be quite at odds with the *Republic*'s, as well as from popular mass media sources such as *Time* and the *Evening News.* The point is that although the media have some influence, the process of persuasion is primarily a social one, rather than being mass-mediated.

The **multistep flow model** assumes that media effects are indirect and are mediated by opinion leaders.

The multistep flow idea is confirmed by recent critical research. People within different social classes make very different interpretations of media. People tend to talk about media with others who are similar to themselves in education, occupation, wealth, and family background. They tend to interpret media content through discussion with key groups of people called *interpretive communities* (Lindlof, 1994), or *peer groups* in Katz and Lazarsfeld's (1955) terminology. These are often natural communities such as families, neighborhoods, unions, and churches, but they also include people who find like-minded people and form a group to interpret and reinforce media messages, such as the many newsgroups on the World Wide Web. Again, the point is that personal influence is more a result of communication with other people than of mass media exposure.

Selective Processes

Another theme of the mass media effects studies that followed World War II was that the selective reception of mass media reduces their impact somewhat. That is, people have a tendency toward *selective exposure:* They avoid messages that are at odds with their existing beliefs. Thus, those who take the "pro-life" position in the abortion debate are not likely to watch a television program featuring "pro-choice" advocates. Even when people expose themselves to discordant content, they tend to distort it through the process of *selective perception.* Thus pro-choice supporters who watch a TV interview with a leader of a right-to-life group are more likely to find additional "proof" that their position is correct than to be converted to the pro-life cause. The term *selective retention* refers to the fact that people's memories of media presentations are also distorted, so that months later someone may remember that "her" side won an abortion debate when in fact her side was humiliated (Sears & Freedman, 1972).

In 1960 Joseph Klapper published an influential review of research on the effects of the mass media that incorporated the postwar research on persuasion, personal influence, and selective processes. Klapper concluded that the media were weak, able to deliver only a few percent of the voters in an election, and able to gain only a few points' worth of market share for advertisers. Even these **limited effects** registered only at the margins, he said, primarily among the uninterested and the uninformed (Klapper, 1960).

Limited effects holds that the effects of the mass media on individuals are slight.

Social Learning Theory

Within a few short years, Klapper's conclusions began to seem unsatisfactory, and the search began for new approaches that could explain the seemingly undeniable influence of the media, particularly television, on the young. In the 1960s, social critics cast about for explanations for mounting violence, increased political unrest, and a perceived decline in public morality, especially among college students. Television was seen as a possible cause, because the college students of that day also constituted the first "TV generation" that had grown up with the medium, and TV was indeed loaded with images of violence and sex. About the same time, there emerged a new theory of mass media effects, **social learning theory,** that lent credence to these claims. Previously (see Chapter 2), we saw how this theory is applied today to media consumption behavior, but it originally entered the field of mass communication research as a means of understanding the effects of exposure to mass media. Based on Albert Bandura's research, the theory explained that viewers imitate what they see on TV through a process known as observational learning. He argued that the "rewards" that television characters receive for their antisocial behavior—including not just the loot from their robberies or the respect of their fellow criminals but also their very appearance on a glamorous medium such as television—encourage imitation (Bandura, 1983).

Social learning theory explains media effects in terms of imitating behavior seen in the media.

Cultivation Theory

Another explanation for the influence of television on violence in America emerged from a group of researchers led by George Gerbner at the University of Pennsylvania. They theorized that heavy exposure to television imparts a worldview that is consistent with the "world" of television (Gerbner & Gross, 1976). According to **cultivation theory,** heavy television viewers are likely to overestimate their own chances of being victims of violent crime. The viewers who adopt this distorted worldview might logically be expected to be more tolerant of violence in their own communities, in their families, and even in their own behavior.

Cultivation theory argues that mass media exposure cultivates a view of the world that is consistent with mediated "reality."

Priming

Priming is another mechanism for explaining media effects (Berkowitz, 1984). According to **priming theory**, the activation of one thought makes it easier to activate related thoughts. Seeing the Roadrunner cartoon character bash the hapless coyote with a hammer makes us more likely to bash our little brother after the show, or so the theory goes. Sometimes even incidental cues may unleash the aggression. The next time we see a hammer and little brother is standing near—look out!! This theory is sometimes offered as an explanation for lurid crimes that are seemingly copied directly from movies or television, such as when those who committed a string of New York subway robberies imitated a movie crime by setting a token booth aflame with flammable liquid (Leland, 1995).

Priming theory states that media images stimulate related thoughts in the minds of audience members.

Other Perspectives

Some theoretical perspectives suggest that the effects of the media are not all bad, however. Social learning theory stresses the importance of punishments as well as rewards in media portrayals (Bandura, 1986). When the bad guys on TV get caught and go to jail, this presumably inhibits viewers from imitating them. The *catharsis hypothesis* argues that media portrayals of sex and violence can actually have positive effects by allowing people to live out their antisocial desires in the fantasy world of the media rather than in the real world (Feshbach & Singer, 1971).

These theories are by no means the only approaches that researchers use to understand the effects of exposure to the media. In recent years, critical theorists have called into question the value of all such attempts to examine media effects, believing that they focus too narrowly on individual behavior and leave out the broader social implications. We will consider this perspective further in the next chapter.

1. **Outline the critical communications perspective.**
2. **Name three theories that contend that mass media have strong effects.**
3. **What are some of the factors that weaken media effects?**
4. **What are examples of media effects that are best explained by persuasion? By social learning theory? By cultivation theory? By priming theory?**

COMMUNICATIONS MEDIA AND ANTISOCIAL BEHAVIOR

Antisocial behavior is behavior that is contrary to prevailing norms for social conduct. It can include unlawful actions, such as murder, hate crimes, rape, and drug abuse, as well as behaviors that most members of society find objectionable even if they are not illegal, such as drunkenness and sexual promiscuity.

Antisocial behavior is behavior contrary to prevailing social norms.

Violence

The effects of violence on television have probably received more attention than any other type of media effect. Effects on children are a special concern, because youngsters have trouble distinguishing between the "real world" and the world of the small screen. To the child's mind, if the Coyote character in the Saturday morning TV cartoon recovers instantly from a bash on the head, then the same should be true for little brother. With their short attention spans, young children are unlikely to associate the legal consequences of violent behavior, which emerge in the dull courtroom scenes at the end of the show, with the eye-catching shootout at the beginning. Given that children spend so much time with television and that much of this viewing is unsupervised by parents, the potential exists for great harm to impressionable young minds (Liebert & Sprafkin, 1988).

Television is indeed packed with violence, as content analyses show (see page 388). Numerous experimental studies conducted in laboratory settings, many patterned after Bandura's Bobo doll study, demonstrate that children can imitate violence they see on television. These studies indicate that televised violence prompts children not only to carry out parallel acts of aggression but also to perform other, novel forms of violent behavior, and it predisposes them to select violent resolutions to conflicts in their daily lives. Also, researchers have found that children will imitate violence even if it is not explicitly reinforced on television (Liebert & Sprafkin, 1988).

Others reject the findings of experimental studies on the grounds that they are conducted under unrealistic conditions (Anderson & Meyer, 1988; Freedman,

MEDIA IMPACT

A Critical View of Media, Violence, and Culture

Critical studies of media impacts, such as violence, focus less on behavioral effects on individuals and more on large-scale cultural impacts, such as permitting some groups to practice violence against other groups. However, some critical scholars also focus on Freudian-style psychological interpretations of motives and implications. For example, one critical analysis of John Hinckley's attempted assassination of Ronald Reagan examined the way in which Hinckley "read" (or interpreted) a violent movie (*Taxi Driver*) and mingled it with his fantasies about actress Jodie Foster and former actor Ronald Reagan (Real, 1989). By noting that Hinckley committed his act of violence on the eve of the Academy Awards ceremony, Real wove an explanation of how the would-be assassin was trying to communicate his unrequited love for Foster. More typical critical approaches might examine changes in the way in which violence toward indigenous Americans was portrayed in Westerns from the 1930s, when violence against "Indians" was uncritically accepted, to the 1960s, when that violence began to be challenged in film treatments, such as *Little Big Man* (see Chapter 5).

Similarly, critical approaches to the study of advertising emphasize the ways that advertising promotes a general pattern of consumption—as opposed to the consumption of specific products, which is the focus of administrative research on advertising—in a way that draws people into a capitalist economic system that may or may not benefit them; the capitalist system itself is under the economic domination of the large corporations that pay for the advertising. Likewise, a critical look at the political effects of mass media might bypass campaign advertisements entirely and instead examine the hidden political messages about obedience to authority, class structure, and gender relations contained in such "nonpolitical" programs as *Sesame Street* and *The Simpsons*. Thus, the critical theorist is able to examine broad questions about the relationship between culture and society that may elude the social scientist.

1984; Milavsky et al., 1982; McGuire,1986). Or, they maintain, experimental results could merely be the result of a sponsor effect: The experimenters implicitly give their subjects "permission" to behave violently by showing them violence in the laboratory environment (Felson, 1996). Field experiments, conducted in real-life settings in which the subjects are less likely to guess that they are being observed, also demonstrate the effects of media violence (Paik & Comstock, 1994), but when natural field observations of violent behavior are used instead of relying on respondents' own imperfect memories, the results are mixed (Wood et al., 1991). One field experiment even found evidence of a catharsis effect that reduces violent tendencies through exposure to fantasy violence (Feshback & Singer, 1971). Historically, the introduction of television in American cities in the 1950s was unrelated to increases in the crime rates in those cities (Hennigan et al., 1982)—a sort of "natural experiment," if you will, that contradicts the notion that TV viewing causes violence.

Survey studies that examine a broader cross-section of the population also tend to show a relationship between violent behavior and viewership of violent television (Paik & Comstock, 1994). Research shows that adult viewers who watch violent programs are likely to hold world views that match the TV portrayals they see (Gerbner, Gross, Morgan, & Signorelli, 1994), a result consistent with cultivation theory. That is, if we see a lot of violence on TV, we are more likely to expect violence in our own lives. However, these relationships are relatively weak outside the laboratory, and they may be statistical artifacts or may be due to factors other than exposure to television violence *per se*, including the differing social characteristics of heavy and light viewers (Hirsch, 1980).

More convincing are longitudinal panel studies in which television viewing at one time is related to violence exhibited at a second time that is days, months, or even years later. Earlier (page 393) we mentioned panel studies by Huesmann (1982) and his associates that indicated that television viewing at an early age is related to violent behavior later in life. But other longitudinal studies have produced complex and contradictory results (Felson, 1996).

It should be obvious by now that the issue of the effects of television violence remains controversial. It is probably safest to conclude that exposure to antisocial television portrayals can have at least short-term effects in promoting violent behavior. Most researchers would add that there are probably long-term effects as well, especially on children. If this is true, recent attempts to label violent content for parents are long overdue. However, they may not be effective unless accompanied by improved parental supervision or automatic content filtering via the V-chip (see page 384). Simply labeling the programs as violent actually attracts more young viewers to the "forbidden fruit" (Bushman & Stack, 1996).

PREJUDICE

Sexism, racism, and other forms of intolerance may also be promoted by the media. Media portrayals often encourage **stereotyping,** or the formation of generalizations about a group of people on the basis of limited information. Stereotypes are harmful when used to define groups of people, particularly when they become rationalizations for treating others unfairly. Furthermore, negative stereotypes may

Stereotyping is the making of generalizations about groups of people on the basis of limited information.

be internalized by members of the groups to which they are applied, undermining their own self-respect. Media can create stereotypes because they are sometimes the only source of information about people who are different from oneself and because they often present a one-sided or distorted view.

For example, content analysis studies show that women are underrepresented in mass media portrayals and that they usually appear in subservient roles or in low-status occupations such as secretary and housewife. To the male viewer, this might somehow make it seem "acceptable" to treat women as inferiors. For their part, women may also get the sense that their group is somehow less important because of their underrepresentation and low status. They may internalize the stereotypes foisted on them by the media—for example, that women who look beautiful have more value than others and that women should sacrifice their careers for their families (Signorelli, 1989). Experimental studies have shown that young girls exposed to a heavy dose of TV shows that portray women in traditional sex roles do tend to limit their own career aspirations to traditionally female occupations such as secretary, nurse, teacher, and housewife (Beuf, 1974; Freuh & McGhee, 1975).

There has been relatively little research on the effects of media stereotypes on minority children, but scholars believe that their life aspirations are affected by the limited media portrayals of minority actors (Clark, 1972). Racially stereotyped television portrayals of minorities may also make white viewers view minorities in more negative ways, such as making them more willing to see African Americans as criminals (Ford, 1997).

These negative effects may occur even when the media attempt to reduce people's prejudices and undermine their stereotypes with satire. The 1970s TV series *All in the Family* was an attempt to poke fun at those who were prejudiced against women, intellectuals, and minorities—indeed against anyone not just like themselves—through the misadventures of the bigoted Archie Bunker. Unfortunately, the real-life "Archie Bunkers" who tuned into the program found Archie to be a sympathetic character. They thought the minorities, women, and wiseguy college students in the program were the butts of the jokes, not Archie. Selective perception, in which we see only what reinforces our firmly entrenched ideas, was evidently very much at work.

Media stereotyping is by no means limited to women and minorities. Blue-collar families are also underrepresented in the media, for example, and when present, they are often portrayed in an unfavorable light that denigrates their lifestyles (consider *The Simpsons*). The same is true of representations of homosexuals, persons with disabilities, the homeless, the mentally ill, and seemingly any group that deviates from a mainstream society dominated by professional, "straight," healthy, and wealthy white males.

Nor are stereotypes limited to conventional mass media. Internet newsgroups and chat rooms are notorious for abusive treatment of female participants—especially in the early days of the Web when few females were on-line—forcing many to assume fake male identities. There are numerous examples to be found in popular CD-ROM games such as *Myst* (save the helpless princess!), and "adult entertainment" sites on the Web offer blatantly sexist content (Dietrich, 1997).

Media stereotypes also apply to many other groups. We can easily summon to mind stock images of serious college students (invariably labeled "nerds" in media lexicon), millionaires, lawyers, doctors, business executives, and law enforcement professionals that have little in common with their real-world counterparts. To some extent, the media cannot function without stereotypes. They are the "picture in our heads" (Lippmann, 1922) that stories are made of, a type of conceptual shorthand that allows viewers to recognize characters immediately and connect with their situations. It is when the negative stereotypes spill over from the flickering screen into our daily lives that they become a concern.

Sexual Behavior

Sex in the mass media erupted as an issue in the 1920s, in the aftermath of a wave of Hollywood sex scandals. Hollywood imposed on itself strict self-censorship standards that now seem ludicrous in retrospect: no cleavage, no navels, separate beds for married couples, no kisses longer than four seconds, cut to the clouds overhead if sex is imminent. When Elizabeth Taylor said the word "virgin" in a 1954 movie, it caused a sensation. Over the next three decades, producers and publishers vied to push the limits of sexually explicit language and behavior even further—and reap the financial benefits at the box office.

The last decades have seen a dramatic increase in the accessibility of highly explicit pornographic material through magazines, home video, and now the Internet. At the same time, social norms have become more harsh against behaviors once-tolerated but now labeled as date rape and sexual harassment. These two trends are clearly on a collision course, raising anew the question of whether the increased exposure to sexually charged media actually fosters inappropriate sexual behavior.

Experimental studies offer a qualified "yes" to this question. When males are exposed to explicit pornography, they are more likely to express negative attitudes toward women, are more likely to think that relatively uncommon sexual practices (such as fellatio and anal intercourse) are widespread, and are likely to be more lenient with rape offenders in hypothetical court cases. In experiments that examine the combined impacts of pornography and violence, a common procedure is to seat the male subjects at an apparatus that supposedly delivers electrical shocks to a female seated in the next room. (This is common practice in psychological experiments on aggression. The shocks are simulated, and the females are confederates of the experimenter who are trained to act as though they are being shocked, so no one really gets hurt.) The males are more likely to administer electric shocks (sometimes even supposedly lethal ones!) after exposure to pornography (Allen, Dalessio, & Brezgel, 1995). However, this may apply only to violent pornography, in which the female models are subject to coercive or sadistic behavior, and then only when women are shown to be enjoying the abuse (Felson, 1996).

In the 1980s, a presidential commission under the Reagan administration (the so-called Meese Commission) spearheaded a clean-up of pornography to remove coercive and violent portrayals (Attorney General of the United States, 1986). Did the Meese Commission go far enough? Some don't think so. Feminists also campaign against any pornography that is *degrading* to women, including, for example, anything that portrays women as subservient or unequal sex partners, shows them as faceless sex objects, or involves bodily invasion by nonhuman species or inanimate objects. Canadian antipornography laws reflect this stricter definition of pornography.

On the other hand, it is possible that the Commission went too far, at least judging by the research we have today. Pornography experiments may be subject to the same "sponsor effects" that plague violence studies: Showing respondents pornographic films communicates permissiveness toward sex, which may unnaturally affect the subjects' behavior in the laboratory environment. For example, the male college students who are willing to administer shocks to female experimenters after viewing pornography might do so because after they are invited by a professor into a university laboratory to view violent pornography, it seems to the male students that the depicted behavior is socially sanctioned. Out in the real world, the availability of pornography in a community does not seem to be related to the incidence of rape in the same area (Gentry, 1991), and sex offenders do not have more exposure to pornography than anyone else (Bauserman, 1996). Unlike access to violent content, which is virtually unavoidable in the media, access to pornography is highly restricted. Thus the mechanism of selective exposure is likely to limit its effects to reinforcing the pre-existing sexual fantasies of those who take the trouble to seek out pornography (Felson, 1996).

Drug Abuse

A generation ago there was concern that movies such as *Easy Rider* glorified the drug scene and contributed to an epidemic of illegal drug use among college students. The media generally heeded these public concerns, if only because drug films were not as profitable as those featuring violence and sex. In movies and television programs about the drug scene today, viewers may see characters handling a white powder, but they seldom see anyone actually consuming the drug.

The abuse of legal drugs is quite another story. Cigarette ads have long been banished from television by law, and although cigarette manufacturers can still use print ads, the content has been restricted. The ads can no longer glorify smoking by showing happy, glamorous people puffing away; the surgeon general's warnings about the hazards of smoking must be displayed; and there can be no imagery that obviously is designed to appeal to children. Hard liquor distillers voluntarily avoid television (although they are rethinking this) but fill magazines with seductive ads for their products. Beer and wine commercials are one of the leading sources of advertising revenue for television, as are ads for over-the-counter drugs, and restrictions on prescription drug ads have been relaxed so that they, too, can appear on television.

Advertisers claim that these ads do not boost overall consumption levels and affect only the relative share of the market that the various brands enjoy. However, studies of children and adolescents provide some evidence that exposure to beer, wine, and cigarette ads is related to their consumption of these products. Meanwhile, young children exposed to over-the-counter drug commercials look on drugs as a way to solve their personal problems, a habit that might carry over to illicit drugs somewhere down the road (Atkin, 1985). Critics have long contended that some of the ads are secretly targeted to young viewers through characters (such as

Old Joe in the Camel cigarette ads) that are carefully crafted to appeal to impressionable young viewers at an age when they are vulnerable to initiating lifelong addictions. Recent revelations of secret cigarette industry marketing studies on children have shown that these critics were right.

The Effects of Computer Media

Antisocial Behavior. As people spend more time with computers, researchers concerned about media effects have naturally turned in that direction. Surprisingly, violent computer games, many of which are far more graphic than television programs, do not seem to stimulate violent behavior in children to the degree that violence on television may (Tapscott, 1998). Perhaps the interactive quality of computer media endows them with a cathartic effect that just passively watching a television program or movie does not.

BLAM!
Violent video games may not be as harmful as conventional television violence.

The Internet also brings pornography, the rantings of hate groups, and information on every conceivable form of aberrant human behavior directly into the home, the local library reading room, and the classroom, where it may be viewed by impressionable children without adult supervision. However, the dynamic newness of the Internet has thus far frustrated attempts by social scientists to measure its effects, or even catalog its content. One study of interactive computer pornography found that it had no effect on either attitudes or aggressive behavior toward women among college freshman males (Barak & Fisher, 1997).

Computer Anxiety. Most research has focused on dysfunctional uses of the computer rather than on the effects of its content. Computer anxiety, also known as cyberphobia and computerphobia, is a debilitating fear of the computer (Kernan & Howard, 1990). By some estimates, it afflicts up to a third of the adult population; people with the most extreme cases suffer from nausea, vertigo, and cold sweats. Their anxiety has several possible origins, including the fear that they will cause damage by pushing the wrong key, concern over the social effects of the computer (such as compromising privacy), fear of personal failure, and an "out of control" feeling that nontechnical persons may experience when faced with a complex technical system. Women and people with relatively low mathematical skills are especially likely to suffer from computer anxiety. Computerphobes do poorly on computer tasks and in computer classes and are dissatisfied computer users.

Addiction. At the other end of the spectrum are those whose compulsive use of the computer might justifiably be called Internet addiction (Grohol, 1996). The

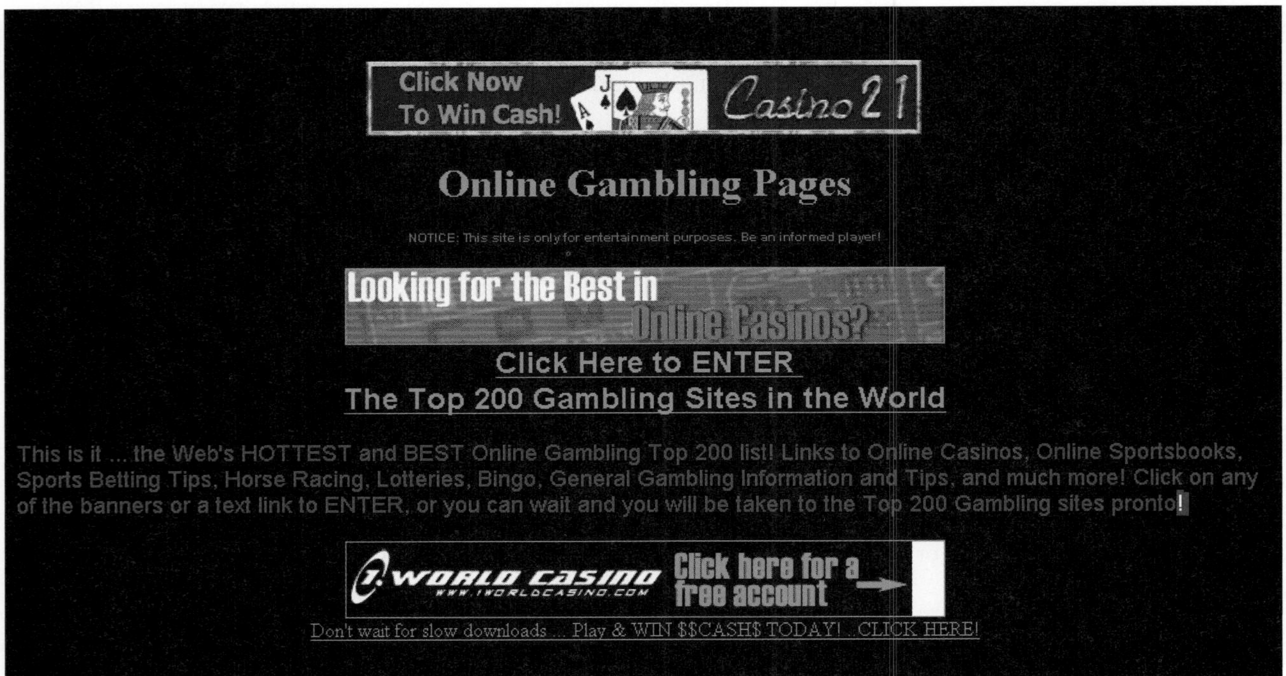

Click Now
To Win Cash!
Casino 21
Online Gambling Pages
NOTICE: This site is only for entertainment purposes. Be an informed player!
Looking for the Best in
Online Casinos?
Click Here to ENTER
The Top 200 Gambling Sites in the World
This is it ... the Web's HOTTEST and BEST Online Gambling Top 200 list! Links to Online Casinos, Online Sportsbooks, Sports Betting Tips, Horse Racing, Lotteries, Bingo, General Gambling Information and Tips, and much more! Click on any of the banners or a text link to ENTER, or you can wait and you will be taken to the Top 200 Gambling sites pronto!
WORLD CASINO
Click here for a free account
Don't wait for slow downloads ... Play & WIN $$CASH$$ TODAY! ..CLICK HERE!

ADDICTIVE?
Gambling sites on the World Wide Web raise concerns about the addictive effects of the Internet on human behavior.

computer has an interactive quality that makes it seem as though it responds to the user's every move. It does not always reward users with the response they hope for, however, but rather keeps them coming back for more—just the kind of pattern known to prompt such obsessive "addictive" behavior as gambling. Video games are often cited in this regard; parents complain about children seemingly becoming addicted to a particular game. The results of an on-line survey of Internet users suggest that tolerance, craving, and withdrawal—all signs of behavioral addiction—are associated with Internet use (Brenner, 1997). There is also anecdotal evidence of adults who have lost everything they own by racking up user fees on interactive games or adult entertainment on the Web. The problem is likely to spread as more activities with well-established addictive qualities, such as gambling and fantasy sports leagues, go on-line. The potentially addictive qualities of virtual reality systems are sometimes even touted by their developers, some of whom promise a "better high than drugs."

Psychologist Sherry Turkle (1995) prefers the metaphor of seduction to that of addiction. She stresses that the holding power of the computer does not come from what is external (like a drug) but rather from what is within people—what they learn about themselves through their infatuation with the computer. What attracts people to the computer, she argues, is its ability to provoke self-reflection, to extend the user's mind into artificial worlds, and to adapt itself to the needs of each user. In this view, habitual computer users are drawn by the appeal of being able to control the world inside the computer, to achieve the illusion of intimacy, to gain confirmation of a sense of selfhood, and to express themselves in the style of their own choosing.

Depression. According to one widely reported recent study (Kraut et al., 1998), the Internet may cause depression among heavy users. The researchers introduced Internet access into 73 homes in Pittsburgh and found that heavy teenage Net surfers exhibited more signs of depression than light users and also showed decreased social involvement and increased loneliness. These investigators argued that the weak social ties formed on the Internet were no substitute for "real" relationships, and that futile efforts to make them play that role lead to isolation and depression.

Educational Impacts. Heavy users of computer games may actually benefit, as well, and be better prepared than others to learn about science and technology. They learn the symbolic codes of computer graphics by playing the games, an increasingly important skill in the Information Age (Greenfield, 1994). Another researcher concluded that video games can be valuable learning tools and that they have no effect on academic performance and do not promote psychological disorders (Emes, 1997).

MEDIA IMPACT

The Social Effects of the Internet

For Further Research:

Communications research is becoming increasingly concerned with the social effects of the Internet, and much of the research *about* the Internet can also be found *on* the Internet. We mentioned a study that revealed a relationship between Internet usage and depression, for example. You can find information about this research at the site of the journal that published it (www.apa.org/journals/amp/amp5391017.html). Another topic of interest is the demographic difference between the "haves" and the "have-nots," on the Web. An example of work in this area is a Vanderbilt University study on the so-called "digital divide" (www.2000.ogsm.vanderbilt.edu/papers/race/science.html). In fact, a great deal of research still focuses on who is using the Web and who is not and on what the most popular Web pages are. For these studies, we refer you to the sites of research organizations that conduct the studies, such as Net Ratings (www.netratings.com). We have found that these are not very stable sites, though. In academia, projects come and go, along with their Web sites, and the commercial ventures are constantly merging and changing names. Hence we leave you with a general Internet search strategy to turn up the latest. Try "(Internet or Web) and (survey or statistics)" with a general Web browser.

WWW

Privacy. Another concern is that growing computer use has negative impacts on personal privacy. It is useful to distinguish between two dimensions of privacy: freedom from unwanted intrusions and freedom from unwanted disclosures of personal information. In the unwanted intrusions category, the receipt of unwanted e-mail, known as spam, is the main concern. Spam is the Information Age equivalent of junk mail, telemarketing, and crank phone calls, all rolled into one. Computers have long been implicated in making unwanted disclosures of personal information through the availability on-line of personal credit histories and the ability of computers to match information between files. The expanding use of the World Wide Web for both entertainment and shopping poses a new threat. Records of your transactions with on-line services, even records of the entertainment programs you consume, could be "turned against you" in the form of high-powered advertising campaigns or direct marketing appeals so finely tuned to your needs that you might find them irresistible (see Chapter 14).

Computer Crime. Finally, computer networks have spawned their own novel forms of antisocial behavior, called *hacking.* Some hackers use computers as a means to commit Information Age versions of age-old crimes, such as theft of electronic funds and sexual and racial harassment. But the "game" of gaining access to secure industrial and governmental computer installations and wrecking their files tempts a growing number of young hackers.

COMMUNICATIONS MEDIA AND PROSOCIAL BEHAVIOR

Prosocial behaviors are those that a society values and encourages.

Prosocial behavior is in a sense the opposite of antisocial behavior. It includes all of those behaviors and positive qualities that many people want to encourage in their children and their society: cooperation, altruism, sharing, love, tolerance, respect, balanced nutrition, contraceptive use, personal hygiene, safe driving, improved reading skills, and so on. We can also include in this list discontinuing antisocial behaviors, such as when an individual decides to stop practicing unsafe sex or to quit smoking, drinking, or reckless driving. Prosocial media attempt to foster prosocial behavior. Such messages fall along a continuum based on the relative mixture of entertainment and informational content. They range from transmitting heavily sugar-coated, subtle messages to explicit, direct educational efforts.

Efforts to put more prosocial programs on television represent the flip side of the "media bashing" ritual that we outlined earlier. Instead of criticizing the media for sex and violence—only to have them retreat behind the First Amendment—why not encourage them to produce more wholesome and educational programs for children? The Children's Television Act of 1990 does just that—it mandates that a certain number of programs designed specifically for children be aired as a condition for broadcast license renewals (see Chapter 14). After years of wrangling over just how much children's programming is enough, what "specifically designed for children" means, and even who children are, meaningful guidelines were finally passed in 1996 (Kunkel, 1997).

Information Campaigns

Information campaigns use the techniques of advertising in an attempt to convince people to adopt prosocial behaviors.

Information campaigns use the techniques of public relations and advertising to "sell" people on prosocial behaviors. They differ from other types of public affairs programming in that they seek to achieve specific changes in their audience, such as heightening public awareness of a health or social problem and changing related attitudes and behaviors. They usually adopt an informal and entertaining style to attract an audience. Perhaps the most familiar manifestations of information campaigns are the public service announcements that populate late-night television, such as the one showing an egg falling on a hot skillet while the narrator intones, "This is your brain. This is drugs. This is your brain on drugs." However, information campaigns take many other forms, including orchestrated celebrity appearances on radio and television talk shows, the pamphlets you find in your doctor's office, and public service advertisements in print media.

Information campaigns have a spotty record of success. Experimental studies show that campaigns sometimes do affect the awareness, attitudes, and even the behavior of their audience. Campaigns can succeed if they have clear objectives and sharply defined target audiences and if they find relevant ways to overcome the indifference of the audience (Mendelsohn, 1973). *Social marketing,* an integrated approach to behavior change that combines well-designed media, interpersonal influence, and carefully managed efforts to introduce recommended products directly into the lives of the target audience, has achieved considerable success in the health communication field (Maibach & Holtgrave, 1995). In the case of a safe-sex campaign, conventional mass media spots might be combined with posters in nightclubs and with the efforts of volunteers who circulate on the dance floor and distribute condoms upon request.

Even when well designed, however, some information campaigns face too many obstacles to have much impact. Many rely on free advertising space, have difficulty reaching their intended audiences, and never have the same impact as a political campaign or product promotion. The public interest groups that produce information campaigns usually expend all their resources in developing the media materials, leaving little remaining for paid media placements that might bring the campaigns to the attention of their true target audiences.

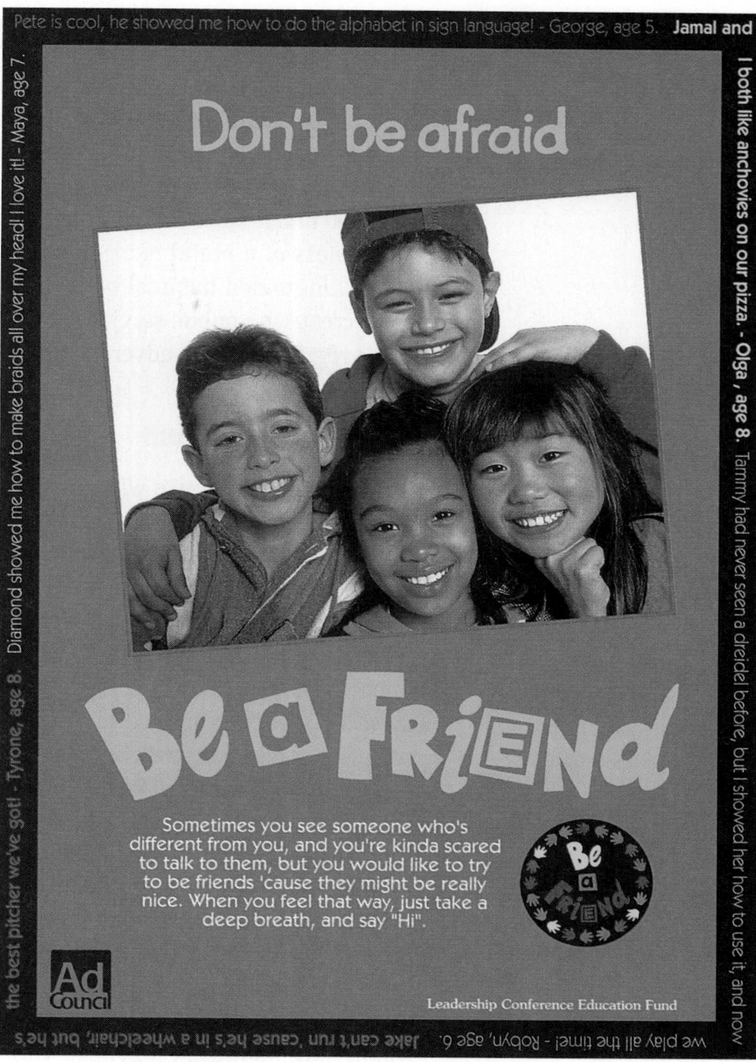

PROSOCIAL.
Public service campaigns, like this one from the Ad Council, are designed to encourage prosocial behavior such as friendliness.

But not all information campaigns are effective to begin with. They are often created by advertising professionals who contribute their time in exchange for a chance to showcase their skills. The results are often eye-catching and memorable ("This is your brain . . .") but seldom achieve their stated goals, because they don't take into account the ability of the audience to process information selectively or because they fail to activate the social networks that apply personal influence. A common mistake is to use strong fear appeals in an effort to dissuade adolescents from engaging in illicit behaviors. Unfortunately, the teens who are most susceptible to these behaviors are also likely to have low self-esteem, which means they will discount or deny the message rather than take it to heart. The adults who are behind the campaigns think strong fear appeals are great ("Yeah, hard hitting. That'll teach them!") but the target audience just makes a joke out of them.

In other cases, campaigns may have foggy objectives or uncertain target audiences, or they may have too many objectives, trying to satisfy multiple agendas ("We want users to stop using, potential users to stop thinking about it, and their parents to drum both messages into their children's heads"). Developers of information campaigns seldom have the resources to fund the detailed background research that goes into successful product commercials. What is more, they try to achieve much more than product advertisements, which merely aim to increase awareness of a brand name or a new product. Information campaigns often target deeply ingrained habitual behaviors, a goal that even the advertising executives who create the public service spots usually admit they cannot readily achieve in their regular product advertisements.

Informal Education

In the next chapter, we will consider the effectiveness of communications media when they are used to present educational materials in formal instructional settings. Media also educate through informal education that focuses on entertaining and enhancing the knowledge of the audience rather than changing its beliefs or social behaviors. Without a "captive audience" of classroom students, informal education efforts must artfully combine the elements of education and entertainment. The best-known example is *Sesame Street.* Since its inception in 1972, *Sesame Street* has proved to be both a popular and an effective means of readying young children for school.

Sesame Street is also an example of another phenomenon that plagues prosocial media, the unintended effect. *Sesame Street* was originally designed to close the gap in school readiness between minority and majority children. Unfortunately, it does just the opposite. Middle-class, white children who watch the show learn more about "words that begin with b" than low-income minority children, and the knowledge gap (see Chapter 13) between the two widens as a result (Cook et al., 1975). Antidrug campaigns also have a habit of backfiring by inadvertently glamorizing abuse or by supplying information that encourages it ("Drugs only *fry* your brain? I thought they *shredded* your brain!").

What about the prosocial effects of entertainment media? Do couch potatoes soak up valuable information from TV quiz shows? Do children imitate altruistic behavior from Smurfs cartoons as readily as they pick up violent behavior from the violent Coyote? Do they learn about anthropology from watching cartoon cavemen on *The Flintstones* or acquire reading skills from the game show *Wheel of Fortune,* as the TV networks sometimes like to claim? We call these effects *incidental learning,* because they are side effects of exposure to entertainment that is otherwise devoid of instructional purpose.

Compared to the investigation of antisocial effects, little research has been done on the prosocial effects of entertainment media. Content analyses of television entertainment programming reveal frequent examples of prosocial behavior, although these instances may be overwhelmed by glorified depictions of aggression (Greenberg et al., 1980). According to some studies, prosocial programs can be highly effective (Huston, 1992; Hearold, 1986), although prosocial effects do not seem to be as predictable and long-lasting as antisocial effects (Liebert & Sprafkin, 1988), which themselves can be quite unpredictable and short-lived.

THE EFFECTS OF ADVERTISING

If the media have such mixed success in influencing behavior, why is there so much advertising? (For more on advertising, see Chapter 11). The answer is that advertisers are happy to achieve far more limited effects than those that concern media watchdog groups. Most advertisers take our consumption behavior as a given and merely seek to influence what particular brand we purchase. First, they seek to increase our *brand awareness* so that we think of their product when we are in the store. Once they have us sold, they try to maintain *brand loyalty* so that we will keep coming back for more. Thus automobile manufacturers do not waste their money convincing us that we need a new car. But they do try to make us think of their product when we are out shopping for a car and convince us to come back to them for our next one (Jeffres, 1986).

Does advertising work? Even with these relatively modest goals, many advertising campaigns are a flop. Sometimes they are outgunned by more powerful campaigns from competitors. In addition, many other factors influence consumer purchases, including special promotional offers, the price of the product, its availability, the way it is packaged, and—let us not forget—the true needs of the consumers and the actual merits of the product! Any of these can negate the effects of the most polished advertising campaign.

Sometimes, too, the campaign is simply ineffective or backfires. Part of the problem lies with the way commercials are tested before they go on the air. If they are highly memorable, they are deemed successful. Only much later do the advertisers find out whether they sell more hamburgers or athletic shoes.

OLD JOE.
Cigarette advertising influences impressionable minds and may encourage young children to acquire an unhealthful lifelong habit.

The effects of television advertising on young children have received a great deal of attention by researchers and policy makers because most children first come into contact with the consumer society through TV. Young children have a difficult time understanding commercials. They confuse the commercials with the programs and react uncritically to the advertising messages (Liebert & Sprafkin, 1988). Advertisers can exploit the gullibility of young viewers by using the hosts of children's shows to hawk their products, selecting deceptive camera angles to make tiny toys appear child-sized, and prompting children to wear down their parents by parroting annoying advertising slogans. Cereal commercials are the worst offenders, promoting unhealthful confections by placing toys in the packages instead of nutrition. Even more serious are the effects of advertising for harmful adult products, such as cigarettes. Before he was forced out of advertisements by the new tobacco advertising code, that smooth "old Joe Camel" in the Camel ads was highly memorable and highly effective in promoting brand awareness among children (Difranza et al., 1991).

There are many successful advertising campaigns, and the best ones can yield substantial increases in market share. However, the average commercial campaign is likely to register an increase in sales of only a few percent. These modest gains nonetheless translate into millions of dollars for mass market products. That, and the hope of the occasional blockbuster campaign, is what keeps the whole system of commercial advertising and mass media afloat.

But now that system is under attack on the Internet, where a new model of advertising is developing. A growing number of information and entertainment sites carry *banners* that direct surfers to Web pages prepared by the product advertisers, where they can find detailed product information, locate the dealer nearest them, or even make their purchase on-line with the click of a mouse button. A new measure of advertising effectiveness is emerging, the *click-through*—that is, the percentage of those visitors responding to the banner ads at the referring site who elect to visit the advertiser's Web site (Briggs & Hollis, 1997).

THE EFFECTS OF POLITICAL COMMUNICATION

Whether we like it or not, political campaigns have largely evolved into advertising campaigns, the candidate being the "product." The techniques of market research and mass persuasion have been applied with a vengeance to politics. The political caucus has given way to the focus group, a type of open-ended interview in which small groups of consumers/voters are prompted by market researchers to reveal their innermost feelings about the products/candidates in front of a hidden TV camera.

What is the net effect of the political ads that glut the airwaves before an election? Surprisingly little, if we look just at the direct effects of the ads on voting behavior. Like ads for commercial products, campaign ads have relatively modest effects, especially those that appear in the final days of the campaign. By that time, most voters have made up their minds, and the processes of selective exposure, selective perception, and selective retention (see page 398) attenuate the effects of the ads. Political commercials cannot convert many voters to the other side at that stage. That leaves the undecided voters, many of whom are likely to stay home anyway. According to the multistep flow model (page 397), the undecided voters who do vote are more likely to be swayed by the people around them than by the candidates' campaign advertising spots. Political communication researchers have largely given up trying to sway votes, concentrating instead on understanding the complex interactions between voters and political systems (McLeod, Kosicki, & McLeod, 1994).

It is ironic that the less important the election, the more important political ads become. This is because voters are unlikely to be aware of candidates or issues outside of the presidential race and one or two other high-profile contests. Most Americans cannot name their own member of the House of Representatives, let alone the name of the challenger or the positions either candidate takes on the issues. Because people are naturally unwilling to vote for an unknown quantity, this often gives incumbents—and candidates with names such as "Kennedy" and

"Trueheart"—a natural advantage. A generation ago, the party label was the accepted way to sort through a field of unknown candidates, but now party loyalty and discipline are in decline. Issues have turned into TV "sound bites." In this vacuum, advertising can be effective. After all, one of the things advertising is good at is establishing name recognition.

What about the other campaign coverage that appears in the media, such as news stories, public opinion polls, public appearances by the candidates, debates, and editorial endorsements? Campaign coverage is inherently more effective than political advertisements because authoritative media sources are generally more credible, or believable, than politicians, and credible sources are more persuasive.

Media coverage sometimes makes political ads effective when the ads become news stories in themselves. The classic example is a television spot run by Lyndon Johnson in the 1964 presidential campaign. The ad showed a little girl picking wildflowers, followed by a picture of the mushroom cloud of a nuclear explosion, implying that opponent Barry Goldwater's "hard-line" military policies would lead to nuclear war. The ad ran only once, but the print and electronic media publicized it in their campaign coverage, greatly extending its reach and lending credibility to the message.

However, selective processes also limit the effectiveness of campaign coverage, just as they limit the effectiveness of campaign ads. Nowhere is this more evident than in presidential debates. Debates are seen through the distorted lens of selective perception to such a degree that who people think won the debate depends almost entirely on which candidate they favored going in. Very few voters are converted to the other side by debates, and most of the shifts in candidate preference are found among those who are undecided or relatively uninterested in the election.

The impact of election polls is also dulled by selective perception; a candidate's "true believers" are likely to discount the credibility of polls rather than to change their preference. This is not to say that polls do not play an important role in the political process. The candidates follow them religiously, constantly reformulating their message and revamping their image to increase their popularity among key blocs of voters. Political contributions also flow in on a rising tide of positive poll numbers and recede when the polls take a downturn. As with paid advertising spots, coverage is likely to be more influential in the less important elections. Editorial endorsements in newspapers follow this rule. They have relatively little impact on elections for national or statewide offices, but they may be the deciding factor for local candidates (Atkin, 1985).

Media coverage does affect voter participation. In minor elections where as few as 10 percent of the eligible voters turn out, if the media focus on an otherwise obscure race, voter participation may soar. If the coverage selectively galvanizes unified blocs of voters, this can have a major impact on the election results, as well.

The media are by no means powerless bystanders in the electoral process; it is just that the effects do not flow directly from the mass media sources that most of us patronize. In accordance with the concept of the multistep flow, *opinion leaders* in our own circle of friends, family, and acquaintances are the true sources of personal influence. They, in turn, are influenced by opinion leaders of their own and by their exposure to elite media sources that most of us do not encounter. They are the "C-SPAN junkies," the people who watch the Sunday newsmaker interviews

1. Give three examples of antisocial behavior that may be caused by television.
2. Does television cause violence, or doesn't it? Explain your answer.
3. Name some examples of prosocial effects of the media.
4. What are the characteristics of successful public information campaigns?
5. Discuss the effects of advertising.
6. How much influence do political campaigns have on the outcomes of elections?

while the rest of the population tunes in the football game. Increasingly, politicians seek to circumvent journalists and media pundits to speak directly to opinion leaders. Using such channels as the Internet and closed-group teleconferences, they deliver their message directly to the influentials, bypassing the media gatekeepers entirely.

Also, recall an earlier discussion (in Chapter 2) of the *gatekeeping* and *agenda setting* functions of the mass media—their ability to define what the important issues are through their choice of the stories they carry. The key issues in many political campaigns are defined by the media before the electioneering begins. In this light, the media may have their most profound effects on *public opinion* between political campaigns, rather than during them.

SUMMARY AND REVIEW

WHY DOESN'T SOMEONE "CLEAN UP" THE MEDIA IF THEY HAVE SO MANY NEGATIVE EFFECTS?

Efforts by the U.S. government to control media content inevitably conflict with the rights of the media to free speech. The media sometimes agree to adopt their own guidelines, such as content ratings or program standards. However, these are voluntary standards that are usually eroded by pressures to make sensational programming in an attempt to reach the largest possible audience. Media spokespersons often question the validity of research that suggests the media's negative effects, and they argue that society's ills have deeper causes than mass media exposure.

WHAT ARE TWO BASIC APPROACHES TO UNDERSTANDING MEDIA EFFECTS?

Media effects are changes in knowledge, attitude, or behavior that result from exposure to the mass media. In the deductive approach, predictions about media effects are derived from theory, and exposure to media content is treated as the causal, or independent, variable that leads to the effects, or the dependent variable. The inductive approach infers the impacts of the media, and theories that explain them are inferred from detailed observations in real-world environments.

WHAT ARE FOUR BASIC METHODS OF RESEARCH ON MEDIA EFFECTS?

Content analysis is used to characterize the content of media systems by enumerating the types of behaviors, themes, and actors that appear in the media, though such analysis cannot be used to make inferences about the actual effects of the media. Experimental research examines the relationship between exposure to media content and audience effects under tightly controlled laboratory conditions that make it possible to rule out competing explanations for the effects that are observed. Survey studies administer questionnaires to large representative samples of subjects in an effort to examine relationships between media exposure and media effects; they take into account a wider range of factors than experimental studies. In ethnographic studies, researchers maintain extended contact with subjects so that they can gain deep insight into social processes and the significance of the media in social systems. Their results, however, may not be generalizable beyond the specific communities they study.

WHAT IS A SAMPLING?

Sampling is a technique that is often used in survey studies. Its goal is to collect responses from a relatively small group of respondents who are statistically representative of the larger population from which the respondents are drawn. The key to good sampling is random selection—that is, giving each member of the population an equal chance of being chosen for study and seeing to it that the sample is drawn from a list that includes all members of the population being studied.

HOW HAVE THEORIES OF MASS MEDIA EFFECTS CHANGED?

Theories of mass media effects have evolved over the years. Early scholars believed the mass media could have immediate and profound effects on their audiences, after the fashion of a speeding bullet or a hypodermic injection. Later, researchers learned that the influence of the mass media is weakened by the intervention of social groups, via a multistep flow process, and by the audience's ability selectively to avoid, misinterpret, or forget content with which they disagree. Social learning theory describes how people can learn behavior from visual media, and cultivation theory shows how people's understanding of the world around them is shaped by media images. Priming theory focuses on the power of media images to activate related thoughts in our own minds. These theories have led to a resurgence of the perception that mass media are relatively powerful influences on society.

WHAT IS THE IMPACT OF THE MASS MEDIA ON ANTISOCIAL BEHAVIOR?

Experimental studies have shown that even relatively short exposure to TV programs featuring violence can provoke violent behavior in viewers, particularly young children. Men exposed to violent pornography harbor more violent feelings toward women. Media also can reinforce sex-role and racial stereotypes that lead to sexism and racism. In general, the mass media can cause a wide variety of antisocial behavior, although the exact nature and extent of these effects remains a subject of research and debate.

WHAT IS THE IMPACT OF THE MASS MEDIA ON PROSOCIAL BEHAVIOR?

Prosocial behaviors are socially desirable acts such as cooperation, sharing, and racial tolerance. Information campaigns seek to convince mass audiences to adopt socially desirable behaviors. Although such campaigns are sometimes effective, they often suffer from poor planning and execution and from limited audience exposure. Furthermore, they must contend with resistance arising from social influence and selective perception among their audiences. Other varieties of prosocial media combine varying degrees of entertainment and educational content, ranging from distance-learning classes to incidental learning from entertainment programs.

WHAT ARE THE EFFECTS OF ADVERTISING AND POLITICAL CAMPAIGNS?

Despite the huge sums of money spent on commercial and political advertisements, their effects are relatively modest; they directly affect perhaps only a few percent of the audience. Those who are affected by advertisements are likely to be those who are relatively uninformed about or uninterested in the product or candidate to begin with. Interpersonal influence and selective perception act to reduce the impact of advertisements on most audiences. Still, that small percent that *is* influenced can translate into millions of dollars in a successful advertising campaign, or into crucial deciding votes in a political race.

Electronic Resources

For up-to-the-minute URLs about *Media and the Individual,* access the MEDIA NOW site on the World Wide Web at:

http://communication.wadsworth.com/

CHAPTER 13

Media and Society

WHAT'S AHEAD

Here, as in Chapter 12, we will examine what research has revealed about the effects of the communications media. Only here we will focus on their broader social implications rather than the effects of specific types of media content on individual users.

WWW

Access the MEDIA NOW site on the World Wide Web at:
http://communication.wadsworth.com/
Choose "Chapter 13" from the selection box to access electronic information and other sites relevant to this chapter.

DETROIT, MICHIGAN, 2010

Hello, is anyone in there?

You can call me DeeVee if you want. You must be Dantaya.

Mr. D.V., Mom says I can play you when she doesn't need you for her new job.

That's right, and I have over 100 million channels and we can call anywhere in the world!

Well, I could use a little help with my arithmetic homework. Mom's so busy now . . .

I have the U-M Elementary Math Tutor Channel, or I can download the M.I.T. Math Buddy program directly to your own computer.

I don't have my own computer. All I have is you, so let's try that You'M tutor.

That's Yew-EM, short for the University of Michigan. A computer simulation of their star quarterback acts as your guide and it's only twenty dollars an hour for a live interactive . . .

No, I don't think Mom can afford that. I know, let's call my gramma in Atlanta. She's real good at math. I'll need to show her my paper, though. Can you do that?

‹Dialing, Mrs. Janetta Johnson, Atlanta, Georgia.› That will be 50 cents a minute for the video.

No! I can do *that* math. That's *thirty* dollars an hour! Don't you have anything for kids that's free?

Certainly! ‹Roadrunner Channel—Sugar Frosties Theater—Beavis & Butt-head Classics—Pee Wee Herman Channel—Michael Jackson Network—Interactive Power Rangers—Toy Store Channel—Child Abuse Victim Support Channel›

No help there! I guess I'll just have to try to do my own arithmetic, MISter DataVision.

Chapter Outline

Understanding Societal Effects
Individual Effects vs. Societal Effects
Social Criticism
Communications Media and Social Inequality
Political Economy
The Knowledge Gap
A Hidden Curriculum?
Race and Gender
Communications Media and Community
The Global Village
Social Fragmentation
Being There
Health and Environment
Communications Media and Culture
Technological Determinism
Cultural Determinism
Mass Media and Mass Culture
Communications Media and Social Institutions
Communications Media and Educational Institutions
Communications Media and Political Institutions
Communications Media and Economic Institutions
Summary and Review

UNDERSTANDING SOCIETAL EFFECTS

Individual Effects vs. Societal Effects

In the last chapter, we reviewed social science research that showed that the various communications media can have powerful effects on their users. Answering the question of societal effects, then, could be as simple as aggregating all of these individual effects across large groups of people, the whole being equal to the sum of its parts.

But it's not that simple. For example, the introduction of television in the United States had no observable relationship to overall crime rates in the cities that were the first to get television (Hennigan et al., 1982), although there may have been a delayed effect on crime 15 years later, when young viewers from the early days of TV entered their adolescence (Centerwall, 1989). Likewise, pornography can encourage sexual aggression toward women, but there is no overall relationship between the availability of pornography and the incidence of rape (Gentry, 1991). Cities that have high levels of television consumption actually have lower crime rates, perhaps because heavy viewers have less opportunity to pick fights with their relatives or to leave their homes looking for trouble (Messner & Blau, 1987). And other countries such as Denmark, with even more permissive pornography laws than the United State have fewer rapes (Kutchinsky, 1991). Yet laboratory experiments suggest that all those people watching all that antisocial behavior on television should add up to nearly immediate and massive increases in antisocial behavior. Given all the violence and sex in the media, we might even be led to ask whether the real question shouldn't be why there is so *little* crime, not why there is so much.

How can we explain these discrepancies? One possibility that we considered in the last chapter is that the laboratory experiments that yield the strongest evidence of individual media effects are just not a good indication of the actual effects of media in society because they are conducted in unrealistic settings. Field experiments with broader populations conducted under more realistic conditions show a more complex pattern of conflicting results, leading some to conclude that the "case" for media effects has not been conclusively proved (Felson,

1996). In other words, the reason why we do not find clear evidence of media effects at the societal level is that they aren't as powerful at the individual level as some may think. Others who have reviewed the same body of research have found it conclusive (Comstock & Paik, 1994).

Alternatively, both sides of the debate on media effects could be right. Perhaps there are many individual effects, but they are neutralized somehow when we look at the big picture. For example, maybe big brother really does think about picking up the hammer when he gets mad at little brother because he saw Coyote hit Road-runner with a cartoon hammer on TV. But big brother may think twice when he remembers the spanking he got the last time the two had a fight, the ice cream cone that little brother shared with him last week, or even how Coyote got clobbered in the end. And for every "bad brother" who actually picks up the hammer, there may be several "good brothers" who do not—and others or who do not even particularly like watching violent cartoons.

Social Criticism

When considering the overall impact of communications media, some scholars prefer to bypass quantitative research methods altogether. They feel that the issues involved are just too big, the social forces too subtle, or perhaps the social scientists' methods too narrow to grasp the real relationships between media and society. Instead, these scholars attempt to find the true significance of the media events by interpreting contemporary trends. Many *critical theorists* (McLuhan, 1964; Schiller, 1981; Mosco, 1982; Postman, 1992) rely on this approach, but so do many other observers who would not label themselves critical theorists (Rheingold, 1993; Negroponte, 1995; Dyson, 1997) and who might rather be known as *futurists* or perhaps simply as scholars. By carefully considering the interplay between media and society, these expert social commentators should be able to figure out not only what is "really going on" but also what is likely to happen in the future. Well, perhaps not always (see Media Watch). Many social critics rely on historical analysis to give us a better understanding of where we are now and what forces have brought us here, although their subjective interpretations of past events may, in the end, be as unreliable as the prognostications of futurists.

For example, one of the very first sweeping technological changes in communications media was the introduction of literacy to oral societies. Anthropologists have documented powerful differences between completely oral societies and literate ones (Goody & Watt, 1991). Literate societies rely less than oral societies on human memories of epic stories, myths, and images to transmit *culture* from one generation to the next. But historical interpretations of these bare facts may differ. Marshall McLuhan (1964) looked at this process and saw *technological determinism* at work. He argued that the changes in society that were brought about by literacy—and especially by the printed word—gave rise to a modern civilization of science and technology. Other social critics look at the same events and see *cultural determinism;* that is, culture is the driving force, and technologies emerge to serve cultural imperatives.

MEDIA WATCH

Forecasting the Telephone

To illustrate the possible pitfalls of the social criticism approach, let us consider some of the various predictions that were made about the telephone in its infancy (de Sola Pool, 1983).

- **The telephone would reduce literacy.** Once relieved of writing letters and thank-you notes people were expected to let their writing skills slide. Actually, the literacy level improved, a result of the expansion of public education.
- **The telephone would be a mass medium.** The earliest demonstrations of the telephone were in fact mass media presentations. But the radio, not the telephone, emerged as the dominant form of audio mass medium.
- **The telephone would revitalize rural areas** by enriching the life of the farm family. Instead, the farm population declined dramatically, as a result of (1) improvements in agricultural technology that reduced its labor-intensiveness and (2) the progressive transition from an agricultural to an industrial economy.
- **Women would benefit,** particularly socially isolated rural women. The feminist critique of the telephone (see the Media Impact box on page 425) argues that just the opposite happened. The spread of the telephone became a further means of confining women in their homes, by making them conduct social relationships through the medium, and of oppressing them when they left their homes, by forcing them into low-status jobs as telephone operators.
- **Suburbanization would accelerate,** because the telephone would make it convenient to move to the suburbs while maintaining employment and social contacts in the city. Suburbanization clearly did take place, although the automobile (and the streetcar before it) probably played a more prominent role.
- **Cities would get bigger.** In one respect, this prediction may have proved true. Prior to the telephone, offices used messengers. Without the phone, the sheer numbers of elevators required to hold all the messengers would have made skyscrapers economically unviable. Without tall buildings, cities could never have grown as they did. However, pneumatic tubes or more efficiently organized office mail systems might also have filled the bill.

These examples show that it is difficult to trace relationships between communications media and social change. When the anticipated effects do not take place, it may be because of other forces that overwhelm them. Likewise, when the observations do hold true, it may turn out that they have little to do with the medium in question. Also note that speculation about media effects is a timeless form: We could easily substitute *television* or *internet* for *telephone* in some of the foregoing statements, and they would read as though they came right out of the word processors of current social critics (Marien, 1996).

Finally, if we wait long enough, many such assertions will come true—and many that seem true now will be proved falsified. Take the prediction that the telephone would become a mass medium. If we had examined it in 1910, before commercial radio service started but when telephone broadcasting trials were under way, we might have concluded that the prediction was accurate. Then by the 1930s, when national radio networks were in full swing, that prediction looked ridiculous. And today, when we see millions accessing the World Wide Web over their telephone lines and dialing 900 numbers, that bit of social criticism looks absolutely clairvoyant.

This is by no means the only example of social critics reaching opposite conclusions. One commentator sees democracy as being enhanced (Rheingold, 1993), whereas others foresee increased authoritarianism (Kroker & Weinstein, 1994) as the inevitable consequence of new communications technology, such as the Internet. Social science offers a way to resolve competing predictions and conflicting results by replicating studies and refining research questions so that competing theories may be tested. Social criticism offers no such claim to definitive answers; rather, it is up to you, the reader, to decide what makes sense to you. Unfortunately, this means that much of what follows will have the tone of "it could be this, but on the other hand, it could be that." (Of course, we saw in the last chapter that social science also can yield ambiguous answers, even on those questions that have attracted the most research attention, including over 30 years of research about the effects of TV violence.)

In the long run, social scientists and social critics will be able to make stronger conclusions about the impacts of various media technologies upon society if they compare, contrast, and build on each other's studies. Anthropology offers the useful notion of triangulation—comparing various kinds of data and information to see if they tend to confirm the same trends or conclusions. If qualitative and quantitative studies confirm similar trends, that adds power to the conclusions of both; if not, both sides should be asking why not, and considering the contradictory evidence offered by other methods of study.

COMMUNICATIONS MEDIA AND SOCIAL INEQUALITY

One of the thorniest issues confronting society is inequality between social groups as defined by wealth, race, and gender. This issue is at the root of many of the political controversies that swirl around the media, and indeed it underlies most of the political debates in a free society. In the last chapter, we saw that the *stereotypes* of females, minorities, and the economically less advantaged that appear in the media may help to perpetuate discrimination and inequality by affecting the attitudes and behavior of individuals.

What are the roots of social inequality? As societies become more complex, they also tend to become more stratified—more divided into unequal social groups or classes (Braudel, 1987). People may be categorized both in terms of their monetary wealth, or economic capital, and in terms of differences in their education and family backgrounds—their "cultural capital" (Bourdieu, 1984). In the past, highly stratified societies were sometimes stable; people simply accepted their roles. Now, in part because of the images of the upper classes that we see in the mass media, and also because of the images of race and class conflict that we see there, almost everyone is aware of the possibility of upward social mobility. Therefore, social stratification tends to produce more crime, more physical violence, and more tensions when people of diverse backgrounds interact (Gitlin, 1995).

Could communications media also be the cure for inequality? Public television programs such as *Sesame Street* and local public libraries and schools try to ensure that all children have access to educational basics through the mass media. The telephone—and soon the Internet—could also improve information access for the economically disadvantaged. But will they?

Political Economy

Not very likely, at least not according to modern-day followers of the nineteenth-century political philosopher Karl Marx (see Chapter 2). Marx argued that conflict between social classes—particularly conflict between owners of "the means of production" (such as factories and newspapers) and those who work for them (such as factory hands and reporters)—underlies all political issues. The industrial societies Marx was writing about, nineteenth-century Germany and Britain, spawned glaring social inequalities. Later, Gramsci (1971) argued that the role of the media was to convince the poor to accept the *hegemony* of ideas that kept the factory owners and newspaper publishers on top of society (Marx, 1967; Mosco, 1996).

Even though current industrialized societies may seem less stratified than in Marx's day, current *political economists* note that the poor, including disproportionate numbers of African American and Hispanic people in the United States, are far less likely to have either phone service (Muller & Schement, 1997) or Internet access (Mosco, 1996). The more critical voices argue that mass media still serve the interests of the ruling class and promote their view of the world (Mosco, 1982; Schiller, 1992) and that social issues in communication technology are still defined by the old class structure (Sussman, 1997). The tendency to turn what was once public information, such as census data, into a commodity that can be bought and sold by private companies, such as market research data bases for large advertisers, is seen as an important means of furthering the dominance of the capitalist ruling classes (Schiller, 1992). The continuing modification of the copyright and patent laws to favor the rights of authors, inventors, and owners is another example (Schement & Curtis, 1997).

The possible relationship between the mass media and social inequality can be illustrated by the following example. When media ads promote buying a new car, that leads workers to accept their role so that they can afford the car, even if they hate their job, feel underpaid, and would really rather ride a bicycle. Although the TV news may cover the strike down at the local plant, the reporters treat it like a football game, reducing it to a game of winners and losers. They never touch on the fundamental issue of the exploitation of the workers by the factory owners and also may neglect to mention that the factory owners sit on the board of directors down at the station. The seemingly diverse and vibrant discussions on the Internet may, overall, still simply be reinforcing, through a novel medium, the very same hegemony of ideas that are present in conventional media (Bromberg et al., 1996). Things are not always as they seem when the interests of the ruling class are at stake.

Meanwhile, the binge of mergers and acquisitions shaking all the communications media industries represents a new wave of consolidation and concentration in the information sector of the economy, this time on a global scale (Haywood, 1995; Harman & McChesney, 1997). This development influences media content in both subtle ways (forewarning advertisers of stories critical of their companies) and unsubtle ways (changes in editorial policy instituted by new management, see Chapter 14). Political economists believe that such actions further reinforce a hegemony of power that acts against the interests of common citizens.

The Knowledge Gap

The question of whether communications media contribute to social inequality has attracted the interest of a number of non-Marxist scholars as well: those who have conducted empirical research to test the so-called **knowledge gap hypothesis.** This perspective makes a distinction between the information "haves" and the "have-nots." The information-rich "haves" are those with superior levels of education and access to resources such as libraries and home computers. The "have-nots" are the information-poor who have inferior levels of education and resource access—and tend to be the economically poor as well (see Figure 13.1). The knowledge gap hypothesis states that the introduction of new information into the population may benefit both groups but that it will benefit the information-rich more, thereby widening the disparity between the two. Many studies have documented that knowledge gaps not only exist but indeed are widened by the media (Gaziano, 1997), even by such well-intentioned efforts as *Sesame Street* that are specifically designed to close the gap.

The **knowledge gap hypothesis** posits that the "information-rich" benefit more from exposure to communications media than the "information-poor."

Knowledge gaps open even when access to the media is equal. When access is unequal, the gaps get wider still. For example, the wealthy and privileged upper

FIGURE 13.1
According to the knowledge gap hypothesis, the introduction of new information technologies will help both the information-rich and the information-poor get richer, in terms of the information they possess, but the rich get richer faster, causing the information gap to widen.

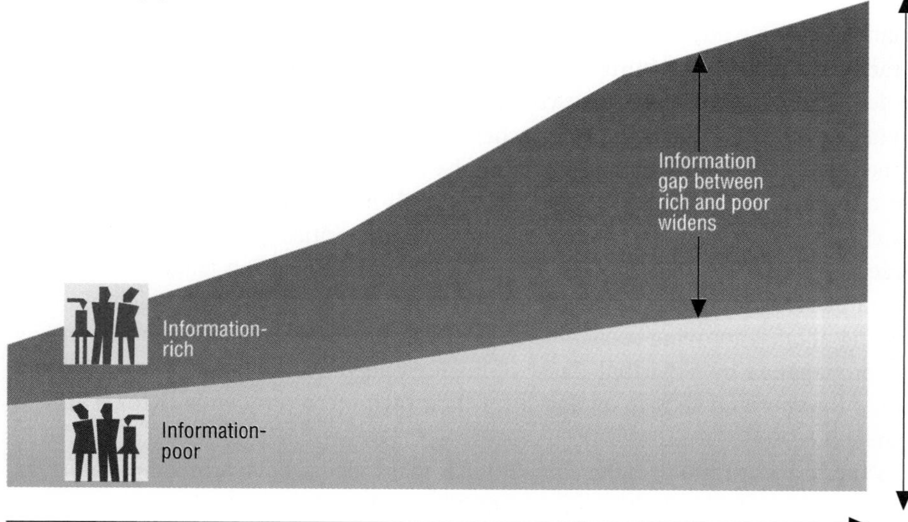

KNOWLEDGE GAP. Well-intentioned efforts to make information more accessible, such as this information kiosk on a university campus, sometimes have the effect of benefiting some groups, such as middle-class college students, more than they benefit others.

classes have easier access to print media because they can afford them more readily and also have more leisure time in which to consume them. Inequalities in access to information technology may therefore further widen the gap between rich and poor (Stoll, 1995; Haywood, 1995.) We saw in previous chapters that access is not at all equal—that the economically disadvantaged are less likely to have telephones, cable television, computers in the home, and Internet connections.

The gaps in access to computers and network services seem to be widening between income and education groups over time (Bikson & Panis, 1997; Novak & Hoffman, 1998; NTIA, 1998), a phenomenon that some commentators call the *digital divide.* The knowledge gap hypothesis suggests that efforts to close the access gap (by placing computers in the schools, for example, or making e-mail available to all) will be at least partially self-defeating. According to this theory, the economically advantaged children (usually white) will still benefit more from the computers in their schools than the economically disadvantaged, predominantly minority children will benefit from the computers in theirs. Of course, if no efforts were made to expand access to the poor, the gap would be even wider, so the sad reality of the digital divide must not be used as an excuse to do nothing.

A Hidden Curriculum?

Others contend that even if we somehow closed the knowledge gap with new computer media, we would still risk perpetuating social inequality. Perhaps computer literacy training is really fulfilling a *hidden curriculum* that imposes the values of the dominant culture by teaching young women and minorities to obey commands and accept repetitive tasks. It also teaches students to accept authority, personified by the adult authority figures who define the computer applications and provide user assistance. According to this argument, well-intentioned efforts to close the knowledge gap by pushing computer literacy for minorities and women only worsen the problem by further conditioning them to accept their "place" in a system of economic exploitation (Roszak, 1994). Likewise, all of the wishful thinking about improving society through the Internet may really be nothing more than propaganda by a "virtual class" of businesspeople and bureaucrats who control the Internet and seek to exploit it for their own mercenary ends (Kroker & Weinstein, 1994).

Other critics argue that the conventional mass media have a hidden agenda of their own. Some think their aim is not to inform and entertain their audiences, but to promote a culture of consumerism and materialism, for the benefit of the advertisers, not the people. From a Marxist perspective, the mass media function to give

MEDIA IMPACT

Women and Telephones, A Feminist Critique

In the words of feminist scholar Lana Rakow (1992), the telephone is a "gendered technology" through which women sustain themselves as women (Moyal, 1988) but also through which they complete gendered work—work that is culturally assigned to women. It is a technology that is embedded in patterns of a social hierarchy that relegates women to certain narrowly defined roles, including that of the household "communications specialist" who maintains social relationships over the telephone. In this view, the stereotype that women have a tendency to spend too much time on the phone is in fact the consequence of their carrying out traditional "female" family roles and also of a society that denies women access to meaningful activities outside the home.

Women have influenced the development of information technologies in other, more subtle ways. The telephone was intended as an instrument of communication for the (male-dominated) business world. At first, telephone companies discouraged "trivial" social use of the telephone (mostly by women) to keep the lines clear for important (male-originated) business calls. However, women staged a quiet rebellion against these restrictions, forcing the redesign of the telephone system. The telephone may have given women new freedom to communicate with the world beyond the home, but at the same time, the communication took place inside the home, perhaps diminishing women's opportunities to make new social contacts outside.

During the 1880s, the job of telephone operator became women's work. Employers believed that women were more docile than men and would be more polite to telephone subscribers—and also more willing to work for low wages. At first, telephone operators enjoyed greater status and better pay than their sisters who worked as retail clerks and factory workers. The Bell System required that their operators be high school graduates, which also contributed to the status of the job. Before 1900, the telephone operator had some autonomy, enjoying the freedom to set her own pace and to frame her own personal greeting for callers.

OPER

This changed swiftly in the early twentieth century, as efficiency experts made the operator's job highly structured and routinized. Operators now had to answer 90 percent of all calls within 4 seconds, and their conversation was limited to some 100 specific expressions in the company rule book.

In the early 1800s, work shifts lasted 11 hours without a break, and employees wore a "headset" the size of a toaster that weighed several pounds. Sexual harassment by male supervisors was rampant. In those days, the "glass ceiling" was more like a "brick roof." Women were never promoted beyond the level of floor supervisor and were allowed to work for the phone company only until their mid-twenties, after which time it was assumed that they would all get married and start families (Martin, 1991).

In response, female operators became active in the labor movement, forming the only international union directed by and composed entirely of women, the Telephone Operator's Department, in 1919. Under the leadership of Julia O'Connor, the Telephone Operator's Department succeeded in winning improvements in working conditions. A strike against New England Telephone backfired when the other, male-dominated telephone unions refused to honor picket lines and male college students were hired as strike-breaking scabs. Later, the hard-won gains in status and pay of the telephone operators declined as they were replaced by automatic switching equipment. The replacement of telephone operators by automatic switching equipment stands today as one of the premiere examples of job displacement by automated systems (Norwood, 1990).

the working classes temporary respite from their labors so that they can be more productive workers (Braverman, 1974).

Race and Gender

Patterns of employment in information industries seem to reflect these gaps. The industries that create information, those that manufacture information technologies, and the occupations that use them are largely dominated by white males.

A generation ago, the Federal Communications Commission instituted equal employment opportunity (EEO) guidelines for broadcasters. Between 1971 and 1997, female employment in broadcasting rose from 23 percent to 41 percent and minority employment from 9 percent to 19 percent, but the U.S. Supreme Court abolished the rules in 1998 (McConnell, 1998a). Although female and minority employees have made substantial progress in lower-level jobs, the executive suites in the mass media industry are still the province of white males. There are only a few notable exceptions, such as Sherry Lansing, chairwoman of Paramount Pictures. Across all media, minority ownership is only 3 percent, up from one-half of 1 percent 20 years ago (McConnell, 1998b).

Matters are no better in computer media. According to the National Science Foundation, only 3 percent of computer specialists are African American. Although women such as Lady Ada Byron Lovelace (patroness of computer inventor Charles Babbage and the world's first computer systems analyst) and Grace Hopper (who is sometimes called "the mother of the computer," see Chapter 8) have played prominent roles in the computer industry, women are seriously underrepresented in computer science fields. Women in computer professions generally earn considerably less than their male colleagues, although this gap is somewhat smaller than the national average across all lines of work (see Davidson & Cooper, 1987; Werneke, 1985; Zientara, 1987; Zimmerman, 1990). Women have also borne the brunt of job losses resulting from the office automation trend, and minority blue-collar workers fill many of the jobs slated for replacement by the modern-day equivalent of slave labor, the robot (Rifkin, 1996).

STOP & REVIEW

1. **What is the difference between individual effects and social effects?**
2. **How does social criticism differ from social science?**
3. **According to political economists, what is the role of the media?**
4. **What does the knowledge gap hypothesis predict about the effects of new information technologies?**
5. **What implications do information technologies have for minorities and women?**

COMMUNICATIONS MEDIA AND COMMUNITY

What impact do communications media have on our most intimate and valued interpersonal and community relationships? When we allocate our free time, media consumption competes with our social and community lives, and it soaks up more and more of our available free time as we grow older (Jeffres, 1987). Television usage, for example, may lower community involvement (Brody, 1990), and virtual communities on the Internet may displace face-to-face relationships

(Spretnak, 1997). People also have a tendency to treat communications media as though they were people, talking back to their television sets and giving their computers affectionate nicknames (Reeves & Nass, 1996); such interactions are a poor substitute for interpersonal relationships. In the last chapter, we reviewed research that showed that the media contain abundant images of dysfunctional social relationships that presumably pollute our social behavior. The media's reliance on stereotypes may also cause us to think too simplistically about other people, impairing our ability to form meaningful human relationships (Miller, 1987).

The Global Village

However, some observers believe that new communications media may build community as much as destroy it. Canadian communications scholar Marshall McLuhan (1964) coined the term *the global village* to describe the changes in communications technology that, to him, seemed to be drawing the entire world together into a kind of electronically mediated small town. "By electricity we everywhere resume person-to-person relations as if on the smallest village scale" (p. 255); and he said that in the 1960s, long *before* the Internet was a reality. The contemporary scholar Howard Rheingold (1994), for one, sees the World Wide Web as an opportunity to form meaningful personal relationships that has been lost since "the malt shop became the mall" (pp. 25–26).

From e-mail to *newsgroups* to *listservs* to *chatrooms* to multi-user role-playing games (see Chapter 9), the Internet presents numerous opportunities to forge social relationships on-line, and users are clearly taking advantage of these opportunities in large numbers (Dyson, 1997; Sproull & Faraj, 1997; Dery, 1996). The Internet thus makes it easier than ever to create "psychological communities" that extend our relationships across time and distance—even to create "virtual communities" of people that know each other only through communication networks.

However, are Internet communities the equivalent of "real" communities? It all depends on how you define *community.* One important characteristic of a community, the ability to create and enforce rules of conduct, seems to be present in Internet chatrooms and newsgroups. However, only Web sites that allow user contributions and direct interaction between users are likely to promote meaningful community (McLaughlin, Osborne, & Ellison, 1997).

Internet relationships may even be superior to "real" ones in certain ways, because they can be formed through the sharing of common needs, free of the inhibiting stigma of observable characteristics such as race, gender, class, and physical handicaps (Mickelson, 1997). Perhaps these qualities can help all of us overcome the social disconnection that has been promoted by suburbanization and by the decline of the extended family and our segmentation into so many target markets by mass media advertisers. There are also efforts to strengthen real-world communities by overlaying them with electronic ones that can facilitate public dialog and reach across social boundaries (Rothenberg, 1996). Indeed, many on-line relationships lead to real-world meetings (Parks & Floyd, 1996).

TECHNOLOGY ***DEMYSTIFIED***

Joining the Luddites

After a frustrating day at the computer, have you ever considered chucking it all and checking out of our high-tech society all together? And maybe taking a pick ax to your PC? You're not alone, and if Neil Postman is too mild for you, you can always join the Luddite Movement! It's named after Ned Ludd, a semi-mythical figure from the early days of the Industrial Revolution who led a revolt against modernization by attacking and destroying the newfangled textile machinery that was Taylorizing, de-skilling and post-Fordizing (see page 442) the workers of the day. Of course, a movement that is against the computer age is a little difficult to locate on a computer network, but if you enter "luddite" as a keyword you will find them. Our favorite is the Luddite Home Page, consisting entirely of the following:

Luddite Home Page
Go Away!
Webmaster Bob Loblaw

Beware, some of what you will find is pretty strong stuff, including directions on how to sabotage some of our favorite Computer Age devices. That counts as an example of one of the possible downsides of the Internet—a postmodern society that splits apart at the seams.

Social Fragmentation

As psychologist Sherry Turkle asks, however, "Is it really sensible to suggest that the way to revitalize community is to sit alone in our rooms, typing at our networked computers?" (Turkle, 1997, p. 235). The potential downside of virtual community is that this trend could lead to a *postmodern* society (Lyotard, 1984). Social groups might turn in on themselves as communication channels proliferate, along with new ideas, and the groups become better able to customize culture for their own interests, to the exclusion of others. With less and less shared information, culture fragments and nation-states could dissolve in chaos. At some point, we would no longer be a nation of Americans, or even of Anglo, African, Asian, or Hispanic Americans, but a disjointed collection of cults and splinter groups. The Internet perhaps accelerates this trend in modern society by divorcing social relationships from physical reality and moving them beyond our local community (Robins, 1996). For example, it appears that one of the effects of the Internet on political campaigns is to help people with extreme opinions find and reinforce each other (Katz, 1996).

Then there are the disturbing tales of how real-life relationships are being destroyed by virtual ones. Families are broken by infidelity with on-line lovers, molesters accost children they lure over the Internet; hate groups and religious cults entice the innocent. And in the last chapter, we reviewed a study (Kraut *et. al.,* 1998) that indicated that heavy Internet use increases social isolation. Virtual communities may thus be communities in name only.

The Internet is not the only means of creating virtual communities, nor is it the first. Recalling our earlier example (see Media Impact on page 420), nineteenth-century social critics expected the telephone to have a negative effect on interpersonal relationships. However, when sociologist Claude Fischer (1992) examined the introduction of the telephone in northern California in the early twentieth century, he concluded that it had actually augmented some forms of local activities, such as the coordination of functions for local clubs and service groups, while interfering with others, such as neighborhood political organizations. Today, the Internet may be having the same impact (Cohill & Kavanaugh, 1997). Thus communications media *can* reinforce community, and to the extent that they have disrupted community life, they perhaps share the blame with other technologies—the automobile and urban transportation systems—and other social forces, such as economic and racial oppression.

Being There

It is certainly true that there is "something missing" when we use mediated communication such as the television or the Internet instead of actually being there ourselves. We miss the nuances of nonverbal cues—gestures, facial expressions, body posture—that help us to understand the deeper meanings of words. This is the concept of *social presence,* or the relative presence or absence of social cues that help convey subtle meanings. This makes electronic media an inferior means of establishing interpersonal relationships. However, they are useful for maintaining relationships over a distance, once these relationships have been established, and for conveying information. Most people say they prefer direct, face-to-face contact when they have something important to say but prefer using the telephone to seek out information. More people save bad news for in-person contacts than they do good news (Dordick & LaRose, 1992). Media with low social presence are adequate for information seeking and problem solving but are less effective when people are resolving conflicts or forming impressions of new acquaintances (Short, Williams, & Christie, 1976). They can also encourage people to communicate more freely, although sometimes the interchange lapses into "flaming" via e-mail, where people use stronger language than they would dare face-to-face (Kiesler, Siegal & McGuire, 1984). And, over time, people found ways to overcome the limited social cues (Walther, 1996).

Health and Environment

Do communications media affect the physical environment as well as the social environment for society? To the extent that their ads induce us to drink alcohol and smoke cigarettes—or even to eat too much junk food or spend too much time lying on the sofa—they might well be deemed public health hazards. However, we saw in the last chapter that commercials are effective only in changing our brand preferences, not in changing our underlying consumption patterns. Thus they may plead "not guilty," but only as long as we do not count the effect that they have on encouraging young children to acquire these bad habits to begin with.

In the late 1990s, a bizarre new category of television health effect emerged: brain seizures. It seems that cartoons with extremely rapidly changing images and extreme colors cause susceptible children to suffer temporary seizures in which they become unconscious and writhe uncontrollably. Hundreds of Japanese children were reportedly stricken (Smillie, 1997).

The print media, too, pose health hazards to society. The paper they are printed on comes from huge paper mills that chew up entire forests, pollute rivers, and foul the air for miles around. Later, print products choke landfills after readers who ignore opportunities to recycle cast them aside.

In contrast, computer media are sometimes heralded as clean technologies that eliminate belching smokestacks. The residents of Silicon Valley and other high-tech corridors might dispute this claim, now that they find high levels of toxic industrial solvents—used in the manufacture of computer chips—in their drinking water.

Computer disposal is also a growing problem. According to one study, there will be 150 million computers in landfills by 2005, enough to cover an acre of land 3.5 miles deep. Computer recyclers now mine discarded computers for valuable materials and reusable computer chips, but there is an increasing need for a "green" computer whose casing and packaging can be recycled. The German government now requires computer makers to reclaim abandoned machines (Lohr, 1993).

Computer power consumption is also significant. In 1993, the Environmental Protection Agency (EPA) began issuing "Energy Star" stickers for machines that "sleep" when they are turned on but are not being actively used. This program could save enough energy to power a small state or two for an entire year. Also on the plus side, *telecommuting* cuts pollution by reducing highway travel.

Extremely low-frequency (ELF) radiation—the kind that electrical power lines emit—also poses an environmental threat. At one point, EPA scientists concluded that ELF was as dangerous as chemical cancer-inducing agents, although this finding was overruled by EPA administrators. Computer video display terminals (VDTs) emit the same type of radiation, and some scientists suspect that this radiation causes cancer and miscarriages in heavy users of computers. Portable telephones have also been implicated as possible triggers of brain cancer. Microwave and satellite communication systems are other sources of electromagnetic radiation that may have health effects. However, there is no proven theory about how electromagnetic fields interact with living tissue. Without this "missing link," scientists are reluctant to blame electromagnetic radiation for health effects or to establish safe exposure levels (Lewis, 1990).

There is far less dispute about repetitive-stress injuries, such as the shooting pains one of your authors gets from tapping a keyboard for hours on end, day after day, relentlessly revising this textbook. Several thousand cases of short- or long-term disabilities resulting from heavy use of computers are reported each year. Computers are also responsible for eyestrain that sometimes results in permanent eye damage. A combination of flickering from the computer screen's scanning pattern and overhead fluorescent lights is the culprit.

COMMUNICATIONS MEDIA AND CULTURE

All communities also have a *culture* in the sense that they cannot function without certain agreed-upon rules for communication and shared underlying values. But can we really say that the concept of "culture" applies to the loose connections and alliances on the Internet? The casual communities of the Internet may have "rules" such as a simple agreement not to write abusive e-mail or "values" such as a shared interest in a particular hobby, but even these minimalist norms are seldom enforced (Sproull & Faraj, 1997). More tellingly, these standards perhaps trivialize the concept of culture. We usually reserve the term *culture* for more deep-seated and longer-lasting values and norms that connect us with society and with the groups that mean the most to us. Culture permeates public festivals, traditions, fine art, and religion. It is also found on television, in books, and at the movies, because popular culture is linked to the values of the wider society.

Technological Determinism

Marshall McLuhan (1964) proposed that communications media technologies *determine* culture in some very basic ways, an idea captured in his famous aphorism "the medium is the message." For example, the invention of the printing press may have led to the rise of the scientific method, and later to our technological society, by forcing thinkers to put their words in linear order and their arguments in a logical progression. This led to thinking about the natural world in the same way, instilling the notion that it, too, had a beginning and an end, a cause and an effect. It is not so much the *content* of the medium that makes a difference, but its technological form.

Neil Postman (1992) argues that computers foster a state of mind and a state of culture that he calls *technopoly,* in which technology is deified and extends its control to all aspects of life. Technopoly compounds the worst excesses of technocracy, in which the scientific method is applied to the improvement of life and also, some think, to the destruction of culture.

A similar theme appears in the writings of French sociologist Jacques Ellul (1990), who argues that the relentless pursuit of technological improvement leads to the social dominance of a technological elite of scientists, engineers, and managers for whom technology becomes an end in itself, devoid of moral foundation. But for Ellul, the technologists' efforts are ultimately ineffective. Technology is a kind of bluff, wherein technologists promise a great deal—much to their own benefit in a society conditioned to welcome technological progress—but deliver very little, not even a truly satisfying evening's entertainment on TV or a true relationship on the Internet.

CULTURAL DETERMINISM. Cultural determinists argue that interactions within social groups, not technology, determine social development.

Cultural Determinism

But does this mean that culture is completely at the mercy of communications technology? We have the ability to transform it to new uses that the inventors and managers of the technology do not anticipate. Users of the French Minitel system—a predecessor of the World Wide Web that uses only text, no graphics—transformed what was intended to be an impersonal instrument of information exchange into a self-organizing community that expressed very personal desires (Lemos, 1996). A century earlier, female users of the American telephone converted it into a social medium, much to the horror of the male engineers who created it for serious business purposes (Fischer, 1992). The Internet was created as an instrument of militaristic domination (see Chapter 8), flourished as a medium for social interchange, but is now being rapidly co-opted by commercialism. Nonetheless, there is a counterculture of "techno-anarchists" who are attempting to maintain a balance of power against commercialization (Bromberg et al., 1996) by such means as electronically attacking the originators of unwanted commercial e-mail.

Not all scholars frame the issue in terms of cultural vs. technological determinism. Some scholars contend that the media reflect culture but do not create it, or that the media merely present us with the symbols that we use to construct culture (Peterson, 1979). Another view is that mass media potentially overwhelm the "true" culture of the people in the interests of perpetuating class hegemony (Carey, 1975).

Mass Media and Mass Culture

How do the mass media shape culture? Views of this relationship have changed over the years. In the early nineteenth century, the so-called English School, led by Matthew Arnold (Raleigh, 1957), held that culture is knowing the best that has been thought in the world. For him, that was embodied in the elite "high culture" media from Western Europe, such as painting, the novel, ballet, opera, and the symphony. According to this school of thought, people moving from the countryside into the cities would become refined by consuming these media. Implicit in this view was the idea that media exist to educate, not entertain. Some present-day critics, such as Neil Postman (1992), still forcefully argue this.

American thinkers such as Ralph Waldo Emerson (Storey, 1993) contested the pre-eminence of European high culture. Emerson focused on the culture that was building in the United States and looked to the future, not the past. American poet Walt Whitman (Kaleb, 1989) described culture as the authentic expression of the "grand common stock" (of American people) that taps the "measureless wealth of latent power and capacity" of the people. These thinkers celebrated the rise of a *popular culture* with media familiar to, and accessible by, the general populace.

The debate about culture took a new turn in the twentieth century as the industrialized mass media reached ever deeper into society, seemingly creating alienated and isolated mass audiences that were cut off from their cultural roots. Critics such as Theodore Adorno (1991) feared that mass-produced cultural goods of low quality were replacing high culture. If people were easily entertained by soap operas, would they ever be enticed to attend a classical opera? A parallel fear was that traditional folk cultures would be replaced by popular culture (Adorno, 1991). The apparent dominance of the mass media fueled a concern that as mass audiences consumed the same popular culture, everyone would begin to think and act alike. For example, they might believe that idealized, antiseptic families such as that portrayed on the popular TV series *Leave It to Beaver* (1957–1963) were a realistic model for how their own families should be (Real, 1989). Neil Postman argued that even the literacy and reasoning skills of Americans were declining as a result of exposure to too much popular culture, particularly television. In his words, we are "amusing ourselves to death" (Postman, 1986).

PROFILE

THOROUGHLY POSTMODERN POSTMAN. In his 1992 book *Technopoly*, social critic Neil Postman warns us how technology can lead us astray.

The Thoroughly Postmodern Postman

Name: Neil Postman

Education: Doctorate in education from Columbia University

Position: University professor and chair of the Department of Culture and Communication at New York University

Style: Engaging, some say rambling, iconoclast

Greatest Achievement: His *Technopoly* is a widely read book on technology and culture.

Most Dubious Achievement: He reportedly refuses to have an e-mail account as an act of protest against the spread of technopoly.

Entry Level: Former school teacher

How He Got to the Top: His 1985 book *Amusing Ourselves to Death: Public Discourse in the Age of Show Business* resonated with scholars who are concerned that popular culture is replacing serious thought. Critical scholars like Postman build their reputation on the basis of their scholarly books rather than through journal publications and grants.

Where Does He Go from Here: His latest work is a critique of modern education methods entitled *The End of Education.*

However, this image of a passive audience, swayed mindlessly by mass media, clashed with what researchers were learning: that people actually use media in a much more active way (see Chapters 2 and 12). Beginning in the late 1940s, researchers realized that people are active and selective in their use of media and their interpretation of it. By the 1960s, the mass media began to reflect this changed idea of the audience by targeting specialized audience segments instead of addressing a mass audience. In retrospect, it appears that the idea of mass culture blinded many social critics to the real differences that exist between people. As an editorial in the British media review *InterMedia* commented, "There never was a mass audience, only ways of seeing people as masses." This interplay of culture and mass media is evident in the way new immigrants to the United States use the mass media today. With media from their home countries available on VCR, audiocassette, and satellite, new immigrant groups remain steeped in their traditional cultures to maintain a sense of identity and ease the pains of acculturation and change (DoBrow, 1989).

STOP & REVIEW

1. **What impact do information technologies have on personal relationships?**
2. **What is a postmodern society?**
3. **What are the environmental impacts of communications media?**
4. **Which explanation do you prefer, technological determinism or cultural determinism? Defend your choice.**
5. **What are some basic approaches to understanding media and culture?**

COMMUNICATIONS MEDIA AND SOCIAL INSTITUTIONS

Society also functions through its institutions. Here we look at the impacts of communications media on educational, political, and economic institutions.

Communications Media and Educational Institutions

Attempts to improve instruction by delivering courses through the mass media are more formally known as *distance education.* Television is perhaps the most familiar distance learning medium for college students at large universities, who watch lecture courses live or on tape via closed-circuit television or public cable systems in their rooms. However, television is by no means the only medium for distance learning. The pioneering Open University in Great Britain relied on radio and print materials in the 1970s before it turned to television. Advanced teleconferencing technologies that combine elements of audio, video, and computer graphics are advancing the state of the art so that some *telecourses* now feature live interactions with students rather than the passive reception of a mass lecture.

The avowed goal of distance education is usually to make instruction more accessible to the learner, something every educator favors. Distance education enables students to take courses at more locations, at different times, and makes it possible to offer them to small groups of students in remote communities. But there is also often a hidden administrative agenda behind distance education: greater economic efficiency through *economies of scale* (Tiffin & Rajasingham, 1995). That sounds good, too, but what it really means is extending the back of the lecture hall electronically to enclose hundreds more students. The drawback, of course, is the lack of any meaningful intellectual relationship between student and teacher. For that matter, who needs teachers? Just roll the tape. Or why not just mail the students the tape, wrapped in a diploma?

As deadly as televised lectures sometimes are, they do seem to work. Numerous research studies have shown that they are as educationally effective as "live" classroom instruction (Johnston, 1987), although they are usually tested under laboratory conditions that make it difficult to fall asleep or channel-hop to MTV. When shown to "nontraditional" students (usually older, working adults) who cannot come to campus for lectures, telecourses sometimes prove more effective than conventional instruction. That is probably because adult learners are often better motivated and more knowledgeable than on-campus students and because they usually take only one course at a time.

The latest trend in distance education is putting courses on the World Wide Web (Hiltz, 1994; Duffy, 1997). There, *virtual courses* on virtually any subject can be found. Universities around the world are vying to become the leaders in cyberspace, even as the first **virtual universities,** institutions with no campuses, no buildings, and no keg parties—come on-line.

Virtual universities put their courses on the World Wide Web.

Web-based education is still in its infancy, so there is no agreement about what a virtual course should be. Many on-line courses are just expanded course outlines or lecture notes published on instructors' home pages. Another approach borrows directly from the *telecourse* model by placing audiotapes or videotapes of classroom lectures on the Web, which appears to be as educationally effective as conventional classroom lectures (LaRose, Gregg, & Eastin, 1999). Another model is to use Internet communication media such as e-mail, newsgroups, and chatrooms to conduct virtual seminars, which may be even *more* effective than conventional instruction (Schutte, 1997). Others seek to take full advantage of the emerging interactive multimedia capabilities of the Internet, immersing learners in a compelling learning environment that is a cross between a video game and a trip to the zoo. Interactive multimedia also appear to be educationally effective (Yaverbaum & Nadarajan, 1996). But what about those keg parties? They're part of higher education, too.

In K–12 schools, observers worry that multimedia glitz may sacrifice education for the sake of entertainment and that the investment in computers just isn't paying off (Bronner, 1997). Students seem to be motivated by computers, but that apparently has not led to better test scores or even to better attendance. Many computers remain locked up in computer labs, and too many teachers simply don't know how to use them. Also, students learn more only when everyone in class has a computer, not when students have to compete for scarce "seat time" on shared computers (Bulkeley, 1997).

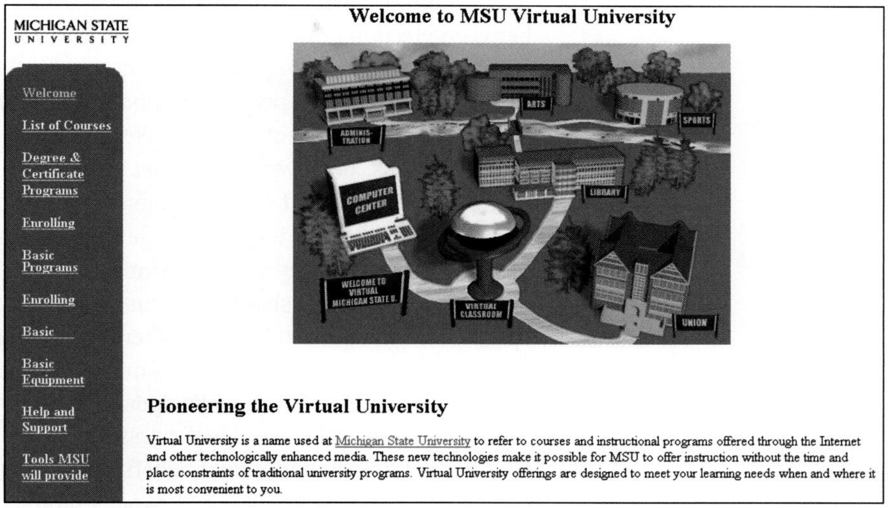

This final point exposes the downside of virtual courses at all levels of education: equal access. Students at well-funded elite universities have better access both to hardware and to assistance than students at less well-endowed institutions. Economically advantaged home learners with the latest in computer technology at their disposal are better able to take advantage of Web courses than the economically disadvantaged. Inner-city schools lag in computer deployment, and African American students have far less access to computers than whites, even after allowing for disparities between races in income and education (Harmon, 1998).

WHAT, NO KEG PARTY? Virtual universities, such as this one at Michigan State University, delivery courses to their students via the World Wide Web.

The Web could also alter the economics of distance education systems, which have always been forced to recoup the cost of production and dedicated distribution channels by attracting hundreds or even thousands of students. Corporations have achieved significant cost savings with Web-based training (King, 1997), but only by counting travel and media costs that universities typically pass on to their students. Web production is relatively cheap, and the user absorbs most of the distribution costs, so it might be possible to break even with relatively small courses. But not if every course tries to be *Myst,* the lavishly produced and wildly popular multimedia computer game. Besides, educators always seem to think that new technology will revolutionize education (Tyack & Cuban, 1995), but it never does.

Communications Media and Political Institutions

Politics is another area wherein the mass media sometimes seem more powerful than they actually may be. We saw in the last chapter that the audience is active in applying *selective exposure, selective attention,* and *selective perception* to media content, and that all these phenomena reduce the individual effects. But the media can affect the political process in other ways than swaying our opinions about the candidates in the last days of an election.

There is growing suspicion that the media do influence voter turnout in a significant way: by making us disenchanted with the entire political process. The constant torrent of political scandals, name calling, and talk show chatter seems to have a numbing effect on the electorate. Or it could be that politics is just turning into a spectator sport, now that the mass media cover it much as they would a sporting event, ignoring the issues for the horse race. It is undeniable that voter participation is falling off and media coverage seems to be playing a part, though how much of a part we do not know (McLeod, Kosicki, & McLeod, 1994).

The mass media may have more important effects on political processes between elections than during them. In earlier chapters we saw how the media serve an *agenda-setting* function. That is, by the topics they choose to cover, they define the issues that people talk about among themselves and that they are likely to perceive as important in future elections. The media are not in complete control of this process, however. They must respond to feedback from their audiences in the form of newsstand sales, ratings, letters to the editor, and their own polls. Some issues resonate with the audience, whereas others fall flat, and the media have to respond if they want to continue selling products for their advertisers. The public agenda is also shaped by a marriage of convenience between politicians, special interests, and the press, wherein the press caters to the agendas of the politicians and the interest groups in order to maintain access to newsmakers (Jeffres, 1986). Also, the public agenda is obviously shaped by such real-world events as wars and economic depression.

The set of commonly held beliefs, attitudes, and misconceptions about the issues of the day is what we call *public opinion.* Like candidate preferences, public opinion is also shaped through interpersonal influence. The publicity attached to polls may help mold public opinion through a process called the *spiral of silence* (Noelle-Neuman, 1984). That is, when we believe that our opinions match the rising tide of public opinion—for example, when we see poll results that support our own opinions—our beliefs are strengthened. Conversely, when we sense that we hold an unpopular belief, we remain silent. Because one of the ways we gauge how popular our own opinions are is by hearing the same opinions voiced by others, a self-perpetuating cycle begins that eventually suppresses the less popular view.

CIVIC FORUM. Santa Monica, California's public electronic network is a model for on-line citizen communication.

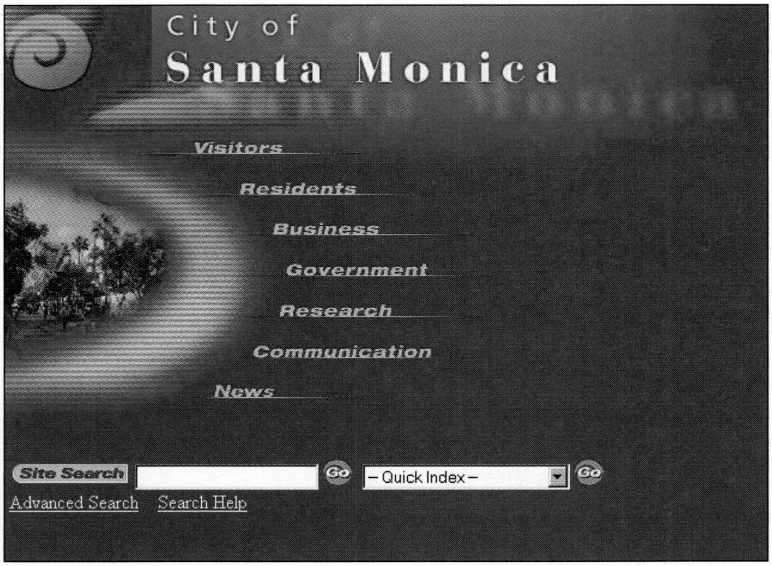

The Internet inspires dreams of a rebirth in political life. One notable example is found in Santa Monica, California, where the Internet is used to open up civic debates by inviting the public to exchange e-mail with city council members. Santa Monica is a relatively wealthy community, so most of its citizens have Internet access, and because free access is available at public locations such as libraries, even the homeless participate (Schmitz, 1997; Rainey, 1998). Internet political newsgroups crackle with political opinions from across the entire political spectrum, unfiltered by mass media gatekeepers and unfettered by establishment opinion makers. In fact, grassroots political organizations are using the Web as an organizing tool. It enables them to communicate easily and inexpensively with potential followers from all over the country and around the world (Friedland, 1996).

But the Internet could also destroy political discourse. It is used as a recruiting tool by hate groups whose extreme views do not promote open dialog (Zickmund, 1997). Attempts to invigorate local politics by fostering public discussion on-line have run afoul of such depressing realities as public indifference and uncivil behavior, even in Santa Monica (Schmitz, 1997). The Internet is still far from being accessible to all, which limits its value as a medium of political communication in an ostensibly egalitarian society. There is also the danger that the political rumors, extremist rantings, and personal innuendo freely traded on the Web will further pollute the political process, not revitalize it. In one infamous incident in 1998, a politically oriented Web site run by an amateur journalist–rumor monger Matt Drudge launched the Monica Lewinsky sex scandal that tied up the political process for months thereafter.

At a deeper level, the spread of information technology has the potential to record and store so much information about us that social control becomes absolute and the mutual trust necessary for political communication becomes impossible (Gandy, 1993). For example, who would check out a book (or a Web site) about Marxism knowing that a record of that transaction might become permanently attached to one's personal data base and be used in some future "witch hunt" for communist sympathizers?

Communications Media and Economic Institutions

Societal Effects of Advertising. The mass media affect the world of business and finance primarily through the advertising they carry. When we examined the individual effects of advertising in the last chapter, we saw that they were surprisingly small, amounting to a change of only a few percentage points in the market shares of products that are advertised (see Chapter 11 for a more detailed discussion of the advertising business). Nonetheless, those percentage points translate into billions of dollars in sales across the economy.

One further effect of advertising is on the consumer's pocketbook. Overall, about 3 percent of the total amount that consumers spend for goods and services goes into advertising. In some product categories—cigarettes and soft drinks, for example—most of the cost of the product is advertising cost. To the extent that the manufacturers establish *brand loyalty,* they can charge more for their products. However, advertising also makes consumers aware of alternative products and special offers, and it generally promotes competition, which helps to keep consumer prices down. In the aggregate, it appears that advertisements are a slight "bargain." That is, they return slightly more to the consumer at the retail level than they take away at the manufacturer level (Jeffres, 1986).

Although ads are not very successful at altering fundamental patterns of consumer behavior (such as "making" us buy a new car when we really don't need one), it is possible that they raise overall levels of consumption. If we are continually exposed to ads with sensuous pictures of gleaming new cars and repeatedly see films and TV shows with glamorous Hollywood stars tooling around in the newest Bulgemobile, doesn't that make our old rust bucket seem all the more shabby to us?

On a broader scale, the advertising barrage may cultivate materialistic values of mass consumption, subtly convincing us that the key to happiness lies in the consumption of consumer goods. The noted economist John Kenneth Galbraith (1967) argues that advertising is a type of propaganda that places consumers on an endless treadmill of work to fulfill wants created by ads, all in the service of large corporations that need to keep their factories running at full capacity. Historically, advertising may be credited with undermining the values of hard work and frugality that were spawned on the American frontier and cultivated by the Great Depression of the 1930s (Ewen & Ewen, 1997). However, it is also possible that consumption causes advertising—that advertising expenditures rise along with the demand for consumer products, which in turn is linked to rising incomes.

The Productivity Paradox. When businesses use computer and telecommunications media, they expect profits to increase. Peter Keen (1988), a noted author and consultant on the topic of information technologies in organizations, points out how businesses can profit from using communications media. For example, film studios can get the edge on the competition by using electronic editing to get summer "blockbuster" motion pictures to the theaters ahead of their rivals. And newspapers create innovative products, such as electronic editions on the World Wide Web and reproductions (for a fee) of their past articles. However, the most important goal of information technology investments is to increase **productivity,** the amount of productive output relative to the inputs—workers, machinery, and other resources—expended to create products.

Productivity is a measure of a firm's output relative to the resources consumed—for example, the number of products each employee makes per hour.

For example, *computer-assisted design/computer-assisted manufacturing (CAD/CAM)* systems help designers visualize new products inside computer workstations. This reduces the need for expensive prototypes. The designs can be sent directly to factory robots so that the entire production process is controlled by computer and telecommunications systems; this is called *computer-integrated manufacturing (CIM)*. By these same means, it is also possible to customize products that were formerly mass produced. "Just-in-time" inventory systems save money on warehousing by closely coordinating deliveries from suppliers to arrive exactly when they are needed. Productivity improvements may also arise from improving internal communication (such as through the use of electronic mail and teleconferencing and by providing more up-to-date information to executives)—and, yes, from reducing the number of workers.

More and more of these methods are finding their way into the conventional mass media as they make their transition to the Information Age. Animated movies such as *A Bug's Life* are now designed, directed, and produced inside powerful computer workstations, combining CAD/CAM and CIM. Customized mass media products are found in the form of "custom publishing" of college textbooks. Cable television pay-per-view movies are just-in-time delivery systems that overcome the "warehousing" problem at the local video store where there are never quite enough copies of the "top renters" to go around. In Hollywood, scripts and audio-visual materials are increasingly whisked from place to place via high-speed networks rather than by production assistants carrying film cans (DiOrio, 1996). In radio stations, automated CD systems or satellite-delivered network radio programs are supplanting announcers and disk jockeys by the hundreds.

A review of some 30 office automation studies by communication researcher Ron Rice revealed a wide range of practices that have the potential for enhancing productivity (Rice & Bair, 1984). These included higher document production rates, fewer separate tasks per activity (such as the elimination of typesetting in newspapers), fewer media transformations (such as from handwriting to printed movie script), lower document production costs, and the elimination of shadow functions (such as telephone tag with your producer) that do not contribute directly to the finished product. Teleconferencing systems also seem to improve productivity by lowering travel expenditures and increasing the efficiency of meetings.

However, actual gains in efficiency have been hard to pinpoint. Thus we encounter the "productivity paradox": Investments in information technology do not yield reliable financial returns. Why? For one thing, the assistance that in-house technicians and unofficial "computer gurus" give their co-workers may more than triple the officially budgeted operating costs of information systems. Some systems create new unproductive activities, such as when newspaper reporters spend more time playing with type fonts than is necessary to write a good article. Organizations sometimes abandon efficient information systems in favor of newer technology before the older systems have paid for themselves. And many information systems never work properly or are abandoned before they are completed (Kirwin & Cappuccio, 1998; Attewell, 1994). Recent research that tracked information technology since the 1950s suggests that until the early 1990s, productivity improvements from information technology were seldom seen at all. It apparently took that long (40 years!) for the majority of businesses to learn how to use computers efficiently and lower the costs of production (Byrnjolfsson & Hitt, 1996).

If information technologies do not always contribute to the corporate "bottom line," why are corporations so eager to adopt them? According to computer sociologist Rob Kling (1980), modernization waves in computer technology assume the character of computerization *movements,* complete with the prophets, zealots, and true believers found in political movements. Communications researchers have found that a similar phenomenon comes into play in corporate decisions about telecommunications technologies. The *social influence model* notes that personal attitudes and interpersonal relationships intrude on the rational financial evaluation of new technologies (Fulk, Schmitz, & Steinfield, 1990).

The Quantity of Work. The pyramid-shaped hierarchical structures of Industrial Age organizations are being swept aside (Toffler, 1990). New metaphorical images are emerging to describe this transformation. The term *flattened pyramid* describes an organization where the middle layers of management have been stripped away, leaving the high-level executives at the apex of the pyramid resting on a wide base of low-level employees (see Figure 13.2). In the "core-and-ring" model, a small core of key employees adds or subtracts temporary employees from the ring as business needs dictate. Then there is the *virtual corporation,* which has only a few full-time employees and no actual place of business other than its corporate

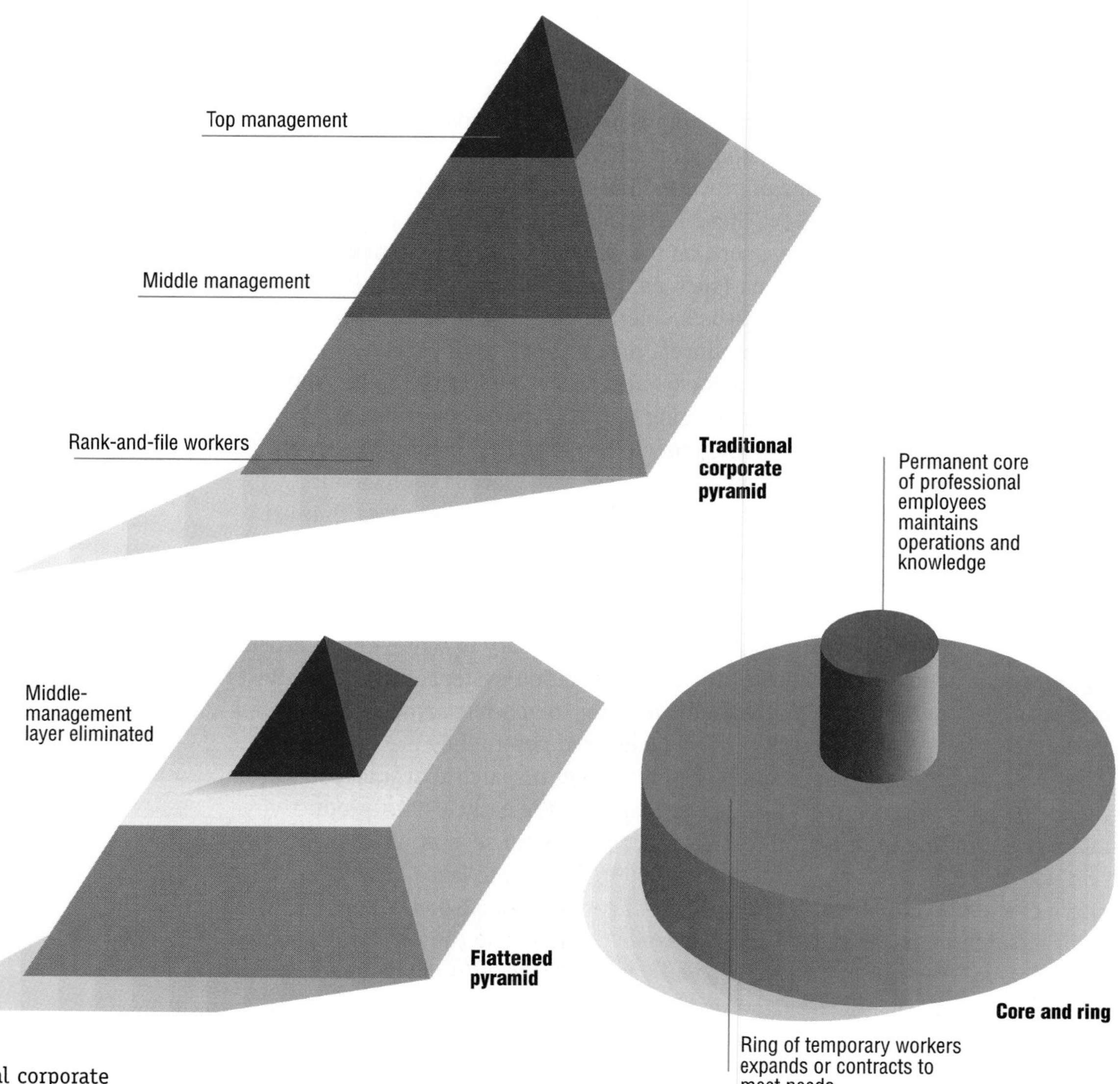

FIGURE 13.2
The traditional corporate pyramid is being replaced by the flattened pyramid and the core-and-ring structure.

communication network infrastructure. The staff communicates via e-mail and teleconferencing and *outsources* everything else by hiring subcontractors to do all the work of design, production, marketing, and distribution (Venkatraman & Henderson, 1998).

Although many conventional mass media institutions cling to the old hierarchical model of the corporate pyramid, there are signs that they are changing with the times. For example, after the "big three" television networks (ABC, NBC, and CBS) changed hands over the last decade, the new managements launched reorganizations that put many of the middle-level managers out of work, essentially flattening the pyramid. Movie studios have long followed the core-and-ring model by adding or subtracting production specialists on a project-by-project basis, and independent film production companies embody the virtual corporation model.

Note that these models all imply fewer full-time employees. Indeed, if we do succeed in improving productivity through information technologies, does that just mean more unemployment? Some experts contend that information technology spells not only the end of a lot of people's jobs but also the end of work itself, as computers take over more and more of the jobs that people do (Aronowitz & DiFazio, 1994; Rifkin, 1995). Examples in the mass media field include newspaper typesetters (replaced by computers), musicians and sound engineers (replaced by electronic synthesizers) and TV newsroom camerapersons (replaced by robotic cameras).

Others are not so sure that employment will decline (Kilborn, 1993; National Commission for Employment Policy, 1986; Perrolle, 1987). If information technology can reduce costs and increase product quality, then there should be an increased demand for more products—and thus higher employment. For example, if computer-generated television programs following *A Bug's LIfe* model catch on, their costs will drop as a result (see Chapter 2); then Hollywood could fill hundreds of new channels with enticing digital entertainment. Then we all might spend more hours watching, which would stimulate demand for yet more channels and generate employment in the television industry. Or the displaced television production staffs who know only analog technology might find employment in new service industries, such as making wedding videos. Historically, fears about higher unemployment resulting from automation have proved unfounded, whether the "new technology" was the textile machinery of the 1790s or computers of the 1990s.

Of course, this information is small comfort to individual workers "automated out of a job" or to the entire classes of workers "automated out of an industry," such as the newspaper typesetters whose skills were rendered obsolete by computerized printing. This phenomenon is euphemistically called *job displacement* by labor economists. The displaced workers are supposed to find new jobs in the service sector, but about half of these new jobs are part-time jobs, and nearly a third of U.S. workers are now "contingent employees" without long-term employment agreements.

Who is being displaced? The United States has seen almost complete elimination of a blue-collar middle class in the span of a single generation. In the automobile industry hundreds of thousands of blue-collar workers have been eliminated by information technology innovations, such as robotic welding machines and paint sprayers (National Commission for Employment Policy, 1986). Thousands of middle managers—the junior assistant vice presidents for Monday morning news programs—once needed to coordinate communications and operations have been replaced by office information systems. And the largely female "pink-collar" employees in clerical occupations—the junior assistant vice presidents' secretaries—are targets for office automation.

The Quality of Work. What will work be like for those who still have it? The new organizational models all imply far less job security. The odds are that today's college students will have several different careers in their lives, not just several different jobs in the same career path with different employers, which was once the normal pattern. And lifelong employment with one employer is a relic of the past.

All of this insecurity could place downward pressure on benefits and wages—except perhaps for the highly skilled elite.

De-skilling is reduction of the skill requirements of a job through mechanization or automation.

Information technology could reduce skill requirements for the average worker, a process known as **de-skilling.** Charles Babbage first envisioned using computers to simplify tasks so that less-skilled—and lower-paid—workers could be used (Braverman, 1974; Schement & Lievrouw, 1987). Today, we call it **Taylorism,** after Frederick Winslow Taylor, the inventor of *scientific management.* Scientific management improves productivity by dictating one "right" way to do each task and specifying exactly how many tasks should be performed per hour.

Taylorism, or scientific management, seeks to improve the efficiency of work by routinizing it.

For example, if we wanted to increase the productivity of sports journalists, we might specify a set of standard lead sentences ("Things looked extremely [pick adjective] for the [city name] nine that day. The score stood [home team score] to [visiting team score] with but an inning left to play"), fire the sportswriter, and hire a college intern to fill in the blanks using reports transmitted on the Associated Press newswire. Then we would hold a stopwatch on the intern to see how many game summaries she could write in an hour and replace her if she fell below the standard for the job.

Fordism is the application of the assembly-line process, reducing work to the endless repetition of a single task.

Fordism, named after Henry Ford, introduced the assembly-line system, in which each employee performs only a single, narrowly defined task over and over again. In our example, we might retain a writer (who need not know anything about sports and writes stock lead sentences for *all* our stories, not just in the sports section) to write the lead sentences, while interns filled in the blanks. Taylorized and Fordized workers do not know how to "make" anything (such as a good sports story). Their knowledge is limited to one small task, so that upward mobility is impossible. Only the owners and their white-collar managers (here, the sports editor) know how to organize those tasks to produce goods and services.

Information technologies amplify Taylorism and Fordism in some distressing ways. First, they make it easier to monitor employees, such as by counting their keystrokes as they type on their computers or by rifling through their e-mail. Second, they extend scientific management from the assembly floor to the office. The advent of *expert systems* and *artificial intelligence* could make scientific management a threat in the executive suite itself.

Post-Fordism de-skills jobs to the point where workers no longer need to be paid a living wage.

De-skilled workers can be paid less and replaced at will, a practice known as **post-Fordism.** Post-Fordism violates the basic social contract initiated by Henry Ford, which was to pay rank-and-file workers a decent living wage so that they could purchase the very products that they assembled. In the post-Fordist society, pay is cut to the point that workers can no longer participate in the consumer economy. In our example, the college intern might be paid so little (or perhaps be paid nothing—it's an internship, after all!) that she could not afford a computer or an Internet connection to read her own sports stories on the Web. Post-Fordism does offer the happy prospect of customized products rather than mass-produced ones, but that is thanks to computer-integrated manufacturing (CIM) techniques (see page 438), not to contented, well-paid workers.

Up-skilling means raising the educational requirements of a job through automation.

Another dismal possibility is that skill requirements will be upgraded to the point where much of the current work force does not possess them. This process is known as **up-skilling.** For example, many TV and film production specialists trained on analog technology cannot easily become a part of the new digital production teams because they lack experience in computer graphics hardware and software.

But there are rays of hope, too, such as work decentralization. Computer networks make it possible to integrate the work products of distant suppliers and far-flung back room (or back lot) operations, moving them farther into the suburbs and even to rural areas. More employees can work where they want to live and thus avoid the stress of commuting and relocating at intervals. For example, the global nature of today's TV and film production industry, combined with a pressing need to relieve traffic congestion, air pollution, and sky-high real estate costs in the Los Angeles basin, has prompted substitution of computer networks for travel.

FORDISM.
Henry Ford built gleaming factories, such as the River Rouge plant shown here, and paid workers a decent wage so that they could buy their own Fords. (Charles Shecter, ***River Rouge Plant,*** 1932, oil on canvas 20 x 24⅛ in. [50.8 × 61.3 cm.], collection of Whitney Museum of American Art, purchase, 32.43.)

The ultimate in work decentralization is **telecommuting,** in which the employee's home office is linked to the workplace. This helps many workers achieve a better balance between the demands of job and family. But there are drawbacks. Working in the home sometimes creates more stress than it relieves, and home workers are less likely to be unionized and are easier to dispose of when no longer needed. A growing number of jobs are being decentralized right out of the country, to developing countries where wages are low and working conditions dismal, a trend that inflicts new pressures on workers in developed economies. A notable example is the near-total export of cartoon animation to countries where animation artists work for a fraction of the going wage in the United States.

Another potential boon to the workers of the future is **re-skilling:** reassigning, to current employees, tasks that were formerly parceled out to specialized workers. The employee, in effect, reclaims the role of the preindustrial craftsperson (Zuboff, 1984) as knowledge becomes the cornerstone for business and social relations (Bell, 1973). For example, desktop publishing puts print publication back within the scope of a single person sitting at a personal computer. It hasn't been that way since the days of the medieval manuscript copyists. These changes rock the very foundations of industrial mass media by restoring control to the workers themselves. It is ironic that information technologies, the crowning achievement of industrial capitalism, may yet fulfill Karl Marx's prophecy. It was he, after all, who pointed out that capitalism creates the contradictions that inevitably lead to its own destruction!

Telecommuting occurs when work is performed in the home and workers are linked by telecommunications networks.

Re-skilling occurs when specialized tasks are reorganized so that a single worker can perform them all.

Electronic Commerce. Thus it is not just the downtrodden typesetter or production assistant whom the information society may displace, after all. Changes wrought by information technology routinely bring entire corporations down and even sweep entire industries into the dustbin of history. Consider the corner newsstands. Where did they go?

Many agree that the most sweeping changes in the way the world does business will come from *electronic commerce,* or the completion of purchases and

Home, Sweet Office

Over 6 million Americans telecommute, and two-fifths of U.S. homes have some type of home office. Telecommuting helps employers retain valued employees who have child-care or elder-care responsibilities or personal disabilities. Job satisfaction rises as workers are relieved of 2-hour commutes and the stress of solving problems that arise from their absence from home. Improved employee satisfaction could translate into increased productivity.

However, there are some pitfalls. Some employees are unable to avoid the temptation of the 5-hour lunch. Some report increased stress from juggling work and family crises at home. Others fear that telecommuting leads to isolation and lack of support at work and that it will throw them off the corporate "fast track." In fact, when we factor in the cost of the the equipment and of training each employee to be a computer troubleshooter, productivity gains shrink alarmingly.

Because commuting costs are absorbed by the employee, they do not affect the employer's "bottom line," and neither party weighs the costs of air pollution and highway construction. Most telecommuters today still have office space downtown, which sits empty most of the time. Computer modems or Digital Subscriber Lines (DSL, see Chapter 9) could greatly increase the quality and ease of access to corporate computer networks. Advances in desktop videoconferencing, in conjunction with faster lines, give remote employees more of a sense of "being there" in the office. Multimedia computers could make it possible to replicate a wide range of office tasks and to facilitate cooperative projects on a computer network (Violino & Stahl, 1993).

The Global Sand Box? Telecommuting has the potential to transform radically the world of work and even society as a whole. Service sector companies from banks to movie studios could become "virtual corporations," little more than a collection of nodes on a worldwide digital network. Downtown office buildings might empty and freeways turn into greenbelt parks. Employees could enjoy a permanent "working holiday," rambling freely about the globe, e-mailing their work from wherever their travels take them. We could all live the life of Steve Roberts, a computer consultant who pedals around the country on a bicycle equipped with four computers, a cellular radio modem, and an on-board satellite link (Carroll, 1992). Employers would benefit, because they would no longer have to maintain expensive office facilities. Upward pressure on salaries might ease, as employees experience lower costs for housing, transportation, and family care. With an end to air pollution and global warming, and with the restoration of the ozone layer, we could all go out and enjoy the sun!

Or the Electronic Sweatshop? Telecommuting could revive the horrors of the Industrial Revolution, when workers toiled long hours for starvation wages at spinning wheels in their homes. When workers supply their own offices and equipment, they are making a capital investment in their employer's corporation. Isn't this tantamount to a massive transfer of wealth from the poor to the rich? Employers might treat such employees as private contractors and eliminate health and retirement benefits. And they might no longer make commitments to employees if they never had to incur moving costs and could replace anyone by putting out a work order "on the Net." Bank clerks in New York City and screenwriters in Hollywood could suddenly find themselves in direct competition with contractors in Bombay. And how would the downtrodden information workers fight these injustices? Without a common physical gathering place, they might be unable to organize themselves into unions or professional associations—or even learn the identities of their co-workers. And what would happen to those empty cities and the people too poor to move out of them?

financial transactions over computer networks, usually the Internet. In preceding chapters, we saw how electronic commerce is already making inroads into markets dominated by book and music retail chains. As newspapers and magazines begin to charge for the on-line versions of their products, electronic commerce is moving to the very core of the mass media industry. The shift of long-distance phone calls away from telephone networks and onto the Internet is another significant development in electronic commerce.

And consumer products are only a small part of electronic commerce today. Computer technology companies, such as the Cisco Corporation, makers of high-speed data switches, rack up billions of dollars per year in sales to corporate customers from their sites on the World Wide Web. Large manufacturing companies, such as Chrysler Corporation, link all of their suppliers and contractors via *electronic data interchange* (EDI) computer networks that completely eliminate the need for sending orders, invoices, and payments through the mail.

HOW ARE THINGS IN THE OFFICE?
Telecommuters who work from home on computer networks are part of a growing trend toward work decentralization.

The ultimate impact of electronic commerce on today's business and financial institutions is hard to predict. It may lead to domination by a handful of companies that control the networks and serve as clearinghouses—but also as bottlenecks and tollgates—for all on-line transactions. Time Warner and AT&T rule. However, a *network marketplace* could also emerge in which suppliers large and small would compete freely, delivering an unprecedented cornucopia of products to consumers and business customers at low, competitive prices. You, the desktop multimedia producer of tomorrow, might compete freely with Paramount Studios when the networks put out a call for new TV shows.

In the process, the media landscape could change radically, although no one today is sure just how. No more newspapers, as newsy Web sites replace metropolitan dailies? Or more newspapers catering to individual needs? No more advertising—and no ad-supported media—as direct sales on the Web become the norm? Or new interactive advertising forms? No more banks (let's start thinking of them as Internet content providers, shall we?) as paper money disappears (Levy, 1994)? Or, will banks become the clearinghouses and guarantors of all on-line transactions? Or will it be Microsoft? Or, it could be you, gentle reader; opportunity knocks.

Careers in the Information Society. What about *your* career? Will you be one of the displaced or de-skilled? The U.S. Department of Labor compiles annual employment projections in its *Occupational Outlook.* Table 13.1 shows the number of people employed in some representative communications media occupations, "average" salaries (actually, either the mean or the median in each field), the

TABLE 13.1 Occupational Outlook in Communications Media

Occupational category	Number of jobs	Typical salary	Growth by 2006	Explanation
Electrical and electronic engineers	367,000	$49,200	Faster than average	Excellent in computers, communications and consumer electronics
Computer systems analysts	506,000	$46,300	Top 3 fastest	Computer technology spurs growth
Radio/TV announcers	52,000	$25,000 *(sm mkt TV)* $199,000 *(lg mkt TV)*	Decline	Many more applicants than jobs
Reporters and correspondents	60,000	$23,300	Decline	Mergers and closures
Photographers and camera operators	154,000	$30,600	Average	Electronic multimedia main growth area but TV and film jobs decline
Actors, directors, and producers	105,000	$13,700 *(actors)* $1500/wk *(directors)* Percentage of gross *(producers)*	Faster than average	Cable TV and home video expanding, growing international market
Broadcast technicians	46,000	$16,400 *(sm mkt TV)* $45,700 *(lg mkt TV)*	Average	Automation will offset expansion of stations
Computer programmers	568,000	$40,100	Faster than average	Technology constantly changes
Telephone operators	319,000	$19,300	Decline	Job cuts from automation and deregulation
Typists and data entry	1,100,000	$20,000	Decline	Office automation
Prepress workers	155,000	$45,800	Decline	Computers make typesetting obsolete, but desktop publishing grows
Line installers and splicers	309,000	$36,600	Average	Telephone and cable rebuilding systems, older workers retire

Source: U.S. Department of Labor, *Occupational Outlook Handbook, 1998–1999 Edition* (Washington, DC: U.S. Government Printing Office). (stats.bls.gov/occname.htm)

outlook for growth in the category by the year 2006, and explanations for anticipated growth or decline.

Generally, the news is worst for blue-collar jobs, such as line installer and broadcast technician, and for pink-collar occupations, such as telephone operator and typist. Reliability improvements in information systems and automation threaten all these livelihoods. White-collar ranks are threatened as well, including news reporters and correspondents and radio and TV announcers. In most white-collar occupations, the outlook is rosier. Most job growth will occur in occupations that require a bachelor's degree. New technologies will keep demand for technical

MEDIA WATCH

What about *Your* Job?

Yes, information technologies are changing the world of work, and not always for the better. But they can also be a valuable tool in furthering your career. Job listings are all over the Internet; just enter "job listings" in a keyword search to see what we mean. Add keyword restrictions for the geographical regions and industries you are interested in to cut the list. Media Line (www.medialine.com) specializes in television industry jobs, for example. It not only lists job openings nationwide but also lets job seekers post their résumés, complete with audio and video audition clips. No experience? No problem. Try "internship openings" along with geographical and industry keywords. Another strategy is to go to the Web sites operated by the organizations you might like to work for. They are also likely to have job and internship postings, many of which may not appear in the other directories. And for general information about career opportunities in various fields, start with the Bureau of Labor Statistics' Occupational Outlook (http://stats.bls.gov/ocohome.htm).

graduates at high levels, especially demand for electrical engineers and systems analysts in communications and computer specialties.

No general expansion of employment in mass media fields is predicted in these forecasts. Industry consolidation spurred by deregulation and a growing reliance on labor-saving computerized production techniques are expected to eliminate many of today's jobs. Mass media fields are already highly competitive at the entry level; tens of thousands of new graduates hope to enter these relatively small fields of employment each year. Unfortunately, experience counts more than education in landing media jobs, and many entry-level positions go to unpaid interns. High turnover rates in media occupations, rather than expansion in the number of jobs available, provide most of the openings. Why the high turnover? Although national media stars get well-publicized multimillion-dollar salaries, rank-and-file actors and television announcers draw salaries that place them near the bottom of the white-collar hierarchy. Small-market media personalities make less than the lowly "cable guy" in the "line installer and splicer" category.

STOP & REVIEW

1. **Would you rather go to a virtual university or a real university? Why?**
2. **What opportunities does the Internet offer for improving political discourse and what barriers does it pose?**
3. **Is advertising good or bad for consumers?**
4. **Do information technologies increase or decrease productivity? Explain.**
5. **What new organizational structures are emerging?**
6. **How do Taylorism, Fordism, and post-Fordism differ?**
7. **Give examples of jobs that have been de-skilled, jobs that have been up-skilled, and jobs that have been re-skilled.**

The best prospects for entering the mass media field are for those who combine strong computer skills with their media talents. For example, digital multimedia production skills are forecasted to be in great demand for technicians and creative positions in the newspaper, television, and film industries as those industries make the transition from conventional mass media to computer media. These trends are reflected in what is expected to be explosive growth in demand for visual artists and designers who are computer-savvy, including the new occupation of "webmaster" that creates and maintains organizational Web sites on the Internet. But there is even hope in the downtrodden occupational category of typesetter—now referred by the more inclusive title of "prepress workers"—where advances in desktop publishing afford new opportunities to those with computer skills.

SUMMARY AND REVIEW

WHAT IS THE DIFFERENCE BETWEEN INDIVIDUAL AND SOCIETAL EFFECTS OF COMMUNICATIONS MEDIA?

Societal effects are not necessarily just the sum total of individual effects. Social statistics (such as the crime rate) do not always agree with expectations based on studies of individual effects. Individual effects apparent in the laboratory may not be observed in real life, especially if behavior is influenced by larger social and cultural values that cannot be reproduced in a controlled environment or that may vary between cultures.

WHAT DOES THE TRADITION OF SOCIAL CRITICISM ADD TO OUR UNDERSTANDING OF SOCIETAL EFFECTS?

Social critics use inductive and interpretive approaches that may help them look beyond the results of empirical research studies to see the bigger picture. For example, early social critics foretold that the telephone would increase illiteracy, revitalize rural life, improve the life of women, increase suburban sprawl, and make cities grow, among other things. However, many of the predictions did not come true, and other technological and social changes may have accounted for the predictions that did come to pass. The same may prove true for the predictions of social critics of today's new communications media.

HOW DO COMMUNICATIONS MEDIA AFFECT SOCIAL EQUALITY?

Information technologies do not benefit all groups in society equally. Women and African Americans may be left behind in the transition to the information economy. The knowledge gap hypothesis predicts that efforts to improve the plight of the disadvantaged through improved access to communications media will instead result in widening the gap between rich and poor. And by learning to use computers for all our work-related and personal needs we may be unwittingly playing into the hands of those who seek economic dominance in the future.

HOW DO COMMUNICATIONS MEDIA AFFECT SOCIAL RELATIONS?

History shows that new communications technologies augment some forms of interpersonal communication while disrupting others. The advent of the information superhighway has the potential for bringing about a situation in which everyone is our neighbor in a small, electronically mediated global village. The virtual communities that have formed on the Internet are an initial indication that new types of human relationships may be created. However, there is the danger that the world could evolve into an extremely fragmented postmodern society in which chaos reigns. Information technologies may also degrade the sense of social presence we experience when we talk to people face to face.

WHAT IS THE RELATIONSHIP BETWEEN COMMUNICATIONS MEDIA AND CULTURE?

There are two opposing views of the interaction between media and culture. According to technological determinism, society is profoundly affected by new communications technology, such as the printing press. The opposing view is that society is culturally determined and that technologies have an impact only in cultures that are receptive to them. Views of mass media and culture have evolved over time. Early writers extolled the high culture of Western Europe and sought to spread it to the masses through the media. Later, American writers such as Emerson and Whitman placed more emphasis on the culture of the masses—on popular culture. Today, there are growing concerns that popular culture is supplanting other cultural values.

DO INFORMATION TECHNOLOGIES CAUSE UNEMPLOYMENT?

Improvements in productivity brought about by applications of information technology have the potential to displace large numbers of jobs. Historically, new waves of industrial technology have increased employment in the long term, and the same is likely to hold true today. In the short term, however, entire categories of workers will be eliminated, and workers with useless skills may be forced to seek unstable contingent employment. Some careers, such as computer systems analyst, actor, director, and producer, will grow rapidly; other categories, such as telephone operator and computer operator, will suffer.

DO COMMUNICATIONS MEDIA MAKE WORK LESS SATISFYING?

In some applications, information technologies increase the twin tendencies of Taylorism and Fordism, de-skilling work to meaningless, repetitive, assembly-line tasks. In the extreme, jobs become so degraded that workers no longer command a decent living wage, a condition called post-Fordism. In other instances, information technology upskills jobs, displacing workers whose skills no longer match job requirements. However, information technologies can also be applied in ways that re-skill jobs, restoring work to a meaningful and dignified pursuit.

HOW ARE COMMUNICATIONS MEDIA CHANGING THE STRUCTURE OF ORGANIZATIONS?

The spread of personal computers and high-speed communications networks is resulting in the decentralization of work in a variety of ways. "Back room" data processing operations that were maintained at corporate headquarters are being relocated to remote areas—sometimes outside the United States—to reduce information processing costs. Other companies outsource operations to independent suppliers, gathering their output and coordinating their efforts with advanced information systems. Telecommuting relocates the workplace to the home environment, while electronic commerce brings the shopping mall to the home via the World Wide Web.

WHAT CHANGES ARE TAKING PLACE IN MEDIA INDUSTRIES AS THE RESULT OF THE SPREAD OF INFORMATION TECHNOLOGIES?

The changes in the media reflect those in other industries. For example, entire animated movies can be created on powerful computer workstations, a capacity that has the potential to lower the cost and time involved in movie production. Media are pioneering new ways to get their products into the home, such as by pay-per-view cable, to stay ahead of the competition. They are also originating new products, such as on-line newspapers. The potential drawback for media professionals is that many existing jobs, such as typesetter and radio disk jockey, may be downgraded to low-wage, monotonous tasks. The quality of work may erode as temporary employment expands and career changing becomes more common. However, some jobs may improve as computer media put the entire production process in the hands of each employee and as new media outlets open to take advantage of the demand spurred by lower costs and more choices.

Electronic Resources

For up-to-the-minute URLs about *Media and Society,* access the MEDIA NOW site on the

http://communication.wadsworth.com/

CHAPTER 14

Media Policy, Law, and Ethics

WHAT'S AHEAD

This chapter concentrates on public policy, law, and ethics. It recaps many of the important social issues covered in previous chapters and puts them into context. Government policy and law focus on content issues, such as sex, violence, and libel in the media, as well as technical standards, competition, ownership, privacy, and copyright. Ethical rules and values guide individuals and professional groups as they make choices on such matters as accuracy, respect for sources' or clients' privacy, and controversial content.

Access the MEDIA NOW site on the World Wide Web at:
http://communication.wadsworth.com/
Choose "Chapter 14" from the selection box to access electronic information and other sites relevant to this chapter.

WASHINGTON, DC, 2010

This hearing of the Senate Committee on Commerce will now come to order! Will the witness please introduce himself?

My name is Red Wormer, and I don't think I need any further introduction.

(Chuckle) I'm sure we all know that Mr. Wormer here is chairman of Wormer Communications, owner of 90 percent of the cable systems and Internet access nodes in the country and over 5000 channels on the Internet.

That's 5132, to be exact, including the one that shows this meeting and the ones that carry your campaign commercials and home pages. And don't forget I also provide phone service to your private offices and run Webcams on all the private alcoves in the Capitol building.

Ahem. Yes, well. Now, Mr. Wormer, it's not true that you're trying to monopolize the telecommunications industry, is it?

No, sir. And I am not trying to destroy family values either.

But what about that Family Fistfight Classics channel?

Well, I believe in our First Amendment right to watch mayhem. Besides, lots of families have fights. We're just reflectin' society by showing their home videos and giving prizes for the best ones . . . as a service to our advertisers, you understand.

Of course you are! But we are also a little concerned that you have taken over the ten biggest banks.

Well, they fell behind on their transaction fee payments to my Home Banking Network. What else could I do?

Perfectly understandable! Perfectly! Will you promise not to do it again?

I promise not to take over the ten biggest banks again.

And the family fistfights?

O.K., no bleeding before 8 P.M. *and* I'll overlook how much the IRS owes my banking network, for now.

Wonderful! Generous! Thank you so much! Meeting adjourned!

Chapter Outline:

Policy, Law, and Ethics in Communications
Key Communications Policies
Freedom of Speech and the First Amendment
Limits on the First Amendment
The Fourth Amendment and Privacy
Patent and Copyright Law: Protecting Intellectual Property
Ownership Issues
Concentration of Ownership
Access to Media and Universal Service
The Radio Acts and Spectrum Management
Defining Technical Standards for Media
The Policymaking Process
Federal Regulation and Policymaking
State and Local Regulation
Lobbies
The Fifth Estate: The Media in the Policy Process
Ethics in the Communications Media
General Considerations in Individual Ethics
Codes of Ethics
Ethical Issues for Media Professionals
Summary and Review

POLICY, LAW, AND ETHICS IN COMMUNICATIONS

The importance of media in public and private life leads to constant concern about what the media are doing and how to guide them. The formation of policy and the passage and enforcement of law involve a collective action of the whole society or its representatives, which requires a good deal of public discussion and the formation of public opinion on what to do. **Policy** reflects government and public consideration of how to structure and regulate social or collective activities, such as those of the media, so that they contribute to the public good. Many groups, such as churches, private companies, industry trade groups, minority groups, and public interest groups, also monitor media performance and lobby the media and the government to change various practices or kinds of content. **Laws** are binding rules passed by legislatures, enforced by the executive power, and applied or adjudicated by courts. Policies are often turned into laws in order to make them legally binding on people and companies. **Standards** are technical characteristics, such as the number of lines on the television screen, that must be agreed on for a technology to be widely manufactured and used.

Policy is a government or public framework for how to structure and regulate media so that they contribute to the public good.

Law is a binding rule enacted, enforced, and interpreted by government legislatures, executive agencies, and courts, respectively.

Standards are technical characteristics that must be agreed on for a technology to be widely manufactured and used.

Ethics are guidelines or moral rules about how professional communicators should behave in situations where their activities may have negative effects on others. **Self-regulation** pertains to communication industry codes and practices of monitoring and controlling the media's performance.

Some issues cut across all these media control mechanisms. For example, sex and violence in the media have been discussed for decades, resulting in government policies such as the FCC's scrutiny of language used on radio, and laws such as the 1996 Telecommunications Act, which required a new ratings system to reflect sex, violence, and objectionable language in television and cable TV offerings. We have also seen examples of industry self-regulation, such as the Hollywood film rating system, and innumerable ethics-based decisions by individual writers and producers about violence and sexual content.

Individual communicators are constantly making ethical decisions beyond what is specifically covered by policy or law. Ethical issues include what kinds of topics to cover, how to respect people's privacy, and how to protect the confidentiality of sources.

MEDIA, POLICY, LAW, AND ETHICS TIME LINE

1644 English poet John Milton calls for freedom of speech in *Aeropagitica*

1710 English Statute of Anne protects authors' and publishers' rights to publish and benefit from it—a precedent for copyright

1733 Peter Zenger trial establishes truth as a defense for press against libel charges

1776 Thomas Paine's pamphlet *Common Sense* challenges British press censorship

1789 Article 1 Section 8 of U.S. Constitution establishes copyright; First Amendment to Constitution enshrines freedom of press; Fourth Amendment protects privacy against unwarranted searches and seizures by government

1798 – 1800 Alien and Sedition Acts temporarily try to limit press criticism of government

1865 International Telecommunication Union formed to set telegraph standards

1890 Sherman Antitrust Act limits monopolies' restraint of trade

1927 Radio Act creates commission to allocate radio frequencies

1934 Communications Act covers broadcasting and telecommunications

1947 Hutchins Commission Report urges social responsibility for media

1957 *Roth vs. United States* permits community level definitions of obscenity

1969 Supreme Court *Red Lion* case cements Fairness Doctrine

1973 Pacifica radio disciplined for broadcasting George Carlin's "Seven Dirty Words You Can't Say on Radio"

1978 National Telecommunications and Information Administration established

1986 Electronic Communications Privacy Act

1996 Telecommunications Act deregulates industries to let them compete; Communications Decency Act declared unconstitutional by Supreme Court

1998 Sonny Bono Copyright Term Extension Act; Children's Online Privacy Protection Act

KEY COMMUNICATIONS POLICIES

Policies governing free speech, privacy, intellectual property, competition, diversity, and access form the basic framework for guiding communications media in the United States.

Freedom of Speech and the First Amendment

The most fundamental U.S. law regarding the content and conduct of media is the **First Amendment.** This reflects an underlying agreement, dating from the American Revolution in 1776, that freedom of speech, both in person and over media, is a basic requirement for the type of political system and society that the writers of the U.S. Constitution wished to create. Many current Americans take freedom of speech for granted, but those who fought in the Revolution and those who wrote the Constitution, such as Jefferson, Franklin, and Paine, were well aware of how few places at that time had freedom of speech and how easily it can be limited.

Ethics are moral rules or rules of conduct that guide one's actions—in specific situations.

Self-regulation refers to industry codes and practices of monitoring the industry's own performance.

The **First Amendment** to the U.S. Constitution guarantees freedom of speech and of the press in the United States.

Reprinted by permission: Tribune Media Services, cartoon by Mike Peters.

STICKS AND STONES! Many governments fear criticism from the press, so they control or censor it. A cartoon such as this, criticizing government or a leader, would not be allowed to run in many countries.

Development of the First Amendment. In the early days of printing in Europe, both church and civil authorities granted licenses to certain guilds or companies to print books, but they also controlled what could be printed. As people began to be concerned about the importance of **freedom of speech** for developing more open societies, such control by licensing came under increasingly severe criticism from writers and philosophers. For example, in 1644 the essayist and poet John Milton wrote a critique of such censorship, called *Aeropagitica,* proclaiming the need for religious free speech.

Protecting Political Speech. Along with economic ideas about the value of a marketplace competition for goods, the idea developed of a **marketplace of ideas** in which different voices could compete for attention. In political terms, John Stuart Mill, Edmund Burke, and other early advocates of democracy promoted the idea of an active, informed citizenry. They pointed to the need for a **free press** to assist in the wide circulation of ideas (Altschull, 1984).

However, in many times and places, before the American Revolution and since, governments have directly censored and controlled media. Sometimes governments want to avoid, or **censor,** criticism. Sometimes they seize control of media to use them as tools in their own plans for development of a society. At a lower level of control, many governments have tried to restrain specific kinds of media content that they consider harmful, such as criticism of rulers. Even Great Britain, the source of many American political traditions, still has laws on the books that permit government to censor media content and require media to publish government statements or announcements.

Under British rule, the American colonies were moving toward protecting free speech and criticism of authority in the press. In the trial of Peter Zenger for libel against the British governor in 1733 (see Chapter 4), his lawyer successfully urged the jury not to rely on British precedents but to consider that the truth of an article was a sufficient defense against libel. Strong support for protecting freedom of speech and of the press continued to developed during the American Revolution against British colonial rule in 1776–1783. Independent newspapers and pamphlets encouraged the American colonists to resist British rule. Benjamin Franklin published pro-independence newspapers, and Thomas Paine wrote pamphlets, such as *Common Sense,* that were widely read. A free press was so important to the American Revolution that it was firmly enshrined in the Declaration of Independence and in the First Amendment to the U.S. Constitution. The First Amendment says

> Congress shall make no law respecting an establishment of religion, or prohibiting the free exercise thereof, or abridging the freedom of speech, or of the press; or the right of the people peaceably to assemble, and to petition the Government for a redress of grievances.

Freedom of speech protects speech and defines and sets limits on indecent or obscene speech.

Marketplace of ideas is the concept that, with free speech, the best ideas will win out in competition with others.

Free press is the extension of freedom of speech to media.

Censorship is control over media content by those in higher authority in a society.

Despite this initial strong stand for freedom of the press, a number of political thinkers in the late 1700s thought freedom should be limited by strong rules against libel and rules about saying things intended to help overthrow or subvert the government. There was a strong attempt to limit "seditious" speech under the 1798 Alien and Sedition Act. Several newspaper writers and editors were charged with sedition in 1798–1800 and were convicted, which, however, did not stop the opposition from winning the 1800 elections. Although the Sedition Law expired without being scrutinized by the Supreme Court, a consensus had grown that people were free to express their thoughts in print. Two other important precedents, that public officials were not protected by libel laws and that the truth of a statement was itself a defense, grew out of a 1804 libel suit against a newspaper by Thomas Jefferson (Blanchard, 1993), confirming the precedent of the Zenger trial.

MEDIA ETHICS

A Question of Ethics

If you plan to be a communications media professional, you may well have to address several kinds of ethical issues. Imagine what you might do in the following situations:

- You are a student reporter for a campus newspaper. One of your professors is on a confidential committee investigating possible financial abuses by the director of athletics. The professor has "leaked" some incriminating information to you, which you can't corroborate, on condition that you won't identify the source. Do you print the information? What do you say about your source?
- You are a student reporter for a radio station. Someone gives you some evidence from electronic mail indicating that a popular professor may be sexually harassing a graduate student. Do you read the mail? Do you write a story on it? Do you mention the professor's name? Do you indicate your source? (While this requires an ethical choice, it is also regulated by the Electronic Communication Privacy Act.)
- You are an aspiring young disk jockey for a local radio station. A record company offers you a block of tickets to a popular, sold-out concert if you will listen to some new recordings from the company label, hoping you will play them. Do you accept? Or does it seem like a conflict of interest? (You should be aware that this is illegal "payola.")
- You are a manager of a telemarketing operation to raise money for your university. You discover that you can use your computerized telephone system to monitor the number of calls per hour that your telemarketing agents are making. Do you use this information to make them work harder? Do you fire those who seem to be making fewer calls?

Limits on the First Amendment

Some kinds of speech are not protected by the First Amendment: defamation, obscenity, plagiarism, invasion of privacy, and inciting insurrection.

Defamation. Defamatory statements (**libel,** if it is written, or *slander,* if it is spoken) are untrue declarations about private citizens that might damage their reputations. Libel means that the information given is false or is intended to damage the reputation of the person being libeled. U.S. legal policy balances libel concerns against the *watchdog* role of the press, which is to expose corruption or incompetence by officials or public figures. In ethics, journalists often have to decide whether a certain kind of story about individuals, or certain treatment of individuals is ethical. For example, was it libelous for tabloid newspapers to speculate on who killed JonBenet Ramsey, especially when discussing specific figures like her parents?

Libel is published harmful or untruthful criticism that intends to damage someone.

Political Speech on the Airwaves and the Fairness Doctrine. Some nations give people who have been criticized a right of reply. That principle has seldom been applied to U.S. print media, because they are numerous and tend to balance each

COMMON SENSE:

ADDRESSED TO THE

INHABITANTS

OF

AMERICA,

On the following interesting

SUBJECTS.

I. Of the Origin and Design of Government in general, with concise Remarks on the English Constitution.

II. Of Monarchy and Hereditary Succession.

III. Thoughts on the present State of American Affairs.

IV. Of the present Ability of America, with some miscellaneous Reflections.

Written by an ENGLISHMAN.

By Thomas Paine

Man knows no Master save creating HEAVEN,
Or those whom choice and common good ordain.
THOMSON.

PHILADELPHIA, Printed
And Sold by R. BELL, in Third-Street, 1776.

COMMON SENSE AGAINST CENSORSHIP.
Publications such as Thomas Paine's challenged British censorship and promoted the American Revolution.

other's excesses. However, the Radio Act of 1927 assumed that the First Amendment goal of promoting a diversity of viewpoints needed regulatory help in the case of radio, where only a few could have direct access to the airwaves. The Act required equal opportunities:

> If any licensee shall permit any person who is a legally qualified candidate for any public office to use a broadcasting station, he shall afford equal opportunities to all other such candidates for that office in the use of such broadcasting station (Sect. 315, Radio Act of 1927).

This principle is still applied to political debates, where all major candidates must be allowed to participate. A far thornier issue has been political advertising, where differences between richer and poorer candidates, financial resources control access to the airwaves via paid political advertising. There, two principles have evolved. First, stations cannot refuse a candidate's advertising. Second, stations have to sell advertising time at their lowest rate to candidates. Congress and the FCC periodically debated requiring broadcast stations to give free time for political debate and candidates' political commercials.

The FCC also developed a concept known as the Fairness Doctrine. Its core idea was that the public has a right to be informed that overrides the right of broadcasters to carry their "own particular views on any matter" (Supreme Court decision in *Red Lion Broadcasting Co. v. FCC,* 395 U.S. 367, 1969). In theory, this concept requires stations to schedule time for controversial programming on issues and then to ensure the expression of opposing views. In practice, the FCC did not really require stations to carry issue-oriented programming, so the rule focused on the right of reply to controversial points of view. By the 1980s, some broadcasters were arguing that the right of reply in the Fairness Doctrine actually led stations to avoid controversial programming. Led by conservative appointees, both the FCC and the Supreme Court questioned the original argument that radio and television stations were so scarce that each of them had a unique responsibility to be fair and balanced. The FCC in 1985 therefore stopped enforcing the doctrine. Congress twice passed bills reinstating the Fairness Doctrine; both were vetoed by President Reagan.

Freedom of Speech; Sex and Obscenity. The First Amendment was originally framed to protect political speech, political criticism, and religious choice. However, the tradition of free speech has gradually been extended to moral issues of sexuality and obscenity. The idea of exercising moral judgment and control on content still has a strong influence in the United States. Although newspapers and newsmagazines have been largely free from censorship on political issues since 1800, books, magazines, radio, film, and television have been subject to content controls on sexuality and language. Novels such as D. H. Lawrence's *Lady Chatterley's Lover* (1928) were widely subjected to censorship in the United States as recently as the 1950s.

In a series of decisions, courts have ruled that moral standards for print and other media cannot be decided on a national basis, because those standards vary among communities. Communities are permitted to develop local standards for treatment of sexuality and *obscenity.* In 1957, in *Roth v. United States,* the U.S. Supreme Court defined obscenity in community-based terms: "whether, to the average person, applying contemporary community standards, the dominant theme of the material taken as a whole appeals to prurient interest." In *Miller v. California* (1973), the Court added that states might prohibit the printing or sale of works "which portray sexual conduct in a patently offensive way, and which, taken as a whole, do not have serious literary, artistic, political or scientific value." For example, some communities define certain books, magazines, and videos as pornographic and restrict their sales to "adult" bookstores.

The late twentieth century saw a sharp decline in the limits placed on **indecency,** which is usually defined somewhat more broadly than obscenity. This was seen as progress for freedom of speech. However, since the 1970s there has been increasing concern about obscenity again. For example, the FCC disciplined the Pacifica radio station in 1973 for broadcasting comedian George Carlin's monolog, "The Seven Dirty Words You Can't Say on Radio." It relied on a definition of indecency as "language that describes, in terms patently offensive as measured by contemporary community standards for the broadcast of the medium, sexual or excretory activities or organs," and its action was upheld by the Supreme Court in 1978 (Heins, 1993:26). (See the Media Impact box.)

Indecency is usually defined as depiction or description of sex or excretion in the media or the arts.

Free-Speech Limits on Broadcasting. The 1934 Communications Act applied the basic idea of protecting freedom of speech to broadcasting:

> Nothing in this Act shall be understood or construed to give the Commission the power of censorship over the radio communications or signals transmitted by any radio station, and no regulation or condition shall be promulgated or fixed by the Commission which shall interfere with the right of free speech by means of radio communication.

These protections of free speech were not changed by the 1996 Telecommunications Act, which notes that FCC authorities or limits not addressed by the 1996 Act are left in place.

However, broadcast media have been more regulated than print media. Access to the airwaves is much more limited than access to speaking, writing, or publishing (see the Media Impact box). By the 1980s, this distinction was reconsidered, as broadcast media became more plentiful.

As we saw in Chapter 5, obscenity and indecency are more limited on broadcasts because they come straight into the home over the airwaves. They are presumed to be more accessible to children, and accessing them does not require the same sort of conscious choice as picking up a book or magazine.

Since the 1978 *Pacifica* decision, there has been a tendency to limit indecency on radio during hours when children are likely to be listening and to create "safe havens" for absolutely free speech from midnight to 6 A.M. So far, the "safe haven" idea has not been applied to broadcast television, which remains more cautious about indecent programming. Cable television channels carry a number of programs that contain indecent material at hours when children are watching, but because cable does not use the public airwaves, it has not been subjected to the same scrutiny by the FCC.

Indecency and the Internet. A new challenge is posed by the Internet, which gives both adults and children potential access to indecent materials. Within the Telecom-

MEDIA IMPACT

George Carlin and "Seven Dirty Words"

The *Pacifica Foundation v. FCC* case (1978) defined a number of key issues relevant to obscenity and indecency. The case centered on whether the Pacifica radio station could play George Carlin's provocative 12-minute monolog about the "seven dirty words you can't say on radio."

The FCC argued that, judged by contemporary community standards, these words are offensive; that broadcasting is an intrusive medium; and that obscenity is separate from indecency. The FCC found that the rules are not overly broad but rather are intended to protect children from "exposure to language that describes, in terms patently offensive as measured by contemporary community standards for the broadcast medium, sexual or excretory activities and organs, at times of the day when there is a reasonable risk that children may be in the audience . . . language which most parents regard as inappropriate for them to hear." The FCC made a later clarification that media can use such words when children are in the audience when they have legitimate artistic, political, or social value (e.g., a Shakespeare play).

Pacifica argued that Sec. 1464 was vague and overboard, that obscenity and indecency are not equal, and that children are in the audience all the time. The Appeals Court agreed with Pacifica's points. It also noted that what is meant by "children" is not sufficiently defined; that one cannot easily discern the degree of legitimate, artistic, political, or social value; that broadcasters can't protect listeners from everything unpleasant; that there is no empirical evidence that filth would flood the air; and that if the majority of audience members disapprove, market forces will remove the station from competition.

The Supreme Court decided (in *FCC v. Pacifica Foundation,* 98 Supreme Court 326, 1978) that the FCC may sanction licensees who use indecent words because broadcasting is the least protected by First Amendment because it enters the privacy of people's homes and children have unusual access to broadcasting. The FCC can review programming after broadcast and can use that review when considering licensing. It noted that Section 1464 of U.S. Code lists "obscene, indecent, or profane" in disjunctive; thus indecency is different from obscenity. It argued that a nuisance "may be merely a right thing in the wrong place. . . ."

For Further Research:

WWW

This box is largely based on a summary of the case contained on a Web site at http://ballmer.uoregon.edu/robinson/j201/carlin.htm, developed by a student for a course where this text was used. If you want to find out more about current issues involving obscenity in the media, you can search the Web for sites like this one, or if you are using InfoTrac College Edition, use keywords such as "Indecency-Radio." A search on those terms found several articles, including one published on October 7, 1996, in *Broadcasting & Cable,* 126(42), 62: "Radio indecency complaints on front burner at FCC; Commission must deal with complaints against stations involved in pending broadcast-group mergers."

munications Act of 1996, the Communications Decency Act (CDA) created a more inclusive definition of objectionable materials under the term *indecency.* Its definition was problematic, however. For example, is the use of the word *breast* indecent in some contexts, like erotica, and not in others, like a discussion of cancer?

The CDA was promptly challenged in court by the American Civil Liberties Union (ACLU), the Electronic Frontier Foundation, and some of the industry actors, such as America Online, who might be held responsible for transmitting indecent material. They argued that the Internet deserves First Amendment protections as broad as those enjoyed by print, rather than the more limited protection given broadcasting. In particular, the restrictions were seen as limiting the free-speech rights of adults too much in an effort to protect children. The Supreme Court agreed and overturned key aspects of the CDA for overly limiting adults' freedom of speech and relying on a definition of indecency that was too vague. Members of Congress have subsequently tried to create more narrowly defined legal restrictions on indecent speech on the Internet aimed at children—restrictions that will not violate the rights of adults. However, another attempt, the Child Online Protection Act, was under review by the Supreme Court as of 1999.

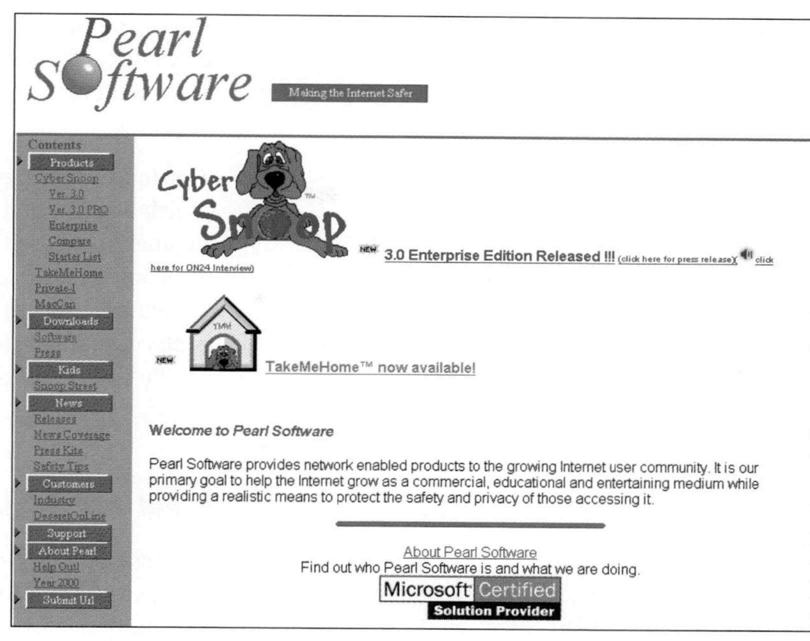

NET FILTER FOR SAFETY? Controversy rages about whether libraries should be allowed, or even required, to use Internet filter or guidance programs to protect children from pornography or other hazards.

The Internet presents new ethical and legal challenges to professionals in news, broadcasting, libraries, and information services about what kinds of materials to permit on interactive services. Some schools and libraries require use of computer filtering programs that screen sexual content on the Internet. Civil liberties groups criticize such programs as restricting the free speech of adults. The American Civil Liberties Union and others showed that breast cancer sites, for example, were often filtered out by such programs because they contained the word *breast,* which was one of the screening criteria. In a key 1998 decision, a District Court ruled against the filtering program in Loudoun County, Virginia. The court ruled that the library "misconstrued the nature of the Internet" and that "the Library Board may not adopt and enforce content-based restrictions on access to protected Internet speech" unless it meets the highest level of constitutional scrutiny (Clausing, April 9, 1998).

Regulation vs. Self-Regulation: TV Violence and the V-Chip. Another response to concerns about controversial content has been proposals for industry self-regulation. In 1993 the television industry proposed voluntary standards about labeling violent programming, but critics felt that simple labeling was not effective. This led Congress to add a provision in the 1996 Telecommunications Act, requiring a *V-chip* to permit television viewers to block out programs rated as containing sex or violence.

The bill represented an interesting combination of regulation and self-regulation, in that it required the industry to come up with a system for rating programs for violence, sex, and language. Film and television industry leaders reluctantly created a rating system in 1997, modeled on the age-based rating of films (see Chapter 6). Critics had hoped for a system that would have a separate rating for levels of sex, violence, and indecent language in each program. Thus the rating represented a compromise between what industry, Congress, and critics wanted.

Other examples of self-regulation include the Motion Picture Association of America's film rating system and the National Association of Broadcasters' self-regulation on the amount of commercial time to be included in various

1. What are the distinctions among policy, law, and ethics?
2. What is censorship?
3. What is the relationship between the marketplace of ideas and freedom of speech?
4. What is the First Amendment?
5. What is libel?
6. What is considered indecent in mass media content?

broadcasting hours. Debate continues on whether self-regulation of Web sites that collect personal information from visitors is adequate or whether federal regulation is required.

Freedom of Commercial Speech. Commercial speech is that which advertises a product or service for profit or for a business purpose. It is entitled to much less protection than noncommercial speech. Misleading commercial speech or commercial speech that proposes unlawful actions has no protection under the law. The Federal Trade Commission monitors **deceptive advertising** in both mass media and on-line media.

The Fourth Amendment and Privacy

Deceptive advertising is advertising that makes misleading or untruthful claims.

Privacy is the right to be protected from unwanted intrusions or disclosure.

Although most Americans assume that they have a right to **privacy,** this right is not so clearly established in law as freedom of speech. The first ten amendments to the U.S. Constitution focus on protecting people from invasions of their privacy by government. Supreme Court Justice Harlan in 1965 said that the constitutional right to privacy derives from the First, Third, Fourth, Fifth, Ninth, and Fourteenth Amendments, although it exceeds the sum of its parts (*Griswold v. Connecticut,* 381 U.S. 479, 499-500, 1965). This broad view of privacy remains controversial, however, and groups like the Electronic Privacy Information Center and the Electronic Freedom Forum have called for clearer, more specific laws to specify privacy rights.

The Fourth Amendment guarantees ". . . the right of the people to be secure in their persons, houses, papers, and effects, against unreasonable searches and seizures." It also states that "no (search) Warrants shall issue but upon probable cause . . . particularly describing the place to be searched, and the persons or things to be seized." On the other hand, people are routinely searched without warrants at airports, for tax information, and in other places by governments.

The right to privacy includes a generalized "right to be let alone," which includes "the individual interest in avoiding disclosure of personal matters." This line of thought forms the basis for many claims to a right to informational privacy (Chlapowski, 1991).

The current threats to privacy come not so much from government, as anticipated in the U.S. Bill of Rights, but from private companies that gather, collate, manipulate, and even sell information about individuals. The private sector intrusion grew with credit bureaus that gather credit information about individuals to sell to banks, loan agencies, and mortgage companies. Companies then began to track sales data about individuals to determine their buying habits and preferences. Magazines, catalogs, and firms that specialized in direct-mail sales also discovered that selling mailing lists of potential customers was a profitable business. Companies gathered and matched different lists or databases to accumulate more information about individuals. The whole process accelerated with the Internet, where many sites gather extensive information from their visitors, which can also be matched with other computer data. The recent controversial practice of coaxing personal or family data out of children before they can play games or get information from Web sites has been outlawed.

The accuracy of computer databases is also becoming a critical issue. Many people already suffer from the consequences of erroneous data in their credit information files. When they apply for a credit card or loan, they may be refused because someone with a similar name or social security number has not made payments.

The United States seems to be moving toward industry self-regulation on the protection of privacy. However, the on-line and consumer database industries have been slow to provide safeguards against encroachments on privacy. In 1998 Vice President Al Gore called for the establishment of an "electronic bill of rights" to prevent new information technology from invading privacy.

Another source of pressure on American industry to develop standards for protecting privacy is the European Union's Data Protection Directive, which became effective in 1998. These rules require that European citizens be told what their personal data will be used for. They have the right to access data about themselves in companies' files, the ability to correct false information, and the opportunity to opt out before personal data are transferred to a third party. Officials in European countries could impose embargoes against transfers of personal data about European citizens to countries, such as the United States, that have privacy protections they consider inadequate (Kaplan, 1998). This forced the United States to move more quickly on creating a privacy protection system that would satisfy European partners, so that electronic commerce would not be impeded.

Some of the movement on privacy issues came from the Federal Trade Commission (FTC), which inspired the passage of a 1998 Children's Online Privacy Protection Act that would require Web publishers to notify visitors about their collection of personal information and would restrict the gathering and use of personal information from children 12 and under. The FTC argued that the legislation was necessary because surveys of child-oriented Internet sites indicate that efforts by Internet companies to regulate themselves on privacy matters have not been adequate (Clausing, September 24, 1998).

The contents of mail and telephone conversations are legally protected. Government criminal investigators can

MEDIA IMPACT

Consumer Privacy Tips

- Periodically review your consumer credit files.
- If you dispute the information in your file, append your own explanation.
- If you want to have your name removed from telemarketing lists, contact the Direct Marketing Association.
- Avoid giving out your social security number except to your employer or government agencies.
- Do not write your telephone number on credit applications, on subscription forms, or even on the checks you cash.
- Assume that everything you say on a cordless or cellular phone can be overheard.
- Assume that all your e-mail from school or work accounts or computers is monitored by those institutions.
- Ask your phone company about Caller ID service.

1. What is the right to privacy?
2. What are the main legal sources of a right to privacy?
3. What challenges do new media present to privacy?

MEDIA IMPACT

Consumer Privacy Rights

A right to privacy has been articulated in a series of decisions by the federal courts and has been extended to information privacy by several pieces of legislation over the last 25 years. All consumers should be aware of their rights under these laws:

The right to inspect. Under the Fair Credit Reporting Act of 1970, consumers have the right to inspect the information contained in a credit agency's file.

The right to challenge. Consumers have the right to challenge the accuracy of the information and to append their own explanations.

The right to updates. Credit agencies must purge items that are more than 7 years old, including records of old arrests and lawsuits.

The right of control. Inquiries for purposes other than hiring, insurance investigations, or credit checks can be made only with the permission of the subject or under a court order. The Privacy Act of 1974 constrains federal agencies—though not state and local government or private companies—from transferring information without consent and from using information for purposes other than that for which it was originally collected.

The right to refuse. The Privacy Act of 1974 stipulates that citizens can refuse to disclose their social security number except where required by law. This limits the use of social security numbers to match data between sources.

The right to notification. The Right to Financial Privacy Act of 1979 requires that federal law enforcement agencies notify individuals when their financial records are subpoenaed. The Privacy Act of 1974 prohibits secret files and requires government agencies to publish descriptions of the files they keep and the types of information they contain each year.

The right to electronic privacy. A 1967 Supreme Court decision held telephone wiretaps unconstitutional, although Congress later legalized wiretaps conducted under court order. The Electronic Communication Privacy Act of 1986 extended this protection to electronic mail messages.

intercept conversations via wiretap, but only with a court warrant, as specified in the Fifth Amendment. The Electronic Communications Privacy Act of 1986 extended wiretap protections to electronic mail, teleconferences, and other new media. However, although e-mail from home computers and personal accounts is protected, e-mail from office or school computers or accounts may be monitored by employers or school officials.

Patent and Copyright Law: Protecting Intellectual Property

Intellectual property rights and the more specific area of copyrights present several policy and ethical problems. **Intellectual property** laws protect patents, copyrights, and trademarks. Copyrights grew out of the tradition of kings granting certain authors and printers the right to publish their works. Originally intended for taxation and control, these rights grew to focus on the authors. The Statute of Anne, passed in England in 1710, said that publishers should benefit from their published works. It also established the idea that such rights should have a limited duration, after which works should pass into the public domain, where all could use them.

Intellectual property is a work of art, writing, film, or software that is created or owned by an individual or company.

Article 1, Section 8 of the United States Constitution authorized a national copyright system to "promote the Progress of Science and useful Arts, by securing for limited Times to Authors . . . the exclusive Right to their . . . Writings." The United States (in 1790) and most developed countries established laws to protect authors' work. With the movement of books across borders, a need for international agreement on copyright became apparent, resulting in the Berne Convention in 1886.

The United States expanded the range of works covered by copyright in 1976 to include computer programs as well as more traditional literature, music, drama, pantomimes, choreography, pictures, graphics, sculptures, motion pictures, audiovisual works, and sound recordings. This list had been earlier expanded in copyright legislation in 1833, 1857, and 1909.

Copyright law tries to make sure that people who create an intellectual product receive the economic benefit from selling, leasing, renting, or licensing their invention, song, play, book, movie, software program, or other work. The premise of this law is that if people do not benefit from their own intellectual or artistic creations, others will not be motivated to create new material. This issue becomes particularly important as we move toward an information economy in which many people's livelihoods will depend directly on creating information.

Copyright is a legal privilege to use, sell, or license intellectual property, such as a book or film.

Policy makers must devise both legal and policy means to help protect intellectual property as technology and society change. For example, many new technologies (from tape recorders, photocopiers, and VCRs to the Internet and electronic mail) make it easier for people to copy books, articles, photographs, music, videos, and programs without paying anything to the creators or to those who have bought the distribution rights. One solution has been to make unauthorized copying a crime. Another has been to make copying technologically more difficult. Policy makers have also issued appeals to personal ethics—asking people not to defraud creators by not paying for use of their creations.

However, this need to protect copyright holders is only half the story. The other side is that users of creative works need reasonable access to them. This is the concept of **fair use.** This permits academic and other noncommercial users to make copies of parts of copyrighted works for personal use and also for purposes of analyzing them in classrooms, in academic publications, or in artistic works, so long as they are not being resold. Limits are imposed on how much of a copyrighted work can be reprinted or redisplayed without incurring the need to pay a license fee.

Fair use permits users to copy parts of copyrighted works for purposes of analyzing them in classrooms, in academic publications, or in artistic works, or personal use, so long as they are not being resold.

Another issue is when copyrights and other intellectual property protections should expire. In 1998, after intense lobbying by companies such as Disney, which was about to lose its copyright on Mickey Mouse, Congress passed the Sonny Bono Copyright Term Extension Act, which extended copyright protection up to the life of the author, plus 70 years.

Information, software, and entertainment products are among America's main exports to the rest of the world. It is particularly difficult to ensure that no one copies these products without paying for their use in international markets. Some countries have permitted practices that the United States considers illegal copying or piracy. Billions of dollars of potential sales have been lost to illegally copied music on CDs, movies on videotape, and computer software.

However, many countries have their own stake in protecting national revenues from intellectual property sales abroad, so international negotiations made much more progress in the late 1990s than in the 1980s. This is true in general trade organizations such as the World Trade Organization, and in more specialized forums, such as the World Intellectual Property Organization (WIPO). Two new WIPO agreements extend copyright protection into digital formats, particularly the Internet and digital storage of music and film. U.S. policymakers are concerned that these two treaties make copyright protection *too* strong, relative to fair use considerations.

1. What is intellectual property?
2. Why is it protected?
3. What challenges do digital media present to copyright law?
4. What are the international aspects of copyright law?

Ownership Issues

The Sherman Antitrust Act and Monopoly. One of the oldest regulatory traditions affecting current developments in the information society is the extent to which concentration of ownership is permitted. In the 1880s, companies in the oil, banking, and railroad industries formed what were called *trusts.* These were either **monopolies,** where a single company controlled an industry, as did the Standard Oil company, or **oligopolies,** where a few companies dominated an industry or a market, as did the railroads.

> **Monopoly** exists when a single firm dominates an industry.

> **Oligopoly** exists when a few firms dominate an industry.

> **Abuse of market power** is exploitation of a dominant or near-monopoly position in a market to keep potential competitors out.

> The **Sherman Antitrust Act of 1890** is the main U.S. law against monopolies or agreements to restrain or limit trade.

Monopoly permitted companies to charge higher prices than would prevail if they had competition. Within oligopolies, potential competitors sometimes agreed to "fix" prices above what they would be with real competition. Monopolists could also force suppliers and business partners to lower prices for parts and materials, because they were the only market for such suppliers. In addition, they used unfair tactics to drive out or keep out would-be competitors. For example, before 1913 the Bell telephone system would refuse to connect competing local telephone companies to long-distance service for local customers, often either forcing those companies into the Bell system or out of business. This kind of activity is an **abuse of market power.**

After widespread realization that monopolistic business practices were hurting public interests, legal and public opinion turned against monopoly and oligopoly. Congress passed the **Sherman Antitrust Act of 1890.** Since then, U.S. courts, charged with enforcing the antitrust laws, and the U.S. Department of Commerce,

MONOPOLY IS NO GAME.
This nineteenth-century cartoon about industry monopolists shows the kind of problem that antitrust laws were enacted to prevent.

charged with prohibiting **restraint of trade,** have both been suspicious of any monopoly.

Nevertheless, in some industries it seemed that competition did not make much sense. For many years, telecommunications seemed like a textbook case of a **natural monopoly**—a business that lends itself to domination by a single firm in each service area because of the immense costs of building an infrastructure, like telephone wires and switches, to supply the service. Telephone monopolies had to submit to rate regulation by state-level public utility commissions to prevent the abuse of their monopoly power (see Chapter 9).

Restraint of trade refers to practices by a company that limit other companies' ability to enter or compete in trade.

A **natural monopoly** is a business or service area that inherently lends itself to domination by a single firm.

Ownership and Diversity. One of the major goals of the Federal Communications Commission since it was established by the Communications Act of 1934 is to promote diversity of content among broadcasters. Due to major barriers to entry in limited frequencies and high costs, relatively few people can actually participate in the broadcast "marketplace of ideas." The FCC decided that it needed to actively promote diversity of content under these conditions.

One continuing issue is whether **diversity of ownership** is linked to **diversity of content.** At several points, policy makers have thought that ensuring diversity of ownership might help diversify content. U.S. policy once gave preference to minorities, local owners, and female applicants for broadcast station licenses in the hope that they would increase diversity and better serve their communities. These preferences were gradually eliminated in the 1980s and 1990s, and minority ownership of broadcast stations remains very low. Furthermore, recent industry consolidation into a few large ownership groups has resulted in many minority owners selling their stations to larger groups (Irving, 1998).

Diversity of ownership implies that media owners are of diverse ethnic backgrounds and gender.

Diversity of content implies a variety of ideas, cultural traditions, and values in media.

MINORITY MEDIA OWNERSHIP FALLING. Larry Irving, Assistant Secretary of Commerce for Communications and Information, has pointed out that minority ownership of media outlets is falling behind in the recent wave of mergers.

Concentration of Ownership

The economics of large-scale communications media industries create situations where the need for massive economies of scale tend to favor the dominance of relatively few firms, such as that of CBS, NBC, and ABC during the heyday of network TV in the 1950s–1970s. This creates oligopolies, where business competition is restricted to a few companies. These few media companies have had a much greater influence on society than would a larger, less concentrated group (Bagdikian, 1993).

Regulatory Implications of Vertical and Horizontal Integration. The concentration of ownership is also reflected in **vertical integration,** which exists when a company owns nearly all aspects of a single industry. For example, the federal government once prohibited the major television networks from producing or owning most of their own programming (Compaigne, 1982). The policy goal was to ensure that a number of production companies would compete with each other, thereby producing more diversity of content. This policy probably succeeded, but the networks complained that such rules, known as the Financial Interest and Syndication (of Fin-Syn) Rules, weakened them too much, particularly in their competition with cable TV (see Chapter 7), and the rules were relaxed in 1992.

Vertical integration concentrates ownership by acquiring companies that are in related businesses, such as program production and distribution.

Horizontal integration concentrates ownership by acquiring companies that are all in the same business, such as several radio stations.

Cross-ownership is ownership of different kinds of media in the same geographical area.

Another form of concentration is **horizontal integration,** in which a company owns many outlets of the same kind of medium. Previous U.S. policies had set first at 7, then at 12, the maximum number of radio or television stations that a single company could own. It was assumed that more diverse ownership—and preferably even more local ownership—would produce more diverse content. The 1996 Telecommunications Act eliminated that limit and raised the proportion of the nation that could be covered by a television network's own stations from 25 percent of homes to 35 percent. For radio, there are no national limits, and local ownership caps increase with market size (see Chapter 5). The 1996 act also deregulated telephone ownership structures to permit new combinations.

Another ownership question has to do with **cross-ownership:** Should a company be allowed to own various kinds of media? Traditionally, U.S. regulators did not allow a single entity to own radio, television, and newspaper media—and, more recently, cable TV and telephony—in the same area to prevent one company from controlling too much content and limiting diversity of ideas.

The 1996 Telecommunications Act largely deregulates vertical and horizontal integration and voids cross-ownership rules, except those preventing ownership of both local television stations and cable television systems. This permits integration of movie studios, broadcast networks, cable providers, and cable channels, for example. Companies have integrated very quickly since 1996, leading a few major firms, such as Disney/ABC, Fox, and Time Warner, to dominate film and television production, film distribution, network and cable TV distribution, and syndication (see Chapters 6 and 7). Some critics now call for police reassessment of the wisdom of unbridled vertical integration (McChesney, 1997). As Chapters 6 and 7 show, there is a rapid erasure of boundaries between film and television production, for example, which is placing more content decisions in fewer hands. Horizontal integration has also run rampant, particularly in the telecommunications industry.

In the past there was no apparent need to create policy about who owns newspapers. Competition between newspapers made government regulation unnecessary. Reduction of that competition makes regulation more likely. When the only two competing newspapers in a city, such as Detroit's *Free Press* and *News,* merge and issue combined editions, under what is called a *Joint Operating Agreement,* diversity of content may suffer (see Chapter 4). U.S. policy on joint operating agreements provides that they are subject to the U.S. Attorney General's Office, as to whether they violate antimonopoly laws.

1. What kinds of links might exist between forms of ownership and issues of media content?
2. What is concentration of ownership?
3. What are vertical and horizontal integration of ownership?
4. What is the Sherman Antitrust Act?
5. How did the 1996 Telecommunications Act affect ownership rules?

Access to Media and Universal Service

Modern societies are increasingly built on the promise that everyone has access to basic telecommunications services, such as the ability to call 911 from home in case of emergency. For most of the twentieth century, **universal service** meant trying to get a telephone into every home. Universal telephone service has largely been met—although many people in low-income and minority communities are still without service.

Universal service is the policy that all Americans should have access to basic telecommunication services.

Now regulators wonder whether plain old telephone service is enough or whether telephone companies should be required to make more advanced digital services, such as the Internet, universal. Given the convenience of using the Internet for mail, shopping, information gathering, and business, many assume that it will become virtually necessary to life in modern America. But only about half of Americans have access to the Internet whether at home, school, or work. That raises questions about whether everyone has equal access to information.

The 1996 Telecommunications Act confirmed that access to basic telephony should be universal, although it is proving difficult to maintain the subsidies even for universal basic phone service in an era of competition. But the FCC hesitated to set a goal of ensuring that all households have access to the Internet. The 1996 Act mandated a commission to make a proposal, which was to subsidize access to the Internet for schools and libraries, so the most people could have at least minimum access through those institutions. To this end, the FCC created a subsidy pool from telecommunications carriers, which could then be given to schools and libraries to make Internet access affordable, particularly in poorer or less advantaged areas. This subsidy was termed the "E-rate." A number of telecommunications companies, as well as fiscal conservatives in Congress, have objected to this kind of subsidy, arguing that the social benefits are not worth the cost. Initial plans for the subsidy were cut back after Congress reduced the funds to be made available and tried to use the funds as a means or lever to impose antipornography filtering. This forced schools and libraries to scale back plans for Internet access for their students and patrons.

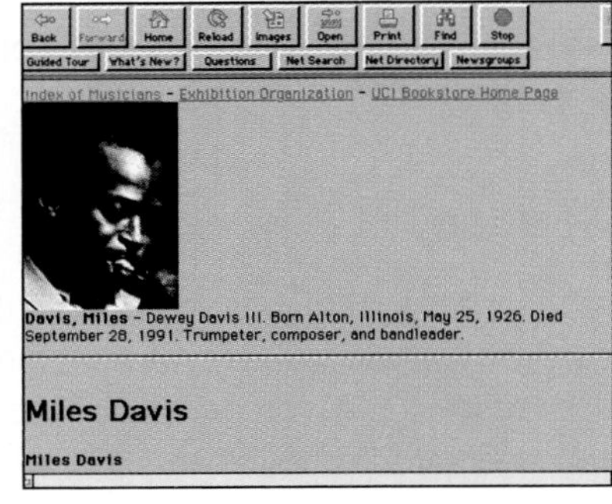

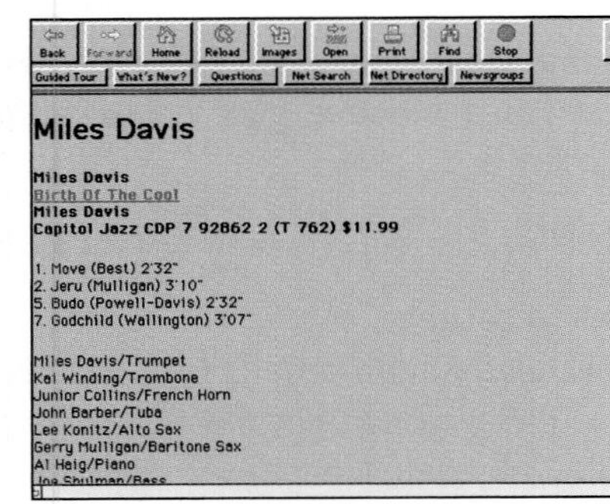

ACCESS FOR ALL?
Those who have access to the Internet can hook into all sorts of resources. Here, for example, are screens taken from the World Wide Web site of the University of California, Irvine. Here the user has accessed a multimedia "exhibit" on jazz.

Frequency allocation is granting the exclusive right to use a radio frequency in a specific area, usually done by government agencies.

License is a permission to operate a service on a specific radio frequency.

Public interest is usually defined for broadcasting in terms of the variety or diversity of programming and the amount of news and public affairs programs carried.

Localism is the practice of giving broadcast stations to all possible local areas and encouraging them to serve local interests.

The Radio Acts and Spectrum Management

One of the main reasons for regulation of broadcasting is the need to allocate the scarce supply of radio and television frequencies among the many competing companies and groups that would like to use them. The growing crowd of radio stations in the United States in the early 1920s soon required some government intervention to **allocate frequencies**—that is, to **license** broadcasting on specific channels (see Figure 5.2). In 1927 the Radio Act established the Federal Radio Commission to administer this process. The much more comprehensive Communications Act of 1934 established the Federal Communications Commission. It determined how close stations could be to each other geographically and still use the same or neighboring frequencies (see Chapters 5 and 7).

Because government regulators were now essentially deciding who got to broadcast, they also had to make rules for allocating and renewing licenses. The main criterion was the **public interest,** but that term was left for the FCC to define. In practice, the FCC tried to promote **localism** by giving stations to cities of a variety of sizes. The FCC later promoted diversity by giving preferential access to minority owners. After the initial rush of AM licenses in the 1920s and 1930s resulted almost entirely in commercial broadcast stations, which emphasized light entertainment, the FCC also began to reserve some licenses in FM and television specifically for noncommercial stations that emphasized education and culture.

After 1980, the conservative Reagan administration appointees to the FCC decided that there was no longer a scarcity of radio stations, given the proliferation of FM stations. They also saw television as competitive, because almost 60 percent of U.S. homes had multichannel cable TV to supplement or replace broadcast television stations (Fowler & Brenner, 1982). Therefore, the **scarcity argument** for regulation was diminished. Furthermore, the pro-business commissioners of the Reagan-era FCC did not think that their predecessors at the FCC had done a particularly good job of picking license applicants. They proposed a lottery to pick applicants at random—or an auction, to "sell" frequencies to the highest bidder. Auctions are increasingly used in two-way radio applications, such as cellular.

The **scarcity argument** maintains that careful government regulation is necessary to allocate and oversee the use of a limited number of frequencies.

The basic uses of radio spectrum frequencies are defined by the International Telecommunications Union (ITU). This body also allocates radio spectrum frequencies to countries, which their governments then allocate internally. Allocation issues are decided at the World Administrative Radio Congress (WARC), held every 4 years, and at regional conferences held in each of the ITU regions every 2 years. It is the WARC that decides, for example, which frequencies will be available for cellular radio service in various countries, which frequencies will be reserved for satellite communication, and how far apart the satellites must be. The regional conferences then deal with communications issues that crop up between neighboring countries.

1. **What is universal service? Why is it important?**
2. **What services need to be universal now? Why?**
3. **Why does the relative scarcity of radio spectrum frequencies require government regulation?**
4. **How has the scarcity argument changed, and how does that change the need for regulation?**
5. **What are the international aspects of frequency allocation?**

Defining Technical Standards for Media

Although issues of ownership and content are more dramatic, the main regulatory function of governments is often more technical. Newspapers can function without any technical regulation, but the situation is different for electronic media. Someone has to design the basic equipment standards for how a television image will be broadcast and received. Someone has to establish basic technical standards so that manufacturers, broadcasters, and audiences will know which channel to tune in to receive a particular station. The FCC works with private companies and with engineering-oriented standards organizations to work out the actual details. Private companies often develop standards for their own equipment, then compete to set the industry-wide standard, such as the 1990s race to set standards for digital television.

Agreement on basic technological standards is important. Standards signal manufacturers when to mass-produce a new technology. But when a technology continues to improve and evolve, when do we say the moment is right to set standards and make one for everyone to buy? In personal computers, for example, the standards have evolved as technology has changed. That is possible because people buy their own computer equipment and do not have to have strict compatibility with everyone else. However, even in computers, standardization is so desirable to users that Microsoft's Windows has become the *de facto* standard.

Standards Bodies. In the United States, telecommunications standards are set in a variety of ways. Some are set nationally, either by the FCC itself or by committees sponsored by the FCC. Some standards are created by industry associations or

HDTV DEBACLE.
Standards can determine the success of technology. The analog Japanese version of high-definition TV, shown here, was rendered obsolete by a U.S. decision to adopt a digital standard.

research groups and are subsequently ratified by the U.S. government. Some standards, like the DOS-Windows computer operating system of Microsoft, evolve from a single company. Sometimes the FCC forces industry to create a working group to resolve a conflict over standards. Examples include the National Television System Committee (NTSC), which set the current U.S. television standard in 1941, and the recent working group that tried to find a new digital high-definition television (HDTV) standard. In recent years, the United States has tended not to set standards for new technologies, but rather has let industry work them out. In some cases, such as cellular telephones and HDTV, this leads to conflicting technical standards. And this make choices confusing for both industry and consumers.

International Regulation and Standards. International regulatory bodies have strongly influenced standards in telecommunications because of the clear need for connections between countries in telephony, fax, and data. The International Telecommunications Union (ITU), first formed in 1865 to standardize telegraph traffic between countries, is the oldest international body in the world. Formed to create standards that would permit people to send a telegram from one country to another, it is now an affiliated agency of the United Nations. The ITU standards process involves negotiation and ratification of technical approaches to providing telecommunications services. Representatives from equipment manufacturers, telecommunications carriers, and national regulatory bodies confer within committees to define the standards.

1. **Why are technical standards important for media and telecommunications development?**
2. **What bodies regulate standards in the United States and internationally?**

THE POLICYMAKING PROCESS

Government policy is made by politicians elected to Congress or state legislatures, lawyers and judges appointed to various courts, and lawyers and economists appointed to regulatory agencies in the government. Corporations also make policy through their own decisions, such as how much advertising to carry, how much

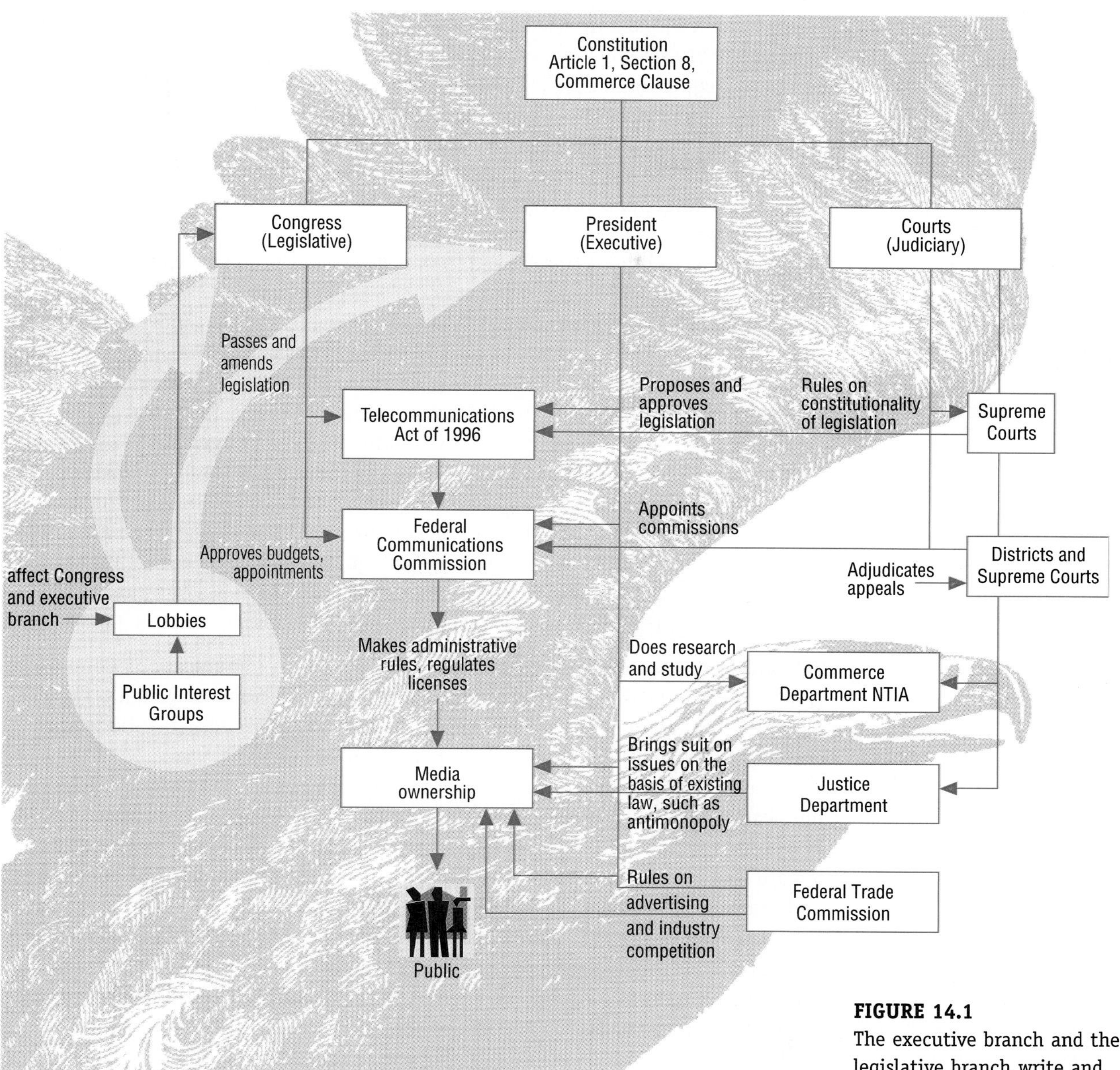

FIGURE 14.1
The executive branch and the legislative branch write and pass media laws such as the Telecommunications Act of 1996. If the laws are challenged, the courts then rule on their constitutionality.

sexual content to show, what kinds of services to offer, and how much to charge. Researchers and journalists may help set the agenda for regulation by bringing issues to the attention of government or corporate policy makers, witness the decades of research done on the effects of television violence on children.

Federal Regulation and Policymaking

All three branches of the federal government play an active role in communications regulation (see Figure 14.1). The fundamental bases for regulating media are laws proposed by the executive branch and Congress. The President works with key executive-branch regulatory agencies, such as the National

Telecommunications and Information Administration (NTIA), to propose legislation, nearly always in close consultation with the Congress. In fact, members of Congress frequently initiate legislation, as well. Congress then considers, alters, and passes the legislation—first in specialized committees, such as the House Telecommunications Subcommittee, and eventually by the full House of Representatives and Senate. Legislation can be modified at all stages. Lobbyists for industries and various public interests also try to affect legislation in favor of their clients at each step of the process. Finally, bills of proposed legislation are either defeated or passed by Congress and then sent to the President, who may either sign or veto them.

The executive branch implements the laws. Cabinet departments monitor industry compliance. For example, the Justice Department examines whether companies are violating the Sherman Antitrust Act. If so, then the department brings a suit against the offender, such as the 1998 suit against Microsoft, in federal courts. Other laws are implemented by executive-branch regulatory agencies, such as the Federal Communications Commission (FCC) and the Federal Trade Commission (FTC). Because actions of the FCC or FTC are taken to federal district courts under the Telecommunications Act of 1996, these courts are often the key media-related element in the judicial branch. Ultimately though, the Supreme Court often hears cases that are appealed from lower courts, especially if there is a question as to whether the law that is being applied violates any principles of the U.S. Constitution.

The Federal Communications Commission. The Federal Communications Commission (FCC) regulates broadcasting, satellite/cable TV, and telecommunications. The FCC Mass Media Bureau oversees licensing and operation of broadcast stations and enforces the regulations imposed on cable TV by Congress.

Market entry rules govern the entry by a new industry or company into a regulated market from which it had previously been excluded.

The FCC's Common Carrier Bureau has primary responsibility for the telecommunications (i.e., telephone) industry. With the 1996 Telecommunications Act, the FCC shifted its focus from direct regulation of telecommunications service prices toward less direct oversight of competition among telecommunications companies and **market entry rules.**

Regional Bell operating companies, or **RBOCs**, are the local telephone companies created by the breakup of AT&T in 1984.

Increasingly, the FCC shares jurisdiction over key issues such as antitrust and monopoly with the Justice Department and Federal Trade Commission. Concerning local telecommunications carriers, such as the **regional Bell operating companies (RBOCs)**, or Baby Bells, the FCC shares jurisdiction with their respective state public utility commissions (PUCs). Cable television regulation is also shared between the FCC and local or state level cable commissions.

Capture theory suggests that regulators are often effectively dominated by the interests of the industry they regulate.

One problem with the FCC and other regulatory agencies is that they may end up attuned more closely to the interests of the industry than to the interests of the public. Critics say that regulators are often effectively *captured* by the industry they regulate—a concept referred to as **capture theory.**

Department of Commerce. The National Telecommunications and Information Administration (NTIA) was established within the Department of Commerce in 1978 to advise on telecommunications policy. In recent years the NTIA helped represent the United States in international bodies, such as the International Telecommunications Union, that set international telecommunications trade policies and make satellite orbit and communication frequency allocations.

Along with the Office of the United States Trade Representative, NTIA has been active in **multilateral trade negotiations.** These include the North American Free Trade Agreement (NAFTA) and the World Trade Organization (WTO). NTIA also negotiates issues such as the settlements of revenues from international phone calls.

Multilateral trade negotiations take place among a number of countries at the same time, usually within an international organization.

Another branch of the Commerce Department, the U.S. Patent and Trademark Office, and the United States Copyright Office of the U.S. Library of Congress are also involved with the World Intellectual Property Organization in addressing international copyright issues in communications media.

The Federal Trade Commission (FTC). The FTC is the regulatory agency charged with domestic trade policy. It is responsible for monitoring trade practices such as advertising. It has held hearings on advertising practices aimed at children. It also investigates companies' actions in restraint of trade. In 1989 it began an investigation of possible **anticompetitive practices** in computer operating systems and programs by Microsoft, Inc.; the investigation was picked up by the Justice Department in 1994.

Anticompetitive practices are those that unfairly use market power to damage potential competitors.

The Justice Department. The Justice Department also plays an important role in the enforcement of general laws that also apply to communications. To enforce the Sherman Antitrust Act, the Justice Department initiated the suit that eventually broke up AT&T, and it is investigating Microsoft. In accordance with the 1996 Telecommunications Act, the Justice Department shares jurisdiction on monopoly issues with the FCC. It monitors competitiveness in important sectors of the information economy, such as monopoly practices in the computer industry, and competition in local TV and radio markets.

The Courts. The judiciary interprets laws made by Congress and rules made by the FCC and other federal agencies to see whether they are consistent with the U.S. Constitution. The Supreme Court and federal district courts are both important in decisions such as freedom-of-speech issues based on the First Amendment, privacy issues based on several amendments, and monopoly issues based on the Sherman Antitrust Act. The Supreme Court is also the ultimate court of appeal for decision by lower courts, so it usually ends up reviewing decisions made in major cases such as the Communications Decency Act. Courts also often interpret and enforce legal decisions. For example, the Third District Court of the District of Columbia supervised the break up of the old Bell system in 1984.

The Congress. It is the U.S. Congress that ultimately writes and rewrites the communications laws of the land. After years of debate, Congress finally replaced the 1934 Communications Act in 1996, because so many crucial issues required substantial definition or redefinition in law, not just regulatory decree or

OPENING NEW MARKETS. The NTIA is trying to get U.S. telecommunications companies into countries such as Japan where there is an imbalance in trade.

judicial interpretation. In 1996, those issues included competition within and across media and telecommunications industries, ownership restrictions, and regulation of violent and sexual content on TV.

Many congressional committees are involved in communications issues. For the 1996 Telecommunications Act, for example, much of the crucial debate and lobbying took place in the House Telecommunications Subcommittee, which shaped the basic provisions that went before the full House of Representatives.

State and Local Regulation

States and municipalities are increasingly involved in the regulation of telecommunication. They have been less involved in mass media, except in cable TV, but that seems to changing as telecommunications and media firms merge and compete.

Public utilities are closely regulated government or private companies, usually monopolies, that provide public services.

For many years, state-level **public utility** commissions regulated local and regional telephone companies' rates. The state regulators promoted the widest possible availability of telephone service at the lowest possible cost. The phone companies they regulate, such as Ameritech, are entering into cable TV, which municipalities usually regulate, and cable TV companies and others are offering local telephone services, which the states regulate.

Deregulation refers to decreasing government oversight in the anticipation that competition will minimize abuses of power.

However, a number of states have drastically reduced their levels of regulatory oversight, becoming laboratories for experiments in deregulation. Some have **deregulated** telecommunications almost entirely by removing most of the restrictions on the nature and scope of activities that such companies engage in and the prices they charge. Nevertheless, after observing considerable price increases for local service, some states, such as Texas, are considering regulating local telephone companies' prices again. One area states and localities are not involved in is regulation of the Internet. Congress has placed a moratorium on local regulation—and taxation—of the Internet in hopes of fostering the growth of the new medium.

Lobbies

Industry and public interest groups lobby to influence proposed legislation in the executive branch and in Congress. Lobbies also try to affect how laws and rules are interpreted and enforced once they are made. For example, since passage of the 1996 Act, telephone companies have lobbied Congress and the President to obtain a less stringent interpretation of the law by the FCC.

Increasingly, telecommunications policy issues cut across industry boundaries, so the powerful lobbies of the publishing and motion picture industries also get involved. These groups not only lobby directly about the substance of legislation and enforcement of laws; they also reinforce their arguments with campaign contributions, and form political action committees (PACs) to lobby and to run advertisements for candidates. Sometimes they even give favorable publicity, travel junkets, or financial deals to politicians in exchange for preferential treatment. For example, "Shortly after Murdoch's HarperCollins publishing company offered House Speaker Newt Gingrich the controversial $4.5 million book deal, Murdoch asked for and got closed door meetings with House Republicans and Pressler's Commerce Committee staff" (Sadler, 1995). The strategy can also backfire. Gingrich later had to give the advance back amid a barrage of negative publicity.

Accuracy of information refers to the media representative's responsibility to ensure that media or information content is truthful, correct, and not deceptive.

Other lobby groups serve the public interest. The American Association of Retired Persons (AARP) and the National Association for the Advancement of Colored People (NAACP) lobby to preserve universal, low-cost "lifeline" local telephone service for older Americans. Meanwhile, telecommunications companies lobbied to reduce or lower their obligation to subsidize universal service. Competing special interests and public interests make it difficult to pass legislation. For example, some public interest groups continue to press for restrictions on television violence, which are resisted strenuously by the National Association of Broadcasters (NAB) and the Motion Picture Association of America (MPAA), whose members produce most television programming.

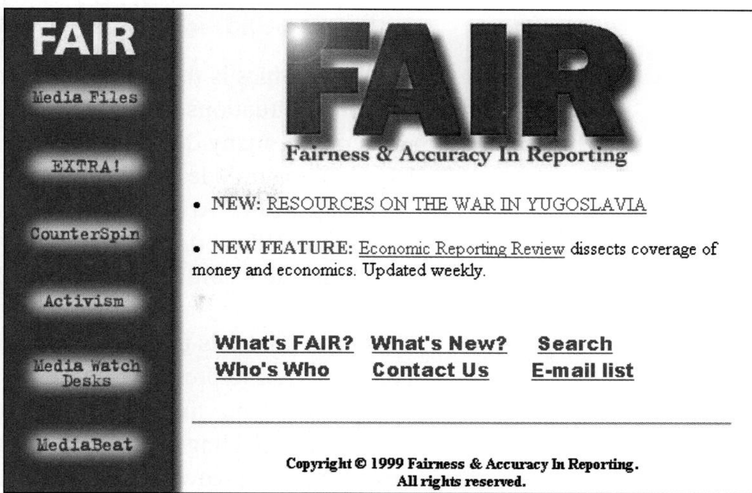

WATCHING THE WATCHDOG PRESS.
Fairness and Accuracy in Reporting tracks what it considers conservative bias in media coverage. Accuracy in Media keeps a similarly watchful eye out for liberal bias.

The Fifth Estate: The Media in the Policy Process

The mass media act as lobbyists for their own interests, either directly in their own channels or through associations such as the NAB and the MPAA. However, media also have a much broader role as the forum in which much of the policy debate takes place.

The news media pursue the goal of reporting such controversies and issues objectively, but they sometimes have a position or agenda of their own. For example, do news media tend to have a generally liberal or generally conservative bias and are they biased for or against specific groups, such as business or the military? Observers disagree. For example, the group Fairness and Accuracy in Reporting [http://www.fair.org/] tracks what it considers conservative bias in media coverage, whereas Accuracy in Media [http://www.aim.org/] tracks perceived liberal bias.

1. How are media laws made and implemented?
2. What are the main institutions in the executive branch that participate in the media policymaking process?
3. What is the role of the courts in media regulation?
4. What is public utility regulation?
5. What is a lobby group? What lobby groups are active in communications media issues?
6. What is the capture theory of regulation?

ETHICS IN THE COMMUNICATIONS MEDIA

Earlier we distinguished policy, law, and regulation, which are public or collective decisions, from ethics, which guide one's personal and professional decisions.

The main ethical issues in communications media revolve around **accuracy** or truthfulness, **fairness** and responsibility of treatment, and privacy for media subjects. Laws, of course, affect many of these areas. Here, however, we consider the ethical dimensions.

Fairness in journalism ethics refers to the media representative's responsibility to select and treat topics and sources ethically.

General Considerations in Individual Ethics

A code of ethics is the moral rules, or rules of conduct, that guide personal actions in specific situations. Although there are ethical guidelines specific to communications media, many decisions are based on people's underlying religious, philosophical, and cultural ideas. The classic principles that people have used in ethical decisions include Aristotle's golden mean, Kant's categorical imperative, situation ethics, and Mill's principle of utility.

Aristotle's golden mean holds that "moral virtue is appropriate location between two extremes."

Aristotle's golden mean holds that "moral virtue is appropriate location between two extremes." Moderation and balance are the key points (Merrill, 1997). This principle leads to media giving balanced points of view or including various points of view to provide balance. Similarly, in making decisions, media organizations may balance the interests of getting a good story against the argument in favor of withholding details in order to safeguard the public interest. For example, news media that cover natural disasters may voluntarily omit details that might panic the public and lead to greater harm.

Kant's categorical imperative says we should act according to rules that we would like to see universally applied.

Immanuel Kant's **categorical imperative** holds that you should "act on that maxim which you will [wish] to become a universal law." That is, act according to rules that you would like to see universally applied (Day, 1991). The idea is that what is good for one person or situation should be good for all, but the categorical imperative also stresses that individuals act according to their own conscience. For example, reporters who would like all other reporters to avoid deception about news sources should avoid such deception themselves.

Situation ethics holds that moral ideas and judgments must be made relative to the situation at hand.

Situation ethics is a more recently evolved idea that conflicts with Kant's categorical imperative and similar universal principles. According to this approach, moral principles are not absolute but relative to the situation at hand. Individuals may trust their intuitive sense of what is right. Situation ethics thus allows specific rules to be broken if the overall purpose is good (Day, 1991). For instance, using illegal, hidden recording devices to document lawbreaking or dangerous practices for a news story might be considered acceptable in this point of view, even though principles and law may both be violated, if revealing the story will serve the public interest. However, most would agree that reporters should not break the law.

Mill's principle of utility holds that we should "seek the greatest happiness for the greatest number."

John Stuart Mill's **principle of utility** holds that we should "seek the greatest happiness for the greatest number." Mill was concerned about what would bring the greatest good for society, which he defined as benefiting the largest number of people (Christians, et al., 1991). People who consider themselves utilitarians look at the consequences of possible actions, consider potential benefits and harms, determine which action would benefit the most people (or harm the fewest), and choose that. As with situation ethics, a reporter could conclude that illegally gathering important information would benefit more people than it would harm.

Codes of Ethics

Rather than relying on abstract basic principles such as "the golden mean," some have tried to come up with more specific sets of guidelines to help individual communicators make ethical decisions. The recommendations of the 1947 Hutchins Commission on social responsibility in the media and the Society of Professional Journalists' Code of Ethics have been quite influential among journalists and broadcasters.

The Hutchins Commission's guidelines were fairly general (see the Media Impact box). The Society of Professional Journalists' Code of Ethics, the current version of which was adopted in 1996, is much more detailed and specific. It attempts to anticipate far more specific situations and to offer journalists guidance on how to deal with them (see the second Media Impact box). If all journalists followed its guidelines, a number of recent ethical missteps would have been avoided. For example, the Code says, "Avoid misleading re-enactments or staged news events. If re-enactment is necessary to tell a story, label it." If television journalists for NBC had followed those guidelines, they could have avoided a famous mistake in 1993, when NBC News staged footage of a GM pickup truck exploding upon collision with another vehicle because they couldn't get the explosion to happen naturally. They compounded the mistake by not initially revealing that the footage was a re-enactment.

MEDIA IMPACT

Social Responsibility and Ethics

Throughout the 1930s and 1940s, critics feared the power of the media, particularly because a few major film studios and radio networks dominated national media and one or two newspapers dominated most cities. Given this concentration of power, study groups such as the Hutchins Commission felt that those within such media had a particular responsibility to society to report in a careful and balanced manner. The Hutchins report in 1947 articulated, for the press, a code of social responsibility with five basic goals:

1. a truthful, comprehensive, and intelligent account of the day's events in a context which gives them meaning;
2. a forum for the exchange of comment and criticism;
3. the projection of a representative picture of the constituent groups in the society;
4. the presentation and clarification of the goals and values of the society;
5. full access to the day's intelligence.

(Blanchard, 1977)

Ethical Issues for Media Professionals

Accuracy of Information. The question of accuracy comes up both in mass media and in new information services. What rules should exist about ensuring the accuracy of information in either a news story or a Web site? Do we need different rules or ethical principles for the two?

In news media, prevailing journalistic ethical principles about the accuracy of information are quite strict. Journalists are not to fabricate evidence, make up quotes, create hypothetical individuals to focus stories around, or create or manipulate misleading photographs. In 1998, two *Boston Globe* columnists, Patricia Smith and Mike Barnicle, fabricated characters and quotes. They were disciplined, but the stories shook journalistic credibility. *National Geographic* was heavily criticized for an even smaller distortion when it used comptuer image-manipulation techniques to move one Egyptian pyramid closer to another to make a more compact cover illustration.

New technologies such as the Internet make it possible for more and more kinds of people to disseminate their own ideas and reporting of events directly to massive audiences. For example, the Drudge Report of entertainment-industry and

MEDIA ETHICS

Society of Professional Journalists' Code of Ethics

Seek Truth and Report It

Journalists should be honest, fair and courageous in gathering, reporting and interpreting information. Journalists should:

Test the accuracy of information from all sources and exercise care to avoid inadvertent error. Deliberate distortion is never permissible.

Diligently seek out subjects of news stories to give them the opportunity to respond to allegations of wrongdoing.

Identify sources whenever feasible. The public is entitled to as much information as possible on sources' reliability.

Always question sources' motives before promising anonymity. Clarify conditions attached to any promise made in exchange for information. Keep promises.

Make certain that headlines, news teases and promotional material, photos, video, audio, graphics, sound bites and quotations do not misrepresent. They should not oversimplify or highlight incidents out of context.

Never distort the content of news photos or video. Image enhancement for technical clarity is always permissible. Label montages and photo illustrations.

Avoid misleading re-enactments or staged news events. If re-enactment is necessary to tell a story, label it.

Avoid undercover or other surreptitious methods of gathering information except when traditional open methods will not yield information vital to the public. Use of such methods should be explained as part of the story.

Never plagiarize.

Tell the story of the diversity and magnitude of the human experience boldly, even when it is unpopular to do so.

Examine their own cultural values and avoid imposing those values on others.

Avoid stereotyping by race, gender, age, religion, ethnicity, geography, sexual orientation, disability, physical appearance or social status.

Support the open exchange of views, even views they find repugnant.

Give voice to the voiceless; official and unofficial sources of information can be equally valid.

Distinguish between advocacy and news reporting. Analysis and commentary should be labeled and not misrepresent fact or context.

Distinguish news from advertising and shun hybrids that blur the lines between the two.

Recognize a special obligation to ensure that the public's business is conducted in the open and that government records are open to inspection.

Source: sss.spj.org/ethics/code

political gossip by independent "columnist" Matt Drudge is released on e-mail lists and a Web site to thousands, sometimes millions, of people. These new "journalists" or communicators don't necessarily follow the same ethical rules as more conventional journalists who work for organizations that encourage following the rules. Internet columnist Drudge, for example, routinely violates the norms of professional journalism, which he considers not a profession but a simple reporting function that anyone can perform who is determined to seek the truth and has a means to publish it such as the Internet (McClintick, 1998). Drudge was the first to release the story about President Clinton's affair with Monica Lewinsky, but a *Brill's Content* review of the 51 stories that Drudge called "exclusive" between January and September 1998 found that at least ten were inaccurately reported or never happened (McClintick, 1998, p. 114).

MEDIA ETHICS

Continued from previous page

Minimize Harm

Ethical journalists treat sources, subjects and colleagues as human beings deserving of respect. Journalists should:

Show compassion for those who may be affected adversely by news coverage. Use special sensitivity when dealing with children and inexperienced sources or subjects.

Be sensitive when seeking or using interviews or photographs of those affected by tragedy or grief.

Recognize that gathering and reporting information may cause harm or discomfort. Pursuit of the news is not a license for arrogance.

Recognize that private people have a greater right to control information about themselves than do public officials and others who seek power, influence or attention. Only an overriding public need can justify intrusion into anyone's privacy.

Show good taste. Avoid pandering to lurid curiosity.

Be cautious about identifying juvenile suspects or victims of sex crimes.

Be judicious about naming criminal suspects before the formal filing of charges.

Balance a criminal suspect's fair trial rights with the public's right to be informed.

Act Independently

Journalists should be free of obligation to any interest other than the public's right to know. Journalists should:

Avoid conflicts of interest, real or perceived.

Remain free of associations and activities that may compromise integrity or damage credibility.

Refuse gifts, favors, fees, free travel and special treatment, and shun secondary employment, political involvement, public office and service in community organizations if they compromise journalistic integrity.

Disclose unavoidable conflicts.

Be vigilant and courageous about holding those with power accountable.

Deny favored treatment to advertisers and special interests and resist their pressure to influence news coverage.

Be wary of sources offering information for favors or money; avoid bidding for news.

Be Accountable

Journalists are accountable to their readers, listeners, viewers and each other. Journalists should:

Clarify and explain news coverage and invite dialogue with the public over journalistic conduct.

Encourage the public to voice grievances against the news media.

Admit mistakes and correct them promptly.

Expose unethical practices of journalists and the news media.

Abide by the same high standards to which they hold others.

Fairness or Responsibility. Journalists and editors constantly make choices about what to cover, as do writers, television and film directors, and even programmers and information service designers and operators. Media people can advance certain companies, people, and causes over others by the decisions they make on whom and what to cover. Ethical issues include favoritism, partisanship, and possibly corruption, bribery, or accepting favors. Should programmers publicize the cause of someone they know or a cause they agree with? Should a reporter who accepts a trip to see a company's new product feel obliged to write about it or write favorably about it (Black, Steele & Barney, 1998)?

A key ethical issue for news reporters and writers is the need to protect the **confidentiality** of their sources. Reporters frequently use as sources people who might be indicted for criminal activity. If a reporter is doing a story on the drug

Confidentiality usually refers to protecting the identity of news sources.

DON'T BE A DRUDGE. Matt Drudge made headlines and gained millions of readers by breaking stories like that of Monica Lewinsky's relationship with President Clinton, but watchdog magazines such as *Brill's Content* questioned his accuracy.

trade, she will end up talking to drug dealers. Because the knowledge the reporter gains from her sources could help convict them, law enforcement officials sometimes try to get evidence from reporters. However, this is one ethical issue on which there is fairly widespread agreement among reporters. The reporter has promised either implicitly or explicitly to keep secret the source's identity and any of the details that could incriminate the source. Reporters take this stance partly for ethical reasons and partly because they could not get information from sources in the future if they could not give a credible promise of confidentiality (Meyer, 1987).

Source attribution refers to methods used to cite sources in a way that reflects their credibility without revealing their identity.

Related to confidentiality and protection of sources is the question of **source attribution**—how to cite sources without revealing their identity. The reporter wants to reveal as much as possible about the competence and position of his or her source in order to bolster the credibility of the quote or the information attributed to the source—and thus that of the whole story. On the other hand, many sources will talk only if they cannot be identified from what is said about them in the story. This issue becomes more complex when the source is a well-known public figure who wants to "**leak**" an idea or a possible policy on which he or she is not yet ready to be quoted. Presidential advisers are constantly leaking ideas about what the President might do about a certain problem; such leaks have become a means of trying out tentative ideas—trial balloons (Merrill, 1998). In 1998, independent counsel Ken Starr's staff, which was investigating President Clinton, was accused of orchestrating leaks to the press that were inappropriate or illegal, including legally sealed grand jury testimony.

Leaks are the release, by officials, of confidential information—often policy ideas or facts about which they do not wish to be quoted.

Several fairly complex methods for describing the general position of a source have been developed—ways to indicate enough of the source's expertise to lend credibility to the story without revealing enough to enable the person to be identified. One of the more famous examples, during the 1972 Watergate investigations that led to the resignation of President Richard Nixon, was a "highly placed official," perhaps a "cabinet-level source," who leaked incriminating details under the code name of Deep Throat. The source would not give information so specific that it revealed his or her identity and the reporters steadfastly protected their source.

WHAT RIGHT TO PRIVACY? Linda Tripp made headlines with her tapes of her initially illegally taped phone conversations with Monica Lewinsky.

Privacy. A more complex ethical dilemma for reporters is respecting the privacy both of potential sources and of people who are subjects of news investigations and reports. Source privacy is largely covered under confidentiality of sources. However, many reporters are little concerned about the privacy of those they are covering. In fact, they have a natural desire to expose and describe the topic of the story. As with sources, it adds legitimacy to a story to provide more details about the people involved.

Some computer-based information might provide input to news stories or media productions. Celebrity gossip reporters could certainly learn a lot by listening to media stars' phone conversations or reading their mail. In 1997–1998, during the investigation of President Clinton's affair with Monica Lewinsky, her supposed confidante Linda Tripp began recording telephone conversations with Lewinsky, first on her own and then at the request of FBI investigators. Tripp's initial recordings of their phone conversations probably violated Lewinsky's right to privacy, but federal investigators with a warrant could then legitimately ask Tripp to keep taping the phone calls. Those tapes were later legally subpoenaed for Ken Starr's investigation. But "reporter" Matt Drudge was certainly on shaky ethical grounds in reporting the contents of illegally taped conversations.

The law on privacy of telephone conversations is clearer than the rules for newer media. As new media develop, are their contents to be considered private, even from reporters? The contents of mail and telephone conversations are now legally protected. Electronic mail, teleconferences, and other new media are now protected under the Electronic Communications Privacy Act of 1986, but clarification of the provisions of that Act seem to be required. In the meantime, reporters, on-line database operators, and Web site designers need to be very careful about both legal and ethical considerations in privacy for the new media.

1. What are the main areas of concern in media ethics?
2. What are some of the classic ethical principles that people apply to issues that arise in media ethics?
3. What is the Society for Professional Journalists' Code of Ethics, and how might it be useful?

SUMMARY AND REVIEW

WHAT ARE THE DISTINCTIONS, IN THE CONTEXT OF THE COMMUNICATIONS MEDIA, AMONG POLICY, LAW, AND ETHICS?

Policy is government and public consideration of how to structure and regulate media so that they contribute to the public good. Public policy involves a collective action of the whole society or its representatives. Laws passed by Congress and enforced by the courts cover some, but not all, of the policy and ethical issues in media. Ethics guide communicators in how to behave in situations where their activities may have a negative impact on others.

WHAT IS THE RELATIONSHIP BETWEEN THE MARKETPLACE OF IDEAS AND FREEDOM OF SPEECH?

The marketplace of ideas reflects the concept that, with free speech, the best ideas will win out in any competition with others. The concept of a free press is the extension of freedom of speech to media.

WHAT IS THE FIRST AMENDMENT?

The First Amendment to the U.S. Constitution says, "Congress shall make no law respecting an establishment of religion, or prohibiting the free exercise thereof, or abridging the freedom of speech, or of the press . . . ." The kinds of speech not protected by the First Amendment are libel, defamation, indecency, plagiarism, invasion of privacy, and inciting insurrection.

WHAT IS LIBEL?

Libel is harmful and untruthful written remarks that damage someone's reputation or good name. To be legally liable, the person or organization accused of libel must be shown to have known that the information was false and that its use was intended to damage the reputation of the person being libeled.

HOW ARE MEDIA AND TELECOMMUNICATIONS STANDARDS SET?

Companies often develop standards for their own equipment and compete to set the industry-wide standard. Industry committees sometimes set collective standards, often when spurred or required by government bodies such as the FCC. Internationally, most standards are set or endorsed by the International Telecommunications Union (ITU).

WHAT IS THE PRIMARY LAW REGULATING ELECTRONIC MEDIA?

The Communications Act of 1934 established the FCC, regulated broadcasting by regulating scarce frequencies, and regulated the monopolies of AT&T and, later, the regional Baby Bells. The 1996 Telecommunications Act encouraged competition between industries such as cable TV and telephony. It relaxed rules on how many stations a group could own and on cross-ownership of broadcasting, cable TV, telephone companies, and movie studios. It deregulated telephony ownership structures, areas of activity, and prices but tried to maintain universal service. The act also proposed restrictions on Internet pornography—since struck down by the Supreme Court—and mandated television content ratings linked to a "V-chip" that could be programmed to block selected signals.

WHAT ASPECTS OF PRIVACY ARE IMPORTANT TO MEDIA?

Reporters must make decisions about when to disturb the privacy of individuals. Even more important in the 1990s, many people are concerned about privacy or control of personal individual information held in consumer credit databases and gathered on the Internet. No overall laws have yet been written on privacy rights, although use of data by government and the interception of messages are controlled by law.

WHAT KINDS OF LINKS MIGHT EXIST BETWEEN FORMS OF OWNERSHIP AND MEDIA CONTENT ISSUES?

Some owners may try to influence content to promote their own ideas and interests. If owners are too much alike, they may not produce diverse content, whereas a greater diversity of ownership may produce more diverse content.

WHAT MAKES FOR A NATURAL MONOPOLY IN MEDIA OR TELECOMMUNICATIONS?

An industry is considered a natural monopoly when competition would not be economically feasible. This is particularly true when the infrastructure for supplying the service is extensive and costly, such as local telephone networks.

WHAT IS THE CAPTURE THEORY OF REGULATION?

Capture theory implies that regulators are often effectively captured by the interests of the industry they regulate. They become dependent on the industry for information, they sometimes work in it before or after government service, and they frequently come to identify with industry players and their goals.

WHY DOES THE RELATIVE SCARCITY OF RADIO SPECTRUM FREQUENCIES NECESSITATE GOVERNMENT REGULATION?

The fact that there are far fewer frequencies than there are people who want to use them, both for broadcasting and for two-way services such as cellular telephony, requires that someone or some agency track who is using what and allocate frequencies in such a way that radio spectrum users do not interfere with each other. Because the scarcity of frequencies requires that some people be given frequencies and others not, rules imposed by governments for allocating and renewing licenses were necessary.

WHAT ARE THE MAIN INSTITUTIONS IN THE MEDIA POLICYMAKING PROCESS?

The main institutions in the executive branch are the Federal Communications Commission (FCC), which regulates most aspects of communication; the National Telecommunications and Information Administration (NTIA), which covers some aspects of policy research and international policy; and the Federal Trade Commission (FTC), which monitors trade and business practices. Congress passes laws about communication. The Justice Department and the court system, particularly the federal district courts, enforce and interpret the existing laws.

WHAT IS A LOBBY GROUP? WHAT ARE THE MAIN LOBBIES THAT ADDRESS COMMUNICATIONS MEDIA ISSUES?

Lobbies are interest or business groups that try to influence lawmaking or enforcement. Some of the main business lobbies are AT&T, the Baby Bells, other telecommunications companies, the large equipment manufacturers, the National Association of Broadcasters, the National Cable Television Association, and the Motion Picture Association of America.

WHAT ARE THE MAIN AREAS OF CONCERN IN MEDIA ETHICS?

The main ethical issues that arise in communications media are accuracy or truthfulness, fairness and responsibility of treatment, privacy for media subjects and people in information services, and respect for the intellectual property or ideas of others.

WHAT ARE SOME OF THE CLASSIC ETHICAL PRINCIPLES THAT PEOPLE APPLY TO ISSUES THAT ARISE IN MEDIA ETHICS?

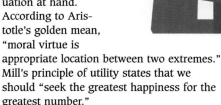

Some are absolute standards. Kant's categorical imperative directs us to act according to rules that we would like to see universally applied. Other principles make judgments more relative to situations. With situation ethics, for example, moral ideas and judgments must be made in the context of the situation at hand. According to Aristotle's golden mean, "moral virtue is appropriate location between two extremes." Mill's principle of utility states that we should "seek the greatest happiness for the greatest number."

WHAT ARE A REPORTER'S ETHICAL RESPONSIBILITIES TO HIS OR HER SOURCES?

Reporters are usually concerned about protecting their sources, but they also need to refer to them as explicitly as possible to increase the credibility of what they write. Confidentiality of sources is crucial to reporters, both to protect those sources and to gain and maintain access to them.

Electronic Resources

For up-to-the-minute URLs about *Media Policy, Law, and Ethics,* access the MEDIA NOW site on the World Wide Web at:

http://communication.wadsworth.com/

CHAPTER 15

Globalization of Communications Media

WHAT'S AHEAD

Some American media companies are moving into the global arena very quickly, such as Time Warner, Disney/ABC, AOL, AT&T, and Microsoft. So are other global players, such as Sony, Bertelsmann, and Seagram, who have bought up major American media companies. Many of these companies see global operations as their main future emphasis. Meanwhile, most countries import newspapers, books, film, music, television, and information services, but more and more countries are not just taking in imports but are also creating their own media and even exporting to other countries. This chapter examines the implications of those global trends.

Access the MEDIA NOW site on the World Wide Web at:
http://communication.wadsworth.com/
Choose "Chapter 15" from the selection box to access electronic information and other sites relevant to this chapter.

MEXICO CITY, 2010

Que pasa, DeeVee?

Good morning, Gloria. Would you like to review your morning schedule?

Sure. Can you scroll current Latin American and Asian media stock prices in a window while we talk?

O.K. At 10 A.M. you have a conference call, with audio translation and subtitles for your charts, to Mimi Chang in Hong Kong and Gordon Banks in New York. At 11 A.M., you requested access to Virtual Studio's sound-mixing service, with access to tracks 1–6 from your last recording session.

Good. Can you ask Jorge Gonzalez, in Santiago, to be on-line at 11:30 to listen to my remix? Oh, one last thing, I am going to do some writing until the call. Can you put the visual at the Brazil–Argentina soccer game in window 1 and the week's top five from the Latino heavy metal channel in window 2?

No problem. Also you should know that Time Warner is bidding $20,000 for the rights to your new album.

That's insulting! I'll distribute it direct from my Web site.

OUTSKIRTS OF MAPUTO, MOZAMBIQUE, 2010

Did you get some batteries for the radio? I want to hear Gloria's latest album.

Sorry, Manuel. It was batteries or a sack of beans. They didn't have the beans the last time I went to the store.

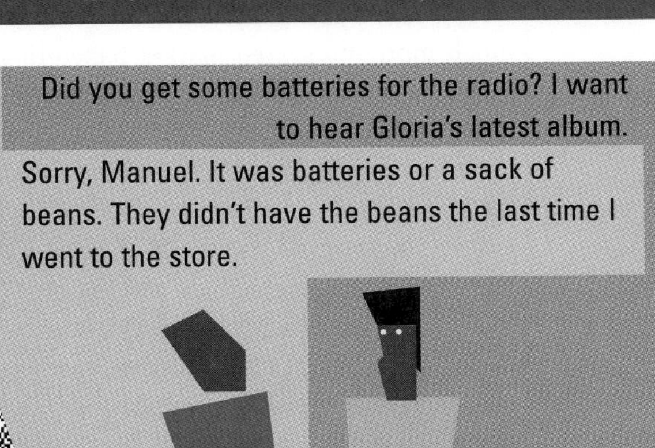

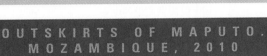

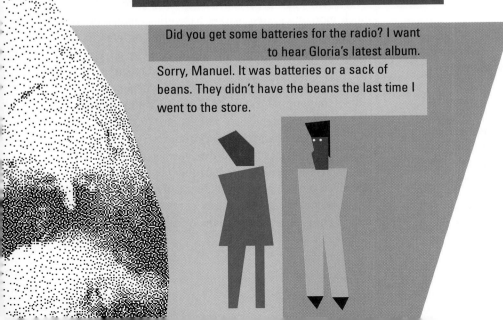

Chapter Outline

Media: Global, Regional, National, Local
Comparisons of National Communications Media Systems
Media and Information Flows
Globalization of Media Companies and Operations
Major Media Systems: National and Global
Newspapers
Magazines and Books
Radio Broadcasting
Music
Film
Television
Cable and Satellite TV around the World
Telecommunications Systems
Computers and Information Services Spreading Slowly Worldwide
The Internet
Telecommunications Industries: Global Providers
Regulation of International Media
Issues in the Globalization of Media
Cultural Imperialism
Free Flow of Information versus Cultural Sovereignty
Trade in Media
Media and National Development
Summary and Review

MEDIA: GLOBAL, REGIONAL, NATIONAL, LOCAL

The global aspect of media is very striking. *Baywatch* was on television in about 60 countries in 1998, while *Titanic* dominated movie and video screens worldwide. Rupert Murdoch's various companies reach about two-thirds of the globe with satellite TV signals and even more countries with movies and TV programs. Global media are not just a Hollywood monopoly anymore. In fact, some major Hollywood companies are now owned by Japanese (Sony), Canadian (Seagrams) and French (Hachette and Havas) companies. Mexican and Brazilian soap operas (*telenovelas*) reach almost as many countries as *Baywatch* and are far more popular in some places, such as Latin America and, interestingly, Eastern Europe and Central Asia (see Figure 15.1).

We are seeing the emergence of global, regional, national, and local media industries, audiences, and regulating political institutions, with a wide variety of ideas, **genres,** and agendas. More countries are competing to sell or broadcast media to others. Some, such as Mexico, Brazil, and Hong Kong, compete worldwide. Brazil sells TV programs to over 100 nations worldwide. Others, such as Egypt and India, dominate "regional" markets characterized by shared geography, language, and culture. American programs remain attractive to world audiences, especially among the wealthy and better educated, who are likely to be more cosmopolitan in their tastes and media exposure.

Genres are types or formats of media content.

Globalization of media is probably most pervasive at the level of media industry models—ways of organizing and creating media. The world is becoming a much more integrated market based in capitalist or commercial economics. This exerts pressures on nations to make media more commercial, supported by advertising, aimed at consumers. The resulting rapid changes, from state and public media to private media dependent on advertising around the world, has had a profound impact well beyond the immediate ratings of *Baywatch* or *X-Files.* As we shall see, most countries produce increasing amounts of their own television, music, and magazines. But if they produce them by drawing on U.S. or French models and genre ideas, then those "national" media products are still at least somewhat globalized. And even if a national soap opera reflects largely local

Globalization refers to the spread worldwide of major media companies and to their serving as models for other countries' media.

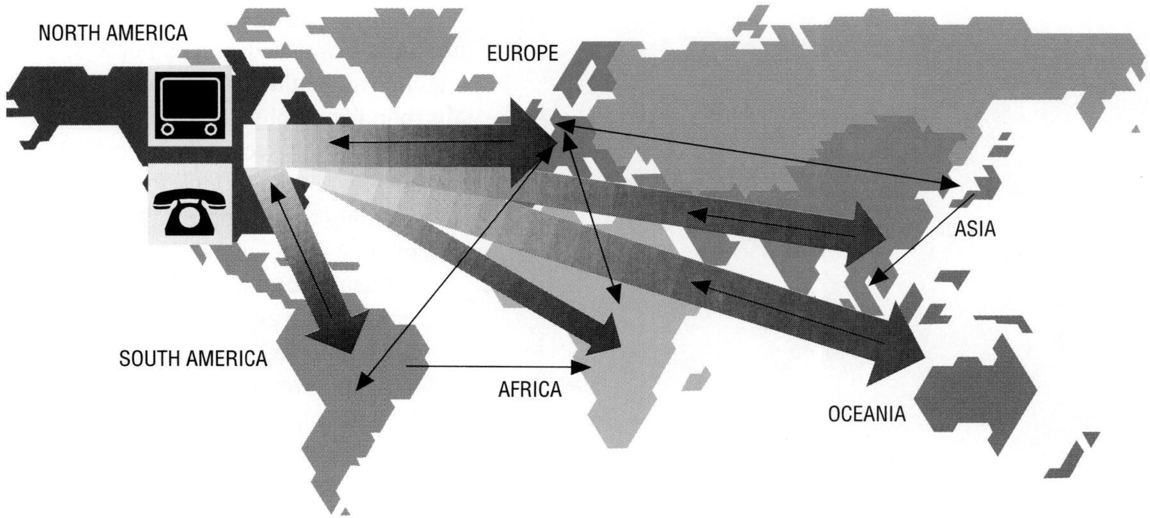

FIGURE 15.1
Although the United States has initially dominated international flows in most media, other countries are beginning to sell more media and information to each other.

culture in its plot and characters, it still helps Colgate-Palmolive and other firms sell soap in yet another part of the global market. Roland Robertson (1992) calls such combinations **glocal**—local productions done with global forms and ideas.

> **Glocal** media are local productions done with global forms and ideas.

Global institutions and companies also have major impact. Global regulators such as the International Telecommunications Union allocate satellite orbits, determine and allocate broadcast frequencies, and define the standards for telephones, faxes, and Internet connections. Global companies, like Rupert Murdoch's News Corporation, not only reach people directly with media but also force competitors to react to them. When Murdoch's Star TV started broadcasting into India, the state television broadcaster had to respond with more competitive entertainment or lose its audience.

Regionalization of media is growing, as well. In several regions of the world (such as Europe, North America, and the Middle East), magazines, newspapers, and books have been transported easily across borders for centuries. Today, radio, television, and satellite television signals also spill directly from one country to its neighbor. Well over half of the Canadian population can directly receive U.S. radio and television signals, for example.

> **Regionalization** refers to media that operate throughout a geographical region.

In the European Union (EU) and the North American Free Trade Agreement (NAFTA—Canada, the United States, Mexico) regions, governments are negotiating agreements on how to handle such media border crossings. The EU went further in 1989 to try to have "television without frontiers." The attempt to produce programming for a Europe-wide television market, promoted heavily by the European Union, is proving difficult, despite the EU's increasing economic and political integration. Europeans are still divided by language and culture. Many still don't want to watch, read, or listen in another language (Schlesinger, 1991). The French still seem to prefer French radio and television to German or British, even if they now have European passports and currency.

IT'S A BAYWATCH WORLD. ***Baywatch*** **is seen in about 140 countries around the world in 32 languages, a sign of the continuing popularity of U.S. media products in world markets.**

Cultural proximity is the desire of audiences to see or hear media products from their own or similar cultures.

Dubbing is the practice of recording a soundtrack in a different language.

Although geographical closeness or proximity helps media cross borders, language and culture seem more important than geography, as the example of Europe shows. It seems that people there and elsewhere tend to look for television programming that is more culturally proximate.

Cultural proximity is the desire for cultural products as similar as possible to one's own language, culture, history, and values. Thus, even though people often like the "cosmopolitan" appeal of European or American television, movies, and music, they tend to choose media from their own culture or one very similar. For example, as soon as VCRs made it possible, the Chinese residents of Malaysia started bringing in Chinese television programs on video and ignoring local broadcast television, which was in the Malay language, stressed Islamic rather than traditional Chinese values, and referred to Malay rather than Chinese history (Boyd, Straubhaar, & Lent, 1989).

Language is a crucial divider of media markets. Increasingly, trade in television between countries is shaped by language (Wildman & Siwek, 1988), and language seems to be shaping music and Internet patterns as well (see below). Language provides a strong natural barrier to media imports. The United States is a prime example. Americans are notorious for wanting to watch or listen in English only, and in television and film, Americans are also very resistant to **dubbing** other language material into English. Most of what little imported television and film Americans watch comes from Great Britain, New Zealand, or Australia, other culturally similar English-speaking countries.

Besides language, other aspects of culture are important in defining audiences: Jokes, slang, historical references, and remarks about current people and events are often culture- and even nation-specific. Such cues, where they are shared across borders, can help build cross-national markets. For instance, Latin American countries used to import American situation comedies. Now they tend to import comedy shows from each other, because the cultural proximity of Spanish-speaking Latin American nations makes slang, jokes, and references to current events easier to understand. Even Brazilian programs, which have to be translated from Portuguese to Spanish, are funnier and more readily comprehensible to other Latin Americans than most U.S. programs because of the similarities in languages, styles, and cultures.

However, Brazilian producers have discovered that when they make too many references to current politics, use too much slang, or otherwise focus too narrowly on current Brazilian issues, their programs are less well received in other parts of Latin America and elsewhere in the world. Hollywood has long experienced the same dilemma. Sometimes a very popular sitcom, such as *Seinfeld,* is too U.S.-specific to export broadly in the global market, whereas a more generic show such as *Baywatch,* featuring action and sex appeal, does better abroad, even after the U.S.

market tires of it. While cultural proximity is a strong factor, audiences in many countries still respond very well to some kinds of imported programs; those whose emphasis is on action, sex, and violence cross cultural boundaries fairly easily.

In many cases, **cultural-linguistic markets** are emerging at a level smaller than global but larger than national. Region-wide music and television markets have emerged in Arabic for the Middle East, Spanish for Latin America, and Chinese in Asia. These markets build on common languages and common cultures that span borders.

Cultural-linguistic markets revolve around language and cultural commonalities.

Just as the United States grew beyond its own market to export globally, a number of companies have grown beyond their original national markets to serve these cultural-linguistic markets. Egyptian television, film, and music dominate much of the Arabic-speaking world. Mexico, Brazil, and Venezuela dominate much of the intra-Latin American trade in film, television, and music, and in *telenovelas* (prime time soap operas), they have become world exporters, with avid fans in Eastern Europe and the Middle East. Similarly, Hong Kong originally dominated much of the Asian market for martial arts and gangster films and television and for pop music. It has become an exporter to the world in the last decade, finally breaking into the U.S. market with Jackie Chan and John Woo movies.

However, although global and cultural linguistic markets for media are all increasingly important, the main point where media are created, regulated, and consumed remains the nation. The vast majority of media companies are structured to serve national markets. National governments have far more effective control over media than regional or global institutions or treaties. And ratings and audience research over the years tend to show that, given a choice, people tend to prefer to see national contents in media (de Sola Pool, 1976; Tracey, 1986; Wilkinson, 1995).

However, nations vary considerably in what they can or will do to create media. Larger, more prosperous nations can create more media content than small, poorer nations. The United States, United Kingdom, and other large or rich countries can afford lavish production values that can overwhelm the modest productions of local media. There can be a contradictory tug of war between cultural proximity and imported production values. Nations that share a large cultural-linguistic community can create more for home and export than can smaller, linguistically isolated nations, such as Albania or Serbia. National governments can help media grow or hinder them. National goals for media, reflected in government policies, are often very different, and they significantly affect how media are structured and what they create.

1. What is globalization?
2. What is cultural proximity?
3. What are cultural-linguistic markets for media?

COMPARISONS OF NATIONAL COMMUNICATIONS MEDIA SYSTEMS

Media systems in various countries can be compared in many ways. A number of scholars have tried to divide world media systems into categories that represent the underlying theories by which various nations have structured their media

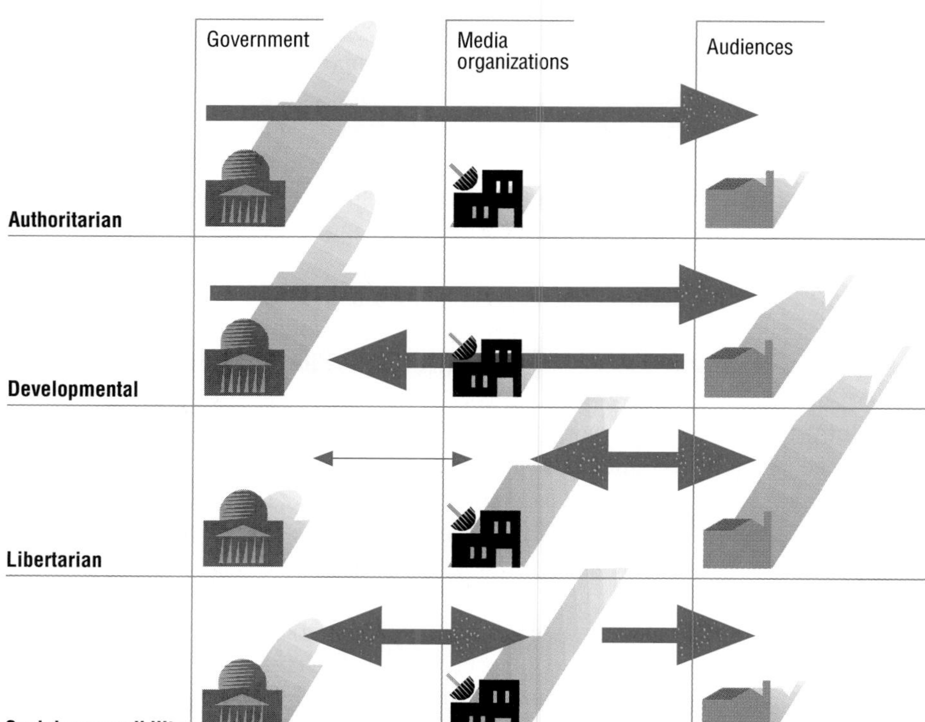

FIGURE 15.2
The role media play in a society depends on the control over information flows given to government, media organizations, and audiences. The arrows indicate the strength and direction of influence. The shadows indicate the power of the actor.

institutions. Most such classifications have reflected the polarization between nations that took shape during the Cold War between the United States and the Soviet Union. For instance, the main initial work in this area, *The Four Theories of the Press,* by Siebert, Schramm, and Peterson (1956), divided media systems into the categories authoritarian, libertarian, social responsibility, and Soviet/totalitarian. Since then, others have suggested a developmental model for Third World or **developing nations.** We will discuss authoritarian, developmental, libertarian, and social responsibility approaches (see Figure 15.2). Because the Soviet "totalitarian" model of media as a tool of the state and the Communist Party has almost disappeared, we will discuss it more briefly. Since the breakup of the Soviet Union in 1991, there seem to be relatively few "totalitarian" media systems left: Cuba, North Korea, Myanmar, Iraq, Afghanistan. Even mainland China's media system is no longer monolithic and centralized enough to be considered totalitarian.

Developing nations are those in Asia, Latin America, the Middle East, and Africa that are struggling to grow economically and to develop socially.

Authoritarian Model. Many governments feel entitled, even obligated, to assert authority and control over mass media. They offer several rationales for this stance. Some governments in poor and politically divided societies feel fragile and unable to assert authority over their citizens if they can't control the media. Other governments are perfectly strong but see media as either a threat or as a tool that they wish to employ to advance their agenda for society.

Governments often censor or prohibit content that they determine to be offensive or counter to what they want to accomplish. Some governments, such as most of the former military regimes of Latin America, censor primarily political news. Others primarily censor moral aspects of entertainment, as when Egypt chops bikini scenes out of "Baywatch." As formerly authoritarian governments in many developing countries become more democratic, they tend to reduce their control over media.

Nazi Germany (1932–1945), the former Soviet Union (1917–1991), and Mao era China (1948–1976) went much further to develop an approach termed **totalitarian,** because the parties in power, such as the Communist Party, saw media as tools of the government in its efforts to develop the economy and society. The party believed that because it was representing the needs and interests of the population, no opposition or divergent views should be allowed. A similar approach was employed by Nazi Germany to control its population and mobilize for World War II. This totalitarian approach differs from "authoritarian systems" in its more pervasive control of society. For example, many Latin American countries have had authoritarian media controls at times, but most media remain private, and government control is often limited to censorship of news and entertainment that the government doesn't like, rather than outright control of media.

Totalitarian systems are those where government owns the media and completely controls them.

Developmental Model. In a number of the developing nations of Africa, Asia, and Latin America, leaders see mass media as a strong social force that should help these nations develop more rapidly and in a planned, efficient way. This belief has led many governments simply to take over and operate electronic media themselves in order to enlist the media in their efforts to promote economic and social development.

What usually distinguishes the developmental approach from the authoritarian is that there is less overall control over content, less censorship, and a tendency to focus on cooperation between media and government for development purposes. This line is a difficult one to draw, however. How much should government compel cooperation from media? Many nations have asked media to cooperate voluntarily with certain government programs in literacy, health, agriculture by communicating ideas to the people. How much should media be able to criticize government programs when they fail, are misguided, or are corrupt?

DEVELOPMENTAL MODEL. Governments in developing countries guide media content to promote national development.

India is an example of a nation with a developmental media approach. Newspapers are private and fairly free, but the government owns and operates radio and television to promote agriculture, health, education, and other goals. In the 1970s, Prime Minister Indira Gandhi, her Congress Party, and their opponents discovered what a powerful political tool television can be. Later, commercial interests, advertisers, and private film industry producers have all pressed for the commercialization of Indian television, which has reduced its developmental orientation.

Free Press/Libertarian Model. Since the eighteenth century, theorists of political democracy have emphasized that people need freedom of expression and speech to become well-informed citizens and voters. In a democracy, media inform voters about what is going on in government and elsewhere so that they can become more involved. To inform the citizens effectively, the press must be free, uncensored, and uncontrolled. The U.S. Constitution specified a libertarian press system, one of the first to eliminate formal government controls.

The print media in most countries tend to be run in a more libertarian manner than do the electronic media. For instance, in the United States, print media are closer than broadcasting media to the libertarian model because of the minimal controls on print. An emerging example of a truly libertarian system is the **Internet,** an international computer network: No central authority makes decisions about content; individuals have the freedom to publish Web pages or post messages; discussion groups talk about whatever they want. However, countries are increasingly making rules about what citizens should do with the Internet, despite the difficulty of enforcing rules on anything as decentralized. China and Singapore both impose filters, or "firewalls," on the Internet to block their citizens' access to outside political material.

The **Internet** is a global network of computer networks.

Social Responsibility Model. This model allows free expression with some limits—either through government regulation or self-regulation by professional ethics. Most mass media are so expensive and difficult to operate that few can make use of this form of "free" expression.

In both print and electronic media, participation in mass media has been effectively limited to professionals, which makes it important that those professionals behave responsibly. The average citizen has essentially delegated his or her freedom of speech to professional reporters and editors. The Internet is beginning to change this, but most people in the world have neither telephone lines nor computers, much less Internet service providers.

MEDIA IMPACT

How Different Media Systems Would Handle a Major Nuclear Disaster

One of the nightmares hanging over many industrialized countries is the possibility of a major environmental disaster such as an accident in a major nuclear power plant or nuclear bomb testing. How would different types of media systems handle such an event?

- *Libertarian.* The U.S. print press reported immediately on the 1979 Three Mile Island nuclear disaster.
- *Social responsibility.* U.S. radio and television in the Three Mile Island area tried not to instill panic in the residents.
- *Authoritarian.* Brazilian military governments in the 1970s–1980s censored reports of problems with nuclear plants being built.
- *Totalitarian.* Soviet media did not report the 1986 Chernobyl reactor disaster for three days while radiation clouds contaminated unsuspecting citizens and farms.
- *Developmental.* Indian media tended to rally to support its government's nuclear bomb tests aimed at scaring rival Pakistan in 1997–1998.

The British Broadcasting Corporation (1922–) is a classic example of operating on a social responsibility model. It is financed by **license fees** to avoid both government and advertiser control. It is a not-for-profit corporation overseen by a commission that sets policy for how it should meet its public service responsibilities. Directors and programmers are guided by a strong internal ethic of responsibility to society, although critics also accuse it of being elitist and out of touch with a diverse British society.

License fees are annual fees, or fees on the sales of radio or television receivers, assessed to pay for public broadcasting.

MEDIA AND INFORMATION FLOWS

Even though nations differ culturally, they are not isolated. As we look at the globalization of media, we see that one of its most obvious implications is an increasing flow of a variety of kinds of media contents between countries. Elements of media, such as books, songs, stories, and news, have always flowed across borders; cultures have never been truly isolated. Even before Gutenberg's printing press, the Christian *Bible* and the Islamic *Koran* had both moved powerfully across a number of countries and cultures.

However, many people worry that modern media move new ideas and values across borders in such quantities, and at such speed, that we have entered a new age of much more pervasive and rapid change in the world's cultures. Marshall McLuhan (1989) looked at the electronic media and anticipated a "global village."

Americanization? What kind of global village might the media construct? Much of what flows across borders originates in Hollywood, so some fear that the "village" will be as Americanized as a San Fernando Valley mall multiplex theater. A major issue is the impact of Hollywood-style material on other cultures. Because Hollywood films, television, and Anglo-American pop music often include sex, violence, drugs, and gender roles and racial images that clash strongly with local values around the world, many people fear its influence, particularly on the young.

1. What is an authoritarian media system?
2. What is a developmental media system?
3. What is a free press or libertarian system?
4. What is the social responsibility model for media?
5. How "Americanized" are media flows between countries?

GLOBALIZATION OF MEDIA COMPANIES AND OPERATIONS

Twenty years ago people talked about Americanization of media in the world. Today people talk more about globalization because it is apparent that although American media play a prominent role in the global scene, media industries from a number of other countries are also heavily involved.

Nine firms dominate the globalized part of the world media system. The five largest are Time Warner (U.S.), Disney (U.S.), Bertelsmann (German), Viacom (U.S.), and Rupert Murdoch's News Corporation (Australian). The other four are AT&T/TCI (U.S.) and three media groups that are all part of much larger industrial

PROFILE

INTERNATIONAL MULTIMEDIA MOGULS. Gerald Levin, chairman of Time Warner, and board member Ted Turner combine to make Time Warner a global media giant.

Global Media Giant

Name: Time Warner. It may not have the flamboyant image of Disney or Murdoch, but Time Warner and its managers have kept merging huge companies to arrive at the top of the global heap.

Formed: In 1989 through the merger of the already large companies Time, Inc. and Warner Communications, Time Warner, then acquired Turner Broadcasting in 1996.

Current Position: Has over 200 subsidiaries worldwide. "In 1996, approximately two-thirds of Time Warner's $25 billion income came from the United States, but that figure is expected to drop to three-fifths by 2000, and eventually to less than one-half" (McChesney, 1997). Music is 20 percent of Time Warner's business. The news division (magazine and book publishing, cable television news) is also about 20 percent. U.S. cable systems account for over 10 percent of income. The other half is largely from its entertainment film, video, and television holdings.

Where Does It Go from Here: "Time Warner has zeroed in on global television as the most lucrative area for growth. Unlike News Corporation, however, Time Warner has devoted itself to producing programming and channels rather than developing entire satellite systems" (McChesney, 1997). However, Time Warner also has significant interests in non-U.S. broadcasting joint ventures. In addition, "Time Warner is one of the largest movie theater owners in the world, with approximately 1000 screens outside the United States and further expansion projected" (McChesney, 1997).

- "HBO International has already established itself as the leading subscription TV channel in the world; it has a family of pay channels and is available in over 35 countries" (McChesney, 1997).
- CNN International, a subsidiary of CNN, is the main global television news channel, reaching over 200 nations. CNN launched a Spanish-language service for Latin America in 1997 and may eventually operate (or participate in joint ventures to establish) CNN channels in French, Japanese, Hindi, Arabic, or other regional languages, but CNN has localized less than some other channels so far.
- TNT/Cartoon Network and Warner channels. Time Warner and Turner were both strong international television forces. Their 1996 merger permits them to use each other's libraries of cartoons, feature films, television programs and other resources. New Time Warner channels can also take advantage of all these holdings plus new productions.
- With the Warner Brothers and New Line Cinema Film studios and their library of more than 6000 films, 25,000 television programs, books, music, and thousands of cartoons, Time Warner is one of the major film producers and distributors in the world.
- Warner Music Group is one of the largest global music businesses; "nearly 60 percent of its revenues come from outside the United States" (McChesney, 1997).

Most of the information for this profile came from a November/December 1997 article, "The Global Media Giants: The nine firms that dominate the world," by Robert McChesney from a Web site maintained by Fairness and Accuracy in Media. If you are using the InfoTrac College Edition and wish to find out more about the big global companies like Time Warner, which have probably acquired several new companies since this was written, check their current situation by searching InfoTrac College Edition for keywords such as international television, music, and film.

corporations: General Electric/NBC (U.S.); Sony/Columbia/TriStar (Japanese); and Seagram/Universal (Canadian) (McChesney, 1997). Of the nine top global media firms, then, four are American (counting News Corp as Australian). These types of companies are growing and globalizing quickly. Time Warner and Disney generated around 15 percent of their income outside of the United States in 1990, a figure that rose to 30–35 percent by 1999.

Behind the top global firms is a second tier of three or four dozen media firms that do between $1 billion and $8 billion yearly in media-related business. These firms tend to have national or cultural-linguistic strongholds or to specialize in specific global niches, as the BBC specializes in news. About half are American (Westinghouse/ CBS, Gannett, the New York Times Co., Hearst, and Comcast). Most of the rest come from Europe (Hachette, Havas, EMI, Reuters, BBC) or Canada (Thomsen, Rogers), and a handful are based in East Asia (NHK, TVB, Fuji, Asahi, Chinese Central TV) and Latin America (TV Globo, Televisa, Cisneros/Venevision). See the accompanying Media Watch box for a more complete listing of the world's main mass media firms. If we stretch the definition of media, we could add Microsoft and AOL.

Some media industries, such as the Hollywood film and TV studios represented by the Motion Picture Export Association of America, have long been global in their operation and scope. They controlled a number of the companies in other countries that distributed and exhibited (in theaters) the films that they produced in the United States. More recently, the ownership of Hollywood itself has become globalized. Sony bought Columbia Pictures (a major film studio), Columbia Pictures Television, and Tri-Star, a major independent production company. The resulting operation has been scrutinized by critics to see whether the kinds of films produced will now reflect Japanese rather than American sensibilities. So far the feeling within Hollywood itself is that ownership is neutral. "It doesn't matter. The product is uniquely American, no matter who owns it," says Paul Kagan, a major entertainment industry consultant (Turner, 1993). 20th Century Fox was purchased by News Corp. of Australia, owned by Rupert Murdoch, who also acquired control of the Fox Television Network. Another Japanese firm, Matsushita, bought Universal Studios but was unable to adapt to Hollywood corporate culture and sold it to Seagram of Canada. The major international media conglomerates are listed in the Media Watch.

MEDIA WATCH

Top Mass Media Firms

Company	Worldwide Sales
United States	
TCI/AT&T	$50 billion
Time Warner	$25 billion
Disney	$24 billion
Viacom	$13 billion
News Corporation	$12 billion
NBC (GE)	$5 billion
Westinghouse/CBS	$5 billion
Advance Publications	$4.9 billion
Gannett	$4.0 billion
Comcast	$4.0 billion
Germany	
Bertelsmann	$15 billion
Kirch Group	$4 billion
Japan	
Sony	$9 billion (media only)
NHK	$5.6 billion
France	
Havas	$8.8 billion
Hachette	$5.3 billion
Canada	
Universal (Seagram)	$7 billion
Thomson	$7.3 billion
Britain	
Reed Elsevier	$5.5 billion
EMI	$5.4 billion
Reuters	$4.1 billion

Source: McChesney (1997). Most sales figures are for 1996 or 1997, but some are as early as 1993. Fairness & Accuracy in Media.

Record companies are similarly structured except that they have a more diverse set of origins and an even more international ownership (see Table 15.1). Major recording companies are based in Great Britain (Thorn, EMI), the Netherlands (Philips), Germany (Bertelsmann), and Japan (Sony). These companies have consolidated across borders. Philips now owns Polygram (formerly of the

TABLE 15.1 The International Music Industry Giants

Company	Home Country	Worldwide Sales (1992)
Sony	Japan	$3.5 billion
Philips/Polygram	Netherlands	$3.3 billion
Time Warner	United States	$3.2 billion
Bertelsmann/RCA	Germany	$2.5 billion
Thorn/EMI	United Kingdom	$2.2 billion
Matsushita/MCA	Japan	$300 million

United Kingdom), Bertelsmann now owns RCA (formerly of the United States), and Seagram/Universal now owns MCA (formerly of Matsushita-Japan). Most of these companies also have large foreign branches that often produce and distribute records within other markets as well as distributing American and European music. As record companies have also been acquired by multinational companies, these firms have become more global and less national in character.

Print media are becoming equally globalized. The publishing industry is highly internationalized, and book publishing houses, magazines, and newspapers are frequently owned across borders. The main actors in print are Rupert Murdoch's News Corp. (Australia), Bertelsmann (Germany), Time Warner (U.S.), and Hachette and Havas (France).

STOP & REVIEW

1. **What are the main reasons why companies buy or start up media in other countries?**
2. **Which companies are the main global owners of media?**
3. **Where are the main global media companies based, besides in the United States?**

MAJOR MEDIA SYSTEMS: NATIONAL AND GLOBAL

Newspapers

Worldwide, newspapers are more often private and subject to less government scrutiny than electronic media. Newspapers do not use public resources, such as the spectrum of radio waves, and unlike broadcast, cable TV, or telephones, they do not require government involvement in setting technical standards. Newspapers do often depend on government controls over newsprint production or importation, but as countries grow more democratic they tend to relax such controls and to treat newsprint as just another business.

In Europe and much of Latin America and Asia, most countries that are inclined toward freedom of the press have privately owned and largely uncontrolled newspapers. This tendency is increasing. In many countries, government and political party print media coexist with "free" print media. But the "free" media are often heavily swayed by advertising and subtle government controls, such as limiting the supply of paper or the advertising budgets of government-owned companies. In a few countries, such as Cuba and North Korea, governments have seen newspapers as a useful tool that they ought to own and control exclusively.

In poorer parts of the developing countries of Asia, Latin America, the Middle East, and Africa, use of newspapers is seriously limited by levels of both education and income. In most of Africa, less than half of the population is literate. Functional literacy in much of Latin America is under 75 percent. Even people who can read may not be able to afford newspapers. Whereas in most European countries the circulation of daily newspapers is about 33 for every 100 people, it is fewer than 2 for every 100 in Africa (see Figure 15.3).

News Flow. News has been flowing across borders in one medium or another for a long time. In Europe, runners, horsemen, ships, carrier pigeons, and the earliest newspapers and newsletters carried political and economic news across borders. Many early newspapers and newsletters installed correspondents in other countries so that they could publish foreign news for their readers.

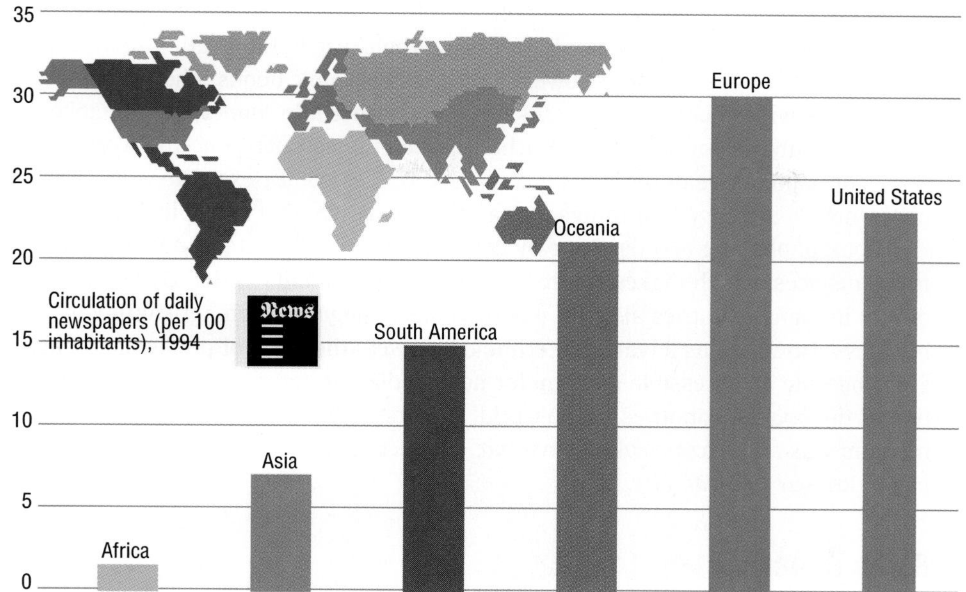

FIGURE 15.3
Newspaper circulation and access are uneven and unequal in different regions of the world, mostly depending on wealth and economic resources.
(*Source:* UNESCO Statistical Yearbook, 1998.)

International news flow took a significant step forward in speed and volume with the development, in the 1840s, of newswire services based on the then-new technology of the telegraph. The Associated Press (AP) developed in 1846 as a cooperative of American newspapers. Reuters grew to cover international news for the British Empire. United Press International (UPI) developed as a rival commercial service. Agence France Presse (AFP) was a joint government-private agency that served primarily France and its former colonies but also grew into a fourth primary international news source.

By the 1970s, a number of critics asserted that the major newswire services had too much control over international news flow. Such services followed standard American and European definitions of what was news: disasters, sensational or unusual events, political upheaval, wars or conflicts, famous personalities, and current (vs. long-term) events. Although this approach fits the Western ideal of the press as a critic and watchdog, it often produces negative coverage and images of other countries. For example, studies show that Arabs receive very negative treatment in American media (Ghareeb, 1983).

Magazines and Books

In many places, particularly developing countries, magazine and book publishing lags behind newspapers. The European habit of newspaper reading spread to local elites with colonization. With scarce resources for printing, many places concentrated on newspapers, which then published essays, fiction, features, and commentaries that might have gone into magazines elsewhere. Anderson (1983) has pointed out that newspapers played a crucial role in the formation of national images and identities in most new nations. Governments frequently supported newspapers, directly or with advertising, because they were felt to be crucial to nation building (Anderson, 1983).

However, book and magazine publishing has gradually increased in most countries. Books demand greater literacy, and their readership is often limited to the middle and upper classes. However, magazines, comic books, photo-novels (magazines with photos and captions, arranged rather like comics), and chapbooks (cheaply bound fiction and poetry) achieve greater penetration into the working and poor populations of developing countries. In Mexico, for example, comics and photo-novels are easy first things to read for people who are newly literate.

Book publishing is often done by government ministries and under government auspices, which makes control over titles and contents easier. Government offices in many countries also put out specialized magazines on agriculture or business. However, as advancing technology lowers the costs of publishing, magazines become an accessible medium for new media entrepreneurs. In Mozambique, one of the poorest countries in the world, the first independent, nongovernment medium was a magazine called *Savanna,* the second a short, faxed daily newspaper, known as *MediaFax.*

Radio Broadcasting

Because the print media's reach is limited in many countries by low literacy and income levels, broadcast media take on increased importance. In the poorest countries, radio is the main mass medium. However, in Africa and South Asia, many people do not even get access to radio, either because the signal doesn't reach them or because they can't afford a receiver. In Mozambique, for example, only about half of its people are covered by a radio signal, and less than a third hear radio often.

International Radio. In some of the poorest countries, where domestic radio stations don't cover all the country, people in remote areas listen to international broadcasters. Such international radio is usually on **short-wave** frequencies that can carry across thousands of miles, compared to the limited range of FM and AM radio. In Africa, people in remote areas listen on short wave to continent-spanning commercial radio stations such as Africa One, as well as to foreign government stations such as the Voice of America, Radio France, and the BBC (Bourgault, 1994).

Short-wave radio broadcasts can carry across oceans by bouncing off the earth's atmosphere.

Most international radio has been broadcast by governments over short wave for largely political and public relations purposes—what has sometimes been called **public diplomacy**—trying to reach and influence public opinion in other countries. The main examples have been Voice of America, Radio Moscow, and Radio Havana. Some international radio has also been broadcast for religious reasons (by Vatican Radio and several American Protestant groups, for instance) and for commercial entertainment, news, and advertising (such as Radio Monte Carlo, run in the Middle East by the French company Sofirad).

Public diplomacy is the use of media to reach people and influence public opinion in other countries.

National Radio. In more developed countries, national and local radio becomes much more important than international radio. Radio tends to be both national and local. Many countries have important national radio networks, which are widely listened to. However, radio in most places is tending to become more local. Radio turns out to be a good local medium because its production costs are only a fraction of those for television.

MEDIA IMPACT

The Cuban–American Radio War

One of the more fiercely fought international radio wars was waged just off the Florida coast. After Fidel Castro led the Cuban Revolution to power in 1959, Cuba and the United States sank into a "cold war" in which radio broadcasting of propaganda seemed to substitute for more active military hostilities following the failure of the Bay of Pigs attack on Cuba. Cuba broadcast its own programs in Spanish and English at the United States. Cuba also provided a base for Soviet radio transmitters for Radio Moscow and Radio Peace and Progress. The United States broadcast at Cuba not only its Spanish Service from the Voice of America but also Radio Swan in the 1960s and a specific anti-Castro service called Radio Marti, starting in 1984, and a television version called TV Marti, starting in 1990. Radio Marti and TV Marti represented an escalation of the radio war by the Reagan administration, which was much more anti-Castro than its predecessors. Radio Marti had a very strong 50,000-watt AM signal, and the Cubans demonstrated an ability to jam it, interfering with several U.S. AM radio stations on the same frequency. TV Marti followed but never functioned well technically.

In 1995, the U.S. government reviewed its whole strategy of international radio and television, in an effort to determine how much to change its propaganda strategy now that the cold war with the former Soviet Union seemed to be over. Radio Marti survived, thanks to intense lobbying by Cuban exiles in the United States, but many other American international radio broadcasts to various countries were shut down.

Radio can cater to the apparently widespread audience desire for local news, local talk shows, and local music. In radio, the urge for cultural proximity by audiences and market segmentation by advertisers favors the very local, although people still want to hear national and global music and news. Local music can reflect local preferences, and local news and talk tend to cover the things that most concern people's daily lives. In the Amazon region, stations play music from local festivals, interspersed with ads. In Lima, Peru, some commercial stations play music in the Quechua Indian language for indigenous people who haven't learned Spanish, accompanied by ads aimed at those people. In contrast, in Bolivia, miners' unions run a number of local radio stations because they don't trust the news on the regular commercial stations. In Wales, some radio stations try to attract people to listening in Welsh in order to help keep the language alive.

Music

The strength of national and local radio has a great deal to do with a revival in local and national music around the globe. The Spice Girls can be heard around the globe on many stations, but others are playing music by local artists as well.

Music around the world seems to be both the most globalized *and* the most localized of media. Travelers to almost any country will hear a great deal of American and European music, but they will also begin to hear an astonishing variety of local music if they listen carefully. Nearly all cultures have a musical tradition linked to religion, festivals or holidays, season changes, work or farming, leisure activities, or other things that people want to celebrate. Such traditional music usually adapts well to being recorded, played on the radio, and sold on CDs and cassettes.

Music Flows. We are seeing the emergence of global, regional, national, and local music industries, with a wide variety of genres and audiences. American, British, and some other European rock and pop music in English is currently popular throughout the world. Many of the same pop singers and groups can be found on the radio and in music stores from Taiwan to Russia to Argentina: the Spice Girls, Madonna, the Backstreet Boys. (When one of the authors took some American students to Chile in 1997, girls outside a television station mobbed one of the students because he looked like one of the Backstreet Boys.) In this sense there is a truly global music industry, based primarily in the United States, that speaks to a globalized youth culture, although local music also remains popular in most countries, too. Cultural-linguistic music markets have emerged in Arabic for the Middle East, in Spanish for Latin America, and in Chinese. Distinct music genres and variations on genres have emerged, such as reggae in Jamaica and samba-reggae in Brazil. Audience tastes tend to be multilayered with many people listening to global music, regional or national music, and local music to suit different needs and interests (Colista & Leshner, 1998).

MUSICAL WORLD. The popularity of "wold music" was first evident in the success of Paul Simon's *Graceland* album and tour.

Governments sometimes require that a certain proportion of nationally produced music be played on radio stations. Some also subsidize national music industries to make sure that local music, or at least some of the rarer forms of it, will be produced. Most often, though, music development has been left to musicians' initiative, market forces, and audience demand. That works fairly well in many countries, because audience members are willing to pay for local and national music, although they also listen to and purchase global music. Music, too, is much cheaper to produce than film or television—so much so that it serves a wide variety of subcultures within and across nations, such as Turkish music among Turkish residents in Germany.

Music also flows across borders more easily in more ways than do films or television. The international music trade is dominated by a few major international companies, such as Sony, Polygram, Philips, and EMI. They import and sell the dominant American and European pop music around the world. In many countries, however, they also record and sell national artists. That gives them something of a stake in promoting those artists, both at home and abroad, when they perceive that there might be an export market. For example, multinational firms record Jamaican reggae, Brazilian samba, and Caribbean salsa and merengue, sell them at home, and also export them to the United States. Furthermore, those international companies are more willing to risk distributing national music recordings than the equivalent television programs, because musical tastes are more diverse and costs (and financial risks) are much lower.

1. Why is the government more likely to operate broadcasting than print media in many countries?
2. How did newspapers develop differently from magazines or books in many countries?
3. How does news flow between countries?
4. Why is music more likely to be produced in a wide variety of countries than film or TV?

Film

Of all the international media examined here, films are perhaps the most globalized and the most difficult to produce on a sustained national basis. First, film is a relatively expensive medium to produce. Even cheap feature films, paying almost nothing to actors and technicians, cost hundreds of thousands of dollars, and an *average* Hollywood film costs $40 million. Second, the economic success of a film is never guaranteed, so it represents an expensive, risky investment to the producer, investors, and other funding sources. Third, the distribution channels that enable a film to make money have been globalized to a degree unlike any of the other media. Films from independent producers or from outside the English-speaking world have a hard time breaking into the international distribution system, which is largely controlled by companies associated with the Hollywood studios through the Motion Picture Export Association of America.

Films of significant quality and interest have been produced in many countries, but few countries are currently producing many feature films. A number of poor nations, such as the Dominican Republic, have produced only one or two feature-length films in their histories—and some have made none at all. Furthermore, film production has slowed down or even stopped in many countries, such as most of Latin America and Africa, as many companies have fallen into debt or suffered other economic crises. In a number of countries where film production had been heavily subsidized, governments have found themselves unable to continue to support it. Some countries, including France and Spain, still continued to subsidize their film industries, but this led to conflicts in trade talks (such as the World Trade Agreement) with the United States, which considers these subsidies an unfair form of protectionism (U.S. Dept. of Commerce, 1998).

The United States has dominated international film production and distribution since World War I (1914–1918). Both world wars disrupted a number of the other major international film producers (Italy, Germany, Japan, France, and Great Britain) and cut their industries off from world trade in films. Hollywood stepped in to occupy world film markets and to set up distribution companies that continue to control global film distribution.

American films have succeeded in a variety of markets around the world for several reasons. One is the enormous size of the U.S. market for movies, which

IMPACT

MEDIA

Titanic Sinks Iranian Culture?

In 1998, the film *Titanic* seemed to be the symbol of American cultural dominance around the world. The film made over $1.2 billion at the box office, over half of that abroad. It has been seen by hundreds of millions of people. In fact, it is impossible to know how many, because illegal videocassettes of the film began to circulate in Iran within days of its U.S. opening—in some cases made by hand-held video cameras taken into movie theaters.

Titanic is a huge hit among many people, particularly young people, in Iran and many other countries. The case of Iran is ironic, however, because the 1979 Iranian revolution brought to power an Islamic government that was specifically motivated by a widespread popular reaction to the perceived excesses of American and Western popular culture in films, TV, and music.

Iran cracked down on Western cultural imports far harder than almost any other place on the globe. Satellite dishes are banned but still widely (if carefully) used. Many Western films on video are banned but are available if the video store owner knows and trusts you. Illegally imported CDs sell briskly. Young women sometimes wear Western clothes hidden underneath their long black robes and veils, or chadors.

The Islamic leadership worries that Western cultural products will affect social and spiritual values, and will divert attention away from Iran's own rich culture. Local filmmakers worry that people might not come to see their movies if many of the imports were not legally prohibited from showing in the theaters.

However, evidence from around the world indicates that effects of imported film and television on deeply held national or local values are hard to demonstrate. However, people's awareness of outside events, fads, and consumer trends is more easily influenced (Elasmar, 1997).

For Further Research:

WWW

Most of the material for this feature was taken from a *Washington Post News Service* story, "Cultural charms seduce even Iran," November 29, 1998. If you are interested in how American films are exported to the rest of the world, you could search the World Wide Web for keywords such as Motion Picture Export Association, or search InfoTrac College Edition.

permits Hollywood to recover most of the costs of films in their domestic release. No other country has such a large and affluent national film audience. Second is the heterogeneous nature of the U.S. audience, which includes diverse groups that demanded simpler, more entertainment-oriented, and more universal films. Because of these elements, Hollywood has been the world's film production center, drawing money and talent from around the world and away from competing film industries abroad, Since the 1920s, Hollywood has drawn actors, directors, writers, and musicians from Europe, Latin America, and Asia (Guback & Varis, 1982).

Furthermore, Hollywood studios, organized under the Motion Picture Export Association of America, have worked together to promote exports and control overseas distribution networks. They have done so with a degree of cooperation or collusion that might be considered anticompetitive and a violation of antitrust laws if it were done domestically but that has been specifically permitted overseas by the U.S. Congress under the Webb-Pomerene Act (Guback, 1986).

Today the United States clearly dominates world film. American films filled over 80 percent of the theater seats in Europe in 1998. Government protection of film industries in other countries is not surprising: They simply want to ensure that national film industries survive. More films are produced in Asia, primarily in Hong Kong and India (which has produced more films than the United States in some years). Egypt is the film center of the Arab world. These countries do show that film industries can be maintained, even in some developing countries, if the domestic market is large or if the film companies produce for a multicountry audience and market. Shared language and culture thus define market segments for international and national filmmakers.

Video. In many countries, films are now most commonly seen on video or on television, rather in cinema houses. In the more affluent parts of most countries, increasing numbers in the middle class and elite have VCRs and satellite or cable TV (Boyd, 1993; McDaniel, 1996).

Television

Compared to print media, television broadcasting in many countries is far more divided among public, governmental, and private ownership. Because broadcasters use the relatively scarce frequencies of the radio spectrum, few channels are available and fewer people or groups can be involved. All governments get involved in planning who gets to own or operate radio or television stations, which also leads them to get involved in controlling content.

FIDEL CASTRO, SUPERSTAR. Since 1959 Castro has used television to mobilize people to support him and his regime. Castro is a charismatic speaker, who often speaks on television for hours. He draws huge audiences, perhaps in part because nothing else is allowed to be on when Castro is.

In Africa, Asia, and Eastern Europe, governments often have owned and operated broadcasting systems in order to control radio and TV. Leaders in these countries want broadcasting to help solve major health, education, and economic problems. Their stated intention has usually been to use radio and television as powerful *tools* to develop their societies, but controlling politics is often the hidden agenda, as well. For example, until dictatorial President Mobuto of Zaire departed power in 1997, the opening of daily television broadcasts showed him descending out of the heavens, framed in light—an effort to add a religious aura to his already considerable power. India's state television, Doordarshan, initially tried to use television to teach better health and agricultural practices to villagers, but urban and middle-class viewers of the single national channel rebelled. Now Doordarshan faces private satellite competition and must be content to insinuate subtle pro-development themes, such as child health care and family planning into soap operas that both urban and rural people like to watch.

Access to television is still very unequal around the globe. In many parts of the world, including much of Africa, most of the population don't see television much, if at all, particularly outside the main cities. In contrast, most people, even among the poor, in Latin America and East Asia (Taiwan, Hong Kong, and so on) have television. Brazilians sometimes say they live in the "land of television."

Public Broadcasting. In many countries, including most of Western Europe, either governments or not-for-profit **public corporations** operate television broadcasting,

Public corporations in broadcasting are not-for-profit companies financed by government or license fees.

with little or no private competition until recently. Their goal has been to use broadcasting to promote education and culture. An example is the BBC (British Broadcasting Corporation) in Great Britain. To a large extent, the public broadcasters in Europe and Japan have outpaced the U.S. Public Broadcasting System (PBS) and National Public Radio in creating more educational, informational, and cultural programming. In fact, PBS uses a good deal of British material, such as "Monty Python," "Absolutely Fabulous," and "Red Dwarf" and increasingly coproduces programs with international public television channels. Until recently, however, in some countries such as Italy, public broadcasters sometimes let political parties, such as Italy's Christian Democrats, control their news and information programs.

State broadcasters are usually supported from government funds. Public radio and television networks, including the BBC, are often been supported by audience *license fees* in order to maintain independence from both government budget control and commercial pressures by advertisers. In Britain and Japan, everyone who owns a radio or a television set pays an annual license fee, That fee goes directly to the public broadcasters (BBC in Britain and NHK in Japan), who use it to finance program production and development.

The Trend toward Private Television Broadcasting. Broadcasting has mostly been privately owned in Canada, Central America, and South America, largely because of the strong influence of the United States. However, government controls over private broadcasters have varied among these countries. In contrast to the minimal controls in the United States, there are strict controls in Canada, where the government has tried to restrict the importation of programs from the United States. Many Latin American governments have exerted strong control over private broadcasters to obtain political support, mostly through economic pressures such as selectively awarding government advertising to supportive broadcasters. In most of the private broadcasting systems, entertainment programming has dominated, although some privately run, nonprofit radio education programs, run by the Catholic Church, have been effective in teaching basic education in Latin America.

There is a general recent tendency in European, Asian, and other countries to increase private commercial broadcasting and reduce government and public ownership. Publics often push for more broadcast choices, while advertisers, both foreign and local, push to be able to put advertising on commercial stations. In response, governments are liberalizing private competition, privatizing some government or public stations, and permitting public stations to use advertising.

Most countries are liberalizing competition in broadcasting by permitting new private companies to enter the market. Many individuals and companies would like to own broadcast stations. Such individuals often come from print publishing, such as Silvio Berlusconi in Italy, who now controls the three major private television networks and used them to help him win the presidency of Italy in 1994.

Privatization of media or telecommunications is the selling of a government operation to private owners.

Many countries are also **privatizing** some public or government broadcast stations and networks. Sometimes this is to reduce government political control over state stations, as when the newly elected socialist president of France, Mitterand, privatized some of France's state television networks because he felt that they had previously been used against him. Sometimes, too, privatizing is done to take broadcasting out of the public budget and make it privately supported through advertising.

Some public broadcasters are feeling budget pressures, which also tends to make them turn to advertising as an alternative source of funding. Putting public media onto a commercial basis to be supported by advertising is often referred to as **corporatization.** British study commissions have even considered putting ads on the BBC, which has been the very prototype of a public station supported by audience license fees. With an increasing number of commercial choices, British viewers are less willing to pay directly for public television, and this puts the BBC under pressure to change its orientation and corporatize.

Corporatization is making a government operation behave like a private company under marketplace rules.

TV News Flows. In the 1970s–1990s, television news flow began to increase steadily in prominence. It began with wire services, such as UPI Television News, and news film sources, such as Visnews from Great Britain, offering filmed (and later video) footage for various national television news operations to use in their newscasts, to supplement wire service coverage. Television news flow increased dramatically as CNN, the BBC, and other satellite-based news operations began to offer entire newscasts and even all-day news coverage across borders, primarily to satellite television receivers and cable television operations.

FOREIGN CORRESPONDENT. Cable News Network (CNN) is carried on television systems around the world.

Television Flows. Television exhibits a much more complicated flow between countries than does film. American television programs are visible globally, but many other producers now sell programs to national and cultural linguistic markets, as well.

At first, U.S. film studios and independent producers sold television programs worldwide with the same economic and cultural advantages that American film producers had enjoyed. In the 1960s–1970s, American films, sitcoms, action adventures, and cartoons flooded into many other countries. A 1972 study for UNESCO found that over half of the countries studied imported over half of their TV programs—mostly entertainment and mostly from the United states. Because television production was expensive and new, not many countries had the equipment, people, or money to produce enough programming to meet their own needs. A few countries decided to limit broadcast hours to what they could fill themselves, but most responded to audience demands for more television by drawing on external sources.

A number of countries, from Great Britain to Taiwan to Canada, have established quotas limiting the amount of imported television programming that can be shown. In 1989, the European Economic Community required member nations to carry at least 50 percent of television programming produced within Europe. Hollywood and U.S. government officials protested these rules at trade talks but did not succeed in blocking them. France has declared its intention to keep import quotas on television to protect its own productions.

American television exports represent a steadily increasing share of television producers' profits. Because many shows now make more money overseas than in the United States, a number of American producers are beginning to shape their programs to anticipate and maximize overseas sales (Waxman, 1998).

MEDIA IMPACT

Soap Operas Around the World

Although American shows are popular worldwide, most people prefer soap operas or serial dramas set in their home countries or regions.

In Latin America, *telenovelas* run in prime time and usually depict romance, family drama, and upward mobility. The archetypal *telenovela* for many was *Simplemente Maria,* about a Peruvian peasant girl who moves to the city, works as a maid, saves money, buys a sewing machine, and becomes a successful seamstress. All sewing machines in Lima sold out after that plot development. *Telenovelas* are also now playing to large audiences in Romania.

Martial arts dramas from Hong Kong and China follow some soap opera themes—romance, love, family intrigues, and rivalries—but add martial arts action, dramatic battles, historical plots, and period costumes. These are popular throughout Asia. Japan makes its own versions, focused on the Samurai era and featuring a similar mix of rugged heroes, beautiful heroines, and battles. These programs are also becoming popular worldwide.

Indian soap operas tend to be more epic, mythological, and even religious. A recent popular soap opera retold the national Hindu religious epic *The Ramayana,* the story of the Hindu gods. It had a powerful effect according to critics, who saw it as reinforcing nationalist Hindu political parties and standardizing throughout India a previously diverse set of versions of *The Ramayana.*

Many of these series are also popular in other markets, especially those that share languages and cultures. *Telenovelas* now sell to all of Latin America; Hong Kong soaps sell in southern China and feature on satellite Star TV; and Indian soaps are popular even in neighboring (and rival) Pakistan. Some of these exporters are also breaking into the global market. Mexican soap operas are popular now in Eastern Europe, and Hong Kong martial arts serials can be seen in Los Angeles dubbed into Spanish.

However, American television programs are also facing increased competition in a number of areas. More nations at virtually all levels of wealth are doing more of their own programming. Production technology costs are going down, groups of experienced technicians and artists have been trained in most countries, and a number of low-cost program forms or genres have been developed, including talk, variety, live music, and game shows. Some countries that have cut back on their film production continue to produce quite a bit of television programming. As ratings in many countries reflect, audiences usually tend to prefer local programming when they can get it.

Cable and Satellite TV around the World

Direct satellite broadcasting is a television or radio satellite service that is marketed directly to home receivers.

Cable TV, which has been familiar to most Americans, Canadians, and some Europeans for years, is now expanding in most other countries of the world. **Direct satellite broadcasting** (DBS) started in Japan and Britain and is rapidly spreading to many other countries, often spanning the borders of neighboring countries.

By the 1990s, cable systems and private satellite TV channels to feed them were blossoming in Europe, Latin America, and Asia. Unlike the latest cable systems in the United States, however, these cable systems delivered what is for the most part a one-way expansion of new video channels, not two-way information services. U.S. cable channels expanded into these new markets. A number of channels quickly became global in reach: CNN, MTV, HBO, ESPN, TNT, Nickelodeon, the Cartoon Network, Discovery, Disney, and others began to sell their existing channels in these countries or even to translate and adapt their U.S. channels to the languages and cultures of the new audiences.

A number of cable channels and DBS services started with a more specific language or regional target. A number of European channels focus on news, music, sports, films, children's shows, and other targeted programming. One satellite television service in Asia, Star TV, owned by Rupert Murdoch, originally targeted the whole of Asia with American (MTV, film), European (BBC, sports) and Chinese-language channels. It has since begun to target more specific markets, such as Taiwan and China, South Asia, Indonesia, and Japan, with more **localized** programming, such as its own adaptations of MTV and more language-specific programs.

Localized media productions are those adapted to local tastes and interests.

Satellite TV and cable television are also beginning to expand in Latin America and the Middle East. Again, channels exported from industrialized nations (CNN, BBC, MTV, and so on) are popular, but several nations (Brazil, Hong Kong, Mexico, Egypt, Saudi Arabia) are developing their own satellite television channels aimed both at national audiences and neighbors within the same cultural-linguistic markets. For example, the Saudi channel Orbit is aimed at Arabs living in Europe as well as the Middle Eastern regional market of Arabic speakers. Some of these regional channels are joint ventures between global and national operations, such as Sky Latin America, which is a regional DBS television operation owned by Murdoch, the U.S. telephone and cable company TCI and AT&T, and the two largest Latin American TV networks, Brazil's TV Globo and Mexico's Televisa.

1. Why did American films come to dominate world film markets?
2. Why did American television also dominate world program markets?
3. What competes with American media products, such as "Baywatch," around the world?
4. Why might American dominance of some world television markets be slipping?
5. Why is television more widely produced around the world than film?

Digital DBS/Cable. Some other countries moved into fully digital television and cable TV before the United States. Japan and some European countries were operating broadcast digital TV early in 1998, and British Sky Broadcasting in Great Britain, owned by Murdoch, initiated 140 channels of fully digital cable TV in 1998.

Telecommunications Systems

Telephone, telegraph, and other telecommunications systems have also developed at different rates in various countries. The United States, Japan, and a few other countries have more than 50 telephones per 100 people and are speeding toward the construction of an Internet (e-mail and World Wide Web) built on the telephone and cable television infrastructures. But some African and South Asian nations have less than 1 telephone per 100 people (see Figure 15.4)—and virutally no cable.

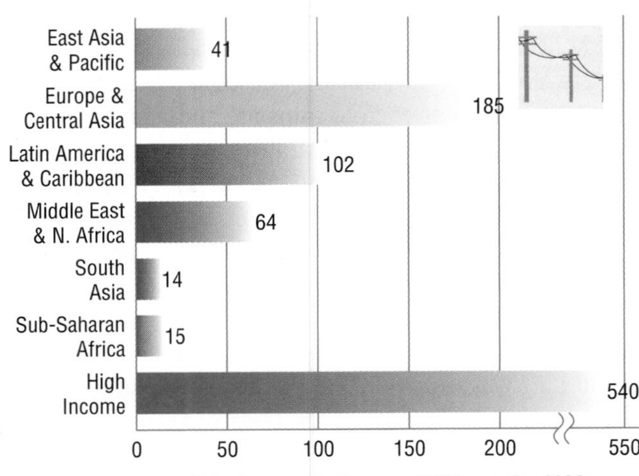

Source: World Bank

FIGURE 15.4
Telephone lines are unequally available around the world, which keeps much of the world's population cut off from telephones, electronic mail, faxes, and other services that use telephone lines.

> **PTT** (postal, telephone, and telegraph) companies are state-owned telecommunications monopolies.

> **Liberalization** in telecommunications or broadcasting policy is the opening up of monopoly services to competition.

Until recently, most telephone systems have been operated by postal, telephone, and telegraph administrations (**PTTs**), state-owned telecommunications monopolies. Governments tended to see telephones as essential to their social and economic development. In many countries, governments have been willing to invest in telephones even when the services are not profitable, such as those to rural areas.

More recently, though, a number of governments have decided to *privatize* their phone companies, or sell them off to private operators. The reasons are usually financial—to reduce debt or gain new resources to expand the phone or information systems. Other reasons for privatization can include trimming the size of government and making the telephone operation more efficient by cutting inefficiencies arising from overgrown, bureaucratic PTTs. This reduces corruption and keeps governments from raking off telephone revenues to support other operations, such as the post office.

NO PHONE AT HOME? In countries such as Argentina, where lines are limited, public pay phones become very important.

Some countries keep the telephone company within the government but still open up some of the newer services, such as cellular telephony, data services, and electronic mail, to competition—a process called **liberalization.** As is true for broadcasting, some countries are also trying to corporatize their telephone companies, making them operate at a profit by marketplace rules.

Some new telephone systems are being built that span national borders. For example, Iridium is a satellite-based telephone system that covers the whole planet with a network of 66 satellites. Satellite service has the ability to bypass all natural barriers, bringing telephone, data, and even Internet service to previously isolated areas. However, the costs of a system capable of allowing direct communication between a satellite and a handset receiver are considerable: An Iridium handset costs around $3000 and monthly service costs $200.

Computers and Information Services Spreading Slowly Worldwide

The production of computers has been limited to a few countries in North America, Europe, and East Asia. The efforts of less industrialized countries, such as Brazil and India, to develop computer industries have often been frustrating and expensive. The use of computers is still highly concentrated in the most industrialized countries because of the relatively high cost of hardware and software and the unequal distribution of income that makes relatively few in the developing world able to afford computers. Even though personal computers can cost less than $400 in the United States, they tend to be more expensive in many other countries. Furthermore, many countries have average monthly incomes well under $200, which makes acquiring even a $400 computer difficult for most of the world's population. Figure 15.5 shows how computers are still concentrated in the industrialized countries, although their use is beginning to spread.

Thus the purchase and use of computers have been spreading worldwide, but unequally. In some countries, only government bureaucrats and a few of the wealthiest professionals and business owners can afford access to computers. In fact, many experts fear that relatively low access to computers will keep businesses and professionals in developing countries from competing in a globalized market where others have a sophisticated computer infrastructure to work with, particularly those in Europe, North America, and East Asia.

Information Services. The concept of information services is relatively new to most countries, However, Europe and Japan have had some experience with what was called videotex. As noted in Chapter 10, videotex was a graphics and text service

MEDIA IMPACT

Bangalore Joins the World Computer Economy

It may have surprised some readers of *Newsweek*'s November 9, 1998, issue to discover that one of the "hot" technology cities in the world is Bangalore, in southern India. Like many technology towns, it has a science-oriented university and a pleasant climate to build on. But so do hundreds of cities around the world. What made Bangalore uniquely successful was a large corps of very well-trained engineers and computer scientists who spoke English and earned a fraction of the salaries of their counterparts in Silicon Valley. American companies, such as Texas Instruments, discovered this in the early 1980s and moved in to take advantage of it. Local and national governments decided to help invest in education and infrastructure, including the telephone system, to help create momentum. Over 250 high-tech firms have either moved in or grown up there since. More trained people poured in from other parts of India.

Another crucial factor is that unlike unsuccessful computer manufacturer Brazil and successful computer manufacturer Taiwan, Bangalore firms concentrated on software rather than hardware. Software requires much less infrastructure (manufacturing capability and capital) than does hardware manufacturing. Software could be created with the resource that Bangalore already had: trained and talented people, resulting from the gradual buildup of scientific personnel at Indian universities over the years.

One danger for India is that many of these talented people may simply move to Silicon Valley or other U.S. technology centers to earn more money. The United States specifically changed immigration rules in 1998 to encourage this "brain drain." However, as salaries rise in Bangalore, and if the all too familiar urban ills of rapid growth don't ruin the city's attractive quality of life, it may continue to provide a crucial center for the growth of high technology in India. Many other developing countries are certainly looking at it to see whether Bangalore is a model that can be adapted.

Source: S. Manzindari, Bangalore, India. *Newsweek,* Nov. 9, 1998, p. 52.

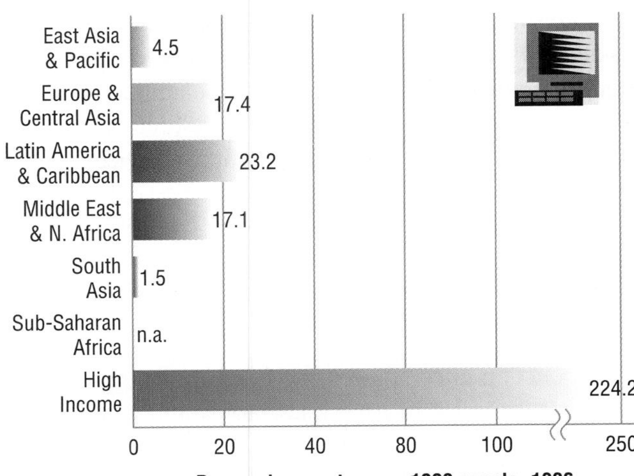

Source: World Bank

FIGURE 15.5
Most people in the world lack access to computers, which also cuts them off from the Internet.

carried over telephone lines, which provided basic databases such as telephone numbers, electronic mail, and a variety of other information like entertainment listings, a forerunner of the World Wide Web.

Videotex succeeded best in France, where it was heavily subsidized and promoted by the government, which gave away millions of "Minitel" terminals in the 1980s, and even required people to use the terminals to get telephone directory information. The French system needed extensive government subsidy for about 6 years before it became profitable. But it introduced millions of people to the idea of information services, well before the Internet had proliferated in the United States, and created the opportunity for a number of private businesses to become information providers through the government system. The challenge in France now is make Minitel compatible with the Internet, so that France's successful system does not backfire and isolate France from the rest of the world.

However, the most significant initial global impact of information services and data communications worldwide was the interconnection of far flung operations of multinational corporations via data networks. In the 1970s and 1980s, well before the Internet brought these kinds of services to ordinary consumers, companies were learning the economic value of sharing data between branches in Japan, the United States and Europe. Even though they had to pay enormous costs to rent special telephone lines to connect computers, the payoff in terms of faster, more accurate internal communications was worth it. Companies began to press in the 1980s and 1990s to connect more and more of their own branches, suppliers and customers throughout the global economy to their networks.

Transborder data flow is the communication of data across political borders.

Transborder Data Flows. Critics such as Herbert Schiller, in a book called *Information in the Age of the Fortune 500* (1981), expressed the fear that **transborder data flows** would be a tool for increasing U.S. corporate power throughout the world, to the detriment of developing and even European economies, political systems, and cultures. One example of how technologies permitted an increase in U.S. control came with the use of satellites to observe resources on the earth. Satellite **remote sensing** could observe the health of the Brazilian coffee crop or

Remote sensing is satellite observation, via photography, infrared photography, and radar, of objects, vegetation, and weather patterns.

even locate copper deposits in Africa. Both the access to satellite signals and the computers required to interpret them were initially very expensive and for a number of years gave corporations an advantage over poor governments (Schiller, 1981). More recently, access has become cheaper, but corporate and military technologies for remote sensing remain more sophisticated than those available to smaller, poorer users.

Transborder data flows permitted some corporations to centralize control over worldwide operations, sometimes causing branches to be downsized, jobs to be moved, and governments to lose tax revenues. However, other observers (Reich, 1991) note that although computers promote U.S. corporate centralization of global operations, computer networks and data transfers also permit low-level jobs such as data entry to be transferred to low-wage nations such as Jamaica, which became an offshore data processing center for many corporations. This situation represents an economic opportunity for some Jamaicans but a loss of jobs for some Americans who had previously done the work.

U.S. dominance is no longer so pronounced, and even the corporations and governments of a number of developing countries are beginning to participate. The arrival of the Internet standardized many of these technologies into a single network that was much cheaper to use, so small business and individual users outside of big business and government can now afford access to rapid, high-capacity international data, text, and graphics communications. However, lack of access to information communication technology still hampers many poorer countries (World Bank, 1998).

The Internet

The Internet has exploded out of the United States into the rest of the world. The idea of sending text, graphics, images, and even music and video via computer has proved attractive almost everywhere. However, the computers and telephone lines that form the backbone of the Internet are in much shorter supply in most other countries. Therefore, the spread of the Internet has been limited outside Japan, Australia, North America, and Northern Europe.

As in the United States, the earliest adopters or users of the Internet around the world have tended to be in universities or governments. Businesses have also moved onto the Internet quickly, particularly those that are affiliated with the major multinational companies. The Internet often permits them to replace expensive private data networks with standard public network connections that give them access to more people, but it also gives them headaches over the security of their data and communications.

In Scandinavia, for example, people have rushed onto the World Wide Web even faster than in the United States. Many college students have Web pages telling about their favorite movies and lyrics to the songs they sing at parties. There are a wide variety of cultural and historical sites, such as Project Runeberg, which has pages on most Scandinavian authors, with sections of their texts. The proportion of small businesses with Web pages is perhaps even larger in Scandinavia than in the United States. Singapore is pushing hard to get all its citizens on

MEDIA IMPACT

The Zapatista Revolution on the Internet

The use of the Internet by the Zapatista Liberation Front in the southern Mexico state of Chiapas has become "one of the most successful examples of the use of computer communications by grassroots social movements" (Zapatistas in Cyberspace, 1998).

This revolutionary group issued a Declaration of War against the Mexican government from the Lacandona Jungle on December 31, 1993, by fax and the Internet. The Zapatistas have explained that their struggle is for work, land, housing, food, health care, education, independence, liberty, democracy, justice, peace, culture, information, security, combating corruption, and protection of the environment.

The Zapatistas don't propose the usual form of revolution: capturing the capital and proclaiming a government. They see a more gradual process: "We think that revolutionary change in Mexico will not be a product of action in just one direction. In other words, it will not be, in the strict sense, an armed revolution or a peaceful revolution . . . the result will be, not one of a party, organization, or coalition of organizations with its triumphant specific social proposals, but a sort of democratic space for the resolution of confrontation between diverse political proposals" (Zapatista declaration, January 20, 1994). Their main method seems to be using modern media, such as the Internet, to create sympathy abroad and exert pressure on the Mexican government to enact reforms and make concessions (Arquilla & Ronfeldt, 1993).

For example, shortly after the Zapatista declaration in January 1994, the Mexican Army moved into the rebel areas to put down the revolt. Impassioned pleas from the Zapatista leaders, foreign anthropologists in the region, and others went out over the Internet asking people to urge the Mexican government to stop the bombardment. One of the authors of this book got seven versions of one of these messages, forwarded by different e-mail groups and lists, within 48 hours of the Mexican government attack. A large number of people did then fax, e-mail, and call Mexican government offices. Concerned about international public opinion, the Mexican government called off the attack and opened negotiations. Hostilities and negotiations have alternated for years subsequently, but the tendency for the government simply to wipe out the Zapatistas militarily has continued to be constrained by Zapatista communications with the outside via Internet, fax, and telephone, which can mobilize international protests.

ACCION ZAPATISTA
http://www.utexas.edu/students/nave/zaps.html
Zapatistas in Cyberspace
http://www.eco.utexas.edu/faculty/Cleaver/zapsincyber.html

About this page]

Zapatista Front of National Liberation

Special Commission for the Promotion of the FZLN in Mexico

English version under construction

Urgent!
Dialogue suspended by the EZLN

THE REVOLUTION WILL NOT BE TELEVISED.
But it will be on the Web, apparently. Revolutionary organizations, such as the Zapatista Front of National Liberation, use the Web to publish their communiqués and to seek supporters.

the Internet, with a high-capacity multimedia network. However, it is not surprising that in fairly prosperous countries, largely well-educated people, many of whom speak English, would start using the Internet. What is more surprising is how many other people around the world are using it.

The Internet has attracted a wide variety of unexpected new users in a variety of countries. Nongovernmental organizations (NGOs), such as human rights groups, environmental activists, churches, labor unions, and political party networks, have found the Internet a useful communications tool (see the Media Impact box). There is a worldwide network of activist groups coordinated by the Institute for Progressive Communications (IPC), which has pioneered opening the Internet to nongovernmental organizations, setting up Internet service providers, and showing groups how to use the Internet to promote social causes—all on a global scale (Frederick, 1993).

The Internet raises a number of new prospects for communication across borders. The structure of the Internet permits anyone with access to a computer and telephone to send or receive electronic mail to or from anyone else on the planet who has an Internet connection. Use of the World Wide Web, with its rich graphics, is much more problematic for many global users, because Internet connections in developing countries may rely on unreliable telephone lines that permit only the slowest connections, making the transmission of graphics impractical. As a result, the Internet in many countries is limited to text information such as e-mail or text pages downloaded via Gopher or other systems.

Although Internet users in developing countries may not be able to see photos or watch music videos over the Internet, they can get access to literally a world of text information. A student in Mexico can read news about his country not only from official sources, but from foreign newspapers, international newswire services, political dissidents (such as the Zapatista Liberation Front), and other sources not approved by his government. Before the Internet, a government such as Mexico would have been able to manipulate press coverage to keep a small group like the Zapatistas largely unknown within Mexico as well as outside. This makes the Internet a revolutionary force in global information flow, as we shall see in the next section. It also makes the Internet the main current challenge for many governments, such as China and Singapore, which are concerned about controlling information flows into their country (see the Technology Trends box). The Chinese and others are working hard on ways to give access to the information people need to participate in a global Information Age economy—while controlling access to politically threatening information and news from the rest of the world. For example, in 1998 the Chinese government charged 30-year-old Shanghai computer software businessman Lin Hai with "inciting the overthrow of state power" by providing 30,000 e-mail addresses to a U.S. Internet magazine called "Big Reference" published by Chinese dissidents. (AP, November 25, 1998).

Telecommunications Industries: Global Providers

The infrastructure for international media and information services has also become increasingly globalized. For transoceanic transmission there are several

TECHNOLOGY *TRENDS*

Political Security: A Closed or an Open Internet— The Great Red Firewall of China

For several years, PRC (People's Republic of China) Public Security Bureau has blocked a few dozen foreign Web sites that carry objectionable material by stopping connect requests at the five major Internet entry points (for example, the academic network control center at Qinghua University) in China. [Note: The full Chinese text of many PRC Internet regulations is available at http://www.edu.cn/law/.] Public security sends the current list of objectionable sites to the entry points periodically, so foreign newspapers or other sites sometimes go on and off the list several times. Chinese officials are well aware that the blocking is neither complete nor insurmountable, but they rely on the fact that most people will not actively seek out objectionable material against government wishes. Some Chinese citizens have said that they would not visit the Embassy Web site (unblocked and also available on the domestic Chinese network at http://www.usembassy-china.org.cn) because officials might frown on visits there.

Blocking Web sites is also not effective because:

- E-mail is generally unaffected by blocking. Chinese-language e-mail magazines such as the Huaxia Digest distributed by China News Digest (http://www.cnd.org) and other organizations are received by thousands of Chinese. News items e-mailed by the Voice of America since early this year are similarly unaffected by net blocks. Dissident organizations outside China collect thousands of e-mail addresses and send them to Chinese netters. One academic said that Chinese are not held responsible for undesirable material that shows up in their e-mail mailbox but might incur a penalty for sending it along to other people.
- The Chinese-language version of Yahoo indexes Chinese-language pages in Hong Kong, Taiwan, the United States, and elsewhere, making the hunt for forbidden information easier for people who do not speak English.
- Those wishing to evade the blockade use alternate routes on the Internet to relay material from blocked Web sites to Web browsers inside China's Great Red Firewall. More and more Chinese users are learning how to access blocked foreign Web sites such as China News Digest, the New York Times, and the VOA home page (http://www.voa.gov). The U.S. State Department home page (http://www.dos.gov) is not blocked, however.
- Enforcement agencies such as the Public Security Bureau appear to lack sufficient technically competent people to monitor the situation.

Quoted from "PRC Internet: Cheaper, More Popular and More Chinese," an October 1998 report from U.S. Embassy Beijing.

worldwide public satellite networks, such as Intelsat, a global consortium of telephone companies that handles much of the world's international telephone and data traffic, and Inmarsat, which handles much of the world's maritime and other mobile communications (see Chapter 9). There are also a number of regional satellite systems, including the Arab League's ArabSat and the European Union's Eutelsat. Quite few national satellite systems also offer telephone and television transmission services to neighboring countries. Privately owned satellite systems, such as PanAmSat, are also increasing in numbers.

Satellites are being at least partially displaced by an emerging set of world and regional fiber optic networks owned by Cable & Wireless of Great Britain, AT&T, and others. Fiber optic cables can carry the same kinds of signals carried by satellites across transoceanic distances, with greater speed and less distortion. Increasingly, for the frequently used routes linking Europe, North America, and Asia, the fiber optic cables are also more cost-efficient.

In another globalizing development, a number of national telecommunications networks are going international. British Telecom has bought up data services in the United States and allied itself with long-distance giant AT&T, after selling earlier interests in MCI. The Baby Bells, France Telecom, Telefonica of Spain, and others are also buying or starting telephone, cellular telephone, and data communications companies in Latin America, Africa, and Asia. These firms have invested in a number of the telephone companies that have been privatized in various nations. They have also eagerly sought to supply new services, such as cellular mobile telephony, in countries where foreign investments have been allowed under newly liberalized rules (Mody, Bauer, & Straubhaar, 1997).

1. **Why did most countries have government telephone companies?**
2. **Why would countries privatize telephone companies?**
3. **Why was videotex a success earlier in France than in the United States? Why is it in danger now?**
4. **Why are some countries trying to limit access to the Internet?**
5. **What are the main global telephone companies?**

REGULATION OF INTERNATIONAL MEDIA

International media and telecommunications systems are regulated differently from national media systems. As with most aspects of **international law,** there is no direct enforcement power, and regulation requires a consensus among nations that the proposed regulations or changes serve their various interests. Failing that, nations tend to assert their self-interest, and the larger, more powerful nations tend to get their way (McPhail, 1989).

International law includes treaties between countries, multicountry agreements, and rules established by international organizations.

One of the few international organizations that has achieved real compromises and real changes is the International Telecommunications Union (ITU). Technical standards have to be established so that users of telegraph, telephone, fax, and electronic mail equipment in various countries can communicate with each other across borders. For instance, the standard for current fax machines was set by the ITU, which has enabled many manufacturers to make equipment that users around the globe can use to send and receive compatible fax messages. One of the main ITU divisions, ITU-T (telecommunications), is primarily involved with technical standards for telecommunications.

The ITU faces some of the same crucial regulatory problems that individual nations must solve within their borders. For example, radio spectrum frequencies have to be allocated to different uses in various nations to avoid interference between users. Even more important, the ITU allocates the space orbits for satellites. This is because satellites occupy orbits that lie above and cross national boundaries. Also, **satellite footprint** areas almost automatically cover multiple countries, requiring international agreements on coverage and standards. Frequency and orbit allocations are routinely recorded by the ITU's B (broadcasting) division and are overseen by periodic World Administrative Radio Conferences that

A **satellite footprint** is the surface area covered by the satellite's signal.

decide ultimately which country gets which orbits and frequencies. Poorer countries have complained since the 1970s that this process favors the larger, more industrialized countries. Spokespersons for developing countries, such as Mustapha Masmoudi from Tunisia, observed that the largest and most powerful 10 percent of the world's countries (particularly the United States and the former U.S.S.R.) controlled the use of 90 percent of the frequencies and orbits (McPhail, 1989). The ITU has responded by creating a third major division, Development, to work with developing countries to accelerate their adoption of new telecommunications and broadcast-related technologies.

ISSUES IN THE GLOBALIZATION OF MEDIA

Among the main issues in globalization of communications media are cultural imperialism, the free flow of information, media trade, and the effects of media on national development.

Cultural Imperialism

Cultural imperialism occurs when some countries dominate others through media exports, advertising, and media institution models.

Unbalanced flow is the unequal flow of media or news between countries.

Perhaps the biggest international issue in communications media has been what many nations call **cultural imperialism,** the unequal flows of film, television, music, news, and information. This **unbalanced flow** bothers many nations on various levels. First, it is seen as a cause of cultural erosion and change. So many media products flow into some countries from the United States that traditionalists fear American ideas, images, and values will replace their own. Some of the fears seem trivial to U.S. observers, as when French authorities fought to keep American words such as "drugstore" and "weekend" from creeping into common use by French people. However, some consequences of media flows can be deadly serious. Some poor countries in Africa saw epidemics of infant diarrhea and death when mothers gave up breast-feeding for bottle-feeding, which they had seen in European and American television programs and advertising. (The problem was caused by mixing infant formula with unsanitary water.)

The cultural imperialism argument has lost some of its force as many countries increase the amount and kinds of media contents they produce. Some governments, such as Brazil and Taiwan, have pressured the national television broadcasters to produce more programming. Others, such as France, subsidize their national film industries to keep them strong. Another solution is to limit media imports, such as the amount of foreign television and film. Many countries have discovered that national and regional television and music production tend to increase more or less naturally, because they are feasible economically and because audiences want them.

Other critics have been more concerned about the economics underlying the flows of media. Underlying the fear of commercial media, in particular, is the idea that they tend

1. What are the limits on international law and international organizations?
2. What are the main organizations involved in the regulation of international media and telecommunications?

to tie countries into a global economy based on advertising and consumption, which offers the poorer countries little and may alienate those in the population who are frustrated by exposure to goods they cannot have.

Free Flow of Information versus Cultural Sovereignty

One of the fears in many countries is that unbalanced media flows will diminish national sovereignty. In contrast, the idea of a free flow of information reflects the basic concept of freedom of speech, whereby all people ought to be as free as possible to both send and receive information across borders. But according to the idea of **national sovereignty**, governments or other domestic forces are entitled to assert national control over natural resources, culture, politics, and so on. Both approaches are established as basic principles in the UNESCO (United Nations Educational Scientific and Cultural Organization) charter and the 1948 U.N. Declaration on Human Rights.

National sovereignty is the policy of keeping domestic forces in control of a nation's economy, politics, and culture.

Those who consider the current international flows of information and culture unequal tend to emphasize national sovereignty as a justification for a country's asserting control over media flows. The United States has opposed many such proposals. It does so in part because American commercial media interests are threatened by proposed restrictions on media sales and flows. But the United States has also opposed certain proposed restrictions on principle. The United States and a number of other nations believe it is important to keep as free a flow of information as possible to promote freedom of speech globally.

Debate raged in UNESCO over these issues in 1976–1979 until the United States decided to withdraw in 1983 in protest over proposed policies that it thought violated the values of the **free flow of information** and journalistic freedom. UNESCO proposed that countries create national policies to balance the flow of information. The United States feared that UNESCO's policies would give too much power to governments, which would be likely to restrict free speech and the free flow of information. The compromise proposal in 1979 in UNESCO was to promote a **free and balanced flow** by helping developing countries build up their own abilities to produce and export media and cultural products.

Free flow of information occurs when information flows as freely as possible between countries.

Free and balanced flow occurs when a country achieves more nearly equal flows of media via the freedom both to produce *and* receive media.

Although this idea received little financial support, a number of developing nations succeeded in producing more media anyway. Some regional news agencies were launched in the Caribbean and Africa, although their impact has been very limited. More recently, the Internet has permitted a much more diverse flow of news, although most major news media continue to use the same old commercial news agencies. As described earlier in this chapter, a number of national media ventures have been started to try to balance the flow of television, film, and music between nations.

Trade in Media

Media flow and trade issues have been raised in regional treaty organizations, such as the European Union (EU) and the North American Free Trade Agreement (NAFTA). The United States tends to see cultural industries as a trade policy issue, because such exports are a significant part of the American balance of trade, compensating for American purchases of Japanese VCRs, radios, and other consumer electronics, for example. European and Canadian governments see these matters partially as a trade issue, desiring to boost their own producers, but they also see a cultural policy issue and believe the distinctness of national cultures ought to be preserved on television, music, and film.

Tariffs are taxes imposed by governments on goods imported from other countries.

Quotas are limits on imports imposed by national governments to keep out foreign films and programs.

The same issue has come up in the General Agreement on Trade and Tariffs (GATT), which was dedicated to lower **tariffs** on trade, and its successor, the World Trade Organization. In the last round of GATT negotiations, concluded in 1993, the United States pushed hard to impose new international trade rules on "audiovisual" materials (television and film) that would keep countries from protecting their own national film and television industries or setting **quotas** to keep imported films and programs out. The European Union rallied around the French, who opposed such a change (existing GATT rules permitted protection and subsidy of film industries) and succeeded in keeping audiovisual materials from being included in more liberal trade rules. At the same time, the European Union has been opening up Europe for greater competition, trade, and non-European investment in telecommunications, since telecommunications is not seen as having the same cultural impact as film and television.

In the late 1990s, the World Trade Organization moved into another crucial area for new digital media: copyright and intellectual property protection. The United States proposed significantly strengthening copyright protection in digital media, such as the Internet and digital recordings (CDs, CD-ROMs, digital audio tape), and a stronger set of protections was agreed on in 1998.

Media and National Development

The other main issue is whether media, information technologies, and telecommunications can be made to serve national development better. As we noted earlier, part of the fear expressed in international debates is that media are primarily serving global commercial interests, not the needs of the populations of the various countries, particularly the poorer populations. Many government planners and social critics feel that most people in developing nations need media that offer more than slick American entertainment and advertising.

Many governments and international organizations, such as UNESCO, have worked hard to create models of using media to promote education, health, agriculture, local religious and cultural values, and so on. Some of these programs have succeeded, particularly radio programs based in rural areas (McAnany, 1980). Television has been less successful in these kinds of efforts, perhaps because its high costs divert programming from local needs.

1. What is cultural imperialism?
2. What are considered unequal flows of media?
3. What is the conflict or tradeoff between national sovereignty and the free flow of information?

The ITU and the World Bank are encouraging national governments and foreign investors to invest more funds in the expansion of developing world telephone and telecommunications systems. World Bank and other research shows that such investment contributes to economic growth.

SUMMARY AND REVIEW

WHY DOES GOVERNMENT OPERATE BROADCASTING MORE THAN PRINT MEDIA IN MANY COUNTRIES?

Print media are easier to start and do not require frequency regulations or standards by governments. Electronic media also have the potential to affect more people. Some governments see electronic media as valuable tools for either development or political control. In some of the poorest countries, governments may be among only a few bodies that have enough money to run broadcasting or telecommunications.

WHAT IS THE PURPOSE OF PUBLIC BROADCASTING?

Public broadcasting is oriented toward providing the public with education and information, balanced with entertainment. Public broadcasting corporations are usually not-for-profit companies financed by government or by license fees paid by everyone who owns a radio or television set.

WHY DID MOST COUNTRIES HAVE GOVERNMENT TELEPHONE COMPANIES IN THE EARLY YEARS OF PHONE SERVICE?

Government-owned and operated PTTs (postal telephone and telegraph administrations) were the telephone companies in nearly all countries. Government monopolies were seen as capable of unifying national services, investing in expansion, and extending services to those not served.

WHY DID COUNTRIES PRIVATIZE TELEPHONE COMPANIES?

Government PTTs came to be seen as inefficient, overstaffed, and incapable of generating the necessary resources for investment. Private companies, both domestic and foreign, were seen as bringing in financial resources and as a more efficient approach to management.

WHY DO AMERICAN FILMS DOMINATE WORLD FILM MARKETS?

American films were made to appeal to a large immigrant audience through a universal and entertainment-oriented style, which made its films easier to accept among diverse international audiences. The United States also benefited from the destruction or blockage of other film producers during World War I and World War II. U.S. producers developed an efficient export cartel, the Motion Picture Export Association of America (MPEAA), which owned much of the world distribution and exhibition structure.

WHY DID AMERICAN TELEVISION ALSO RISE TO DOMINATE WORLD PROGRAM MARKETS?

U.S. television programs were produced primarily by the MPEAA film studio companies, which gave them the benefit of an existing international distribution structure. American television also used many of the popular techniques and formulas of Hollywood film producers, which gave their productions much of the same universal entertainment appeal. Many other countries found that showing American television programs was cheaper than the cost of local production and provided an easy solution to filling schedules.

WHAT IS THE IMPACT OF AMERICAN MEDIA PRODUCTS AROUND THE WORLD?

American television programs, films, and music are very popular, particularly among young people, but people fear that American ideas, images, and values will replace those of their own cultures. Actual effects seem to have been less than was anticipated, because many people do not watch American programs much, and they tend to interpret them in their own way.

WHY MIGHT AMERICAN DOMINANCE OF SOME WORLD TELEVISION MARKETS BE SLIPPING?

As technology costs for television production decline and experience in producing shows increases, people in many countries are finding it easier to make their own shows. Furthermore, once countries develop television genres that are popular at home and in nearby cultural linguistic markets, audiences tend to prefer the local programs.

WHAT ARE SOME OF THE MAIN CULTURAL DIFFERENCES AMONG TELEVISION PROGRAMS FROM VARIOUS COUNTRIES?

Soap operas, variety shows, and music and talk shows tend to be more prominent in programming abroad than in the United States. Some countries are too small to produce certain kinds of programming. Smaller countries tend to focus on these lower-cost genres.

WHY DO MORE COUNTRIES PRODUCE MUSIC THAN TELEVISION?

Recorded music is cheaper to produce than television shows. Musical preferences are often more localized within countries and to subcultures defined by age, ethnicity, and religion. Thus there is demand for a large, diverse set of artists and recording companies.

WHAT ARE THE MAIN REASONS WHY COMPANIES BUY OR START UP MEDIA IN OTHER COUNTRIES?

The trend to extend successful products into foreign markets sometimes leads companies to get involved in global distribution systems. Investing in film distributors and theater chains guarantees that the owners' films will be distributed. In radio, television, cable, and satellite television systems, some companies buy into or start up foreign stations or networks to sell programming, to get into a profitable business, or to guarantee that their cable program channels will be carried.

WHICH COMPANIES ARE THE MAIN GLOBAL OWNERS OF MASS MEDIA?

The main companies are Time Warner (U.S.), Disney-ABC (U.S.), Rupert Murdoch's News Corp. (Australia), Hachette (France), Bertelsmann (Germany), AT&T/TCI (U.S.), and NBC (U.S.). Companies beyond traditional mass media, such as Microsoft and AOL, should be considered, too.

WHAT ARE THE LIMITS ON INTERNATIONAL LAW AND INTERNATIONAL ORGANIZATIONS?

International law is just a collection of treaties between countries, multilateral agreements or treaties between groups of countries, and rules set by international organizations. The problem is that they all rely on voluntary compliance and consensual behavior by individual governments.

WHAT ARE THE MAIN ORGANIZATIONS INVOLVED IN THE REGULATION OF INTERNATIONAL MEDIA AND TELECOMMUNICATIONS?

The main regulator is the ITU (International Telecommunications Union), which has telecommunication, broadcasting, and development divisions. It allocates frequencies and satellite orbits (through the World Administrative Radio Conferences) to countries and, together with the International Standards Organization, sets international standards for telecommunications. UNESCO (United Nations Educational, Scientific and Cultural Organization) has been the main forum for debate in which a number of countries have protested the unbalanced flows of media and news between countries.

The EU (European Union) is increasingly important in setting standards, establishing rules about media production and flow, and creating regional markets for information and media industries. The World Trade Organization has also become important in debates about trade in media products and information services.

WHAT IS CULTURAL IMPERIALISM?

Cultural imperialism is an unbalanced relationship in culture and media between countries. The main specific issue is unequal flows of film, news, television programs, cable channels, and music from the United States to other countries. Other aspects include the globalization of media ownership, foreign investment in national media, and the use of foreign media models. International media flows seem to become more balanced as other countries produce and export more, although the United States still exports a great deal of media and information and imports relatively little. This tendency toward balance is more notable in music and television than in film or news.

WHAT IS THE CONFLICT OR TRADEOFF BETWEEN NATIONAL SOVEREIGNTY AND THE FREE FLOW OF INFORMATION?

The United States has promoted the free flow of information as an international extension of its national values about freedom of speech and press. The United States and many other countries feel that the free flow of information will reduce conflict and increase understanding. Other countries complain that, in practice, the free flow of ideas permits the United States to dominate international flows of media. They argue that they should have national control or sovereignty over flows of media in order to ensure more balance in the flow. However, giving such power to government raises the prospects of censorship and control of information.

Electronic Resources

For up-to-the-minute URLs about *Globalization of Communications Media,* access the MEDIA NOW site on the World Wide Web at:

http://communication.wadsworth.com/

Credits

CHAPTER 1: 4: Shelley Gazin/Corbis-Bettmann; 6: ©1999 Cable News Network. All Rights Reserved. Used by permission of CNN; 7: Nina Berman/SIPA Press; 10: Reuters/Gregg Newton/Archive Photos; 11: Reuters/Ken Cedeno/Archive Photos; 12: Edward Hicks, Residence of David Twining, 1787. Courtesy of Abbey Adlrich Rockefeller Folk Art Center, Williamsburg, VA; 14: (left) Corbis-Bettmann; (right) The Granger Collection; 17: Photofest; 18: Official White House Photo; 20: Courtesy of Eidos Interactive; 25: ©1999 The New York Times Company. Reprinted by Permission.
CHAPTER 2: 35: Craig McClain; 44: Forest McMullin/Black Star; 46: Photofest; 47: Porter Gifford/Gamma Liaison; 49: Photofest; 52: David Frazier; 53: Courtesy of Apple Computers.
CHAPTER 3: 60: Archivo de Stato Siena, Italy, Scala/Art Resource, NY; 63: Archive Photos; 64: The Granger Collection; 66: UPI/Corbis-Bettmann; 68: Jonathan Elderfield/Gamma Liaison; 69: Peter Stackpole/Life Magazine/©Time, Inc.; 75: SoftBook reader image used courtesy of SoftBook® Press, Inc. www.softbook.com 650-463-1800. SoftBook R is a registered trademark of SoftBook Press, Inc.; 76: Copyright ©1999 Microsoft Corporation; 77: Bryce Lankard/Gamma Liaison; 79: Courtesy of Zero City; 82: Amazon.com is a registered trademark of Amazon.com, Inc. in the US and/or in other countries. ©1999 Amazon.com. All rights reserved.
CHAPTER 4: 97: The Granger Collection; 98: The Granger Collection; 99: Archive Photos; 102: The Granger Collection; 109: Courtesy of MediaFax; 110: Excite (personalize your content) and the Excite logo are trademarks of Excite, Inc. and may be registered in various jurisdictions. Excite screen display copyright 1995-1999 Excite, Inc.; 116: ©G. B. Trudeau. Reprinted with permission by the Universal Press Syndicate. All rights reserved; 119: Reuters/Tim Aubry/ Archive Photos; 124: The Gamma Liaison Network/Liaison.
CHAPTER 5: 132: The Granger Collection; 133: Corbis-Bettmann; 134: David Sarnoff Collection; 142: Amalie Rothschild/Corbis-Bettmann; 147: Courtesy of MP3.com; 151: The Granger Collection; 153: Joseph Sia/Archive Photos; 155: Evan Agostini/Gamma Liaison.
CHAPTER 6: 173: Corbis-Bettmann; 175: Springer/Bettmann Film Archive; 178: Photofest; 181: Photofest; 182: Fred Prouser/SIPA Press; 185: ©Disney Enterprises, Inc./Pixar Animation Studios/Photofest; 193: David Frazier; 197: David Frazier.
CHAPTER 7: 203: Photofest; 206: Courtesy of the Broadcast Pioneer's Library, University of Maryland, College Park; 208: Corbis-Bettmann; 211: Photofest; 213: Courtesy of Black Entertainment Television; 217: ©1990 Capital Cities/ABC, Inc./Photofest; 218: Helayne Seidman/SIPA Press; 224: Reuters/Fred Prouser/Archive Photos; 233: David Frazier; 236: Bohdan Hrynewych/Stock Boston; 241: Reuters/Sam Mircovich/Archive Photos.
CHAPTER 8: 248: Photodisc; 257: The Computer Museum; 259: Eric Neurath/Stock Boston; 264: Source: UCLA Gateway Home Page. Reproduced with permission of The Regents of the University of California; 267: Laima Druskis/Stock Boston; 276: Courtesy of www.lyrics.ch.
CHAPTER 9: 280: Randy Taylor/Liaison; 284: Library of Congress; 285: Courtesy of HBO. HBO and Home Box Office are registered service marks of Time Warner Entertainment Company, L.P.; 289: (top) AT&T Archives; (bottom) Dale C. Spartas/Gamma Liaison; 293: AT&T Archives; 297: Mike Yamashita/Gamma Liaison; 299: AT&T Archives; 302: NY Post-David Rentas (New York Post)/Corbis.
CHAPTER 10: 317: The Granger Collection; 319: The Granger Collection; 328: Courtesy of the Pillsbury Company; 331: Courtesy of Alaska Wilderness League. ©1999 Survivors of the Exxon Valdez Oil Spill. Photos ©Gary Braasch; 334: (top) Dwight Carter; (bottom) UPI/Corbis-Bettmann.
CHAPTER 11: 350: The Granger Collection; 351: The Granger Collection; 354: Copyright ©1994 Mazda Motor of America, Inc. Used by permission; 361: ©1997 David Lubarsky; 370: Craig McClain; 372: Courtesy of PepsiCola Company; 381: Courtesy of PepsicCola Company.
CHAPTER 12: 386: Craig McClain; 390: Courtesy of Albert Bandura; 405: Seth Resnick/Stock Boston; 406: Courtesy of NetVentures, Inc.; 409: Courtesy of the Advertising Council of America; 411: Jacques Chenet/Woodfin Camp & Associates.
CHAPTER 13: 424: Bob Daemmrich/Stock Boston; 431: ©Michael Newman/Photo Edit; 433: Jerry Bauer; 435: Copyright Michigan State University Board of Trustees. Used with permission; 436: Courtesy of the City of Santa Monica; 445: Courtesy of IBM.
CHAPTER 14: 454: Reprinted by Permission: Tribune Media Services, Cartoon by Mike Peters; 456: Corbis-Bettmann; 459: Courtesy of Pearl Software, Inc.; 465: The Granger Collection; 466: Courtesy of the National Telecommunications Information Administration; 468: Used with permission and courtesy of University of California, Irvine, bookstore. Photos by Ray Avery; 470: Robert Wallis/SIPA Press; 473: George Hunter/Tony Stone Images; 475: Courtesy of FAIR; 478: Copyright ©1997 Society of Professional Journalists; 480: Lawrence Schwartzwald/ Gamma Liaison; 481: Robert Giroux/Gamma Liaison.
CHAPTER 15: 491: Milind A. Ketkar/Dinodia Picture Agency; 494: Agence France Presse/Corbis-Bettmann; Peter Magubane/Liaison; 503: Reuters/Corbis-Bettmann; 505: ©1994 CNN. All rights reserved; 508: Christian Science Monitor; 508, 510: Figs. 15.4, 15.5 Copyright ©1998 The World Bank. Used by permission; 512: Courtesy of FZLN.

Glossary

Abuse of market power is exploitation of a dominant or near-monopoly position in a market to keep potential competitors out.

Account executives are the liaisons between the agency and the client.

An **accreditation program** is a voluntary certification program.

Accuracy of information refers to the media representative's responsibility to ensure that media or information content is truthful, correct, and not deceptive.

Acoustic is sound that is not electronically amplified.

Advertising is communication that is paid for and is usually persuasive in nature.

Advertising agencies are independent organizations that create promotional campaigns on behalf of advertisers.

Advertising managers coordinate the advertiser's efforts across all of its products.

Advertising media are the communication channels that carry messages to consumers.

The **advertising plan** is a written document outlining the objectives and strategies for a product's advertising.

Affiliate fees are monthly per-subscriber fees that cable networks charge to local cable operators for the right to carry their programs.

Affiliate stations take programming and advertising from a network.

Affiliates in broadcasting are stations that contract to use the programming of and share advertising/financing with a network.

Agenda setting is the ability of the media to determine what is important.

AM or **amplitude modulation** refers to the fact that the sound information is carried in the height, or amplitude, of the radio wave.

Analog communication uses continuously varying signals corresponding to the light or sounds originated by the source.

Anticompetitive practices are those that unfairly use market power to damage potential competitors.

Antisocial behavior is behavior contrary to prevailing social norms.

Aristotle's golden mean holds that "moral virtue is appropriate location between two extremes."

Audience segment is a subgroup of consumers with specialized tastes and media habits.

Audiotape is magnetic tape used for recording audio.

Audits are formal assessments of the internal and external forces affecting an organization.

B-movies are cheaply and quickly made genre films.

Backlist books are those which are not being currently promoted by a publisher but are still in print.

Basic cable includes the local channels, distant stations, and satellite signals that cable operators offer for a basic monthly fee.

Bits, short for *b*inary dig*its,* are the basic 1s and 0s of computer data.

Bluegrass developed from English, Scottish, and Irish roots with similar instrumentation and ballad forms.

Blues is an African American musical tradition based primarily on guitar and distinctive plaintive lyrics.

Box office receipts are the money made from selling tickets to movies in theaters, not counting video, television, etc.

A product's name, design, and symbols constitute a **brand,** which distinguishes it from other products.

Brand loyalty is the consumer's propensity to make repeat purchases of a specific brand of product.

Brand managers are in charge of one specific product.

Broadcast fax services send faxes of news and information to the media.

Broadcast transcription services transcribe radio and television coverage.

Browsers are the computer programs that display information found on the Web.

The **bullet model,** ***or** **hypodermic model,*** posits powerful, direct effects of the mass media.

Business video programs are created by organizations for their employees and customers.

The **buying motive** explains the consumer's desire to purchase particular products.

A **byte** is (usually) eight computer bits. Each byte can represent a single numerical digit or letter of the alphabet.

Capture theory suggests that regulators are often effectively dominated by the interests of the industry they regulate.

CD-ROM (compact disc read-only memory) drives hold discs that store large amounts of computer data and work, similar to compact disc music players.

Cellular radio is a mobile telephone service that subdivides service areas into many small cells to maximize the number of users.

Censorship is control over media content by those in higher authority in a society.

Chain broadcasting refers to radio networks and their control over talent and affiliated stations.

Channel surfing uses remote controls to browse briefly through a number of channels, viewing short bits of each.

Chapbooks were cheaply bound books or pamphlets of poetry or prose aimed at a broader audience, much like early paperbacks.

Chilling effect is when fairness rules inhibit stations from airing controversial programs.

Classified ads are brief newspaper advertisements, usually one column wide.

Coaxial cable is the high- capacity wire used for cable television transmission.

Communications media include all forms of communication mediated through mechanical or electronic channels.

Compact discs (CDs) are digitally encoded recordings that are played back by lasers.

Competition exists when several companies supply the same market.

Computer animation is the use of computers rather than hand drawing and coloring in film animation.

Computers are electronic data processing machines.

Concentration of ownership occurs when media are owned by a small number of individuals, government agencies, or corporations.

Confidentiality usually refers to protecting the identity of news sources.

Conglomerates are companies made up of diverse parts, usually across several media industries.

A **consent decree** is an agreement by the subject of an antitrust suit to change practices without formally admitting guilt.

Consolidation refers to a reduction in the number of media outlets and a concentration of the ownership of media among fewer owners.

In a **consumer culture,** social status is largely defined by the acquisition of goods and services.

Content analysis is a quantitative description of the content of the media.

Convergence is the integration of mass media, computers, and telecommunications into a common technological and institutional base.

Copy testing evaluates the effectiveness of advertisements.

Copyright royalty fee is a payment legally required for use of another person's intellectual property.

Copyright is a legal privilege to use, sell, or license intellectual property, such as a book or a film.

Copywriters write the text of advertisements.

Corantos, the ancestors of newspapers, were irregular news sheets that appeared around 1600 in Holland and England and covered foreign affairs.

Corporate underwriting on PBS television stations is financial support of programs in return for a mention of the underwriter on the air.

Corporatization is making a government operation behave like a private company under marketplace rules.

Correlations are statistical measures of association between two or more variables.

Cost per thousand (CPM) is a way of comparing advertising costs in terms of the price paid to reach 1000 members of the target audience.

Creative strategy is a written statement about what advertising must say in order to achieve marketing objectives.

The **Creel Committee** built public support for U.S. involvement in World War I.

Crisis communications are designed to ameliorate the public relations impact of crises.

Critical studies explains society in terms of the interrelationships among audiences, media, and culture.

Cross-ownership is ownership of different kinds of media in the same geographical area.

Cross-subsidize applies revenues from a profitable area to a less profitable one.

Cultivation theory argues that mass media exposure cultivates a view of the world that is consistent with mediated "reality."

Cultural imperialism occurs when some countries dominate others through media exports, advertising, and media institution models.

Cultural proximity is the desire of audiences to see or hear media products from their own or similar cultures.

Cultural-linguistic markets revolve around language and cultural commonalities.

In the **cultural studies** view, communication is a process in which the source and the receiver jointly create the meaning of the message.

Culture is a system of images and symbols shared by a group.

Custom publishing refers to creating customized versions of print newspapers, magazines, or books for particular audiences.

Database marketing is used when advertisers store information about consumers so that they can personalize messages.

DBS (direct broadcast satellite) is a satellite service that is sold directly to home subscribers.

De-skilling is reduction of the skill requirements of a job through mechanization or automation.

Deceptive advertising is advertising that makes misleading or untruthful claims.

Demographic channels are designed to appeal to audiences with shared demographic characteristics.

Demographic segmentation is based on social or personal characteristics, such as age, sex, education, or income.

Dependent variables are the consequences, or effects, of media exposure.

Deregulation refers to decreasing government oversight in the anticipation that competition will minimize abuses of power.

Desktop publishing is the composition, layout, and sometimes printing of materials using a personal computer.

Developing nations are those in Asia, Latin America, the Middle East, and Africa that are struggling to grow economically and to develop socially.

Diffusion is the process whereby innovations spread in a social system.

Digital audio broadcasting (DAB) is the transmission of radio programs in digital format.

Digital communication converts sound, pictures, and text into computer-readable formats by breaking them up into strings of ones and zeros.

Digital compression reduces the number of computer bits that have to be transmitted.

Digital subscriber line (DSL) is a high-speed digital phone service that can transmit audio, video, and computer data over conventional phone lines.

Digital television is television that is transmitted in a digital format.

Digital versatile disc (DVD) technology is a higher- capacity descendant of compact disc (CD) technology that fully integrates computer, audio, and video storage.

Digital means computer readable.

Digitizing means making an image or text computer- readable, as with a scanner.

Dime novels were inexpensive paperback novels that aimed at a mass readership.

Direct Broadcast Satellite (DBS) is a system of transmitting television signals from satellites directly to compact home receivers.

Direct marketing is a form of advertising in which an immediate response is requested from the customer.

Disc jockey is a radio station announcer who plays records and often emphasizes delivery and personality.

Distant signals are cable channels imported from major television markets.

Diurnos, direct ancestors of daily newspapers, gave daily reports and tended to be more focused on domestic events.

Diversity of content implies a variety of ideas, cultural traditions, and values in media.

Diversity of ownership implies that media owners are of diverse ethnic backgrounds and gender.

Dubbing is the practice of recording a soundtrack in a different language.

Economics is a theory that explains society in terms of the production, distribution, and consumption of goods and services.

Economies of scale result in reduced per-unit costs when large numbers of copies are manufactured.

Electromagnetic recording rearranges the magnetic fields of metallic particles in the tape according to the electrical current produced by a microphone.

Electronic commerce is the ability to offer goods, advertise, and complete purchases on-line.

Electronic press kits are CD-ROM or Internet versions of printed press kits.

Elite are better educated, more affluent, higher status audiences who have earlier, wider access to media.

Encryption means the writing of a message in a secret code.

Environmental monitoring tracks and weighs the environment in which a given institution operates.

In the **era of creativity,** advertisers emphasized entertainment as well as information.

Ethics are moral rules of conduct that guide one's actions in specific situations.

Ethnography is a naturalistic research method in which the observer obtains detailed information from personal observation or interviews over extended periods of time.

Experimental research studies the effects of media in carefully controlled situations that manipulate media exposure and content.

Fair use permits users to copy parts of copyrighted works for purposes of analyzing them in classrooms, in academic publications, or in artistic works, or personal use, so long as they are not being resold.

Fairness in journalism ethics refers to the media representative's responsibility to select and treat topics and sources ethically.

Feature films are longer story films, usually over 1½ hours.

The **Federal Trade Commission (FTC)** is the major regulator of advertising thought to be deceptive.

Fiber optic cable systems use light instead of electricity to communicate.

Film studios are production companies that have achieved considerable stability or success over time, often by relying on the same directors and actors.

Filtering software automatically prevents Web users from visiting pornographic Web sites.

Fin-Syn or Financial interest in Syndication Rules by FCC kept networks from producing or owning most of their programming to increase diversity.

The **First Amendment** to the U.S. Constitution guarantees freedom of speech and of the press in the United States.

First-run distribution for films is to movie theaters, usually followed by video, cable TV, TV, etc.

Floppy disc drives store computer data on a flexible ("floppy") plastic disc coated with a magnetized film.

FM or **frequency modulation** means that the sound information is carried in variations in the frequency of the radio wave.

Focus groups are small group interviews intended to explore consumer reactions in depth.

Fordism is the application of the assembly-line process, reducing work to the endless repetition of a single task.

Free and balanced flow occurs when a country achieves more nearly equal flows of media via the freedom both to produce *and* receive media.

Free flow of information occurs when information flows as freely as possible between countries.

Free press is the extension of freedom of speech to media.

Freedom of speech protects political speech, defines and sets limits on indecent or obscene speech.

Frequency allocation is granting exclusive right to use a radio frequency in a specific area, usually done by government agencies.

Frequency bands are parts of the electromagnetic spectrum authorized for a particular purpose.

Frequency interference takes place when two broadcasts are on the same frequency so that they interfere with one another.

Frequency is the number of cycles that waves complete in a set amount of time.

A **front group** works on behalf of another organization whose direct involvement might be controversial.

Full-service agencies offer a wide range of advertising services, including research, strategy development, and media placement.

Functionalism is the theory of communications media that explains them in terms of their basic social functions.

Gatekeepers decide what will appear in the media.

Gatekeeping is deciding what will appear in the media.

General audience means that the audience is made up of a large group of people from all walks of life.

General-audience channels contain a variety of program types for a wide audience.

Generalizability is the degree to which research procedures and samples may be generalized to the real world.

Genre channels feature programs of a certain type, such as movies or sports events.

Genres are formats of media content that enable writers and audiences to understand each others' expectations.

Geodemographic clustering categorizes consumers based on the demographic characteristics common to the area in which they live.

Globalization refers to the spread worldwide of major media companies and to their serving as models for other countries' media.

Glocal media are local productions done with global forms and ideas.

Gospel originated as southern Protestant religious music, with distinctive but related African American and white forms.

Gross refers to the overall revenue of films from box office distribution before expenses are deducted.

Group owners own a number of broadcast stations but do not always provide them with common programming, as a network would.

Hegemony is an underlying consensus of ideology that favors a system that serves the interests of a dominant group in society.

Helical scanning stores video frames at a slant, like cutting up tape and stacking it slantwise.

Hertz (Hz) is a measure of the frequency of a radio wave in cycles per second.

High-definition television (HDTV) is a form of digital television that provides a wider and more detailed picture than conventional TV.

Horizontal integration is concentrating ownership by acquiring companies all in the same business.

http (Hypertext transfer protocol) is the Internet protocol used to transfer files over the Web.

Hypertext markup language (HTML) is the programming language used to create pages on the Web.

Hypertext is a system for linking different texts and images within a computer document or over a network.

Indecency is usually defined as depiction or description of sex or excretion in the media or the arts.

Independence in media usually refers to freedom from governmental control, not from owners or advertisers.

Independent filmmakers ("indies") usually produce fewer films than the majors and at much less cost- often a few million dollars.

Independent variables are the causes of media effects.

Independents are those stations not affiliated with a network.

The **Industrial Revolution** produced a situation in which more products are manufactured than can be consumed.

Information campaigns use the techniques of advertising in an attempt to convince people to adopt prosocial behaviors.

In the **information society,** exchange of information is the predominant economic and social activity.

Information workers produce, process, or distribute information as their primary work activity.

Integrated marketing communication (IMC) assures that the use of all commercial media and messages is clear, consistent, and achieves impact.

Intellectual property is a work of art, writing, film, or software that is created or owned by an individual or company.

Interactive communication uses feedback to modify a message as it is presented.

International law includes treaties between countries, multicountry agreements, and rules established by international organizations.

The **Internet** is a global network of computer networks.

Internet 2 is the "next generation" Internet.

Internet service providers (ISPs) are the companies that provide connections to the Internet.

Internet TV allows consumers to watch television and then access on-line advertising from the same TV set.

Joint operation agreements occur when competing newspapers share facilities, costs, administrative structure, and advertising, while maintaining editorial independence.

Kant's categorical imperative says we should act according to rules that we would like to see universally applied.

The **knowledge gap hypothesis** posits that the "information-rich" benefit more from exposure to communications media than the "information-poor."

Labels of record companies are particular names for a group of recordings that usually follows a consistent line of music.

Law is a binding rule enacted, enforced, and interpreted by government legislatures, executive agencies, and courts, respectively.

The **law of supply and demand** describes the relationship among the supply of products, profits, prices, and consumer demand.

Leaks are the release, by officials, of confidential information-often policy ideas or facts about which they do not wish to be quoted.

Libel is a harmful and untruthful criticism by media that intends to damage someone.

Liberalization in telecommunications or broadcasting policy is the opening up of monopoly services to competition.

License fees are annual fees, or fees on the sales of radio or television receivers, assessed to pay for public broadcasting.

License is a permission to operate a service on a specific radio frequency.

Licensing is an agreement granting permission to use a copyrighted or trademarked work, for an agreed-on fee.

Lifestyle channels are targeted to audiences with certain common interests.

Lifestyle segmentation categorizes people on the basis of their attitudes, interests, and opinions.

Limited effects holds that the effects of the mass media on individuals are slight.

Local area networks (LANs) are high-speed computer networks that link computers within a department, a building, or a campus of buildings.

Local market monopoly in the newspaper industry is a market served by only a single daily newspaper.

Local origination is cable programming created within the community by the cable operator.

Localism is the practice of giving broadcast stations to all possible local areas and encouraging them to serve local interests.

Localized media productions are those adapted to local tastes and interests.

Magazine was a colonial-era term for a warehouse; print magazines were storehouses of various materials from books, pamphlets, and newspapers.

Major film producers are the larger studios, each of which produces 15-25 movies per year.

Manuscript originally meant written or copied by hand.

Market entry rules govern the entry by a new industry or company into a regulated market from which it had previously been excluded.

Marketing managers are in charge of a family of products for an advertiser.

Marketplace of ideas is the concept that, with free speech, the best ideas will win out in competition with others.

Mass communication is one-to-many, with limited audience feedback.

Media departments negotiate on behalf of the advertiser to buy space from media companies.

Media effects are changes in knowledge, attitudes, or behaviors resulting from media exposure.

Media literacy is the ability to use advertising and other forms of media in optimal ways in everyday life.

Media relations focuses on establishing and maintaining good relations with the media.

Media representatives are intermediaries between advertising agencies and media outlets.

Media research compiles data about media consumption for the advertising industry.

A **merger** is the economic joining of two or more previously unrelated companies.

Microwave is a high-capacity system that transmits information between relay towers on highly focused beams of high-frequency radio waves.

Mill's principle of utility holds that we should "seek the greatest happiness for the greatest number."

Miscellanies were magazines that carried a wide variety of contents.

Modems convert digital data to analog signals for transmission over analog networks such as the public telephone network.

Monopoly exists when a single firm dominates an industry.

Motion pictures are the technical means for taking a series of photographs at a constant speed to portray motion.

MPAA ratings is a movie rating system instituted in 1968.

MPAA (Motion Picture Association of America) is a sales and lobby organization that represents the major film studios.

Muckraking is journalism that investigates scandal, "raking up the muck" of dirty details.

Multilateral trade negotiations take place among a number of countries at the same time, usually within an international organization.

Multimedia systems integrate text, audio, and video and let the user select the presentation mode.

Multiple system operators (MSOs) are cable companies that operate systems in two or more communities.

The **multistep flow model** assumes that media effects are indirect and are mediated by opinion leaders.

Musical traditions are genres passed along from one generation to another.

Must carry is the requirement that cable operators carry all locally available broadcast TV signals.

Narrowcasting directs media channels to specific segments of the audience.

National sovereignty is the policy of keeping domestic forces in control of a nation's economy, politics, and culture.

A **natural monopoly** is a business or service area that inherently lends itself to domination by a single firm.

Networks are groups of stations that centralize the production and distribution of programming and ads.

New journalism relied on investigative reporting, big headlines, crusading for causes, and sensational stories.

Nickelodeon is a phonograph or player piano operated by inserting a coin, originally a nickel.

Novels are long prose fiction narratives, dealing with human experience and a sequence of events.

NTSC (National Television Systems Committee) developed the U.S. television standard in 1941.

O&O's are local stations owned and operated by corporations that also own networks.

Obscene speech depicts sexual conduct in a way that appeals to prurient interests in a manner that is "patently offensive" to community standards, and lacks serious artistic, political, or scientific value.

Oligopoly exists when a few firms dominate an industry.

On-line databases are Internet sources of news and research provided by for- profit and nonprofit organizations.

One-voice marketing assures that all commercial messages have continuity of theme.

Opinion leaders are people who try to influence media coverage.

Oral traditions are poetry, stories, ballads, and other pre-media forms of culture passed orally from one generation to another.

Packet switching breaks digital information up into individually addressed chunks, or packets, so that many users can share a single channel.

Partisan refers to media with clear support for one particular political party, or certain leaders and ideas.

Patent pool was several companies sharing technologies that had been awarded government protection via a formal patent.

Patent is a written document that secures to an inventor for a number of years the exclusive right to make, use, or sell an invention.

Pay TV is the practice of charging cable customers an extra monthly fee to receive a specific channel, usually movies or sports.

Pay-per-view is when cable subscribers order a specific program and pay a separate fee just to receive that one show.

Payola occurred when record companies gave gifts or even bribes to key DJs to get their records played.

PBS is the Public Broadcasting Service, which offers news and other programming to radio stations.

Penny arcades were commercial entertainment areas with coin-operated sound and film nickelodeons and other amusements.

Penny Press were daily newspapers after 1830 that sold for one cent and were aimed at a mass audience.

Personal computers are computers for individual users.

Persuasion is the use of convincing arguments to change people's beliefs, attitudes, or behaviors.

A **picture tube** fires an electron gun at dots on the inside of the TV screen. These dots glow with varying intensity to create an image.

Pitch letters are designed to interest editors and reporters in covering a topic from a given perspective or "angle."

Plagiarism is using the exact language or a very close paraphrase of another writer or speaker without citing them as the source.

Playlists are the songs picked to fit the radio station's format and target audience.

Policy is a government or public framework for how to structure and regulate media so that they contribute to the public good.

Political press refers to media that are clearly engaged in political comment or struggle.

Popular culture includes art and entertainment that is widely shared by a population.

Popularization is the process of making a medium appeal to a much broader audience across social classes.

Post-Fordism de-skills jobs to the point where workers no longer need to be paid a living wage.

Press bureau is the office of an organization charged with disseminating information to the media.

Press clipping services "clip" newspaper stories.

A **press release** summarizes news and information in a form that is preferred by the media.

Priming theory states that media images stimulate related thoughts in the minds of audience members.

Privacy is the right to be protected from unwanted intrusions or disclosure.

Private networks are privately owned telecommunications networks.

Privatization of media or telecommunications is the selling of a government operation to private owners.

Productivity is a measure of a firm's output relative to the resources consumed-for example, the number of products each employee makes per hour.

Propaganda is the intentional influence of attitudes and opinions.

Prosocial behaviors are those that a society values and encourages.

Protocols are sets of rules for computer communication that govern such functions as physical interconnection, addressing, routing, error checking, and data formatting.

PTT (postal, telephone, and telegraph) companies are state-owned telecommunications monopolies.

Public access is cable programming created by community residents and organizations without the involvement of the cable operator.

Public corporations in broadcasting are not-for- profit companies financed by government or license fees.

Public diplomacy is the use of media to reach people and influence public opinion in other countries.

Public interest is usually defined for broadcasting in terms of the variety or diversity of programming and the amount of news and public affairs programs carried.

Public opinion is the aggregate view of the general population.

Public relations are organized activities intended to favorably influence the opinions and behavior of the public.

Public relations agencies are for-profit consulting firms staffed by public relations professionals.

A **public relations counsel** is a person who provides professional public relations advice.

Public relations news services electronically disseminate PR news to the media.

The **Public Relations Society of America (PRSA)** is the main professional organization in public relations.

Public utilities are closely regulated government or private companies, usually monopolies, that provide public services.

Publicity is the key function of public relations directed to obtaining free, favorable media coverage.

Quotas are limits on imports imposed by national governments to keep out foreign films and programs.

Radio Act of 1912 was the initial government regulation for licensing of transmitters.

Radio Act of 1927 created a Federal Radio Commission, defined the broadcast band, standardized frequency designations, and limited the number of stations operating at night, when AM signals carry farther.

Radio format is a programming approach, often linked to music genres, news, or talk, focused on a particular audience.

Radio waves are composed of electromagnetic energy and rise and fall in regular cycles.

Ragtime is an early form of jazz most frequently played on the piano.

Ratings are audience surveys that show what proportions of all households with a television are watching a specific show.

Re-skilling occurs when specialized tasks are reorganized so that a single worker can perform them all.

Readability studies assess how well publications achieves their goals.

Regional Bell operating companies (RBOCs) are the local telephone operating companies of which AT&T divested itself in 1984.

Regionalization refers to media that operate throughout a geographical region.

Relationship marketing is when consumers develop a strong preference for a brand through one-to-one communication.

Remote sensing is satellite observation, via photography, infrared photography, and radar, of objects, vegetation, and weather patterns.

Reputation management involves managing an institution's public image.

Research organizations compile statistics about consumers and their media habits and evaluate advertising messages.

Restraint of trade refers to practices by a company that limit other companies' ability to enter or compete in trade.

Right of reply gives time to present opposing views on broadcast stations when only one side has been aired.

Royalty is a fee required to use another person's intellectual property.

A **satellite footprint** is the surface area covered by the satellite's signal.

A **satellite media tour** is a press briefing broadcast via satellite.

Satellite systems are microwave systems on which the relays are in Earth's orbit instead of on towers.

Scanning is the method that makes TV pictures out of a series of 525 separate picture lines.

The **scarcity argument** maintains that careful government regulation is necessary to allocate and oversee the use of a limited number of frequencies.

Scoop is an exclusive that beats other newspapers in covering a story.

Search engines let the user search for specific text, audio, and video within a computer document or site, or over a network, like the World Wide Web.

Segmentation is the trend toward targeting specialized audiences in the newspaper, magazine, radio, and other media industries.

Selective binding allows publishers to create multiple versions of the same publication.

Self-regulation refers to industry codes and practices of monitoring the industry's own performance.

Semiotic analysis is the science of signs, of how meaning is generated in media "texts."

Share of the audience is the proportion of those actually watching at that moment, *not* of the whole potential audience.

Sheet music is print reproduction of song lyrics and musical notation for people to perform.

The **Sherman Antitrust Act of 1890** is the main U.S. law against monopolies or agreements to restrain or limit trade.

Short-wave radio broadcasts can carry across oceans by bouncing off the earth's atmosphere.

Silent films conveyed plot with expressions, actions, and subtitles, before sound technology.

Situation comedies feature a group of characters in a comic situation dealing with new tensions or issues each episode.

Situation ethics holds that moral ideas and judgments must be made relative to the situation at hand.

SMATV (satellite master antenna television) is a TVRO system serving an entire apartment building or housing complex from a central satellite antenna.

SMCR is a model of the communication process that analyzes the exchange of information as it passes back and forth from the *source* to the *message* to the *channel* to the *receiver,* and back to the source.

Social learning theory explains human behavior in terms of how we learn through our own experience or the experience of others.

Software consists of the programs and codes that instruct computers what to do.

Source attribution refers to methods used to cite sources in a way that reflects their credibility without revealing their identity.

Standards are technical characteristics that must be agreed on for a technology to be widely manufactured and used.

The **star system** was the film studios' use of stars' popularity to promote their movies.

Stereotyping is the making of generalizations about groups of people on the basis of limited information.

Story films, or **movies,** introduced the idea of telling a story, usually fictional, with a plot and characters.

Subscription libraries lent books to the public for a fee or a regular subscription.

A **superstation** is a distant signal that is distributed nationally via satellite.

Survey studies make generalizations about a population of people by addressing questions to a sample of that population.

Syndicated programs are rented or licensed by their producers to other companies for broadcast, distribution, or exhibition.

Syndication is a rental or licensing of media products by their producers to other media companies for broadcast, distribution, or exhibition.

Syndicators rent or license radio programs to other media companies for broadcast.

Tabloids are sensationalist and feature bold headlines, shocking photos, focused on divorce, murder, and crime.

Talent in media refers to the newspeople, actors, and singers in front of the microphones and cameras.

Talkies were films with synchronized soundtracks, which emphasized dialog, singing, and music.

Target audiences are groups that share the same product needs and media usage habits.

Tariffs are taxes imposed by governments on goods imported from other countries.

Taylorism, or scientific management, seeks to improve the efficiency of work by routinizing it.

TCP/IP (transmission control protocol/Internetworking protocol) is the basic protocol used by the Internet.

The **Telecommunications Act of 1996** is the legislation that opened the U.S. telecommunications industry to competition.

Telecommuting occurs when work is performed in the home and workers are linked by telecommunications networks.

Theatrical films are those released for distribution in movie theaters.

Theories are general principles that can be used to explain things.

Toll broadcasting was charging someone to carry a radio program or advertisement, parallel to long-distance or "toll" telephone calls.

Top 40 is a radio format that plays only top single records, the top 40 on record sales charts.

Totalitarian systems are those where government owns the media and completely controls them.

Transborder data flow is the communication of data across political borders.

TVRO (television receive only) is a backyard satellite receiver that lets individual homes receive the same channels that are intended for cable systems.

UHF stands for ultra high frequency channels 14 to 69.

Unbalanced flow is the unequal flow of media or news between countries.

Universal service is the policy that all Americans should have access to basic telecommunication services.

Up-skilling means raising the educational requirements of a job through automation.

URLs (uniform resource locators) are the addresses of pages of content on the Web.

Usage-based segmentation divides consumers according to their amount of consumption.

Uses and gratifications is the theory that predicts media usage according to the human needs that they satisfy.

Vacuum tubes can amplify and precisely modulate a weak signal by controlling the flow of electrical charges inside the tube.

Variety shows combine a number of elements such as comedy, music, games, interviews, and amateur try-outs.

Vaudeville was a stage show of mixed specialty acts, such as songs, dances, skits, comedy, and acrobatics.

A **video news release (VNR)** is a video version of a traditional printed press release.

VCRs (videocassette recorders) are home videotape machines.

Vernacular is the everyday language that people speak, like German, compared to official religious or governmental languages, like Latin in the European Middle Ages.

Vertical integration concentrates ownership by acquiring companies that are in related businesses, such as program production and distribution.

VHF stands for very high frequency television in channels 2 to 13.

Victrola was the trade name for an early phonograph that became a common name.

The **V-chip** is an electronic tool for automatically filtering out violence or adult programming on television.

Videotex services delivered text and graphics through telephone networks.

Virtual bookstores, like Amazon.com, sell books via the Internet and may have no physical retail stores at all.

Virtual reality gives users the sense that they are "inside" a computer- generated reality.

Virtual universities put their courses on the World Wide Web.

A **Web cast** is a real-time PR event or press briefing broadcast over the Internet.

Web pages are the individual locations, or sites, where information is found on the Web.

Wide area networks connect distant users to centralized computer systems.

Windows are times in the film release sequence for showing films in theaters, on pay per view, and so on.

Wire services are news services that supply a variety of newspapers, named originally for their use of the telegraph and its wires.

The **World Wide Web** (the "Web," for short) is the portion of the Internet that links users to graphical, audio, and video information.

Yellow journalism was sensationalistic use of photos and headlines, focusing on personality, scandal and human interest stories.

'Zines are very narrowly focused, even personal, magazines or Web sites usually produced by non-professionals.

References

Adorno, T., & Horkheimer, M. (1972). The culture industry: Enlightenment as mass deception. In *The Dialectics of Enlightenment.* New York: Herder and Herder.

Allen, M., Dalessio, D., & Brezgel, K. (1995). A meta analysis summarizing the effects of pornography. Aggression after exposure. *Human Communication Research,* 22(2), 258–283.

Allen, R. (1992). *Channels of discourse, reassembled.* Chapel Hill, NC: University of North Carolina Press.

Alsop, R., (ed.) (1997). *The Wall Street Journal almanac, 1998.* New York: Ballantine Books.

Altheide, D. (1974). *Creating reality.* Beverly Hills, CA: Sage.

Altschull, H. (1995). *Agents of power,* 2nd ed. New York: Longman.

Anderson, B. (1983). *Imagined communities: Reflections on the origin and spread of nationalism.* London: Verso.

Anderson, J., & Meyer, T. (1988). *Mediated communication.* Newbury Park, CA: Sage.

Ang, I. (1985). *Watching* Dallas. New York: Methuen.

AP (Associated Press). (1998). China maintains tight control of Internet. November 15.

Applegate, E. (1993). The development of advertising, 1700–1900. In Sloan, W., Stovall, J., & Startt, J. (eds.), *The media in America,* 2nd ed. Scottsdale, AZ: Publishing Horizons.

Arfin, F. (1994). *Financial public relations.* Philadelphia: Trans-Atlantic.

Aronowitz, S., & DiFazio, W. (1994). *The jobless future: Sci-tech and the dogma of work.* Minneapolis: University of Minnesota Press.

Arquilla, J., & Ronfeldt, D. (1993). Cyberwar is coming! *Comparative Strategy,* 12(2), 141–165.

Atkin, C. (1985). *The effects of mass media: Readings in mass communication and society.* East Lansing: Department of Communication, Michigan State University.

Attewell, P. (1994). Information technology and the productivity paradox. In Harris, D. (ed.)., *Organizational linkages: Understanding the productivity paradox.* Washington, DC: National Academy Press.

Attorney General of the United States. (1986). *Final report of the Attorney General's Commission on Pornography.* Washington, DC: U.S. Government Printing Office.

Auletta, K. (1991). *Three blind mice: How the TV networks lost their way.* New York: Random House.

———. (1997, Nov. 17). Demolition Man. *New Yorker,* 17(35), 40–45.

Bacard, A. (1995). *The computer privacy handbook.* Berkeley, CA: Peachpit Press.

Bagdikian, B. (1993). *The media monopoly,* 4th ed., Boston: Beacon Press.

Baldwin, T., & McVoy, D (1983). *Cable communications.* Englewood Cliffs, NJ: Prentice-Hall.

Baldwin, T., McVoy, D., & Steinfield, C. (1996). *Convergence: Integrating media, information & communication,* Thousand Oaks, CA: Sage.

Bandura, A. (1965). Influence of models' reinforcement contingencies on the acquisition of imitative responses. *Journal of Personality and Social Psychology,* 1, 589–595.

———. (1983). Psychological mechanisms of aggression. In Geen, R., & Connerstien, E. (eds). *Aggression: Theoretical and Empirical Reviews.* New York: Academic Press.

———. (1986). *Social foundations of thought and action.* Englewood Cliffs, NJ: Prentice-Hall.

Bank, D. (1997, September 11). Changing picture: The advent of digital broadcasting makes the convergence of television and PCs a real possibility. *Wall Street Journal,* R15.

———. (1997, September 15). Microsoft's WebTV unit to introduce process that uses web to enhance TV. *Wall Street Journal,* Ae.

Bannon, L. (1998, March 19). Turning points: Great moments in technology and film. *Wall Street Journal,* R4–6.

Barak, A., & Fisher, W. (1997). Effects of interactive computer erotica on men's attitudes and behavior toward women: An experimental study. *Computers in Human Behavior,* 13(3), 353–369.

Barnouw, E. (1966). *A history of broadcasting in the United States.* New York: Oxford University Press.

———. (1990). *Tube of plenty: the evolution of American television,* 2nd rev. ed. New York: Oxford University Press.

Baudrillard, J. (1983). *Simulations.* New York: Semiotext.

Bauserman, R. (1996). Sexual aggression and pornography: A review of correlational research. *Basic and Applied Social Psychology,* 18(4), 405–427.

Beatty, S. (1998, August 20). Companies push for much bigger, more-complicated on-line ads. *Wall Street Journal,* B10.

Bell, D. (1973). *The coming of post-industrial society.* New York: Basic Books.

Bell, G., & Gray, N. (1997). The revolution yet to happen. In Denning, P., & Metcalfe, R. *Beyond calculation: The next fifty years of computing.* New York: Springer-Verlag.

Belz, C. (1972). *The story of rock.* New York: Harper & Row.

Benson, K., & Whitaker, J. (1990). *Television and audio handbook.* New York: McGraw-Hill.

Benton Foundation (1996). Public Interest advocates, universal service, and the Telecommunications Act of 1996. Available at http://www.benton.org /Library/Advocates /advocates.html

Berger, A. (1992a). *Media analysis techniques.* Newbury Park, CA: Sage.

———. (1992b). *Popular culture genres.* Newbury Park, CA: Sage.

Berkowitz, L. (1984). Some effects of thought on anti- and pro-social influences of media effects. *Psychological Bulletin,* 95, 410–427.

Bernays, E. (1961). *Crystallizing public opinion.* Norman: University of Oklahoma Press.

Bernstein, C., & Woodward, B. (1974). *All the President's men.* New York: Simon & Schuster.

Bertrand, K. (1998, March/April). An unqualified success: Inside & out. *Integrated Marketing & Promotion,* 22–27.

Beuf, A. (1974). Doctor, lawyer, household drudge. *Journal of Communication,* 24(2), 142–145.

Biagi, S. (1998). *Media impact.* Belmont, CA: Wadsworth.

Bikson, T., & Panis, C. (1997). Computers and connectivity: Current trends. In Kiesler, S. (ed.) *Culture of the Internet.* Mahwah, NJ: Lawrence Erlbaum.

Biocca, F. (1997). The cyborg's dilemma: Progressive embodiment in virtual environments. *Journal of Computer-Mediated Communication,* 3(2). Available at: http://www.ascusc.org/jcmc/vol3/issue2 /biocca2.html

Biocca, F., Lauria, R., & McCarthy, M. (1996). Virtual reality. In Grant, A. (ed.), *Communication technology update,* 5th ed. Boston: Focal Press, 176–195.

Bittner, J. (1982). *Broadcast law and regulation.* Englewood Cliffs, NJ: Prentice-Hall.

Black, J., Steele, B., & Barney, R. (1998). *Doing ethics in journalism.* Greencastle, IN: Society for Professional Journalists.

Blanchard, M. (1977). The Hutchins Commission, the press and the responsibility concept. *Journalism monographs; no. 49.* Minneapolis: Association for Education in Journalism.

———. (1993). Freedom of the press. In Sloan, W., Stovall, J., & Startt, J. (eds.), *The media in America.* Scottsdale, AZ: Publishing Horizons.

Blanton, J. (1996, March 26). A novel medium: Hypertext fiction. *Wall Street Journal,* RIO.

Bleifuss, J. (1994, March 20). New angles from the spin doctors. *New York Times,* F13.

Bouman, H., & Christofferson, M. (eds.). (1992). *Relaunching videotext.* Boston, MA: Kluwer Academic Publishers.

Bourdieu, P., (1984). *Distinction: A social critique of the judgement of taste.* Cambridge, MA: Harvard University Press.

———. (1998). *On television.* New York: New Press.

Bourgault, L. (1994). *Mass media in sub-Saharan Africa.* Bloomington, IN: Indiana University Press.

Bowen, B. (1999). Four puzzles in adult literacy: Reflections on the National Adult Literacy Survey. *Journal of Adolescent & Adult Literacy. 42*(4), 314–324.

Boyd, D., Straubhaar, J., & Lent. J. (1989). *The videocassette recorder in the third world.* New York: Longman.

Braestrup, P. (1977). *Big story: How the American press and television reported and interpreted the crisis of Tet 1968 in Vietnam and Washington.* Boulder, CO: Westview Press.

Braudel, F., (1987). *A history of civilizations.* New York: Penguin.

Braverman, A. (1996, December 3). The roadmaps of the Internet. *CS First Boston Industry Report.*

Braverman, H. (1974). *Labor and monopoly capitalism.* New York: Monthly Review Press.

Brenner, V. (1997). Psychology of compter use. XLVII. Parameters of Internet use, abuse and addiction: The first 90 days of the Internet usage survey. *Psychological Reports,* 80, 879–882.

Briere, D. (1993). Communications services: An overview. In *Managing voice networks.* Delran, NJ: McGraw-Hill Information Services.

Briggs, R., & Hollis, N. (1997). Advertising on the Web: Is there response before click-through? *Journal of Advertising Research,* 37(2), 33–45.

Brinidey, J.(1997, July 21). Companies' quest: Lend them your ears. *New York Times, Cg.*

Britt, S., Adams, S., & Miller, A. (1972). How many advertising exposures per day? *Journal of Advertising Research,* 12, 3–9.

Brockway, A., Chadwick, T., & Hall, D. (1997). Persistence of vision: Moving images through the ages. Available at: http://www.iup.edu/~gcfg/vision/frames.html

Brody, G. (1990). Effects of television viewing on family interactions: An observational study. *Family Relations,* 29, 216–220.

Bromberg, H., Campana, M. Deisman, W., Lee, R., McLeod, R., Pardoe, T., & Tyrell, M. (1996). Contradictions in cyberspace: Collective response. In Shields, R. (ed.) *Cultures of the Internet.* Thousand Oaks, CA: Sage.

Brooks, J. (1976). *Telephone: The first hundred years.* New York: Harper & Row.

Broom, G., & Dozier, D. (1991). *Using research: Methodological foundations.* New York: Dryden Press.

———. (1989). *Using research in public relations: Applications to program management.* Englewood Cliffs, NJ: Prentice-Hall.

Brosnon, J. (1974). *Movie magic.* Scranton, PA: The Haddon Craftnien.

Brynjolfsson, E., & Hitt, L. (1996). Paradox lost? Firm-level evidence on the returns to information systems spending. *Management Science,* 42(4), 541–558.

Bulkeley, W. (1997, November 11). Hard lessons. *Wall Street Journal,* R1.

Burnett, J., & Moriarty, S. (1998). *Marketing communications: An integrated approach.* Upper Saddle River, NJ: Prentice-Hall.

Busman, B., & Stack, A. (1996). Forbidden fruit versus tainted fruit: Effects of warning labels on attraction to television violence. *Journal of Experimental Psychology—Applied,* 2(3), 207–226.

Cable Television Advertising Bureau (1997). 1997 Cable TV facts. Available at http://www.mabinter national.com /infofact.htm

———. (1998). 1997 cable TV facts on access CAB. Available at: http://www.cabletvadbureau.com/infofact.html

CableLabs (1997). Available at www.cablelabs.org.

Cairncross, F. (1997). *The death of distance: How the communcations revolution will change our lives.* Cambridge, MA: Harvard Business School Press.

Calica, B., & Newson, G. (1996, January 2). When did you get multimedia? *NewMedia,* 48–52.

Carey, J. (1972). Politics of the Electronic Revolution or 1989 Commas Culture? Urban, IL: University of Illinois.

Carlebach, M. (1997). *American photojournalism comes of age.* Washington, D.C.: Smithsonian Instution Press.

Carter, T. (1991). Paper and block printing—From China to Europe. In Crowley, D., & Heyer, P. (eds.), *Communication in history.* New York: Longman.

Carvajal, D. (1996, April 28). Do it-yourselfers carve out a piece of the publishing pie. *New York Times,* Al.

———. (1998, March 9). There's room for every book in a virtual bookstore. *New York Times,* Cybertimes section.

Cauley, L. (1996, September 16). In the loop. *Wall Street Journal,* R21.

Cavazos, E. (1994). *Cyberspace and the law: Your rights and duties in the on-line world.* Cambridge, MA: M.I.T. Press.

Center, A. (1983). The truth is in the consequence. Address to the Arthur W. Page Society, April 15, University of Texas at Austin.

Center, A., & Jackson, P. (1990). *Public relations practices: Managerial case studies and problems,* 4th ed. Englewood Cliffs, NJ: Prentice-Hall.

Centerwall, B. (1989). Exposure to television as a cause of violence. In Comstock, G. (ed.), *Public communication and behavior.* Orlando, FL: Academic Press.

CERN (1998). Available at: http://wwwcn.cern.ch/pdp/ns/ben/TCPHIST.html

Chapman, S. (1998, September 3). Don't unleash the cybercensors on libraries. *Chicago Tribune Internet Edition.* Available at: http://chicagotribune.com

Chartrand, S. (1998, October 19). Congress extends protection for Goofy and Gershwin. *New York Times Cybertimes Edition.*

Chlapowski, F. (1991). The constitutional protection of informational privacy. *Boston University Law Review,* 71, 133.

Chomsky, N., & Herman, E. (1988). *Manufacturing consent: The political economy of the mass media.* New York: Pantheon Books.

Christians, C., Rotzoll, K., & Fackler, M. (1991). *Media ethics: Cases and moral reasoning,* 3rd ed. New York: Longman.

Ciotta, R. (1998). Baby you should drive this car. In Wickham, K. (ed.) *OnLine Journalism.* Boulder, CO: Coursewise Publishing.

Clark, C. (1972). Race, identification and television violence. In Comstock, G., Rubenstein, E., & Murray, J. (eds.), *Television and social behavior,* vol. 5. Washington, DC: U.S. Government Printing Office.

Clausing, J. (1998, April 9). In rejecting dismissal of filtering case, judge sets high standard for libraries. *New York Times Cybertimes Edition.*

———. (1998, September 24). Senate panel debates children's on-line privacy. *New York Times Cybertimes Edition.*

Cohill, A., & Kavanaugh, A. (1997). *Community networks: Lessons from Blacksburg, Virginia.* Boston: Artech House.

Cole, B. (1991). *After the breakup.* New York: Columbia University Press.

Cole, J. (1997, March 18). New satellite era looms just over the horizon. *Wall Street Journal,* B1.

Colista, C., & Leshner, G. (1998). Traveling music: Following the path of music through the global market. *Critical Studies in Mass Communication,* (15), 181–194.

Compaigne, B. (1982). *Who owns the media? Concentration of ownership in the mass communication industry.* New York: Crown.

Cook, T., Appleton, H., Conner, R., Shaffer, A., Tamkin, G., & Weber, S. (1975). *Sesame Street revisited: A case study in evaluation research.* New York: Russell Sage Foundation.

Cuneo, A., & Petrecca, L. (1998, March 30). The best agencies. *Advertising Age,* S1–11.

Cutlip, S. (1995). *Public relations history: From the seventeenth to the twentieth century.* Hillsdale, NJ: Erlbaum.

———. (1994). *The unseen power: Public relations, a history.* Hillsdale, NJ: Erlbaum.

Cutlip, S., Center, A., & Broom, G. (1985). *Effective public relations,* 6th ed. Englewood Cliffs, NJ: Prentice-Hall.

cyberatlas (1998). Available at: http://www.cyberatlas.com

Czitrom, D. (1982). *Media and the American mind.* Chapel Hill, NC: University of North Carolina Press.

Dates, J., & Barlow, W. (1997). Does mass media realistically portray African American culture? No. In Alexander, A., & Hanson, J. (eds.), *Taking sides: Clashing views on controversial issues in mass media and society.*Guilford, CT: Dushkin/Brown & Benchmark.

Davidson, M., & Cooper, C. (1987). *Women and information technology.* New York: Wiley.

Davis, B. (1994, March 22). Clipper Chip is your friend, NSA contends. *Wall Street Journal,* B1.

Davis, K. (1985). *Two-bit culture.* Boston: Houghton Mifflin.

Day, L. (1991). *Ethics in media communications: Cases and controversies.* Belmont, CA: Wadsworth.

de Sola Pool, I. (1983). *Forecasting the telephone: A retrospective technology assessment of the telephone.* Norwood, NJ: Ablex.

DeBarros, A. (1998, June 7). Radio's historic change: Amid consolidation, fear of less diversity, choice. *USA Today,* A1-2.

December, J. (1996). Units of analysis for Internet communication. *Journal of Communication,* 46(1), 14–38.

Dery, M. (1996). *Escape velocity: Cyberculture at the end of the century.* New York: Grove Press.

Dessauer, J. (1981). *Book publishing—What it is, what it does,* 2nd ed. New York: R. R. Bowker.

Dietrich, D. (1997). (Re)-Fashioning the techno-erotic woman: Gender and textuality in the cybercultural matrix. In Jones, S. (ed.), *Virtual culture.* Thousand Oaks, CA: Sage.

Difranza, Jr., Richards, J., Paulman, P., Wolfgillespie, N., Fletcher, C., Jaffe, R., & Murray, D. (1991). RJR Nabisco's cartoon camel promotes Camel cigarettes to children. *Journal of the American Medical Association,* 266(22), 3149–3153.

DiOrio, C. (1996, April 16). PacBell direct dials H'wood. *Hollywood Reporter,* 1.

Dizard, W. (1993). *The coming information age.* New York: Longman.

———. (1997). *Old media, new media.* New York: Longman.

Dobrow, J. (1989). Away from the Mainstream? VCRs and Ethnic Identity. In Levy, M., (ed.) *The VCR Age.* Thousand Oaks, CA: Sage.

Dominick, J. (1993). *The dynamics of mass communication,* 4th ed. New York: McGraw-Hill.

Dordick, H., & LaRose, R. (1992). *The telephone in daily life: A study of personal telephone use.* East Lansing, MI: Department of Telecommunication.

Dordick, H., & Wang, G. (1993). *The information society: A retrospective view.* Newbury Park, CA: Sage.

Dortch, S. (1996). Going to the Movies. *American Demographics,* 18(12), A–7.

Downing, J., Mohammadi, A., & Sreberny-Mohammadi, A. (1990). *Questioning the media: A critical introduction.* Newbury Park, CA: Sage.

Duffy, J. (1997). *College On-line: How to take college courses without leaving home.* New York: Wiley.

Duncan, T., & Moriarty, S. (1997). *Driving brand value: Using integrated marketing to manage profitable stakeholder relationships.* New York: McGraw-Hill.

Durocher, D. (1998, Nov. 3). The Times-Mirror Shuffle. *American Journalism Review.* AJR NewsLink. Available at: http://ajr.newslink.org/ajrby48.html

Dutton, W., Rogers, E., & Jun, S. (1987). The diffusion and impacts of information technology in households. In Zorkoczy, P., *Oxford surveys in information technology* (vol. 4). New York: Oxford University Press.

Dyson, E. (1997). *Release 2.0: A design for living in the digital age.* New York: Broadway Books.

Eastman, L. (1993). *Broadcast/cable programming.* Belmont, CA: Wadsworth.

Eastman, S., Head, S., & Klein, L. (1989). *Broadcast/cable programming: strategies and practices,* 3rd ed. Belmont, CA: Wadsworth.

Editor and Publisher Web site. (1998). Available at: http://www.naa.org.info.facts.html

Eighmey, J., & McCord, L. (1998). Adding value in the information age: Uses and gratifications of sites on the World Wide Web. *Journal of Business Research,* 41(3), 187–195.

Ellis, J. (1990). *A history of film,* 3rd ed. Englewood Cliffs, NJ: Prentice-Hall.

Ellul, J. (1964). *The technological society.* New York: Knopf.

Emes, C. (1997). Is Mr. Pac Man eating our children? A review of the effect of video games on children. *Canadian Journal of Psychiatry,* 42(4), 409–414.

Engleberg, S. (1993. March 17). A new breed of hired hands cultivates grass-roots anger. *New York Times,* A1.

Evans, C. (1981). *The making of the micro: A history of the computer.* New York: Van Nostrand Reinhold.

Everett, G. (1993). The age of new journalism, 1883–1900. In Sloan, W., Stovall, J., & Startt, J. (eds.), *Media in America: A history,* 2nd ed. Scottsdale, AZ: Publishing Horizons.

Ewen, S. (1976). *Captains of consciousness.* New York: McGraw Hill.

———. (1996). *PR! A social history of spin.* New York: Basic Books.

Ewen, S., & Ewen, E. (1992). *Channels of desire—Mass images and the shaping of American Consciousness.* Minneapolis: University of Minnesota Press.

Fagen, M. (ed.). (1975). *A history of engineering and science in the Bell System: The early years, 1875–1925.* Murray Hill, NJ: Bell Telephone Laboratories.

Featherstone, M. (1990). Perspectives on consumer culture. *Sociology,* 24.

Federal Communications Commission (1997). 1997 *monitoring report,* Section I. Available at: http://www.fcc.gov/Bureaus/Common_Carrier/Reports/FCC-State_Link/monitor.html

Federal Trade Commission (1998). Privacy on line: A report to Congress. Available at: http://www.ftc.gov/reports/privacy3/toc.htm

Federman, J. (1998). *National television violence study.* vol. 3, *Executive summary.* Santa Barbara, CA: University of California Santa Barbara, Center for Communication and Social Policy.

Felson, R. (1996). Mass media effects on violent behavior. *Annual Review of Sociology,* 22, 103–128.

Feshbach, S., & Singer, R. (1971). *Television and aggression.* San Francisco: Jossey-Bass.

Feurey, J. (1986). Video news releases. In *New technology and public relations.* New York: Institute for Public Relations.

Fife, M. (1984). Minority ownership and multiple ownership in the deregulated broadcast marketplace. Paper presented at the Telecommunications Policy Research Conference, Airlie, Virginia.

Fischer, C. (1992). *America calling.* Berkeley: University of California Press.

Fitzgerald, (1998, August 3). Beyond advertising *Advertising Age,* 1,14.

Fleming, S., & McLaughlin, M. (1993, July 12). ADSL: The on-ramp to the information highway. *Telephony,* 111–114.

Folkerts, J., & Teeter, D. (1994). *Voices of a nation: A history of mass media in the United States.* New York: Macmillan.

Ford, T. (1997). Effects of stereotypical television portrayals of African-Americans on person perception. *Social Psychology Quarterly,* 60(3), 266–275.

Fortini-Campbell, L. (1992). *Hitting the sweet spot: How consumer insights can inspire better marketing and advertising.* Chicago: The Copy Workshop.

Fox, S. (1984). *The mirror makers: A history of American advertising.* London: Heinemann.

Frederick, H. (1993). *North American NGO networking on trade and immigration: Computer communications in cross border coalition building.* Unpublished paper, Benson Latin American Collection, University of Texas, Austin.

Freedman, J. (1984). Effect of television violence on aggressiveness. *Psychological Bulletin,* 96(2), 227–246.

Freiberger, P., & Swaine, M. (1984). *Fire in the valley: The making of the personal computer.* Berkeley, CA: Osborne/McGraw-Hill.

Freuh, T., & McGhee, P. (1975). Traditional sex role development and the amount of time spent watching television. *Developmental Psychology,* 11(1), 109.

Friedland, L. (1996). Electronic democracy and the new citizenship. *Media, Culture and Society,* 18, 185–212.

Frost, R. (1996). The electronic Gutenberg fails to win mass appeal. *Wall Street Journal.*

Fulk, J., Schmitz, J., & Steinfield, C. (1990). A social influence model of technology use. In Fulk, J., & Steinfield, C. (eds.), *Organizations and communication technology.* Thousand Oaks, CA: Sage.

The future of advertising: New approaches to the attention economy. (1997). Washington, DC: The Aspen Institute.

Gandy, O. (1982). *Beyond agenda setting: Information subsidies and public policy.* Norwood, NJ: Ablex.

———. (1993). *The panoptic sort.* Boulder, CO: Westview.

Gaziano, C. (1997). Forecast 2000: Widening knowledge gaps. *Journalism and Mass Communication Quarterly,* 74(2), 237–264.

Gentry, C. (1991). Pornography and rape: An empirical analysis. *Deviant Behavior,* 12, 277–288.

Gerbner, G., Gross, L., Morgan, M., & Signorelli, N. (1994). Growing up with television: The cultivation perspective. In Bryant, J., & Zillmann, D., *Media effects: Advances in theory and research.* Hillsdale, NJ: Lawrence Erlbaum.

Ghareeb, E. (1983). *Split vision: The portrayal of Arabs in the media.* Washington, D.C. American-Arab Affairs Council.

Gitlin, T. (1983). *Inside prime time.* New York: Pantheon Books.

———. (1995). *The twilight of common dreams.* New York: Henry Hold.

Gladwell, M. (1998, July 6). The spin myth. *The New Yorker,* 66–73.

Gomery, D. (1991). *Movie history: A survey.* Belmont, CA: Wadsworth.

Gramsci, A. (1971). *Selections from the prison notebooks.* New York: International Publishers.

Greenberg, B., *et al.* (1980). Antisocial and prosocial behaviors on television. In Greenberg, B. (ed.), *Life on television: Content analysis of U.S. TV drama.* Norwood, NJ: Ablex.

Greenfield, P. (1994). Video games as cultural artifacts. *Journal of Applied Developmental Psychology,* 15(1), 3–12.

Grefe, E. (1986). Relational data base management. In *New technology and public relations.* New York: Institute for Public Relations.

Grohol, J. (1996). Psychology of the Internet research and theory: Internet additions. Available at: http://www.cmhc.com/mlists/research

Grossberg, L. (1993). Can cultural studies find true happiness in communication? *Journal of Communication,* 43, 89–97.

Gruley, B. (1997, March 11). TV stations, satellite firms reach pact. *Wall Street Journal,* A2.

———. (1997, April 3). FCC prepares for rollout of digital TV. *Wall Street Journal,* B2.

Gruley, B., & Robichaux, M. (1997, April 1). Justices uphold "must carry" broadcast rules. *Wall Street Journal,* B1.

Guback, T., & Varis, T. (1982). Transnational communication and cultural industries. Paris: *UNESCO Reports and Papers on Mass Communication 92.*

Hall (1980). "Encoding/Decoding," in Hall, S., Hobson, D., Lowe, A., & Willis. P., eds. *Culture, Media Language.* London: Hutchinson.

Hamlin, S. (1995, September 6). Time flies, but where does it go? *New York Times,* B1

Hansell, S. (1998, August 16). Big Web sites to track steps of users. *New York Times,* cybertimes edition.

Hardy, Q. (1996, September 16). Wireless wagers. *Wall Street Journal,* R18.

Harmon, A. (1997, December 7). The self-appointed cops of the Information Age. *New York Times,* A-1.

———. (1998, April 17). Blacks less likely to have access to Internet, study shows. *New York Times,* A1.

Harris, T.(1993). *Marketer's guide to public relations: How today's top companies are using the new PR to gain a competitive edge.* New York: John Wiley.

Harrison, E. (1993). *Going green: How to communicate your company's environmental commitment.* Homewood, IL: Irwin.

Harrison, S. (1990). Pedagogical ethics for public relations and advertising. *Journal of Mass Media Ethics,* 5, 256–262.

Hart, M. (1990). *Drumming at the edge of magic.* New York: HarperCollins.

Harte, L., Levine, R., & Prokup, S. (1997). *Cellular and PCS: The big picture.* New York: McGraw-Hill.

Haywood, T. (1995). *Info-rich/info-poor: Access and exchange in the global information society.* West Sussex, England: Bowker/Saur.

Head, S., Sterling, C., & Schofield, L. (1994). *Broadcasting in America,* 7th ed. Boston: Houghton Mifflin.

Hearold, S. (1986). A synthesis of effects of television on social behavior. In Comstock, G. (ed.), *Public communication and behavior,* vol. I. New York: Academic Press.

Heins, M. (1993). *Sex, sin and blasphemy.* New York: New Press.

Hennigan, K., Del Rosario, M., Heath, L., Cook, T., Wharton, J., & Calder, B. (1982). The impact of the introduction of television on crime in the United States. *Journal of Personality and Social Psychology,* 42, 461–477.

Herman, E., & McChesney, R. (1997). *The global media: The new missionaries of global capitalism.* Washington: Cassell.

Hiebert, R. (1966). *Courtier to the crowd: The story of Ivy L. Lee and the development of public relations.* Iowa City, IA: Iowa State University Press.

Hiltz, S. (1994). *The virtual classroom: Learning without limits via computer networks.* Norwood, NJ: Ablex.

Hirsch, P. (1980). The "scary world" of the nonviewer and other anomalies: A reanalysis of Gerbner *et al.*'s findings on cultivation analysis. *Communication research,* 7, 403–456.

Holzmann, G., & Pherson, B. (1994). The early history of data networks. Available at: http://www.it.kth.se/docs/early_net/toc.html

Houston, P. (1993, March 16). Phone frenzy in the Capitol. *Los Angeles Times,* A1.

Hovland, C., Lumsdane, A., & Sheffield, F. (1949). *Experiments on mass communications.* Princeton, NJ: Princeton University Press.

Howard, C., & Mathews, W. (1997). *On deadline: Managing media relations,* 3rd ed. Prospect Heights, IL: Waveland.

Hudson, H. (1990). *Communication satellites: Their development and impact.* New York: Free Press.

Huesmann, L., (1982). Television violence and aggressive behavior. In Pearl, D., Bouthliet, L., & Lazar, J. (eds.) *Television and behavior: Ten years of scientific progress and implications for the eighties.* Washington, DC: National Institute for Mental Health.

Huesmann, L., & Eron, L. (1986). The development of aggression in American children as a consequence of television violence viewing. In authors (eds.) *Television and the aggressive child.* Hillsdale, NJ: Lawrence Erlbaum.

Huntzicker, W. (1993). The frontier press 1800–1900. In Sloan, W., Stovall, J., & Startt, J. (eds.), *Media in America: A history,* 2nd ed. Scottsdale, AZ: Publishing Horizons.

Huston, A., *et al.* (1992). *Big world, small screen: The role of television in American society.* Omaha: University of Nebraska Press.

Hynds, E. (1980). *American newspapers in the 1980s.* New York: Hastings House.

InterMedia. (1989). There Never Was a Mass Audience . . . *Intermedia,* (17)2.

Institute for Alternative Journalism (October 1997). *The synergy report (25 select case studies).* Available at: http://www.fourthestate.com/synergy.html

Irving, L. (1998, September 18). *Minority commercial broadcast ownership report.* National Telecommunications and Information Administration. Washington, D.C.

Janal, D. (1998). *On-line marketing handbook.* New York: Wiley.

Jeffres, L. (1986). *Mass media processes and effects.* Prospect Heights, IL: Waveland Press.

Jensen, E., & Graham, E. (1993, October 26). Stamping out TV violence: A losing fight. *Wall Street Journal,* B1.

Jerram, P. (1997, June 2). Energize your brand. *New Media,* 35–42.

Johnston, C. (1995, November 24). Anonymity on line? It depends who's asking. *Wall Street Journal,* B1.

Johnston, J. (1987). *Electronic learning.* Hillsdale, NJ: Lawrence Erlbaum.

Jones, C. (1996). *Winning with the news media.* Tampa, FL: Video Consultants, Inc.

Jones, S. (1992). *Rock formation: Music, technology and mass communication.* Newbury Park, CA: Sage.

Kaplan, C. (1998, October 9). Strict European privacy law puts pressure on U.S. *New York Times Cybertimes Edition.*

Kateb, G. (1989). *Walt Whitman and the cultural democracy.* New Brunswick, NJ: Rutgers Unviersity.

Katz, E., & Lazarsfeld, P. (1955). *Personal influence.* New York: Free Press.

Katz, E., & Wedell, G. (1976). *Broadcasting in the third world.* Cambridge, MA: Harvard University Press.

Keen, P. (1988). *Competing in time.* New York: Harper.

Keller, J. (1996, September 19). The "new" AT&T faces daunting challenges. *Wall Street Journal,* B1.

Kernan, M., & Howard, G. (1990). Computer anxiety and computer attitudes: An investigation of construct and predictive validity issues. *Educational and Psychological Measurement,* 50, 681–690.

Kerwin, B. & Cappuccio, D. (1998). Technology migrations toting up the hidden costs. *Data Communications,* 27(7), 31–33.

Kiesler, S., Siegal, J., & McGuire, T. (1984). Social psychological aspects of computer-medited communication. *American Psychologist,* 39(10), 1123–1134.

Kilborn, P. (1993, March 15). New jobs lack the old security in time of "disposable workers." *New York Times,* A1.

Kim, J. (1996, October 30). Net use strains phone lines. *USA Today,* A1.

———. (1997). Teaching over the 'net. *Computerworld,* 31(20), 59–61.

Klapper, J. (1960). *The effects of mass communication.* New York: Free Press.

Kling, R. (1980). Social analyses of computing: Theoretical perspectives in recent empirical research. *Computing Surveys,* 12(1), 61–110.

Knight, A. (1979). *The liveliest art.* New York: New American Library.

Kottak, C. (1990). *Prime time society.* Belmont, CA: Wadsworth.

Kraut, R., Patterson, M., Lundmark, V., Kiesler, S., Mukophadhyay, T., & Scherlig, W. (1998). Internet paradox: A social technology that reduces social involvement and psychological well-being? *American Psychologist,* 53(9), 10171031.

Kroker, A., & Weinstein, M. (1994). *Data trash: The theory of the virtual class.* New York: St. Martin's.

Kunkel, D. (1998, May). Policy battles over defining children's educational television. (Children and Television). *The Annals of the American Academy of Political and Social Science,* 57(15), 37.

Kutchinsky, B. (1991). Pornography and rape: Theory and practice? Evidence from crime data in four countries where pornography is easily available. *International Journal of Law and Psychiatry,* 14(1–2), 47–64.

Landler, M. (1995, December 26). Multiple family phone lines, a post-postwar U.S. trend. *New York Times,* A1.

Langdale, J. (1991). *Internationalization of Australia's service industries.* Canberra: Australian Government Publishing Service.

LaRose, R. (1999). *Understanding personal telephone behavior.* In Sawhney, H., & Barnett, G., (eds.), *Progress in communication science,* Vol. XV: *Advances in telecommunication theory and research.* Norwood, NJ: Ablex.

LaRose, R., & Atkin, D. (1988). Satisfaction, demographic and media environment predictors of cable subscription. *Journal of Broadcasting and Electronic Media,* 32(4), 403–413.

LaRose, R., Gregg, J., & Eastin, M. (1999). Audiographic telecourses for the Web. An experiment. *Journal of Computer Mediated Communication.* 4(2). Available at: http://www.ascusc.org/jcmc/vol4/issue2/larose.htm

Lazarsfeld, P. (1941). Remarks on adminstrative and critical communication research. *Studies in Philosophy and Social Science,* 9, 2–16.

Lefkowitz, M., Eron, L., Walder, L., & Huesmann, L. (1972). Television violence and child aggression: A follow-up study. In Comstock, G., & Rubenstein, E. (eds.), *Television and social behavior,* vol. 3. Washington, DC: U.S. Government Printing Office.

Leiss, W., Kline, S., & Jhally, S. (1990). *Social communication in advertising.* Ontario: Nelson Canada.

Leland, J. (1995, December 11). Violence, reel to real. *Newsweek,* 46–48.

Lemos, A. (1996). The labyrinth of Minitel. In Shields, R. (ed.) *Cultures of the Internet.* Thousand Oaks, CA: Sage.

Letter to Congress explaining FTC's new deception policy, (1983). *Advertising Compliance Service.* Westport, CT: Meckler Publishing.

Levy, S. (1994). E-money. *Wired,* 2(12), 124–129.

———. (1996, September 16). The Internet crash scare. *Newsweek,* 96.

Lewis, P. (1990, July 8). Worries about radiation continue, as do studies. *New York Times,* F8.

Lewis, T. (1991). *Empire of the air.* New York: Harper.

Liebert, R., & Sprafkin, J. (1988). *The early window.* New York: Pergamon Press.

Liebes, T., & Katz, E. (1989). *The export of meaning: Cross-cultural readings of* Dallas. New York: Oxford University Press.

Limmer, J. (ed.). (1981). *The Rolling Stone illustrated history of rock and roll.* New York: Random House.

Lindlof, T. (1995). *Qualitative communications research methods.* Thousand Oaks, CA: Sage.

Lippmann, W. (1922). *Public opinion.* New York: Macmillan.

Livingstone, S. (1998). *Making sense of television: The pyschology of audience interpretation,* 2nd ed. New York: Routledge.

Loeffler, R. (1993). *A guide to preparing cost-effective press releases.* Binghamton, NY: Haworth Press.

Lohr, S. (1993, April 14). Recycling answer sought for computer junk. *New York Times,* A1.

Lyotard, J. (1984). *The postmodern condition.* Manchester, England: Manchester University Press.

MacDonald, J. (1979). *Don't touch that dial! Radio programming in American life from 1920 to 1960.* Chicago: Nelson-Hall.

Maibach, E., & Holtgrave, D.(1995). Advances in public health communication. *Annual Review of Public Health,* 16, 219–238.

Mandell, S.(1990). Computer crime. In Ermann, M., Williams, M., & Gutierrez, C. (eds.) *Computers, ethics and society.* New York: Oxford University Press.

Manheim, J. (1991). *All of the people, all of the time: Strategic communications & American politics.* Armonk, NY: M.E. Sharpe.

Mannes, G. (1996).The birth of cable TV. *Invention and Technology,* 12(2), 42–50.

Marcuse, H. (1964). *One-dimensional man.* Boston: Beacon Press.

Marien, M. (1996). New communications technology: A survey of impacts and issues. *Telecommunications Policy,* 20(5), 375–387.

Markus, L. (1990). Toward a "critical mass" theory of interactive media. In Fulk, J., & Steinfield, C. (eds.), *Organizations and communication technology.* Thousand Oaks, CA: Sage.

Marriott, M. (1999, January 7). "If only DeMille had owned a desktop." *New York Times,* Circuits.

Marsh, H. (1993). The contemporary press. In Sloan, W., Stovall, J., & Startt, J. (eds.), *Media in America: A history,* 2nd ed. Scottsdale, AZ: Publishing Horizons.

Martin, D., & Coons, D. (1998). *Media flight plan.* Provo, UT: Deer Creek Publishing.

———. (1998a, April 20). Court KO's EEO. *Broadcasting & Cable,* 6 .

Martin, M. (1991). *"Hello, central?" Gender, technology and culture in the formation of telephone systems.* Montreal, Canada: McGill-Queen's University Press.

Martin-Barbero, J. (1993). *Communication, culture, and hegemony: From the media to the mediations.* Newbury Park, CA: Sage.

Martinez, B. (1997, September 11). The holy grail: Cellular Visions's grasp may exceed its reach, but it's a quest worth watching. *Wall Street Journal,* R26.

Marx, K. (1967). *Capital, a critique of political economy,* vol. 1. New York: International Publishers.

Mast, G., & Kawin, B. (1996). *The movies: A short history.* Needham Heights, MA: Simon & Schuster.

McAnany, E. (1980). *Communication in the rural third world: The role of information in development.* New York: Praeger.

McChesney, R. (1996). The Internet and U.S. communication policy-making in historical and critical context. *Journal of Communication,* 46(1), 98–124.

———. (1997). *Corporate Media and the Threat to Democracy.* New York: Seven Stories Press.

———. (November 1997). The global media giants: The nine firms that dominate the world. *EXTRA! The magazine of Fairness and Accuracy in Media.* (http://www.fair.org/extra/index)

———. (1993). Critical communication research at the crossroads. In Levy, M. & Gurevitch, M. (eds.), *Defining media studies.* New York: Oxford University Press.

McClintick, D. (1998, November). Town crier for the new age. *Brill's Content,* 113–127.

———. (1998b, July 20). Minority ownership: A not-much-progress report. (Department of Commerce report on minority ownership of media). *Broadcasting & Cable,* 7.

McCourt, J. (1998). Satisfaction guaranteed. *Video Store,* 20(46), 12–7.

McCracken, H. (1997, November). The new set-top boxes. *PCWorld,* 169–174.

McGovern, P. (1993, August 6). Plug in for productivity. *New York Times,* F7.

McGuire, W. (1986). The myth of massive media impact: Savagings and salvagings. In Comstock, G. (ed). *Public communication and behavior.* New York: Academic Press.

McKearns, J. (1993). The emergence of modern media, 1900–1945. In Sloan, W., Stovall, J., & Startt, J. (eds.), *Media in America: A history,* 2nd ed. Scottsdale, AZ: Publishing Horizons.

McLaughlin, M., Osborne, K., & Ellison, N. (1997). Virtual community in a telepresence environment. In Jones, S. (ed.), *Virtual community.* Thousand Oaks, CA: Sage.

McLeod, J., Kosicki, G., & McLeod, D. (1994). The expanding boundaries of political communication effects. In Bryant, J., & Zillman, D. (eds.) *Media effects.* Hillsdale, NJ: Lawrence Erlbaum.

McLuhan, M. (1964). *Understanding media.* New York: McGraw-Hill.

McLuhan, M., & Powers, B. (1989). *The global village: Transformations in world life and media in the 21st century.* New York : Oxford University Press, 1989.

McPhail, T. (1989). *Electronic colonialism.* Newbury Park, CA: Sage.

McQuail, D. (1987). *Mass communications theory—An introduction,* 2nd ed., Beverly Hills, CA: Sage.

MediaMetrix (1997, December). New Media Watch. Available at http://www.mediametrix.com/

MediaPost Communications. (1998). Synopsis of @d:tech, p. 1; www.medipost.com

Media Studies Journal (1996, Spring/Summer). "Media Mergers." Media Studies Center. Available at: http://www.mediastudies.org/nymeger.html

Mendelsohn, H. (1973). Some reasons why information campaigns can succeed. *Public Opinion Quarterly,* 37, 50–61.

Merli, J. (1998, January 5). Listening while driving most popular. *Broadcasting & Cable,* 128 (1) 40.

Merrill, J. (1997). *Journalism ethics: Philosophical foundations for news media.* New York: St. Martin's Press.

Messner, S., & Blau, J. (1987). Routine leisure activity and rates of crime: A macro-level analysis. *Social Forces,* 65, 1035–1052.

Meyer, P. (1987). *Ethical journalism.* New York: Longman.

Mickelson, K. (1997). Seeking social support: Parents in electronic support groups. In Kiesler, S. (ed.), *Culture of the Internet.* Mahwah, NJ: Lawrence Erlbaum.

Middleton, K. & Chamberlin, B. (1994). *Law of public communication,* 3rd ed. London: Longman.

Milavsky, J., Kessler, R., Stipp, H., & Rubens, W. (1982). Television and aggression: Results of a panel study. In Perarl, D., Bouthliet, L., & Lazar, J. (eds.), *Television and behavior: Ten years of scientific progress and implications for the eighties,* vol. 2. Washington, DC: National Institute for Mental Health.

Miller, G. (1987). A neglected connection: Mass media exposure and interpersonal communication process. In Gumpert, G., & Cathcart, R. (eds.) *Intermedia: Interpersonal communication in a media world,* 3rd ed. New York: Oxford University Press.

Miller, T., & Clemente, P. (1997). 1997 American Internet User Survey. New York: FIND/SVP Emerging Technologies Research Group. Available: http://etrg.findsvp.com/internet/findf.html

Millman, S. (1984). *A history of engineering & science in the Bell System: Communications sciences, 1925–1980.* Murray Hill, NJ: AT&T Bell Laboratories.

Mody, B., Bauer, J., & Straubhaar, J. (1995). *Telecommunications politics: Ownership and control of the information highway in developing countries.* Hillsdale, NJ: Lawrence Earlbaum.

Moore, G. (1996). Nanometers and gigabucks—Moore on Moore's Law. University Video Corporation Distinguished Lecture. Available at: http://www.uvc.com/

Morley, N. (1986). *Family television: Cultural power and domestic leisure.* London: Routledge.

Morley, D. (1992). *Television, audiences and cultural studies.* New York: Routledge.

Morse, R. (1985). Videotex USA. In Zarkoczy, *Oxford surveys in information technology,* vol. 2. New York: Oxford University Press.

Mosco, V. (1982). *Pushbutton fantasies: Critical perspectives on videotex and information technology.* Norwood, NJ: Ablex.

———. (1989). *The pay-per society: Computers and communication in the information age.* Norwood, NJ: Ablex.

———. (1996). *The political economy of communication.* Thousand Oaks, CA: Sage.
Moyal, A. (1988). *Women and the telephone in Australia: Study of a national culture.* Paper presented to the International Communication Association, Dublin, Ireland.
Mueller, M. & Schement, J. (1995). *Universal service from the bottom up: A profile of telecommunications access in Camden, New Jersey.* New Brunswick, NJ: Rutgers University School of Communication, Information and Library Studies.
Murphy, J., & Hofacker, C. (1997, June 21). Move over '.com'! There's a whole world of good domain names. *New York Times,* CyberTimes section.
Muto, S. (1995, September 15). From here to immodesty: Milestones in the toppling of TV's taboos. *Wall Street Journal,* B1.
Nash, E. (1992). *The direct marketing handbook,* 2nd ed. New York: McGraw-Hill.
National Cable Television Association (1998). Available at: http://www.ncta.com/directory.html
National Commission for Employment Policy. (1986). *Computers in the workplace: Selected issues.* Washington, DC: U.S. Government Printing Office.
Negroponte, N. (1996). *Being digital.* New York: Knopf.
NetRatings (1999). Current reports. Available at: http://www.netratings.com/sample.htm
Network Solutions, Inc. (1998). The history of the Internet. Available at: http://csis.swac.edu/~thomas/CSIS105/Internic.guide/Internet.History/history/sld01.html
Newcomb, H. (1992). *Television: A critical view, 5th Ed.* New York: Oxford University Press.
Newsom, D. & Carrell, B. (1995). *Public relations Writing: Forms and style,* 4th ed. Chicago, IL: Probus.
Newsom, D., *et al.* (1993). *This is PR: The realities of public relations,* 5th ed. Belmont, CA: Wadsworth.
Noam, E. (1983). *Telecommunications regulation today and tomorrow.* New York: Law and Business.
———. (1996). Going beyond spectrum auctions. Available at: http://www.columbia.edu/dlc/wp /citi/citinoam22.html
Noelle-Neumann, E. (1984). *The spiral of silence: Public opinion—our social skin.* Chicago: University of Chicago Press.
Nora, S., & Minc, N. (1980). *The computerization of society.* Cambridge, MA: M.I.T Press.
Norwood, S. (1990). *Labor's flaming youth.* Urbana: University of Illinois Press.
Novak, T., & Hoffman, D. (1998). Bridging the digital divide. Available at http://www2000.ogsm.vanderbilt.edu/papers/race/science.html
NPD (1997, December). Softrends topsellers ranked on unit sales. Available at: http://www.npd.com/corp/products/product_indsoft97.htm
NTIA (National Telecommunications and Information Administration) (1998). *Falling Through the Net II.* Washington, DC: NTIA. Available at: http: //www.ntia.doc.gov/ntiahome/net2/falling.html
O'Keefe, S. (1996). *Publicity on the Internet.* New York: Wiley.
O'Neill, E. (ed.). (1985). *A history of engineering and science in the Bell System: Transmission technology, 1925–1975.* Murray Hill, NJ: Bell Telephone Laboratories.
Olasky, M. (1987). *Corporate public relations & American private enterprise.* Hillsdale, NJ: Erlbaum.
Orwall, B. (1997, April 29). Ticketmaster sues Microsoft Corp. over Internet link. *New York Times,* B8.
Overbeck, W. (1998). *Major principles of media law,* 1997–1998 ed. Fort Worth, TX: Harcourt Brace College Publishers.
Owen, B., & Wildman, S. (1992). *Video economics.* Cambridge, MA: Harvard University Press.
Paik, H., & Comstock, G. (1994). The effects of television violence on social behavior: A metanalysis. *Communication Research.* 21, 516–545.
Palmgreen, P., & Rayburn, J. (1985). An expectancy-value approach to media gratifications. In Rosengren, K., Wenner, L., & Palmgreen, P. (eds.). *Media gratifications research: Current perspectives.* Thousand Oaks, CA: Sage.
Parks, M., & Floyd, K. (1996). Making friends in cyberspace. *Journal of Communication,* 46(1), 80–97.
Parsons, P., & Frieden, R. (1998). *The cable and satellite television industries.* Needham Heights, MA: Allyn and Bacon.
Pavlik, J. (1987). *Public relations: What research tells us.* Newbury Park, CA: Sage.
———. (1998). *New media technology: Cultural and commercial perspectives,* 2nd Ed. Boston: Allyn and Bacon.
Payne, D. (1993). The age of mass magazines, 1900–present. In Sloan, Stovall, & Startt (eds.). *Media in America: A history,* 2nd ed. Scottsdale, AZ: Publishing Horizons.
Peal, D., & Savitz, K. (1997). *Official America Online Internet guide.* New York: McGraw-Hill.
Perrolle, J. (1987). *Computers and social change: Information, property and power.* Belmont, CA: Wadsworth.
Pew Research Center (1999). *The Internet News Audience Goes Ordinary.* Available at: http://www.people-press.org/tech98sum.htm
Picard, R. (1989). *Media economics: Concepts and issues.* Thousand Oaks, CA: Sage.
Pinsdorf, M. (1986). *Communicating when your company is under siege: Surviving public crisis.* New York: Free Press.
Pipher, M. (1994). *Reviving Ophelia: Saving the Selves of Adolescent Girls.* New York: Ballantine Books.
Pope, K. (1998, April 3). TV plans to use new digital capacity to improve picture, not add channels. *Wall Street Journal,* A4.
Postman, N. (1986). *Amusing ourselves to death: Public discourse in the age of show business.* New York: Penguin Books.
———. (1992). *Technopoly.* New York: Knopf.
Pulley, B. (1998, January 31). On Antigua it's sun, sand and 1-800 betting. *New York Times,* CyberTimes section.
Quick, R. (1997, January 22). "Framing" muddies issue of content ownership. *Wall Street Journal,* B6.

———. (1997, September 12). Is the Internet outgrowing its volunteer traffic cops? *Wall Street Journal,* B5.

———. (1998, February 5). Internet incident raises concern over control. *Wall Street Journal,* B6.

———. (1998, February 6). Don't expect your secrets to get kept on the Internet. *Wall Street Journal,* B6.

Rafaeli, S. (1988). Interactivity: From new media to communication. In Hawkins, Pingree, & Weimann (eds.), *Advancing communication sciences,* Vol. 16. Beverly Hills, CA: Sage.

Raleigh, I. *Matthew Arnold and American Culture.* Berkeley: University of California Press.

Rainey, R. (1998, September 8). Santa Monica seeking a return to on-line civic forum of yore. *New York Times,* 16.

Rajeev, P., & Lonial, S. (1990). Advertising to children: Findings and implications. *Current Research and Issues in Advertising, 12,* 231–274.

Rakow, L. (1992). *Gender on the line.* Urbana: University of Illinois Press.

Ramstad, E. (1998, February 26). Audionet scores by tapping a mundane medium. *Wall Street Journal,* B8.

Raney, R. (1998, Feburary 11). E-Mail sender convicted of civil rights violation. *New York Times,* CyberTimes section.

Real, M. (1989). *Super media: A cultural studies approach.* Thousand Oaks: Sage.

Reeves, B., & Nass, C. (1996). *The media equation.* New York: Cambridge University Press.

Reich, R. (1991). *The work of nations.* New York: Knopf.

Research on the effects of television on children (1977). National Science Foundation, 45.

Rheingold, H. (1993). *The virtual community: Homesteading on the electronic frontier.* Reading, MA: Addison-Wesley.

Rice, R., & Bair, J. (1984). New organizational media and productivity. In R. Rice & Associates (eds.), *The new media.* Beverly Hills, CA: Sage.

Richtel, M. (1998, March 5). Usenet death penalties: The long arm of the self-appointed law. *New York Times,* CyberTimes section.

Rifkin, J. (1995). *The end of work: The decline of the global labor force and the dawn of the post-market era.* New York: Tarcher & Putnam.

Rigdon,J. (1997, February 28). The letter P in your home PC just might mean potted plant. *Wall Street Journal,* B1.

Riley, S. (1993). American magazines, 1740–1900. In Sloan, W., Stovall, J., & Startt, J. (eds.) *Media in America: A history,* 2nd ed. Scottsdale, AZ: Publishing Horizons.

Rivers, W., & Schramm, W. (1980). *Responsibility in mass communication.* New York: Harper & Row.

Robins, K. (1996). Cyberspace and the world we live in. In Dovey, J. (ed.), *Fractal dreams.* London: Lawrence & Wishart.

Robinson, J., Levy, M., & Davis, D. (1986). *The main source: Learning from television news.* Beverly Hills: Sage Publications.

Roche, B. (1993). The development of modern advertising, 1900-present. In Sloan, W., Stovall, J., & Startt, J. (eds.), *The media in America,* 2nd ed. Scottsdale, AZ: Publishing Horizons.

Rogers, E. (1986). *Communication technology—The new media in society.* New York: Free Press.

———. (1995). *Diffusion of innovations,* 4th Ed. New York: Free Press.

Rose, B. (1998, March 19). Digital distortions. *Wall Street Journal,* R6.

Rosenbaum, M. (1994). *Selling your story to Wall Street: The art & science of investor relations.* Chicago, IL: Probus.

Roszak, T. (1994). *The cult of information,* 2nd ed. Berkeley, CA: University of California Press.

Rotheberg, R. (1996, December). The age of spin. *Esquire,* 73.

———. (1996, February). Life in cyburbia. *Esquire,* 56–64.

Sadler, R. (1995, February 20). "Big Bird and Barney." Posted on cyber-rights@cpsr.org. http://www.cpsr.org/cpsr/lists/listserv_archives /cyber-rights/950224

Sandage, C., Fryburder, V., & Rotzoll, K. (1989). *Advertising theory and practice.* New York: Longman.

Scarborough Research Corporation. (1998). Available at: http://www.scarborough.com

Schement, J., & Lievrouw, L. (eds.). (1987). *Competing visions, complex realities: Social aspects of the information society.* Norwood, NJ: Ablex.

Schement, J., & Curtis, T. (1995). *Tendencies and tensions of the information age.* New Brunswick, NJ: Transaction Publishers.

Schiller, H. (1969). *Mass communications and American empire.* New York: A. M. Kelley.

———. (1976). *Communication and cultural domination.* Armonk, NY: Sharpe.

———. (1981). *Information in the age of the Fortune 500.* Norwood, NJ: Ablex.

———. (1989). *Culture, Inc.: The corporate takeover of public expression.* New York: Oxford University Press.

Schindler, G. (ed.). (1982). *A history of engineering and science in the Bell System: Switching technology, 1925–1975.* Murray Hill, NJ: Bell Telephone Laboratories.

Schlesinger, P. (1991). *Media, state and nation.* Newbury Park, CA: Sage.

Schmitz, J. (1997). Structural relations, electronic media, and social change: The public electronic network and the homeless. In Jones, S. (ed.), *Virtual Culture.* Thousand Oaks, CA: Sage.

Schramm, W. (1982). *Men, women, messages and media.* New York: Harper & Row.

———. (1988). *The story of human communication: Cave paintings to micro-chip.* New York: HarperCollins.

Schudson, M. (1984). *Advertising, the uneasy persuasion.* New York: Basic Books.

Schutte, J. (1997). Virtual teaching in higher education: The new intellectual superhighway or just another traffic jam? Available at: http://www.csun.edu/sociology/virexp.htm

Sears, D., & Freedman, J. (1972). Selective exposure to information: A critical review. In Schramm, W., & Roberts, D. (eds.), *The process and effects of mass communication.* Chicago: University of Illinois Press.

Seitel, F. (1997). *The practice of public relations,* 7th ed. Englewood Cliffs, NJ: Prentice Hall.

Seiter, E. (1992). Semiotics, structuralism, and television. In Allen, R. (ed.), *Channels of discourse, reassembled.* Chapel Hill, NC: University of North Carolina Press.

Shaw, D. (1998, March 30). Cooperation within *Times* Viewed with Trepdiation. *Los Angeles Times* Special Reports. Available at: http://www.timesoc.com/HOME/NEWS /REPORTS/THEWALL/t000030398.1.html

Shefrin, D. (1993). Rediscovering an olde technology: Facsimile newspaper lessons of invention and failure. In Pavlik, J., & Dennis, E. (eds.), *Demystifying media technology.* Mountain View, CA: Mayfield Publishing.

Shoemaker, P. (1991). *Gatekeeping.* Newbury Park, CA: Sage.

Short, J., Williams, E., & Christie, B. (1976). *The social psychology of telecommunications.* New York: Wiley.

Sieber, U. (1986). *The international handbook of computer crime.* New York: Wiley.

Siebert, F., Peterson, T., & Schramm, W. (1956). *The four theories of the press.* Urbana, IL: University of Illinois Press.

Signorelli, N. (1989). Television and conceptions about sex roles: Maintaining conventionality and the status quo. *Sex Roles,* 21(5–6), 341–360.

Simon, R., & Wylie, F. (1994). *Cases in public relations management.* Lincolnwood, IL: NTC Business.

Sirgy, M. (1998). *Integrated marketing communication: A systems approach.* Upper Saddle River. NJ: Prentice-Hall.

Sloan, W., Stovall, J., & Startt, J. (eds.). (1993). *Media in America: A history,* 2nd ed. Scottsdale, AZ: Publishing Horizons.

Smillie, B. (1997, December 18). Japanese TV cartoon show stuns hundreds. *Lansing State Journal,* 15A.

Smith, A. (1980). *Good-bye, Gutenberg.* New York: Oxford University Press.

Smythe, T. (1993). The press in industrial America. In Sloan, W., Stovall, J., & Startt, J. (eds.), *Media in America: A history,* 2nd ed. Scottsdale, AZ: Publishing Horizons.

Software Publisher's Association (1997). 1996 personal computer application software sales pass $10 billion for the first time. Available at: http://www.spa.org/research /releases/1996NA.htm

Spohn, D. (1997). *Data network design.* New York: McGraw-Hill.

Spretnak, C. (1997, July). Resurgence of the real. *UTNE Reader,* 59–63, 106.

Sproull, L., & Faraj, S. (1997). Atheism, sex, and databases: The net as a social technology. In Kiesler, S. (ed.), *Culture of the Internet.* Mahwah, NJ: Lawrence Erlbaum.

Steeves, H. (1993). Creating imagined communities: Development communication and the challenge of feminism. In Levy, M., & Gurevitch, M. (eds.), *Defining media studies.* New York: Oxford University Press.

Stephens, M. (1989). *A history of news.* New York: Penguin.

Sterling, C., and Kittross, J. (1990). *Stay tuned—A concise history of American broadcasting,* 2nd Ed. Belmont, CA: Wadsworth.

Sterngold, J. (1998, December 29). Prime-time TV's growing racial divide frustrates industry's blacks. *New York Times.* Arts section.

Stevens, E. (1998, December). Mouse•ke•fear. *Brill's Content,* 1(5), 94.

Stoll, C. (1995). *Silicon snake oil: Second thoughts on the information superhighway.* New York: Doubleday.

Storey, J. (1993). *An introductory guide to cultural theory and popular culture.* Athens, GA: University of Georgia Press.

Stout, D., & Mouritsen, R. (1987). Prosocial behavior in advertising aimed at children. *Southern Speech Communication Journal,* 53, 159–174.

Straubhaar, J. *et al.* (1992). The emergence of a Latin American market for television programs. Paper presented at International Comunications Association Conference, Miami.

Stump, M., & Jessell, H. (1988, November 21). Cable: The first forty years. *Broadcasting,* 37–49.

Sussman, G. (1997). *Communication, technology and politics in the information age.* Thousand Oaks, CA: Sage.

Tebbel, J. (1969a). *The compact history of the American newspaper.* New York: Hawthorne Books

———. (1969b). *The American magazine: A compact history.* New York: Hawthorne Books.

Tech Law Journal (1998). Judge denies motion to dismiss Loudoun blocking software case. Available at: http: //www.techlawjournal.com/censor/80408.htm

Temin, P. (1987). *The fall of the Bell System.* New York: Cambridge University Press.

Thelist (1998). Thelist of internet access providers. Available at: http://www.thedirectory.org/

Tiffin, J., & Rajasingham, L. (1995). *In search of the virtual class.* New York: Routledge.

Toffler, A. (1990). *Powershift.* New York: Bantam Books.

Tracey, M. (1988). Popular culture and the economics of global television. *Intermedia.* (2), 9–25.

Trade Point (1995). U.S. global trade outlook. Available at: http://www.i-trade.com/dir03/mrktinfo /usglobal/

Tucker, E., & Stout, D. (1998, August). *Advertising ethics and pedagogy: Findings from the 1995 Advertising Division membership survey.* Paper presented at the annual meeting of the Association of Journalism and Mass Communication (AEJMC), Baltimore, MD.

Tucker, K. (1994). *Public relations writing: An issue-driven behavioral approach,* 2nd ed. Englewood Cliffs, NJ: Prentice-Hall.

Turkle, S. (1995). *Life on the screen: Identity in the age of the Internet.* New York: Simon & Schuster.

Turner, R. (1993, March 26). Hollyworld. *Wall Street Journal Reports,* R1.

Tyack, D., & Cuban, L. (1995). *Tinkering toward utopia: A century of public school reform.* Cambridge, MA: Harvard University Press.

Tye, L. (1997). *The father of spin: Edward L. Bernays and the birth of public relations.* New York: Crown.

U.S. Census (1993). Level of access and use of computers. Available at: http://www.census.gov/population/socdemo/computer/compusea.txt

U.S. Dept. of Commerce. (1998). *France—Economy—Trade Barriers.*

University Consortium for Advanced Internet Design (1998). Internet 2 home page. Available at: http://www.internet2.edu/

Venkatraman, N., & Henderson, J. (1998). Real strategies for virtual organizing. *Sloan Management Review,* 40(1), 33–49.

Veronis, Suhler & Associates. (1997). *VS&A communications industry forecast.* New York: Veronis, Suhler & Associates.

Volgelstein, F. (1998, February 2). A really big disconnect. You call this reform? Try getting a phone line in the sticks.*U.S. News & World Report,* 39.

Walter, J. (1996). Computer mediated communication: Impersonal, interpersonal and hypersonal. *Communication Research* 23(1),3–41.

Warlaumount, H. (1996). Advertising: Social institution in the American marketplace. In Sloan, W., Staples C., Gonsenbach, W., & Stovall, J. (eds.) *Mass communication in the information age.* Northport, AL: Vision Press.

Waxman, S. (1998, November 29). As Hollywood looks afar, minorities often lose out. *Washington Post News Service* in *Austin American-Statesman,* November 29, G-1.

Weber, T. (1996, December 9). Who uses the Internet? *Wall Street Journal,* R6.

Weiner, R. (1996). *Webster's new world dictionary of media and communications,* 3rd ed. New York: Macmillan.

Weiss, M. (1988). *The clustering of America.* New York: Harper.

Wells, W., Burnett, J., & Moriarty, S. (1995). *Advertising principles and practice.* Engelwood Cliffs, NJ: Prentice-Hall.

Werneke, D. (1985). Women: The vulnerable group. In Forester, T. (ed.), *The information technology revolution.* Cambridge, MA: M.I.T. Press.

Whetmore, E. (1981). *The magic medium: An introduction to radio in America.* Belmont, CA: Wadsworth.

White, D. (1949). The gate-keeper: A case study in the selection of news. *Journalism Quarterly,* 27.

Wiggins, R. (1997, October 13). Corralling your content. *NewMedia,* 40–45.

Wilcox, D., & Nolte, L. (1994). *Public relations writing and media techniques,* 2nd ed. New York: HarperCollins.

Wildman, S., & Siwek, S. (1988). *International trade in films and television programs.* Cambridge, MA: Ballinger.

Wilkinson, K. (1995). *Where culture, language and communication converge: The Latin-American cultural linguistic market. University of Texas–Austin.* Ph.D. thesis.

Wimmer, R., & Dominick, J. (1997). *Mass media research,* 5th ed. Belmont, CA: Wadsworth.

Wittenberg, E. & Wittenberg, E. (1994). *How to win in Washington.* Oxford, England: Blackwell.

Wood, J. (1994). *Gendered lives: Communication, gender and culture.* Belmont, CA: Wadsworth.

World Bank. (1998). *Knowledge for development.* Washington, DC.

Wright, C. (1974). Functional analysis and mass communications revisited. In Blumler, J., & Katz, E. (eds.), *The uses of mass communications.* Beverly Hills: Sage.

Wulforst, H. (1982). *Breakthrough to the computer age.* New York: Scribner's.

Wynter, L. (1998, December 24). Business & Race. *Wall Street Journal.*

Yale, D. (1991). *The publicity handbook.* Lincolnwood, IL: NTC Business.

Yaverbaum, G., & Nadarajan, U. (1996). Learning basic concepts of telecommunications: An experiment in multimedia learning. *Computers in education,* 26(4), 215–224.

Young, J. (1988). Steve Jobs: *The journey is the reward.* Glenview, IL: Scott, Foresman.

ZapNet, "Zapatistas in Cyberspace," (1998). Available at: http://www.eco.utexas.edu/faculty/Cleaver/zapsincyber.html

Zelezny, J. (1993). *Communications law.* Belmont, CA: Wadsworth.

Zickmund, S. (1997). Approaching the radical other: The discursive culture of cyberhate. In Jones, S. (ed.), *Virtual culture.* Thousand Oaks, CA: Sage.

Zientara, M. (1987). *Women, technology and power.* New York: American Management Association.

Zimmerman, J. (1990). Some effects of the new technology on women. In Ermann, M., Williams, M., & Gutierrez, C. (eds.), *Computers, ethics and society.* New York: Oxford University Press.

Zuboff, S. (1984). *In the age of the smart machine.* New York: Basic Books.

Zuckman, H., & Gaynes, M. (1983). *Mass communications law,* 2nd ed. St. Paul, MN: West Publishing.

Index

Access fees, 307
as media revenue source, 41
Accreditation programs, in public relations, 342
Accuracy, 475
of computer databases, 461
of information, 474
of news reporting, 120–121, 122, 477–479
Addiction. *See also* Drug abuse
to Internet, 405–406
Addressable converters, 293
Advertisers, 350, 358–359. *See also* Local advertisers; National advertisers; National spot advertisers; Regional advertisers
Advertising, 348–379
audiences for, 371–373
on basic cable television, 235
in broadcast media, 37
on cable television, 228, 232
and children, 375–376, 411
corporate, 369
corrective, 379
critical studies of, 400
deception in, 460
in early American newspapers, 96
ethics issues in, 374–379
genres of, 366–371
history of, 348–353
in industrial societies, 14
industry organization of, 357–366
information campaigns as, 408–410
jamming of, 357
in mass media, 34–35
as media revenue source, 38, 39–40
on network television, 232, 233
in newspapers, 103, 111, 112
personalized, 354
political economy and, 42–43
as profession, 350–352
public television and, 40–41
on radio, 134–135, 136, 139
revenues of magazines, 79
social impact of, 411–412, 437–438
technological trends in, 353–357
time line of, 349
virtual, 356
Advertising agencies, 350, 357
best, 359
future of, 355
organization of, 359–361
Affiliates
of radio stations, 157–158, 162
of television networks, 212, 232–233
African American music, 149, 150–151
African American press, 104
early history of, 97
African American radio, 141, 151
African Americans
in commercials, 376
in computer media, 426
computer usage by, 267
corporate discrimination against, 340
in educational institutions, 435
lobbying on behalf of, 475
in public relations, 334
in television, 210–211
African American television, 213, 216–217, 229, 238
Agence France Presse (AFP), 98, 115
Agenda setting
in communications media, 16, 43–44, 424–426, 436
opinion leaders and, 45
in political campaigns, 414
Alternative television programs, 212–213
American Association for Public Opinion Research,
surveying guidelines by, 392
American Broadcasting Corporation (ABC)
corporate acquisition of, 216, 217
origins of, 136
ownership of, 236
as television network, 205–206, 208, 210
Americanization, of global media, 493
American Revolution, 62, 95–96, 316, 453
American Telephone and Telegraph (AT&T)
in cable TV industry, 237
divestiture of, 284, 287–288
interactive broadband networks and, 294
origins of, 283
public relations of, 319–320
toll broadcasting by, 134–135
US government versus, 284
America Online (AOL), 11, 110, 253, 271, 273, 275
Amplitude modulation (AM), 140, 142, 146, 147, 155
Analog communication, 20, 23–26, 146, 293–295
Analog systems, 21, 144, 223–224, 225
Animation, 176, 226–227
computer, 184–186, 438–439
Antisocial behavior, 273–274, 399–408
Apple computers, 251, 252, 253, 256, 258–259, 309
Applets, 257
Aristotle's golden mean, 476
ARPANET (Advanced Research and Projects network), 251, 252, 283, 286
Artificial intelligence (AI), 19, 422
Associated Press (AP), 104, 115, 250, 251, 326
origins of, 95, 98, 108
Atanasoff, John Vincent, 250, 251
Audiences
for advertising, 362, 363–366, 371–373
in advertising sales, 39–40
for audio media, 158–160
books for mass, 83–85
for cable television, 238
in critical communication theory, 387
for film media, 194–195
for films, 179–180
magazines for mass, 67–69, 83–85
magazines for specialized, 78–80
for mass newspapers, 97–100, 117
media profit motive and, 37
for multichannel media, 238–239
for Penny Press, 99
for popular music, 149–155
for public relations, 333–337, 337–339
quality of, 41
relationship of media to, 46–47
for television, 210–211, 237–239
Audio media, 130–163
audiences for, 158–160
ethics issues for, 160–163
genres of, 149–155
history of, 130–143
policy issues for, 160–163
recent industry organizational trends in, 155–158
technological trends in, 144–149
Audiotape, 222. *See also* Digital audiotape (DAT); Magnetic tape
Audits, in public relations, 342–343
Automatic switching, 292–293

Backlists, with virtual bookstores, 74, 83
Bandura, Albert, 385, 389–391, 398
Bangalore, computer economy of, 509
Barnes & Noble, 82, 83
BASIC (beginner's all-purpose symbolic instruction
code) computer language, 251, 252, 257
Basic cable, 213, 235
Bell, Alexander Graham, 282–283, 288–289, 291
Bell Telephone Company, 283. *See also* American Telephone and Telegraph (AT&T)
Bernays, Edward L., 314, 315, 318–319
Berne Copyright Convention, 197, 463
Bias
in mass media, 44–45
among media professionals, 45
in survey studies, 394
Bible. *See also* Gutenberg Bible
public relations and, 315–316
readership of, 84
transnational publication of, 493
Black Entertainment Television (BET), 213, 229
Blacklisting, McCarthyism and, 208–209
Books
in agricultural societies, 13
censorship of, 87–89
concentration of ownership of publishers of, 81–82, 85–86
custom publishing of, 72
electronic, 75
genres of, 77–78
globalization and, 497–498
hardback, 69–70
history of, 59
in industrial societies, 13
for mass audiences, 83–85
as mass medium, 58–60
paperback, 70–71
popularization of, 64–65
targeted, 71
technology trends in publishing of, 71–76
time line of, 59

  top North American publishers of, 82
  twentieth-century publishing of, 69–71
  in vernacular languages, 59
Bookstores, 70–71, 82
  virtual, 73–74, 83
Box office receipts
  in movie industry, 177
  top ten movies by, 194
  video rentals and sales versus, 181–182
Brand awareness, 370, 411
Brand loyalty, 370, 411, 437
Brands, in advertising, 358
British Broadcasting Corporation (BBC), 504
  license fees of, 493
  origins of, 137, 221
Broadcast fax services, in public relations, 325
Broadcast media. *See also* Audio media; Music; Radio; Recorded music; Television
  digitization of, 25–26
  economics of, 37
  equal employment opportunity guidelines for, 426
  free speech limits on, 457
  genres of, 141
  history of sound, 133–135
  narrowcasting by, 41–42
Broadcast Music Incorporated (BMI), 163
Broadcast transcription services, 338
Browsers, 17, 257
Bullet model, of media effects, 395–397
Business
  media policymaking by, 470–471
  public relations in, 316–320, 333. *See also* Corporate public relations
Business communications services, 298, 299–300
Business Wire, 337–338

Cable Act of 1984, 214, 285
Cable Act of 1992, 285–286
Cable modems, 295, 299
Cable networks, history of, 213–215
Cable News Network (CNN), 213, 505
Cable Satellite Public Affairs Network (C-SPAN), 213, 413–414
Cable television. *See also* Basic cable; Coaxial cable; Fiber optic cable; Wireless cable
  alternative television programming on, 212–213
  audiences for, 238
  backyard, 214–215
  broadcast television versus, 238–239
  converters for, 293
  digital compression in, 23
  digitization of, 25
  FCC regulation of, 210
  film distribution through, 191–192
  genre channels in, 228–229
  globalization and, 506–507
  industry organization of, 234–235
  infrastructure for, 285
  movies on, 180–182
  narrowcasting by, 41–42, 228
  network television versus, 207, 215–219
  organization of, 303
  origin of, 205
  ownership of, 236–237
  pay-per-view on, 230
  scrambling of, 285–286
  switching and, 293
  technology of, 222–223
  Telco TV versus, 294
  usage of, 300
  US government versus, 285
  wireless, 286
Caller ID service, 293, 298
Capture theory, 472
Careers, media convergence in changing, 7, 8, 441–442, 445–448
Carlin, George, 162, 453, 457, 458
Cartoons, 175, 176
Castro, Fidel, 499, 503
Catalog sales, 369, 370
Categorical imperative, 476
Catharsis hypothesis, of media effects, 399
Catholic Legion of Decency, movie censorship by, 172–173
CD-ROM format, 253, 256
  book indexes in, 76
  book publishing in, 74
  reference books in, 78
Cellular radio services, 286, 297
Cellular telephones, 52–53, 297, 303
Censorship, 454
  First Amendment rights and, 87–89
  on Internet, 272–273
  invisible, 44
  of movies, 172–173, 179–180, 195–196
  Paine against, 456
  in television industry, 240–241
Centrex (central exchange) service, 299
Chain bookstores, 70–71, 82
Chain broadcasting, 139, 162
Chain newspapers, 103, 104, 105, 107, 115, 118
Chain stores, 82, 89, 156
Channels
  in digital systems, 22–23
  in SMCR model, 15, 16
  for Web pages, 17, 261
Chat rooms
  on Internet, 108, 263, 427
  in public relations, 329
Children. *See also* V-chips
  advertising and, 375–376, 411
  cigarette ads targeted at, 404–405, 411
  effects of mass media on, 384–386
  media stereotyping and, 402
  public relations for, 323
  TV violence and, 241–242, 389–391, 399–401, 408
Children's On-Line Protection Act of 1998, 273, 459
Children's Television Act of 1990, 241–242, 408
Children's Television Advertising Practice Act, 375
China
  book censorship and, 89
  origin of printing in, 58
  politics on Internet and, 514
Christian Broadcasting Network (CBN), 213
Christianity, public relations of, 315
Cigarette advertising
  children and, 404–405, 411
  as promoting drug abuse, 404–405
Circuits
  dedicated, 22
  packet switching and, 296, 307
Civil War, 95
  American industrial growth following, 100
  magazine publishing during, 63, 64
  newspaper coverage of, 99
CLASS (custom local area signaling services), 298
Classified ads, 349
Classrooms. *See* Educational institutions
Clear Channel Communications, 143
Client review, in advertising, 360
Clinton, William Jefferson, 10, 47, 73, 106, 119, 120, 121–123, 480, 481
Coaxial cable, 222
  fiber optic cable versus, 222–223
  technology of, 290
Cold war
  newspapers during and after, 106–107
  television newscasting and, 208
Colleges. *See* Educational institutions
Color
  in film media, 178, 184
  in television, 209
Color fading, in film media, 199
Columbia Broadcasting System (CBS), 143
  corporate acquisition of, 216, 217
  origins of, 136
  as television network, 205–206, 207–208, 210
Columbia Pictures, 176
  Sony and Tri-Star and, 193
  television and, 179
Comedy movies, 188
Comedy shows, 206, 226. *See also* Situation comedies
Commercials. *See also* Advertising
  for children, 375–376
  lifestyle promotion by, 375
Commission system, in advertising, 350
Common carrier, 284, 306
Communication
  in agricultural societies, 12–13
  analog, 20
  critical theory of, 387
  cultural studies view of, 18
  digital, 20
  in industrial societies, 13–14
  in information society, 14–15
  mass, 16
  oral, 12
  in preagricultural societies, 12
  SMCR model of, 15–17
  via Internet, 17–18
Communications Act of 1934, 135, 160, 284, 306, 457, 465, 468
Communications Decency Act of 1996, 251, 385
  challenge to, 457–459
  Internet and, 273
Communications infrastructure, 282–309
  history of, 282–288
  industry organization for, 300–305
  policy issues concerning, 305–309
  security of, 308–309
  services of, 298–300
  technology for, 288–298

time line of, 283
usage of, 300
Communications media, 10–12, 418–448
American usage of, 4
antisocial behavior and, 399–408, 418–419
community and, 426–430
comparisons of national, 489–493
culture and, 430–433
development of, 12–15
digitization in, 23–26
ethics issues in, 475–481
federal regulation of, 471–474
genres of, 298–300
individual versus societal effects of, 418–419
interactive, 10
occupation outlook in, 445–446
opinion leaders in, 45
ownership patterns of, 35–37
policy issues for, 452, 453–470
policymaking in, 470–475
prosocial behavior and, 408–411, 418–419
relationship of audiences to, 46–47
in social criticism, 419–421
social inequality and, 421–426
social institutions and, 433–448
as supporting political status quo, 43
technical standards for, 469–470
theories of, 32–33
Community antenna television (CATV) service, 291
origins of, 205, 206
Compact disc (CD) technology, 6, 24, 25, 145, 253
book publishing via, 74–76
records versus, 142, 143
Competitive local exchange carriers (CLECs), 288, 302
CompuServe, 11, 110, 253, 326
Computer animation, 184–186
Computer-integrated manufacturing (CIM), 438
Computer media, 250–278. *See also* Digital revolution; Personal computers
adverse health effects of, 430
convergence with mass media of, 5–12
ethics issues for, 270–278
genres of, 261–266
globalization and, 509–511
history of, 250–254
industry organization of, 268–270
in newsgathering, 108–109, 110–111
policy issues for, 270–278
power of, 20
print media as, 72
productivity increases via, 438–439
recent technological trends in, 254–261
self-efficacy and, 50
social effects of, 405–408
social issues for, 270–278
time lines of, 5, 251
using, 267–268
Computer networks, 5–6, 11. *See also* Internet; World Wide Web (WWW)
crimes against, 407–408
origins of, 251–252
Computers. *See also* Personal computers
adverse health effects of, 430
in advertising, 352, 354–357
early, 250–251
educational institutions and, 434–435
energy-saving, 430
future of, 257–261, 259
generations of, 254
hardware technology of, 254–256
in intelligent networks, 293
invention of, 250
power consumption of, 430
recycling and disposal of used, 430
in relationship marketing, 368
software technology of, 256–257
thought control of, 258
.com Web sites, 265
Concentration of ownership, 422–423, 466–467. *See also* Ownership patterns
among book publishers, 81–82, 85–86
of communications infrastructure, 305–306
in movie industry, 177–179, 193
among newspapers, 118
in radio industry, 161–162
in television industry, 219, 239–240
Confidentiality, in journalism, 479–480
Conglomerates
copyright protection for, 87
in film industry, 191–193
in newspaper publishing, 107
in publishing industry, 86
Connectionless networks, 22
Consolidation, 422–423
in broadcast industry, 143
in computer hardware industry, 268
in computer industry, 270–271
of film industry, 193
of global media firms, 495–496
of magazine industry, 80–81
of magazine publishers, 85–86
of newspaper publishers, 104, 107, 118
in television industry, 219
Consumer privacy, 461, 462
"Consumption values," advertising that promotes, 374–375
Contemporary hit radio (CHR), 151, 153
Content analysis, 387–388
of media stereotyping, 402
in research on antisocial behavior, 400
"Content customization" software, 198
Content providers, 269–270
Conversations
interactivity of, 19
in telephone system, 24
Copyright Act of 1790, 62
Copyright Act of 1976, 87
Copyright law, history of, 463–464
Copyright protection, 40, 86–87, 463–464
in computer industry, 276–278
fair use and, 87, 277, 463
in film industry, 196–197, 198
origins of, 62
in recordings and radio, 163
Copyright royalty fees
as media revenue source, 40
in recording industry, 141
Corporate public relations, 337–339
adverse Internet effects on, 330–331
ethics issues in, 339–343
Internet in, 327–329
principles of, 319–320
Corporation for Public Broadcasting, 233
Council of Public Relations Firms, 338
Counseling firms, 319
Courts. *See* Judicial Branch
Creel Committee, 318–319
Crime, media effects on, 418–419
Crime movies, 188
Crisis communications, 320
Critical mass, in diffusion of innovation, 53
Critical research, 387
Critical studies approach, 32
in media studies, 42–47
to media violence, 400
Critical theorists, 386
on communications media, 419–421
on women and telephones, 425
Cross-ownership, 466
Cross-subsidies, in cable TV industry, 240
Cuba, American radio versus, 499
Cultivation theory, of media effects, 396, 398
Cultural criticism, 432–433
of communications media, 45–46
Cultural determinism, communications media and, 419, 431–432
Cultural imperialism, 516–517
Cultural studies view of communication, 18, 32
Culture. *See also* Genres
in communication, 18, 419, 430–433
consumer, 349–350
defined, 430–431
fragmentation of, 428–429
media shaping of, 42, 46–47, 384–414, 430–433
popular, 367–368, 432
Customer premise equipment (CPE), 304
Cyberspace media, in public relations, 329

Daily newspapers, 112–115
Databases. *See also* Online databases
right to privacy and, 460–462
Data networks, 257–258, 510–511
Data Protection Directive, privacy and, 461
Declaration of Principles (Lee), 318
Declaration of Principles (PRSA), 321
Decoders
in SMCR model, 15, 16, 18
for Web pages, 17
Defamation, First Amendment and, 455
De Forest, Lee, 131, 133, 147, 289
Democracy
communications media and, 421, 491–493
free press and, 454
Demographic channels, 229
Demographic characteristics
defining market segments with, 17
of television audiences, 238
Demographic segmentation, 371–372, 372–373
Department of Commerce, media regulation by, 472–473
Depression, Great
motion pictures and, 174
newspapers and, 104–105
Deregulation, of telecommunications, 474
De-skilling, 442
Desktop computers. *See* Personal computers
Desktop filmmaking, 186
Desktop publishing, 20, 69, 72, 443. *See also*

Electronic publishing
Developing nations, media in, 490, 496–518
Developmental model, of mass media, 490, 491, 492
DHTML (Dynamic HTML), 261
Diffusion, 51–53, 205
Digital audio broadcasting (DAB), 25–26, 147–148
Digital audiotape (DAT), 146
Digital cable, 295
Digital carriers, 291, 295–296
Digital compression, 22–23, 286
in digital cable, 295
of tape recordings, 146
of video signals, 223, 224
Digital conversion, 21, 23–26
Digital data services (DDS), 299
Digital media, 6–8, 21, 23–26, 145. *See also* Compact disc (CD) technology
Digital networks, 293–297
Digital revolution, 20–26
Digital Subscriber Line (DSL), 24, 295, 298–299
computers with, 258
interactive broadband networks and, 294
Digital television, 6, 22–23, 223–225. *See also* High-definition television (HDTV)
computers in, 259
in foreign countries, 507
Digital transmission, 291
in cellular radio, 297
packet switching in, 22
quality of, 21–22
Digital versatile discs (DVDs), 24, 25, 146, 187, 198, 261
book publishing via, 74–76
film piracy and, 197
Digitization, 21–22, 72
in communications media, 23–26
in film preservation, 199
Direct Broadcast Satellite (DBS) systems, 25, 148, 214–215, 235, 286, 303, 506
Direct mail, 369
Direct marketing, 352, 368–370
Direct sales, as media revenue source, 38, 39
Disney studio, 179, 193, 236
computer animation at, 185
extension of copyrights owned by, 464
as global media firm, 493, 495
suppression of investigative journalism by, 241
television and, 178, 207
Distance education, 434–435
Distant signals, with cable television, 212–213
Distribution, 34. *See also* Cable television; Globalization; Mass distribution
first-run, 181
of magazines, 81
of motion pictures, 174–177, 179–180, 191–193, 196, 501–503
narrowcasting in, 42
of newspapers, 106–107
of recorded music, 156
of television programming, 230–231
Divestiture, of AT&T, 284, 287–288
DIVX standard, 197
DNS (domain name service) protocol, 263
Domain names, 264–265
Drudge, Matt, 121, 122, 437, 478, 480
Drudge Report
Clinton-Lewinsky scandal in, 122, 480
unethical material in, 477–478
Drug abuse, mass media as promoting, 404–405
Dubbing, 488
Dumont, Allen, 204, 220
Dumont Network, 205

Eastman Kodak, 178, 184
Economic disadvantage. *See* Poverty
Economic institutions, communications media and, 437–448
Economics, 32. *See also* Media economics
Economic success, mass production and distribution in, 33–35
Economies of scale, 33–35
in distance education, 434
printing press and, 60
within radio networks, 136
Edison, Thomas Alva, 131, 132, 144
invention of motion picture camera by, 170, 182–183
movie patents of, 171
public relations by, 317
talking pictures invented by, 173
Education
of elite classes, 58
informal, 410–411
of journalists, 123
for media literacy, 379
Educational software, 266
Educational television, 241–242. *See also* Public Broadcasting Service (PBS)
.edu Web sites, 264
Elections, media effects on, 412–414, 435–437
Electromagnets, 148
in recording technology, 144, 145
in telegraph and telephone, 288–289
in TV picture tube, 220, 221
Electronic commerce, 111, 265, 266, 272
impact on publishing of, 73–76
technological changes in, 443–445
Web sites for, 266
Electronic Communications Privacy Act of 1986, 276, 462, 481
Electronic data interchange (EDI), 445
Electronic Data Systems (EDS), 304
Electronic magazines, 73, 76, 79
in public relations, 329
Electronic publishing, 86. *See also* Desktop publishing
ELF (extremely low frequency) radiation, as environmental threat, 430
E-mail (electronic mail), 262, 267
flaming via, 429
in public relations, 328
Employee relations, 332, 438–448
Employment patterns, in mass media, 426
Encoders, in SMCR model, 15, 16, 18
Encryption software, 274
ENIAC (electronic numerical integrator and calculator), 250–251, 256
Entertainment, 47
early books as, 60
incidental learning from, 410
as mass media function, 49
Environment, communications media as affecting, 429–430
Environmental monitoring, 342–343
Environmental Protection Agency (EPA), 430
Equal employment opportunity (EEO) guidelines, for broadcasters, 426
Era of creativity, in advertising, 349, 353
E-rate subsidy, 467
Ethernet, origin of, 252
Ethics, 374, 452, 453, 475–481
in advertising, 374–379
in audio media industry, 160–163
codes of, 476–477
in communications infrastructure industry, 305–309
in computer industry, 270–278
in film industry, 195–199
general guidelines for, 476
for media professionals, 45, 216, 455, 477–481
in newspaper publishing, 118–124
of public relations, 320–321
rules for, 378
social responsibility in, 477
in survey studies, 392
in television broadcasting, 239–244
time line of, 453
Ethnographic research, 393–395
European Union (EU), 487–488, 517–518
Evaluation
of audiences, 373
in public relations, 335, 342–343
Event marketing, 369. *See also* Media events; Special events
Executive Branch, media regulation by, 471, 472–473
Experimental research
of antisocial behavior, 400–401
on mass media effects, 389–391
on media stereotyping, 402
Expert systems, 442

Facsimile transmission. *See also* Fax machines
in news delivery systems, 109–110
Fairness, 475
in journalism, 479–481
in public relations, 340
Fairness and Accuracy in Reporting group, 475
Fairness Doctrine
in political speech, 455–456
in television, 243–244
Fair use of copyrighted materials, 87, 277, 463
Farmers. *See* Agricultural societies
Farnsworth, Philo, 204, 205, 221
Fax machines, 109. *See also* Broadcast fax services
Federal Communications Commission (FCC), 469
cable television and, 212, 214
equal employment opportunity guidelines by, 426
Fairness Doctrine by, 456
interactive broadband networks and, 294
media regulation by, 472
origins of, 135, 468
public television and, 211–212
radio regulation by, 160–161
"seven dirty words" and, 458

standards established by, 469–470
telephone monopoly and, 284
television regulation by, 204–205, 210
universal service and, 467
Federalist Papers, 62–63, 96, 316
Federal Radio Commission (FRC), 135, 147, 468
Federal Trade Commission (FTC)
anticompetitive practices investigated by, 473
deceptive advertising and, 378–379
privacy and, 461
Federal Trade Commission Act of 1914, 378
Feedback, 15, 16, 17–18, 19–20
Fiber optic cable, 222–223, 286
satellites versus, 514–515
Fiber optics, 23, 291–292
technology of, 292
Fiction. *See* Mass-market fiction; Novels; Science fiction
Fidelity
of FM radio, 141–142
high, 144–145
of recordings, 140
File transfer protocol (FTP), 262, 263
Film media, 170–199
audiences for, 194–195
color, 178, 184
digitization of, 24–25
ethics issues for, 195–199
genres of, 187–190
globalization and, 501–503
history of, 170–182
policy issues for, 195–199
preservation of, 197–199
recent industry organizational trends in, 190–193
social issues for, 195–199
special effects in, 184
standardization of, 183–184
technological trends in, 182–187
television versus, 177–179
time line of, 171
Film studios, 172, 174–177, 190, 191
Filtering programs, 23, 88, 273, 492
First Amendment
censorship and, 87–89
and children's television, 242
freedom of speech and, 118–119, 384, 453–460
and Internet, 273
origins of, 95–96
in radio broadcasting, 162–163
Floppy disc drives, 252, 256
Ford, Henry, 442, 443
Fordism, 442
Ford Motor Company, Internet publicity against, 330
Foreign-language newspapers, 99–100
Foreign Web sites, 265
Formula programming, 216–217
Fourth Amendment, 460–462
Fox Broadcasting Corporation, 217–218, 236
Fox studio. *See* Twentieth Century-Fox
Framing, 44–45, 277
Franklin, Benjamin, 62, 67, 96, 316, 454
advertising in publications of, 349
as early American publisher, 61–62
on freedom of the press, 95–96
as newspaper editor, 94
Freedom fund, ethical decision-making and, 378
Freedom of access, 88. *See also* Universal service
Freedom of speech, 454
First Amendment and, 118–119, 384, 453–460
in radio broadcasting, 162–163
Free press model, of mass media, 491–492
Freeware, 269
Frequency allocations. *See also* Spectrum allocation
for radio broadcasting, 135, 468–469
for television broadcasting, 220–221
Frequency modulation (FM), 141
invention of, 147
and radio audience segmentation, 152–153
radio broadcasting fidelity with, 141–142
rock music genres for, 153–155
television frequency bands and, 220–221
Front groups, in public relations, 319
Full-service agencies, in advertising, 359
Functionalism, 32, 33

Gannett chain, 105, 114
founding of, 103
USA Today and, 107, 112
Gatekeeping
in communications media, 16, 44–45
by newspapers, 123–124
in political campaigns, 414
Gender, 425, 426. *See also* Women
General Electric (GE), 236
as global media firm, 494
NBC acquisition by, 216
Genres, 486
of advertising, 366–371
of audio media, 149–155
of books, 77–78
of broadcast media, 141
in communications media, 45–46
of communications services, 298–300
of computer media, 261–266
of film media, 187–190
of film media (tables), 188, 189, 190
of magazines, 65, 78–80
of newspaper contents, 116–117
of public relations functions, 329–333
of radio music, 149–151, 151–155, 158–159
of radio music (chart), 159
of software, 266
of television, 225–230
of television (tables), 226, 227, 229
Geodemographic clustering, 372–373
Globalization, 486, 487–489
issues in, 516–518
of mass media, 486–518
time line of, 487
Global media firms, 493–496
Global providers, of telecommunications, 513–515
Global village, 427, 493
Glocal media, 487
Good corporate citizens, in public relations, 319–320
Government
media versus, 340
relationships of mass media to, 489–493
Government relations, 332, 333
.gov Web sites, 264
GPS (geopositioning satellite) systems, 298
Graphics
digitization of, 21, 72
in publications, 71–72
on Web pages, 262–263
Great Depression
motion pictures and, 174
newspapers and, 104–105
Group mediation, 387
Group ownership, of radio stations, 157
Groups, musical, 155–156
Group W radio stations, 143
Gutenberg, Johannes, 13, 58, 59, 60
Gutenberg Project, The, 74

Hacking, 275, 408
Hand-copied books, 13, 58–60
Handing off, in cellular radio, 297
Hard disc drives, 255–256
"Hard-sell" advertising, 352–353
Hardware, 254–256
industry organization for, 268
Hays Office, movie censorship and, 172–173, 174, 179–180
Headends, 290
Health, communications media as affecting, 429–430
Hearst, William Randolph, 95, 100, 101–102, 104, 385
yellow journalism and, 102–103
Hegemony, 43
Hidden curriculum, within communications media, 424–426
High-definition television (HDTV), 7, 8, 25, 199, 223–224. *See also* Digital television
standards for, 470
High fidelity recording, 144–145
"High-risk" programming, 388
High schools. *See* Educational institutions
Hollywood, California
globalization and, 495, 501–503
as moviemaking center, 171–172, 174, 178–179, 190
sex scandals in, 403
television programming from, 206–207, 211
Home Box Office (HBO), 180, 235, 285
origin of, 213
Home pages, 110. *See also* Web pages
Home shopping, 357, 369
Home video, 181–182, 215
film distribution through, 191–193
technology for, 223
Honesty, in ethics, 378
Hopper, Grace Murray, 256–257, 426
Horizontal integration
in cable TV industry, 237
in computer industry, 271
in movie industry, 196
regulation of, 466–467
Household appliances, computer chips in, 259
Households, computers in, 267–268
Households using television (HUTs), 364
HTML (Hypertext Markup Language), 251, 254, 257, 261, 262–263

http (hypertext transfer protocol), 263–264
Hutchins Commission, ethics guidelines by, 477
Hypercard, 253, 257
Hypertext, 74, 253. *See also* HTML (Hypertext Markup Language)
Hypodermic model, of media effects, 395–397

IAB (Internet Architecture Board), 270
IBM (International Business Machines), 251, 253
IETF (Internet Engineering Task Force), 270
Illiteracy
in agricultural societies, 13
and book and magazine readership, 84–85
in industrial societies, 14
during Middle Ages, 59
modern, 12
Illustrations. *See* Graphics
Immigrants, newspapers for, 99–100, 104
Impulse technology, in advertising, 354
Incidental learning, from mass media, 410
Indecency, 457, 458
freedom of speech and, 457
Internet and, 457–459
in radio broadcasting, 162–163
Independent filmmakers, 179–180
George Lucas as, 182
organization of, 191
Independent local telephone carriers, 301–302
Independent newspapers, 94–95
Independent television stations, 212
network television versus, 215–219
programming for, 233
India, 491, 509
Indians. *See* Native American press
Individual effects, of communications media, 418–419
Industrial Revolution, 5, 13
development of American advertising during, 349–350
development of printing during, 58, 60
Luddites versus, 428
Industrial societies
economies of scale in, 34
information workers in, 14
Infinity, 143, 157–158
Howard Stern with, 158
Infomercials, 369
Informatics, 10
Information
in advertising, 366–367
free flow of, 517
interpretation of, 48
Information campaigns, 408–410
Information services, 270
global, 509–510
Information society, 4, 14–15
careers in, 445–448
economies of scale in, 34
employment in, 438–448
knowledge gap in, 423–424
women's influence on, 425
Information superhighway, 5, 11–12, 287. *See also* Internet; World Wide Web
Information workers, 4, 14
Ink, in public relations, 333
INMARSAT, 303
Innovations, diffusion of, 51–53, 205
Input/output, for computers, 256
Integrated marketing communication (IMC), 353
Intellectual property, copyright protection of, 86–87, 163, 196–197, 198, 276–278, 463–464
Intelligent networks, 293, 298
INTELSAT, 303
Interactive broadband networks, 294
Interactive communication, 10, 19–20
Interactivity, 19–20, 74, 265
in Internet advertising, 354–356
Interexchange carriers (IXCs), 301
Interfaced scanning, 225
International Association of Business Communicators (IABC), 338, 341
International film distribution, 501–503
International law, 515–516
International media, regulation of, 515–516
International music flow, 500–501
International news flow, 496–497, 505
International News Service, 104
International publishing, 497–498
International radio, 498
International record carriers (IRCs), 301
International standards, for communications media, 470
International Telecommunications Union (ITU)
communications standards by, 470
in international media regulation, 515, 516
in national development, 518
radio frequency allocation by, 469
International telephony, via Internet, 307
International television, 505–506
Internet, 5, 251. *See also* World Wide Web (WWW)
accuracy of reporting on, 477–479
addiction to, 405–406
adverse public relations via, 330–331
advertising agencies on, 355
as advertising medium, 363
America Online and, 11
antisocial behavior on, 273–274, 405
as cause of depression, 407
censorship on, 272–273
Chinese blocking of, 514
Clinton-Lewinsky scandal on, 121–123, 480
connection options for, 296
content providers on, 269–270
copyright protection of music and, 163
in cultural determinism, 432
data networks and, 257–258
digital recordings on, 147, 148–149
digital television via, 224–225
in direct marketing, 369–370
electronic commerce on, 111, 443–445
e-mail with, 262
encryption on, 274
entertainment via, 49
filtering programs for, 23
globalization and, 511–513
as global village, 427
governance of, 271–272
indecency and, 457–459
as information medium, 48
intellectual property rights and, 276–278
international telephony via, 307
as libertarian medium, 492
long-distance telephony via, 307
in mass communication, 17–18
in media convergence, 5–6, 7
media research conducted on, 389
as newsgathering technology, 108
online databases on, 326
organization of, 303
origins of, 251–252, 283, 286–287
ownership of, 270
packet switching in, 22
political institutions and, 436–437
political security and, 514
protocols in, 22, 261–264
in public relations, 327–329, 330–331
public subsidies for, 41
and publishing industry, 85–86
publishing on, 73–76
scandals reported on, 437
security on, 308–309
sexual material on, 88
social impact of, 9, 10
technology of advertising on, 354–356
universal service and, 308, 468
usage of, 267–268
user privacy on, 274–276
virtual bookstores on, 73–74, 82, 83
virtual communities on, 49
virtual universities on, 434
World Wide Web and, 254
Zapatista Liberation Front on, 512, 513
Internet 2, 296–297
Internet telephony, 11–12, 261, 288
Interpersonal relationships, 428–429
Intranets, 304, 328
Investigative journalism, 95, 99, 100, 101, 105, 106, 119–120
corporate suppression of, 241
simulations in, 243, 244
in Watergate scandal, 106–107
Invisible censorship, 44
"Invisible hand," 33
IRC (Internet relay chat) protocol, 263
Iridium network, 298, 303, 508–509
ISDN (integrated services digital network) lines, 295–296, 298–299
ISOC (Internet Society), 270
ISPs (Internet service providers), 264, 265–266, 269, 288, 302

Jamming of advertising, 357
Java computer language, 257, 258
Job displacement, in mass media, 441
Job security, effects of technological advances on, 441–442
Joint operation agreements, among newspapers, 118
Journalism. *See also* Investigative journalism; Newspapers; Photojournalism; Society of Professional Journalists; Wire services; Yellow journalism
confidentiality in, 479–480
education for, 123
fairness in, 479–481
in public relations, 338
television, 240–241, 243–244
Journals, for public relations industry, 338
Judicial Branch, media regulation by, 471, 472,

473
Justice Department, media regulation by, 473

KDKA radio station, 133–134
Knight–Ridder chain, 105
Knowledge gap hypothesis, 423–424
Ku Klux Klan, 171–172, 273

Labels
of record companies, 141, 156
warning, 162, 197
Large companies. *See also* Concentration of ownership; Consolidation; Corporatization; Ownership patterns
advertising by, 358
market power of, 35–37
mass media as supporting, 43
Lasers, in fiber optic systems, 291–292
Latin America. *See also* Globalization
mass media in, 490, 491
Latin music, 154–155
Law, 452
international, 515–516
mass media and, 452–481
time line of, 453
Leaks, political, 480
Leased lines, 299
Lee, Ivy Ledbetter, public relations practiced by, 317–318
LEO (low earth orbit) satellites, 297–298
Letterboxing, 199
Lewinsky, Monica, 73, 106, 119, 120, 121–123, 437, 481
Libel, 95, 455
First Amendment and, 119
via Internet, 330–331
in Zenger trial, 94–95, 454
Libertarian model, of mass media, 490, 491–492
Liberty Media, 214
Libraries, 59, 61
computerization of, 76
freedom of access to books in, 88
License fees, BBC financed by, 493, 504
Licensing, 468. *See also* Radio licensing
of computer software, 269
of recorded music, 163
Lifestyles
defining market segments with, 17
media convergence in changing, 7, 8
narrowcasting and, 42
Lifestyle segmentation, 372
Links, in Web pages, 18, 262–263
Linotype machines, 71, 108
Listservs, 108, 262, 329, 427
Literacy
and book and magazine readership, 84–85
communications media and, 419
of elite classes, 58–59
in industrial societies, 14
in Latin, 59
rise of magazines and, 65
telephones and, 420
Lithography, in printing, 71–72
Lobbying groups, 45
laws influenced by, 474–475
in public relations, 332
Local access and transport area (LATA) zones, 301
Local area networks (LANs), 251–252, 296
in private networks, 304
technology of, 305
Local exchange carriers (LECS), 301–302
Localism
in foreign countries, 507
in radio licensing, 468–469
Local market monopoly, by newspapers, 118
Local media, 106, 487–489
Local origination, of television programming, 214
Local retailers, advertising by, 358–359
Local telephony, carriers for, 301–302
Local television stations, video news releases for, 324
Loew's/MGM studio, 174, 175
CBS acquisition by, 216
competition from television and, 177
ownership consolidation of, 193
Long-distance telephony
carriers for, 301
origin of, 289
ownership and control of, 305–306
switching in, 292–293
via Internet, 307
Long-term memory, in computers, 255–256
Luddites, 428
Lumiére brothers, 170, 183

Macintosh computers, 253. *See also* Apple computers
Magazines
as advertising medium, 361–362, 363
censorship of, 87–89
circulation and annual advertising revenues of, 79
consolidation of publishers of, 80–81, 85–86
distribution of, 81
early American, 62–66
electronic, 73, 76, 329
genres of, 65, 78–80
globalization and, 497–498
history of, 59, 61
on Internet, 73
for mass audiences, 67–69, 83–85
men's, 84, 85
muckraking by, 65–66
newsmagazines, 68–69
personally published ('zines), 69, 70
popularization of, 64–65
postal distribution of, 62, 65
targeted, 67–68
technology trends in publishing of, 71–76
television and, 68–69
time line of, 59
top-selling men's and women's, 84
twentieth-century, 65–66
women's, 63, 65, 69, 84, 85
Magnetic tape. *See also* Audiotape
for music recording, 139–140, 144–145
Mall intercepts, in advertising research, 365–366
Management
in public relations, 336
scientific, 442
Manual switching, 292
Marconi, Guglielmo, 131, 146–147
invention of radio by, 132
Marconi Wireless Telegraph Company, 132
Sarnoff at, 133, 134
Marginal costs, of mass media, 33–35
Marketing, 34
in advertising, 368–370
competition in, 35–37
Marketing managers, 358
Marketing research, 363–364
Marketplace of ideas, 454, 465
Market power, of large companies, 35–37
Market segments, narrowcasting to, 17, 41–42
Marxism, 32, 42, 422
on mass media, 424–426
Mass culture, mass media and, 432–433
Mass distribution, 33–35
Mass-market fiction, 70, 77–78
Mass media
in agricultural societies, 13
American usage of, 4
contemporary view of, 17–20
content analysis of, 387–388
conventional view of, 15–17
corporate structures within, 438–441
corporations versus, 340
critical studies of, 42–47
cultural time line of, 385
globalization of, 486–518
glocal, 487
government versus, 340
in industrial societies, 13–14
job displacement in, 441
law and, 452–481
lobbying by, 475
mass cultural effects of, 432–433
mass production and distribution for, 33–35
national development and, 518
occupational outlook in, 445–448
political campaigns in, 412–414
political power of, 43–44, 435–437
public relations via, 321–322
regionalization of, 487–488
relationship of audiences to, 46–47
segmentation of, 67
as serving ruling classes, 43
social impact of changes in, 9
societal functions of, 47–49, 384–414
telephone as, 420
Mass media firms, globalization of, 493–496
Mass newspapers, 97–103
Mass production, 12–13, 33–35, 438
McCarthyism, 89, 119, 208–209
McLuhan, Marshall, 419, 427, 431
Meat Inspection Act of 1906, 66
Media. *See* Audio media; Broadcast media; Communications media; Computer media; Digital media; Film media; Mass media; Multimedia systems; Print media; Recording media
Media behavior, social learning of, 49–50
Media buyers, in advertising, 361
Media convergence, 4, 5–12
changing careers and lifestyles and, 7, 8
changing regulations in, 8–9
Internet in, 5–6
within media industries, 7–8, 26
new vocabulary for, 10–12
personal computers in, 6–7, 8

social impact of, 9
World Wide Web and, 10
Media departments, of ad agencies, 360–361
Media Distribution Services (MDS), 325, 338
Media economics, 32, 33–42
Media effects, 386. *See also* Mass media
advertising as, 411–412
antisocial behavior as, 399–408
content analysis of, 387–388
political, 412–414, 435–437
prosocial behavior as, 408–411
theories of, 395–399
time line of, 385
Media evaluation model, 373
Media literacy, 379
Media One, 214
Media relations, 331–333
Media representatives, 350
in advertising, 362
Media research, 364. *See also* Nielsen Media Research
Media revenue, sources of, 38–41
Media usage, statistics on American, 4
Meese Commission, on sex in media, 403–404
MEO (middle earth orbit) satellites, 298
Messages
in packet switching, 296
in SMCR model, 15, 16
in Web pages, 17
Metro Goldwyn Mayer (MGM) studio. *See* Loew's/MGM studio
Metropolitan daily newspapers, 112, 113–115
Micropublishing, 116
Microsoft Corporation, 11, 251
antitrust action against, 9, 270–271, 473
DOS software from, 253
founding of, 252
monopoly practices of, 36
online publications of, 76
Microwave transmitters, 222, 289–291
Middle Ages, literacy during, 59–60
Middle-of-the-road (MOR) radio format, 151
.mil Web sites, 264
Minnesota Mining and Manufacturing (3M), magnetic tape invented by, 139–140
Minority groups, 242–243
advertising targeted at, 376
media ownership by, 466
media stereotyping of, 402
telephone usage among, 300
Minority presses, 96–97
Mobile telephones, 286, 297–298, 303
Modems (modulator-demodulators), 251
cable, 295, 299
in digital networks, 293–295
Modem taxes, 307
Modified final judgment (MFJ), 284
Money transfers, on Internet, 274
Monopoly, 35–37, 464
in British broadcasting, 137
in cable TV industry, 240
in computer industry, 270–271
liberalization of, 508
local market, 118
muckraking about, 66
natural, 465
from newspaper mergers, 104
by RBOCs, 305–306
of Technicolor, 184
of telephone service, 284
Morse, Samuel F. B., 250, 251, 282, 288
Motion Picture Association of America (MPAA), 475
movie ratings by, 180, 195–196
video piracy of movies and, 180, 196–197
Motion picture camera, invention of, 170, 182–183
Motion Picture Export Association of America (MPEAA), 180, 495, 501
Motion Picture Patents Company (MPPC), 171
Motion Picture Producers and Distributors of America, movie censorship and, 172–173
Motion pictures, 170. *See also* Movies
distribution of, 174–177, 179–180, 181, 191–193
history of, 170–182
television genres from, 226–227
Movable type, 13, 58. *See also* Typesetting
Movie ratings, 195–196
Movies, 171. *See also* Motion pictures
big-budget, 178
independently produced, 179–180
made-for-TV, 181, 207
panning and scanning of, 199
silent, 170–173
with sound, 173–174, 183, 188–190
on television, 178
top ten moneymaking, 194
Movie theaters
film audiences in, 194
new technology for, 186–187
Muckraking, 65–66, 99
Multichannel Multipoint Distribution Service (MMDS), 223
Multimedia computers, 253, 259–260
Multimedia publications, as genre, 78
Multimedia systems, 25, 26, 435
Multimedia Web sites, 265
Multiple system operators (MSOs), 214, 234, 239–240, 285
Multipoint distribution systems (MDS), 286
Murdoch, Rupert, 89, 107, 218, 495
in film industry, 193
Fox network and, 217
Music
alternative, 154
genres of popular, 149–155
globalization and, 500–501
origins of, 130
popular, 138–139
radio broadcasting of, 137–139
recorded, 131–132
Must carry rules, 214, 306
Muybridge, Eadweard, 170, 182–183
Narrowcasting, 17, 41–42, 213, 228
National advertisers, on television, 232
National Association of Broadcasters (NAB), 475
National Broadcasting Corporation (NBC)
corporate acquisition of, 216, 217
origins of, 134, 136, 351
ownership of, 236
as television network, 205–206, 207
National Investor Relations Institute (NIRI), 338
National media, 487–489
National Public Radio, 158, 161
National radio, in foreign countries, 498–499
National spot advertisers, on television, 232, 233
National Telecommunications and Information Administration (NTIA), 471–472, 472–473
National Television Systems Committee (NTSC),
television broadcast standards by, 204, 220, 470
Native American press, 96–97, 98
Natural monopoly, 465
Nazis
Ivy Lee and, 318
propaganda by, 396
totalitarian media of, 491
NBC Blue network, 136
NBC Red network, 136
Negroponte, Nicholas, 111, 123, 124
Netscape, Microsoft versus, 271
Netscape Communicator, 262
.net Web sites, 264
Network computers, 258–259
Network marketplace, 445
Networks. *See* Cable networks; Communications
infrastructure; Computer networks; Data networks; Intelligent networks; Internet; Private networks; Radio networks; Telephone
networks; Television networks; World Wide Web
News broadcasts
Fairness Doctrine in, 243–244
globalization of, 505
owner interference with, 240–241
simulations in, 243, 244
television, 208, 216, 226, 240–241, 244
News Corporation, 107, 236
in film industry, 193
as global media firm, 493, 495
Newsgroups
on Internet, 108, 427
in public relations, 329
Newsletters, 70, 80, 116
as newspaper precursors, 94
for public relations industry, 338
via fax machine, 109
Newsmagazines, 68–69
as genre, 78
Newspapers, 80, 94–124
accuracy of, 120–121, 122
as advertising medium, 361–362, 363
antislavery, 97
audiences for, 117
"by authority" publishing of, 94–95
chain, 103, 104, 105, 107, 115, 118
circulation of national, 113
in colonial America, 94–96
daily, 112–115
distribution of, 106–107
early American, 61–62
ethics issues for, 118–124
ethnic, 104
foreign-language, 99–100
gatekeeping by, 123–124
genres of, 116–117

global circulation of, 497
globalization and, 496–497
history of, 94–107
for immigrants, 99–100, 104
local, 106
for minorities, 96–97
muckraking by, 65–66, 99
peak circulation of, 105–106
Penny Press and rise of mass, 97–100
personalized, 110–111
policy issues for, 118–124
for public relations industry, 338
radio versus, 105
recent industry organizational trends in, 112–116, 467
rise of yellow journalism in, 99–103
tabloid, 104
technological improvements in publishing of, 107–111
television versus, 105
time line of, 95
during twentieth century, 103–107
weekly, 115
wire services for, 98
New York City
Pulitzer's newspapers in, 101
telegraph lines in, 284
television programming from, 207
Tweed Ring in, 99, 100
New York Times, The, 107, 112–113
Ochs and, 102
online, 116, 117
on slavery, 99
tabloid journalism in, 120
Time magazine and, 68
versus Tweed Ring, 99, 100
on World Wide Web, 25
Noise
digitized removal of, 21–22
in Internet, 18
in SMCR model, 16
Nongovernmental organizations (NGOs), on Internet, 513
Nonlinear editing, 186, 222
Nonprofit enterprises, in public relations, 333
North American Free Trade Act (NAFTA), 473, 487–488, 517–518
Novels
dime, 64–65
genres of, 46
history of, 77
impact of printing press on, 60–61
interactive, 74

Objectivity, in news reporting, 122
Obscenity. *See also* Sexually explicit material
freedom of speech and, 456–457
in radio broadcasting, 162–163
Occupational outlook, in information society, 445–448
Ochs, Adolph, *New York Times* and, 102
Octopus network, 251–252
Office work, in telecommuting, 444, 445
Offset printing, 72
Oligopoly, 35–37, 464
from newspaper mergers, 104
One-voice marketing, 366–367
Online databases
in public relations, 326
right to privacy and, 460–462
Online services, 253. *See also* America Online (AOL);
CompuServe
Opinion leaders, 45
in multistep flow, 397
in political campaigns, 413–414
Optical character recognition (OCR) software, 76
Oral traditions
books and, 58
among homeless people, 12
.org Web sites, 264
Outsourcing
in private networks, 304
by virtual corporations, 440
Owned-and-operated (O&O) stations
radio programming for, 136
television programming for, 231
Ownership patterns. *See also* Concentration of ownership
among book publishers, 81–82
for cable television, 234–235, 236–237, 239–240
of communications infrastructure, 305–306
of communications media, 35–37, 465
in computer industry, 271–272
of Internet, 270
media profit motive and, 37–38
for network television, 236, 239–240
for radio stations, 157–158, 160–162

Packet networks, 22, 296
Packet switching, 22, 23, 24, 296, 307
Page, Arthur W., public relations practiced by, 319–320
Pagination software, 72
Paging services, 297
Paperback books, 60, 70–71
mass-market, 77
Paperback publishers, during twentieth century, 70–71
Parallel processing, 254
Paramount Studios, 174, 175
competition from television and, 177–178
UPN network initiated by, 218–219
Parental guidelines, for television, 241–242
Patent pools, 132
Patents, 463
in computer industry, 276
for motion pictures, 171
for television, 221
Payola scandal, 140, 141
Pay-per-use television, 43
Pay-per-view (PPV) television, 230, 235
Pay telephones, in developing countries, 508
Pay TV, 213, 235
Penny Press, 65, 67
advertising in, 350
early history of, 97–100, 350
People meters, in advertising, 364–365
Periodicals. *See* Magazines
Personal Communication Services (PCS), 24, 286, 297
Personal computers, 5–6, 268. *See also* Desktop publishing; Internet; World Wide Web (WWW)
as digital communications medium, 25
digital television and, 225
hardware technology of, 254–256
history of, 252–253
Internet and, 17–18
magazines about, 81
in media convergence, 6–7, 8
in newsgathering, 108
in public relations, 325–326
reinvention and, 53
software technology of, 256–257
using, 267–268
Personal data assistant (PDA), 259
Personal productivity software, 266
Persuasion. *See also* Propaganda
experimental studies of, 396–397
Phonograph, origins of, 131, 132, 144
Photocopying, desktop publishing by, 72
Phototypesetting, 108. *See also* Photoengraving
PICS (Platform for Internet Content Selection), 273
Pictures. *See* Graphics
Piracy
of cable TV, 309
of movies, 180, 196–197
on World Wide Web, 277–278
Policy issues, 452, 453–470
for audio media, 160–163
in computer industry, 270–278
for film media, 195–199
for newspapers, 118–124
for print media, 85–89
in television broadcasting, 239–244
time line of, 453
Policymaking, 470–475
Political communication, social effects of, 412–414
Political economists, 33, 42–43, 422–423
Political institutions. *See also* Government; United States government
communications media and, 435–437
Political power
early American newspapers versus, 94–96
of Internet, 514
of mass media, 43–44, 387, 422–423
muckraking versus, 65–66
Political speech
Fairness Doctrine and, 455–456
protection of, 454–455
Polling, in survey studies, 394
Pollution, telecommuting as reducing, 430
Popular culture, 432
in advertising, 367–368
Popularization
of media, 64
of radio, 137–138
Popular music, 132, 138–139
genres of, 149–155
Pornography. *See* Sexually explicit material
Portals, 111, 266
Positioning, in advertising, 366–367
Positioning statement, 360
Postal Act of 1879, 65
Post-Fordism, 442
Postman, Neil, 431, 432, 433
Post office
book rates established by, 70

magazine distribution by, 62, 65
Post-production process, in film media, 186
Poverty
communications media and, 421–422
computer usage and, 267
hidden media curriculum for, 424–426
knowledge gap and, 423–424
lifeline telephone service and, 307–308
political economy of, 422
telephone usage and, 300
PPP (point-to-point protocol), 263
Preservation, of film media, 197–199
Press. *See also* Newsletters; Newspapers
freedom of, 95–96, 316, 340, 454
Press bureaus, 317
Press clipping services, 338
Press releases, 320, 322
Prestel videotex service, 251, 253
Price fixing, 36
Prime Time Access Rule, 212
Priming theory, of media effects, 396, 399
Principle of utility, 476
Printing, origin of, 58–60
Printing press, 14
impact of, 60–61
invention of rotary, 71
Print media, 58–89. *See also* Books; Magazines; Newspapers
adverse health effects of, 430
advertising in, 350
audiences for, 83–85
computerization of, 72
digitization of, 24
foreign, 492
genres and forms of, 65, 77–80
history of, 58–71
history of American, 61–69
policy issues for, 85–89
recent industry organizational trends in, 80–83
recent technological trends within, 71–76
technology of advertising in, 354
Privacy, 460
advertising and, 377
consumer, 461, 462
Fourth Amendment and, 460–462
on Internet, 274–276, 407, 437
in journalism, 481
of newsmakers, 119
Private branch exchanges (PBXs), 293
Private networks, 304
virtual, 299
Privatization, 504
of telephone companies, 508
of television broadcasting, 504–505
PR Newswire, 337–338
Prodigy, origins of, 110
Production, 34. *See also* Mass production
of motion pictures, 174–177, 178–179, 179–180, 190, 196
of television programming, 230–231, 232–234
Production Code, movie censorship and, 173
Profit motive
for communications media, 37–38
media revenue and, 38–41
in social learning theory, 51
in television industry, 219
Progressive Era, muckraking during, 65–66
Promotional costs, for films, 192
Promotional videos, 322
Propaganda, 46, 385
advertising as, 351
effectiveness of, 396
origins of, 315–316
Prosocial behavior, 408–411
Protocols
in Internet, 22, 261–264
for Internet 2, 297
in telephone system, 24
PTTs (postal, telephone, and telegraph administrations), 508
Public access channels, 214
Public Broadcasting Act of 1967, 211
Public Broadcasting Service (PBS)
corporate underwriting of, 233–234
economic support for, 43
globalization and, 504
media profit motive and, 37–38
radio broadcasting by, 155, 161
subsidies for, 40–41
television broadcasting by, 211–212, 234
Public data networks, 299–300
Public diplomacy, radio in, 498
Public information, in public relations, 332
"Public interest" standard
private interests versus, 339–341
in radio licensing, 160, 468–469
Publicity, 317, 369
Publicity Bureau, The, 317
Publicity firms, first, 317
Public media systems
economic support for, 43
globalization and, 503–504
media profit motive and, 37–38
for radio broadcasts, 158
Public opinion, 316
communications media and, 436
Public relations (PR), 314–343
audiences for, 333–337, 337–339
corporate, 337–339
defined, 316, 329–331
ethics issues in, 320–321, 339–343
forms of, 329–333
history of, 314–321
industry trends in, 337–339
information campaigns as, 408–410
Internet in, 327–329, 330–331
origins of modern, 315–316
personal computers in, 325–326
public issues of, 333–337
social impact of, 318–319
social issues in, 339–343
successful, 334, 335–337
technological trends in, 321–329
time line of, 315
via mass media, 321–322
Public relations activities, 337
Public relations agencies, 320
Public relations campaigns, 335
Public relations counsels, 318
Public relations firms, 337–339
Public relations news services, 325
Public Relations Society of America (PRSA), 321
code of ethics of, 341
professionalism fostered by, 342
Public relations tools, 333
Public service
information campaigns as, 409
media profit motive and, 37–38
Public subsidies, as media revenue source, 38, 40–41
Public support, in public relations, 336
Public utilities, state and local regulation of, 474
Publishing. *See* Books; Custom publishing; Desktop publishing; Magazines; Newspapers; Print media; Web pages
Publishing houses
concentration of ownership of, 81–82, 85–86
during twentieth century, 69–71
Puffery, 377–379
Pulitzer, Joseph, 95, 100–103
Punishment, media violence and, 390, 399
Pure Food and Drug Act of 1907, 66

Qualitative methods, in media research, 386–387, 389
Quality
of digital transmissions, 21–22
of television audiences, 41
Quantitative methods. *See also* Content analysis
in media research, 386–387
Quotas, in global trade, 518

Race, in communications media, 426
Racing wires, 250
Radio, 5
as advertising medium, 351, 361, 363
AM transmission of, 146
copyright protection for, 163
digital technology in, 6, 25–26
First Amendment and, 162–163
globalization and, 498–499
intellectual property rights and, 163
invention of, 131, 132
music broadcasts on, 137–139
newspapers versus, 105
ownership of, 161–162
public relations via, 321
regulation of, 160–161
short-wave, 498
television genres from, 225–226
television versus, 139
time line of, 131
Radio Act of 1912, 132, 135
Radio Act of 1927, 135, 136, 456, 468
Radio Corporation of America (RCA)
origins of, 132
Sarnoff and, 134
toll broadcasting by, 135
Radio formats, 141
chart of, 159
genres of, 151–155, 158–159
specialized, 141–143
Radio licensing, 132, 160–161, 468–469
Radio networks, 136–139
changing ownership patterns and, 162
genre programming for, 151
television networks from, 205–210
Rate-of-return regulation, 284
Ratings. *See also* Movie ratings

by television audiences, 210, 364
of TV violence, 241
Reading
audience reception through, 47
by-category breakdown of, 84
among elite classes, 58–59
selective, 117
Receivers
in cultural studies view of communication, 18
with Internet, 17
in SMCR model, 16
Recorded music, 131–132
copyright protection for, 163
distribution of, 156
globalization of, 495–496
radio broadcasting of, 137–139, 139–141
time line of, 131
Recording companies, 156
globalization of, 495–496
Recording media. *See also* Victrola
digitization of, 25
technology of, 144–146
Record player, origins of, 131
Records
compact discs versus, 142
origins of, 131, 144
recording speeds of, 140–141
technological innovations in, 140–141
Regional advertisers, on television, 232, 233
Regional Bell operating companies (RBOCs), 301–302, 307
monopoly ownership by, 305–306
regulation of, 472
Relationship marketing, 368
Remote access protocols, 263
Remote sensing, 510–511
Remote TV controls, 237
Repeater amplifier, 289
Repetitive-stress injuries, 430
Republic studio, 176, 177–178
Research
on media effects, 386–395
in public relations, 335, 342–343
Research organizations, for advertising, 357, 363–366
Residential communications services, 298–299
Re-skilling, 443
Restraint of trade, 465
Revenue. *See* Media revenue
RKO (Radio-Keith-Orpheum) studio, 174, 176, 179
competition from television and, 177–178
Rock 'n' Roll, 150–155
genres of, 153–155
history chart of, 152
origins of, 140, 150
Rotary press
invention of, 71, 95
in mass newspaper publishing, 98, 108
Royalties. *See* Copyright royalty fees
Rural areas, telephones and, 420

Sabotage, of Internet, 309
SABRE airline reservation system, 251
Sampling, copyright protection and, 163
Sampling methods, 394
Satellite broadcasting, public relations via, 322–323
Satellite carriers, 303
Satellite footprints, 515–516
Satellite master antenna television (SMATV), 214–215, 291
Satellite media tours (SMTs), 322–323
Satellites
fiber optic cables versus, 514–515
low earth orbit, 297–298
in microwave transmission, 290–291
in news delivery systems, 109
remote sensing from, 510–511
Satellite television, 25, 214–215, 222, 285–286
basic cable delivered by, 235
globalization and, 506–507
Scandals. *See also* Sexual scandals; Watergate scandal
media reporting of, 436
newspaper coverage of, 99, 100, 119, 120
Scanners, digitizing photographs with, 72
Scanning system. *See also* Panning and scanning of films
helical, 223
in television, 204, 221, 225
Scarcity argument, in radio licensing, 469
Scholarly presses, as genre, 78
Schools. *See* Educational institutions
Science fiction, 45–46, 71
Scientific management, 442
Scrambling, of cable TV, 285–286
Scripps–Howard chain, 103, 104, 105
Search engines, 23, 76, 254, 265
Security
of communications infrastructure, 308–309
political, 514
Segmentation
in advertising, 362
demographic, 371–372, 372–373
lifestyle, 372
of magazines, 78–80
of media, 67
of newspapers, 104
of radio, 142, 152–153
of television, 242–243
usage-based, 371
Selective attention, 46, 435
Selective binding, in advertising, 354
Selective effects, of media, 396, 397–398
Selective exposure, 46, 397–398, 435
Selective perception, 46, 398, 435
media stereotyping and, 402
Selective reading, 117
Selective retention, 398
Self-censorship
of movies, 172, 195–196, 198
of television, 240–241
Self-regulation, 452, 453
privacy and, 461
of TV violence, 459–460
Semiotic analysis, 387
of communications media, 45–46
Set-top boxes, 225, 259
Sexual behavior, mass media as influencing, 403–404
Sexual language, in movies, 403
Sexually explicit material
in experimental research, 391
First Amendment rights and, 87–89, 384–386
freedom of speech and, 456–457
on Internet, 273
social effects of, 418
Sexual references, 384
in domain names, 265
in mass media, 385
in movies, 172–173, 179, 195–196
in radio broadcasting, 162–163
in television, 216
Sexual scandals, 66, 106, 119, 121–123, 403
effects of reporting of, 437
tabloid journalism of, 120
Shareware, 269
Sherman Antitrust Act of 1890, 283, 472, 473
monopoly and, 464–465
Short-wave radio, 498
Signaling, 293. *See also* Distant signals
in pre-industrial societies, 282
Silent films, 170–173
era of, 172, 183
genres of, 188
"talkies" versus, 173
Site licenses, 269
Situation analysis, 360
Situation comedies (sitcoms), 207–208, 210, 227–228
recent, 217
social impact of, 210
Situation ethics, 476
Skimming, 117
Slander, 455
First Amendment and, 119
SLIP (serial line interface protocol), 263
SMCR (Source-Message-Channel-Receiver) model,
15–18
Soap operas, 206, 226
worldwide popularity of, 506
Social cognitive theory, 49
Social impact
of advertising, 411–412
of computer industry, 270–278
of Internet, 9, 10
of mass media, 384–414
of political communication, 412–414
of public relations, 318–319, 343
of television, 207–210
Social inequality. *See also* Poverty
communications media and, 421–426
Social institutions, communications media and, 433–448
Social learning theory, 32, 33, 49–51
diffusion of innovation in, 51–53
media effects in, 396, 398
uses and gratifications perspective versus, 50–51
Social responsibility model, 33, 477
of journalism, 479–481
of mass media, 490, 492–493
Societal media functions, 47–49, 418–419, 437–448
Society of Professional Journalists, code of ethics of, 340, 477, 478–479
Society of Professional Journalists Code, 244
Software, 253, 256–257
from Bangalore, 509

genres of, 266
industry organization for, 269
for public relations management, 325–326
Sonny Bono Copyright Term Extension Act of 1998, 87, 277, 464
Sources
checking multiple, 122
in cultural studies view of communication, 18
news, 115–116
in SMCR model, 15, 16
of Web pages, 17
Spamming, 272, 274, 407
Spanish–American War
Hearst and, 101, 385, 395–396
yellow journalism during, 101, 102
Special effects, 184–186
Special events, in public relations, 328, 332
Special-interest magazines, as genre, 78
Spectrum allocation, 308, 468–469
Spin, 44, 319
Spiral of silence, public opinion and, 436
Sponsors, of television shows, 352
Standards, 452, 469–470
Stars, movie, 172, 173
Star Wars, 176, 181, 182, 187
computerized special effects in, 184
computer special effects in, 24
State governments, media policymaking by, 474
Stereotypes, 421
advertising and, 376
community relations and, 427
in mass media, 401–403
sexual, 403–404, 425
Storage devices, 268
Story films, 171. *See also* Movies
Streaming, 261
Studeo agency, 355
Studio Era, in movie industry, 174–177
Studios. *See* Film studios
Subscription libraries, origin of, 61
Subscriptions. *See also* Digital Subscriber Line (DSL)
as media revenue source, 38, 39
Subscription television (STV), 286
Subsidies. *See also* Cross-subsidies; Public subsidies
to support communications infrastructure, 306–307
Supercomputers, 268
Superstations, 213, 229, 230
Supreme Court. *See* Judicial Branch
Surveillance, 47
as mass media function, 47–48
Survey studies
of antisocial behavior, 401
ethnographic research versus, 393–395
in media research, 391–393
sampling methods in, 394
unethical, 392
Suspense movies, 189
Switchboard operators, 293, 425
Switching, 292–293. *See also* Packet switching
replacement of telephone operators with, 425
Syndicated television programs, 212
Syndication
as media revenue source, 40
of motion pictures, 196
of radio programming, 142–143, 151
in television industry, 219, 231, 233
of television shows, 210, 211, 212
Syndicators, 40
as newspaper sources, 115–116
of radio shows, 158

Tabloid newspapers, 104, 119, 120
"Talkies," 173–174, 183
genres of, 188–190
Tape recorders
digital, 146
technology of, 144–145
Target audiences
for advertising, 371
for cigarette ads, 404–405
Target market profile, 360
Tariffs
in global trade, 518
for telephone service, 284
Taxation, 272, 307
Taylorism, 442
Technicolor, 178, 184
Techno-anarchists, 432
Technological determinism, communications media and, 419, 431–432
Tele-Communications, Inc. (TCI), 214, 237, 239–240
as global media firm, 494, 495
interactive broadband networks and, 294
Telecommunications Act of 1996, 5, 8–9, 143, 157, 161, 219, 242, 251, 287–288, 308, 457, 471, 473, 474
industry reorganization following, 300–301, 305–306
interactive broadband networks and, 294
Internet and, 273
ownership patterns regulated by, 466–467
universal service and, 467
V-chips and, 459–460
Telecommunications systems. *See also* Internet; Post office; Telegraph; Telephone; World Wide Web
globalization and, 507–509
global providers of, 513–515
Telecommuting, 443
office environment for, 444, 445
as reducing pollution, 430
Teleconferencing, 299–300, 438, 439
Telegraph. *See also* American Telephone and Telegraph (AT&T)
as first electronic information service, 250
globalization and, 507–509
invention of, 250, 251, 282, 283, 288
mass newspapers and, 98
technology of, 288
wireless, 131
Telemarketing, 369
Telephone. *See also* American Telephone and Telegraph (AT&T)
in cultural determinism, 431–432
early predictions about, 420
globalization and, 507–509
invention of, 282–283, 288–289
long-distance calling with, 289
mobile, 286
privatization of, 508
in public relations, 326–327
in relationship marketing, 368
in survey studies, 394
technology of, 288–289
usage of, 300
women and, 420, 425
Telephone networks
business services with, 298, 299–300
Internet as, 11–12
residential services with, 298–299
Teletypesetting, in newspaper production, 108
Television, 204–244
as advertising medium, 351–352, 361, 363
advertising terminology for, 364–365
as affecting health, 429–430
audiences for, 237–239
children's, 241–242
children's advertising on, 375–376
children and violence on, 241–242, 389–391, 391–393, 399–401
community relations and, 426–427
digital, 6
in direct marketing, 369
distance education via, 434
effectiveness of, 398
ethics issues for, 216, 239–244
film versus, 177–179, 179–180
genres of, 225–230
globalization and, 503–506
history of, 204–219
integration of film with, 193
magazines and, 68–69
minority ownership in, 242–243
multichannel distribution of, 223
narrowcasting by, 41–42
newspapers versus, 105
parental guidelines for, 241–242
policy issues for, 239–244
public relations via, 321–322
radio versus, 139
recent industry organizational trends in, 230–237
social impact of, 207–210
technological trends in, 219–225
time line of, 205
video news releases via, 323–324
Television networks
affiliate stations of, 212, 232–233
competitors of, 215–219
history of, 205–210, 210–215, 215–219
ownership of, 236
programming strategies of, 231–232
VHF/UHF restrictions on, 205
Television receive-only (TVRO) installations, 214, 285, 286, 291
Television receivers, 219–222
Television stations
first, 204
proliferation of American, 204–205
Television transmitters, 219–222
Telnet protocol, 263
Textbooks, 74, 77
Texts
media presentations as, 45–46, 47
readability of computerized, 74
Three-dimensional (3D) movies, 187
Time-Life, Inc.
history of, 80

ownership consolidation with Warner Brothers, 193
Time Warner, 236, 237. *See also* Warner Brothers
as global media firm, 493–494, 495
as multiple system operator, 214
WB television network initiated by, 218–219
Toll broadcasting, 135
T1 digital carrier system, 291, 299
Top 40 radio, 140, 141, 151–152, 153
Totalitarian media, 490, 491, 492
Trade, global, 517–518
Transmission. *See* Digital transmission; Facsimile transmission; Microwave transmitters; Radio transmitters; Television transmitters
Transmission Control Protocol/Internetworking Protocol (TCP/IP), 22, 261–264, 296
Truthfulness, of news reporting, 120–121
T3 digital carrier system, 299
Turing test, 19
Turner, Ted, 9, 191, 214, 237, 494
film colorization by, 199
superstations and, 213
Twentieth Century-Fox, 174, 175
competition from television and, 177
integration of television and film by, 193
Typesetting, technological advances in, 71, 72, 108, 439

UHF (ultra high frequency) television band, 205, 220–221
development of, 212, 213
network television and, 215, 217
Unbalanced flow, in international media, 516–517
United Artists, 176
origin of, 173
ownership consolidation of, 193
television and, 179
United Paramount Network (UPN), 218–219
ownership of, 236
United States
as agricultural society, 13
by-category reading breakdown for, 84
copyright protection in, 463–464
displacement of blue-collar workers in, 441
founding of, 316
freedom of the press in, 95–96, 454–455
history of public relations in, 316–321
as information society, 14
level of advertising in, 375
media globalization and, 487–489
media usage in, 4
motion-picture industry dominance of, 501–503
newspaper publishing in, 94–124
public television in, 211–212
radio regulation and licensing in, 160–162
versus Microsoft, 270–271
United States Congress, media legislation by, 471–472, 473–474
United States government. *See also* Post office
communications media standards by, 469–470
ethical advertising and, 378–379
Internet and, 272, 273
Justice Department investigation of Microsoft, 36
media oversight by, 33
media policymaking by, 470–474
media policymaking by (chart), 471
spectrum allocation by, 308
telecommunications regulation by, 8, 9, 287–288
television regulation by, 204–205
versus AT&T, 284
versus cable television, 285
Universal service, 307–308, 467
media access via, 467–468
with telephones, 283
Universal Studios, UPN network initiated by, 218–219
Universities. *See* Educational institutions
Up-skilling, 442–443
Urbanization, 14, 420
URLs (universal resource locators), 262–263
domain codes for, 264–265
Usage-based segmentation, 371
Usage fees, as media revenue source, 39
USA Today, 95, 112
style-setting by, 106–107
and television, 114
Usenet, 262, 329
Utility, principle of, 476

Vacuum tube, 133, 147, 254
Variety shows, 206–207, 210, 226
Vaudeville, 137, 206–207
V-chips, 5, 9, 10, 23, 242, 459–460. *See also* Children
in Telecommunications Act of 1996, 384–386
Vertical integration, 174
in cable TV industry, 237, 240
in computer industry, 271
among movie studios, 174–177, 196
regulation of, 466–467
VHF (very high frequency) television band, 205, 220
on cable networks, 214
Viacom, 236
as global media firm, 493, 495
UPN network initiated by, 218–219
Video cassette recorders (VCRs)
diffusion of, 51–52, 215
helical scanning in, 223
movies on, 180
Video compression, 23, 223, 224
Video games. *See also* Pong video game
addiction to, 406
children and violence in, 391–392, 405
educational impact of, 407
Video Home System (VHS) players, 223
Video media. *See also* Film media; Motion pictures; Television
business services for, 299–300
globalization and, 503
movies on, 180–182
residential services for, 299
time line of, 171
Video teleconferencing, 299–300
Videotex services, 110, 251, 253, 509–510
Vietnam War
movies during, 179
newspapers during, 106
television broadcasting of, 209, 210
Violence
in computer media, 405
experimental research on, 389–391
in mass media, 384–386, 386, 399–401
media content analysis of, 387–388
in movies, 195–196, 198
survey research on, 391–393
in television, 216, 241–242, 459–460
Virtual advertising, 356
Virtual bookstores, 73–74, 83
Virtual communities, 49
Virtual corporations, 439–440, 444
Virtual courses, 434
Virtual film studios, 186
Virtual private networks, 299
Virtual reality, 187, 259, 260
Virtual relationships, real-life relationships versus, 428
Virtual universities, 434, 435
VRML (virtual reality markup language), 261

Waldenbooks, 82, 83
Warner Brothers, 174, 175
cartoons from, 176
early talking pictures by, 173
industry integration by, 196
ownership consolidation of, 193
television and, 177–178, 179, 207
Warning labels, 197, 241
War propaganda, 351, 396
Watergate scandal, 66, 95, 119–120
investigative reporting in, 106–107
Web casts, 328
Web pages, 5, 110
addictive behavior toward, 406
addresses of, 264–265
copyright violations on, 277
designing, 262–263
domain codes for, 264–265
interactivity of, 19
marginal costs of, 34–35
in media convergence, 5–6
narrowcasting through, 41
as newspaper sources, 115
"rogue," 328
SMCR model of, 17–18
uses of and gratifications from, 50
Westerns
as movie genre, 189
on radio, 137
on television, 206, 207–208
Wide area networks (WANs), 252
Widescreen film, 178, 183–184
Williams, Terrie, 334
Windows, films released through, 192
Windows operating system, as computer industry standard, 469
Wireless cable, 286
Wireless infrastructure, 285–286
Wireless telegraph, invention of, 131
Wire services, 108
monopolies among, 104
as newspaper sources, 115
origins of, 98, 250
Wiretaps, 461–462
Women
advertising targeted at, 376

in computer media, 426
media stereotyping of, 402, 403–404, 425
telephones and, 420, 425
Women Executives in Public Relations (WEPR), 338
Women in Communications Incorporated (WICI), 338
Women's magazines, 85
early American, 63, 65
specialization among, 69
top-selling, 84
World Administrative Radio Conferences, in international media regulation, 515–516
World Administrative Radio Congress (WARC), 469
World Intellectual Property Organization (WIPO), 464
World Trade Organization (WTO), 473
World War I
newspapers and, 104–105
propaganda during, 351, 396
public relations during, 319
radio and, 133–134
World War II
advertising following, 351–352
computers during, 250–251
films about, 189
newspapers and, 104–105
propaganda during, 396
public relations during, 318–319
radio and, 138–139
studio system during and after, 177
television during, 204
World Wide Web (WWW), 5, 12. *See also* Internet
book publishing via, 74
browser software for, 257
copyright protection and, 40, 87, 276–278
direct marketing on, 369–370
electronic commerce on, 445
future of, 261
magazine publishing on, 69, 76
in media convergence, 5–6
narrowcasting through, 41
newspapers on, 110–111
New York Times on, 116
origins of, 254
print media on, 24, 25
radio listening and, 160
search engines for, 76
search engines on, 23
self-publishing on, 86
sexual material on, 88
social impact of, 10
surveillance via, 48
telephones and, 420
virtual universities on, 434, 435
Zapatista Liberation Front on, 512, 513
Writing
origin of, 58
as profession, 59

Xerox Corporation, personal computers at, 252
XML (extensible markup language), 261

Yellow journalism, 99, 102–103
during Spanish–American War, 101
Youth cultures, radio formats for, 158–159

Zapatista Liberation Front, on Internet, 512, 513
Zenger, John Peter, 94–95, 96, 316, 453, 454
Zworykin, Vladimir, 204, 205, 206, 221